ISBN: 978-965-550-554-2

2 ' land the ' ye and ' heaven`s the ' ye ' from as Allah ' create ' whom head in 1
' around ' on ' dark and , and thus and ' nought ' whom`ed the ' land the and
Water the ' around ' on ' you flutter from , from as Allah ' spirit is and ' deep`ing
4 light`ing ' became as and ' light`ing ' became as ' from as Allah ' say as and ' 3
' good`ing ' for ' light`ing the ' ye ' from as Allah ' look as and '
' between in and ' light`ing the ' between in ' from as Allah ' separate as and
call ' dark of and ' day as ' light`ing of ' from as Allah ' call as and ' 5 dark the
one ' day as ' is morn ' became as and ' twilight ' became as and ' the night`s '
' Water the ' middle`ing in ' expanse`s ' became as ' from as Allah ' say as and ' 6
' do as and ' 7 Water of ' Water ' between in ' separate`s from ' became as and
' Water the ' between in ' separate as and ' expanse`s the ' ye ' from as Allah
' above ' which ' Water the ' between in and ' expanse`s of ' under from ' which
' expanse`s of ' from as Allah ' call as and ' 8 so ' became as and ' expanse`s of
' 9 two ' day as ' is morn ' became as and ' twilight ' became as and ' heaven`s
to ' heaven`s the ' under from ' Water the ' rim`ing as ' from as Allah ' say as and
' 10 so ' became as and ' wither`ed the ' saw`ed and ' one ' place`ing '
' Water the ' ditch`ed of and ' Land ' wither`ed of ' from as Allah ' call as and
' say as and ' 11 good`ing ' for ' from as Allah ' look as and ' from as Sea ' call
' seed ' seed`s from ' grass ' develop ' land the ' develop you ' from as Allah
' on ' and in ' and seed ' which ' and has kind ' fruit ' do`ed ' fruit ' tree and
' grass ' develop ' land the ' spring you and ' 12 so ' became as and ' land the
and seed ' which ' fruit ' do`ed ' tree and , and the has kind ' seed ' seed`s from
' 13 good`ing ' for ' from as Allah ' look Then . and the has kind ' and in '
' 14 as three`s ' day as ' is morn ' became as and ' twilight ' became as and
' expanse`s in ' you and light`ing from ' became as ' from as Allah ' say as and

' between in ' separate`s the of and ' land the ' on ' light`s the of ' heaven`s the
' evidence`ing of ' and became and ' the night`s the ' between in and ' day as the
' and became and ' 15 from as Year and ' from week of and ' from as season from of and
' on ' light`s the of ' heaven`s the ' expanse`s in ' you and light`ing from of
' two ' ye ' from as Allah ' do as and ' 16 so ' became as and ' land the
' great`ing the ' light`ing them ' ye ' from as great the ' you and light`ing them
you rule from of ' small the ' light`ing them ' ye and ' day as the ' you rule from of
' from ye ' give as and ' 17 from as in star`ing the ' ye and ' the night`s the '
' 18 land the ' on ' light`s the of ' heaven`s the ' expanse`s in ' from as Allah
' between in ' separate`s the of and ' the night`s in and ' day as in ' rule of and
' for ' from as Allah ' look as and ' dark the ' between in and ' light`ing the
' day as ' is morn ' became as and ' twilight ' became as and ' 19 good`ing
' soul ' breed ' Water the ' and breed as ' from as Allah ' say as and ' 20 as four`s
' expanse`s ' around ' on ' land the ' on ' put fly`ing as ' fly`ing and ' the life
' from as has monster the ' ye ' from as Allah ' create as and ' 21 heaven`s the
' which ' you crawl the ' life`ed the ' soul ' all ' ye and ' from as great the
' wing ' fly`ing ' all ' ye and ' them as has kind ' Water the ' and breed
' bless as and ' 22 good`ing ' for ' from as Allah ' look Then . and the has kind
ye ' and fill and , and increase and , and apart ' say of ' from as Allah ' from ye
' 23 land in ' increase`ed as ' fly`ing the and ' from as sea in ' Water the '
' 24 as five`s ' day as ' is morn ' became as and ' twilight ' became as and
' the has kind ' the life ' soul ' land the ' spring you ' from as Allah ' say as and
' became as and ' the has kind ' land the ' and you life and ' crawl and ' cattle`ed
' the has kind ' land the ' you life ' ye ' from as Allah ' do as and ' 25 so
' ground`ed the ' crawl ' all ' ye and ' the has kind ' cattle`ed the ' ye and

' say as and ' (26 good`ing ' for ' from as Allah ' look Then . and the has kind

' our liken`ing are and ' our image in ' ground ' the make ' from as Allah

' heaven`s the ' fly`ing in and ' sea the ' you squirm in ' and up as and

on ' crawl the ' crawl the ' all in and ' land the ' all in and ' cattle`ed in and

' and image in ' ground the ' ye ' from as Allah ' create as and ' (27 land the '

from ye ' create ' female`ed and ' male ' and ye ' create ' from as Allah ' image in

' from as Allah ' them of ' say as and ' from as Allah ' from ye ' bless as and ' (28

the and footstool and ' land the ' ye ' and fill and , and increase and , and apart

' all in and ' heaven`s the ' fly`ing in and ' sea the ' you squirm in ' and up and '

' be`th ' from as Allah ' say as and ' (29 land the ' on ' you crawl the ' life`ed the

' around ' on ' which ' seed , seed ' grass ' all ' ye ' relate ' as set has

, seed ' tree ' fruit ' and in ' which ' tree the ' all ' ye and ' land the ' all

' land the ' you life ' all of and ' (30 eat`ed of ' be`s as ' relate ' seed

which ' land the ' on ' ing`crawl ' all of and ' heaven`s the ' fly`ing ' all of and

became as and ' eat`ed of ' grass ' green ' all ' ye ' the life ' soul ' and in '

' be`th and ' do`ed ' which ' all ' ye ' from as Allah ' look as and ' (31 so '

day as ' is morn ' became as and ' twilight ' became as and ' especially ' good`ing

as six the '

INTRODUCTION 2

finish and ' (2 from mass ' all and ' land the and ' heaven`s the ' and finish and ' (1
' do`ed ' which ' and you are fill ' as six the ' day as in ' from as Allah '
' which ' and you are fill ' all from ' as seven`s the ' day as in ' desist as and
holy as and ' as seven`s the ' day as ' ye ' from as Allah ' bless as and ' (3 do`ed
' create ' which ' and you are fill ' all from ' desist ' and in ' for ' and ye '
' heaven`s the ' you and bore and you ' to`ed ' (4 you concoct of ' from as Allah
from as Allah ' be`ing as ' you concoct ' day as in ' from create thus ' land the and
' be`s as ' suspend ' field`ed the ' at gift ' all and ' (5 ' land and ' heaven`s '
' not ' for ' sprout as ' suspend ' field`ed the ' grass ' all and ' land in
' whither`s ' from fog and ' land the ' on ' from as Allah ' Jehovah ' rain`s the
' land the ' has from ' went`ed ' fog and ' (6 ground`ed the ' ye ' serve of
Jehovah ' mould as and ' (7 ground`ed the ' around ' all ' ye ' moisten`ed the and
' puff and ' ground`ed the ' has from ' dust ' Men the ' ye ' from as Allah '
(8 the life ' soul of ' Men the ' became as and ' from as life ' you blow ' now`s in
site and ' east from ' has till in ' garden ' from as Allah ' Jehovah ' fix as and '
' Jehovah ' sprout as and ' (9 mould ' which ' ground the ' ye ' there '
' desire has ' tree ' all ' ye ' ground`ed the ' has from ' from as Allah
' from as life the ' tree and ' eat from of ' good`ing and ' look`ed from of
' (10 evil and ' good`ing ' knowledge the ' tree and ' garden the ' middle`ing in
there from and ' garden the ' ye ' drunk`ing the of ' Eden from ' out ' river and
Pishon ' one the ' there ' (11 from as head ' four`ed I of ' be`s and ' disperse as '
' which ' the of as sand the ' land ' all ' ye ' ing`surround the ' that`ing '
' especially ' good`ing ' that`ing the ' land the ' gold and ' (12 gold the ' there
' two the ' river the ' there and ' (13 onyx the ' stone and ' at separate the ' there
' (14 joy`ing ' land ' all ' ye ' ing`surround the ' that`ing ' has and gush`s

' you east ' enter the ' that`ing ' of sting ' as three`s the ' river the ' there and
' took as and ' 15 forth ' that`ing ' as four`s the ' river the and ' which`ing
' Eden ' garden in ' and rest`ed as and ' Men the ' ye ' from as Allah ' Jehovah
' on ' from as Allah ' Jehovah ' command as and ' 16 guard`ed of and ' serve`ed of
tree from and ' 17 eat you ' eat ' garden the ' tree ' all from ' say of ' Men the
' for ' and her from ' eat you ' not ' evil and ' good`ing ' knowledge the '
' Jehovah ' say as and ' 18 die`ing you ' die`ing ' and her from ' are eat ' day as in
' do`ed I ' and alone of ' Men the ' whom`ing the ' good`ing ' not ' from as Allah
' till`ing ' from as Allah ' Jehovah ' mould and , 19 and over are ' aid ' and of
fly`ing ' all ' ye and ' field`ed the ' you life ' all ' ye ' ground`ed the ' her
and of ' call as ' what ' you see of ' Men the ' to ' came as and ' heaven`s the '
name ' that`ing ' the life ' soul ' Men the ' and of ' call as ' which ' all and ,
' fly`ing of and ' cattle`ed the ' all of ' you name ' Men the ' call as and ' 20
' come ' not ' Men of and ' field`ed the ' you life ' all of and ' heaven`s the
on ' the stupefy you ' from as Allah ' Jehovah ' made Then . 21 and over are ' aid
' close as and ' him you rib from ' sister ' took as and ' slept as and ' Men the '
' rib the ' ye ' from as Allah ' Jehovah ' perform and ' 22 am has under ' flesh
' to ' the came`ing as and ' resemble I of ' Men the ' has from ' took of ' which
' as might from ' might ' move the ' such ' Men the ' say as and ' 23 Men the
' the man I from ' for ' resemble I ' call as ' such of ' as flesh from ' flesh and
ye and , and as father ' ye ' man I ' forsake as ' so ' on ' 24 such ' the take
' flesh of ' them two from ' and be`s and , and wife in ' cleave and , and mother '
and wife and ' Men the ' from as tote`ing ' them two ' and became as and ' 25 one
and six beset ' not and ,

INTRODUCTION 3

Gen 3:1-3:13

’ which ’ field`ed the ’ you life ’ all from ’ tote`ing ’ be`s ’ serpent the and ’ 1

’ for ’ anger ’ Woman the ’ to ’ say as and ’ from as Allah ’ Jehovah ’ do`ed

2 ’ garden the ’ tree ’ all from ’ and eat you ’ not ’ from as Allah ’ say

’ garden the ’ tree ’ fruit from ’ serpent the ’ to ’ Woman the ’ say you and

garden the ’ middle`ing in ’ which ’ this the ’ tree the ’ fruit from and ’ 3 eat has

’ and reach ’ not and , and her from ’ and eat you ’ not ’ from as Allah ’ say ’

’ Woman the ’ to ’ serpent the ’ say as and ’ 4 has and die`ing you ’ turn ’ and in

day as in ’ for ’ from as Allah ’ known ’ for ’ 5 has and die`ing you ’ die`ing ’ not

’ your as has eye ’ and clear shall ’ and her from , from are eat ’

’ 6 evil and ’ good`ing ’ as known ’ from as Allah are ’ complete as became and

’ for and ’ eat from of ’ tree the ’ good`ing ’ for ’ Woman the ’ look you and

bereave`s the of ’ tree the ’ desire has and ’ from as has eye of ’ that`ing ’ lust`ed

’ the man I of ’ also ’ has set and ’ eat you and ’ and fruit from ’ took you and ’

’ them two ’ as has eye ’ the has clear you and , 7 and eat as and ’ people`ed

’ the fig ’ am on ’ and sew as and ’ them ’ they`s town`s ’ for ’ and known and

’ voice`ing ’ ye ’ and hear as and ’ 8 you and restrain ’ them of ’ concoct as and

’ day as the ’ spirit is of ’ garden in ’ are hymm from ’ from as Allah ’ Jehovah

from as Allah ’ Jehovah ’ around from ’ and wife and ’ ground the ’ came at whom and

’ to ’ from as Allah ’ Jehovah ’ call as and ’ 9 garden the ’ tree ’ middle`ing in ’

’ are voice`ing ’ ye ’ say as and ’ 10 the sure`s ’ if ’ say as and ’ ground the

’ for whither ’ from and town`s ’ for ’ dread I and ’ garden in ’ as you hear

’ from and town`s ’ for ’ walk ’ my nation the ’ who ’ say as and ’ 11 came at I and

’ eat ’ as except of ’ are as whom command ’ which ’ tree the ’ has them ’ ye`ed

the set has ’ which ’ Woman the ’ ground the ’ say as and ’ 12 you eat ’ and her from

’ 13 eat and ’ tree the ’ has from ’ vessel ’ gave`ed ’ that`ing ’ as stand ’

' you as do ' such ' what ' resemble I of ' from as Allah ' Jehovah ' say as and

14 ' say as and ' eat and ' as has lift`s the ' serpent the ' Woman the ' say you and

execrate`ing ' such ' you as do ' for ' serpent the ' to ' from as Allah ' Jehovah

' on ' field`ed the ' you life ' all from and ' cattle`ed the ' all from ' ye`ed '

15 ' are as life ' week ' all ' eat you ' dust and ' walk you ' are grace will

' Woman the ' between in and ' are between in ' whom fire ' the enemy I and

' that`ing ' the seed ' between in and ' are seed ' between in and

16 ' heel ' and has overwhelm too you ' ye`ed and ' head ' are over whelm too as

' are shall vex ' increase`ed I ' increase`ed the ' say ' Woman the ' to and

' to and ' from as son ' as bore you ' shall vex in ' are s`shout`ing the and

17 ' Men of and ' against ' rule as ' that`ing and ' are you long`ing ' are man I

tree the ' has from ' eat you and ' are wife ' voice`ing of ' you hear ' for ' say

' and her from ' eat you ' not ' say of ' are as whom command ' which '

' the has eat you ' shall vex in ' are cross`ing in ' ground`ed the ' the execrate`ing

18 ' sprout`s you ' evermore, evermore and ' end`ing and ' are as life ' week ' all

19 eat you ' nose`s ' you sweat in ' field`ed the ' grass ' ye ' you eat and ' walk

you take ' her`ed from ' for ' ground`ed the ' to ' are carry`ing ' till ' fight '

20 ' call as and ' carry`ing you ' are dust ' to and ' ye`ed ' dust ' for '

' all ' mother ' whom`ed the ' that`ing ' for ' Eve ' and wife ' there ' ground the

21 ' and wife of and ' Men of ' from as Allah ' Jehovah ' do as and ' life

22 ' from as Allah ' Jehovah ' say as and ' from arm as and ' town`ing ' you and coat

' good`ing ' knowledge of ' and her from ' one are ' be`s ' ground the ' behold

' tree from ' also ' take and ' and hand ' send as ' turn ' the time and ' evil and

23 ' and the send as and ' from on`ing of ' life and ' eat and ' from as life the

' ground`ed the ' ye ' serve of ' Eden ' garden from ' from as Allah ' Jehovah

' nigh as and ' ground the ' ye ' exact as and ' 24 there from ' took of ' which
' devour ' ye and ' from as Cherub`ing the ' ye ' Eden ' garden of ' east from
' tree ' way ' ye ' guard of ' you overthrow complete the ' desolate the
from as life the

INTRODUCTION 4

' bore you and ' pregnant and ' and wife ' Eve ' ye ' known ' men the and ' 1
2 ' further and ' Jehovah ' ye ' man I ' as whom nest ' say you and ' Cain ' ye
' evil`ed ' Abel ' became as and ' Abel ' ye ' him brother ' ye ' you bore of
3 ' end from ' became as and ' ground`ed ' serve ' be`s ' Cain and ' flock
Jehovah of ' bestow`ed ' ground`ed the ' fruit from ' Cain ' came as and ' from week
4 ' and flock ' you and first from ' that`ing ' also ' came`s the ' Abel and '
' to and ' Abel ' to ' Jehovah ' salvation and ' has the as milk from and
5 ' save`ed ' not ' and you bestow ' to and ' Cain ' to and ' and you bestow
6 ' Jehovah ' say as and ' him turn ' and fell and ' especially ' Cain of ' delay and
7 ' are as turn ' and made has ' what of and ' walk ' hole`ed ' what of ' Cain ' to
' improve`s you ' not ' mother and ' arise ' improve`s you ' mother ' forward`ing
rule you ' ye`ed and ' and you long`ing ' struck to and ' crouch ' you sin ' open of
8 ' stroll has ' him brother ' Abel ' to ' Cain ' say as and ' and in '
Cain ' rise as and ' field`ed in ' complete him the in ' became as and ' field`ed the
9 ' to ' Jehovah ' say as and ' and kill`ed as and ' him brother ' Abel ' to '
' as you known ' not ' say as and ' are as brother ' Abel ' where`s ' Cain
10 ' you as do ' what ' say as and ' for whither ' as brother ' ing`guard the
ground`ed the ' has from ' Eli ' from as cry ' are as brother ' as blood ' voice`ing
11 rid`ed ' which ' ground`ed the ' has from ' ye`ed ' execrate`ing ' the time and '
12 ' are hand from ' are as brother ' as blood ' ye ' you take ' edge`ed ' ye '
' walk ' power`ed ' set ' further ' not ' ground`ed the ' ye ' serve you ' for
13 ' Jehovah ' to ' Cain ' say as and ' land in ' be`s you ' wander and ' keep
14 ' day as the ' near ' you exact ' behold ' help`ing from ' as low`ing ' great`ing
as whom became and ' demolish I ' are around from and ' ground`ed the ' around ' above
15 ' as has kill as ' as come ' all ' be`s and ' land in ' wander and ' keep '

' from as you swear too ' Cain ' kill ' all ' so of ' Jehovah ' if ' say as and
' group`ing the ' as except of ' ye`ing ' Cain of ' Jehovah ' site and ' rise as
' dwell and ' Jehovah ' as before from ' Cain ' out and ' 16 and come ' all ' and ye
' and wife ' ye ' Cain ' known and ' 17 Eden ' you east ' wander`ing ' land in
' town`s ' son`ed ' became as and ' Enoch`ing ' ye ' bore you and ' pregnant and
' 18 Enoch`ing ' and son ' there are ' town`s the ' there ' ye ' call as and
Mehujael ' ye ' bore as ' my town`s and ' Irad ' ye ' Enoch of ' bore him and
' of I buck`ing from and ' of I buck`ing from ' ye ' bore as ' to life`s from and '
' from as women ' twosome ' Lamech ' if ' took as and ' 19 Lamech ' ye ' bore as
' bore you and ' 20 shade`ed ' you two the ' there and ' till`ed ' sister the ' there
' tent ' dwell ' as father ' be`s ' that`ing ' Jabal ' ye ' till`ed
' be`s ' that`ing ' ing`produce ' him brother ' there and ' 21 nest`ed from and
' that`s ' also ' Zillah and ' 22 ing`crave and ' harp`ing ' handle ' all ' as father
of iron and ' copper has ' devise ' all ' hammer ' Cain ' Tubal ' ye ' bore`ed as
him women of ' Lamech ' say as and ' 23 pleasant`ed ' Cain ' Tubal ' sister`ing and '
the ear`s the ' Lamech ' as women ' as voice`ing ' has hear ' Zillah and ' till`ed '
as you connect of ' boy and ' as wound of ' as you kill ' man I ' for ' as you say '
' from as seven ' Lamech and ' Cain ' rise as ' from as you swear too ' for ' 24
' bore you and ' and wife ' ye ' till`ing ' ground ' known and ' 25 swear`ed too and
' from as Allah ' vessel ' Seth ' for ' Seth ' name ' ye ' call you and ' son
' also ' Seth of and ' 26 Cain ' and kill ' for ' Abel ' under ' after ' seed
' ing`block ' yet ' Enosh ' name ' ye ' call as and ' son ' bore as ' that`ing
' Jehovah ' spice ' call of

’ from as Allah ’ create ’ day as in ’ ground ’ you bore and you ’ report ’ this (1
’ female`ed and ’ male ’ (2 and ye ’ do`ed ’ from as Allah ’ liken`ing in ’ ground
’ ground ’ from there ’ ye ’ call as and ’ from ye ’ bless as and ’ from create
’ each and ’ from as three ’ ground ’ life as and ’ (3 from create the ’ day as in
’ ye ’ call as and ’ and image are ’ and liken`ing in ’ bore him and ’ the Year
’ and bore`s and the ’ as after ’ ground ’ week ’ and became as and ’ (4 Seth ’ name
’ from as son ’ bore him and ’ the Year ’ you and hundred ’ eight`ed ’ Seth ’ ye
’ life ’ which ’ ground ’ week ’ all ’ and became as and ’ (5 daughter`th`ing and
’ (6 die as and ’ the Year ’ from as three and ’ the Year ’ you and hundred ’ nine
’ ye ’ bore him and ’ the Year ’ each and ’ from two ’ five ’ Seth ’ life as and
’ Enosh ’ ye ’ and bore`s and the ’ as after ’ Seth ’ life as and ’ (7 Enosh
’ bore him and ’ the Year ’ you and hundred ’ eight`ed and ’ from two ’ seven
’ Seth ’ week ’ all ’ and became as and ’ (8 daughter`th`ing and ’ from as son
die as and ’ the Year ’ you and hundred ’ nine and ’ the Year ’ ten`ed ’ from twosome
(10 Cainan ’ ye ’ bore him and ’ the Year ’ from as nine ’ Enosh ’ life as and ’ (9
’ five ’ Cainan ’ ye ’ and bore`s and the ’ as after ’ Enosh ’ life as and ’
’ bore him and ’ the Year ’ you and hundred ’ eight`ed and ’ the Year ’ ten`ed
’ Enosh ’ week ’ all ’ and became as and ’ (11 daughter`th`ing and ’ from as son
life as and ’ (12 die as and ’ the Year ’ you and hundred ’ nine and ’ from two ’ five
’ (13 Mahalalael ’ ye ’ bore him and ’ the Year ’ from as seven ’ Cainan ’
’ Mahalalael ’ ye ’ and bore`s and the ’ as after ’ Cainan ’ life as and
’ bore him and ’ the Year ’ you and hundred ’ eight`ed and ’ the Year ’ from as four I
ten ’ Cainan ’ week ’ all ’ and became as and ’ (14 daughter`th`ing and ’ from as son
’ life as and ’ (15 die as and ’ the Year ’ you and hundred ’ nine and ’ from two ’
’ ye ’ bore him and ’ the Year ’ from as six and ’ from two ’ five ’ Mahalalael

descend ' ye ' and bore`s and the ' as after ' Mahalalael ' life as and ' 16 descend
bore him and ' the Year ' you and hundred ' eight`ed and ' the Year ' from as three '
' Mahalalael ' week ' all ' and became as and ' 17 daughter`th`ing and ' from as son '
' the Year ' you and hundred ' eight`ed and ' the Year ' from as nine and ' five
' the Year ' from as six and ' from twosome ' descend ' life as and ' 18 die as and
' as after ' descend ' life as and ' 19 Enoch`ing ' ye ' bore him and
' the Year ' from as eight and ' five ' Enoch`ing ' ye ' and bore`s and the
' from as son ' bore him and ' the Year ' you and hundred ' seven and
' seven ' descend ' week ' all ' and became as and ' 20 daughter`th`ing and
die as and ' the Year ' you and hundred ' eight`ed and ' the Year ' from as four I and
' bore him and ' the Year ' from as six and ' five ' Enoch`ing ' life as and ' 21
' from as Allah the ' ye ' Enoch`ing ' walk he as and ' 22 Methuselah ' ye
the Year ' you and hundred ' three ' Methuselah ' ye ' and bore`s and the ' as after
week ' all ' and became as and ' 23 daughter`th`ing and ' from as son ' bore him and '
' you and hundred ' three and ' the Year ' from as six and ' five ' Enoch`ing '
' from as Allah the ' ye ' Enoch`ing ' walk he as and ' 24 the Year
' life as and ' 25 from as Allah ' and ye ' took of ' for ' our whither`s and
' 26 Lamech ' ye ' bore him and ' the Year ' from as six and ' seven ' Methuselah
' three ' Lamech ' ye ' and bore`s and the ' as after ' Methuselah ' life as and
' bore him and ' the Year ' you and hundred ' six and ' the Year ' from as five and
' Methuselah ' week ' all ' and became as and ' 27 daughter`th`ing and ' from as son
' 28 die as and ' the Year ' you and hundred ' seven and ' the Year ' from as ten
' 29 son ' bore him and ' the Year ' from as five and ' three ' Lamech ' life as and
' our from rest as ' this ' say of ' Noah ' name ' ye ' call as and
' ground`ed the ' has from ' our as hand ' has and vex from and ' our as work from

' as after ' Lamech ' life as and ' 30 Jehovah ' the execrate ' which
bore`s him and ' the Year ' you and hundred ' six ' Noah ' ye ' and bore`s and the
' Lamech ' week ' all ' and became as and ' 31 daughter`th`ing and ' from as son '
' the Year ' you and hundred ' six and ' the Year ' from as five and ' three
' the Year ' you and hundred ' five ' son ' Noah ' became as and ' 32 die as and
Japheth ' ye and ' hot ' ye and ' there ' ye ' Noah ' bore him and

' around ' on ' increase of ' ground the ' sick the ' for ' became as and ' 6
' as son ' see as and ' 2 them of ' and bore as ' daughter`th`ing and ' ground`ed the
' be`th ' you good ' for ' ground the ' daughter`th`ing ' ye ' from as Allah the
' 3 and choose ' which ' all from ' from as women ' them of ' acquire as and
from on`ing of ' Men in ' as spirit is ' judge`ing as ' not ' Jehovah ' say as and
' hundred`ed ' and week ' and became and ' flesh ' that`ing ' additional in '
' land in ' him the ' from as fall the and ' 4 the Year ' from as ten and
as son ' and came as ' which ' so ' as after ' also and ' them the ' from as sea in
them of ' and bore him and ' ground the ' daughter`th`ing ' to ' from as Allah the '
' 5 there the ' as person ' from on`ing from ' which ' from as strong the ' them`ed '
' all and ' land in ' ground the ' bad ' increase`ed ' for ' Jehovah ' look as and
' 6 day as the ' all ' evil ' only ' and heart ' you and reckon from ' mould
' vex whom and ' land in ' ground the ' ye ' do`ed ' for ' Jehovah ' comfort as and
' which ' ground the ' ye ' wipe`ed I ' Jehovah ' say as and ' 7 and heart ' to
' till ' cattle`ed ' till ' men from ' ground`ed the ' around ' above ' as you create
' for ' as you comfort ' for ' heaven`s the ' fly`ing ' till and ' crawl
' to`ed ' 9 Jehovah ' as has eye in ' grace ' come ' Noah and ' 8 from as whom do
' be`s ' from as complete ' just`s ' man I ' Noah ' Noah ' you bore and you
' 10 Noah ' are hymm the ' from as Allah the ' ye ' him ing`generation in
ye and ' hot ' ye and ' there ' ye ' from as son ' three`ed ' Noah ' bore`s him and
' from as Allah the ' as before ' land the ' eradicate you and ' 11 Japheth '
land the ' ye ' from as Allah ' look as and ' 12 violence ' land the ' fill you and
and way ' ye ' flesh ' all ' you corrupt the ' for ' eradicate`ed has ' be`th and '
came ' flesh ' all ' end ' Noah of ' from as Allah ' say as and ' 13 land the ' on '
' them around from ' violence ' land the ' fill`ed ' for ' as before '

you box ’ walk ’ do`ed ’ 14 land the ’ ye ’ from you corrupt from ’ face behold and
’ box`ed the ’ ye ’ do`ed you ’ from as nest ’ brimstone ’ as tree ’
’ 15 is palm in ’ outside`ing from and ’ you house from ’ ye`ed ’ you is palm and
’ mother`ed ’ you and hundred ’ three ’ ye`ed ’ do`ed you ’ which ’ this and
’ from as three and ’ the large ’ mother`ed ’ from as five and ’ box`ed the ’ lenghten
mother`ed ’ to and ’ the box of ’ do`ed you ’ noon ’ 16 the you rise`ing ’ mother`ed
’ the sector ’ box`ed the ’ open and ’ the above of from ’ the has perfect ’
’ 17 do`ed you ’ from as three`s and ’ from two ’ from as under ’ there`s you
’ on ’ Water ’ flood`ing the ’ ye ’ came`s from ’ as behold`th ’ as whither and
’ spirit is ’ and in ’ which ’ flesh ’ all ’ eradicate`s the of ’ land the
’ 18 expire'ing ’ land in ’ which ’ all ’ heaven`s the ’ under from ’ from as life
’ box`ed the ’ to ’ brought and ’ are ye ’ as covenant`s ’ ye ’ as you verify and
’ 19 are ye ’ are as son ’ as women and ’ are wife and ’ are as son and ’ ye`ed
’ all from ’ from two ’ flesh the ’ all from and ’ life`ed the ’ all from and
’ female`ed and ’ male ’ are ye ’ you and life the of ’ box`ed the ’ to ’ came`s you
’ has from and ’ and the has kind ’ fly`ing the ’ has from ’ 20 and be`s as
’ ground`ed the ’ on ’ crawl ’ which ’ all from and ’ the has kind ’ cattle`ed the
’ are as to ’ and came as ’ all from ’ from two ’ and them as has kind
’ which ’ eat from ’ all from ’ walk ’ took ’ ye`ed and ’ 21 you and life the of
’ 22 eat`ed of ’ them of and ’ walk ’ be`s and ’ are as to ’ you gather and ’ eat as
’ so ’ from as Allah ’ and ye ’ command`ed ’ which ’ accord ’ Noah ’ do as and
do`ed

1 ' all and ' ye`ed ' came ' Noah ' to ' from as Allah ' Jehovah ' say as and '
' as before ' just`s ' as you seen ' are ye ' for ' box`ed the ' to ' are you house
2 ' the clean`ing the ' cattle`ed the ' all from ' this the ' evermore`ing in
' has from and ' female`ed and ' male ' the seven ' the seven ' walk ' implicate
' male ' from two ' from two ' that`s ' clean`ed ' not ' which ' cattle`ed the
3 the seven ' clean`ing the ' heaven`s the ' fly`ing from ' also and ' female`ed and
' around ' on ' seed ' you and life the of ' female`ed and ' male ' the seven '
4 ' for whither ' the seven ' till`ing ' from week of ' for ' land the ' all
' from as four I and ' day as ' from as four I ' land the ' on ' rain`s from
' which ' substance`ing the ' all ' ye ' as you life from and ' the night`s
5 ' which ' accord ' Noah ' do as and ' ground`ed the ' around ' above ' as whom do
6 ' the Year ' you and hundred ' six ' son ' Noah and ' Jehovah ' and command`ed
7 ' Noah ' came as and ' land the ' on ' Water ' be`s ' flood`ing the and
' box`ed the ' to ' and ye ' him son ' as women and ' and wife and ' him son and
8 ' the clean`ing the ' cattle`ed the ' has from ' flood`ing the ' who ' around from
' has from and ' clean`ed ' the has whither`s ' which ' cattle`ed the ' has from and
9 from two ' from two ' ground`ed the ' on ' crawl ' which ' all and ' fly`ing the
' which are ' female`ed and ' male ' box`ed the ' to ' Noah ' to ' and came '
10 you seven of ' became as and ' Noah ' ye ' from as Allah ' Jehovah ' command`ed
11 ' land the ' on ' him the ' flood`ing the ' as from and ' from week the '
' new in ' Noah ' as life of ' the Year ' you and hundred ' six the ' you Year in
' this the ' day as in ' new of ' day as ' ten ' the seven in ' two the
' increase`ed ' deep`ing ' you and purpose`s ' all ' and divide has
12 ' tifon the ' became as and ' and open has ' heaven`s the ' you and in light and
13 ' the night`s ' from as four I and ' day as ' from as four I ' land the ' on

’ Japheth and ’ Ham and ’ there and ’ Noah ’ came ’ this the ’ day as the ’ might in
to ’ from ye ’ him son ’ as women ’ you three and ’ Noah ’ wife and ’ Noah ’ as son
’ all and ’ the has kind ’ life`ed the ’ all and ’ them`ed ’ 14 box`ed the ’
’ land the ’ on ’ crawl the ’ crawl the ’ all and ’ the has kind ’ cattle`ed the
’ all ’ bird`ing ’ all ’ and the has kind ’ fly`ing the ’ all and ’ and the has kind
’ from two ’ from two ’ box`ed the ’ to ’ Noah ’ to ’ and came as and ’ 15 wing
’ 16 from as life ’ spirit is ’ and in ’ which ’ flesh the ’ all from
flesh ’ all from ’ female`ed and ’ male ’ female`ed and ’ male ’ from as came the and
Jehovah ’ close as and ’ from as Allah ’ and ye ’ command`ed ’ which are ’ and came ’
’ on ’ day as ’ from as four I ’ flood`ing the ’ became as and ’ 17 and till in ’
’ box`ed the ’ ye ’ and lift as and ’ Water the ’ and increase as and ’ land the
’ Water the ’ and strong as and ’ 18 land the ’ above ’ high you and
’ on ’ box`ed the ’ are hang and ’ land the ’ on ’ especially ’ and increase as and
’ on ’ especially ’ especially ’ and strong ’ Water the and ’ 19 Water the ’ around
’ from as peak`ed the ’ from as mountain the ’ all ’ and conceal as and ’ land the
’ mother`ed ’ ten`ed ’ five ’ 20 heaven`s the ’ all ’ under ’ which
from as mountain the ’ and conceal as and ’ Water the ’ and strong ’ the above of from
’ fly`ing in ’ land the ’ on ’ crawl the ’ flesh ’ all ’ expire`ing as and ’ 21
’ on ’ breed the ’ breed the ’ all in and ’ the life in and ’ cattle`ed in and
’ spirit is ’ you blow ’ which ’ all ’ 22 ground the ’ all and ’ land the
’ wipe as and ’ 23 and die ’ thus choose ’ which ’ all from ’ now`s in ’ from as life
’ men from ’ ground`ed the ’ around ’ on ’ which ’ substance`ing the ’ all ’ ye
and wipe as and ’ heaven`s the ’ fly`ing ’ till and ’ crawl ’ till ’ cattle`ed ’ till
box`ed in ’ and ye ’ which and ’ Noah ’ sure ’ remain as and ’ land the ’ has from ’
day as ’ each and ’ from as five ’ land the ’ on ’ Water the ’ and strong as and ’ 24

' life`ed the ' all ' ye and ' Noah ' ye ' from as Allah ' is remember as and ' 1

' cross as and ' box`ed in ' and ye ' which ' cattle`ed the ' all ' ye and

' 2 Water the ' and appease as and ' land the ' on ' spirit is ' from as Allah

' heaven`s the ' you and in light and ' deep`ing ' you and purpose`s ' and halt as and

' Water the ' and dwell and ' 3 heaven`s the ' has from ' tifon the ' finish`er and

' Water the ' and lack as and ' and carry and ' and walk the ' land the ' above

' box`ed the ' rest you and ' 4 day as ' each and ' from as five ' the end from

suggestive ' on ' new of ' day as ' ten ' the seven in ' as seven`s the ' new in

' till ' and lack and ' and walk the ' him the ' Water the and ' 5 me spittle the '

' as head ' see has ' new of ' one in ' as ten`s in ' as ten`s the ' new the

' day as ' from as four I ' end from ' became as and ' 6 from as mountain the

send as and ' 7 do`ed ' which ' box`ed the ' window`ing ' ye ' Noah ' open as and

' you wither ' till ' carry`ing and ' out`ing ' out and ' twilight the ' ye '

and ye from ' the Dove`ing the ' ye ' send as and ' 8 land the ' above ' Water the

' not and ' 9 ground`ed the ' around ' above ' Water the ' toast the ' you see of '

him to ' carry you and ' foot`ed ' sole ' rest`ing from ' the Dove`ing the ' come`ed

' send as and ' land the ' all ' around ' on ' Water ' for ' box`ed the ' to '

box`ed the ' to ' him to ' ye`ed ' came as and ' the took as and ' and hand ' ye

' send ' add and ' from as after ' from week ' you seven ' till`ing ' wait and ' 10

' him to ' came you and ' 11 box`ed the ' has from ' the Dove`ing the ' ye

' torn ' olivet`s ' on`ed ' be`th and ' twilight ' time of ' the Dove`ing the

' 12 land the ' above ' Water the ' toast ' for ' Noah ' known and ' edge`ed in

ye ' send as and ' from as after ' from week ' you seven ' till`ing ' wait as and

' 13 till`ing ' him to ' the carry`ing ' the add ' not and ' the Dove`ing the '

has and head`s in ' the Year ' you and hundred ' six and ' crush came ' became as and

' repent as and ' land the ' above ' Water the ' and desolate ' new of ' one in '

' and desolate ' be`th and ' look as and ' box`ed the ' conceal`ed from ' ye ' Noah

' from as ten and ' the seven in ' two the ' new in and ' (14 ground`ed the ' around

Noah ' to ' from as Allah ' word as and ' (15 land the ' wither`ed ' new of ' day as

' are as son and ' are wife and ' ye`ed ' box`ed the ' has from ' issue ' (16 say of '

' are ye ' which ' life`ed the ' all and ' (17 are ye ' are as son ' as women and

' crawl the ' all in and ' cattle`ed in and ' fly`ing in ' flesh ' all from

' land in ' and breed and ' are ye ' issue alas ' land the ' on ' crawl the

' him son and ' Noah ' out and ' (18 land the ' on ' and increase and ' and apart and

' all and ' life`ed the ' all and ' (19 and ye ' him son ' as women and ' and wife and

' land the ' on ' ing`crawl ' crawl the ' all and ' fly`ing the

' Noah ' son as and ' (20 box`ed the ' has from ' and out ' them as you at family of

' cattle`ed the ' all from ' took as and ' Jehovah of ' sacrifice from

offer`ing ' went and ' clean`ing the ' fly`ing the ' all from and ' the clean`ing the

' odour has the ' smell`s ' ye ' Jehovah ' smell as and ' (21 sacrifice from in '

' accurse of ' till`ing ' yield I ' not ' and heart ' to ' Jehovah ' say as and

' ground the ' heart ' mould ' for ' ground the ' cross`ing in ' ground`ed the ' ye

' ye ' you and smitten of ' till`ing ' yield I ' not and ' him youth from ' evil

' seed ' land the ' week ' all ' till ' (22 as whom do ' which are ' life ' all

' from day as and ' winter and ' end`s and ' Ham and ' cold`ing ' reap`s and

and desist as ' not ' the night`s and

' say as and ' him son ' ye and ' Noah ' ye ' from as Allah ' bless as and ' 1

2 ' land the ' ye ' and fill and ' and increase and ' form put ' them of

' you life ' all ' on ' be`s as ' from are dismay and ' from are I drop`ing and

' crawl you ' which ' all in and ' heaven`s the ' fly`ing ' all ' on and ' land the

3 and as set has ' from are hand in ' sea the ' as squirm ' all in and ' ground`ed the

' green are ' eat`ed of ' be`s as ' relate ' life ' that`ing ' which ' crawl ' all '

and blood ' and soul in ' flesh ' sure ' 4 total ' ye ' relate ' as set has ' grass

' from are as you soul of ' from are blood ' ye ' sure and ' 5 and eat you ' not '

ground the ' hand from and ' and has search I ' the life ' all ' hand from ' search I

pour ' 6 ground the ' soul ' ye ' search I ' him brother and ' man I ' hand from '

' image in ' for ' pour as ' and blood ' Men in ' ground the ' blood '

' form put ' from ye and ' 7 ground the ' ye ' do`ed ' from as Allah

' say as and ' 8 thus ' and increase and ' land in ' and breed and ' and increase and

' as whither and ' 9 say of ' and ye ' him son ' to and ' Noah ' to ' from as Allah

' ye and ' from are ye ' as covenant`s ' ye ' rise`s from ' as behold`th

' which ' life`ed the ' soul ' all ' ye and ' 10 your as after ' from are seed

' land the ' you life ' all in and ' cattle`ed in and ' fly`ing in ' from are ye

' 11 land the ' you life ' all of ' box`ed the ' as out ' all from ' from are ye

till`ing ' hew as ' not and ' from are ye ' as covenant`s ' ye ' as you verify and

' till`ing ' be`s as ' not and ' flood`ing the ' as they ' flesh ' all '

such ' from as Allah ' say as and ' 12 land the ' eradicate`s the of ' flood`ing the

' as between in ' gave ' as whither ' which ' covenant`s the ' ye`ing '

' which ' life`ed the ' soul ' all ' between in and ' your as between in and

' as set has ' as arch ' ye ' 13 from on`ing ' ing`generation of ' from are ye

' between in and ' as between in ' covenant`s ' loop`ing ' whom`ed the and ' cloud in

' sight`ed has and ' land the ' on ' cloud ' as cloud in ' be`s and ' (14 land the
' which ' as covenant`s ' ye ' as you is remember and ' (15 cloud in ' arch the
' life`ed the ' soul ' all ' between in and ' your as between in and ' as between in
' Water the ' till`ing ' be`s as ' not and ' flesh ' all in ' from are ye ' which
' arch the ' whom`ed the and ' (16 flesh ' all ' eradicate the of ' flood`ing of
' from on`ing ' covenant`s ' the is remember I of ' am sight`s and ' cloud in
' all in ' life`ed the ' soul ' all ' between in and ' from as Allah ' between in
such ' Noah ' to ' from as Allah ' say as and ' (17 land the ' on ' which ' flesh
' between in and ' as between in ' as arch the ' which ' covenant`s the ' ye`ing '
' Noah ' as son ' and became as and ' (18 land the ' on ' which ' flesh ' all
' Japheth and ' Ham and ' there ' box`ed the ' has from ' from as spring became
' Noah ' as son ' to`ed ' three`ed ' (19 Canaan ' as father ' that`ing ' Ham and
' man I ' Noah ' wait and ' (20 land the ' all ' scatter'ed ' to'ed from and
' has from ' drink as and ' (21 vineyard ' fix as and ' ground`ed the
' (22 and tent`ed ' middle`ing in ' rent as and ' merry as and ' has intoxicate the
' my told and ' him father ' skin`ing ' ye ' Canaan ' as father ' Ham ' look as and
' ye ' Japheth and ' Shem ' took as and ' (23 outside`ing in ' him brother ' two of
' and walk as and ' them two ' ridge ' on ' and site`s and ' raiment`ed
' them as father ' skin`ing ' ye ' and conceal as and ' whom has after
' (24 see ' not ' them as father ' skin`ing and ' whom has after ' them around and
' do`ed ' which ' ye ' known and ' and has intoxicate from ' Noah ' awake as and
, serve ' Canaan ' execrate`ing ' say as and ' (25 small the ' and son ' and of
' Jehovah ' bless`ing ' say as and ' (26 him brother of ' be`s as ' from as serve
' Japheth ' (27 and from of ' serve ' Canaan ' became as and ' Shem ' as Allah
Canaan ' became as and ' Shem ' as tent in ' nigh as and ' Japheth of ' from as Allah

’ three ’ flood`ing the ’ as after ’ Noah ’ life as and ’ 28 and from of ’ serve ’
all ’ and became as and ’ 29 the Year ’ from as five and ’ the Year ’ you and hundred
’ the Year ’ from as five and ’ the Year ’ you and hundred ’ nine ’ Noah ’ week ’
die as and

' Japheth and ' hot ' there ' Noah ' as son ' you bore and you ' to`ed and ' 1
' as son ' 2 flood`ing the ' as after ' from as son ' them of ' and bore him and
' ing`Meshech and ' Tubal and ' Javan and ' Madai and ' Magog and ' Gomer ' Japheth
' 4 Togarmah and ' Riphath and ' Ashkenaz ' Gomer ' as son and ' 3 Tiras and
' from as group ' Tarshish`s and ' Elishah ' between`ing ' as son and
' hence`s ' and disperse has ' to`ed from ' 5 from as ing`Dodan and
' and tongue of ' man I ' from you and land in ' from nation`ing the
' joy`ing ' hot ' as son and ' 6 them nation`ing in ' complete and at family of
' drunkard ' joy`ing ' as son and ' 7 Canaan and ' Put and ' from as Mizra and
the Raama ' as son and ' Sabtecha`ed and ' the Raama and ' the Sabta and ' Havilah and
' that`ing ' Nimrod`ing ' ye ' bore`s and the ' Joy'ing and ' 8 Deden and ' Sheba '
strong`ing ' be`s ' that`ing ' 9 land in ' strong`ing ' you and became of ' sick the
' strong`ing ' Nimrod`ing are ' say as ' so ' on ' Jehovah ' as before ' hunt`s '
' and you king from ' you as head ' became you and ' 10 Jehovah ' as before ' hunt`s
' 11 Shinar ' land in ' the has all and ' stronghold and ' lengthen and ' mingle
' ye ' son as and ' which`ing ' out ' that`s the ' land the ' has from
' ye and ' 12 at all ' ye and ' town`s ' you and large ' ye and ' the and progeny`s
' that`s ' at all ' between in and ' the and progeny`s ' between in ' has drip
' from as Lud ' ye ' bore as ' from as Mizra and ' 13 great`ed the ' town`s the
' 14 from as Naphtuh ' ye and ' from as Lehab ' ye and ' from as s`Anam ' ye and
there from ' and out ' which ' from as Casluhim ' ye and ' from as Pathrus ' ye and
' ye ' bore as ' Canaan and ' 15 from as Caphtor ' ye and ' from as Philista '
' as Jebus`ing the ' ye and ' 16 crush the ' ye and ' and first`ing ' has and hunt`s
ye and ' as Hivite the ' ye and ' 17 as Girgashite the ' ye and ' as Amar the ' ye and
' ye and ' as Arvad the ' ye and ' 18 as Sina the ' ye and ' as Arkite`ing the '

' and scatter'ed ' after and ' as Hamath the ' ye and ' as Zimar the
' as Canaan the ' border`ing ' became as and ' (19 as Canaan the ' you and at family
' Euphrates ' river ' great`ing the ' river the ' till ' from as Mizra ' river from
' hot ' as son ' to`ed ' (20 shall after the ' sea the ' till and
(21 them nation`ing in ' from you land in ' from you tongue of ' from you at family of
' Obara ' as son ' all ' as father ' that`ing ' also ' bore as ' Shem of and '
' Asshur and ' Elam ' there ' as son ' (22 great`ing the ' Japheth ' as brother
Hul`s and ' tree`ing ' highland ' as son and ' (23 Aram and ' Lud and ' Arpachshand and
' send and ' send ' ye ' bore as ' Arpachshand and ' (24 Mash`er and ' Gether and '
' there ' from as son ' two ' and bore as ' Obara of and ' (25 Obara ' ye ' bore as
' there and ' land the ' divid`ed has ' and week in ' for ' divid ' one the
extract ' ye and ' Almodad ' ye ' bore as ' Joktan and ' (26 Joktan ' him brother
' s`Uzal ' ye and ' Hadoram ' ye and ' (27 moon ' ye and ' Hazarmavath ' ye and '
' (29 Sheba ' ye and ' Abimael ' ye and ' of in eye ' ye and ' (28 Diklah ' ye and
' as son ' to`ed ' all ' Jobab ' ye and ' Havilah ' ye and ' ing`Ophir ' ye and
' the report ' here came ' lift they ' from sojourn from ' became as and ' (30 Joktan
' complete and at family of ' there ' as son ' to`ed ' (31 east the ' mountain
' to`ed ' (32 them nation`ing of ' from you and land in ' from you and tongue of
' them nation`ing in ' from you bore and you of ' Noah ' as son ' you and at family
as after ' land in ' from nation`ing the ' hence`s ' and disperse has ' to'ed from and
flood`ing the '

' from as word and ' sister ' lip`ed ' land the ' all ' became as and ' 1
the divide ' and come as and ' east from ' from go in ' became as and ' 2 from as one
' to ' man I ' and say as and ' 3 there ' and dwell and ' Shinar ' land in '
' the burn has and ' from as son of ' the white has ' handover`ed ' and shepherd is
' heass the and ' has father of ' white`ed the ' them of ' became you and ' burn`ed of
' our of ' the son has ' handover`ed ' and say as and ' 4 heass of ' them of ' be`s
there ' our of ' do`ed has and ' heaven`s in ' and head and ' great from and ' town`s
' Jehovah ' descend and ' 5 land the ' all ' around ' on ' scatter`ing ' turn '
' as son ' and son ' which ' great from the ' ye and ' town`s the ' ye ' you see of
' sister ' lip`ed and ' one ' people ' behold ' Jehovah ' say as and ' 6 ground the
defense as ' not ' the time and ' you concoct of ' dream the ' this and ' from all of
' up`ed has ' handover`ed ' 7 you concoct of ' plan as ' which ' all ' lag '
' ye ' man I ' and hear as ' not ' which ' from as ordain ' there ' the mix has and
' on ' there from ' from ye ' Jehovah ' drive Then ' 8 and shepherd is ' you lip
' 9 town`s the ' ye ' you and white ' and forbare as and ' land the ' all ' around
' there ' for ' mingle ' there`ed ' call ' so ' on ' great from the ' ye and
' there from and ' land the ' all ' you lip ' ye ' Jehovah ' mingle
' to`ed ' 10 land the ' all ' around ' on ' Jehovah ' from drive`s the
' ye ' bore him and ' the Year ' each ' son ' there ' there ' you bore and you
' there ' life as and ' 11 flood`ing the ' after ' from as you year ' Arpachshad
' you and hundred ' five ' Arpachshad ' ye ' and bore`s and the ' as after
all ' and became as and ' daughter`th`ing and ' from as son ' bore him and ' the Year
' Arpachshand and ' 12 die as and ' the Year ' you and hundred ' six ' there ' week '
send ' ye ' bore him and ' the Year ' each and ' from as three and ' five ' life
' three ' send ' ye ' and bore`s and the ' as after ' Arpachshad ' life as and ' 13

’ from as son ’ bore him and ’ the Year ’ you and hundred ’ three and ’ from two
’ eight`ed ’ Arpachshad ’ week ’ all ’ and became as and ’ daughter`th`ing and
14 die as and ’ the Year ’ you and hundred ’ four I and ’ the Year ’ from as three and
bore him and ’ the Year ’ each and ’ the Year ’ from as three ’ send ’ life as and ’
Obara ’ ye ’ and bore`s and the ’ as after ’ send ’ life as and ’ 15 Obara ’ ye ’
’ bore him and ’ the Year ’ you and hundred ’ three and ’ from two ’ three ’
’ three ’ send ’ week ’ all ’ and became as and ’ daughter`th`ing and ’ from as son
16 die as and ’ the Year ’ you and hundred ’ four I and ’ the Year ’ from as three and
’ the Year ’ each and ’ from as three and ’ four I ’ Obara ’ life as and ’
’ and bore`s and the ’ as after ’ Obara ’ life as and ’ 17 divid ’ ye ’ bore him and
’ the Year ’ from as you and hundred and ’ the Year ’ from as seven ’ divid ’ ye
’ week ’ all ’ and became as and ’ daughter`th`ing and ’ from as son ’ bore him and
’ 18 die as and ’ the Year ’ you and hundred ’ four I and ’ from two ’ four I ’ Obara
’ 19 tend ’ ye ’ bore him and ’ the Year ’ from as three ’ divid ’ life as and
from two ’ nine ’ tend ’ ye ’ and bore`s and the ’ as after ’ divid ’ life as and
’ from as son ’ bore him and ’ the Year ’ from as you hundred and ’
’ nine ’ divid ’ week ’ all ’ and became as and ’ daughter`th`ing and
’ 20 die as and ’ the Year ’ from as you and hundred and ’ from as three and
’ the Year ’ each and ’ from as three and ’ from twosome ’ tend ’ life as and
’ as after ’ tend ’ life as and ’ 21 tendril`ing ’ ye ’ bore him and
from as you hundred and ’ from two ’ seven ’ tendril`ing ’ ye ’ and bore`s and the
’ and became as and ’ daughter`th`ing and ’ from as son ’ bore him and ’ the Year ’
’ the Year ’ from as three and ’ nine ’ tendril`ing ’ week ’ all
’ tendril`ing ’ life as and ’ 22 die as and ’ the Year ’ from as you hundred and
’ 23 Nahor ’ ye ’ bore him and ’ the Year ’ each and ’ the Year ’ from as three

' Nahor ' ye ' and bore`s and the ' as after ' tendril`ing ' life as and
' daughter`th`ing and ' from as son ' bore him and ' the Year ' from as you hundred
' the Year ' from as three ' nine ' tendril`ing ' week ' all ' and became as and
' nine ' Nahor ' life as and ' 24 die as and ' the Year ' from as you hundred and
' Nahor ' life as and ' 25 old ' ye ' bore him and ' the Year ' from as seven and
' from as six and ' from two ' nine ' old ' ye ' and bore`s and the ' as after
all ' and became as and ' daughter`th`ing and ' from as son ' bore him and ' the Year
' the Year ' each and ' the Year ' from as four I and ' eight`ed ' Nahor ' week '
' ye ' bore him and ' the Year ' from as seven ' old ' life as and ' 26 die as and
' old ' you bore and you ' to`ed and ' 27 Haran ' ye and ' Nahor ' ye ' Abram
Haran and ' Haran ' ye and ' Nahor ' ye and ' Abram ' ye ' bore`s and the ' old
' old ' around ' on ' Haran ' die as and ' 28 Lot ' ye ' bore`s and the '
' 29 from as Chald ' well`ing ' and you bore and from ' land in ' him father
' wife ' there ' from as women ' them of ' Nahor and ' Abram ' took as and
' Haran ' daughter ' the king ' Nahor ' wife ' there and ' as captain ' Abram
as captain ' became you and ' 30 the sculpture ' as father and ' the king ' as father
' ye ' old ' took as and ' 31 bore as ' nihil ' whither`s ' exterminate'ed '
' ye and ' and son ' son ' Haran ' son ' Lot ' ye and ' and son ' Abram
Nahor and ' Abram ' wife ' and daughterinlaw`ing ' the king ' ye and ' as captain
' you walk of ' from as Chald ' Ur from ' from ye ' and spring as and ' him son '
' 32 there ' and dwell and ' parch ' till ' and came as and ' Canaan ' land`ed
' from as four I and ' from two ' five ' old ' week ' and became as and
parch in ' old ' die as and ' the Year ' from as you hundred and

' are land from ' walk ' walk ' Abram ' to ' Jehovah ' say as and ' (1
' land the ' to ' are as father ' you house from and ' are decree split`ing from and
' are bless I and ' great`ing ' nation`ing of ' are do I and ' (2 are look I ' which
' are as bless from ' bless`ed I and ' (3 bless`ed ' be`s and ' rug ' great`ed I and
' all ' against ' and bless has and ' light I ' are as accurse from and
' word ' which are ' Abram ' walk as and ' (4 ground`ed the ' you and at family
from two ' five ' son ' Abram and ' Lot ' and ye ' walk as and ' Jehovah ' him to
' took as and ' (5 parch from ' and you issue in ' the Year ' from as seven and '
ye and ' him brother ' son ' Lot ' ye and ' and wife ' as captain ' ye ' Abram
' which ' soul the ' ye and ' and property ' which ' from property`ing ' all '
' and came as and ' Canaan ' land`ed ' you walk of ' and out and ' parch in ' concoct
' ridge ' place`ing ' till ' land in ' Abram ' cross as and ' (6 Canaan ' land`ed
' look as and ' (7 land in ' yet ' as Canaan the and ' the ing`appear ' oak`ing ' till
' land the ' ye ' donkey ' are seed of ' if ' say as and ' Abram ' to ' Jehovah
(8 him to ' speak`ed the ' Jehovah of ' sacrifice from ' there ' son as and ' such the
' to ' you house of ' east from ' mountain`ed the ' there from ' leave as and '
' east from ' eye the and ' Water ' to ' you house ' and tent`ed ' extent and
' (9 Jehovah ' spice ' call as and ' Jehovah of ' sacrifice from ' there ' son as and
became as and ' (10 south`ed the ' go`ing and ' walk`ing the ' Abram ' onward as and
there ' guest`ing of ' the from as Mizra ' Abram ' descend and ' land in ' hunger '
approach`s the ' which are ' became as and ' (11 land in ' hunger the ' honour ' for '
be`th ' and wife ' as captain ' to ' say as and ' the from as Mizra ' came`ing of '
' be`s and ' (12 ye ' look`ed from ' Japheth ' Woman ' for ' as you known ' oh '
' such ' and wife ' and say and ' from as Mizra the ' are ye ' and look as ' for
' as sister ' oh ' as say ' (13 and life as ' are ye and ' near ' and kill and

’ the you life and ’ are cross`ing in ’ vessel ’ improve as ’ purpose of ’ ye
the from as Mizra ’ Abram ’ came`ing are ’ became as and ’ 14 are sake in ’ as soul
’ that`s ’ beautiful`ed ’ for ’ Woman the ’ ye ’ from as Mizra the ’ see as and ’
ye`ed ’ and glory as and ’ Pharaoh ’ as captain ’ ye`ed ’ see as and ’ 15 especially
’ Abram of and ’ 16 Pharaoh ’ he house ’ Woman the ’ took you and ’ Pharaoh ’ to ’
’ herd and ’ flock ’ if ’ became as and ’ the cross`ing in ’ improve`s the
’ you and slave and ’ from as serve and ’ especially ’ honour ’ purchase`ed
’ touch as and ’ 17 from as Camel and ’ you and donkey and ’ from as heass`ing and
’ and you house ’ ye and ’ from as great ’ from as touch ’ Pharaoh ’ ye ’ Jehovah
’ Abram of ’ Pharaoh ’ call as and ’ 18 Abram ’ wife ’ as captain ’ word ’ on
’ you proclaim ’ not ’ what of ’ vessel ’ you as do ’ such ’ what ’ say as and
’ that`s ’ as sister ’ you say ’ what of and ’ 19 that`s ’ are wife ’ for ’ vessel
took ’ are wife ’ be`th ’ the time and ’ resemble I of ’ vessel ’ ye`ed ’ took I and
and send as and ’ from as person ’ Pharaoh ’ and Mosthigh ’ command as and ’ 20 led ’
and blood ’ Lot and ’ if ’ which ’ all ’ ye and ’ and wife ’ ye and ’ and ye ’

' all and ' and wife and ' that`ing ' from as Mizra from ' Abram ' went and ' 1

especially ' honour ' Abram and ' 2 south`ed the ' and people ' Lot and ' if ' which

' him march of ' walk as and ' 3 gold in and ' silver in ' purchase``ed in '

' be`s ' which ' place`ing the ' till ' to ' you house ' till and ' south from

' between in and ' to ' you house ' between in ' begin`ed in ' and tent`ed ' there

' there ' do`ed ' which ' sacrifice them ' place`ing ' to ' 4 eye the

also and ' 5 Jehovah ' spice ' Abram ' there ' call as and ' the has and head`s in

6 from as tent and ' herd and ' flock ' be`s ' Abram ' ye ' enter the ' Lot of '

' be`s ' for ' together as ' desist of ' land the ' from ye ' help`ed ' not and '

' 7 together as ' desist of ' and all as ' not and ' increase ' from property`ing

' Abram ' purchase`ed ' pastoral ' between in ' increase`s ' became as and

as Periz the and ' as Canaan the and ' Lot ' purchase`ed ' pastoral ' between in and

' oh ' to ' Lot ' to ' Abram ' say as and ' 8 land in ' dwell ' yet '

' between in and ' are as between in and ' as between in ' the much`s ' be`s you

' from as brother ' from as person ' for ' are pastoral ' between in and ' pastoral

' oh ' disperse the ' are as before ' land the ' all ' forward`ing ' 9 and us I

' mother and ' the right`s the and ' the of left the ' mother ' as on from

him has eye ' ye ' Lot ' lift as and ' 10 the of as left the and ' the right`s the

' and all`ed ' for ' has desend the ' circle ' all ' ye ' look as and '

' ye and ' scorch ' ye ' Jehovah ' eradicate ' as before ' moisten`ed from

the Zoar ' here came ' from as Mizra ' land are ' Jehovah ' garden are ' Gomorrah`ed

onward as and ' has desend the ' circle ' all ' ye ' Lot ' if ' choose as and ' 11

' Abram ' 12 him brother ' above ' man I ' and disperse as and ' east from ' Lot '

' tent as and ' circle the ' as town in ' dwell ' Lot and ' Canaan ' land in ' dwell

' from as sin and ' from as evil ' scorch ' as person and ' 13 scorch ' till

' as after ' Abram ' to ' say ' Jehovah and ' 14 especially ' Jehovah of
' look`ed and ' are as has eye ' oh ' lift ' and people from ' Lot ' disperse the
' south`ed and ' the north`ing ' there ' ye`ed ' which ' place`ing the ' has from
look`ed ' ye`ed ' which ' land the ' all ' ye ' for ' 15 sea`ed and ' east`ed and
' as you there and ' 16 from on`ing ' till ' are seed of and ' the has give I ' walk '
' man I ' all him ' mother ' which ' land the ' dust are ' are seed ' ye
' rise`ing ' 17 right`ed ' are seed ' also ' land the ' dust ' ye ' you and her of
' walk ' for ' large`ed of and ' the lenghten of ' land in ' are hymm the
' as oak`ing in ' dwell and ' came as and ' Abram ' tent as and ' 18 the has give I
' sacrifice from ' there ' son as and ' Hebron`ing in ' which ' appear from
Jehovah of

Ellasor ' king ' Arioch ' Shinar ' king ' Amraphel ' week in ' became as and ' 1
' concoct ' 2 from nation`ing ' king ' Tidal and ' Elam ' king ' Chedorlaomer '
' king ' Birsha ' ye and ' scorch ' king ' evil in ' ye ' fight`ed from
' from as Zeboy ' king ' Shemebar and ' ground`ed ' king ' Shinab and ' Gomorrah`ed
valley ' to ' and connect ' to`ed ' all ' 3 little ' that`s ' worthless ' king and
the Year ' ten`ed ' from twosome ' 4 salt the ' sea ' that`ing ' from as field the '
' 5 and rebel ' the Year ' ten`ed ' three in and ' Chedorlaomer ' ye ' and serve '
' from as king the and ' Chedorlaomer ' came ' the Year ' ten`ed ' four I in and
' you and Astar in ' from as decease the ' ye ' and struck and ' and ye ' which
' from week that ' ye and ' cattle ' from as beast`ing the ' ye and ' from as horn
till ' gate`s ' from mount in ' as hole the ' ye and ' 6 from as city`s ' the vain in
' and dwell and ' 7 is wilderness the ' on ' which ' has I apart ' Ram`s '
' and struck and ' holy ' that`s ' discern from ' has eye ' to ' and came as and
' dwell the ' as Amar the ' ye ' also and ' as Amalek the ' field`ed ' all ' ye
' Gomorrah`ed ' king and ' scorch ' king ' out and ' 8 constant ' has and sever in
' that`ing ' worthless ' king and ' from as Zeboy ' king and ' ground`ed ' king and
from as field the ' valley in ' fight`ed from ' from ye ' and are town as and ' little
' from nation`ing ' king ' Tidal and ' Elam ' king ' Chedorlaomer ' ye ' 9
' the four I ' Ellasor ' king ' Arioch and ' Shinar ' king ' Amraphel and
' you and well ' from as field the ' valley and ' 10 five`ed the ' ye ' from as king
' Gomorrah`ed ' king and ' scorch ' king ' and flee as and ' heass ' you and well
' 11 sign ' mountain`ed ' from as remain has the and ' there`ed ' and fell and
all ' ye and ' Gomarrah`ed and ' scorch ' property`ing ' all ' ye ' acquire as and
' all ' ye and ' Lot ' ye ' acquire as and ' 12 and walk as and ' from eat '
' that`ing and ' and walk as and ' Abram ' as brother ' son ' and property`ing

' Abram of ' my told and ' escape`s the ' came as and ' 13 Sodom in ' dwell
' as Amar the ' appear from ' as oak`ing in ' nigh ' that`ing and ' as cross the
' as on in ' them and ' from Aner ' as brother and ' of and testicle ' as brother
' him brother ' carry`ed has ' for ' Abram ' hear as and ' 14 Abram ' covenant`s
ten ' eight`ed ' and you house ' as bore`s as ' him dedicate`s ' ye ' only as and
' part as and ' 15 judge ' till ' chase as and ' you and hundred ' three and '
' from struck and ' him serve and ' that`ing ' the night`s ' them as on
' 16 steward my of ' of left from ' which ' the hide`ing ' till ' from chase as and
' him brother ' Lot ' ye ' also and ' property`ing the ' all ' ye ' dwell and
' ye and ' from as women the ' ye ' also and ' carry`s the ' and property`ing and
and carry`ing ' as after ' and you call of ' scorch ' king ' out and ' 17 people the
' from as king the ' ye and ' sheaf of ' evermore are ' ye ' group`ing the from '
' 18 king the ' valley ' that`ing ' resemble`ing the ' valley ' to ' and ye ' which
' has intoxicate and ' fight ' issue`s alas ' whole ' king ' just ' as king and
' ye ' and bless`ed as and ' 19 has and mosthigh ' divinity ' priest ' that`ing and
' nest`ed ' has and mosthigh ' divinity ' Abram ' bless`ing ' say as and ' Abram
garden from ' which ' has and mosthigh ' to ' bless`ing and ' 20 land and ' heaven`s
' say as and ' 21 all from ' ten from ' if ' give as and ' are hand in ' are balm '
' property`ing the and ' soul the ' vessel ' give`ed ' Abram ' to ' scorch ' king
' as you high`s the ' scorch ' king ' to ' Abram ' say as and ' 22 walk ' took
' nest`ed ' has and mosthigh ' to ' from as Allah the ' Jehovah ' to ' as hand
' shoe ' tendril`ing ' till and ' thread`ing ' mother ' 23 land and ' heaven`s
' for whither ' say you ' not and ' walk ' which ' all from ' took I ' mother and
' and eat ' which ' only ' as beyond in ' 24 Abram ' ye ' as you ten the
' near ' and walk the ' which ' from as person the ' part and ' from as youth the

from part ' and took as ' them ' appear from and ' of and testicle and ' from Aner

' Abram ' to ' Jehovah ' word ' be`s ' these`ed ' from as word the ' after ' 1
garden from ' for whither ' Abram ' look as you ' to ' say of ' vision`ed from in
' Abram ' say as and ' 2 especially ' increase`ed I ' are merry and ' walk '
' ing`enter ' for whither and ' vessel ' has set ' what ' Jehovah ' as master
' 3 Eliezer ' steward my ' that`ing ' as you house ' steward ' son and ' as raise`s
son ' be`th and ' seed ' the set has ' not ' vessel ' behold ' Abram ' say as and
' him to ' Jehovah ' word ' be`th and ' 4 near ' possess as ' as you house '
' out ' which ' mother ' for ' this ' are posess as ' not ' say of
' and ye ' issue him and ' 5 are posess as ' that`ing ' are as bowel from
' report and ' the heaven`s the ' oh ' scan the ' say as and ' the outside`ing the
' if ' say as and ' from ye ' report of ' able you ' mother ' from as in star`ing the
' if ' the reckon as and ' Jehovah in ' beleive the and ' 6 are seed ' be`s as ' here
' which ' Jehovah ' as whither ' him to ' say as and ' 7 just`ed
' land the ' ye ' walk ' set of ' from as Chald ' Ur from ' are as you issue alas
' know ' height`ed ' Jehovah ' as master ' say as and ' 8 the net`ness of ' such the
' the calf ' vessel ' took`ed ' him to ' say as and ' 9 the has possess I ' for
' survive ' three from ' Ram`s and ' you three from ' Goat and ' you three from
' section as and ' to`ed ' all ' ye ' if ' took as and ' 10 of shear`ing and
' you call of ' and section ' ye ' man I ' give as and ' are section`ing ' from ye
' descend and ' 11 section ' not ' from as bird`ing the ' ye and ' and shepherd is
' 12 Abram ' from ye ' dwell and ' from as carcase the ' on ' swoop`s the
' on ' the fall ' stupefy`ed you and ' came`ing of ' sun the ' became as and
and Mosthigh ' you fall ' great`ed ' the dark ' the from hence ' be`th and ' Abram
' are seed ' be`s as ' guest ' for ' perceive ' known ' Abram of ' say as and ' 13
' four I ' from ye ' and low and ' from and serve and ' them of ' not ' land in

' which ' nation`ing the ' ye ' also and ' (14 the Year ' you and hundred

' property`ing in ' and out ' so ' as after and ' for whither ' judge ' and serve as

' from and peace in ' are as you father ' to ' income`ing ' ye`ed and ' (15 great`ing

' as four`s ' evermore`ing and ' (15 the good`ing ' the carry`s in ' bury you

(17 be`th ' till ' as Amar the ' low`ing ' whole ' not ' for ' be`th ' and dwell`ing

' flame`ing ' be`th and ' be`s ' dawn`ed and ' came`ed ' sun the ' became as and '

' from as desert the ' between in ' Obara ' which ' fire ' torch`s and ' smoke

covenant`s ' Abram ' ye ' Jehovah ' hew ' that`ing the ' day as in ' (18 these`ed

' river from ' such the ' land the ' ye ' as set has ' are seed of ' say of '

' ye ' (19 Euphrates ' river ' great`ing the ' river the ' till ' from as Mizra

' ye and ' (20 as has and east the ' ye and ' as tracker the ' ye and ' as nest`s the

' ye and ' (21 from as decease the ' ye and ' as Periz the ' ye and ' as Heth the

' ye and ' as Girgashite the ' ye and ' as Canaan the ' ye and ' as Amar the

as Jebus`ing the ' ye and ' as Hivite the

THE TORAH SCROLL 16

Gen 16:1-16:12

the slave ’ the maybe ’ if ’ bore`ed as ’ not ’ Abram ’ wife ’ as captain and ’ 1
’ Abram ’ to ’ as captain ’ say you and ’ 2 abide ’ there`ed and ’ whom Mizra ’
’ to ’ oh ’ came ’ you bore from ’ Jehovah ’ as kept have ’ oh ’ be`th
’ Abram ’ hear as and ’ her`ed from ’ son`ed I ’ as maybe I ’ as you slave
’ ye ’ Abram ’ wife ’ as captain ’ took you and ’ 3 as captain ’ voice`ing of
Abram ’ desist of ’ from two ’ ten ’ end from ’ he slave ’ whom Mirza the ’ abide
resemble I of ’ if ’ the man I ’ Abram of ’ ye`ed ’ has set and ’ Canaan ’ land in ’
’ conceive`ly the ’ for ’ look you and ’ pregnant and ’ abide ’ to ’ came as and ’ 4
’ to ’ as captain ’ say you and ’ 5 am has eye in ’ he strong ’ voice you and
’ as you slave ’ as set has ’ for whither ’ are as on ’ as violence ’ Abram
’ am has eye in ’ voice I and ’ conceive`ly the ’ for ’ look you and ’ are bosom at in
Abram ’ say as and ’ 6 are as between in and ’ as between in ’ Jehovah ’ discern as
’ nihil ’ as do ’ are as hand in ’ are you slave ’ be`th ’ as captain ’ to ’
’ shout you and ’ as captain ’ the low you and ’ are as has eye in ’ good`ing the
’ has eye ’ on ’ Jehovah ’ messenger from ’ the come as and ’ 7 the around from
’ say as and ’ 8 captain`ing ’ way in ’ has eye the ’ on ’ word from in ’ Water the
’ whither`ed and ’ brought ’ victual`ed ’ hence`ing ’ as captain ’ you slave ’ abide
’ for whither ’ as you strong ’ as captain ’ around from ’ say you and ’ as walk you
’ to ’ as carry`ing ’ Jehovah ’ messenger from ’ nihil ’ say as and ’ 9 you shoot
’ nihil ’ say as and ’ 10 the as hand ’ under ’ as low you the and ’ are you strong
not and ’ are seed ’ ye ’ increase`ed I ’ increase`ed the ’ Jehovah ’ messenger from
’ are behold ’ Jehovah ’ messenger from ’ nihil ’ say as and ’ 11 much ’ report as ’
for ’ Ishmael ’ name ’ ye ’ you call and ’ son ’ you bore as and ’ mountain`ed
ground ’ wild`ed ’ be`s as ’ that`ing and ’ 12 are as low ’ to ’ Jehovah ’ hear ’
’ him brother ’ all ’ around ’ on and ’ and in ’ all ’ friend`s ’ all in ’ and hand ’

' to ' ye`ed ' Eli`ed ' word the ' Jehovah ' there ' call you and ' 13 nigh as
seen ' as after ' as you seen ' from worship ' also the ' drop`ed I ' for ' seen`ed
' between in ' be`th ' seen ' Jawbone ' well ' well of ' call`ed ' so ' on ' 14
' son ' Abram of ' abide ' bore you and ' 15 hail ' between in and ' holy
' abide ' bore`ed as ' which ' and son ' there ' ye ' Abram ' call as and
' from two ' six and ' the Year ' from as eight ' son ' Abram and ' 16 Ishmael
Abram of ' Ishmael ' ye ' abide ' you bore in

' from two ' nine and ' the Year ' from as nine ' son ' Abram ' became as and ' (1

' to ' as whither ' him to ' say as and ' Abram ' to ' Jehovah ' look as and

the give I and ' (2 from as complete ' be`ing and ' as before ' are hymm the ' almighty

' the increase I and ' are between in and ' as between in ' as covenant`s '

' him turn ' on ' Abram ' fell and ' (3 especially ' especially in ' are ye`ing

' be`th ' as whither and ' (4 say of ' from as Allah ' and ye ' word as and

(5 from nation`ing ' shall them ' father of ' whom became and ' are ye ' as covenant`s

' rug ' be`s and ' Abram ' rug ' ye ' till`ing ' call as ' not and '

' (6 are as set has ' from nation`ing ' shall them ' father ' for ' Abraham

' are as set shall ' especially ' especially in ' are ye ' as you fruit the and

' as you verify and ' (7 and out ' with from ' from as king and ' from nation`ing of

are seed ' between in and ' are between in and ' as between in ' as covenant`s ' ye

' from on`ing ' covenant`s of ' from ing`generation of ' are as after '

' (8 are as after ' are seed of and ' from as Allah of ' walk ' you and became of

' land ' ye ' are as after ' are seed of and ' walk ' as set has and

' from on`ing ' you hold of ' Canaan ' land ' all ' ye ' are as pilgrimage

to ' from as Allah ' say as and ' (9 from as Allah of ' them of ' as whom became and

' are seed and ' ye`ed ' guard you ' as covenant`s ' ye ' ye`ed and ' Abraham '

' which ' as covenant`s ' such ' (10 from ing`generation of ' are as after

' are seed ' between in and ' your as between in and ' as between in ' and guard you

' (11 male ' all ' relate ' circumcise`ing the ' are as after

' whom`ed the and ' from are you foreskin ' flesh ' ye ' complete circumcise has and

' son and ' (12 your as between in and ' as between in ' covenant`s ' loop`ing

' male ' all ' relate ' split`ing as ' from week ' you eight

' silver ' you purchase and ' you house ' bore`s as ' from are as generation of

13 ' that`ing ' are seed from ' not ' which ' foreign ' son ' all from
' you purchase and ' are you house ' as bore`s as ' split`ing as ' circumcise`ing the
' covenant`s of ' your flesh in ' as covenant`s ' whom`ed the and ' are silver
' flesh ' ye ' split`ing as ' not ' which ' male ' foreskin and ' 14 from on`ing
that`s the ' soul the ' hew`ed shall ' as eight`s the ' day as in ' and you foreskin
' from as Allah ' say as and ' 15 broken ' as covenant`s ' ye ' am people from '
' there`ed ' ye ' call you ' not ' are wife ' as captain ' Abraham ' to
' also and ' ye`ed ' as you bless and ' 16 there`ed ' Sarah ' for ' as captain
' whom`ed the and ' the him you bless and ' son ' walk ' her`ed from ' as set has
' 17 and became as ' her`ed from ' from as people ' as king and ' from nation`ing of
' and heart in ' say as and ' Isaac and ' him turn ' on ' Abraham ' fell and
' Sarah ' mother and ' bore`s him I ' the Year ' you hundred`ed ' son of the
' to ' Abraham ' say as and ' 18 bore you ' the Year ' from as nine ' daughter the
' say as and ' 19 are as before ' am decide ' Ishmael ' Levi ' from as Allah the
' son ' walk ' you bore as ' are wife ' Sarah ' be`th ' mourn ' from as Allah
' as covenant`s ' ye ' as you verify and ' Isaac ' name ' ye ' you call and
Ishmael of and ' 20 him after ' and seed of and ' from on`ing ' covenant`s of ' and ye
' and ye ' as you fruit the and ' and ye ' as you bless ' be`th ' are as you hear '
' ten ' from two ' especially ' especially in ' and ye ' as whom increase the and
' ye and ' 21 great`ing ' nation`ing of ' him set shall ' bore`s him ' from as help`s
' Sarah ' walk ' bore you ' which ' Isaac ' ye ' from definite ' as covenant`s
' word of ' finish and ' 22 you after the ' Year`ed in ' this the ' season from of
' Abraham ' took as and ' 23 Abraham ' above ' from as Allah ' went and ' and ye
' ye and ' and you house ' as bore`s as ' all ' ye and ' and son ' Ishmael ' ye
' Abraham ' you house ' as person in ' male ' all ' and silver ' you purchase ' all

’ day as the ’ might in ’ complete foreskin ’ flesh ’ ye ’ Circumcise as and
’ son ’ Abraham and ’ (24 from as Allah ’ and ye ’ word ’ which are ’ this the
’ flesh ’ and circumcise thus ’ from as Year`ed ’ nine and ’ from as nine
’ the Year ’ ten`ed ’ three ’ son ’ and son ’ Ishmael and ’ (25 and you foreskin
’ day as the ’ might in ’ (26 and you foreskin ’ flesh ’ ye ’ and circumcise thus
’ all and ’ (27 and son ’ Ishmael and ’ Abraham ’ circumcise`ing has ’ this the
each ’ silver ’ you purchase and ’ you house ’ bore`s as ’ and you house ’ as person
and ye ’ and circumcise has ’ foreign ’ son ’

THE TORAH SCROLL 18

Gen 18:1-18:14

' that`ing and ' appear from ' as oak`ing in ' Jehovah ' him to ' look as and ' (1

' him has eye ' lift as and ' (2 day as the ' hot are ' tent the ' open ' dwell

' from as settle ' from as person`ing ' three`ed ' be`th and ' look as and

' tent the ' open from ' from you call of ' run as and ' look as and ' and Mosthigh

' oh ' mother ' as master ' say as and ' (3 land`ed ' the and humble`ly as and

' above ' and cross you ' oh ' to ' your as has eye in ' grace ' as you come

' your as foot ' and wash and ' Water ' less ' oh ' took as ' (4 are serve

' fight ' bit ' the took I and ' (5 tree the ' under ' and stay the and

' so ' on ' for ' and cross you ' after ' your in heart ' and support and

' which are ' do`ed you ' so ' and say as and ' your serve ' on ' from you cross

' say as and ' Sarah ' to ' tent`ed the ' Abraham ' soon as and ' (6 you word

' as do and ' as knead`ing ' flour ' mill ' measurement`s ' three ' as soon

' herd ' son ' took as and ' Abraham ' run ' herd the ' to and ' (7 you and bake

' you concoct of ' soon as and ' youth the ' to ' give as and ' good`ing and ' faint

' which ' herd the ' son ' ye and ' milk and ' curdle`ed ' took as and ' (8 and ye

' under ' them as on ' stand ' that`ing and ' them as before ' give as and ' do`ed

' are wife ' Sarah ' where`s ' him to ' and say as and ' (9 and eat as and ' tree the

' are as to ' carry`ing I ' carry`ing ' say as and ' (10 tent in ' be`th ' say as and

' you hear ' Sarah and ' are wife ' Sarah of ' son ' be`th and ' the life ' while

from as elder ' Sarah and ' Abraham and ' (11 him after ' that`s and ' tent the ' open

' manner ' Sarah of ' you and became of ' forbare ' from as sea in ' from as came '

' as after ' say of ' approach`ed in ' Sarah ' laugh you and ' (12 from as women are

' (13 elder ' as master and ' the pleasure ' vessel ' whom`ed the ' as zero in

say of ' Sarah ' laugh`ed ' this ' what of ' Abraham ' to ' Jehovah ' say as and

wonderful became ' (14 as you elder ' as whither and ' bore I ' from believe ' cook '

the life ' while ' are as to ' carry`ing I ' season from of ' word ' Jehovah from '
' for ' as you laugh ' not ' say of ' Sarah ' lie you and ' 15 son ' Sarah of and '
' there from ' and rise as and ' 16 you laugh ' for ' not`ed ' say as and ' look`ed as
walk the ' Abraham and ' scorch ' around ' on ' and gaze as and ' from as person the
' as whither ' amount`ed the ' say ' Jehovah and ' 17 from send of ' from people '
be`s as ' him the ' Abraham and ' 18 do`ed ' as whither ' which ' ye ' Abraham from
' all ' and in ' and bless has and ' might`ing and ' great`ing ' nation`ing of '
' which ' purpose of ' him you known ' for ' 19 land the ' as nation`ing
' him after ' and you house ' ye and ' him son ' ye ' Abraham ' command`ed as
' discern from and ' just`ed ' you concoct of ' Jehovah ' way ' and guard and
' word ' which ' ye ' Abraham ' on ' Jehovah ' came`s the ' purpose of
' for ' Gomarrah`ed and ' scorch ' you yell ' Jehovah ' say as and ' 20 and Mosthigh
oh ' up`ed I ' 21 especially ' the alone are ' for ' from you sin and ' increase`ed
mother and ' all`ed ' concoct ' Eli ' came`ed the ' he cry are the ' look`ed I and '
' from as person`ing the ' there from ' and turn as and ' 22 the know ' not '
' as before ' stand ' and has till`ing ' Abraham and ' Sodom`ed ' and walk as and
' just`s ' join`ed you ' cook ' say as and ' Abraham ' adduce and ' 23 Jehovah
' from as just`s ' from as five ' man ' as maybe I ' 24 evil`ness ' people
place`ing of ' lift you ' not and ' join`ed you ' cook ' town`s the ' middle`ing in
' 25 approach`ed in ' which ' from as just`s the ' from as five ' purpose of '
' just`s ' whom them of ' this the ' word are ' you and work ' walk ' the profane`s
' walk ' the profane`s ' evil`ness are ' just`s are ' be`s and ' evil`ness ' people
' say as and ' 26 discern from ' success`ed ' not ' land the ' all ' ing discern the
' middle`ing in ' from just`s ' from as five ' Sodom in ' come I ' mother ' Jehovah
' 27 from cross`ing in ' place`ing the ' all of ' as you help and ' town`s the

to ’ word of ’ as you slack the ’ oh ’ be`th ’ say as and ’ Abraham ’ low as and
’ has and lack as ’ as maybe I ’ 28 ashes and ’ dust ’ for whither and ’ as master ’
’ ye ’ the five in ’ eradicate`s sacred ’ the five ’ from just`s the ’ from as five
’ there ’ come I ’ mother ’ eradicate`s I ’ not ’ say as and ’ town`s the ’ all
say as and ’ him to ’ word of ’ till`ing ’ add and ’ 29 the five and ’ from as four I
’ not ’ say as and ’ from as four I ’ there ’ has and come as ’ as maybe I ’ him to ’
delay ’ oh ’ to ’ say as and ’ 30 from as four I the ’ cross`ing in ’ eradicate`s I
from as three ’ there ’ has and come as ’ as maybe I ’ the word I and ’ as master of ’
’ 31 from as three ’ there ’ come I ’ mother ’ eradicate`s I ’ not ’ say as and ’
as maybe I ’ as master ’ to ’ word of ’ as you slack the ’ oh ’ be`th ’ say as and
’ eradicate`s I ’ not ’ say as and ’ from as ten ’ there ’ has and come as ’
’ as master of ’ delay ’ oh ’ to ’ say as and ’ 32 from as ten the ’ cross`ing in
’ ten`ed ’ there ’ has and come as ’ as maybe I ’ move the ’ sure ’ the word I and
’ walk as and ’ 33 ten`ed the ’ cross`ing in ’ eradicate`s I ’ not ’ say as and
’ carry ’ Abraham and ’ Abraham ’ to ’ word of ’ all`ed ’ which are ’ Jehovah
and place of

' twilight in ' Sodom`ed ' from as messenger them ' two ' and came as and ' 1
' rise as and ' Lot ' look as and ' scorch ' gate in ' dwell ' Lot and
' say as and ' 2 land`ed ' toward`s ' the and humble`ly as and ' from you call of
' your serve ' you house ' to ' oh ' and repent`ing ' as master ' oh ' be`th
' from you ridge the and ' your as foot ' and wash and ' and stop`s and
' large`ing in ' for ' not ' and say as and ' from are way of ' from you walk the and
' him to ' and repent as and ' especially ' height ' urge as and ' 3 stop`s has
' feast`ed ' them of ' do as and ' and you house ' to ' and came as and
as person and ' and lay as ' suspend ' 4 and eat as and ' anger`ed ' unleaven`ing and
' youth from ' you house the ' on ' and converge ' scorch ' as person ' town`s the '
Lot ' to ' and call as and ' 5 the end from ' people the ' all ' elder ' till and
' and came ' which ' from as person`ing the ' where`s ' him to ' and say as and '
' comprehend`ed and ' our as to ' from spring`s the ' the night`s the ' are as to
' and close ' door the and ' open'ed the ' Lot ' them as to ' out and ' 6 from ye
' oh ' be`th ' 8 and evil you ' as brother ' oh ' to ' say as and ' 7 him after
' man I ' and known ' not ' which ' daughter`th`ing ' twosome ' vessel
' behold of ' concoct and ' your as to ' has ye`ed ' oh ' the issue`s and I
' to ' these`ed ' from as person of ' only ' your as has eye in ' good`ing are
' 9 as ing`city ' shade in ' and came ' so ' on ' for ' word ' and do you
' came ' one the ' and say as and ' the forward ' Ill`ed ' and say as and
' walk ' alarm's ' time`ed ' discern`ing ' also ' discern as and ' guest`ing of
' and adduce and ' especially ' Lot in ' man I in ' and urge as and ' lag
' energy ' ye ' from as person`ing the ' and send as and ' 10 door the ' is carry of
' door the ' ye and ' he house the ' them as to ' Lot ' ye ' and came`s as and
' you house the ' open ' which ' from as person the ' ye and ' 11 and close

' great`ing ' till and ' small from ' from as dazzle`ing in ' and smitten
' from as person the ' and say as and ' 12 open the ' come of ' and not as and
' inlaw ' talk ' walk ' who ' till`ing ' Lot ' to ' from as messenger them
' town`s in ' walk ' which ' all and ' are as daugther`th and ' are as son and
' from as eradicate`s from ' for ' this the ' 13 place`ing the ' has from ' issue alas
' ye ' from you cry ' great`ed ' for ' this the ' place`ing the ' ye ' and us I
out and ' 14 the eradicate`s the of ' Jehovah ' and has send as and ' Jehovah ' around
' say as and ' him daughter`th ' as take ' him inlaw ' to ' word as and ' Lot '
' for ' this the ' place`ing the ' has from ' and issue ' and rise`ing
' laugh from are ' became as and ' town`s the ' ye ' Jehovah ' eradicate`s from
' and hurry`s as and ' on`ed ' black the ' when are and ' 15 him inlaw ' as has eye in
ye and ' are wife ' ye ' took ' rise`ing ' say of ' Lot in ' from as messenger them
' join`ed you ' turn ' you and come has the ' are as daughter`th`ing ' twosome '
' and strength as and ' them`ed complete as and ' 16 town`s the ' low`ing in
twosome ' hand in and ' and wife ' hand in and ' and hand in ' from as person`ing the
' alas ing`out and ' and Mosthigh ' Jehovah ' you pity in ' him daughter`th '
' became as and ' 17 town`s of ' outside`ing from ' and the rest`s as and
on ' rescue the ' say as and ' the outside`ing the ' from ye ' from issue`s alas are
circle the ' all in ' stand you ' to and ' are as after ' glance`s ' to ' are soul '
' Lot ' say as and ' 18 join`ed you ' turn ' rescue the ' mountain`ed the '
' grace ' are serve ' come ' oh ' be`th ' 19 as master ' oh ' to ' them as to
' as stand ' you as do ' which ' are bow ' great you and ' are as has eye in
rescue the of ' able I ' not ' for whither and ' as soul ' ye ' you and life the of
' be`th ' 20 as die and ' evil`ed the ' as has cleave you ' turn ' mountain`ed the '
that`s and ' there`ed ' flee`ing of ' the approach`ing ' such the ' town`s the ' oh

' that`s ' is gain from ' forward`ing ' there`ed ' oh ' rescue`ed I ' is gain from '
' as you help ' be`th ' him to ' say as and ' 21 as soul ' the life you and
' ye ' as overthrow ' as except of ' this the ' word of ' also ' are as turn
not ' for ' there`ed ' rescue the ' mountain from ' 22 you word ' which ' town`s the
' call ' so ' on ' there`ed ' are came ' till ' word ' you concoct of ' able I '
' Lot and ' land the ' on ' out ' sun the ' 23 is gain`ing ' town`s the ' there
' Gomorrah`ed ' on and ' scorch ' on ' rain`s the ' Jehovah and ' 24 the Zoar ' came
' 25 heaven`s the ' has from ' Jehovah ' each ' fire and ' you as brimstone
' circle the ' all ' ye and ' these ' from as town the ' ye ' overthrow as and
' 26 ground`ed the ' sprout and ' from as town the ' as dwell ' all ' ye and
' 27 salt ' settle`s ' became you and ' and as after from ' and wife ' glance and
there ' stand ' which ' place`ing the ' to ' is morn in ' Abraham ' ridge as and
Gomarrah`ed and ' scorch ' around ' on ' gaze as and ' 28 Jehovah ' around ' ye '
' on`ed ' be`th and ' look as and ' circle the ' land ' all ' around ' on and '
' became as and ' 29 has footstool the ' is and mere`s are ' land the ' is and mere`s
' is remember as and ' circle the ' watch ' ye ' from as Allah ' eradicate`s the in
' middle`ing from ' Lot ' ye ' send as and ' Abraham ' ye ' from as Allah
' thick ' dwell ' which ' from as town the ' ye ' overthrow in ' overthrow`ed the
' twosome and ' blemish ' dwell and ' is gain`ing from ' Lot ' went and ' 30 Lot
dwell and ' is gain`ing in ' desist of ' dread ' for ' and people ' him daughter`th
' 31 and people ' him daughter`th ' twosome and ' that`ing ' the cave in '
' elder ' our as father ' the little`s the ' to ' the first`s the ' say you and
land the ' all ' way are ' our as on ' came`ing of ' land in ' whither`s ' man I and
' the lay shall ' between`s ' our as father ' ye ' moisten`ed has ' here`s of ' 32
' 33 seed ' our as father from ' the life has and ' and people

’ the night`s in ’ between`s ’ has am father ’ ye ’ the has as moisten you and
not and ’ am father ’ ye ’ lay you and ’ the first`s the ’ came you and ’ that`ing
’ you tomorrow from ’ became as and ’ (34 the rise`ing in and ’ the lay in ’ known ’
’ as you lay ’ be`th ’ the little`s the ’ to ’ the first`s the ’ say you and
’ also ’ between`s ’ and has moisten has ’ as father ’ ye ’ lastnight
’ the life has and ’ and people ’ as lay ’ as came and ’ the night`s the
’ the night`s in ’ also ’ the has as moisten you and ’ (35 seed ’ our as father from
’ the little`s the ’ rise you and ’ between`s ’ has am father ’ ye ’ that`ing the
’ (36 the rise`ing in and ’ the lay in ’ known ’ not and ’ and people ’ lay you and
’ (37 has am father from ’ Lot ’ daughter`th`ing ’ twosome ’ the has as pregnant and
’ Moab ’ name ’ ye ’ call you and ’ son ’ the first`s the ’ bore you and
’ also ’ the little`s the and ’ (38 day as the ’ till ’ Moab ’ as father ’ that`ing
that`ing ’ as people ’ son ’ name ’ ye ’ call you and ’ son ’ bore`ed as ’ that`s
day as the ’ till ’ Ammon ’ as son ’ as father ’

' dwell and ' south the ' land`ed ' Abraham ' there from ' onward as and ' 1
' 2 Gerar in ' guest as and ' captain`ing ' between in and ' holy ' between in
' send as and ' that`s ' as sister ' and wife ' Sarah ' to ' Abraham ' say as and
' came as and ' 3 Sarah ' ye ' took as and ' expatriate ' king ' Abimelech
' if ' say as and ' the night`s the ' dream`ing in ' Abimelech ' to ' from as Allah
' that`s and ' you take ' which ' Woman the ' on ' concern`ing ' die ' are behold
' say as and ' Eli`ed ' approach ' not ' Abimelech and ' 4 marry ' you marry`s
' that`ing ' forward`ing ' 5 kill you ' just`s ' also ' nation`ing the ' as master
' drop`ed I ' that`ing ' also ' that`s and ' that`s ' as sister ' vessel ' say
as palm ' has and innocent in and ' as in heart ' complete in ' that`ing ' as brother
' dream`ing in ' from as Allah the ' him to ' say as and ' 6 such ' as whom do '
' you as do ' are in heart ' complete in ' for ' as you known ' for whither ' also
' vessel ' the sin`ing from ' are ye`ing ' for whither ' also ' are held and ' such
' carry the ' the time and ' 7 Eli`ed ' touch of ' are as set has ' not ' so ' on
are till in ' praise whom and ' that`ing ' prophet`s ' for ' man that ' wife ' ye
die`ing ' for ' opinion ' carry`s from ' are whither`s ' mother and ' the life and '
' Abimelech ' ridge as and ' 8 walk ' which ' all and ' ye`ed ' die`ing you '
' all ' ye ' word as and ' him serve ' all of ' call as and ' is morn in
' all ' and dread as and ' them as ear in ' these`ed ' from as word the
say as and ' Abraham of ' Abimelech ' call as and ' 9 especially ' from as person the
brought the ' for ' walk ' as you sin ' what and ' our of ' you as do ' what ' if '
' which ' from as work ' great`ed ' sin`ed ' as you king from ' on and ' mosthigh '
' to ' Abimelech ' say as and ' 10 as stand ' you as do ' shall do as ' not
' 11 this the ' word the ' ye ' you as do ' for ' you seen ' what ' Abraham
' whither`s ' only ' as you say ' for ' as you dread ' for ' Abraham ' say as and

word ' on ' as shall kill and ' this the ' place`ing in ' from as Allah ' you dread
as father ' daughter ' that`s ' as sister ' from believe`ed ' also and ' 12 as wife '
resemble I of ' vessel ' became you and ' Ami ' daughter ' not ' sure ' that`ing '
' from as Allah ' near ' seduce`ed the ' which are ' became as and ' 13
' nihil ' say and ' as you bore and from ' as bitter and ' as father ' you house from
' place`ing the ' all ' to ' as stand ' has as do you ' which ' are bow ' this
' 14 that`ing ' as brother ' vessel ' as say ' there`ed ' prophet`ing ' which
' herd and ' flock and ' silver ' thousand ' Abimelech ' took as and
' if ' dwell and ' Abraham of ' give as and ' you and slave and ' from as serve and
are as before ' as land ' be`th ' Abimelech ' say as and ' 15 and wife ' Sarah ' ye
' be`th ' say ' Sarah of and ' 16 carry ' are as has eye in ' good`ing in '
' walk ' that`ing ' be`th ' are as brother of ' silver ' thousand ' as set has
' total ' ye and ' are ye ' which ' all of and ' from as has eye ' garment`ing
' from as Allah the ' to ' Abraham ' praise whom and ' 17 you ing`behalf and
' and wife ' ye and ' Abimelech ' ye ' from as Allah ' decease as and
' Jehovah ' festival ' festival ' for ' 18 and bore as and ' him you mother`ed and
word ' on ' Abimelech ' you house of ' compassion ' all ' till in ' from as Allah
Abraham ' wife ' Sarah '

THE TORAH SCROLL 21

' Jehovah ' do as and ' say ' which are ' Sarah ' ye ' punish ' Jehovah and ' (1
' Abraham of ' Sarah ' bore you and ' pregnant and ' (2 word ' which are ' Sarah of
' (3 from as Allah ' and ye ' word ' which ' season from of ' him elder of ' son
' which ' if ' child has the ' and son ' there ' ye ' Abraham ' call as and
' Isaac ' ye ' Abraham ' Circumcise as and ' (4 Isaac ' Sarah ' if ' bore`ed as
' and ye ' command`ed ' which are ' from week ' you eight ' son ' and son
' ye ' if ' bore alas in ' the Year ' each ' son ' Abraham and ' (5 from as Allah
from as Allah ' vessel ' do`ed ' laugh`ed ' Sarah ' say you and ' (6 and son ' Isaac
' Abraham of ' utter ' who ' say you and ' (7 vessel ' Isaac ' hear the ' all '
him elder of ' son ' if ' as you bore as ' for ' Sarah ' from as son ' the suck`s the
' feast`ed ' Abraham ' do as and ' wean as and ' boy the ' great as and ' (8
' Sarah ' look you and ' (9 and son ' Isaac ' ye ' wean the ' day as in ' great`ing
(10 laugh from ' Abraham of ' bore`ed as ' which ' whom Mirza the ' abide ' son ' ye
' ye and ' such the ' mother`ed the ' ye ' exact ' Abraham of ' say you and '
' as son ' people ' such the ' mother`ed the ' son ' possess as ' not ' for ' son`ed
' Abraham ' as has eye in ' especially ' word the ' evil as and ' (11 Isaac ' people
' to ' Abraham ' to ' from as Allah ' say as and ' (12 and son ' concern`ing ' on
' which ' all ' are you mother ' on and ' youth the ' on ' are as has eye in ' sore
' call as ' Isaac in ' for ' the voice`ing in ' hear ' Sarah ' are as to ' say you
' nation`ing of ' such the ' mother`ed the ' son ' ye ' also and ' (13 seed ' walk
' ridge as and ' (14 that`ing ' are seed ' for ' and has there`s I ' great`ing
' give as and ' Water ' hotspring and ' fight ' took as and ' is morn in ' Abraham
' send`ed as and ' boy the ' ye and ' ridge`ed ' on ' there ' abide ' to
' and all as and ' (15 seven ' well ' word from in ' have set and ' are hang and
one ' under ' boy the ' ye ' hurl you and ' hotspring the ' has from ' Water the

' over from ' nihil ' carry you and ' are hang and ' 16 from as humble the '
' cat`ed ' to ' drop`ed I ' for ' arch ' grind`ing from are ' the get`s the
' voice`ed ' ye ' lift you and ' over from ' carry you and ' boy the ' die`ing in
call as and ' youth the ' voice`ing ' ye ' from as Allah ' hear as and ' 17 sob and
say as and ' heaven`s the ' has from ' abide ' to ' from as Allah ' messenger from '
' from as Allah ' hear ' for ' as dread you ' to ' abide ' walk ' what ' nihil '
as lift ' as rise`ing ' 18 there ' that`ing ' which in ' youth the ' voice`ing ' to
' for ' and in ' are hand ' ye ' as strength`s the and ' youth the ' ye '
ye ' from as Allah ' clear as and ' 19 and has there`s I ' great`ing ' nation`ing of
' ye ' fill you and ' are hang and ' Water ' well ' look you and ' am has eye '
' became as and ' 20 youth the ' ye ' moisten you and ' Water ' hotspring the
' word from in ' dwell and ' great as and ' youth the ' ye ' from as Allah
' has I apart ' word from in ' dwell and ' 21 arch ' increase`ed ' became as and
' 22 from as Mizra ' land from ' Woman ' and mother ' if ' took you and
captain ' Phicol and ' Abimelech ' say as and ' that`s the ' time in ' became as and
which ' all in ' are people ' from as Allah ' say of ' Abraham ' to ' and mass '
' from as Allah in ' vessel ' swear`ed too the ' the time and ' 23 do`ed ' ye`ed '
' as over of and ' as progeny`s of and ' vessel ' is moisten you ' mother ' be`th
' as stand ' do`ed you ' are people ' as whom do ' which ' my spare are and
' Abraham ' say as and ' 24 thus ' he guest ' which ' land the ' people and
on ' Abimelech ' ye ' Abraham ' power`s alas and ' 25 swear too I ' for whither
' 26 Abimelech ' as serve ' and tear ' which ' Water the ' well ' concern`ing '
' word the ' ye ' do`ed ' who ' as you known ' not ' Abimelech ' say as and
' for whither ' also and ' vessel ' you proclaim ' not ' ye`ed ' also and ' this the
' flock ' Abraham ' took as and ' 27 day as the ' as zero in ' as you hear ' not

' 28 covenant`s ' them two ' and hew as and ' Abimelech of ' give as and ' herd and
' flock the ' drink`ing in are ' seven ' ye ' Abraham ' establish as and
seven ' be`th ' what ' Abraham ' to ' Abimelech ' say as and ' 29 has alone`ed of
say as and ' 30 has alone`ed of ' grip the ' which ' these`ed ' drink`ing in are the '
' as hand from ' implicate ' drink`ing in are the ' seven ' ye ' for ' Abraham '
' well the ' ye ' as forth at ' for ' till`ed of ' vessel ' be`s you ' cross`ing in
' for ' seven ' well ' that`ing the ' place`ing of ' call ' so ' on ' 31 such the
' well in ' covenant`s ' and hew as and ' 32 them two ' and swear too has ' there
' and dwell and ' and mass ' captain ' Phicol and ' Abimelech ' rise as and ' seven
seven ' well in ' grove ' Abraham ' fix as and ' 33 from as Philista ' land ' to
' guest as and ' 34 from on`ing ' to ' Jehovah ' spice ' there ' call as and '
from as increase ' from week ' from as Philista ' land in ' Abraham

' from as Allah the and ' these`ed ' from as word the ' after ' became as and ' 1
' say as and ' Abraham ' him to ' say as and ' Abraham ' ye ' flee`ed
' are darl`s as ' ye ' are son ' ye ' oh ' took ' say as and ' 2 as behold`th
' am ing`appear the ' land ' to ' walk ' led ' Isaac ' ye ' you love ' which
' which ' from as mountain the ' one ' on ' on`ed of ' there ' and on`ed the and
' ye ' saddle as and ' is morn in ' Abraham ' ridge as and ' 3 are as to ' say
' Isaac ' ye and ' and ye ' him youth ' two ' ye ' took as and ' and heass`ing
' to ' walk as and ' rise as and ' on`ed ' as tree ' divide as and ' and son
' day as in ' 4 from as Allah the ' if ' say ' which ' place`ing the
' ye ' look as and ' him has eye ' ye ' Abraham ' lift as and ' as three`s the
' sparkle ' him youth ' to ' Abraham ' say as and ' 5 get from ' place`ing the
walk`ed has ' youth the and ' as whither and ' heass`ing the ' people ' talk ' relate
' 6 your as to ' the carry`ing has and ' the and humble`ly has and ' here ' till '
' Isaac ' on ' site and ' on`ed the ' as tree ' ye ' Abraham ' took as and
' you of knife the ' ye and ' fire the ' ye ' and hand in ' took as and ' and son
' Abraham ' to ' Isaac ' say as and ' 7 together as ' them two ' and walk as and
say as and ' as son ' as behold`th ' say as and ' as father ' say as and ' him father
' 8 on`ed of ' Lamb the ' where`s and ' from as tree the and ' fire the ' be`th '
' on`ed of ' Lamb the ' if ' look`ed as ' from as Allah ' Abraham ' say as and
' to ' and came as and ' 9 together as ' them two ' and walk as and ' as son
' there ' son as and ' from as Allah the ' if ' say ' which ' place`ing the
tie as and ' from as tree the ' ye ' pile as and ' sacrifice them ' ye ' Abraham
' above from ' sacrifice them ' on ' and ye ' site and ' and son ' Isaac ' ye '
' ye ' took as and ' and hand ' ye ' Abraham ' send as and ' 10 from as tree of
messenger from ' him to ' call as and ' 11 and son ' ye ' slay of ' you of knife the

say as and ' Abraham ' Abraham ' say as and ' heaven`s the ' has from ' Jehovah '
' youth the ' on I ' are hand ' send you ' to ' say as and ' 12 as behold`th '
' dread ' for ' as you known ' time`ed ' for ' the noth`ing ' if ' do you ' to and
' are darl`s as ' ye ' are son ' ye ' hedge at ' not and ' ye`ed ' from as Allah
' look as and ' him has eye ' ye ' Abraham ' lift as and ' 13 apportion from
' walk as and ' him horn in ' entwine in ' hold has ' after ' Ram`s ' be`th and
' under ' on`ed of ' and went`ed and ' Ram`s the ' ye ' took as and ' Abraham
' that`ing the ' place`ing the ' there ' ye ' Abraham ' call as and ' 14 and son
look`ed as ' Jehovah ' blemish ' day as the ' say as ' which ' look`ed as ' Jehovah
' has from ' you two ' Abraham ' to ' Jehovah ' messenger from ' call as and ' 15
' for ' Jehovah ' state ' as you swear too has ' house ' say as and ' 16 heaven`s the
ye ' hedge at ' not and ' this the ' word the ' ye ' you as do ' which ' because
' are bless I ' bless`ing ' for ' 17 apportion from ' are darl`s as ' ye ' are son '
' as in star`ing are ' are seed ' ye ' increase`ed I ' increase`ed the and
' possess and ' sea the ' you lip ' on ' which ' of sand are and ' heaven`s the
' all ' are seed in ' and bless sacred and ' 18 him enemy I ' gate ' ye ' are seed
' dwell and ' 19 as voice`ing in ' you hear ' which ' heel ' land the ' as nation`ing
to ' together as ' and walk as and ' and rise as and ' him youth ' to ' Abraham
' became as and ' 20 seven ' well in ' Abraham ' dwell and ' seven ' well '
' be`th ' say of ' Abraham of ' my told and ' these`ed ' from as word the ' as after
' 21 are as brother ' Nahor of ' from as son ' that`s ' also ' the king ' bore`ed as
' ye and ' him brother ' spoil`ing ' ye and ' and first`ing ' tree`ing ' ye
' ye and ' and vision ' ye and ' Chald ' ye and ' 22 highland ' as father ' Kemuel
' bore`s and the ' Bethuel and ' 23 Bethuel ' ye and ' by hand ' ye and ' s`Pildash
' as brother ' Nahor of ' the king ' bore`ed as ' to`ed ' eight`ed ' Rebekeh ' ye

' bore you and ' Reumah ' there`ed and ' and concubine as put and ' 24 Abraham

' ye and ' badger ' ye and ' from gush ' ye and ' butcher ' ye ' that`s ' also

bruise`ed

’ from as ten and ’ the Year ’ hundred`ed ’ Sarah ’ as life ’ and became as and ’ 1
’ Sarah ’ die you and ’ 2 Sarah ’ as life ’ two ’ from two ’ seven and ’ the Year
’ Canaan ’ land in ’ Hebron`ing ’ that`s ’ valley ’ to ’ four that ’ city`s in
’ rise as and ’ 3 the weep`ing of and ’ Sarah of ’ fret of ’ Abraham ’ came as and
4 say of ’ crush ’ as son ’ to ’ word as and ’ and die ’ around ’ above ’ Abraham
you hold ’ vessel ’ and give ’ your people ’ for whither ’ sojourn you and ’ guest ’
’ 5 as before from ’ extent ’ ye ’ bury`ed I and ’ your people ’ bury ’
’ our hear ’ 6 not`ing ’ say of ’ Abraham ’ ye ’ crush ’ as son ’ and low as and
’ choose from in ’ our middle`ing in ’ ye`ed ’ from as Allah ’ lift`s has ’ as master
’ not ’ and bury ’ ye ’ and her from ’ man I ’ are die ’ ye ’ bury ’ our as bury
’ Abraham ’ rise as and ’ 7 are die ’ bury from ’ with from ’ all`ed as
’ word as and ’ 8 crush ’ as son of ’ land the ’ people of ’ the and humble`ly as and
’ extent ’ ye ’ bury of ’ from are soul ’ arise as ’ mother ’ say of ’ from ye
’ son ’ Ephron`ing in ’ vessel ’ and entreat and ’ as shall hear ’ as before from
which ’ fold`ed them ’ you cave ’ ye ’ vessel ’ give as and ’ 9 as Heth the ’ noon
vessel ’ reward`ed as ’ fill ’ silver in ’ and field`ed ’ the end in ’ which ’ if ’
middle`ing in ’ dwell ’ Ephron`ing and ’ 10 bury ’ you hold of ’ your middle`ing in ’
’ Abraham ’ ye ’ as Heth the ’ Ephron`ing ’ low as and ’ crush ’ as son ’
not ’ 11 say of ’ and town`s ’ gate ’ as came ’ all of ’ crush ’ as son ’ as ear in
’ cave`ed the and ’ walk ’ as set has ’ field`ed the ’ as has hear ’ as master ’
am set has ’ as people ’ as son ’ as has eye of ’ am set has ’ walk ’ and in ’ which
’ people ’ as before ’ Abraham ’ and humble`ly as and ’ 12 are die ’ bury ’ walk ’
say of ’ land the ’ people ’ as ear in ’ Ephron`ing ’ to ’ word as and ’ 13 land the
’ field`ed the ’ silver ’ as set has ’ as has hear ’ if ’ ye`ed ’ mother ’ sure ’
’ low as and ’ 14 there`ed ’ extent ’ ye ’ bury`ed I and ’ apportion from ’ took

land ’ as has hear ’ as master ’ 15 not`ing ’ say of ’ Abraham ’ ye ’ Ephron`ing
’ are between in and ’ as between in ’ silver ’ weigh ’ you and hundred ’ four I ’
’ to ’ Abraham ’ hear as and ’ 16 bury ’ are die ’ ye and ’ that`ing ’ what
’ which ’ silver the ’ ye ’ Ephron`ing of ’ Abraham ’ weigh as and ’ Ephron`ing
’ silver ’ weigh ’ you and hundred ’ four I ’ crush ’ as son ’ as ear in ’ word
’ fold`ed from in ’ which ’ Ephron`ing ’ field`ed ’ rise as and ’ 17 trade of ’ Obara
and in ’ which ’ cave`ed the and ’ field`ed the ’ appear from ’ around ’ on ’ which
’ and border`ing ’ all in ’ which ’ field`ed in ’ which ’ tree the ’ all and ’
all in ’ crush ’ as son ’ as has eye of ’ purchase`ed of ’ Abraham of ’ 18 surround`s
’ ye ’ Abraham ’ bury ’ so ’ as after and ’ 19 and town`s ’ gate ’ as came ’
’ around ’ on ’ fold`ed them ’ field`ed ’ you cave ’ to ’ and wife ’ Sarah
field`ed the ’ rise as and ’ 20 Canaan ’ land in ’ Hebron`ing ’ that`ing ’ appear from
’ each ’ bury ’ you hold of ’ Abraham of ’ and in ’ which ’ cave`ed the and ’
crush ’ as son

THE TORAH SCROLL 24

' ye ' bless ' Jehovah and ' from as sea in ' came ' elder ' Abraham and ' 1
' elder ' and serve ' to ' Abraham ' say as and ' 2 all in ' Abraham
' under ' are hand ' oh ' there`s ' if ' which ' all in ' rule the ' and you house
' heaven`s the ' as Allah ' Jehovah in ' are swear`s too I and ' 3 as soft
' as son of ' Woman ' implicate ' not ' which ' land the ' as Allah and
' sojourn as ' for whither ' which ' as Canaan the ' daughter`th`ing from
' as you bore and from ' to and ' as land ' to ' mother ' for ' 4 and approach in
' him to ' say as and ' 5 Isaac of ' as son of ' Woman ' you take and ' walk you
' to ' as after ' you walk of ' Woman the ' want`ed ' not ' as maybe I ' serve the
which ' land the ' to ' are son ' ye ' carry`s I ' carry be ' such the ' land the
turn ' walk ' guard the ' Abraham ' him to ' say as and ' 6 there from ' you out '
' heaven`s the ' as Allah ' Jehovah ' 7 there`ed ' as son ' ye ' carry`s you '
' land from and ' as father ' you house from ' as has take ' which
vessel ' swear too has ' which and ' vessel ' word ' which and ' as you bore and from
' send as ' that`ing ' such the ' land the ' ye ' donkey ' are seed of ' say of '
8 there from ' as son of ' Woman ' you take and ' are as before ' and messenger from
' are as after ' you walk of ' Woman the ' want`ed ' not ' mother and '
' not ' as son ' ye ' only ' such ' as you swear too from ' you innocent and
' soft ' under ' and hand ' ye ' serve the ' site and ' 9 there`ed ' carry`s you
' 10 this the ' word the ' on ' if ' swear too as and ' him master ' Abraham
' him master ' as camel from ' from as Camel ' ten`ed ' serve the ' took as and
' rise as and ' and hand in ' him master ' good`ing ' all and ' walk as and
' 11 Nahor ' town`s ' to ' from as river ' highland ' to ' walk as and
' well ' on I ' town`s of ' outside`ing from ' from as Camel the ' bless as and
' say as and ' 12 you and draw the ' grip ' time of ' twilight ' time of ' Water the

' as before ' oh ' call`ed the ' Abraham ' as master ' as Allah ' Jehovah
' be`th ' (13 Abraham ' as master ' people ' bow ' do`ed and ' day as the
' as person ' daughter`th`ing and ' Water the ' has eye ' on ' settle ' for whither
' which ' youth`ed the ' be`s and ' (14 Water ' draw of ' you and out ' town`s the
drink`ed ' say`ed and ' the drink I and ' are pail ' oh ' as lean ' Eli`ed ' say
' are serve of ' ing`monitor the ' ye`ed ' the moisten I ' are as Camel ' also and '
' as master ' people ' bow ' you as do ' for ' know ' obey`ed ' Isaac of
' to ' word of ' all`ed ' suspend ' that`ing ' became as and ' (15 Abraham
' son ' Bethuel of ' bore`ed as ' which ' you out ' Rebekeh ' be`th and ' and heart
(16 ridge`ed ' on ' the pail and ' Abraham ' as brother ' Nahor ' wife ' the king
' the bride`ing ' especially ' look`ed from ' you good`ing ' youth`ed the and '
' pail`ed ' fill you and ' the low`s the ' up you and ' known`ed ' not ' man I and
' say as and ' the you call of ' serve the ' run as and ' (17 on you and
' say you and ' (18 are pail from ' Water ' less ' oh ' face as swallow`s the
' hand`ed ' on ' pail`ed ' up and assent ' soon you and ' as master ' drink`ed
' say you and ' and you and moisten the of ' perfect and ' (19 and moisten`ed you and
' soon you and ' (20 laid of ' fail ' mother ' till ' draw I ' are as Camel of ' also
' to ' till`ing ' run you and ' drunk`ing the ' on I ' pail`ed ' up and assent
' man that and ' (21 him Camel ' all of ' draw you and ' draw of ' well the
' Jehovah ' prosper`s be ' knowledge of ' devise`s from and ' nihil ' were drink from
' from as Camel the ' fail ' which are ' became as and ' (22 not ' mother ' and way
' and weigh from ' divide ' gold ' jewelry ' man that ' took as and ' laid`ing of
' the as hand ' on ' from as bracelet`s ' two and ' anger`ed ' on ' site and
' ye ' who ' daughter ' say as and ' (23 from weight from ' gold ' ten`ed
place`ing ' are as father ' you house in ' man the ' vessel ' oh ' as my nation the

' for whither ' Bethuel ' daughter ' him to ' say you and ' 24 stop`s of ' our of '
' also ' him to ' say you and ' 25 Nahor of ' bore`ed as ' which ' the king ' son
' place`ing ' also ' our people ' increase ' that`ing number ' also ' similar
' 27 Jehovah of ' the and humble`ly as and ' man that ' stoop as and ' 26 stop`s of
' not ' which ' Abraham ' as master ' as Allah ' Jehovah ' bless`ing ' say as and
' Abraham ' as master ' affirm ' and faithful and ' and found at ' forsake
28 as master ' as brother ' you house ' Jehovah ' as grace has ' way in ' for whither
' mother`ed ' you house of ' my tell and ' youth`ed the ' run you and '
' son of ' name and ' brother ' Rebekah of and ' 29 these`ed ' from as word are
' 30 has eye the ' to ' the outside`ing the ' man that ' to ' son of ' run as and
' ye and ' jewelry the ' ye ' and you see are ' became as and
' ye ' and hear are and ' and sister ' as hand ' on ' from as bracelet`s the
' man that ' Eli ' word ' here ' say of ' and sister ' Rebekeh ' as word
' on ' from as Camel the ' on ' stand ' be`th and ' man that ' to ' came as and
' stand you ' what of ' Jehovah ' bless`ing ' came`ing ' say as and ' 31 has eye the
' place`ing and ' you house the ' as whom turn ' for whither and ' outside`ing in
' open as and ' he house the ' man that ' came as and ' 32 from as Camel of
' from as Camel of ' that`ing number and ' similar ' give as and ' from as Camel the
33 and ye ' which ' from as person the ' as foot and ' him foot ' wash of ' Water and
' mother ' till ' eat ' not ' say as and ' eat of ' him before ' from joy Then '
' Abraham ' serve ' say as and ' 34 word ' say as and ' as word ' as you word
' great as and ' especially ' as master ' ye ' bless ' Jehovah and ' 35 for whither
' from as serve and ' gold and ' silver and ' herd and ' flock ' if ' give as and
Sarah ' bore you and ' 36 from as heass`ing and ' from as Camel and ' you and slave and
' give as and ' he`ing elder ' as after ' as master of ' son ' as master ' wife '

' say of ' as master ' as has swear`s too as and ' 37 if ' which ' all ' ye ' if
' which ' as Canaan the ' daughter`th ing from ' as son of ' Woman ' implicate ' not
' you house ' to ' not ' mother ' for ' 38 and land in ' dwell ' for whither
as son of ' Woman ' you take and ' as you at family ' to and ' walk you ' as father
as after ' Woman the ' walk you ' not ' as maybe I ' as master ' to ' say and ' 39
send as ' him before ' as you walk he the ' which ' Jehovah ' Eli ' say as and ' 40
' Woman ' you take and ' are way ' proper`s the and ' are ye ' and messenger from '
' yet ' 41 as father ' you house from and ' as you at family from ' as son of
' as you at family ' to ' income`ing ' for ' as oath from ' emission`ed you
42 as oath from ' emission`s ' whom became and ' walk ' and give as ' not ' mother and
' as Allah ' Jehovah ' say and ' has eye the ' to ' day as the ' came I and '
' which ' as way ' proper`s from ' oh ' are man ' mother ' Abraham ' as master
' has eye ' on ' settle ' for whither ' be`th ' 43 am on ' walk the ' for whither
' as you say and ' draw of ' you issue became ' what on the ' be`s and ' Water the
say`ed and ' 44 are pail from ' Water ' less ' oh ' as has as moisten the ' Eli`ed
' that`s ' draw I ' are as Camel of ' also and ' drink`ed ' ye`ed ' also ' Eli '
' as whither ' 45 as master ' son of ' Jehovah ' power`s and the ' which ' Woman the
' you out ' Rebekeh ' be`th and ' as heart ' to ' word of ' the eat ' suspend
' say and ' draw you and ' the low`s the ' up you and ' ridge`ed ' on ' the pail and
' 46 are pail from ' Water ' time from ' oh ' as has as moisten the ' Eli`ed
also and ' drink`ed ' say you and ' am above ' pail`ed ' up and assent ' soon you and
' from as Camel the ' also and ' wife and ' the moisten I ' are as Camel '
say you and ' ye ' who ' daughter ' say and ' ye`ed ' ask I and ' 47 he moisten the
' the king ' if ' bore`ed as ' which ' Nahor ' son ' Bethuel ' daughter '
' on ' from as bracelet`s the and ' anger`ed ' on ' jewelry the ' there`s I and

' bless I and ' Jehovah of ' the and humble`ly I and ' stoop I and ' 48 the as hand
way in ' as grace has the ' which ' Abraham ' as master ' as Allah ' Jehovah ' ye
' 49 and son of ' as master ' as brother ' daughter ' ye ' you take ' faithful '
' ye ' faithful and ' bow ' from as do ' ridge as ' mother ' the time and
' vessel ' and hand direct ' not ' mother and ' vessel ' and hand direct ' as master
son of ' low as and ' 50 of left the ' to ' or ' right`s the ' to ' turn`ed I and
' able has ' not ' word the ' out ' Jehovah from ' and say as and ' Bethuel and '
' are as before ' Rebekeh ' be`th ' 51 good`ing ' or ' evil ' are as to ' word
word ' which are ' are as master ' son of ' Woman ' the became you and ' led ' took
' ye ' Abraham ' serve ' hear ' which are ' became as and ' 52 Jehovah '
' issue him and ' 53 Jehovah of ' land`ed ' the and humble`ly as and ' them as word
' from as fortune in and ' gold ' as all and ' silver ' weapon ' serve the
' am brother of ' gave ' you and has pleasant and ' Rebekeh of ' give as and
' that`ing ' and drink as and ' and eat as and ' 54 the mother of and
' and rise`ing as and ' and tarry`s and ' and people ' which ' from as person the and
' Ahijah ' say as and ' 55 as master of ' as shall send ' say as and ' is morn in
' ten`ing ' or ' from week ' and has ye ' youth the ' inhabitant ' mother`ed and
' near ' and after you ' to ' them as to ' say as and ' 56 walk you ' after ' new
' to ' the eat and ' as shall send ' as way ' ye ' prosper`s the ' Jehovah and
edge`ed ' ye ' ask`ed has and ' youth of ' call has ' and say as and ' 57 as master
people ' as walk you the ' Eli`ed ' and say as and ' Rebekeh of ' and call as and ' 58
' Rebekeh ' ye ' and send as and ' 59 walk I ' say you and ' this the ' man that '
ye and ' Abraham ' serve ' ye and ' he blameless as from ' ye and ' from sister`ing
' nihil ' and say as and ' Rebekeh ' ye ' and bless as and ' 60 him person '
' possess as and ' thus increase ' as thousand of ' became`ing ' ye ' and has sister

’ Rebekeh ’ rise you and ’ 61 him hateful ’ him enemy I ’ gate ’ ye ’ are seed
’ from as Camel the ’ on ’ the has ride you and ’ am you youth and
Rebekeh ’ ye ’ serve the ’ took as and ’ man that ’ as after ’ the has walk you and
Jawbone ’ well ’ came`ing from ’ word from in ’ came ’ Isaac and ’ 62 walk as and ’
’ Isaac ’ out and ’ 63 south the ’ land in ’ sojourn as ’ that`ing and ’ seen ’
’ him has eye ’ lift as and ’ twilight ’ you and before ’ field`ed in ’ humble`ing of
’ Rebekeh ’ lift you and ’ 64 from as came ’ from as Camel ’ be`th and ’ look as and
65 wean the ’ above ’ made you and ’ Isaac ’ ye ’ look you and ’ am has eye ’ ye
’ enter the ’ this of the ’ man that ’ who ’ serve the ’ to ’ say you and ’
’ as master ’ that`ing ’ serve the ’ say as and ’ our you call of ’ field`ed in
Isaac of ’ serve the ’ report as and ’ 66 conceal set and ’ veil`s the ’ took you and
’ Isaac ’ the came`s as and ’ 67 do`ed ’ which ’ from as word the ’ all ’ ye ’
if ’ became you and ’ Rebekeh ’ ye ’ took as and ’ and mother ’ Sarah ’ tent`ed the
and mother ’ as after ’ Isaac ’ comfort as and ’ love`ed as and ’ resemble I of ’

' 2 Keturah ' there`ed and ' Woman ' took as and ' Abraham ' add and ' 1

' ye and ' Medan ' ye and ' Jokshan ' ye and ' Zimran`ing ' ye ' if ' bore you and

' ye ' bore as ' Jokshan and ' 3 humble'ing ' ye and ' Ishbak ' ye and ' Midian

' Letushim and ' Asshurim`s ' him the ' Dedan ' as son and ' Dedan ' ye and ' Sheba

' Hanoch`ing and ' ashes and ' Ephah ' Midian ' as son and ' 4 Leummim and

Abraham ' give as and ' 5 Keturah ' as son ' to`ed ' all ' Eldaah and ' Abida and

' as son of and ' 6 and son ' Isaac of ' if ' which ' all ' ye '

' Abraham ' gave ' Abraham of ' which ' from as concubine as put the

' and has till`ing in ' and son ' Isaac ' above ' from send as and ' you and present

' as life ' two ' week ' to`ed and ' 7 east`ed ' land ' to ' east`ed ' life

' the Year ' from as seven and ' the Year ' each ' life ' which ' Abraham

' the carry`s in ' Abraham ' die as and ' expire`ing as and ' 8 from two ' five and

' 9 him people ' to ' gather as and ' from week ' seven and ' elder ' the good`ing

' you cave ' to ' him son ' Ishmael and ' Isaac ' and ye ' and bury as and

on ' which ' as Heth the ' noon ' son ' Ephron`ing ' field`ed ' to ' fold`ed them

' each ' Abraham ' nest`ed ' which ' field`ed the ' 10 appear from ' around '

' 11 and wife ' Sarah and ' Abraham ' bury`ing ' there`ed ' crush ' as son

ye ' from as Allah ' bless as and ' Abraham ' die`ing ' as after ' became as and

' 12 seen ' Jawbone ' well ' people ' Isaac ' dwell and ' and son ' Isaac '

' bore`ed as ' which ' Abraham ' son ' Ishmael ' you bore and you ' to`ed and

' you name ' to`ed and ' 13 Abraham of ' Sarah ' you slave ' whom Mirza the ' abide

' first`ing ' from you bore and you of ' from garlic'ing in ' Ishmael ' as son

' Mishma and ' 14 Mibsam and ' Adbeel and ' Kedad and ' Nebajoth`ing ' Ishmael

' 16 east`ed and ' Naphish ' Ietur ' Tema`ed and ' Hadad ' 15 Mash`er and ' Dumah and

' them and yard in ' from you name ' to`ed and ' Ishmael ' as son ' them ' to`ed

17 ' from faithful of ' from as help`s ' ten ' from two ' complete row`s in and
' from as three and ' the Year ' each ' Ishmael ' as life ' two ' to`ed and
' gather as and ' die as and ' expire`ing as and ' from two ' seven and ' the Year
' captain`ing ' till ' the of Hivite from ' and nigh as and ' 18 him people ' to
all ' around ' on ' the ox`ing I ' here came ' from as Mizra ' around ' on ' which
' Abraham ' son ' Isaac ' you bore and you ' to`ed and ' 19 fall ' him brother '
' son ' Isaac ' became as and ' 20 Isaac ' ye ' bore`s and the ' Abraham
' Bethuel ' daughter ' Rebekeh ' ye ' and you took in ' the Year ' from as four I
' if ' as Aram the ' son of ' you and brother ' highland ' Padan from ' as Aram the
' for ' and wife ' behalf of ' Jehovah ' to ' Isaac ' pray as and ' 21 resemble I of
' Rebekeh ' pregnant and ' Jehovah ' if ' pray as and ' that`s ' exterminate'ed
' say you and ' approach`ed in ' from as son the ' and struggle whom and ' 22 and wife
' ye ' search of ' are hang and ' for whither ' this ' what of ' so ' mother
' are womb in ' from nation`ing ' two ' nihil ' Jehovah ' say as and ' 23 Jehovah
' mother of and ' and disperse as ' are as bowel from ' from as mother of ' two and
' and fill as and ' 24 little`s ' serve as ' increase and ' harden as ' from fill
' out and ' 25 the womb in ' from as twin`ing ' be`th and ' you bore of ' the week
' and call as and ' gate ' you big are ' fail ' as has and Men ' has and head`s the
' and hand and ' him brother ' out ' so ' as after and ' 26 concoct ' name
' son ' Isaac and ' Jacob ' name ' and call as and ' concoct ' heel in ' you hold
' and great as and ' 27 from ye ' you bore in ' the Year ' from as six
' man I ' hunt`s ' known ' man I ' concoct ' became as and ' from as youth the
' love as and ' 28 from as tent ' dwell ' complete ' man I ' Jacob and ' field`ed
' you love ' Rebekah and ' him animal ' and hunt`s ' for ' concoct ' ye ' Isaac
' concoct ' came as and ' proud`s has ' Jacob ' proud as and ' 29 Jacob ' ye

' to ' concoct ' say as and ' 30 fly`s ' that`ing and ' field`ed the ' has from

' ground`ing the ' ground`ing the ' has from ' oh ' as has greed`s the ' Jacob

' 31 Edom ' name ' call ' so ' on ' for whither ' fly`s ' for ' this the

' 32 vessel ' are you first`ing ' ye ' day as are ' the sale ' Jacob ' say as and

' what of and ' die`ing of ' ing`enter ' for whither ' be`th ' concoct ' say as and

' vessel ' swear`ed too the ' Jacob ' say as and ' 33 the first`ing ' vessel ' this

' and you first`ing ' ye ' sale as and ' if ' swear too as and ' day as are

' from as lentile ' proud`s has and ' fight ' Esau of ' gave ' Jacob and ' 34 Jacob of

ye ' concoct ' spoil as and ' walk as and ' rise as and ' drink as and ' eat as and

the first`ing the '

' hunger the ' alone of from ' land in ' hunger ' became as and ' (1
to ' Isaac ' walk as and ' Abraham ' week in ' be`s ' which ' has and head`s the
' him to ' look as and ' (2 the is guest ' from as Philista ' king ' Abimelech '
' which ' land in ' nigh ' the from as Mizra ' spinach ' to ' say as and ' Jehovah
' are people ' be`s I and ' such the ' land in ' guest`ing ' (3 are as to ' say
' all ' ye ' donkey ' are seed of and ' walk ' for ' are bless I and
' which ' the swear`ing too the ' ye ' as you verify and ' these ' you and land the
ye ' as whom increase the and ' (4 are as father ' Abraham of ' as you swear too has
' ye ' are seed of ' as set has and ' heaven`s the ' as in star`ing are ' are seed '
' all ' are seed in ' and bless sacred and ' these`ed ' you and land the ' all
' are as father ' Abraham ' hear ' which ' heel ' (5 land the ' as nation`ing
' as you command from ' as you guard from ' guard as and ' as voice`ing in
' (7 Gerar in ' Isaac ' dwell and ' (6 as you protect`ing and ' as statute`ing
' as sister ' say as and ' and wife ' on ' place`ing the ' as person ' and ask as and
' as has and kill as ' turn ' that`s ' as wife ' say of ' dread ' for ' that`s
' look`ed from ' you good`ing ' for ' Rebekeh ' on ' place`ing the ' as person
' there ' if ' and lengthen ' which are ' for ' became as and ' (8 that`s
' till in ' from as Philista ' king ' Abimelech ' gaze as and ' from week the
' Rebekeh ' ye ' laugh from ' Isaac ' be`th and ' look as and ' window`ing the
' be`th ' sure ' say as and ' Isaac of ' Abimelech ' call as and ' (9 and wife
' say as and ' that`s ' as sister ' you say ' are hence and ' that`s ' are wife
' say as and ' (10 am on ' faithful`ing ' turn ' as you say ' for ' Isaac ' him to
' one ' lay ' less are ' our of ' you as do ' such ' what ' Abimelech
' (11 guilty ' our as on ' brought the and ' are wife ' ye ' people the
' touch the ' say of ' and people the ' all ' ye ' Abimelech ' command as and

' Isaac ' seed as and ' 12 die him ' die`ing ' and wife in and ' this the ' man I in
' hundred`ed ' that`s the ' Year`ed in ' come as and ' that`s the ' land in
' man that ' great as and ' 13 Jehovah ' and bless`ed as and ' from as Barley
' 14 especially ' great ' for ' till ' great and ' walk`ing the ' walk as and
the serve and ' herd ' nest`ed from and ' flock ' purchase`ed ' if ' became as and
' all and ' 15 from as Philista ' and ye ' and jealous as and ' increase`ed '
' Abraham ' week in ' him father ' as serve ' and scout ' which ' you and well the
' 15 dust ' from and fill as and ' from as Philista ' from and closeup ' him father
you might ' for ' and has people from ' walk ' Isaac ' to ' Abimelech ' say as and
' encamp and ' Isaac ' there from ' walk as and ' 17 especially ' and her from '
' scout as and ' Isaac ' dwell and ' 18 there ' dwell and ' expatriate ' inherit in
Abraham ' week in ' as serve ' and scout ' which ' Water the ' you and well ' ye
' die`ing ' as after ' from as Philista ' from and closeup as and ' him father '
' call ' which ' you name are ' you name ' behold of ' call as and ' Abraham
' inherit in ' Isaac ' as serve ' and scout as and ' 19 him father ' behold of
' and increase`s as and ' 20 from as life ' Water ' well ' there ' and come as and
' Water the ' our of ' say of ' Isaac ' pastoral ' people ' expatriate ' pastoral
21 and people ' and oppress you the ' for ' oppress ' well the ' there ' call as and
' am on ' also ' and increase`s as and ' you after ' well ' and scout as and '
and scout as and ' there from ' leave as and ' 22 accurse`ed ' there`ed ' call as and
' there`ed ' call as and ' am on ' million ' not and ' you after ' well '
' our of ' Jehovah ' large`s the ' time`ed ' for ' say as and ' you and large
' 24 seven ' well ' there from ' went and ' 23 land in ' and has fruitful and
' say as and ' that`ing the ' the night`s in ' Jehovah ' him to ' look as and
are ye ' for ' look as you ' to ' are as father ' Abraham ' as Allah ' for whither

' are seed ' ye ' as whom increase the and ' are as you bless and ' for whither '
' sacrifice from ' there ' son as and ' 25 as serve ' Abraham ' cross`ing in
' and pasture as and ' and tent ' there ' extent and ' Jehovah ' spice ' call as and
gerar from ' him to ' walk the ' Abimelech and ' 26 well ' Isaac ' as serve ' there
' say as and ' 27 and mass ' captain ' Phicol and ' alas evil from ' you hold and '
' complete hateful ' from ye and ' Eli ' from ye in ' why`ing ' Isaac ' them as to
' see ' and say as and ' 28 from are ye from ' as shall send you and ' near
' oh ' be`s you ' say has and ' are people ' Jehovah ' be`s ' for ' our as look
' are between in and ' our as between in ' and give`s and between in ' to`ed
evil`ed ' our people ' do`ed you ' mother ' 29 are people ' covenant`s ' hew`ed shall
' only ' are people ' our as do ' which are and ' are our touch ' not ' which are '
' bless`ing ' ye`ed ' time`ed ' from and peace in ' are send has and ' good`ing
' 31 and drink as and ' and eat as and ' feast`ed ' them of ' do as and ' 30 Jehovah
' him brother of ' man I ' and swear too as and ' is morn in ' and ridge`s as and
' and ye from ' and walk as and ' Isaac ' from send as and ' and evil`ed of
' and came as and ' that`ing the ' day as in ' became as and ' 32 from and peace in
' which ' well the ' concern`ing ' on ' if ' and fortune as and ' Isaac ' as serve
' ye`ed ' call as and ' 33 Water ' and has come ' if ' and say as and ' and scout
' day as the ' till ' seven ' well ' town`s the ' there ' so ' on ' the seven
took as and ' the Year ' from as four I ' son ' concoct ' became as and ' 34 this the
' Bashemath ' ye and ' as Heth the ' Beer ' daughter ' Judith ' ye ' Woman '
' spirit is ' grief ' the has became`s you and ' 35 as Heth the ' Elon`ing ' daughter
Rebekah of and ' Isaac of

' him has eye ' the has as middle'ed and ' Isaac ' elder ' for ' became as and ' 1
' say as and ' great`ing the ' and son ' concoct ' ye ' call as and ' you see from
' oh ' be`th ' say as and ' 2 as behold`th ' him to ' say as and ' as son ' him to
' lift ' the time and ' 3 as die`ing ' day as ' as you known ' not ' as you elder
' field`ed the ' spring ' are arch and ' are crooked`s ' are weapon ' oh
' from as flavor from ' vessel ' do`ed and ' 4 the hunt`s ' vessel ' the hunt`ing and
cross`ing in ' eat`ed and ' vessel ' the you came`s the and ' as you love ' which are
' you hear ' Rebekah and ' 5 faithful`ing ' suspend in ' as soul ' are bless you '
' field`ed the ' concoct ' walk as and ' and son ' concoct ' to ' Isaac ' word in
' Jacob ' to ' drop`ed I ' Rebekah and ' 6 came`s the of ' hunt`s ' hunt`ing of
' to ' word from ' are as father ' ye ' as you hear ' be`th ' say of ' son`ed
' do`ed and ' hunt`s ' vessel ' the came`s the ' 7 say of ' are as brother ' concoct
Jehovah ' as before ' the are bless I and ' eat`ed and ' from as flavor from ' vessel
' as voice`ing in ' hear ' as son ' the time and ' 8 as die`ing ' as before '
' flock the ' to ' oh ' walk ' 9 are ye ' command`ed from ' as whither ' which of
' from as good`ing ' from as Goat ' as kid ' two ' there from ' vessel ' ercort
10 love ' which are ' are as father of ' from as flavor from ' from ye ' do`ed I and
are bless as ' which ' cross`ing in ' eat and ' are as father of ' brought the and '
' and mother ' Rebekeh ' to ' Jacob ' say as and ' 11 and die`ing ' as before '
' 12 part ' man I ' for whither and ' gate`s ' man I ' as brother ' concoct ' be`th
' him has eye in ' as whom became and ' as father ' as has refrain`ing ' as maybe I
' not and ' the accurse ' mosthigh ' as you came the and ' have fraud from are
' as son ' are you accurse ' mosthigh ' and mother ' if ' say you and ' 13 bless`ed
took as and ' walk as and ' 14 vessel ' took ' led ' as voice`ing in ' hear ' sure
' from as flavor from ' and mother ' do you and ' and mother of ' came as and '

' as fabric ' ye ' Rebekeh ' took you and ' 15 him father ' love ' which are
' you house in ' ye`ed ' which ' you desire the ' great the ' son`ed ' concoct
as kid ' ing`skin`ing ' ye and ' 16 small the ' son`ed ' Jacob ' ye ' arm you and
' you smooth at ' on and ' him hand ' on ' the arm`s the ' from as Goat the '
fight the ' ye and ' from as flavor from the ' ye ' has set and ' 17 him is neck did
' him father ' to ' came as and ' 18 son`ed ' Jacob ' hand in ' he do ' which '
' 19 as son ' ye`ed ' who ' as behold`th ' say as and ' as father ' say as and
' are first`ing ' concoct ' for whither ' him father ' to ' Jacob ' say as and
' eat`ed and ' carry`ed ' oh ' rise`ing ' Eli ' you word ' which are ' as whom do
' Isaac ' say as and ' 20 are soul ' as has bless you ' cross`ing in ' as hunt`s from
' for ' say as and ' as son ' come of ' you soon ' this ' what ' and son ' to
' to ' Isaac ' say as and ' 21 as before ' are as Allah ' Jehovah ' call`ed the
' as son ' this ' ye`ed the ' as son ' are lastnight`ing and ' oh ' Ill`ed ' Jacob
' him father ' Isaac ' to ' Jacob ' adduce and ' 22 not ' mother ' concoct
' Jacob ' voice`ing ' voice`ing the ' say as and ' and the refrain`ing and
' for ' and knew are the ' not and ' 23 concoct ' as hand ' from as hand the and
' you and gate`s ' him brother ' concoct ' as hand are ' him hand ' him the
say as and ' concoct ' as son ' this ' ye`ed the ' say as and ' 24 and bless`ed as and
' hunt`s from ' eat`ed and ' vessel ' the I'll`s the ' say as and ' 25 as whither '
' eat as and ' if ' adduce and ' as soul ' are bless you ' purpose of ' as son
' Isaac ' him to ' say as and ' 26 drink as and ' between`s ' if ' came as and
' adduce and ' 27 as son ' vessel ' moisten`ed and ' oh ' Ill`ed ' him father
' him fabric ' smell`s ' ye ' smell as and ' if ' moisten as and
' smell`s are ' as son ' smell`s ' and look`ed ' say as and ' and bless`ed as and
' walk ' give as and ' 28 Jehovah ' and bless`ed ' which ' fill ' field`ed the

' land the ' as has there from and ' heaven`s the ' dew from ' from as Allah the
' from as people ' are and serve as ' 29 possess you and ' grain ' increase and
' strong`s ' be`ing ' from as mother of ' walk ' prostate humble`ly as and
' are mother ' as son ' walk ' prostate humble`ly as and ' are as brother of
became as and ' 30 bless`ing ' are as bless from and ' execrate`ing ' are of execrate
' sure ' became as and ' Jacob ' ye ' bless of ' Isaac ' all`ed ' which are '
' concoct and ' him father ' Isaac ' around ' each ' Jacob ' out ' out
' that`ing ' also ' do as and ' 31 and hunt`s from ' came ' him brother
' him father of ' say as and ' him father of ' came as and ' from as flavor from
' cross`ing in ' and son ' hunt`s from ' eat as and ' as father ' rise`s as
' who ' him father ' Isaac ' him to ' say as and ' 32 are soul ' as has bless you
' 33 concoct ' are first`ing ' are son ' as whither ' say as and ' ye`ed
' say as and ' especially ' till ' great`ed ' shudder`ed ' Isaac ' shudder as and
' eat and ' vessel ' came as and ' hunt`s ' hunt the ' that`ing ' although`ing ' who
be`s as ' bless`ing ' also ' and bless`ed I and ' income`ing ' suspend in ' all from
' cry as and ' him father ' as word ' ye ' concoct ' hear are ' became as and ' 34
' him father of ' say as and ' especially ' till ' the drop and ' great`ed ' cry`ed
' are as brother ' came ' say as and ' 35 as father ' as whither ' also ' as has bless
call ' for`ing the ' say as and ' 36 are you bless ' ye ' took as and ' craft`ed in
' as you first ' ye ' from as move ' this ' as has heel as and ' Jacob ' name '
' forward ' say as and ' as you bless ' took of ' time`ed ' be`th and ' took of
' Esau of ' say as and ' Isaac ' low as and ' 37 bless`ed ' vessel ' you beside
' as set has ' him brother ' all ' ye and ' walk ' him you there ' strong`s ' behold
' the all and ' him you laid ' possess you and ' grain and ' from as serve of ' if
him father ' to ' concoct ' say as and ' 38 as son ' do`ed I ' what ' although`ing

' also ' as has bless ' as father ' walk ' that`s ' sister ' bless`ed the '
' 39 against as and ' and voice`ing ' concoct ' lift as and ' as father ' as whither
' as eight from ' be`th ' him to ' say as and ' him father ' Isaac ' low as and
' 40 above from ' heaven`s the ' dew from and ' are sojourn from ' be`s as ' land the
be`s and ' serve you ' are as brother ' ye and ' the life you ' are desolate ' on and
' above ' and on`ing ' you break and ' up`s you ' big you ' which are '
' bless`ed the ' on ' Jacob ' ye ' concoct ' hate as and ' 41 are is neck did
' and heart in ' concoct ' say as and ' him father ' and bless ' which
' Jacob ' ye ' the kill I and ' as father ' mourn ' week ' and approach as
' son`ed ' concoct ' as word ' ye ' Rebekeh of ' my told and ' 42 as brother
' small the ' son`ed ' Jacob of ' call you and ' send you and ' great`ing the
' walk ' comfort complete ' are as brother ' concoct ' be`th ' him to ' say you and
' rise`ing and ' as voice`ing in ' hear ' as son ' the time and ' 43 are kill of
and people ' desist as and ' 44 the Charan ' as brother ' son of ' to ' walk ' shoot
are as brother ' hotspring ' carry`ing you ' which ' till ' from as one ' from week '
' ye ' forget and ' with from ' are as brother ' anger ' carry`ing ' till ' 45
what of ' there from ' are as you take and ' as you send and ' if ' you as do ' which
' to ' Rebekeh ' say you and ' 46 one ' day as ' from are two ' also ' Eshcol '
' mother ' crush ' daughter`th`ing ' around from ' as life in ' as you end ' Isaac
' to`ed are ' crush ' daughter`th`ing from ' Woman ' Jacob ' took of
from as life ' vessel ' what of ' land the ' daughter`th`ing from

' and ye ' bless as and ' Jacob ' to ' Isaac ' call as and ' (1

' Woman ' implicate ' not ' if ' say as and ' and command`ed as and

he house ' highland ' the plateau ' walk ' rise`ing ' (2 Canaan ' daughter`th`ing from

' Woman ' there from ' walk ' ercort ' are mother ' as father ' Bethuel '

' almighty ' to and ' (3 are mother ' as brother ' son of ' daughter`th`ing from

' whom became and ' are increase as and ' are apart as and ' are ye ' bless as

' Abraham ' you bless ' ye ' walk ' give as and ' (4 from as people ' assemble of

' land ' ye ' are net`ness of ' are ye ' are seed of and ' walk ' are as father

' (5 Abraham of ' from as Allah ' Jehovah ' gave ' which ' are as pilgrimage

' to ' highland ' the plateau ' walk as and ' Jacob ' ye ' Isaac ' send as and

' Jacob ' mother ' Rebekeh ' as brother ' as Aram the ' Bethuel ' son ' son of

' Jacob ' ye ' Isaac ' bless ' for ' concoct ' look as and ' (6 concoct and

' Woman ' there from ' if ' you take ' highland ' the plateau ' and ye ' send and

implicate ' not ' say of ' and Mosthigh ' and command as and ' and ye ' and bless in

him father ' to ' Jacob ' hear as and ' (7 Canaan ' daughter`th`ing from ' Woman '

' look as and ' (8 highland ' the plateau ' walk as and ' and mother ' to and '

' Isaac ' as has eye in ' Canaan ' daughter`th`ing ' you and evil ' for ' concoct

' ye ' took as and ' Ishmael ' to ' concoct ' walk as and ' (9 him father

' you and brother ' Abraham ' son ' Ishmael ' daughter ' you dance

' Jacob ' out and ' (10 resemble I of ' if ' him women ' on ' you and prophet`s

' entreat as and ' (11 the Charan ' walk as and ' you walk of ' seven ' well from

' took as and ' sun the ' came ' for ' there ' tarry and ' place`ing in

' lay as and ' him you head from ' site and ' place`ing the ' as stone from

' altar ' staircase ' be`th and ' dream as and ' (12 that`ing the ' place`ing in

' as messenger from ' be`th and ' the heaven`s the ' reach`s ' and head and ' land`ed

' Jehovah ' be`th and ' 13 and in ' from as descend and ' from as on ' from as Allah
' Abraham ' as Allah ' Jehovah ' as whither ' say as and ' and Mosthigh ' settle
' am on ' lay ' ye`ed ' which ' land the ' Isaac ' as Allah and ' are as father
land the ' dust are ' are seed ' be`s and ' 14 are seed of and ' the has give I ' walk
' south`ed and ' the north`ing and ' east`ed and ' sea`ed ' you grow and '
' ground`ed the ' you and at family ' all ' against ' and bless has and
' and as you guard and ' are people ' for whither ' be`th and ' 15 are seed in and
' such the ' ground`ed the ' to ' are as desist the and ' walk you ' which ' all in
' which ' ye ' as whom do ' mother ' which ' till ' are forsake I ' not ' for
certain ' say as and ' and sleep from ' Jacob ' awake as and ' 16 walk ' as you word
17 as you known ' not ' for whither and ' this the ' place`ing in ' Jehovah ' man '
' this the ' place`ing the ' terror has ' what ' say as and ' dread as and '
' gate ' this and ' from as Allah ' you house ' mother ' for ' this ' whither`s
stone the ' ye ' took as and ' is morn in ' Jacob ' ridge as and ' 18 heaven`s the
' establish`ed from ' ye`ed ' site and ' him you head from ' there ' which '
' place`ing the ' there ' ye ' call as and ' 19 head`ed ' on ' eight ' cast and
' there ' the almond`ing ' from to`ing and ' to ' you house ' that`ing the
' say of ' vow ' Jacob ' evermore as and ' 20 the has and head`s of ' town`s the
' this the ' way in ' as has guard and ' as stand ' from as Allah ' be`s as ' mother
' fabric and ' eat of ' fight ' vessel ' gave and ' ing`enter ' for whither ' which
be`s and ' as father ' you house ' to ' from and peace in ' as desist and ' 21 arm of
' which ' such the ' stone the and ' 22 from as Allah of ' vessel ' Jehovah '
' all and ' from as Allah ' you house ' be`s as ' establish`ed from ' as you there
walk ' and has ten I ' ten ' vessel ' has set ' which

’ (2 east ’ as son ’ land`ed ’ walk as and ’ him foot ’ Jacob ’ lift as and ’ (1
’ three`ed ’ there ’ be`th and ’ field`ed in ’ well ’ be`th and ’ look as and
’ that`s the ’ well the ’ has from ’ for ’ am on ’ from as crouch ’ flock ’ as drove
’ (3 well the ’ edge ’ on ’ great`ed ’ stone the and ’ from as drove the ’ draught as
’ from as drove the ’ from pastoral the ’ all ’ there`ed ’ and gather has and
’ ye ’ draught the and ’ well the ’ edge ’ above ’ stone the ’ ye ’ and sake and
’ well the ’ edge ’ on ’ stone the ’ ye ’ and carry`s the and ’ flock the
’ whither`s from ’ as brother ’ Jacob ’ them of ’ say as and ’ (4 the place`ing of
’ them of ’ say as and ’ (5 and us I ’ parch from ’ and say as and ’ from ye
’ (6 and has known ’ and say as and ’ Nahor ’ son ’ son of ’ ye ’ from you known the
’ from and peace ’ and say as and ’ if ’ from and peace the ’ them of ’ say as and
’ say as and ’ (7 flock the ’ people ’ came`ed ’ and daughter ’ Rachel ’ be`th and
’ gather the ’ time ’ not ’ great`ing ’ day as the ’ till`ing ’ behold ’ them of
’ and say as and ’ (8 tend ’ and all and ’ flock the ’ draught the ’ purchase`ed the
’ from pastoral the ’ all ’ and gather as ’ which ’ till ’ able has ’ not
’ well the ’ edge ’ above ’ stone the ’ ye ’ and sake and ’ from as drove the
from people ’ word from ’ and has till`ing ’ (9 flock the ’ and has as moisten the and
’ evil`ed ’ for ’ am father of ’ which ’ flock the ’ people ’ came`ed ’ Rachel and ’
daughter ’ Rachel ’ ye ’ Jacob ’ look`ed ’ which are ’ became as and ’ (10 that`s
’ as brother ’ son of ’ flock ’ ye and ’ and mother ’ as brother ’ son of ’
’ edge ’ above ’ stone the ’ ye ’ exile and ’ Jacob ’ adduce and ’ and mother
’ (11 and mother ’ as brother ’ son of ’ flock ’ ye ’ moisten as and ’ well the
’ and voice`ing ’ ye ’ lift as and ’ Rachel of ’ Jacob ’ moisten as and
’ am father ’ as brother ’ for ’ Rachel of ’ Jacob ’ my told and ’ (12 against as and
’ my tell and ’ run you and ’ that`ing ’ Rebekeh ’ son ’ for and ’ that`ing

’ son ’ Jacob ’ hear ’ ye ’ son of ’ hear are ’ became as and ’ 13 am father of
’ if ’ kiss as and ’ if ’ embrace as and ’ and you call of ’ run as and ’ and sister
’ all ’ ye ’ Laban of ’ report as and ’ and you house ’ to ’ alas came`s as and
’ as might ’ sure ’ son of ’ if ’ say as and ’ 14 these`ed ’ from as word the
’ say as and ’ 15 from week ’ new ’ and people ’ dwell and ’ ye`ed ’ as flesh and
reason ’ as has you serve and ’ ye`ed ’ as brother ’ as smitten ’ Jacob of ’ son of
’ twosome ’ Laban of and ’ 16 are hew feel ’ what ’ vessel ’ the proclaim`s ’
Rachel ’ small`ed the ’ there and ’ not’ed ’ great`ed the ’ there ’ daughter`th`ing
’ Japheth ’ whom`ed the ’ Rachel and ’ you and faint ’ not’ed ’ as has eye and ’ 17
’ Rachel ’ ye ’ Jacob ’ love as and ’ 18 look`ed from ’ Japheth and ’ figure
small`ed the ’ are daughter ’ Rachel in ’ from two ’ seven ’ are serve I ’ say as and
’ ye`ed ’ as set from ’ walk ’ ye`ed ’ as set ’ good`ing ’ son of ’ say as and ’ 19
seven ’ Rachel in ’ Jacob ’ serve as and ’ 20 as stand ’ carry`ed ’ after ’ man I of
’ from as one ’ from week are ’ him has eye in ’ and became as and ’ from two ’
ye ’ came`ed the ’ son of ’ to ’ Jacob ’ say as and ’ 21 ye`ed ’ and you love in
’ gather as and ’ 22 Eli`ed ’ the came`ing I and ’ week ’ and fill ’ for ’ as wife ’
’ 23 feast`ed ’ do as and ’ place`ing the ’ as person ’ all ’ ye ’ son of
’ and daughter ’ not’ed ’ ye ’ took as and ’ twilight in ’ became as and
’ give as and ’ 24 Jacob ’ Eli`ed ’ came as and ’ him to ’ ye`ed ’ came as and
’ and daughter ’ Leah of ’ and you slave ’ trickle’ed ’ ye ’ nihil ’ son of
’ not’ed ’ that`s ’ be`th and ’ is morn in ’ became as and ’ 25 slave`ed of
’ forward`ing ’ vessel ’ you as do ’ such ’ what ’ son of ’ to ’ say as and
say as and ’ 26 as has beguile`s ’ what of and ’ are people ’ as you serve ’ Rachel in
’ the little`s the ’ set of ’ our place`ing in ’ so ’ success`ed ’ not ’ son of ’
’ walk ’ the give has I and ’ such ’ seven ’ fill ’ 27 the first`s the ’ as before

seven ' till`ing ' as stand ' serve you ' which ' the serve in ' such ' ye ' also
' seven ' fill as and ' so ' Jacob ' do as and ' 28 you and after ' from two '
' 29 resemble I of ' if ' and daughter ' Rachel ' ye ' if ' give as and ' such
' and you slave ' Bilhah ' ye ' and daughter ' Rachel of ' son of ' give as and
' also ' love as and ' Rachel ' to ' also ' came as and ' 30 slave`ed of ' nihil
' from two ' seven ' till`ing ' and people ' serve as and ' fill`ed ' Rachel ' ye
' not'ed ' the hateful`ing ' for ' Jehovah ' look as and ' 31 you and after
' pregnant and ' 32 exterminate'ed ' Rachel and ' the compasion ' ye ' open as and
' for ' Reuben ' name ' ye ' call you and ' son ' bore you and ' not'ed
' as has love as ' time`ed ' for ' as eye`th in ' Jehovah ' look`ed ' for ' drop`ed I
' for ' say you and ' son ' bore you and ' till`ing ' pregnant and ' 33 as man I
also ' vessel ' give as and ' for whither ' the hateful`ing ' for ' Jehovah ' hear
' till`ing ' pregnant and ' 34 Simeon ' name ' ye ' call you and ' this ' ye '
' Eli ' as man I ' the if as ' move the ' time`ed ' say you and ' son ' bore you and
' name ' call ' so ' on ' from as son ' three`ed ' if ' as you bore as ' for
' move the ' say you and ' son ' bore you and ' till`ing ' pregnant and ' 35 Levi
' Judah ' name ' call`ed ' so ' on ' Jehovah ' ye ' thank and I
you bore from ' stand you and

THE TORAH SCROLL 30

Gen 30:1-30:15

' jealous you and ' Jacob of ' bore`ed as ' not ' for ' Rachel ' look you and ' 1

' vessel ' handover`ed ' Jacob ' to ' say you and ' the sister`ing in ' Rachel

' anger ' delay and ' 2 for whither ' die`ed ' whither`s ' mother and ' from as son

' which ' for whither ' from as Allah ' under the ' say as and ' Rachel in ' Jacob

' as faithful ' be`th ' say you and ' 3 womb ' fruit ' are as bowel from ' keep from

' also ' the son I and ' as bless ' on ' bore you and ' Eli`ed ' came ' Bilhah

' he slave ' Bilhah ' ye ' if ' has set and ' 4 her`ed from ' for whither

' Bilhah ' pregnant and ' 5 Jacob ' Eli`ed ' came as and ' resemble I of

from as Allah ' as has judge ' Rachel ' say you and ' 6 son ' Jacob of ' bore you and

' so ' on ' son ' vessel ' give as and ' as voice`ing in ' hear ' also and '

' Bilhah ' bore you and ' till`ing ' pregnant and ' 7 judge ' name ' call`ed

' Naphtali ' Rachel ' say you and ' 8 Jacob of ' two ' son ' Rachel ' you slave

' as you finish ' also ' as sister`ing ' people ' as you lace has ' from as Allah

' the stand ' for ' not'ed ' look you and ' 9 Naphtali ' name ' ye ' call you and

' ye`ed ' has set and ' he slave ' trickle'ed ' ye ' took you and ' you bore from

' not'ed ' you slave ' trickle'ed ' bore you and ' 10 resemble I of ' Jacob of

' name ' ye ' call you and ' fabric ' not'ed ' say you and ' 11 son ' Jacob of

13 Jacob of ' two ' son ' not'ed ' you slave ' trickle'ed ' bore you and ' 12 fortune

' daughter`th`ing ' as has and captain I ' for ' as which in ' not'ed ' say you and '

' reap`s ' week in ' Reuben ' walk as and ' 14 which ' name ' ye ' call you and

' came as and ' field`ed in ' from as ing`mandrake ' come as and ' from as wheat

monster ' not'ed ' to ' Rachel ' say you and ' and mother ' not'ed ' to ' from ye

' less the ' nihil ' say you and ' 15 are son ' as ing`mandrake from ' vessel ' oh '

' as ing`mandrake ' ye ' also ' you take and ' as man I ' ye ' are you took

under ' the night`s the ' are people ' lay as ' so of ' Rachel ' say you and ' as son

' field`ed the ' has from ' Jacob ' came as and ' 15 are son ' as ing`mandrake '
' Eli ' say you and ' and you call of ' not'ed ' issue you and ' twilight in
' as ing`mandrake in ' are as you merry ' merry ' for ' the night`s the ' income`ing
' hear as and ' 17 that`ing the ' the night`s in ' people`ed ' lay as and ' as son
' son ' Jacob of ' bore you and ' pregnant and ' not'ed ' to ' from as Allah
' which ' as merry ' from as Allah ' gave ' not'ed ' say you and ' 18 as five`s
' 19 Issachar ' name ' ye ' call you and ' as man I of ' as you slave ' as set has
' 20 Jacob of ' as six ' son ' bore you and ' not'ed ' till`ing ' pregnant and
' good`ing ' confer ' near ' from as Allah ' as has confer ' not'ed ' say you and
' six`ed ' if ' as you bore as ' for ' as man I ' as has of secrete as ' move the
' bore`ed as ' after and ' 21 Zebulun ' name ' ye ' call you and ' from as son
' is remember as and ' 22 Dinah ' there`ed ' ye ' call you and ' daughter
' open as and ' from as Allah ' Eli`ed ' hear as and ' Rachel ' ye ' from as Allah
' gather ' say you and ' son ' bore you and ' pregnant and ' 23 the compasion ' ye
' Joseph ' name ' ye ' call you and ' 24 as you put hole ' ye ' from as Allah
' which are ' became as and ' 25 after ' son ' vessel ' Jehovah ' add ' say of
' son of ' to ' Jacob ' say as and ' Joseph ' ye ' Rachel ' bore`ed as
ye ' give`ed ' 26 as land ' to and ' as place`ing ' to ' the eat and ' as has send
' thick ' are ye ' as you serve ' which ' as bore`s as ' ye and ' as women '
' which ' as you serve ' ye ' you known ' ye`ed ' for ' the eat and
' as you come ' oh ' mother ' son of ' him to ' say as and ' 27 are as you serve
' Jehovah ' as has bless as and ' as you sense has ' are as has eye in ' grace
' 29 the give I and ' mosthigh ' are merry ' the female ' say as and ' 28 are sake in
' ye and ' are as you serve ' which ' ye ' you known ' ye`ed ' him to ' say as and
' walk ' be`s ' which ' less ' for ' 30 near ' are as purchase ' be`s ' which

as foot of ' are ye ' Jehovah ' bless as and ' increase of ' grow as and ' as before
' 31 as you house of ' for whither ' also ' do`ed I ' extent ' the time and '
' vessel ' has set ' not ' Jacob ' say as and ' walk ' donkey ' what ' say as and
' this the ' word the ' ye ' vessel ' do`ed you ' mother ' the noth`ing
' are flock ' all in ' cross I ' 32 guard I ' are flock ' evil`ed I ' the carry`ing I
' spot`ing and ' stud`ing ' resemble ' all ' there from ' wriggle ' day as the
' stud and ' spot`ing and ' from as sheep in ' hot`ing ' resemble ' all and
' as you just ' house ' the answer and ' 33 as merry ' be`s and ' from as Goat in
' all ' are as before ' as merry ' on ' income`ing ' for ' tomorrow ' day as in
' hot`ing and ' from as Goat in ' spot`ing and ' stud`ing ' and has whither`s ' which
behold and ' son of ' say as and ' 34 near ' that`ing ' steal`ing ' from as sheep in
' that`ing the ' day as in ' repent as and ' 35 are as word are ' be`s as ' not`ing '
' ye and ' from as spot`ing the and ' from as tie`ing the ' from as buck`s the ' ye
' all ' you and spot`ing the and ' you and stud`ing the ' from as Goat the ' all
' give as and ' from as sheep in ' hot`ing ' all and ' and in ' son of ' which
' and asleep in ' from week ' you three ' way ' site and ' 36 him son ' hand in
' son of ' flock ' ye ' evil`ed ' Jacob and ' Jacob ' between in and
' Jacob ' to ' from as Allah ' messenger from ' say as and ' you survive has the
' lift ' say as and ' as behold`th ' say as and ' Jacob ' say as and ' dream`ing in
' from as hegoat`ing the ' all ' ye ' look`ed and ' are as has eye ' oh
' from as stud`ing ' from as tie`ing ' flock the ' on ' from mosthigh the
' do`ed ' son of ' which ' all ' ye ' as you seen ' for ' from as up`ing in and
' there ' you anoint ' which ' to ' you house ' these ' for whither ' walk
' the time and ' vow ' there ' vessel ' you vow ' which and ' establish`ed from
' land ' to ' carry`ing and ' such the ' land the ' has from ' issue ' rise`ing

' stick ' Jacob ' if ' took as and ' 37 bell ' good`ing I and ' are as father
' from thick ' peel as and ' has and chestnut and ' almond`ing and ' bread ' white`ed
' on ' which ' son of the ' pill from ' you and white ' you and peel
' peel ' which ' you and stick the ' ye ' sat as and ' 38 you and stick the
flock the ' penetrate`ed you ' which ' Water the ' you and drunk in ' from as stick in
' penetrate`ed in ' the has hot as and ' flock the ' behalf of ' laid`ing of '
' you and stick the ' on I ' flock the ' the totem`ing as and ' 39 laid`ing of
' from as stud`ing ' from as tie`ing ' flock the ' the has bore you and
' give as and ' Jacob ' disperse`s ' from as sheep the and ' 40 from as spot`ing and
' son of ' flock in ' hot`ing ' all and ' tie`ing ' Ram`s ' flock the ' around
' flock ' on ' unveil ' not and ' and alone of ' from as drove ' if ' drink as and
' site`s and ' you and bind them ' flock the ' hot as ' all in ' be`s and ' 41 son of
' from as stick in ' flock the ' as has eye of ' you and stick the ' ye ' Jacob
' not ' flock the ' feeble`s the in and ' 42 you and stick in ' the has hot as of
' from as bind the and ' Laban of ' from as feeble`ing the ' and be`s and ' site`s
if ' became as and ' especially ' especially ' man that ' grow as and ' 43 Jacob of
from as Camel and ' from as serve and ' you and slave and ' you and increase ' flock '
from as heass`ing and '

1 ' Jacob ' took of ' say of ' son of ' as son ' as word ' ye ' hear as and '
' do`ed ' our as father of ' which from and ' our as father of ' which ' all ' ye
2 ' around ' ye ' Jacob ' look as and ' this the ' honour`ing the ' all ' ye
3 from and three ' past`ing are ' and people ' our from whither`s ' be`th and ' son of
' land ' to ' carry`ing ' Jacob ' to ' Jehovah ' say as and '
4 ' are people ' be`s I and ' are you bore and from of and ' are as you and father
' to ' field`ed the ' Leah of and ' Rachel of ' call as and ' Jacob ' send as and
5 ' around ' ye ' for whither ' look`ed ' behold of ' say as and ' and flock
' from and three ' past`ing are ' Eli ' our from whither`s ' for ' so as father
6 for ' has you known ' the give I and ' as stand ' be`s ' as father ' as Allah and
7 mock ' so as father and ' so as father ' ye ' as you serve ' as power ' all in '
' from apportion ' you ten ' as you merry from ' ye ' change the as and ' house '
8 ' mother ' as stand ' mischief`s of ' from as Allah ' Jehovah ' and gave ' not and
' all ' and bore as and ' are merry ' be`s as ' from as stud`ing ' say as ' here
be`s as ' from as tie`ing ' say as ' here ' mother and ' from as stud`ing ' flock the
9 ' shade Then ' from as tie`ing ' flock the ' all ' and bore as and ' are merry '
vessel ' give as and ' your as father ' purchase`ed ' ye ' from as Allah ' Jehovah
10 ' as has eye ' lift I and ' flock the ' hot as ' time in ' became as and '
from mosthigh the ' from as hegoat`ing the ' be`th and ' dream`ing in ' look`ed I and
11 ' from as up`ing in and ' from as stud`ing ' from as tie`ing ' flock the ' on '
' Jacob ' dream`ing in ' from as Allah the ' messenger from ' Eli ' say as and
12 ' look`ed and ' are as has eye ' oh ' lift ' say as and ' as behold`th ' say and
' flock the ' on ' from mosthigh the ' from as hegoat`ing the ' all ' ye
ye ' as you seen ' for ' from as up`ing in and ' from as stud`ing ' from as tie`ing
13 ' to ' you house ' these ' for whither ' walk ' do`ed ' son of ' which ' all '

there ' vessel ' you vow ' which and ' establish`ed from ' there ' you anoint ' which
' such the ' land the ' has from ' issue ' rise`ing ' the time and ' vow '
' Rachel ' low you and ' 14 are you bore and from ' land ' to ' carry`ing and
the inherit and ' part ' our of ' till`ing the ' if ' the has say you and ' leah and
' you and as foreign are ' forward`ing ' 15 our as father ' you house in '
' ye ' eat`ing ' also ' eat as and ' our sale ' for ' if ' our reckon has
' from as Allah ' Jehovah ' shade`s the ' which ' ten the ' all ' for ' 16 our silver
' all ' the time and ' our as son of and ' that`ing ' our of ' our as father from
' Jacob ' rise as and ' 17 do`ed ' from as Allah ' are as to ' say ' which
' 18 from as Camel the ' on ' him son ' ye and ' him women ' ye ' lift as and
which ' and property`ing ' all ' ye and ' and purchase`ed ' all ' ye ' lead as and
' highland ' plateau in ' property ' which ' our money ' purchase`ed ' property '
' walk the ' Laban and ' 19 Canaan ' land`ed ' him father ' Isaac ' to ' came`ing of
' from as cure the ' ye ' Rachel ' steal you and ' and flock ' ye ' it shear of
as Aram the ' son of ' heart ' ye ' Jacob ' steal as and ' 20 am father of ' which
shoot as and ' 21 that`ing ' shoot ' for ' if ' my nation the ' as zero in ' until '
' river the ' ye ' cross as and ' rise as and ' if ' which ' all and ' that`ing '
' Laban of ' my told and ' 22 Gilead the ' mountain ' him turn ' ye ' site and
' ye ' took as and ' 23 Jacob ' shoot ' for ' as three`s the ' day as in
' from week ' you seven ' way ' him after ' chase as and ' and people ' him brother
to ' from as Allah ' came as and ' 24 Gilead the ' blemish ' and ye ' cleave as and
guard the ' if ' say as and ' the night`s the ' dream`ing in ' as Aram the ' son of '
' 25 evil ' till ' good`ing from ' Jacob ' people ' word you ' turn ' walk '
' blemish ' and tent ' ye ' slap ' Jacob and ' Jacob ' ye ' son of ' catch and
son of ' say as and ' 26 Gilead the ' blemish ' him brother ' ye ' slap ' Laban and

' lead you and ' as in heart ' ye ' steal you and ' you as do ' what ' Jacob of '
' you secrecy has ' what of ' 27 desolate ' whom`ing sheep ' as daughter`th`ing ' ye
' are send I and ' vessel ' you proclaim ' not and ' near ' steal you and ' shoot of
' not and ' 28 harp`ing in and ' tambourine in ' from as flesh and ' rejoice`ed in
' time`ed ' as daughter`th`ing of and ' as son of ' kiss of ' as give too permit
' you concoct of ' as hand ' divinity ' man ' 29 you and do ' you silly the
' Eli ' say ' lastnight ' your as father ' as Allah and ' evil ' your people
' till ' good`ing from ' Jacob ' people ' word from ' walk ' guard the ' say of
' silver has ' for ' you walk the ' walk the ' the time and ' 30 evil
' ye ' you steal ' what of ' are as father ' you house of ' the you silver has
for ' as you dread ' for ' Laban of ' say as and ' Jacob ' low as and ' 31 as Allah
' 32 as people from ' are as daughter`th`ing ' ye ' tear you ' turn ' as you say '
' over ' am decide ' not ' are as Allah ' ye ' come you ' which ' people
known ' not and ' walk ' ercort ' as stand ' what ' walk ' recognize ' our as brother
' free as and ' son of ' came as and ' 33 from you steal ' Rachel ' for ' Jacob '
' you maid`ed ' twosome ' tent in and ' not'ed ' tent in and ' Jacob ' tent in
' came as and ' not'ed ' tent from ' out and ' come ' not and ' you and slave the
' from as cure the ' ye ' the take ' Rachel and ' 34 Rachel ' tent in
' grope as and ' them as on ' carry you and ' wean the ' first ' from deposite and
am father ' to ' say you and ' 35 come ' not and ' tent the ' all ' ye ' son of
' rise`ing of ' able I ' not`ing ' for ' as master ' as has eye in ' delay ' to '
' not and ' free as and ' vessel ' from as women the ' way ' for ' are around from
' Laban in ' contend and ' Jacob of ' delay and ' 36 from as cure the ' ye ' come
' what and ' as trespass ' what ' Laban of ' say as and ' Jacob ' low as and
' all ' ye ' you grope ' for and ' 37 as after ' you infame ' for ' as you sin

over ' here ' there`s ' are you house ' weapon ' all from ' you come ' what ' weapon

' (38 our two ' between in ' and decide are him and ' are as brother and ' as brother '

' are as Rachel ' are people ' for whither ' the Year ' from as ten ' this

(39 as you eat ' not ' are flock ' as Ram`s and ' and bereave ' not ' are as goat and

' reconcil`ed I ' for whither ' are as to ' as brought the ' not ' torn`ed '

' as you steal`ing and ' day as ' as you steal`ing ' the has seek you ' as hand from

' at cold and ' desolate ' as has eat ' day as in ' as whom became ' (40 the night`s

' vessel ' this ' (41 as purpose`s ' as sleep ' my endure and ' the night`s in

' ten`ed ' four I ' are as you serve ' are you house in ' the Year ' from as ten

' are flock in ' from two ' six and ' are as daughter`th`ing ' twosome in ' the Year

not`s ' if ' (42 from apportion ' you ten ' as you merry from ' ye ' change you and

vessel ' be`s ' Isaac ' startle and ' Abraham ' as Allah ' as father ' as Allah '

have toil ' ye and ' as poor ' ye ' as has you send ' from only`s ' time`ed ' for '

' low as and ' (43 lastnight ' power him and ' from as Allah ' look`ed ' as palm '

' as daughter`th`ing ' daughter`th`ing the ' Jacob ' to ' say as and ' son of

' ye`ed ' which ' all and ' as flock ' flock the and ' as son ' from as son the and

' to`ed of ' do`ed I ' what ' as daughter`th`ing of and ' that`ing ' vessel ' look`ed

walk`ed ' the time and ' (44 and bore as ' which ' behold as son of ' or ' day as the

' beyond ' be`s and ' ye`ed and ' as whither ' covenant`s ' hew`ed has '

' stone ' Jacob ' took as and ' (45 are between in and ' as between in

' him brother of ' Jacob ' say as and ' (46 establish`ed from ' the high`s as and

' heap ' concoct as and ' from as stone ' acquire as and ' from as stone ' and pickup

' fear ' son of ' if ' call as and ' (47 heap the ' on ' there ' and eat as and

' son of ' say as and ' (48 till ' heap ' if ' call ' Jacob and ' I you and record

' on ' day as the ' are between in and ' as between in ' till ' this the ' heap the

espy as ' say ' which ' thus espy them and ' 49 till ' heap ' name ' call ' so
' man I ' is camouflage ' for ' are between in and ' as between in ' Jehovah '
' mother and ' as daughter`th`ing ' ye ' vouch`ed ' mother ' 50 alas evil from
our people ' man I ' whither`s ' as daughter`th`ing ' on ' from as women ' implicate
say as and ' 51 are between in and ' as between in ' till ' from as Allah ' look`ed '
which ' altar`ed the ' be`th and ' this the ' heap the ' be`th ' Jacob of ' son of '
' heap the ' till ' 52 are between in and ' as between in ' as whom ' you dread '
' cross I ' not ' as whither ' mother ' altar`ed the ' till`ed and ' this the
' cross you ' not ' ye`ed ' mother and ' this the ' heap the ' ye ' are as to
53 the evil of ' such the ' altar`ed the ' ye and ' this the ' heap the ' ye ' Eli
' our as between in ' and discern as ' Nahor ' as Allah and ' Abraham ' as Allah '
' him father ' startle in ' Jacob ' swear too as and ' them as father ' as Allah
' call as and ' blemish ' sacrifice ' Jacob ' sacrifice as and ' 54 Isaac
blemish ' and tarry`s and ' fight ' and eat as and ' fight ' eat of ' him brother of
' him son of ' kiss as and ' is morn in ' son of ' ridge as and ' 55
' dwell and ' walk as and ' them ye ' bless as and ' him daughter`th`ing of and
and place`ing of ' son of

' and in ' and entreat as and ' and way of ' walk the ' Jacob and ' 1
' boost ' which are ' Jacob ' say as and ' 2 from as Allah ' as messenger from
that`ing the ' place`ing the ' there ' call as and ' this ' from as Allah ' the camp
' to ' him before ' from as messenger from ' Jacob ' send as and ' 3 from as camp '
' command as and ' 4 Edom ' field`ed ' gate`s ' land`ed ' him brother ' concoct
' say ' here ' Esau of ' as master of ' has and say you ' here ' say of ' from ye
' 5 time`ed ' till ' after and ' as you guest ' son of ' people ' Jacob ' are serve
' serve and ' flock ' heass`ing and ' captain`ing ' vessel ' became as and
' grace ' come of ' as master of ' fortune`s the of ' send`ed I and ' the slave and
say of ' Jacob ' to ' from as messenger them ' and dwell and ' 6 are as has eye in
' walk the ' also and ' concoct ' to ' are as brother ' to ' and has came '
dread as and ' 7 and people ' man I ' you and hundred ' four I and ' are you call of
' which ' people the ' ye ' allot and ' if ' mould and ' especially ' Jacob '
' two of ' from as camel the and ' herd the ' ye and ' flock the ' ye and ' and ye
' camp`ed the ' to ' concoct ' came`ing as ' mother ' say as and ' 8 you and camp
' remain behold ' camp`ed the ' be`s and ' and smitten`ed and ' sister the
' Abraham ' as father ' as Allah ' Jacob ' say as and ' 9 the escape`s of
' carry`ing ' Eli ' say the ' Jehovah ' Isaac ' as father ' as Allah and
' 10 are people ' the good`s hence and ' are you bore and from ' to and ' are land of
which ' you mother the ' all from and ' from as my spare the ' all from ' as you small
' ye ' as you cross ' as stick in ' for ' are serve ' ye ' you as do '
' 11 you and camp ' two of ' as whom became ' the time and ' this the ' has desend the
dread ' for ' concoct ' hand from ' as brother ' hand from ' oh ' as has shade`s the
' on ' maid ' as stable and ' came`ing as ' turn ' and ye ' for whither '
' are people ' good`s hence ' good became ' you say ' ye`ed and ' 12 from as son the

report as ' not ' which ' sea the ' of sand are ' are seed ' ye ' as you there and
' took as and ' that`ing the ' the night`s in ' there ' tarry and ' 13 much '
' 14 him brother ' Esau of ' bestow`ed ' and hand in ' came the ' has from
' from as ewe ' from as ten ' from as buck`s and ' from as you hundred ' from as Goat
' from as Camel ' 15 from as ten ' from as Ram`s and ' from as you hundred
' you and bullock ' from as three ' them as son and ' you and suck`s from
' from as ten ' you and give I ' ten`ed ' from as bullock and ' from as four I
' drove ' drove ' him serve ' hand in ' give as and ' 16 ten`ed ' from as town`s and
' spirit is and ' as before ' and cross ' him serve ' to ' say as and ' and alone of
' command as and ' 17 drove ' between in and ' drove ' between in ' and deposite`s
' as brother ' concoct ' are meet as ' for ' say of ' has and head`s the ' ye
' who of and ' walk you ' whither`ed and ' ye`ed ' kind ' say of ' are ask and
that`s ' bestow`ed ' Jacob of ' are serve of ' you say and ' 18 are as before ' to`ed
our as after ' that`ing ' also ' be`th and ' Esau of ' as master of ' the send`ing '
also and ' as three`s the ' ye ' also ' two the ' ye ' also ' command as and ' 19
' word are ' say of ' from as drove the ' as after ' from as enter the ' all ' ye '
' 20 and ye ' from are come in ' concoct ' to ' shall word you ' this the
' for ' our as after ' came ' Jacob ' are serve ' be`th ' also ' from you say and
' as before ' you enter the ' rest`ed from in ' him turn ' the atone I ' say
' 21 around ' linger ' as maybe I ' him turn ' cat`ed ' so ' as after and
the night`s in ' stop ' that`ing and ' him turn ' on ' bestow`ed the ' cross you and
' that`ing the ' the night`s in ' rise as and ' 22 camp`ed in ' that`ing the '
ye and ' him you slave ' twosome ' ye and ' him women ' twosome ' ye ' took as and
' 23 spew the ' cross from ' ye ' cross as and ' him bore as ' ten ' one '
all ' ye ' cross as and ' inherit the ' ye ' from cross as and ' from took as and

' man I ' float as and ' and alone of ' Jacob ' survive as and ' (24 if ' which '

if ' finish ' not ' for ' look as and ' (25 black the ' offer`ing ' till ' and people

' Jacob ' soft ' palm ' slap and ' and soft ' palm in ' expire as and '

' black the ' on`ed ' for ' as has send ' say as and ' (26 and people ' and float thus

' say as and ' (27 as has you bless ' mother ' for ' are send I ' not ' say as and

say as ' Jacob ' not ' say as and ' (28 Jacob ' say as and ' rug ' what ' him to

' people ' you as captain ' for ' Israel ' mother ' for ' rug ' till`ing '

' Jacob ' ask as and ' (29 able you and ' from as person ' people and ' from as Allah

' ask you ' this ' what of ' say as and ' rug ' oh ' the proclaim`s ' say as and

' there ' Jacob ' call as and ' (30 there ' and ye ' bless as and ' as there of

' to ' inner`s ' from as Allah ' as you seen ' for ' to and turn ' place`ing the

' which are ' sun the ' if ' appear as and ' (31 as soul ' shade give and ' inner`s

' so ' on ' (32 and soft ' on ' rib`ing ' that`ing and ' to and turn ' ye ' Obara

on ' which ' help`ed the ' fortune`s ' ye ' Israel ' as son ' and eat as ' not

' soft ' palm in ' touch ' for ' this the ' day as the ' till ' soft the ' palm '

help`ed the ' fortune`s in ' Jacob

' came ' concoct ' be`th and ' look as and ' him has eye ' Jacob ' lift as and ' 1

' ye ' allot and ' man I ' you and hundred ' four I ' and people and

' twosome ' on and ' Rachel ' on and ' not'ed ' on ' from as bore as the

' has am bore as ' ye and ' you and slave the ' ye ' site and ' 2 you and slave the

' ye and ' from as has after ' am bore as and ' not'ed ' ye and ' the has and head`s

them as before ' Obara ' that`ing and ' 3 from as has after ' Joseph ' ye and ' Rachel

' and accost ' till ' from as move ' seven ' land`ed ' the and humble`ly as and '

and embrace`ed as and ' and you call of ' concoct ' run as and ' 4 him brother ' till

lift as and ' 5 and wept and ' and moisten`ed as and ' and neck did ' on ' fell and '

' ye and ' from as women the ' ye ' look as and ' him has eye ' ye '

' say as and ' walk ' to`ed ' who ' say as and ' from as bore as the

' 6 are serve ' ye ' from as Allah ' favor ' which ' from as bore as the

' has am bore as and ' be`th ' you and slave the ' the has I`ll you and

' am bore as and ' not'ed ' also ' I`ll you and ' 7 the has as and humble`ly you and

' Rachel and ' Joseph ' presence ' after and ' prostate humble`ly as and

this the ' camp`ed the ' all ' walk ' who ' say as and ' 8 prostate humble`ly as and

' 9 as master ' as has eye in ' grace ' come of ' say as and ' as you meet ' which '

' walk ' became as and ' as brother ' increase ' vessel ' man ' concoct ' say as and

' as you come ' oh ' mother ' oh ' to ' Jacob ' say as and ' 10 walk ' which

' on ' for ' as hand from ' as bring from ' you take and ' are as has eye in ' grace

' from as Allah ' around ' as you and look are ' are as turn ' as you seen ' so

' as brought the ' which ' as you bless ' ye ' oh ' took ' 11 as accept you and

' all ' vessel ' man ' for and ' from as Allah ' as has grace ' for ' walk

' walk`ed has and ' the go ' say as and ' 12 took as and ' and in ' urge as and

' for ' known ' as master ' him to ' say as and ' 13 are over of ' the eat and

’ offer`ing ’ herd the and ’ flock the and ’ from as faint ’ from as bore as the
flock the ’ all ’ and die and ’ one ’ day as ’ from as you and knock and ’ mosthigh
’ as whither and ’ and serve ’ as before ’ as master ’ oh ’ cross as ’ 14
’ as before ’ which ’ the messenger from the ’ foot of ’ as tender of ’ flow`ed ye
’ as master ’ to ’ came`ing I ’ which ’ till ’ from as bore as the ’ foot of and
’ has from ’ are people ’ oh ’ the seat`s I ’ concoct ’ say as and ’ 15 the Seir
’ grace ’ come I ’ this ’ what of ’ say as and ’ near ’ which ’ people the
’ concoct ’ that`ing the ’ day as in ’ dwell and ’ 16 as master ’ as has eye in
’ if ’ son as and ’ the booth`ing ’ go ’ Jacob and ’ 17 the Seir ’ and way of
there ’ call ’ so ’ on ’ Succoth`ing ’ do`ed ’ and purchase`ed of and ’ you house
’ town`s ’ from and peace ’ Jacob ’ came as and ’ 18 Succoth`ing ’ place`ing the ’
’ encamp and ’ highland ’ Padan from ’ and came in ’ Canaan ’ land in ’ which ’ ridge
’ field`ed the ’ you smooth at ’ ye ’ nest as and ’ 19 town`s the ’ around ’ ye
’ as father ’ heass`ing ’ as son ’ hand from ’ and tent ’ there ’ permit`ed ’ which
sacrifice from ’ there ’ establish as and ’ 20 the balance`s ’ the hundred in ’ ridge
Israel ’ as Allah ’ to ’ if ’ call as and ’

' Jacob of ' bore`ed as ' which ' not`ed ' daughter ' Dinah ' issue you and ' 1
2 ' ridge ' ye`ed ' look as and ' land the ' daughter`th`ing in ' sight`ing the of
' ye`ed ' took as and ' land the ' lift`s has ' as Hivite the ' heass`ing ' son
3 ' Dinah in ' and soul ' cleave you and ' the because and ' ye`ed ' lay as and
' heart ' on ' word as and ' youth`ed the ' ye ' love as and ' Jacob ' daughter
4 ' took ' say of ' him father ' heass`ing ' to ' ridge ' say as and ' youth`ed the
5 ' for ' hear ' Jacob and ' resemble I of ' such the ' boy`ed the ' ye ' vessel
' ye ' him the ' him son and ' and daughter ' Dinah ' ye ' unclean
6 out and ' cubit ' till ' Jacob ' devise`s the and ' field`ed in ' and purchase`ed
7 ' as son and ' and ye ' word of ' Jacob ' to ' ridge ' as father ' heass`ing '
' and vex whom and ' from hear are ' field`ed the ' has from ' and came ' Jacob
' do`ed ' the foolish ' for ' especially ' them of ' delay and ' from as person the
8 ' success`ed ' not ' so and ' Jacob ' daughter ' ye ' lay of ' Israel in
and soul ' the delight ' as son ' ridge ' say of ' from ye ' heass`ing ' word as and
9 ' resemble I of ' if ' ye`ed ' oh ' and give ' your daughter in '
ye and ' our of ' and give you ' your as daughter`th ' and has ye ' our under the and
10 ' and inhabitant ' and give I and ' relate ' and took you ' our as daughter`th '
' the and trade and ' sparkle ' your as before ' be`s you ' land the and
11 Ahijah ' to and ' am father ' to ' ridge ' say as and ' thus ' and hold the and
12 donkey ' Eli ' and say you ' which and ' your as has eye in ' grace ' come I '
' present`ed and ' especially ' mountain from ' mosthigh ' and increase the '
' ye ' vessel ' and give and ' Eli ' and say you ' which are ' the give I and
13 ' ridge ' ye ' Jacob ' as son ' and low as and ' resemble I of ' youth`ed the
and unclean ' which ' and word as and ' craft`ed in ' him father ' heass`ing ' ye and
14 ' able has ' not ' them as to ' and say as and ' from sister ' Dinah ' ye '

' and has sister ' ye ' set of ' this the ' word the ' ye ' you concoct of
' sure ' 15 our of ' that`s ' talk hole ' for ' the foreskin ' if ' which ' man I of
' and storeup`ing ' and as he ' mother ' relate ' ye`ing has ' such in
' ye ' and gave and ' 16 male ' all ' relate ' Circumcise`ing the of
' our of ' took has ' your as daughter`th ' ye and ' relate ' our as daughter`th
' 17 one ' people are of ' our as became and ' from are ye ' and has dwell and
' our take and ' Circumcise`ing the of ' our as to ' and hear you ' not ' mother and
' them as word ' and improve as and ' 18 our walk the and ' our daughter ' ye
' 19 heass`ing ' and son ' ridge ' as has eye in and ' heass`ing ' as has eye in
daughter in ' please ' for ' word the ' you concoct of ' youth the ' after ' not and
' 20 him father ' you house ' all from ' honour has ' that`ing and ' Jacob '
' from town`s ' gate ' to ' and son ' Shechem and ' heass`ing ' came as and
' from as person the ' 21 say of ' from town`s ' as person ' to ' and word as and
' land in ' and dwell and ' and has ye ' them ' from as whole ' these`ed
' from as hand ' you and large ' be`th ' land the and ' ye`ed ' and trade as and
' from as women of ' our of ' took has ' from daughter`th ' ye ' them as before
' and ye`ing as ' such in ' sure ' 22 them of ' gave ' our as daughter`th ' ye and
' people of ' you and became of ' and has ye ' desist of ' from as person the ' our of
' them ' which are ' male ' all ' our of ' circumcise`ing the in ' one
' all and ' from has money and ' them as purchase ' 23 from as circumcise has
' them of ' the ye`ing has ' sure ' them ' our of ' forward`ing ' from you cattle
' ridge ' to and ' heass`ing ' to ' and hear as and ' 24 and has ye ' and dwell and
' male ' all ' and circumcise as and ' and town`s ' gate ' as out ' all ' and son
' as three`s the ' day as in ' became as and ' 25 and town`s ' gate ' as out ' all
' Jacob ' as son ' two ' acquire as and ' from as pain ' complete him the in

' and came as and ' and desolate ' man I ' Dinah ' as brother ' Levi and ' Simeon
' heass`ing ' ye and ' 26 male ' all ' and kill as and ' safe ' town`s the ' on
' ye ' acquire as and ' desolate ' as by ' and kill ' and son ' ridge ' ye and
' and came ' Jacob ' as son and ' 27 and out and ' ridge ' you house from ' Dinah
' and unclean ' which ' town`s the ' loot as and ' from as profane the ' on
' ye and ' from herd ' ye and ' from flock ' ye ' 28 from sister`ing
' field`ed in ' which ' ye and ' town`s in ' which ' ye and ' them as heass`ing
' ye and ' from children ' all ' ye and ' from of life ' all ' ye and ' 29 and take
' 30 you house in ' which ' all ' ye and ' loot as and ' sparkle ' them as woman
' near ' complete disturb ' Levi ' to and ' Simeon ' to ' Jacob ' say as and
' as Periz in and ' as Canaan in ' land the ' ing`dwell in ' as has man I handover of
' mosthigh ' and gather has and ' report from ' extent ' as whither and
' 31 as you house and ' as whither ' as you destory has and ' as shall smitten and
our sister`ing ' ye ' success`ed ' the harlot`ing the ' and say as and

THE TORAH SCROLL 35

' to ' you house ' on`ed ' rise`ing ' Jacob ' to ' from as Allah ' say as and ' 1

' speak`ed the ' divinity ' sacrifice from ' there ' do`ed and ' there ' sojourn

' say as and ' 2 are as brother ' concoct ' around from ' are shoot in ' are as to

and repent`s the ' and people ' which ' all ' to and ' and you house ' to ' Jacob

' and clean the and ' your middle`ing in ' which ' foreign the ' as Allah ' ye '

the on shall ' the rise`ing has and ' 3 from are as you raiment ' and change`s the and

' low`ed the ' divinity ' sacrifice from ' there ' do`ed I and ' to ' you house '

' which ' way in ' as stand ' became as and ' as splendor ' day as in ' near

' as Allah ' all ' ye ' Jacob ' to ' and give as and ' 4 as you walk the

' which ' from as jewelry the ' ye and ' from hand in ' which ' foreign the

' which ' the these`s ' under ' Jacob ' from ye ' hidden as and ' them as ear in

' on ' from as Allah ' you crush ' became as and ' leave as and ' 5 ridge ' people

' as after ' and chase ' not and ' them as you surround`s ' which ' from as town the

Canaan ' land in ' which ' the almond`ing ' Jacob ' came as and ' 6 Jacob ' as son

and people ' which ' people the ' all and ' that`ing ' to ' you house ' that`ing '

' to ' place`ing of ' call as and ' sacrifice from ' there ' son as and ' 7

' from as Allah the ' him to ' and heap`ed has ' there ' for ' to ' you house

' the word`ing ' die you and ' 8 him brother ' around from ' and shoot in

' under ' to ' you house of ' under from ' bury you and ' Rebekeh ' you suck from

' look as and ' 9 weep`ing ' oak`ing ' name ' call as and ' oak`ing the

' highland ' Padan from ' and came in ' till`ing ' Jacob ' to ' from as Allah

' rug ' from as Allah ' if ' say as and ' 10 from as Allah ' and ye ' bless as and

' Israel ' mother ' for ' Jacob ' rug ' till`ing ' call as ' not ' Jacob

' if ' say as and ' 11 Israel ' name ' ye ' call as and ' rug ' be`s as

' the increase and ' apart`ed ' almighty ' to ' as whither ' from as Allah

' from as king and ' with from ' be`s as ' from nation`ing ' assembly and ' nation`ing
Abraham of ' as set has ' which ' land the ' ye and ' 12 and out ' are as change from
' donkey ' are as after ' are seed of and ' the has give I ' walk ' Issac of and '
' which ' place`ing in ' from as Allah ' him on from ' went and ' 13 land the ' ye
' place`ing in ' establish`ed from ' Jacob ' establish as and ' 14 and ye ' word
' libation ' am on ' sculpture and ' stone ' you altar ' and ye ' word ' which
' place`ing the ' there ' ye ' Jacob ' call as and ' 15 eight ' am on ' cast and
' leave as and ' 16 to ' you house ' from as Allah ' there ' and ye ' word ' which
came`ing of ' land the ' you sieve ' till`ing ' became as and ' to ' you house from
' 17 the you bore in ' hard you and ' Rachel ' bore you and ' forth`ed I '
' nihil ' say you and ' the you bore in ' the you and hard thus ' became as and
' 18 son ' walk ' this ' also ' for ' as dread you ' to ' you bore as them
son ' name ' call you and ' die`ed ' for ' the soul ' you issue in ' became as and
Rachel ' die you and ' 19 Benjamim`s ' if ' call ' him father and ' as whither`ing '
' 20 fight ' you house ' that`s ' forth`ed I ' way in ' bury you and '
' that`s ' the you bury ' on ' establish`ed from ' Jacob ' establish as and
' Israel ' onward as and ' 21 day as the ' till ' Rachel ' you bury ' you altar
' 22 drove ' great from of ' not`ed the from ' and tent`ed ' extent and
' Reuben ' walk as and ' that`s the ' land in ' Israel ' nigh in ' became as and
' Israel ' hear as and ' him father ' concubine as put ' Bilhah ' ye ' lay as and
' not'ed ' as son ' 23 ten ' from two ' Jacob ' as son ' and became as and
' Issachar and ' Judah and ' Levi and ' Simeon and ' Reuben ' Jacob ' first`ing
' as son and ' 25 Benjamim`s and ' Joseph ' Rachel ' as son and ' 24 Zebulun and
' trickle'ed ' as son and ' 26 Naphtali and ' judge ' Rachel ' you slave ' Bilhah
' which ' Jacob ' as son ' to`ed ' which and ' fortune ' not'ed ' you slave

' Isaac ' to ' Jacob ' came as and ' 27 highland ' plateau in ' if ' and bore as
guest ' which ' Hebron`ing ' that`s ' four that ' city`s ' appear from ' him father
' each ' Isaac ' week ' and became as and ' 28 Isaac and ' Abraham ' there '
' die as and ' Isaac ' expire`ing as and ' 29 the Year ' from as eight and ' the Year
' and bury as and ' from week ' seven and ' elder ' him people ' to ' gather as and
him son ' Jacob and ' concoct ' and ye

’ concoct ’ (2 Edom ’ that`ing ’ concoct ’ you and bore you and ’ to`ed and ’ (1
’ till`ed ’ ye ’ Canaan ’ daughter`th`ing from ’ him women ’ ye ’ took of
’ low`ed ’ daughter ’ Oholibamah ’ ye and ’ as Heth the ’ Elon`ing ’ daughter
’ daughter ’ you dance ’ Bashemath ’ ye and ’ (3 as Hivite the ’ Zibeon ’ daughter
Esau of ’ till`ed ’ bore you and ’ (4 `you and house has ’ you and brother ’ Ishmael
’ (5 Reuel ’ ye ’ bore`ed as ’ you dance ’ Bashemath and ’ Eliphaz ’ ye ’
bald ’ ye and ’ eternal as ’ ye and ’ Jeush`ing ’ ye ’ bore`ed as ’ Oholibamah and
’ (6 Canaan ’ land in ’ if ’ and bore as ’ which ’ concoct ’ as son ’ to`ed ’
’ ye and ’ him son ’ ye and ’ him women ’ ye ’ concoct ’ took as and
’ ye and ’ and you house ’ you and soul ’ all ’ ye and ’ him daughter`th
’ which ’ our money ’ all ’ ye and ’ and you cattle ’ all ’ ye and ’ and purchase`ed
’ around from ’ Canaan ’ land from ’ to ’ walk as and ’ Canaan ’ land in ’ property
you carry from ’ increase ’ from property`ing ’ be`s ’ for ’ (7 him brother ’ Jacob
’ arise of ’ them as guest`ing from ’ land ’ all`ed as ’ not and ’ together as ’
’ gate`s ’ blemish ’ concoct ’ dwell and ’ (8 them as purchase ’ around from ’ from ye
’ concoct ’ you and bore you and ’ to`ed and ’ (9 Edom ’ that`ing ’ concoct
’ concoct ’ as son ’ you name ’ to`ed ’ (10 gate`s ’ blemish ’ Edom ’ as father
you dance ’ Bashemath ’ son ’ Reuel ’ concoct ’ wife ’ till`ed ’ son ’ Eliphaz
’ Amar`ing ’ Teman ’ Eliphaz ’ as son ’ and became as and ’ (11 concoct ’ wife ’
’ concubine as put ’ whom`ed the ’ Timma and ’ (12 Kenaz and ’ Gatam and ’ and espy and
’ to`ed ’ Amalek ’ ye ’ Eliphaz of ’ bore you and ’ concoct ’ son ’ Eliphaz of
’ bring ’ Reuel ’ as son ’ to`ed and ’ (13 concoct ’ wife ’ till`ed ’ as son
’ Bashemath ’ as son ’ him the ’ to`ed ’ victual`ed and ’ there`ed ’ Zerah and
’ Oholibamah ’ as son ’ him the ’ to`ed and ’ (14 concoct ’ wife ’ you dance
’ Esau of ’ bore you and ’ concoct ’ wife ’ Zibeon ’ daughter ’ low`ed ’ daughter

' as thousand`ing ' to`ed ' 15 bald ' ye and ' eternal as ' ye and ' Jeush`ing ' ye
' Teman ' thousand`ing ' concoct ' first`ing ' Eliphaz ' as son ' concoct ' as son
' 16 tracker ' thousand`ing ' Zep`ing ' thousand`ing ' Amar`ing ' thousand`ing
' to`ed ' Amalek ' thousand`ing ' Gatham ' thousand`ing ' bald ' thousand`ing
' 17 till`ed ' as son ' to`ed ' Edom ' land in ' Eliphaz ' as thousand`ing
' thousand`ing ' bring ' thousand`ing ' concoct ' son ' Reuel ' as son ' to`ed and
' to`ed ' victual`ed ' thousand`ing ' rejoice`ed ' thousand`ing ' emerge
' Bashemath ' as son ' to`ed ' Edom ' land in ' Reuel ' as thousand`ing
concoct ' wife ' Oholibamah ' as son ' to`ed and ' 18 concoct ' wife ' you dance
to`ed ' bald ' thousand`ing ' eternal as ' thousand`ing ' Jeush`ing ' thousand`ing '
' to`ed ' 19 concoct ' wife ' low`ed ' daughter ' Oholibamah ' as thousand`ing '
20 Edom ' that`ing ' concoct ' them as thousand`ing ' to`ed and ' concoct ' as son
' Lotan ' land the ' as sojourn as ' as hole the ' gate`s ' as son ' to`ed and '
' Ezert and ' s`statisfy`ing and ' 21 Anah and ' Zibeon and ' Shobal and
' land in ' gate`s ' as son ' as hole the ' as thousand`ing ' to`ed ' s`statisfy and
' they became and ' cavedweller ' Lotan ' as son ' and became as and ' 22 Edom
' Olvan ' Shobal ' as son ' to`ed and ' 23 Timma ' Lotan ' sister`ing and
' Zibeon ' as son ' to`ed and ' 24 Onam and ' Shepho`ing ' Ebal and ' Manahath and
' from week that ' ye ' come ' which ' low`ed ' that`ing ' Anah and ' where`s and
' 25 him father ' Zibeon of ' from as heass`ing the ' ye ' and Berat ' word from in
' 26 low`ed ' daughter ' Oholibamah and ' s`Dishon`ing ' low`ed ' as son ' to`ed and
Cheren and ' Ithran and ' Eshbah and ' has desire ' s`Dishon`ing ' as son ' to`ed and
' as son ' to`ed ' 28 Akan and ' Zaavan`ing and ' Bilhan ' Ezer ' as son ' to`ed ' 27
' as hole the ' as thousand`ing ' to`ed ' 29 master and ' tree`ing ' Dishon`s
thousand`ing ' Zibeon ' thousand`ing ' Shobal ' thousand`ing ' Lotan ' thousand`ing

' thousand`ing ' Ezer ' thousand`ing ' s`Dishon`ing ' thousand`ing ' 30 low`ed '
' land in ' them as thousand`ing of ' as hole the ' as thousand`ing ' to`ed ' Dishon`s
' Edom ' land in ' and king ' which ' from as king the ' to`ed and ' 31 gate`s
' Edom`ing in ' king as and ' 32 Israel ' as son of ' king ' king ' as before
' 33 handover`ed judge ' and town`s ' there and ' burn`ing ' son ' worthless
' emerge ' son ' Jobab ' him under ' king as and ' worthless ' die as and
' enrich ' him under ' king as and ' Jobab ' die as and ' 34 defence`ed from
Hadad ' him under ' king as and ' enrich ' die as and ' 35 as Teman`s the ' land from
' Moab ' field`ed in ' as Midian`s the ' ye ' here them ' single ' son '
him under ' king as and ' Hadad ' die as and ' 36 whom Avim ' and town`s ' there and
' him under ' king as and ' raiment`ed ' die as and ' 37 Masrekah from ' raiment`ed '
' king as and ' Saul ' die as and ' 38 river the ' you and large from ' Saul
' son ' favor ' marry ' die as and ' 39 Achbor ' son ' favor ' marry ' him under
' and scream ' and town`s ' there and ' Hadad ' him under ' king as and ' Achbor
40 gold ' who ' daughter ' my rain ' daughter ' Mehetabel ' and wife ' there and
' complete and at family of ' concoct ' as thousand`ing ' you name ' to`ed and '
' thousand`ing ' Timma ' thousand`ing ' from garlic'ing in ' from you place`ing of
to`ed ' thousand`ing ' Oholibamah ' thousand`ing ' 41 set as ' thousand`ing ' Olvah
' Teman ' thousand`ing ' tracker ' thousand`ing ' 42 has turn`s ' thousand`ing '
' from town`s ' thousand`ing ' Magdiel ' thousand`ing ' 43 Mibzar ' thousand`ing
' land in ' complete and at family of ' Edom ' as thousand`ing ' to`ed
Edom ' as father ' concoct ' that`ing ' from you hold

Canaan ' land in ' him father ' as guest`ing from ' land in ' Jacob ' dwell and ' 1
' ten`ed ' seven ' son ' Joseph ' Jacob ' you and bore and you ' to`ed ' 2
' youth ' that`ing and ' flock in ' him brother ' ye ' evil`ed ' be`s ' the Year
' him father ' as women ' trickle'ed ' as son ' ye and ' Bilhah ' as son ' ye
' 3 them as father ' to ' evil`ed ' from slander ' ye ' Joseph ' came as and
from as elder ' son ' for ' him son ' all from ' Joseph ' ye ' love ' Israel and
' see as and ' 4 from as tunic ' you coat ' if ' do`ed as and ' if ' that`ing '
' him son ' all from ' them as father ' love ' and ye ' for ' him brother
' him word ' and all as ' not and ' and ye ' and hateful as and ' him brother
him brother of ' my told and ' dream`ing ' Joseph ' dream as and ' 5 from and peace of
and hear ' them as to ' say as and ' 6 and ye ' hateful ' till`ing ' and Joseph and '
' and us I ' be`th and ' 7 as you dream ' which ' this the ' dream`ing the ' oh '
' be`th and ' field`ed the ' middle`ing in ' from as sheave ' from as sheave from
' the governor`s you ' be`th and ' the settle ' also and ' as you sheave ' rise`ed
' 8 as you sheave of ' the has as and humble`ly you and ' your as you sheave
' mother ' our as on ' king you ' king`ing the ' him brother ' if ' and say as and
' on ' and ye ' hateful ' till`ing ' and Joseph and ' and son ' rule you ' rule`ing
' after ' dream`ing ' till`ing ' dream as and ' 9 him word ' on and ' him you dream
' as you dream ' be`th ' say as and ' him brother of ' and ye ' report as and
' ten ' one and ' moon the and ' sun the ' be`th and ' till`ing ' dream`ing
' to ' report as and ' 10 vessel ' from as and humble`ly from ' from as in star`ing
say as and ' him father ' and in ' reproof as and ' him brother ' to and ' him father
' came`ing the ' you dream ' which ' this the ' dream`ing the ' what ' if '
' are as brother and ' are mother and ' as whither ' prophet`ing
' and in ' and jealous as and ' 11 land`ed ' walk ' you and humble`ly the of

' and walk as and ' 12 word the ' ye ' guard ' him father and ' him brother
say as and ' 13 ridge in ' them as father ' flock ' ye ' you tend of ' him brother
' ridge in ' from as evil ' are as brother ' forward`ing ' Joseph ' to ' Israel '
say as and ' 14 as behold`th ' if ' say as and ' them as to ' are send I and ' walk`ed
' ye and ' are as brother ' from and peace ' ye ' look`ed and ' oh ' walk ' if '
' and the send as and ' word ' as has carry`ing the and ' flock the ' from and peace
' man that ' alas come as and ' 15 ridge`ed ' came as and ' Hebron`ing ' valley from
' what ' say of ' man that ' and ask`ed as and ' field`ed in ' seduce`ed ' be`th and
' seek from ' for whither ' as brother ' ye ' say as and ' 16 seek you
say as and ' 17 from as evil ' them ' the put hence ' vessel ' oh ' the proclaim`s
walk`ed has ' from as say ' from as you hear ' for ' victual`ed ' and go ' man that '
' from come as and ' him brother ' as after ' Joseph ' walk as and ' Dothan`s '
' approach as ' suspend in and ' get from ' and ye ' see as and ' 18 Dothan`s in
' and say as and ' 19 and die`s the of ' and ye ' and conspire you as and ' them as to
20 came ' this of the ' you and dream the ' marry ' be`th ' him brother ' to ' man I
' one in ' alas hurl shall ' and the kill shall ' follow ' the time and '
the look shall ' and he eat ' evil`ed ' the life ' our say and ' you and empty`ing the
' Reuben ' hear as and ' 21 him you dream ' and became as ' what '
' 22 soul ' and has strike ' not ' say as and ' from hand from ' and shade`ed as and
' and hurl`s the ' blood ' and pour you ' to ' Reuben ' them as to ' say as and
' to ' friend`s ' word from in ' which ' this the ' empty`ing the ' to ' and ye
' from hand from ' and ye ' shade`s the ' purpose of ' and in ' and send you
Joseph ' came ' which are ' became as and ' 23 him father ' to ' and carry`s the of
ye ' and you coat ' ye ' Joseph ' ye ' and pull`s as and ' him brother ' to '
' alas took as and ' 24 and Mosthigh ' which ' from as tunic the ' you coat '

whither`s ' only`s ' empty`ing the and ' the empty`ing the ' and ye ' and hurl as and

' and lift as and ' fight ' eat of ' and dwell and ' 25 Water ' and in '

' came`ed ' from as Ishmeal ' you manner ' be`th and ' see as and ' them as has eye

' Lot and ' balm and ' you smite ' from as lift has ' them as Camel and ' Gilead from

to ' Judah ' say as and ' 26 the from as Mizra ' up`s alas of ' from as walk alas

' our as brother ' ye ' kill has ' for ' profit ' what ' him brother '

' and has sale shall ' follow ' 27 and blood ' ye ' our as conceal and

' for ' and in ' be`s you ' to ' and has hand and ' from as Ishmeal of

' 28 him brother ' and hear as and ' that`ing ' our flesh and ' our as brother

and remove as and ' from as trade ' from as Midian ' from as person ' and cross as and

' ye ' and sale as and ' empty`ing the ' has from ' Joseph ' ye ' and went and '

' ye ' and came`s as and ' silver ' from as ten in ' from as Ishmeal of ' Joseph

be`th and ' empty`ing the ' to ' Reuben ' dwell and ' 29 the from as Mizra ' Joseph

' dwell and ' 30 him fabric ' ye ' rend as and ' empty`ing in ' Joseph ' whither`s '

' as whither and ' and has whither`s ' boy the ' say as and ' him brother ' to

' Joseph ' you coat ' ye ' acquire as and ' 31 came ' as whither ' whither`ed

' you coat the ' ye ' and dip as and ' from as Goat ' gate`s ' and slay as and

' from as tunic the ' you coat ' ye ' and send as and ' 32 blood in

and has come ' such ' and say as and ' them as father ' to ' the and came`s as and

' 33 not ' mother ' that`s ' are son ' you coat the ' oh ' recognize '

' evil`ed ' the life ' that`s ' as son ' you coat ' say as and ' the pasture`s as and

' him you raiment ' Jacob ' rend as and ' 34 Joseph ' torn ' torn ' and he eat

' from week ' and son ' on ' mourn whom and ' him has die in ' moisten ' site and

' him daughter`th ' all and ' him son ' all ' and rise as and ' 35 from as increase

to ' wander ' for ' say as and ' comfort you no ' refuse as and ' and comfort of

36 ' him father ' and ye ' against as and ' the ask`ing ' mourn ' as son '
' the from as Mizra ' Joseph ' to ' and ye ' and sale ' from as midian`s the and
from as butcher the ' captain ' Pharaoh ' officer`s ' Potiphar of

' each ' Judah ' descend and ' that`s the ' time in ' became as and ' (1
' (2 the hole's ' name and ' Adullam ' man I ' till ' extent and ' him brother
save`ing ' name and ' as Canaan ' man I ' daughter ' Judah ' there ' look as and
' son ' bore you and ' pregnant and ' (3 Eli`ed ' came as and ' the took as and '
' son ' bore you and ' till`ing ' pregnant and ' (4 town ' name ' ye ' call as and
' till`ing ' further and ' (5 has whither`ing ' name ' ye ' call you and
' be`s and ' peace`ed ' name ' ye ' call you and ' son ' bore you and
' Woman ' Judah ' took as and ' (6 and ye ' the you bore in ' the secrete's are in
' town ' became as and ' (7 constant ' there`ed and ' and first`ing ' town of
(8 Jehovah ' and die`ed as and ' Jehovah ' as has eye in ' evil ' Judah ' first`ing
' are as brother ' wife ' to ' came ' Onan of ' Judah ' say as and '
' known and ' (9 are as brother of ' seed ' rise`s the and ' ye`ed ' brotherinlaw and
' came ' mother ' be`s and ' seed the ' be`s as ' if ' not ' for ' has whither`ing
' seed ' gave ' as except of ' land`ed ' eradicate and ' him brother ' wife ' to
' do`ed ' which ' ye ' Jehovah ' as has eye in ' evil as and ' (10 him brother of
' and daugtherinlaw ' Tamar of ' Judah ' say as and ' (11 and ye ' also ' die as and
' peace`ed ' great as ' till ' are as father ' you house ' the widow I ' captive
' him brother are ' that`ing ' also ' die`ing as ' turn ' say ' for ' as son
' (12 am father ' you house ' carry you and ' constant ' are hang and
' wife ' save`ing ' daughter ' die you and ' from week the ' and increase as and
' and flock ' as it shear ' on I ' went and ' Judah ' comfort as and ' Judah
my told and ' (13 he portion ' as Adullam the ' and shepherd is ' Hirah and ' that`ing
' on`ed ' are fatherinlaw ' be`th ' say of ' and daugtherinlaw ' Tamar of '
' as fabric ' repent you and ' (14 and flock ' shear of ' he portion
' put elude you and ' veil`s in ' conceal set and ' am above ' the you and widow I

' for ' he portion ' way ' on ' which ' from as has eye ' open in ' carry you and
resemble I of ' if ' gave`ed ' not ' that`s and ' peace`ed ' great ' for ' sight`ed
' for ' the prostitute`ing ' the reckon as and ' Judah ' look`ed as and ' 15
' say as and ' way the ' to ' Eli`ed ' extent and ' 16 the around ' garment`ed
' for ' known ' not ' for ' are as to ' came`ing I ' oh ' handover`ed
income`ing ' for ' vessel ' has set ' what ' say you and ' that`s ' and daugtherinlaw
' has from ' from as Goat ' kid ' send I ' for whither ' say as and ' 17 Eli '
' 18 are send ' till ' shall in town ' has set ' mother ' say you and ' flock the
' say you and ' walk ' donkey ' which ' shall in town the ' what ' say as and
' give as and ' are hand in ' which ' are down and ' are lace`s and ' are signet`s
' are hang and ' rise you and ' 19 if ' pregnant and ' Eli`ed ' came as and ' nihil
the you and widow I ' as fabric ' arm you and ' am above ' the veil`s ' repent you and
' hand in ' from as Goat the ' kid ' ye ' Judah ' send as and ' 20
' hand from ' shall in town the ' you take ' as Adullam the ' and shepherd is
' the place`ing ' as person ' ye ' ask as and ' 21 come`ed ' not and ' Woman the
' way the ' on ' from as has eye in ' that`s ' holy`ed the ' where`s ' say of
' to ' dwell and ' 22 the holy ' spoil`ed ' whom`ed the ' not ' and say as and
place`ing the ' as person ' also and ' the as you come ' not ' say as and ' Judah
' Judah ' say as and ' 23 the holy ' spoil`ed ' whom`ed the ' not ' and say '
ye ' as you send ' be`th ' spoil`ing of ' the became has ' turn ' nihil ' implicate
' became as and ' 24 the you come ' not ' ye`ed and ' this the ' kid the '
' whore`ed ' say of ' Judah of ' my told and ' from as new ' you three from are
from as coitus`ing of ' mountain`ed ' be`th ' also and ' are daughterinlaw ' constant
' that`s ' 25 burnt you and ' the and issue`s alas ' Judah ' say as and '
' man I of ' say of ' the fatherinlaw ' to ' the send ' that`s and ' grip and from

' oh ' recognize ' say you and ' mountain`ed ' for whither ' if ' to`ed ' which
25 ' these`ed ' down`ed the and ' from as lace`s the and ' you signet`s the ' kind
' so ' on ' for ' apportion from ' just`ed ' say as and ' Judah ' recollect and
' till`ing ' add ' not and ' as son ' the Shilo of ' am set has ' not
' be`th and ' the you bore ' time in ' became as and ' 27 the knowledge of
' give as and ' the you bore in ' became as and ' 28 the womb in ' from as twin`ing
' two ' and hand ' on ' bind you and ' you bore as them ' took you and ' hand
and hand ' sit`s are ' became as and ' 29 the and has head`s ' out ' this ' say of
' our are as on ' you grow ' what ' say you and ' him brother ' out ' be`th and '
him brother ' out ' so ' as after and ' 30 grow ' name ' ye ' call as and ' grow
emerge ' name ' call as and ' two the ' and hand ' on ' which '

' Potiphar ' and the bought and ' the from as Mizra ' up alas ' Joseph and ' 1
' hand from ' as Mizra ' man I ' from as butcher the ' captain ' Pharaoh ' officer`s
Jehovah ' became as and ' 2 there`ed ' alas cart`s the ' which ' from as Ishmeal the
' became as and ' proper`s from ' man I ' became as and ' Joseph ' ye '
Jehovah ' for ' him master ' look as and ' 3 as Mizra the ' him master ' you house in
' proper`s from ' Jehovah ' do`ed ' that`ing ' which ' all and ' and ye '
' him master ' him has eye in ' grace ' Joseph ' come as and ' 4 and hand in
' all and ' and you house ' on ' alas my appoint as and ' and ye ' minister as and
' it hundred ' became as and ' 5 and hand in ' gave ' if ' man ' which
' if ' man ' which ' all ' on and ' and you house in ' and ye ' hand appoint the
' Joseph ' sake in ' as Mizra the ' you house ' ye ' Jehovah ' bless as and
' you house in ' if ' man ' which ' all in ' Jehovah ' you bless ' became as and
' not and ' Joseph ' hand in ' if ' which ' all ' forsake as and ' 6 field`ed in and
able I ' that`ing ' which ' fight the ' mother ' for ' the noth`ing ' and ye ' known
7 look`ed from ' the beautiful and ' figure ' beautiful`ed ' Joseph ' became as and '
' wife ' lift you and ' these`ed ' from as word the ' after ' became as and '
8 ' as people ' the lay ' say you and ' Joseph ' to ' am has eye ' ye ' him master
' not ' as master ' behold ' him master ' wife ' to ' say as and ' refuse as and
' gave ' if ' man ' which ' all and ' you house in ' the noth`ing ' near ' known
' this the ' you house in ' great`ing ' and has whither`s ' 9 as hand in
' mother ' for ' the noth`ing ' apportion from ' dark ' not and ' apportion from
' evil`ed the ' do`ed I ' are hence and ' and wife ' ye ' which in ' are ye`ing
' became as and ' 10 from as Allah of ' as you sin and ' such the ' great`ed the
' Eli`ed ' hear ' not and ' day as and ' day as ' Joseph ' to ' the word are
' became as and ' 11 people`ed ' you and became of ' beside`ed ' lay of

' you concoct of ' he house the ' Joseph ' came as and ' this the ' day as the are
' as person from ' man I ' whither`s and ' you house in ' and you are fill
' him fabric in ' and handle'ed you and ' 12 you house in ' there ' you house the
flee as and ' hand`ed in ' him fabric ' forsake as and ' as people ' the lay ' say of
' forsake ' for ' he see are ' became as and ' 13 the outside`ing the ' out and '
' 14 the outside`ing the ' out and ' flee as and ' hand`ed in ' him fabric
' see ' say of ' them of ' say you and ' he house ' as person of ' call you and
lay of ' Eli ' came ' and son ' laught of ' as Obara ' man I ' our of ' came`s the
and hear are ' became as and ' 15 great`ing ' voice`ing in ' call I and ' as people '
' him fabric ' forsake as and ' call I and ' as voice`ing ' as you high`s the ' for '
rest you and ' 16 the outside`ing the ' out and ' flee as and ' as beside ' as hand in
' 17 and you house ' to ' him master ' came`ing ' till ' beside`ed ' him fabric '
' Eli ' came ' say of ' these`ed ' from as word are ' him to ' word you and
' 18 house ' laught of ' our of ' brought the ' which ' as cross the ' serve the
' forsake as and ' call I and ' as voice`ing ' as high`s the are ' became as and
' became as and ' 19 the outside`ing the ' flee as and ' as beside ' him fabric
' him to ' Deborah ' which ' and wife ' as word ' ye ' him master ' hear are
' delay and ' are serve ' vessel ' do`ed ' these`ed ' from as word are ' say of
' to ' and give`ed as and ' and ye ' Joseph ' as master ' took as and ' 20 now
' king the ' as bound`ing ' which ' place`ing ' prison the ' you house
' 21 prison the ' you house in ' there ' became as and ' from as bound`ing
give as and ' bow ' him to ' extent and ' Joseph ' ye ' Jehovah ' became as and
' give as and ' 22 prison the ' you house ' captain ' as has eye in ' and grace '
' all ' ye ' Joseph ' hand in ' prison the ' you house ' captain
' which ' all ' ye and ' prison the ' you house in ' which ' from as bound`ing the

' you house ' captain ' whither`s ' 23 do`ed ' be`s ' that`ing ' there ' from as do
' Jehovah ' which in ' and hand in ' the noth`ing ' all ' ye ' look`ed ' prison the
proper`s from ' Jehovah ' do`ed ' that`ing ' which and ' all and ' and ye

’ moisten`ed from ’ and sin ’ these`ed ’ from as word the ’ after ’ became as and ’ 1
2 ’ from as Mizra ’ king of ’ them as master of ’ the cook and ’ from as Mizra ’ king
’ captain ’ on ’ him officer`s ’ two ’ on ’ Pharaoh ’ angry as and
’ from ye ’ give as and ’ 3 from as cook`ing ’ captain ’ on and ’ from as steward the
’ you house ’ to ’ from as butcher the ’ captain ’ you house ’ guard from in
’ punish as and ’ 4 there ’ bound`ing ’ Joseph ’ which ’ place`ing ’ prison the
’ from ye ’ minister as and ’ from ye ’ Joseph ’ ye ’ from as butcher the ’ captain
’ dream`ing ’ and dream as and ’ 5 guard from in ’ from week ’ and became as and
shall interpret are ’ man I ’ one ’ the night`s in ’ and dream ’ man I ’ them two
which ’ from as Mizra ’ king of ’ which ’ the cook and ’ steward`ed the ’ and dream ’
Joseph ’ them as to ’ came as and ’ 6 prison the ’ you house in ’ from as bound`ing ’
ask as and ’ 7 from as wroth ’ from behold and ’ from ye ’ look as and ’ is morn in ’
’ you house ’ guard from in ’ and ye ’ which ’ Pharaoh ’ as officer`s ’ ye ’
’ 8 day as the ’ from as evil ’ your as turn ’ why`ing ’ say of ’ him master
and ye ’ whither`s ’ interpret and ’ our dream ’ dream`ing ’ him to ’ and say as and
’ from as Allah of ’ forward`ing ’ Joseph ’ them as to ’ say as and ’
’ captain ’ report as and ’ 9 vessel ’ oh ’ and report ’ from as has interpret
’ if ’ say as and ’ Joseph of ’ and dream ’ ye ’ from as steward the
’ three`ed ’ vine in and ’ 10 as before ’ vine ’ be`th and ’ as dream`ing in
’ discharge`ed ’ offer`ed ’ you bud are ’ that`s and ’ from as tendril`ing
’ Pharaoh ’ cup are and ’ 11 from as grape ’ am you bereave I ’ and roast`s the
on I ’ from ye ’ me squeeze and ’ from as grape the ’ ye ’ took I and ’ as hand in
12 ’ Pharaoh ’ palm ’ on ’ cup are the ’ ye ’ give I and ’ Pharaoh ’ conceal`ing ’
’ you three ’ and has interpret ’ this ’ Joseph ’ if ’ say as and
’ you three ’ till`ing in ’ 13 them ’ from week ’ you three ’ from as tendril`ing the

’ are so ’ on ’ are carry`s the and ’ are head ’ ye ’ Pharaoh ’ linger ’ from week
’ discern from are ’ and hand in ’ Pharaoh ’ conceal`ing ’ set`ed has and
’ mother ’ for ’ 14 and steward`ed ’ you became`s ’ which ’ has and head`s the
’ oh ’ dual`s and ’ walk ’ improve as ’ which are ’ are ye ’ as has you is remember
’ Pharaoh ’ to ’ as has you is remember the and ’ bow ’ as stand
’ steal`ing ’ for ’ 15 this the ’ you house the ’ has from ’ as has issue alas and
as whom do ’ not ’ talk ’ also and ’ from as Obara the ’ land from ’ as you steal has
’ captain ’ look as and ’ 16 empty`ing in ’ near ’ name ’ for ’ the noth`ing ’
’ anger ’ Joseph ’ to ’ say as and ’ interpret ’ good`ing ’ for ’ from as cook
’ on ’ cavedweller ’ as Osier ’ three`ed ’ be`th and ’ as dream`ing in ’ as whither
’ Pharaoh ’ eat from ’ all from ’ has him on the ’ Osier in and ’ 17 as head
’ has from ’ above ’ from ye ’ eat ’ fly`ing the and ’ anger`ed ’ do`ed from
’ this ’ say as and ’ Joseph ’ low as and ’ 18 as head ’ above ’ Osier the
’ 19 them ’ from week ’ you three ’ from as Osier the ’ you three ’ and has interpret
’ are head ’ ye ’ Pharaoh ’ linger ’ from week ’ you three ’ till`ing in
fly`ing the ’ eat and ’ tree the ’ on ’ are ye`ing ’ that hang and ’ are as on from
’ as three`s the ’ day as in ’ became as and ’ 20 are as on from ’ are flesh ’ ye ’
’ him serve ’ all of ’ feast`ed ’ do as and ’ Pharaoh ’ ye ’ you bore alas ’ day as
captain ’ head ’ ye and ’ from as steward the ’ captain ’ head ’ ye ’ lift as and
’ captain ’ ye ’ dwell and ’ 21 him serve ’ middle`ing in ’ from as cook ’
’ on ’ cup are the ’ ye ’ give as and ’ and steward`ed ’ on ’ from as steward the
’ which are ’ that hang ’ from as cook ’ captain ’ ye and ’ 22 Pharaoh ’ palm
’ from as steward the ’ captain ’ male ’ not and ’ 23 Joseph ’ them of ’ interpret
and the forget as and ’ Joseph ’ ye

THE TORAH SCROLL 41

Gen 41:1-41:12

' dream ' Pharaoh and ' from week ' from as you year ' end from ' became as and ' 1
' channel the ' has from ' be`th and ' 2 channel the ' on ' stand ' be`th and
' look`ed from ' you and beautiful ' you and bullock ' seven ' offer`ing
seven ' be`th and ' 3 and at came ' the flourish`s you and ' flesh ' ye`ing plump and
' has from ' behold as after ' offer`ing ' you and after ' you and bullock '
' flesh ' you and thin and ' look`ed from ' you and evil ' channel the
' 4 channel the ' you lip ' on ' you and bullock the ' beside ' the has stand you and
' appear`ed the ' you and evil ' you and bullock the ' the has eat you and
' you and beautiful ' you and bullock the ' seven ' ye ' flesh the ' you thin and
' slept as and ' 5 Pharaoh ' awake as and ' ye`ing plump the and ' appear`ed the
' the stalk ' offer`ing ' from as corn ' seven ' be`th and ' you two ' dream as and
' from as corn ' seven ' be`th and ' 6 you and good`ing and ' ye`ing plump ' one
' 7 behold as after ' you and sprout ' east`s ' you blast`s and ' you and thin
' seven ' ye ' you and thin the ' from as corn the ' the has worthless you and
' awake as and ' you and fill`ing the and ' ye`ing plump the ' from as corn the
' move you and ' is morn in ' became as and ' 8 dream`ing ' be`th and ' Pharaoh
' as from engrave ' all ' ye ' call as and ' send as and ' and spirit is
' ye ' them of ' Pharaoh ' report as and ' am wise ' all ' ye and ' from as Mizra
' 9 Pharaoh of ' from ye`ing ' is assent put ' whither`s and ' and as dream
' ye ' say of ' Pharaoh ' ye ' from as steward the ' captain ' word as and
' on ' angry ' Pharaoh ' 10 day as the ' is as remember from ' as whither ' as sin
' captain ' you house ' guard from in ' near ' give as and ' him serve
' the dream has and ' 11 from as cook ' captain ' ye and ' near ' from as butcher the
' man I ' that`ing and ' as whither ' one ' the night`s in ' dream`ing
' youth ' and has ye ' there and ' 12 our dream ' and dream ' shall interpret are

' if ' report has and ' from as butcher the ' captain of ' serve ' as Obara

' and dream are ' man I ' our as you dream ' ye ' our of ' interpret as and

' near ' be`s ' so ' our of ' interpret ' which are ' became as and ' 13 interpret

' Pharaoh ' send as and ' 14 hang`ed ' and ye and ' as so ' on ' carry`s the

' empty`ing the ' has from ' alas run`s as and ' Joseph ' ye ' call as and

' 15 Pharaoh ' to ' came as and ' him you raiment ' change as and ' shave as and

' interpret and ' as you dream ' dream`ing ' Joseph ' to ' Pharaoh ' say as and

hear you the ' say of ' are as on ' as you hear ' as whither and ' and ye ' whither`s

' Pharaoh ' ye ' Joseph ' low as and ' 16 and ye ' interpret of ' dream`ing '

' from and peace ' ye ' the because ' not ' from as Allah ' as beyond in ' say of

' as behold`th ' as dream in ' Joseph ' to ' Pharaoh ' word as and ' 17 Pharaoh

' channel the ' has from ' be`th and ' 18 channel the ' you lip ' on ' stand

' you and beautiful and ' flesh ' ye`ing plump ' you and bullock ' seven ' offer`ing

you and bullock ' seven ' be`th and ' 19 and at came ' the flourish`s you and ' figure

' you and evil and ' you and weak ' behold as after ' offer`ing ' you and after '

' priest`ed ' as you seen ' not ' flesh ' you and only and ' especially ' figure

you and bullock the ' the has eat you and ' 20 evil of ' from as Mizra ' land ' all in

' you and bullock the ' seven ' ye ' you and evil the and ' you and only the '

' to ' the has came you and ' 21 ye`ing plump the and ' you our and head`s the

has approach`ed ' to ' and came ' for ' acknowledge has ' not and ' has approach`ed

look`ed I and ' 22 awake I and ' begin`ed in ' which are ' evil ' has am appear and '

' one ' the stalk ' offer`ing ' from as corn ' seven ' be`th and ' as dream in '

' from as corn ' seven ' be`th and ' 23 you and good`ing and ' you and fill`s

' you and sprout ' east`s ' you and blast`s and ' you and thin ' you and shrink

you and thin the ' from as corn the ' the has worthless you and ' 24 has them as after

' to ' say and ' you and good`ing the ' from as corn the ' seven ' ye '
25 to ' Joseph ' say as and ' vessel ' cheer`s ' whither`s and ' from who engrave the
from as Allah the ' which ' ye ' that`ing ' one ' Pharaoh ' dream`ing ' Pharaoh '
26 ' you and bullock the ' seven ' Pharaoh of ' my nation the ' do`ed '
' from as corn the ' seven and ' be`th ' from two ' seven ' you and good`ing the
27 ' that`ing ' one ' dream`ing ' be`th ' from two ' seven ' you and good`ing the
' you and evil the and ' you and only the ' you and bullock the ' seven and
' seven and ' be`th ' from two ' seven ' behold as after ' offer`ing the
and became as ' east`s the ' you and blast`s and ' you and thin the ' from as corn the
28 ' to ' as you word ' which ' word the ' that`ing ' hunger ' two ' seven '
29 Pharaoh ' ye ' look`ed the ' do`ed ' from as Allah the ' which ' ye ' Pharaoh
' land ' all in ' great`ing ' seven ' you and came ' from two ' seven ' be`th '
30 ' behold as after ' hunger ' two ' seven ' and rise and ' from as Mizra
hunger the ' the all and ' from as Mizra ' land in ' seven the ' all ' forget shall
31 ' around from ' land in ' seven the ' acknowledge as ' not and ' land the ' ye '
32 ' especially ' that`ing ' honour ' for ' so ' as after ' that`ing the ' hunger the
ready`ing ' for ' from as move ' Pharaoh ' to ' dream`ing the ' you two ' on`ed and
' from as Allah the ' soon from and ' from as Allah the ' affirm ' word the '
33 ' man I ' Pharaoh ' if ' look`ed as ' the time and ' and you concoct of
34 ' from as Mizra ' land ' on ' and he gift as and ' wise and ' understand`ing
' land the ' on ' from as my appoint ' punish as and ' Pharaoh ' do`ed as and
35 ' seven the ' two ' seven in ' from as Mizra ' land ' ye ' five as and
' from as Year the ' seven ' eat ' all ' ye ' and collect as and
' empty ' and aggregate as and ' these`ed ' you and came the ' you and good`ing the
36 ' be`s and ' and guard as and ' form as town in ' eat ' Pharaoh ' hand ' under

' which ' hunger the ' two ' seven of ' land of ' has and my apoint of ' eat the
' land the ' hew you ' not and ' from as Mizra ' land in ' the has became`s you
as has eye in and ' Pharaoh ' as has eye in ' word the ' improve as and ' (37 hunger in
' come behold ' him serve ' to ' Pharaoh ' say as and ' (38 him serve ' all '
' say as and ' (39 and in ' from as Allah ' spirit is ' which ' man I ' this are
' are ye`ing ' from as Allah ' acknowledge`s the ' as after ' Joseph ' to ' Pharaoh
ye`ed ' (40 with`ing are ' wise and ' understand`ing ' whither`s ' such ' all ' ye
only ' as people ' all ' guide ' reverse`s ' on and ' as you house ' on ' be`s you '
look`ed ' Joseph ' to ' Pharaoh ' say as and ' (41 with from ' great I ' throne the '
Pharaoh ' repent as and ' (42 from as Mizra ' land ' all ' on ' are ye ' as set has '
Joseph ' hand ' on ' ye`ed ' give as and ' and hand ' above ' and you ring ' ye '
' on ' gold the ' collar`s ' site and ' six ' as fabric ' and ye ' arm as and '
' if ' which ' care`ed the ' you ride from in ' and ye ' ride Then ' (43 and neck did
' land ' all ' on ' and ye ' gave`ing and ' bless I ' him before ' and call as and
' Pharaoh ' as whither ' Joseph ' to ' Pharaoh ' say as and ' (44 from as Mizra
and foot ' ye and ' and hand ' ye ' man I ' elevate`s ' not ' are adorn of in and
' Joseph ' there ' Pharaoh ' call as and ' (45 from as Mizra ' land ' all in '
' as Put ' daughter ' you bush I ' ye ' if ' give as and ' at probe ' as you north
' land ' on ' Joseph ' out and ' resemble I of ' whither ' priest ' hair
' and stand in ' the Year ' from as three ' son ' Joseph and ' (46 from as Mizra
' as before from ' Joseph ' out and ' from as Mizra ' king ' Pharaoh ' as before
' land the ' do you and ' (47 from as Mizra ' land ' all in ' cross as and ' Pharaoh
' all ' ye ' collect as and ' (48 from as grasp of ' seven the ' two ' seven in
' land in ' seven the ' and be`s ' which ' from as Year the ' seven ' eat
town`s the ' field`ed ' eat ' form as town in ' eat ' give as and ' from as Mizra

Joseph ' aggregate as and ' 49 the middle`ing in ' gave ' am you surround`s ' which '
forbare ' for ' till ' especially ' increase`ed the ' sea the ' of sand are ' empty '
two ' and bore`s as ' Joseph of and ' 50 report from ' whither`s ' for ' report of '
' bore`ed as ' which ' hunger the ' sleep ' income`ing ' suspend in ' from as son '
' call as and ' 51 whither`ing ' priest ' hair ' as Put ' daughter ' you bush I ' if
' as has women ' for ' Manasse`ed ' first`ing the ' there ' ye ' Joseph
' 52 as father ' you house ' all ' ye and ' as of people ' all ' ye ' from as Allah
from as Allah ' as has apart the ' for ' Ephraim ' call ' two the ' there ' ye and
' which ' seven the ' two ' seven ' the deplete`s you and ' 53 as poor ' land in '
hunger the ' two ' seven ' the has as begin and ' 54 from as Mizra ' land in ' be`s
' all in ' hunger ' became as and ' Joseph ' say ' which are ' came`ing of '
' 55 fight ' be`s ' from as Mizra ' land ' all in and ' you and land the
' to ' people the ' cry as and ' from as Mizra ' land ' all ' hunger you and
' follow ' from as Mizra ' all of ' Pharaoh ' say as and ' from bread of ' Pharaoh
' hunger the and ' 56 smoke`ing you ' relate ' say as ' which and ' Joseph ' to
' which ' all ' ye ' Joseph ' open as and ' land the ' around ' all ' on ' be`s
' hunger the ' strength as and ' from as Mizra of ' buy`s as and ' empty ' cattle
the from as Mizra ' and came ' you and land the ' all and ' 57 from as Mizra ' land in
land the ' all in ' hunger the ' strength ' for ' Joseph ' to ' is carry of '

' say as and ' from as Mizra in ' buy ' man ' for ' Jacob ' look as and ' 1

' as you hear ' be`th ' say as and ' 2 see as set ' what of ' him son ' to ' Jacob

' our of ' and buy and ' there`ed ' and up ' from as Mizra in ' buy ' man ' for

' as brother ' and up as and ' 3 die`ing has ' not and ' the life has and ' there from

' Benjamim`s ' ye and ' 4 from as Mizra from ' empty ' is carry of ' ten`ed ' Joseph

turn ' say ' for ' him brother ' ye ' Jacob ' send ' not ' Joseph ' as brother

' is carry of ' Israel ' as son ' and came as and ' 5 harm`ing ' and whither value '

' 6 Canaan ' land in ' hunger the ' be`s ' for ' from as came the ' middle`ing in

buy`s them ' that`ing and ' land the ' on ' supervise`s the ' that`ing ' Joseph and

' Joseph ' as brother ' and came as and ' land the ' people ' all of '

' ye ' Joseph ' look as and ' 7 land`ed ' toward`s ' if ' prostate humble`ly as and

' word as and ' them as to ' foreign whom and ' from recollect and ' him brother

' from ye in ' whither`s from ' them as to ' say as and ' you and hard ' from ye

' Joseph ' recollect and ' 8 eat ' is carry of ' Canaan ' land from ' and say as and

' is remember as and ' 9 and the recognize ' not ' them and ' him brother ' ye

them as to ' say as and ' them of ' dream ' which ' you and dream the ' ye ' Joseph

from ye in ' land the ' skin`ing ' ye ' you see of ' from ye ' from as foot from '

' and came ' are as serve and ' as master ' not ' him to ' and say as and ' 10

from as so ' and us I ' one ' man I ' as son ' and has all ' 11 eat ' is carry of

' say as and ' 12 from as foot from ' are as serve ' him the ' not ' and us I '

' 13 you see of ' from ye in ' land the ' skin`ing ' for ' not ' them as to

as son ' and us I ' from as brother ' are as serve ' ten ' from two ' and say as and

' our as father ' ye ' small the ' be`th and ' Canaan ' land in ' one ' man I '

' Joseph ' them as to ' say as and ' 14 and has whither`s ' one the and ' day as the

from ye ' from as foot from ' say of ' your as to ' as you word ' which ' that`ing

’ victual`ed ’ and issue you ’ mother ’ Pharaoh ’ life ’ and prove you ’ such in ’ 15
’ and send ’ 16 be`th ’ small the ’ your as brother ’ came`ing in ’ mother ’ for
’ from ye and ’ your as brother ’ ye ’ took as and ’ one ’ from with
’ from are ye ’ you mother the ’ your as word ’ and prove as and ’ and bound the
’ from ye ’ from as foot from ’ for ’ Pharaoh ’ life ’ not ’ mother and
’ him father ’ ye ’ forsake of ’ youth the ’ all him ’ not ’ and say as and
’ to ’ from ye ’ gather as and ’ 17 die and ’ him father ’ ye ’ forsake and
’ day as in ’ Joseph ’ them as to ’ say as and ’ 18 from week ’ you three ’ guard from
as whither ’ from as Allah the ’ ye ’ him spirit ’ concoct ’ such ’ as three`s the
’ bound as ’ one the ’ your as brother ’ from ye ’ from as so ’ mother ’ 19 dread ’
ye ’ and came`s the and ’ follow ’ from ye and ’ from are guard from ’ you house in
’ small the ’ your as brother ’ ye and ’ 20 your house`ly ’ has and hunger ’ buy ’
’ not and ’ your as word ’ and believe as and ’ Eli ’ has and came`s you
’ to ’ man I ’ and say as and ’ 21 so ’ concoct as and ’ has and die`ing you
’ which ’ our as brother ’ on ’ and us I ’ heaven`s I ’ mourn ’ him brother
’ not and ’ our as to ’ and has grace you thus ’ and soul ’ splender in ’ our as look
’ 22 such the ’ the phenomenon ’ all ’ our as on I ’ came`ed ’ so ’ on ’ our hear
’ as you word ’ as you say ’ forward`ing ’ say of ’ from ye ’ Reuben ’ low as and
’ from you hear ’ not and ’ boy in ’ and sin you ’ to ’ say of ’ your as to
’ for ’ and known ’ not ’ them and ’ 23 search has ’ be`th ’ and blood ’ also and
’ away as and ’ 24 from you between in ’ translater`s the ’ for ’ Joseph ’ hear
’ them as to ’ word as and ’ them as to ’ dwell and ’ against as and ’ them as on from
them as has eye of ’ and ye ’ bound as and ’ Simeon ’ ye ’ spy from ’ took as and
’ empty ’ them as all ’ ye ’ and fill as and ’ Joseph ’ command as and ’ 25
’ set of and ’ draught ’ to ’ man I ’ them as silver ’ ye ’ carry`s the of and

' ye ' and lift as and ' 25 so ' them of ' do as and ' way of ' hunt`ed ' them of
' open as and ' 27 there from ' and walk as and ' them as heass ' on ' from buy
' lodge`ing in ' and heass of ' that`ing number ' set of ' draught ' ye ' one the
and under from I ' as animal ' that`ing ' be`th and ' and silver ' ye ' look as and
' be`th ' also and ' as silver ' carry alas ' him brother ' to ' say as and ' 28
' man I ' and shudder as and ' from heart ' out and ' as under from I in ' that`ing
' 29 our of ' from as Allah ' do`ed ' such ' what ' say of ' him brother ' to
' Canaan ' land`ed ' them as father ' Jacob ' to ' and came as and
word ' 30 say of ' from ye ' you and befall ' all ' ye ' if ' and fortune`s as and
' give as and ' you and hard ' and has ye ' land the ' as master ' man that '
' him to ' say has and ' 31 land the ' ye ' from as foot from are ' and has ye
ten ' from two ' 32 from as foot from ' our as became ' not ' and us I ' from as so
' one the and ' our as father ' as son ' and us I ' from as brother '
' land in ' our as father ' ye ' day as the ' small the and ' and has whither`s
' such in ' land the ' as master ' man that ' our as to ' say as and ' 33 Canaan
' and rest`s the ' one the ' your as brother ' from ye ' from as so ' for ' know
' 34 and all and ' and took ' your house`ly ' has and hunger ' ye and ' near
' for ' the know and ' Eli ' small the ' your as brother ' ye ' and came`s the and
' ye ' from ye ' from as so ' for ' from ye ' from as foot from ' not
' 35 and trade you ' land the ' ye and ' relate ' donkey ' your as brother
' man I ' be`th and ' them bottle ' from as dribble`s ' them ' and became as and
' you and bundle ' ye ' see as and ' draught in ' and silver ' bundle`ing
' say as and ' 36 and dread as and ' them as father and ' them`ed ' them as silver
' Joseph ' from you bereave ' near ' them as father ' Jacob ' them as to
' Benjamim`s ' ye and ' and has whither`s ' Simeon and ' and has whither`s

’ to ’ Reuben ’ say as and ’ 37 stop`ed are ’ him the ’ mosthigh ’ and took you
’ not ’ mother ’ die`s you ’ as son ’ two ’ ye ’ say of ’ him father
’ as whither and ’ as hand ’ on ’ and ye ’ give`ed ’ are as to ’ and has came`s I
your people ’ as son ’ descend ’ not ’ say as and ’ 38 are as to ’ and has carry`s I
alas call and ’ remain has ’ and alone of ’ that`ing and ’ die ’ him brother ’ for ’
’ ye ’ from you up alas and ’ thus ’ and walk you ’ which ’ way in ’ harm`ing ’
the ask`ing ’ has and food`s ’ as you carry`s

1 2 eat of ' fail ' which are ' became as and ' land in ' honour ' hunger the and '
' say as and ' from as Mizra from ' and came`s the ' which ' buy the ' ye '
3 ' eat ' less ' our of ' and buy ' and carry`ing ' them as father ' them as to
' man that ' and son ' repeat ' repeat ' say of ' Judah ' him to ' say as and
4 ' from are ye ' your as brother ' as zero in ' around ' see you ' not ' say of
' up`ed has ' and has ye ' our as brother ' ye ' send from ' are man ' mother
5 ' not ' send from ' are whither`s ' mother and ' eat ' walk ' the buy has and
as zero in ' around ' see you ' not ' our as to ' say ' man that ' for ' spikenard
6 ' what of ' Israel ' say as and ' from are ye ' your as brother '
' relate ' till`ing the ' man I of ' fortune`s the of ' vessel ' from you mischief
7 ' our of ' man that ' ask ' Saul ' and say as and ' brother
' life ' your as father ' till`ing the ' say of ' and has you bore and from of and
' from as word the ' edge ' on ' if ' over`s and ' brother ' relate ' man the
' ye ' and up`s alas ' say as ' for ' shaken ' till`ing became ' these`ed
8 ' the send ' him father ' Israel ' to ' Judah ' say as and ' your as brother
' the life has and ' walk`ed has and ' the rise`ing has and ' near ' youth the
9 ' our children ' also ' ye`ed ' also ' and us I ' also ' die`ing has ' not and
' not ' mother ' and has seek you ' as hand from ' and son restore ' for whither
as you sin and ' are as before ' him you sat the and ' are as to ' him you came`s the
10 ' for ' our the from return`ed ' not ' if ' for ' from week the ' all ' walk '
11 Israel ' them as to ' say as and ' from as move ' this ' and has carry ' time`ed
' and took ' concoct ' such ' although`ing ' so ' mother ' them as father '
' man I of ' and up`s alas and ' from are as all in ' land the ' you prune from
' from as womb ' Lot and ' you smite ' honey ' less and ' balm ' less ' bestow`ed
12 ' ye and ' from are hand in ' and took ' care`ed ' silver and ' from as nut and

' and carry`s you ' from are as under from I ' as animal ' carry and them ' silver the

' your as brother ' ye and ' 13 that`s ' the error ' as maybe I ' your as hand in

' almighty ' to and ' 14 man that ' to ' and carry`ing ' and rise`ing and ' and took

' relate ' send and ' man that ' as before ' from as compassion ' relate ' permanent

' which are ' as whither and ' Benjamim`s ' ye and ' after ' your as brother ' ye

' ye ' from as person the ' acquire as and ' 15 as you bereave ' as you bereave

' from hand in ' and take ' silver ' the has there and ' such the ' bestow`ed the

' the from as Mizra ' and up as and ' and rise as and ' Benjamim`s ' ye and

' ye and ' from ye ' Joseph ' look as and ' 16 Joseph ' as before ' and stand as and

' ye ' came the ' and you house ' on ' which of ' say as and ' Benjamim`s

near ' for ' stable and ' butcher ' butcher and ' he house the ' from as person the

' man that ' do as and ' 17 from as noon in ' from as person the ' and eat as '

' from as person the ' ye ' man that ' came as and ' Joseph ' say ' which are

' and came alas ' for ' from as person the ' and dread as and ' 18 Joseph ' he house

' carry and them ' silver the ' word ' on ' and say as and ' Joseph ' he house

' from as came and from ' and us I ' begin`ed in ' our as under from I in

' you take and ' our as on ' fall sacred of and ' our as on ' sake sacred of

' to ' and adduce and ' 19 our as heass`ing ' ye and ' from as serve of ' and has ye

' open ' him to ' and word as and ' Joseph ' you house ' on ' which ' man that

' our up as ' descend ' as master ' house ' and say as and ' 20 you house the

' to ' and has came ' for ' became as and ' 21 eat ' is carry of ' begin`ed in

' silver ' be`th and ' our as under from I ' ye ' open`ed has and ' lodge`ing the

' and weight from in ' our silver ' and under from I ' as animal ' man I

' after ' silver and ' 22 and has hand in ' and ye ' carry`s has and

' not ' eat ' is carry of ' and has hand in ' and has take ' and has up and the

' say as and ' 23 our as under from I in ' our silver ' there ' who ' and has known
' as Allah and ' your as Allah ' and look as you ' to ' relate ' from and peace
' your as under from came ' has and prize ' relate ' gave ' from are as you father
' 24 Simeon ' ye ' them as to ' issue him and ' Eli ' came ' from are silver
give as and ' Joseph ' he house ' from as person the ' ye ' man that ' came as and
' that`ing number ' give as and ' them as foot ' and wash as and ' Water '
' came`ing ' till ' bestow`ed the ' ye ' and column`s and ' 25 them as heass`ing of
' 26 fight ' and eat as ' there ' for ' and hear ' for ' from as noon in ' Joseph
' bestow`ed the ' ye ' if ' and came`s as and ' he house the ' Joseph ' came as and
' 27 land`ed ' if ' prostate humble`ly as and ' he house the ' from hand in ' which
' from and peace the ' say as and ' from and peace of ' them of ' ask as and
' 28 life ' and has till`ing the ' from you say ' which ' elder the ' your as father
' and has till`ing ' our as father of ' are serve of ' from and peace ' and say as and
' from as Allah of ' that`ing the ' man that ' bless`ing ' say as and ' life
' him has eye ' lift as and ' 29 prostate humble`ly as and ' and stoop as and
' say as and ' and mother ' son ' him brother ' Benjamim`s ' ye ' look as and
' say as and ' Eli ' from you say ' which ' small the ' your as brother ' this the
and yearn has ' for ' Joseph ' soon as and ' 30 as son ' are grace as ' from as Allah
' came as and ' group`ing in of ' seek as and ' him brother ' to ' him compassion '
' out and ' him turn ' wash as and ' 31 there`ed ' against as and ' within`ed the
' if ' and site`s and ' 32 fight ' and there`s ' say as and ' contain you as and
' from as eat the ' from as mizra of and ' from alone of ' them of and ' and alone of
' eat of ' from as Mizra the ' has and able as ' not ' for ' from alone of ' and ye
from as Mizra of ' that`s ' the abominate you ' for ' fight ' from as Obara the ' ye
little`s the and ' and you first`s are ' first`s the ' him before ' and dwell and ' 33

' to ' man I ' from as person the ' and what whom and ' and you little`s are '

' them as to ' him turn ' each ' arise from ' lift as and ' 34 and shepherd is

esteem`ing ' five ' taunt ' arise they ' Benjamim`s ' arise from ' increase you and

and people ' and merry as and ' and drink as and '

' ye ' fill ' say of ' and you house ' on ' which ' ye ' command as and ' 1
' arise ' has and able as ' which are ' eat ' from as person the ' under from I
' as hill`s ' ye and ' 2 and under from I ' as animal ' man I ' silver ' there`s and
' ye and ' small the ' under from I ' as animal ' there`s you ' silver the ' hill`s
' herd the ' 3 word ' which ' Joseph ' word are ' do as and ' and buy ' silver
' 4 from am heass`ing and ' them`ed ' and send ' from as person the and ' light`ing
' say ' Joseph and ' and get`s the ' not ' town`s the ' ye ' and out ' them
' from as person the ' as after ' chase ' rise`ing ' and you house ' on ' which of
evil`ed ' from you whole ' what of ' them as to ' you say and ' from you drawl the and
' as master ' belong`ed ' which ' this ' forward`ing ' 5 the good`ing ' under '
' which ' from you mischief ' and in ' serpent as ' serpent ' that`ing and ' and in
' ye ' them as to ' word as and ' additional as and ' 6 from whom do
' word as ' what of ' him to ' and say as and ' 7 these`ed ' from as word the
' are as serve of ' the profane`s ' these`ed ' from as word are ' as master
' and has come ' which ' silver the ' behold ' 8 this the ' word are ' you and work
' land from ' are as to ' and has carry`s and the ' our as under from I ' as animal
' or ' silver ' are as master ' you house from ' steal has ' are hence and ' Canaan
' also and ' die him ' are as serve from ' and ye ' come as ' which ' 9 gold
' also ' say as and ' 10 from as serve of ' as master of ' the became has ' and us I
' be`s as ' and ye ' come as ' which ' that`ing ' so ' your as word are ' time`ed
' and soon as and ' 11 from as emission`ing ' and as he ' from ye and ' serve ' vessel
' and open as and ' land`ed ' and under from I ' ye ' man I ' and cart`s as and
' small in and ' sick the ' great`ing in ' free as and ' 12 and under from I ' man I
and rend as and ' 13 Benjamim`s ' under from I in ' hill`s the ' come as and ' all`ed
' and heass`ing ' on ' man I ' and load as and ' from you and raiment '

' him brother and ' Judah ' came as and ' 14 the town`s the ' and dwell and
' and fell and ' there ' and has till`ing ' that`ing and ' Joseph ' he house
' work`ed the ' what ' Joseph ' them of ' say as and ' 15 land`ed ' him before
' serpent ' for ' from you known ' forward`ing ' from whom do ' which ' this the
' what ' Judah ' say as and ' 16 as storeup`ing ' which ' man I ' serpent as
' just`ous has ' what and ' word has ' what and ' as master of ' say has
' and behold`th ' are as serve ' low`ing ' ye ' come ' from as Allah the and
hill`s the ' come has ' which ' also ' and us I ' also ' as master of ' from as serve
' such ' you and work ' vessel ' the profane`s ' say as and ' 17 and hand in '
vessel ' be`s as ' that`ing ' and hand in ' hill`s the ' come has ' which ' man that
' 18 your as father ' to ' from and peace of ' lug ' from ye and ' serve '
' oh ' word as ' as master ' house ' say as and ' Judah ' him to ' adduce and
' are serve in ' nose ' delay ' to and ' as master ' as ear in ' word ' are serve
' say of ' him serve ' ye ' ask ' as master ' 19 Pharaoh are ' with`ing are ' for
' man ' as master ' to ' say has and ' 20 brother ' or ' father ' relate ' man the
' him brother and ' small ' from as elder ' bore him and ' elder ' father ' our of
' him father and ' and mother of ' and alone of ' that`ing ' survive as and ' die
' Eli ' alas cart`s the ' are as serve ' to ' say you and ' 21 and love
not ' as master ' to ' say has and ' 22 and Mosthigh ' as has eye ' the guilty`s and
' ye ' forsake and ' him father ' ye ' forsake of ' youth the ' all him '
' descend ' not ' mother ' are as serve ' to ' say you and ' 23 die and ' him father
' you see of ' has and yield`s you ' not ' from are ye ' small the ' your as brother
' our as father ' are serve ' to ' our as on ' for ' became as and ' 24 around
' our as father ' say as and ' 25 as master ' as word ' ye ' if ' over`s and
' able has ' not ' say has and ' 26 eat ' less ' our of ' and buy ' and carry`ing

' our up as and ' and has ye ' small the ' our as brother ' man ' mother ' you up of
' our as brother and ' man that ' around ' ye ' you see of ' able has ' not ' for
' as father ' are serve ' say as and ' (27 and has ye ' and has whither`s ' small the
as wife ' vessel ' bore`ed as ' from two ' for ' from you known ' from ye ' our as to
' not and ' torn ' torn ' sure ' say and ' as ye from ' one the ' out and ' (28
' affirm ' this ' ye ' also ' from you take and ' (29 be`th ' till ' him you seen
' as you carry`s ' ye ' from you up alas and ' harm`ing ' alas call and ' around
' are serve ' to ' as you heavy ' the time and ' (30 the ask`ing ' evil`ed in
' and soul and ' and has as ye ' and has whither`s ' youth the and ' as father
' whither`s ' for ' and you see are ' be`s and ' (31 and soul in ' the bind`ing
' ye ' are as serve ' and up`s alas and ' die and ' and has ye ' youth the
' for ' (32 the ask`ing ' has and food`s ' our as father ' are serve ' you carry`s
' mother ' say of ' him father ' affirm ' youth the ' ye ' twilight ' are serve
' all ' as father of ' as you sin and ' are as to ' and has came`s I ' not
serve ' youth the ' under ' are serve ' oh ' dwell ' the time and ' (33 from week the
' sure`s ' for ' (34 him brother ' people ' went`ed ' youth the and ' as master of '
' turn ' near ' and has whither`s ' youth the and ' as father ' to ' on`ed I
as father ' ye ' come as ' which ' evil`ed in ' cat`ed

THE TORAH SCROLL 45

Gen 45:1-45:11

' from as settle the ' all of ' contain you no ' Joseph ' finish ' not and ' 1

' him on from ' man I ' all ' and issue`s alas and ' call as and ' and Mosthigh

him brother ' to ' Joseph ' acknowledge you thus ' and ye ' man I ' stand ' not and

' from as Mizra ' and hear as and ' wept in ' and voice`ing ' ye ' give as and ' 2

' him brother ' to ' Joseph ' say as and ' 3 Pharaoh ' you house ' and hear as and

' and all as ' not and ' life ' as father ' till`ing the ' Joseph ' as whither

' 4 and as turn from ' and amaze has ' for ' and ye ' answer`ing of ' him brother

' and adduce and ' Eli ' oh ' and I'll ' him brother ' to ' Joseph ' say as and

' near ' from you sale ' which ' your as brother ' Joseph ' as whither ' say as and

' delay ' to and ' and vex you ' to ' the time and ' 5 the from as Mizra

' the life from of ' for ' be`th ' near ' from you sale ' for ' your as has eye in

' from as you year ' this ' for ' 6 your as before ' from as Allah ' as has send

' which ' from two ' five ' till`ing and ' land the ' approach in ' hunger the

' from as Allah ' as has send as and ' 7 reap`s and ' divise`s ' whither`s

' land in ' whom remain ' relate ' there`s of ' your as before

not ' the time and ' 8 great`ed ' the escape`s of ' relate ' you and life the of and

' from as Allah the ' for ' be`th ' near ' from you send ' from ye '

' all of ' master`ing of and ' Pharaoh of ' father of ' as has there`s as and

' and travel ' and soon ' 9 from as Mizra ' land ' all in ' rule and ' and you house

' Joseph ' are son ' say ' here ' him to ' from you say and ' as father ' to

Eli ' up`ed ' from as Mizra ' all of ' master`ing of ' from as Allah ' as has there

' whom became and ' has I`ll ' land in ' desist as and ' 10 stand you ' to '

' are as son ' as son and ' are as son and ' ye`ed ' Eli ' approach`ing

are ye ' as you of fed and ' 11 walk ' which ' all and ' are herd and ' are flock and

' ye`ed ' occupy you ' turn ' hunger ' from two ' five ' till`ing ' for ' there '

you see ' your as has eye ' be`th and ' (12 walk ' which ' all and ' are you house and
' is wilderness the ' as edge ' for ' Benjamim`s ' as brother ' as has eye and '
' as honour`ing ' all ' ye ' as father of ' from you told the and ' (13 your as to
' from you soon and ' from you seen ' which ' all ' ye and ' from as Mizra in
as is issue`ing ' on ' fell and ' (14 be`th ' as father ' ye ' from you up alas and
' on ' against`ed ' Benjamim`s and ' against as and ' him brother ' Benjamim`s '
them as on ' against as and ' him brother ' all of ' kiss as and ' (15 him is neck did
' voice`ing the and ' (16 and ye ' him brother ' and word ' so ' as after and '
' Joseph ' as brother ' and came ' say of ' Pharaoh ' you house ' hear has
' (17 him serve ' as has eye in and ' Pharaoh ' as has eye in ' improve as and
' such ' are as brother ' to ' say ' Joseph ' to ' Pharaoh ' say as and
land`ed ' and came and ' and all and ' from are town`s in ' ye ' and lade ' concoct
' your house`ly ' ye and ' your as father ' ye ' and took and ' (18 Canaan '
' land ' good`ing ' ye ' relate ' the give I and ' Eli ' and came and
whom`ed command ' ye`ed and ' (19 land the ' milk ' ye ' and eat and ' from as Mizra
' you and calf ' from as Mizra ' land from ' relate ' and took ' concoct ' such '
' ye ' from you lift has and ' your as women of and ' your children of
' on ' spare`ing you ' to ' your as low`s and ' (20 from brought and ' your as father
' (21 that`ing ' relate ' from as Mizra ' land ' all ' good`ing ' for ' your as all
' Joseph ' them of ' give as and ' Israel ' as son ' so ' concoct as and
' (22 way of ' hunt`ed ' them of ' give as and ' Pharaoh ' edge ' on ' you and calf
' Benjamim`s of and ' you and raiment ' you and lock`s ' man I of ' gave ' from all of
' (23 you and raiment ' you lock`s ' five and ' silver ' you and hundred ' three ' gave
' from as lift has ' from as heass`ing ' ten`ed ' such are ' send ' him father of and
' arise`ing has ' you and give I ' ten and ' from as Mizra ' land ' good`ing from

send as and ’ 24 way of ’ him father of ’ has and victual and ’ from bread and ’ empty
’ to ’ them as to ’ say as and ’ and walk as and ’ him brother ’ ye ’
’ and came as and ’ from as Mizra from ’ and went and ’ 25 way in ’ and tremble set
’ if ’ and fortune as and ’ 26 them as father ’ Jacob ’ to ’ Canaan ’ land`ed
’ land ’ all in ’ rule ’ that`ing ’ for and ’ life ’ Joseph ’ till`ing ’ say of
’ 27 them of ’ believe`s the ’ not ’ for ’ and heart ’ cride as and ’ from as Mizra
them as to ’ word ’ which ’ Joseph ’ as word ’ all ’ ye ’ him to ’ and word as and
and ye ’ arise of ’ Joseph ’ send ’ which ’ you and calf the ’ ye ’ look as and ’
’ Israel ’ say as and ’ 28 them as father ’ Jacob ’ spirit is ’ life you and ’
’ and has look I and ’ the walk I ’ life ’ as son ’ Joseph ’ till`ing ’ increase
faithful`ing ’ suspend in

seven ' the well ' came as and ' if ' which ' all and ' Israel ' onward as and ' 1
' 2 Isaac ' him father ' as Allah of ' from as sacrifice ' sacrifice as and '
' the night`s the ' you and appear in ' Israel of ' from as Allah ' say as and
for whither ' say as and ' 3 as behold`th ' say as and ' Jacob ' Jacob ' say as and
' the up from ' look as you ' to ' are as father ' as Allah ' these '
' 4 there ' are there`s I ' great`ing ' nation`ing of ' for ' the from as Mizra
reinstate I ' for whither and ' the from as Mizra ' are people ' wander ' for whither
' 5 are as has eye ' on ' and hand ' whom too as ' Joseph and ' on`ed ' also '
ye ' Israel ' as son ' and lift as and ' seven ' well from ' Jacob ' rise as and
' them as woman ' ye and ' from children ' ye and ' them as father ' Jacob '
' acquire as and ' 6 and ye ' arise of ' Pharaoh ' send ' which ' you and calf in
land in ' and property ' which ' from property`ing ' ye and ' them as purchase ' ye
and ye ' and seed ' all and ' Jacob ' the from as Mizra ' and came as and ' Canaan '
' daughter`th`ing and ' him daughter`th ' and ye ' him son ' as son and ' him son ' 7
to`ed and ' 8 the from as Mizra ' and ye ' came`s the ' and seed ' all and ' him son
' Jacob ' the from as Mizra ' from as came the ' Israel ' as son ' you name '
' Enoch`ing ' Reuben ' as son and ' 9 Reuben ' Jacob ' first`ing ' him son and
' Jemuel ' Simeon ' as son and ' 10 Carmi and ' Hezron`ing and ' Pallu`ing and
' 11 whom Canaan the ' son ' Saul and ' Zohar and ' Jachin and ' Ohad and ' Jamin and
' Judah ' as son and ' 12 Merari and ' Kohath ' Gershon`ing ' Levi ' as son and
' town ' die as and ' Zerah and ' Pharez and ' Shilo`ed and ' Onan and ' town
' Hezron`ing ' grow ' as son ' and became as and ' Canaan ' land in ' Onan and
Shomron`ing and ' Job and ' Phuvah and ' Tola ' Issachar ' as son and ' 13 Hamul and
' as son ' to`ed ' 15 Jahleel and ' Elon`ing and ' Sered ' Zebulun ' as son and ' 14
' Dinah ' ye and ' highland ' plateau in ' Jacob of ' bore`ed as ' which ' not`ed

three and ' from as three ' him you and son and ' him son ' soul ' all ' and daughter

' watch ' Ezbon and ' Shuni and ' Haggi and ' Ziphion ' fortune ' as son and ' 16

Jeshui and ' Jeshuah and ' right`ed ' which ' as son and ' 17 Areli and ' Arodi and

' connect ' Beriah ' as son and ' from sister ' Serah and ' Beriah and '

' Leah of ' son of ' gave ' which ' trickle'ed ' as son ' to`ed ' 18 Malchiel and

' 19 soul ' ten`ed ' six ' Jacob of ' to`ed ' ye ' bore you and ' and daughter

' bore him and ' 20 Benjamim`s and ' Joseph ' Jacob ' wife ' Rachel ' as son

' you bush I ' if ' bore`ed as ' which ' from as Mizra ' land in ' Joseph of

Ephraim ' ye and ' Manasse`ed ' ye ' whither ' priest ' hair ' as Put ' daughter

Naaman and ' Gera ' Ashbel and ' first and ' worthless ' Benjamim`s ' as son and ' 21

' to`ed ' 22 wander and ' from as pure and ' from as lip ' head and ' as brother '

ten`ed ' the four I ' soul ' all ' Jacob of ' bore`ed as ' which ' Rachel ' as son

' Jahziel ' Naphtali ' as son and ' 24 enrich`s ' judge ' as son and ' 23

' which ' Bilhah ' as son ' to`ed ' 25 whole`ing and ' mould and ' as garden`ing and

' Jacob of ' to`ed ' ye ' bore you and ' and daughter ' Rachel of ' son of ' gave

' Jacob of ' came`ed the ' soul the ' all ' 26 the seven ' soul ' all

' Jacob ' as son ' as women ' alone of from ' and soft ' as out ' the from as Mizra

' and bore as ' which ' Joseph ' as son and ' 27 six and ' from as six ' soul ' all

' Jacob ' you house of ' soul the ' all ' from two ' soul ' from as Mizra in ' if

' send ' Judah ' ye and ' 28 from as seven ' the from as Mizra ' came`ed the

' the Goshen ' him before ' ye`ing mountain`ing of ' Joseph ' to ' him before

' and you ride from ' Joseph ' bound as and ' 29 has I`ll ' land`ed ' and came as and

him to ' look`ed as and ' the Goshen ' him father ' Israel ' you call of ' went and

' him is neck did ' on ' against as and ' him is neck did ' on ' fell and '

' move the ' the die`ing I ' Joseph ' to ' Israel ' say as and ' 30 till`ing

’ 31 life ’ are till`ing ’ for ’ are as turn ’ ye ’ as you seen ’ as after
’ on`ed I ’ him father ’ you house ’ to and ’ him brother ’ to ’ Joseph ’ say as and
’ you house and ’ as brother ’ him to ’ say`ed and ’ Pharaoh of ’ the fortune`s I and
’ from as person the and ’ 32 Eli ’ and came ’ Canaan ’ land in ’ which ’ as father
’ from flock and ’ him the ’ purchase`ed ’ as person ’ for ’ flock ’ pastoral
’ for ’ be`s and ’ 33 and came`s the ’ them of ’ which ’ all and ’ from herd and
’ from you say and ’ 34 your as work ’ what ’ say and ’ Pharaoh ’ relate ’ call as
’ till and ’ our as youth`ing from ’ are as serve ’ him the ’ purchase`ed ’ as person
’ cross`ing in ’ our as you and father ’ also ’ and us I ’ also ’ time`ed
’ all ’ from as Mizra ’ you abominate you ’ for ’ has I`ll ’ land in ’ and inhabitant
flock ’ evil`ed

as father ' him to ' say as and ' Pharaoh of ' my told and ' Joseph ' came as and ' 1
' them of ' which ' all and ' from herd and ' from flock and ' as brother and '
the lease and ' 2 has I`ll ' land in ' from behold and ' Canaan ' land from ' and came
' from sat as and ' from as person ' the five ' and people ' took of ' him brother '
' what ' Joseph ' him brother ' to ' Pharaoh ' say as and ' 3 Pharaoh ' as before
also ' are as serve ' flock ' evil`ed ' Pharaoh ' to ' and say as and ' your as work
' Pharaoh ' to ' and say as and ' 4 our as you and father ' also ' and us I '
flock of ' shepherd is from ' whither`s ' for ' and has came ' land in ' guest`ing of
' Canaan ' land in ' hunger the ' honour ' for ' are as serve of ' which '
say as and ' 5 has I`ll ' land in ' are as serve ' oh ' and carry as ' the time and
' and came ' are as brother and ' are as father ' say of ' Joseph ' to ' Pharaoh '
land the ' good who in ' that`s ' are as before ' from as Mizra ' land ' 6 are as to
' and carry as ' are as brother ' ye and ' are as father ' ye ' carry alas '
sick`s ' as person ' height ' joy`s the ' you known ' mother and ' has I`ll ' land in
' 7 vessel ' which ' on ' purchase`ed ' as captain ' from you there and '
' as before ' alas stand as and ' him father ' Jacob ' ye ' Joseph ' came as and
' to ' Pharaoh ' say as and ' 8 Pharaoh ' ye ' Jacob ' bless as and ' Pharaoh
' to ' Jacob ' say as and ' 9 are as life ' two ' week ' your`ed ' Jacob
' the Year ' each and ' from as three ' as guest`ing from ' two ' week ' Pharaoh
' not and ' as life ' two ' week ' him the ' from as evil and ' less
' week in ' as you and father ' as life ' two ' week ' ye ' and drawal`s the
' out and ' Pharaoh ' ye ' Jacob ' bless as and ' 10 them as guest`ing from
' ye and ' him father ' ye ' Joseph ' carry him and ' 11 Pharaoh ' as before from
good who in ' from as Mizra ' land in ' hold`ed ' them of ' give as and ' him brother
' 12 Pharaoh ' command`ed ' which are ' skip from evil ' land in ' land the '

' all ' ye and ' him brother ' ye and ' him father ' ye ' Joseph ' of walk for and
whither`s ' from bread and ' 13 children the ' as by ' fight ' him father ' you house
' land ' the hang and ' especially ' hunger the ' honour ' for ' land the ' all in '
' pickup as and ' 14 hunger the ' around from ' Canaan ' land and ' from as Mizra
' from as Mizra ' land in ' come behold ' silver the ' all ' ye ' Joseph
' Joseph ' came as and ' from as buy ' them ' which ' buy in ' Canaan ' land in and
' land from ' silver the ' complete as and ' 15 Pharaoh ' he house ' silver the ' ye
to ' from as Mizra ' all ' and came as and ' Canaan ' land from and ' from as Mizra
' die`ing has ' what of and ' fight ' our of ' handover`ed ' say of ' Joseph '
' ascribe ' Joseph ' say as and ' 16 silver the ' however ' for ' are fortune has
' mother ' your as purchase in ' fight ' relate ' the give I and ' your as purchase
Joseph ' to ' them as purchase ' ye ' and came`s as and ' 17 silver the ' however
' purchase`ed in and ' from as Horse`ing in ' fight ' Joseph ' them of ' give as and '
' from as heass`ing in and ' herd the ' purchase`ed in and ' flock the
that`s the ' Year`ed in ' them as purchase ' all in ' from bread in ' from flow as and
Year`ed in ' him to ' and came as and ' that`ing the ' Year`ed the ' from set and ' 18
' for ' as master from ' my power has ' not ' if ' and say as and ' you two the '
' as master ' to ' cattle`ed the ' nest`ed from and ' silver the ' complete ' mother
' mother ' as zero in ' as master ' as before ' remain has ' not
' die`ing has ' what of ' 19 our as you ground and ' our as you nation`ing
and has ye ' nest`ed ' our as you ground ' also ' and us I ' also ' are as has eye of
' and us I ' be`s shall ' from bread in ' our as you ground ' ye and '
' seed ' give and ' Pharaoh of ' from as serve ' our as you ground and
' 20 deposite ' not ' ground`ed the and ' die`ing has ' not and ' the life has and
' for ' Pharaoh of ' from as Mizra ' you ground ' all ' ye ' Joseph ' nest as and

' them on ' strength ' for ' and field`ed ' man I ' from as Mizra ' and sale
' people the ' ye and ' 21 Pharaoh of ' land the ' became you and ' hunger the
the end from ' from as town of ' from as serve of ' and ye ' cross`s the ' serve`s the
' you ground ' only ' 22 and the end ' till and ' from as Mizra ' border`ing '
Pharaoh ' each ' from as priest of ' law ' for ' nest`ed ' not ' from as priest the
not ' so ' on ' Pharaoh ' them of ' gave ' which ' from law ' ye ' and eat and '
' people the ' to ' Joseph ' say as and ' 23 from you ground ' ye ' and sale '
' your as you ground ' ye and ' day as the ' from are ye ' as whom nest ' behold
' 24 ground`ed the ' ye ' from you seed and ' seed ' relate ' that ' Pharaoh of
' Pharaoh of ' you as five`s ' from set has and ' the you income`ing in ' be`s and
' field`ed the ' seed of ' relate ' be`s as ' you and hand the ' four I and
' eat of and ' from are house`ly in ' which of and ' from are eat of and
' grace ' come has ' our you life the ' and say as and ' 25 your children of
' 26 Pharaoh of ' from as serve ' our as became and ' as master ' as has eye in
you ground ' on ' this the ' day as the ' till ' law of ' Joseph ' ye`ed ' site and
' from as priest the ' you ground ' only ' five`ing of ' Pharaoh of ' from as Mizra '
' land in ' Israel ' dwell and ' 27 Pharaoh of ' whom`ed the ' not ' them alone of
' form beautiful and ' thus ' and hold as and ' has I`ll ' land in ' from as Mizra
' from as Mizra ' land in ' Jacob ' life as and ' 28 especially ' and increase as and
' him life ' two ' Jacob ' week ' and became as and ' the Year ' ten`ed ' seven
' and approach as and ' 29 the Year ' each and ' from as four I and ' from two ' seven
' say as and ' Joseph of ' and son of ' call as and ' die`ing of ' Israel ' week
' oh ' there`s ' are as has eye in ' grace ' as you come ' oh ' mother ' if
' faithful and ' bow ' as stand ' oh ' dual`s and ' as soft ' under ' are hand
' people ' as you lay and ' 30 from as Mizra in ' as has bury you ' oh ' to

as has you bury and ’ from as Mizra from ’ as has you lift has and ’ as you and father

’ 31 are as word are ’ do`ed I ’ for whither ’ say as and ’ from you bury in ’

’ if ’ swear too as and ’ vessel ’ swear`ed too the ’ say as and

down`ed the ’ head ’ on ’ Israel ’ the and humble`ly as and

' Joseph of ' say as and ' these`ed ' from as word the ' as after ' became as and ' 1
' and people ' him son ' two ' ye ' took as and ' sick`ed ' are as father ' be`th
be`th ' say as and ' Jacob of ' my told and ' 2 Ephraim ' ye and ' Manasse`ed ' ye
' dwell and ' Israel ' strength whom and ' are as to ' came ' Joseph ' are son '
speak`ed ' almighty ' to ' Joseph ' to ' Jacob ' say as and ' 3 down`ed the ' on
' say as and ' 4 near ' bless as and ' Canaan ' land in ' the almond`ing in ' Eli '
' are as whom increase the and ' are as multiply ' as behold`th ' Eli
' land the ' ye ' as set has and ' from as people ' assemble of ' are as set shall
' the time and ' 5 from on`ing ' you hold ' are as after ' are seed of ' such the
' till ' from as Mizra ' land in ' walk ' from as bore and behold ' are as son ' two
' Manasse`ed and ' Ephraim ' them ' vessel ' the from as Mizra ' are as to ' as came
which ' are kindred when and ' 6 vessel ' and became as ' Simeon are and ' Reuben are
them as brother ' there ' on ' and became as ' walk ' them as after ' you bore alas '
' Padan from ' as came in ' as whither and ' 7 from you inherit in ' and call as '
' way in ' Canaan ' land in ' are mother ' Rachel ' mosthigh ' die`ed ' highland
' bury`ed I and ' forth`ed I ' came`ing of ' land the ' you sieve ' till`ing in
Israel ' look as and ' 8 fight ' you house ' that`s ' forth`ed I ' way in ' there
' Joseph ' say as and ' 9 walk ' to`ed ' who ' say as and ' Joseph ' as son ' ye '
spoil`ed ' from as Allah ' vessel ' gave ' which ' them ' as son ' him father ' to
' as has eye and ' 10 from bless I and ' Eli ' oh ' from took ' say as and '
' adduce and ' you see of ' all him ' not ' elder`ed from ' and honour`ed ' Israel
say as and ' 11 them of ' embrace as and ' them of ' moisten as and ' him to ' from ye
' be`th and ' as you praise ' not ' are as turn ' look`ed ' Joseph ' to ' Israel '
' issue him and ' 12 are seed ' ye ' also ' from as Allah ' near ' look`ed the
land`ed ' now`s of ' prostate humble`ly as and ' him bless ' affirm ' from ye ' Joseph

' and right`s in ' Ephraim ' ye ' them two ' ye ' Joseph ' took as and ' 13

' right`s from ' and of left in ' Manasse`ed ' ye and ' Israel ' of left from

and right`s ' hand ' ye ' Israel ' send as and ' 14 him to ' adduce and ' Israel

' ye and ' little`s the ' that`ing and ' Ephraim ' head ' on ' belong`ed and '

Manasse`ed ' for ' him hand ' ye ' bereave ' Manasse`ed ' head ' on ' and of left

' from as Allah the ' say as and ' Joseph ' ye ' bless as and ' 15 first`ing the '

Isaac and ' Abraham ' him before ' as you and father ' and walk the sacred ' which

' day as the ' till ' as has till`ing from ' near ' evil`ed the ' from as Allah the '

ye ' bless as ' evil ' all from ' near ' redeem the ' messenger them ' 16 this the

' there and ' as there ' cattle ' call as and ' these`ed ' from as youth the '

' increase of ' and squirm as and ' Isaac and ' Abraham ' as you and father

' him father ' whom too as ' for ' Joseph ' look as and ' 17 land the ' approach in

' him has eye in ' evil as and ' Ephraim ' head ' on ' and right`s ' hand ' ye

' head ' above ' ye`ed ' wriggle`s of ' him father ' hand ' are from whom and

' him father ' to ' Joseph ' say as and ' 18 Manasse`ed ' head ' on ' Ephraim

' on ' are right`s ' there`s ' first`ing the ' this ' for ' as father ' so ' not

' as son ' as you known ' say as and ' him father ' refuse as and ' 19 and head

great as ' that`ing ' also and ' people of ' be`s as ' that`ing ' also ' as you known

' and seed and ' and her from ' great as ' small the ' him brother ' from to`ing and '

' day as in ' from bless as and ' 20 from nation`ing the ' fill ' be`s as

' are there`s as ' say of ' Israel ' bless as ' against ' say`ing of ' that`ing the

' Ephraim ' ye ' site and ' Manasseh are and ' Ephraim are ' from as Allah

for whither ' be`th ' Joseph ' to ' Israel ' say as and ' 21 Manasse`ed ' as before

to ' from are ye ' carry`s the and ' your people ' from as Allah ' be`s and ' die '

' ridge ' walk ' as set has ' as whither and ' 22 from are as you father ' land '

' as Amar the ' hand from ' as you take ' which ' are as brother ' on ' one

as you seek and ' as desolate in

' and gather the ' say as and ' him son ' to ' Jacob ' call as and ' 1
you as after in ' from are ye ' call as ' which ' ye ' relate ' the fortune`s I and
' and hear and ' Jacob ' as son ' and hear and ' and collect the ' 2 from week the '
' as power ' ye`ed ' as first`ing ' Reuben ' 3 your as father ' Israel ' to
' 4 harsh ' preserve and ' arise ' preserve ' as whither`ing ' you as head and
' as lay from ' whom on ' for ' survive you ' to ' Water are ' you bubble
' Levi and ' Simeon ' 5 on`ed ' as couch`ing ' you profane ' yet ' are as father
' to ' ing`Sodom in ' 6 them as hew from ' violence ' weapon ' from as brother
' for ' as honour`ing ' unite as ' to ' from assemble in and ' as soul ' income`ing
' and exterminate ' from has and race and ' man I ' and kill ' from anger in
' for ' from you cross at and ' harsh ' for ' toward ' big`ing ' 7 captain`ing
' Judah ' 8 Israel in ' from drive`s I and ' Jacob in ' from part I ' the arch
' put town in ' are as hand ' are as brother ' are menstrate him ' ye`ed
' 9 are as father ' as son ' walk ' prostate humble`ly as and ' are as enemy I
' crouch ' leg ' whom on ' as son ' torn from ' Judah ' the lion ' guest`ing
correct`ing ' not ' 10 and has rise`s as ' who ' the wildcat`s are and ' the lion are
' for ' till ' him foot ' son`s from ' prescribe from and ' Judah from ' tribe '
' 11 from as people ' and you bossom`ed ' if and ' the peace`s ' came`ing as
' and has ye`ing ' as son ' the hiss of and ' the town`s ' vine of ' as bound`ing
' from as grape ' blood in and ' and arm`ing ' has house`s ' immersion
' Laban and ' has who`s ' from as has eye ' and as utter`s at ' 12 and the garment`ing
' that`ing and ' nigh as ' from week ' put sand of ' Zebulun ' 13 milk from ' from two
' 14 has and hunt`s ' until ' and veil as and ' you and as whither ' put sand of
' 15 from as ordain them ' between in ' crouch ' from as guest ' heass`ing ' Issachar
' for ' land the ' ye and ' the good`ing ' for ' the bestow`ing ' look as and

' cargo`ing ' became as and ' charge of ' and ridge ' extent and ' pleasant`ed
' (17 Israel ' as tribe ' one are ' and people ' judge`s as ' judge ' (16 serve
' manner ' mosthigh ' has and snap`s ' way ' mosthigh ' serpent ' judge ' be`s as
' (18 after`ing ' and ride ' fell and ' skip`ing ' as heel ' bite the
' gash`ing ' fortune ' (19 Jehovah ' as you stedfast`ing ' are you Joshua`ing of
' eight`ed ' which from ' (20 heel ' fortune`s as ' that`ing and ' and has compress`s
' Naphtali ' (21 king ' as has till from ' permanent ' that`ing and ' and from bread
' Euphrates ' son ' (22 is lip`ing ' as say ' has ligue the ' the send`ing ' the to`s
' the pace ' as little's ' you built ' has eye ' mosthigh ' Euphrates ' son ' Joseph
' and the increase`s as and ' and spittle`ed from as and ' (23 captain`ing ' mosthigh
and arch ' has whom came ' carry you and ' (24 arrow`s ' as on in ' and hate`ed as and
' Jacob ' chief `s ' as hand from ' him hand ' as seed`ing ' and gilt as and '
are aid as and ' are as father ' to from ' (25 Israel ' stone ' evil`ed ' there from
' above from ' heaven`s ' you bless ' are bless as and ' almighty ' ye and ' to '
compassion and ' from as field ' you bless ' under ' you crouch ' deep`ing ' you bless
' you bless ' on ' and strong ' are mother and ' are as father ' you bless ' (26
' the has became`s you ' from on`ing ' you hill ' ye`ing you ' till ' as mountain`ing
' Benjamim`s ' (27 him brother ' consecrate`s ' my crown of and ' Joseph ' head of
(28 strip ' part as ' twilight of and ' adorn ' eat as ' is morn in ' torn as ' yellow
' word ' which ' such and ' ten ' from two ' Israel ' as tribe ' to`ed ' all '
' which ' man I ' from ye`ing ' bless as and ' them as father ' them of
' say as and ' from ye`ing ' command as and ' (29 from ye ' bless ' and you bless are
' to ' near ' and bury ' as people ' to ' gather has ' as whither ' them as to
' Ephron`ing ' field`ed in ' which ' cave`ed the ' to ' as you and father
' on ' which ' fold`ed them ' field`ed in ' which ' the cave in ' (30 as Heth the

' ye ' Abraham ' nest`ed ' which ' Canaan ' land in ' appear from ' around
31 ' bury ' you hold of ' as Heth the ' Ephron`ing ' each ' field`ed the
' there`ed ' and wife ' Sarah ' ye and ' Abraham ' ye ' and bury ' there`ed and
' as you bury ' there`ed and ' and wife ' Rebekeh ' ye and ' Isaac ' ye ' and bury
' and in ' which ' cave`ed the and ' field`ed the ' purchase`ed ' 32 not'ed ' ye
' him son ' ye ' you command of ' Jacob ' finish and ' 33 crush ' as son ' each
' gather as and ' expire`ing as and ' down`ed the ' to ' him foot ' gather as and
him people ' to

' and Mosthigh ' against as and ' him father ' around ' on ' Joseph ' fell and ' 1
' ye ' him serve ' ye ' Joseph ' command as and ' 2 if ' moisten as and
' and embalm as and ' him father ' ye ' emblam of ' from as decease the
' from as four I ' if ' and fill as and ' 3 Israel ' ye ' from as decease the
and ye ' and wept and ' from as embalm the ' week ' and fill as ' so ' for ' day as
and weep`s ' week ' and cross as and ' 4 day as ' from as seven ' the from as Mizra '
' oh ' mother ' say of ' Pharaoh ' you house ' to ' Joseph ' word as and '
' Pharaoh ' as ear in ' oh ' and word ' your as has eye in ' grace ' as you come
' say of ' and die`ing ' as before ' as has swear`s too the ' as father ' 5 say of
' land in ' vessel ' as net`s are ' which ' as bury in ' die ' for whither ' be`th
bury`ed I and ' oh ' on`ed I ' the time and ' as has bury you ' there`ed ' Canaan
' 6 the carry`ing I and ' as has swear`s too the ' which are ' as father ' ye '
' which are ' are as father ' ye ' bury and ' on`ed ' Pharaoh ' say as and
and went and ' him father ' ye ' bury of ' Joseph ' went and ' 7 are swear`s too the
' as elder ' all and ' and you house ' as elder ' Pharaoh ' as serve ' all ' and ye '
' him brother and ' Joseph ' you house ' all and ' 8 from as Mizra ' land
' from herd and ' from flock and ' from children ' only ' him father ' you house and
' also ' ride ' also ' and people ' went and ' 9 has I`ll ' land in ' and forsake
' 10 especially ' honour ' camp`ed the ' became as and ' from as excrement
' cross in ' which ' thorntree the ' threshingfloor ' till ' and came as and
' honour and ' great`ing ' fret from ' there ' and fret as and ' has desend the
' 11 from week ' you seven ' mourn ' him father of ' do as and ' especially
' mourn the ' ye ' as Canaan the ' land the ' sojourn as ' look as and
' this ' honour ' mourn ' and say as and ' thorntree the ' threshingfloor in
' which ' from as Mizra ' mourn ' there`ed ' call ' so ' on ' from as Mizra of

' which are ' so ' him son ' if ' concoct as and ' 12 has desend the ' cross in
and bury as and ' Canaan ' land`ed ' him son ' and ye ' and lift as and ' 13 fast`ing
ye ' Abraham ' nest`ed ' which ' fold`ed them ' field`ed ' you cave in ' and ye '
' on ' as Heth the ' Ephron`ing ' each ' bury ' you hold of ' field`ed the '
' that`ing ' the from as Mizra ' Joseph ' dwell and ' 14 appear from ' around
him father ' ye ' bury of ' and ye ' from mosthigh the ' all and ' him brother and
for ' Joseph ' as brother ' see as and ' 15 him father ' ye ' and bury ' as after '
' Joseph ' and has hate as ' if ' and say as and ' them as father ' die '
' which ' evil`ed the ' all ' ye ' our of ' carry`s as ' carry the and
' say of ' Joseph ' on I ' and command as and ' 16 and ye ' our of also
' here ' 17 say of ' and die`ing ' as before ' command`ed ' are as father
' are as brother ' trespass ' oh ' lift ' the thou`th ' Joseph of ' has and say you
' oh ' lift ' the time and ' are and of also ' evil`ed ' for ' from you sin and
' Joseph ' against as and ' are as father ' as Allah ' as serve ' trepass of
' and fell and ' him brother ' also ' and walk as and ' 18 him to ' from word in
say as and ' 19 from as serve of ' walk ' and behold`th ' and say as and ' him before
' from as Allah ' under the ' for ' and look as you ' to ' Joseph ' them as to '
' evil`ed ' mosthigh ' from you reckon ' from ye and ' 20 as whither
' you and do`ed ' purpose of ' the good`ing of ' reckon`ed ' from as Allah the and
' the time and ' 21 increase ' people ' you and life the of ' this the ' day as are
' ye and ' from are ye ' all eat ' for whither ' and look as you ' to
22 from heart ' on I ' word as and ' from ye`ing ' comfort as and ' from are children
' him father ' you house and ' that`ing ' from as Mizra in ' Joseph ' dwell and '
' Joseph ' look as and ' 23 from two ' ten and ' hundred`ed ' Joseph ' life as and
' son ' Machir ' as son ' also ' from as three`s ' from as son ' Ephraim of

Joseph ' say as and ' 24 Joseph ' as bless ' on ' week in ' and bore as ' Manasse`ed
punish as ' punish ' from as Allah the and ' die ' for whither ' him brother ' to '
' to ' such the ' land the ' has from ' from are ye ' on`ed the and ' from are ye '
' 25 Jacob of and ' Isaac of ' Abraham of ' swear too has ' which ' land the
' punish as ' punish ' say of ' Israel ' as son ' ye ' Joseph ' swear too as and
victual`ed ' as bone have ' ye ' from whom on the and ' from are ye ' from as Allah
' from two ' ten and ' hundred`ed ' son ' Joseph ' die as and ' 26 from are ye '
' from as Mizra in ' stream`ing in ' site as and ' and ye ' and embalm as and

' the from as Mizra ' from as came the ' Israel ' as son ' you name ' to`ed and (1

' Simeon and ' Reuben ' (2 and came ' and you house and ' man I ' Jacob ' ye

' judge ' (4 Benjamim`s and ' Zebulun and ' Issachar and ' (3 Judah and ' Levi and

' as out ' soul ' all ' and became as and ' (5 which and ' fortune ' Naphtali and

' (6 from as Mizra in ' be`s ' Joseph and ' soul ' from as seven ' Jacob ' soft

that`ing the ' magnificent`ing ' all and ' him brother ' all and ' Joseph ' die as and

' and increase as and ' and bread as and ' form put ' Israel ' as son and ' (7

' (8 from ye ' land the ' fill you and ' especially ' especially in ' and might as and

' ye ' known ' not ' which ' from as Mizra ' on ' new ' king ' rise as and

' Israel ' as son ' people ' be`th ' and people ' to ' say as and ' (9 Joseph

' if ' the wise you has ' handover`ed ' (10 and her from ' might`ing and ' increase

' fight`ed from ' alas has call you ' for ' be`s and ' increase`ed as ' turn

' and son ' fight has and ' our as hateful ' on ' that`ing ' also ' join and shall

' as captain ' and Mosthigh ' and site`s and ' (11 land the ' has from ' on`ed and

' from you and charge in ' and complete and low ' purpose of ' from as burden

' s`Pithon`ing ' ye ' Pharaoh of ' you and has castimage ' watch ' and son as and

' so ' and ye ' and because ' which are and ' (12 skip from evil ' ye and

(13 Israel ' as son ' around from ' and end as and ' grow as ' so and ' thus apart as

' (14 fracture in ' Israel ' as son ' ye ' from as Mizra ' and serve as and '

' s`heass in ' hard`ed ' the serve in ' them as life ' ye ' and poison as and

' all ' ye ' field`ed in ' serve`ed ' all in and ' from as son of in and

' king ' say as and ' (15 fracture in ' cattle ' and serve ' which ' from you serve

sister the ' there ' which ' whom`ing Obara the ' you and bore who of ' from as Mizra

so bore house ' say as and ' (16 the scream'ing ' you two the ' there and ' the happy '

' mother ' from as stone the ' on ' has whom look and ' whom`ing Obara the ' ye '

' that`s ' daughter ' mother and ' and ye ' has die the and ' that`ing ' son
' ye ' you and bore as them ' the has dread you and ' 17 the you life and
' king ' has am to ' word ' which are ' concoct ' not and ' from as Allah the
' call as and ' 18 from as bore as the ' ye ' the has life`s you and ' from as Mizra
' behold of ' say as and ' you and bore who of ' from as Mizra ' king ' Pharaoh
' ye ' the has life`s you and ' this the ' word the ' ye ' has whom do ' why`ing
' Pharaoh ' to ' you and bore as them ' the has say you and ' 19 from as bore as the
' for ' whom`ing Obara the ' whom`ing Mirza the ' from as women are ' not ' for
' you and bore as them ' has am to ' income`ing ' suspend in ' be`th ' you and life
' you and bore who of ' from as Allah ' improve as and ' 20 and bore as and
' became as and ' 21 especially ' and might as and ' people the ' and increase as and
' do as and ' from as Allah the ' ye ' you and bore as them ' and look as ' for
' say of ' and people ' all of ' Pharaoh ' command as and ' 22 integrity`s ' them of
' channel`ed the ' from as cross of ' bore`ing became ' son the ' all
shall life you ' daughter the ' all and ' has and the hurl`s you

' daughter ' ye ' took as and ' Levi ' you house from ' man I ' walk as and ' 1
for ' and ye ' look you and ' son ' bore you and ' Woman the ' pregnant and ' 2 Levi
' not and ' 3 from as moon ' three`ed ' and the north you and ' that`ing ' good`ing '
' you box ' and mother ' if ' took you and ' and north`s the ' till`ing ' all`ed as
ye ' thus ' there you and ' pitch in and ' s`heass in ' the heass you and ' swallow
' 4 channel the ' you lip ' on ' join`ing in ' there you and ' boy the '
if ' success`ed ' what ' you opinion`ed of ' get from ' and sister ' locator you and
am you youth and ' channel the ' on ' wash of ' Pharaoh ' daughter ' up you and ' 5
' box`ed the ' ye ' look you and ' channel the ' hand ' on ' you walk the '
' 6 took`ed you and ' faithful`ed ' ye ' send you and ' join`ing the ' middle`ing in
' youth ' be`th and ' boy the ' ye ' and look`ed you and ' open`ed you and
' say you and ' Pharaoh ' daughter ' and Mosthigh ' pity you and ' against`ed
daughter ' to ' and sister ' say you and ' 7 this ' from as Obara the ' as boy from
' has from ' you suck from ' Woman ' walk ' as you call and ' walk I the ' Pharaoh '
' nihil ' say you and ' 8 boy the ' ye ' walk ' suck you and ' whom Obara the
' ye ' call you and ' what on the ' are hang and ' for of ' Pharaoh ' daughter
ye ' as bear`s the ' Pharaoh ' daughter ' nihil ' say you and ' 9 boy the ' mother
' ye ' donkey ' as whither and ' vessel ' alas suck the and ' this the ' boy the '
' 10 and bosom`ed give and ' boy the ' ye ' Woman the ' took you and ' are merry
' Pharaoh ' daughter ' to ' and came`ed you and ' boy the ' youth the ' great as and
say you and ' Moses ' name ' ye ' call you and ' son of ' nihil ' became as and
' became as and ' 11 him the whom too from ' Water the ' has from ' for '
' him brother ' to ' out and ' Moses ' great as and ' them the ' from as sea in
' with`ed ' as Mizra ' man I ' look as and ' from you and charge in ' look as and
look as and ' here and ' here ' turn as and ' 12 him brother from ' as Obara ' man I

and the hidden as and ' as Mizra the ' ye ' struck and ' man I ' whither`s ' for '
' from as person ' two ' be`th and ' two the ' day as in ' out and ' 13 of sand in '
fellow ' middle`ed ' what of ' evil`ness of ' say as and ' quarrel`s ' from as Obara
' our as on ' ing`discern of and ' captain ' man I of ' rug ' who ' say as and ' 14
' as Mizra the ' ye ' you kill ' which are ' say ' ye`ed ' as has kill of the
' 15 word the ' acknowledge has ' certain ' say as and ' Moses ' dread as and
' ye ' kill of ' seek as and ' this the ' word the ' ye ' Pharaoh ' hear as and
Midian ' land in ' dwell and ' Pharaoh ' around from ' Moses ' shoot as and ' Moses
' daughter`th`ing ' seven ' Midian ' priest of and ' 16 well the ' on ' dwell and '
' ye ' the has fill you and ' the has frail you and ' the has came you and
' 17 has am father ' flock ' ye ' drunk`ing the of ' from as trough the
' Moses ' rise as and ' from and exact as and ' from pastoral the ' and came as and
' the has came you and ' 18 from flock ' ye ' moisten as and ' has deliver`s as and
' came ' has you soon ' why`ing ' say as and ' has am father ' Reuel ' to
' hand from ' our shade`s the ' as Mizra ' man I ' the has say you and ' 19 day as the
' ye ' moisten as and ' our of ' frail`ed ' frail`ed ' also and ' from pastoral the
' this ' what of ' and hence and ' him daughter`th ' to ' say as and ' 20 flock the
to him and ' 21 fight ' eat as and ' if ' has call ' man that ' ye ' has dowry have
' the bird`ing ' ye ' give as and ' man that ' ye ' desist of ' Moses '
' ye ' call as and ' son ' bore you and ' Moses of ' 22 Moses of ' and daughter
' 23 am foreign ' land in ' as whom became ' guest ' say ' for ' Gershom ' name
king ' die as and ' them the ' from as increase the ' from as sea in ' became as and
serve`ed the ' has from ' Israel ' as son ' and brother`th as and ' from as Mizra '
' from as Allah the ' to ' from you save`ing ' on you and ' and yell as and '
' from you groan ' ye ' from as Allah ' hear as and ' 24 serve`ed the ' has from

ye and ’ Abraham ’ ye ’ and covenant`s ’ ye ’ from as Allah ’ is remember as and

Israel ’ as son ’ ye ’ from as Allah ’ look as and ’ 25 Jacob ’ ye and ’ Isaac ’

from as Allah ’ known and ’

' priest ' and inlaw ' and preserve ' flock ' ye ' evil`ed ' be`s ' Moses and ' 1

' came as and ' is wilderness the ' after ' flock the ' ye ' lead as and ' Midian

' him to ' look as and ' 2 the ing desolate ' from as Allah the ' mountain ' to

' bush`ed the ' middle`ing from ' fire ' you bright in ' Jehovah ' messenger from

' bush`ed the and ' abhorrence ' burn ' bush`ed the ' be`th and ' look as and

' oh ' the bound`ing ' Moses ' say as and ' 3 eat ' and has whither`s

' not ' why`ing ' this the ' great`ing the ' appear`ed the ' ye ' look`ed I and

' repent ' for ' from as Allah ' Jehovah ' look as and ' 4 bush`ed the ' burn as

' bush`ed the ' middle`ing from ' from as Allah ' him to ' call as and ' you see of

' to ' say as and ' 5 as behold`th ' say as and ' Moses ' Moses ' say as and

' for ' are as foot ' above ' are as shoe ' peace ' from worship ' approach you

' holy ' you ground ' and Mosthigh ' ing`stand ' ye`ed ' which ' place`ing the

' as Allah ' are as you and father ' as Allah ' for whither ' say as and ' 6 that`s

' Moses ' is cloth as and ' Jacob ' as Allah and ' Isaac ' as Allah and ' Abraham

' say as and ' 7 from as Allah the ' to ' scan`s the from ' dread ' for ' him turn

' which ' as people ' poor ' ye ' as you seen ' and look`ed ' Jehovah

' him presence ' around from ' as you hear ' from you cry ' ye and ' from as Mizra in

' and shade`s the of ' wander`ed and ' 8 him pain`ing from ' ye ' as you known ' for

' land the ' has from ' and offer`ing the of and ' from as Mizra ' hand from

' you secrete ' land ' to ' the large and ' the good`ing ' land ' to ' that`s the

' as Heth the and ' as Canaan the ' place`ing ' to ' honey and ' milk

' as Hivite the and ' as Girgash the and ' as Periz the and ' as Amar the and

' came`ed ' Israel ' as son ' you cry ' be`th ' the time and ' 9 as Jebus the and

' from as Mizra ' which ' affict the ' ye ' as you seen ' also and ' Eli

Pharaoh ' to ' are send I and ' walk`ed ' the time and ' 10 from ye ' from as affict

11 ' from as Mizra from ' Israel ' as son ' as people ' ye ' you spring the and '
' walk I ' for ' for whither ' who ' from as Allah the ' to ' Moses ' say as and
from as Mizra from ' Israel ' as son ' ye ' spring`s I ' for and ' Pharaoh ' to
' for ' ye`ing the ' walk ' this and ' are people ' be`s I ' for ' say as and ' 12
' people the ' ye ' are issue`s alas in ' are as you send ' for whither
' mountain the ' on ' from as Allah the ' ye ' shall serve you ' from as Mizra from
' for whither ' be`th ' from as Allah the ' to ' Moses ' say as and ' 13 this the
' as Allah ' them of ' as you say and ' Israel ' as son ' to ' came
' what ' vessel ' and say and ' your as to ' as has send ' your as you and father
' Moses ' to ' from as Allah ' say as and ' 14 them as to ' say ' what ' name
' Israel ' as son ' to ' say you ' here ' say as and ' be`s I ' which ' be`s I
' to ' from as Allah ' till`ing ' say as and ' 15 your as to ' as has send ' be`s I
' as Allah ' Jehovah ' Israel ' as son ' to ' say you ' here ' Moses
' as Allah and ' Isaac ' as Allah ' Abraham ' as Allah ' from are as you father
' this and ' from on`ing of ' as there ' this ' your as to ' as has send ' Jacob
' ye ' you gather and ' walk ' 16 evermore`ing and ' evermore of ' as is remember
' as Allah ' Jehovah ' them as to ' you say and ' Israel ' as son ' as elder
' Isaac and ' Abraham ' as Allah ' Eli ' speak`ed ' from are as you father
' as concoct the ' ye and ' from are ye ' as you punish ' punish ' say of ' Jacob and
' as low from ' from are ye ' on`ed I ' say`ed and ' 17 from as Mizra in ' relate
' as Amar the and ' as Heth the and ' as Canaan the ' land ' to ' from as Mizra
' to ' as Jebus the and ' as Hivite the and ' as Girgash the and ' as Periz the and
' are voice`ing of ' and hear and ' 18 honey and ' milk ' you secrete ' land
' from as Mizra ' king ' to ' Israel ' as elder and ' ye`ed ' brought and
' the pick ' from as as Obara the ' as Allah ' Jehovah ' him to ' from you say and

' from week ' you three ' way ' oh ' walk`ed has ' the time and ' our as on
' as whither and ' (19 our as Allah ' Jehovah of ' the sacrifice has and ' word from in
' from as Mizra ' king ' from are ye ' permanent ' not ' for ' as you known
' ye ' as you send and ' (20 the strength ' hand in ' forward`ing ' walk the of
' all in ' from as Mizra ' ye ' as whom smitten and ' as hand
' so ' as after and ' and approach in ' do`ed I ' which ' as you and wonderful has
' this the ' people the ' grace ' ye ' as set has and ' (21 from are ye ' send as
' not ' shall walk you ' for ' be`s and ' from as Mizra ' as has eye in
' and shepherd is ' each ' Woman ' the ask and ' (22 from as only ' shall walk you
' he house ' you pilgrimage and ' the you nigh from ' he tend ' each ' Woman and
on ' from you there and ' you and raiment and ' gold ' as all and ' silver ' weapon
' ye ' from you pluck and ' your as daughter`th ' on and ' your as son '
from as Mizra

' vessel ' and believe`s as ' not ' behold and ' say as and ' Moses ' low as and ' (1
' speak`ed ' not ' and say as ' for ' as voice`ing in ' and hear as ' not and
' are hand in ' this ' what ' Jehovah ' him to ' say as and ' (2 Jehovah ' are as to
' land`ed ' and the hurl`s the ' say as and ' (3 down`ed ' say as and
' Moses ' flee as and ' serpent of ' became as and ' land`ed ' and the hurl`s as and
hold and ' are hand ' send ' Moses ' to ' Jehovah ' say as and ' (4 and as turn from
' became as and ' and in ' strength as and ' and hand ' send as and ' and tail in '
are as to ' speak`ed ' for ' and believe`s as ' purpose of ' (5 and palm in ' below`ed
' as Allah and ' Abraham ' as Allah ' from you and father ' as Allah ' Jehovah '
' came the ' till`ing ' if ' Jehovah ' say as and ' (6 Jacob ' as Allah and ' Isaac
' and bosom at in ' and hand ' came as and ' are bosom at in ' are hand ' oh
' you leper from ' and hand ' be`th and ' and bosom at from ' the spring`s as and
' dwell and ' are bosom at ' to ' are hand ' carry the ' say as and ' (7 snow are
' be`th and ' and bosom at from ' the spring`s as and ' and bosom at ' to ' and hand
' walk ' and believe`s as ' not ' mother ' be`s and ' (8 and flesh are ' carry`ed
' has and head`s the ' ye`ing the ' voice`ing of ' and hear as ' not and
' be`s and ' (9 shall after the ' ye`ing the ' voice`ing of ' and believe`s the and
' these`ed ' evidence`ing the ' two of ' also ' and believe`s as ' not ' mother
' as Water from ' you take and ' are voice`ing of ' shall hear as ' not and
' which ' Water the ' and became and ' wither`ed the ' you pour and ' channel the
' (10 you carry as in ' blood of ' and became and ' channel the ' has from ' implicate
from as word ' man I ' not ' as master ' house ' Jehovah ' to ' Moses ' say as and
it hundred ' also ' from and three from ' also ' past`ing from ' also ' for whither '
' speech`ing ' honour and ' talk ' honour ' for ' are serve ' to ' are word '
or ' Men of ' talk ' there ' who ' him to ' Jehovah ' say as and ' (11 for whither

' town`ing ' or ' clear ' or ' devise ' or ' sheave ' site`ing ' who '
' for whither and ' walk ' the time and ' 12 Jehovah ' for whither ' forward`ing
' 13 word you ' which ' are as whom mountain`ing and ' reverse`s ' people ' be`s I
' delay and ' 14 send you ' hand in ' oh ' send ' as master ' house ' say as and
' are as brother ' Aaron ' forward`ing ' say as and ' Moses in ' Jehovah ' anger
' be`th ' also and ' that`ing ' word as ' word ' for ' as you known ' Levi the
' 15 and mind in ' rejoice and ' are look and ' are you call of ' out ' that`ing
' him animal ' from as word the ' ye ' herein and ' him to ' you word and
' and talk`s ' people and ' reverse`s ' people ' be`s I ' for whither and
' word and ' 16 smoke`ing you ' which ' ye ' from are ye ' as whom mountain`ing and
' by`ed ' walk ' be`s as ' that`ing ' be`s and ' people the ' to ' walk ' that`ing
' this the ' down`ed the ' ye and ' 17 from as Allah of ' if ' be`s you ' ye`ed and
' 18 ing`evidence the ' ye ' and in ' do`ed you ' which ' are hand in ' implicate
if ' say as and ' and inlaw ' and preserve ' to ' dwell and ' Moses ' walk as and
' which ' as brother ' to ' the carry`ing I and ' oh ' the walk I '
' say as and ' from as life ' from till`ing the ' look`ed I and ' from as Mizra in
' to ' Jehovah ' say as and ' 19 from and peace of ' walk ' Moses of ' and preserve
' all ' and die ' for ' the from as Mizra ' carry`ing ' walk ' Midian in ' Moses
' Moses ' took as and ' 20 are soul ' ye ' from as seek them ' from as person the
' heass`ing the ' on ' from ride as and ' him son ' ye and ' and wife ' ye
' down`ed ' ye ' Moses ' took as and ' from as Mizra ' land`ed ' dwell and
' Moses ' to ' Jehovah ' say as and ' 21 and hand in ' from as Allah the
' all ' ye ' look`ed ' the from as Mizra ' carry`ing of ' are you walk in
' from dual`s and ' are hand in ' as you there ' which ' from as ing`wonder the
' not and ' and heart ' ye ' strength I ' as whither and ' Pharaoh ' as before

’ say ’ here ’ Pharaoh ’ to ’ you say and ’ (22 people the ’ ye ’ send as
’ ye ’ send ’ are as to ’ say and ’ (23 Israel ’ as first`ing ’ as son ’ Jehovah
’ for whither ’ be`th ’ and send of ’ refuse you and ’ as has serve as and ’ as son
’ lodge`ing in ’ way in ’ became as and ’ (24 are first`ing ’ are son ’ ye ’ kill
’ took you and ’ (25 and die`s the ’ seek as and ’ Jehovah ’ and the meet as and
’ reach and ’ son`ed ’ you foreskin ’ ye ’ hew you and ’ boulder ’ the bird`ing
’ (26 vessel ’ ye`ed ’ from as blood ’ inlaw ’ for ’ say you and ’ him foot of
’ from as blood ’ inlaw ’ drop`ed I ’ yet ’ and numb`ed ’ heal and
’ you call of ’ walk ’ Aaron ’ to ’ Jehovah ’ say as and ’ (27 you and circumcise of
’ blemish ’ and the meet as and ’ walk as and ’ word`ed them ’ Moses
’ ye ’ Aaron of ’ Moses ’ my told and ’ (28 if ’ moisten as and ’ from as Allah the
which ’ ing`evidence the ’ all ’ ye and ’ and send ’ which ’ Jehovah ’ as word ’ all
ye ’ and gather as and ’ Aaron and ’ Moses ’ and walk as and ’ (29 and command`ed ’
’ all ’ ye ’ Aaron ’ word as and ’ (30 Israel ’ as son ’ as elder ’ all ’
’ do as and ’ Moses ’ to ’ Jehovah ’ word ’ which ’ from as word the
’ people the ’ and believe as and ’ (31 people the ’ as has eye of ’ ing`evidence the
’ for and ’ Israel ’ as son ’ ye ’ Jehovah ’ punish ’ for ’ and hear as and
prostate humble`ly as and ’ and stoop as and ’ from as low ’ ye ’ look`ed

THE TORAH SCROLL 5

here ' Pharaoh ' to ' and say as and ' Aaron and ' Moses ' and came ' after and ' 1
' reef as and ' as people ' ye ' send ' Israel ' as Allah ' Jehovah ' say '
' hear I ' which ' Jehovah ' who ' Pharaoh ' say as and ' 2 word from in ' vessel
' Jehovah ' ye ' as you known ' not ' Israel ' ye ' send of ' and voice`ing in
' as Allah ' and say as and ' 3 send I ' not ' Israel ' ye ' also and
' way ' word`ed them ' oh ' walk`ed has ' our as on ' call has ' from as Obara the
' Jehovah of ' the sacrifice has and ' word from in ' from week ' you three
say as and ' 4 desolate in ' or ' word in ' and has entreat as ' turn ' our as Allah
' and hair`s you ' Aaron and ' Moses ' what of ' from as Mizra ' king ' them as to '
' 5 from are as you charge of ' follow ' and as work from ' people the ' ye
' land the ' affirm ' time`ed ' from as increase ' behold ' Pharaoh ' say as and
' Pharaoh ' command as and ' 6 from you charge from ' from ye ' from desist the and
' ye and ' people in ' from as presence the ' ye ' that`ing the ' day as in
' similar ' set of ' has and gather and you ' not ' 7 say of ' him ing`officer
' them ' from and three ' past`ing are ' from as white the ' Laban of ' people of
' you has middle from ' ye and ' 8 similar ' them of ' and forage as and ' and walk as
' from and three ' past`ing ' from as do ' them ' which ' from as white the
' for ' and her from ' and withdraw you ' not ' them as on ' and deposite`s
' walk`ed has ' say of ' from as cry ' them ' so ' on ' them ' from as encourage
' on ' serve`ed the ' honour you ' 9 our as Allah of ' the sacrifice has
' as word in ' and save as ' not and ' thus ' and save as and ' from as person the
' him ing`officer and ' people the ' as presence ' and out and ' 10 false
' say ' here ' say of ' people the ' to ' and word as and ' and say as and
and took ' follow ' from ye ' 11 similar ' relate ' gave ' as has whither`s ' Pharaoh
' withdraw has ' whither`s ' for ' and come you ' which from ' similar ' relate '

' land ' all in ' people the ' drive Then ' 12 word ' from are you serve from
' from as presence the and ' 13 son you of ' hard ' forage of ' from as Mizra
' day as ' word ' your as work ' fail ' say of ' people in ' from as and issue
' 14 relate ' gave ' son you the ' you and became in ' which are ' and day as in
' them as on ' name ' which ' Israel ' as son ' as ing`officer ' and struck and
' from are law ' complete as all ' not ' why`ing ' say of ' Pharaoh ' as presence
' 15 day as the ' also ' past`ing ' also ' from and three ' past`ing are ' Laban of
Pharaoh ' to ' and cry as and ' Israel ' as son ' as ing`officer ' and came as and
' whither`s ' similar ' 16 are as serve of ' here ' do`ed you ' what of ' say of '
' concoct ' our of ' from as say ' from as white and ' are as serve of ' gave
' say as and ' 17 are people ' you sin and ' your`s from ' are as serve ' be`th and
' from as say ' from ye ' so ' on ' from as encourage ' from ye ' from as encourage
' and serve ' follow ' the time and ' 18 Jehovah of ' the sacrifice has ' walk`ed has
and give you ' from as white the ' so you and ' relate ' gave as ' not ' son you and
' say of ' evil`ed in ' from ye ' Israel ' as son ' as ing`officer ' see as and ' 19
' 20 and day as in ' day as ' word ' from are as white from ' and withdraw whom ' not
' from as settle ' Aaron ' ye and ' Moses ' ye ' and entreat as and
' and say as and ' 21 Pharaoh ' around ' each ' from you issue in ' from you call of
' which ' discern as and ' from are mosthigh ' Jehovah ' look`ed as ' them as to
' Pharaoh ' as has eye in ' and encamp is ' ye ' from you abhorrence the
' 22 our kill of ' and energy in ' desolate ' set of ' him serve ' as has eye in and
' bad`ed the ' what of ' as master ' say as and ' Jehovah ' to ' Moses ' dwell and
as brought ' yet from and ' 23 as has you send ' this ' what of ' this the ' people of
' this the ' people of ' mischief ' are there in ' word of ' Pharaoh ' to '
are people ' ye ' you rescue ' not ' recover and

’ which ’ ye ’ saw`ed ’ ye`ed ’ time`ed ’ Moses ’ to ’ Jehovah ’ say as and ’ 1
’ hand in and ’ from send as ’ the strength ’ hand in ’ for ’ Pharaoh of ’ do`ed I
2 from as Allah ’ Jehovah ’ word as and ’ and land from ’ from exact as ’ the strength
3 to ’ look`ed I and ’ Jehovah ’ as whither ’ him to ’ say as and ’ Moses ’ to ’
’ as there and ’ almighty ’ route ’ Jacob ’ to and ’ Isaac ’ to and ’ Abraham ’
4 ’ ye ’ as arch the ’ also and ’ them of ’ as you opinion and has ’ not ’ Jehovah
’ land ’ ye ’ Canaan ’ land ’ ye ’ them of ’ set of ’ from ye ’ as covenant`s
5 as you hear ’ as whither ’ also and ’ thus ’ and guest ’ which ’ them as pilgrimage
’ from as serve from ’ from as Mizra ’ which ’ Israel ’ as son ’ you groan ’ ye ’
6 as son of ’ say ’ so of ’ as covenant`s ’ ye ’ the is remember I and ’ from ye
’ under from ’ from are ye ’ as you issue alas and ’ Jehovah ’ as whither ’ Israel ’
from you serve from ’ from are ye ’ as you rescue and ’ from as Mizra ’ you and charge
’ am and permit ’ seed`ing in ’ from are ye ’ as you redeem and ’
7 vessel ’ from are ye ’ as you take and ’ from as great ’ from as discern from in and
’ complete known and ’ from as Allah of ’ relate ’ as whom became and ’ people of ’
’ from are ye ’ issue`s and them ’ your as Allah ’ Jehovah ’ as whither ’ for
8 ’ from are ye ’ as you came the and ’ from as Mizra ’ you and charge ’ under from
Abraham of ’ ye`ed ’ set of ’ as hand ’ ye ’ as you help ’ which ’ land the ’ to
’ the occupy from ’ relate ’ ye`ed ’ as set has and ’ Jacob of and ’ Isaac of ’
9 ’ Israel ’ as son ’ to ’ so ’ Moses ’ word as and ’ Jehovah ’ as whither
’ the serve from and ’ spirit is ’ reap from ’ Moses ’ to ’ and hear ’ not and
’ and her from ’ oh ’ forbare ’ Moses ’ to ’ and say as and ’ hard`ed
’ ye ’ serve ’ our of ’ good`ing ’ for ’ from as Mizra ’ ye ’ the serve shall
10 ’ to ’ Jehovah ’ word as and ’ word from in ’ our die`ing from ’ from as Mizra
11 ’ from as Mizra ’ king ’ Pharaoh ’ to ’ word ’ came ’ say of ’ Moses

' Moses ' word as and ' 12 and land from ' Israel ' as son ' ye ' send as and
' Eli ' and hear ' not ' Israel ' as son ' behold ' say of ' Jehovah ' as before
from as ordain ' foreskin ' as whither and ' Pharaoh ' as has hear as ' are hence and
' from command as and ' Aaron ' to and ' Moses ' to ' Jehovah ' word as and ' 13
' issue`s alas of ' from as Mizra ' king ' Pharaoh ' to and ' Israel ' as son ' to
' as head ' to`ed and ' 14 from as Mizra ' land from ' Israel ' as son ' ye
Enoch`ing ' Israel ' first`ing ' Reuben ' as son ' from you and father ' you house
' 15 Reuben ' you and at family ' to`ed ' Carmi and ' Hezron`ing ' Pallu`ing and '
' Zohar and ' Jachin and ' Ohad and ' Jamin and ' Jemuel ' Simeon ' as son and
' 16 Simeon ' you and at family ' to`ed ' whom Canaan the ' son ' Saul and
Kohath and ' Gershon`ing ' from you bore you of ' Levi ' as son ' you name ' to`ed and
' each and ' from as three and ' seven ' Levi ' as life ' two and ' Merari and '
from you at family of ' as hear and ' as son of ' Gershon`ing ' as son ' 17 the Year
Uzziel and ' has and connect and ' noon as and ' from sheaf ' Kohath ' as son and ' 18
' 19 the Year ' each and ' from as three and ' three ' Kohath ' as life ' two and '
' you and at family ' to`ed ' as feel`ing and ' as dance ' Merari ' as son and
honour him ' ye ' from sheaf ' took as and ' 20 from you bore and you of ' Levi the
' ye and ' Aaron ' ye ' if ' bore you and ' resemble I of ' if ' and aunt '
' six ' from sheaf ' as life ' two and ' from sister`ing ' Miriam ' ye and ' Moses
' bald ' Izhar ' as son and ' 21 the Year ' each and ' from as three and
s`Elzaphan and ' ask as from ' Uzziel ' as son and ' 22 as male and ' cride has and
' daughter ' Elisheba ' ye ' Aaron ' took as and ' 23 as demolish and '
' resemble I of ' if ' pocket`ing has ' you and brother ' freewill as people
' Eleazar ' ye ' that`ing as father ' ye and ' freewill ' ye ' if ' bore you and
' Ablassaph and ' Elkanah and ' bound`s ' bald ' as son and ' 24 Ithamar ' ye and

' took of ' Aaron ' son ' Eleazar and ' 25 as Korah the ' you and at family ' to`ed
' if ' bore you and ' resemble I of ' if ' Putiel ' daughter`th`ing from ' if
' from Levi the ' you and father ' as head ' to`ed ' Phinehas ' ye
' say ' which ' Moses and ' Aaron ' that`ing ' 26 complete and at family of
' land from ' Israel ' as son ' ye ' and issue`s alas ' them of ' Jehovah
Pharaoh ' to ' from as word from the ' them ' 27 from you mass ' on ' from as Mizra
' land from ' Israel ' as son ' ye ' issue`s alas of ' from as Mizra ' king '
' day as in ' became as and ' 28 Aaron and ' Moses ' that`ing ' from as Mizra from
' Jehovah ' word as and ' 29 from as Mizra ' land in ' Moses ' to ' Jehovah ' word
' king ' Pharaoh ' to ' word ' Jehovah ' as whither ' say`ing of ' Moses ' to
' say as and ' 30 are as to ' word ' as whither ' which ' all ' ye ' from as Mizra
' from as ordain ' foreskin ' as whither ' behold ' Jehovah ' as before ' Moses
Pharaoh ' Eli ' as has hear as ' are hence and

from as Allah ' are as set has ' look`ed ' Moses ' to ' Jehovah ' say`ing Then ' 1
' ye`ed ' 2 are prophet`s ' be`s as ' are as brother ' Aaron`ing and ' Pharaoh of '
' are as brother ' Aaron`ing and ' are command I ' which ' all ' ye ' word you
3 ' and land from ' Israel ' as son ' ye ' send and ' Pharaoh ' to ' word as
ye ' as whom increase the and ' Pharaoh ' heart ' ye ' hard`ed I ' as whither and
' not and ' 4 from as Mizra ' land in ' as you lip'ing ' ye and ' as ing`evidence '
' from as Mizra in ' as hand ' ye ' as set has and ' Pharaoh ' your as to ' hear as
' Israel ' as son ' as people ' ye ' as you mass ' ye ' as you issue alas and
and known and ' 5 from as great ' from as discern from in ' from as Mizra ' land from
' as hand ' ye ' as contact in ' Jehovah ' as whither ' for ' from as Mizra ' all '
' Israel ' as son ' as people ' ye ' as you issue alas and ' from as Mizra ' on
' command`ed ' which are ' Aaron and ' Moses ' do as and ' 6 from middle`ing from
' the Year ' from as eight ' son ' Moses and ' 7 concoct ' so ' from ye ' Jehovah
Pharaoh ' to ' from word in ' the Year ' from as eight and ' three ' son ' Aaron and
9 say of ' Aaron ' to and ' Moses ' to ' Jehovah ' word as and ' say as and ' 8
or ' ye`ing ' relate ' and give ' say of ' Pharaoh ' your as to ' word as ' for '
' hurl the and ' are down ' ye ' took ' Aaron ' to ' you say and ' you lip`ing '
' Moses ' came as and ' 10 has monster of ' became as and ' Pharaoh ' as before
command`ed ' which are ' so ' concoct as and ' Pharaoh ' as before ' to ' Aaron and
' Pharaoh ' as before ' and staff from ' ye ' Aaron ' hurl as and ' Jehovah '
' also ' call as and ' 11 has monster of ' became as and ' him serve ' as before and
' also ' concoct as and ' from as witchcraft from of and ' from as wise of ' Pharaoh
' 12 so ' them as lean of in ' from as Mizra ' as from engrave ' them
' and became as and ' and staff from ' man I ' and hurl`s as and
' ye ' Aaron ' down`ed ' worthless as and ' from as has monster of

' hear ' not and ' Pharaoh ' heart ' strength as and ' 13 from you and down
' Jehovah ' word as and ' say as and ' 14 Jehovah ' word ' which are ' them as to
' 15 people the ' ye ' send of ' refuse ' Pharaoh ' heart ' honour ' Moses ' to
' Water`ed the ' out ' that`ing ' be`th ' is morn in ' Pharaoh ' to ' walk
' down`ed the and ' channel the ' you lip ' on ' and you call of ' you settle and
' you say and ' 16 are hand in ' implicate ' serpent of ' reverse the has ' which
' say of ' are as to ' as has send ' from as Obara the ' as Allah ' Jehovah ' him to
' not ' be`th and ' word from in ' as has serve as and ' as people ' ye ' send
' for ' perceive ' such in ' Jehovah ' say ' here ' 17 here ' till ' you hear
' which ' staff from in ' with`ed ' for whither ' be`th ' Jehovah ' as whither
blood of ' and overthrow has and ' channel in ' which ' Water the ' on ' as hand in
' channel the ' abhor and ' die`ing you ' channel in ' which ' squirm`ed the and ' 18
' channel the ' has from ' Water ' laid`ing of ' from as Mizra ' and weary and
Jehovah ' him to ' and say as and ' Pharaoh ' to ' Aaron and ' Moses ' walk as and
' ye ' send ' say of ' are as to ' and has send ' from as Obara the ' as Allah '
' till ' you hear ' not ' be`th and ' word from in ' as has serve as and ' as people
' Jehovah ' as whither ' for ' perceive ' such in ' Jehovah ' say ' here ' here
Water the ' on ' as hand in ' which ' staff from in ' with`ed ' for whither ' be`th
' which ' squirm`ed the and ' blood of ' and overthrow has and ' channel in ' which '
' from as Mizra ' and weary and ' channel the ' abhor and ' die`ing you ' channel in
Moses ' to ' Jehovah ' say as and ' 19 channel the ' has from ' Water ' laid`ing of
' are hand ' ye ' staff has and ' are down ' ye ' took ' Aaron ' to ' say '
' them as Nile ' on and ' from you and river ' on ' from as Mizra ' as Water ' on
and became as and ' them as Water ' the ditch ' all ' on and ' them as pond ' on and
' from as Mizra ' land ' all in ' blood the ' became as and ' blood '

' Moses ' so ' concoct as and ' 20 from as stone in and ' from as tree in and
' and staff from in ' elevate and ' Jehovah ' command`ed ' which are ' Aaron and
' Pharaoh ' as has eye of ' channel in ' which ' Water the ' ye ' struck and
' which ' Water the ' all ' and reverse am and ' him serve ' as has eye of and
' die`ed ' channel in ' which ' squirm`ed the and ' 21 blood of ' channel in
' laid`ing of ' from as Mizra ' and all as ' not and ' channel the ' abhor as and
' land ' all in ' blood the ' became as and ' channel the ' has from ' Water
' from as Mizra ' as from engrave ' so ' concoct as and ' 22 from as Mizra
them as to ' hear ' not and ' Pharaoh ' heart ' strength as and ' them as lean of in
' to ' came as and ' Pharaoh ' turn as and ' 23 Jehovah ' word ' which are '
' and scout as and ' 24 such of ' also ' and heart ' Seth ' not and ' and you house
not ' for ' laid`ing of ' Water ' channel the ' you surround`s ' from as Mizra ' all
' and fill as and ' 25 channel the ' as Water from ' laid`ing of ' and all as '
channel the ' ye ' Jehovah ' group`ing the ' as after ' from week ' you seven

' you say and ' Pharaoh ' to ' came ' Moses ' to ' Jehovah ' say as and ' 1

' as people ' ye ' send ' Jehovah ' say ' here ' him to ' you word and

' for whither ' be`th ' send of ' ye`ed ' refuse ' mother and ' 2 as has serve as and

' breed and ' 3 from as opinion bird in ' are border`ing ' all ' ye ' defeat

' are house`ly in ' and came and ' and travel ' from as opinion bird ' channel the

' as you neighbor and ' are mattress ' on and ' are as lay from ' as within in and

' are as flame`ing in and ' are people in and ' are as serve

all in and ' are people in and ' against`ed and ' 4 are as you and remain from in and

Aaron and ' Moses ' came as and ' from as opinion bird the ' lug as ' are as serve '

' ye ' send ' Jehovah ' say ' here ' him to ' and word as and ' Pharaoh ' to '

' be`th ' send of ' ye`ed ' refuse ' mother and ' as has serve as and ' as people

' from as opinion bird in ' are border`ing ' all ' ye ' defeat ' for whither

' and came and ' and travel ' from as opinion bird ' channel the ' as captain and

' are as mattress ' on and ' are as lay from ' as within in and ' are house`ly in

' are as flame`ing in and ' are people in and ' are as serve ' as you neighbor and

are as serve ' all in and ' are people in and ' jungle ' are as you remain from in and

' say ' Moses ' to ' Jehovah ' say as and ' 5 from as opinion bird the ' lug as '

' you and river the ' on ' are down in ' are hand ' ye ' permit`ed ' Aaron ' to

' ye ' on the and ' from as pond the ' on and ' from as channel the ' on and

' to ' Moses ' say as and ' from as Mizra ' land ' on ' from as opinion bird the

' opinion bird the ' on you and ' are down in ' are hand ' ye ' permit`ed ' Aaron

' on ' and hand ' ye ' Aaron ' extent and ' 6 from as Mizra ' land ' on

' ye ' conceal you and ' opinion bird the ' on you and ' from as Mizra ' as Water

from as Mizra ' from who engrave the ' so ' concoct as and ' 7 from as Mizra ' land

' land ' on ' from as opinion bird the ' ye ' and went and ' them as lean of in '

' say as and ' Aaron of and ' Moses of ' Pharaoh ' call as and ' 8 from as Mizra
' from as opinion bird the ' repent as and ' Jehovah ' to ' and pray`s the
' people the ' ye ' send`ed I and ' as people from and ' apportion from
' Pharaoh ' to ' Moses ' say as and ' 9 Jehovah of ' and sacrifice as and
' are as serve of and ' walk ' pray`s I ' extent of ' mosthigh ' is renown the
' with from ' from as opinion bird the ' hew`s the of ' are people of and
' only ' are people from and ' are as serve from and ' are house`ly from and
' say as and ' tomorrow of ' say as and ' 10 the has remain you ' channel in
our as Allah ' Jehovah are ' whither`s ' for ' perceive ' purpose of ' are as word are
' are house`ly from and ' with from ' from as opinion bird the ' and chasten ' 11
12 the has remain you ' channel in ' only ' are people from and ' are as serve from and
' to ' Moses ' cry as and ' Pharaoh ' affirm ' Aaron and ' Moses ' out and '
' 13 Pharaoh of ' there ' which ' from as opinion bird the ' word ' on ' Jehovah
' from as opinion bird the ' and die as and ' Moses ' word are ' Jehovah ' do as and
' has from and ' you and yard the ' has from and ' from house`ly the ' has from
' from as heass ' from as heass ' from ye ' and aggregate as and ' 14 you and field the
' whom`ed the ' for ' Pharaoh ' look as and ' 15 land the ' abhor you and
' them as to ' hear ' not and ' and heart ' ye ' honour the and ' spirit`ed is the
' to ' say ' Moses ' to ' Jehovah ' say as and ' 15 Jehovah ' word ' which are
' dust ' ye ' smitten and ' are down in ' are hand ' ye ' permit`ed ' Aaron
' concoct as and ' 17 from as Mizra ' land ' all in ' lice`s of ' be`s and ' land the
ye ' struck and ' and staff from in ' and hand ' ye ' Aaron ' extent and ' so
' all ' cattle`ed in and ' Men in ' lice`s the ' became you and ' land the ' dust '
' 18 from as Mizra ' land ' all in ' from as so ' be`s ' land the ' dust
' issue`s alas of ' them as lean of in ' from who engrave the ' so ' concoct as and

' Men in ' lice`s the ' became you and ' and all as ' not and ' lice`s the ' ye

' Pharaoh ' to ' from who engrave the ' and say as and ' (19 cattle`ed in and

' not and ' Pharaoh ' heart ' strength as and ' that`s ' from as Allah ' have flinger

' to ' Jehovah ' say as and ' (20 Jehovah ' word ' which are ' them as to ' hear

' be`th ' Pharaoh ' as before ' reside you the and ' is morn in ' ridge the ' Moses

' Jehovah ' say ' here ' him to ' you say and ' Water`ed the ' issue him ' that`ing

' are whither`s ' mother ' for ' (21 as has serve as and ' as people ' ye ' send

' against ' send`ed from ' as behold`th ' as people ' ye ' send from

' twilight the ' ye ' are house`ly in and ' are people in and ' are as serve in and

' also and ' twilight the ' ye ' from as Mizra ' house`ly ' and fill and

' day as in ' as swift`s the and ' (22 am on ' them ' which ' ground`ed the

' am on ' stand ' as people ' which ' has I`ll ' land ' ye ' that`ing the

' for ' perceive ' purpose of ' twilight ' there ' whom`ing the ' as except of

' distinct`ing ' as you there and ' (23 land the ' approach in ' Jehovah ' as whither

' be`s as ' tomorrow of ' are people ' between in and ' as people ' between in

' Pharaoh ' to ' Aaron and ' Moses ' came as and ' this the ' ye`ing the

' as people ' ye ' send ' Jehovah ' say ' here ' him to ' and say as and

' as people ' ye ' send from ' are whither`s ' mother ' for ' as has serve as and

' are people in and ' are as serve in and ' against ' send from ' as behold`th

' from as Mizra ' house`ly ' and fill and ' twilight the ' ye ' are house`ly in and

' am on ' them ' which ' ground`ed the ' also and ' twilight the ' ye

' which ' has I`ll ' land ' ye ' that`ing the ' day as in ' as swift`s the and

' twilight ' there ' whom`ing the ' as except of ' am on ' stand ' as people

' land the ' approach in ' Jehovah ' as whither ' for ' perceive ' purpose of

are people ' between in and ' as people ' between in ' distinct`ing ' as you there and

’ so ’ Jehovah ’ do as and ’ (24 this the ’ ye`ing the ’ be`s as ’ tomorrow of ’

’ you house and ’ Pharaoh ’ he house ’ especially ’ honour ’ twilight ’ came as and

’ land the ’ eradicate you and ’ from as Mizra ’ land ’ all in and ’ him serve

’ Aaron of and ’ Moses ’ to ’ Pharaoh ’ call as and ’ (25 twilight the ’ around from

’ say as and ’ (26 land in ’ your as Allah of ’ and sacrifice ’ follow ’ say as and

’ you and abominate you ’ for ’ so ’ you concoct of ’ ready`ing ’ not ’ Moses

sacrifice has ’ behold ’ our as Allah ’ Jehovah of ’ the sacrifice has ’ from as Mizra

’ not and ’ them as has eye of ’ from as Mizra ’ you abominate you ’ ye ’

’ word from in ’ walk`ed has ’ from week ’ you three ’ way ’ (27 our throw as

’ say as ’ which are ’ our as Allah ’ Jehovah of ’ and has sacrifice`ed has and

’ from are ye ’ send I ’ for whither ’ Pharaoh ’ say as and ’ (28 our as to

’ get the ’ only ’ word from in ’ your as Allah ’ Jehovah of ’ from you sacrifice and

’ say as and ’ (29 as till in ’ and pray`s the ’ you walk of ’ and get`s you ’ not

’ as you pray the and ’ are people from ’ issue him ’ for whither ’ be`th ’ Moses

’ him serve from and ’ Pharaoh from ’ twilight the ’ chasten ’ Jehovah ’ to

’ as except of ’ mock ’ Pharaoh ’ add ’ to ’ only ’ tomorrow ’ and people from and

’ affirm ’ Moses ’ out and ’ (30 Jehovah of ’ sacrifice of ’ people the ’ ye ’ send

’ Moses ’ word are ’ Jehovah ’ do as and ’ (31 Jehovah ’ to ’ pray as and ’ Pharaoh

and people from and ’ him serve from and ’ Pharaoh from ’ twilight the ’ repent as and

’ also ’ and heart ’ ye ’ Pharaoh ’ honour as and ’ (32 one ’ remain has ’ not ’

people the ’ ye ’ send ’ not and ’ such the ’ move in

' you say and ' Pharaoh ' to ' came ' Moses ' to ' Jehovah ' say as and ' 1
send ' from as Obara the ' as Allah ' Jehovah ' say ' here ' him to ' you word and
send of ' ye`ed ' refuse ' mother ' for ' 2 as has serve as and ' as people ' ye '
' Jehovah ' hand ' be`th ' 3 height ' strength`s from ' are till`ing and '
' from as Horse`ing in ' field`ed in ' which ' are as purchase in ' the became`ing
' word ' flock in and ' is morn in ' from as camel in and ' from as heass`ing in and
' purchase`ed ' between in ' Jehovah ' I made`ed the and ' 4 especially ' honour
' die`ing as ' not and ' from as as Mizra ' purchase`ed ' between in and ' Israel
' ing`congregate ' Jehovah ' site and ' 5 word ' Israel ' as son of ' all from
' land in ' this the ' word the ' ye ' Jehovah ' success`ed ' tomorrow ' say of
' here ' him to ' and say as and ' Pharaoh ' to ' Aaron and ' Moses ' came as and
' as people ' ye ' send ' from as Obara the ' as Allah ' Jehovah ' say
' are till`ing and ' send of ' ye`ed ' refuse ' mother ' for ' as has serve as and
' are as purchase in ' be`s ' Jehovah ' hand ' be`th ' height ' strength`s from
' from as heass`ing in and ' from as Horse`ing in ' field`ed in ' which
' especially ' honour ' word ' flock in and ' is morn in ' from as camel in and
' between in and ' Israel ' purchase`ed ' between in ' Jehovah ' wonderful the and
' Israel ' as son of ' all from ' die`ing as ' not and ' from as Mizra ' purchase`ed
6 ' land in ' this the ' word the ' ye ' Jehovah ' success`ed ' tomorrow ' word
' die as and ' you tomorrow from ' this the ' word the ' ye ' Jehovah ' do as and
' not ' Israel ' as son ' the purchase from and ' from as Mizra ' purchase`ed ' all
' the purchase from ' die ' not ' be`th and ' Pharaoh ' send as and ' 7 one ' die
send ' not and ' Pharaoh ' heart ' honour as and ' one ' till ' Israel ' as son
' Aaron`ing ' to and ' Moses ' to ' Jehovah ' say as and ' 8 people the ' ye '
' has footstool ' sheet`s ' your as fist ' fill`ing ' relate ' and took

' be`s and ' 9 Pharaoh ' as has eye of ' the heaven`s the ' Moses ' and sprinkle and
' on and ' ground the ' on ' be`s and ' from as Mizra ' land ' all ' on ' float of
' land ' all in ' you and have blain I ' bud ' botch`s of ' cattle`ed the
' has footstool the ' sheet`s ' ye ' acquire as and ' 10 from as Mizra
' Moses ' and ye ' sprinkle as and ' Pharaoh ' as before ' and stand as and
' Men in ' bud ' you and have blain I ' botch`s ' became as and ' the heaven`s the
' stand of ' from who engrave the ' and all as ' not and ' 11 cattle`ed in and
' botch`s the ' be`s ' for ' botch`s the ' around from ' Moses ' as before
' ye ' Jehovah ' strength as and ' 12 from as Mizra ' all in and ' they engrave in
' to ' Jehovah ' word ' which are ' them as to ' hear ' not and ' Pharaoh ' heart
' is morn in ' ridge the ' Moses ' to ' Jehovah ' say as and ' 13 Moses
' say ' here ' him to ' you say and ' Pharaoh ' as before ' reside you the and
' as people ' ye ' send ' from as Obara the ' as Allah ' Jehovah
' all ' ye ' send ' as whither ' such the ' move in ' for ' 14 as has serve as and
' are people in and ' are as serve in and ' against of ' on I ' as you pestilence
' 15 land the ' all in ' as storeup`ing ' whither`s ' for ' perceive ' cross`ing in
' ye and ' are ye`ing ' sure and ' as hand ' ye ' as you send ' time`ed ' for
' from to`ing and ' 16 land the ' has from ' slash you and ' word in ' are people
ye ' are as sight the ' cross`ing in ' are as you stand the ' such ' cross`ing in
are till`ing ' 17 land the ' all in ' as there ' report ' purpose of and ' as power '
' as behold`th ' 18 from send ' as except of ' as people in ' of exalt`ing from '
' be`s ' not ' which ' especially ' honour ' hail ' tomorrow ' while ' rain`s from
' till and ' situate`ed became ' day as the ' widow ' from as Mizra in ' and your`ed
all ' ye and ' are as purchase ' ye ' it shelter ' send ' the time and ' 19 time`ed
' which ' cattle`ed the and ' ground the ' all ' field`ed in ' walk ' which '

them as on ' descend and ' he house the ' gather as ' not and ' field`ed in ' come as

' Pharaoh ' to ' Aaron and ' Moses ' came as and ' 20 and die and ' hail the '

send ' from as word the ' as Allah ' Jehovah ' say ' here ' him to ' and say as and

' as whither ' such the ' move in ' for ' as has serve in and ' as people ' ye '

' are as serve in and ' against of ' on ' as you pestilence ' all ' ye ' send

' as storeup`ing ' whither`s ' for ' perceive ' cross`ing in ' are people in and

are ye ' sure and ' as hand ' ye ' as you send ' time`ed ' for ' land the ' all in

' land the ' has from ' slash you and ' word in ' are people ' ye and '

' cross`ing in ' are as you stand the ' such ' cross`ing in ' from to`ing and

' all in ' as there ' report ' purpose of and ' as power ' ye ' are as sight the

from send ' as except of ' as people in ' of exalt`ing from ' are till`ing ' land the

which ' especially ' honour ' hail ' tomorrow ' while ' rain`s from ' as behold`th '

' position`ed the ' day as from of ' from as Mizra in ' and your`ed ' be`s ' not '

' are as purchase ' ye ' it shelter ' send ' the time and ' time`ed ' till and

' cattle`ed the and ' ground the ' all ' field`ed in ' walk ' which ' all ' ye and

' descend and ' he house the ' gather as ' not and ' field`ed in ' come as ' which

' Jehovah ' word ' ye ' dread the ' and die and ' hail the ' them as on

' and purchase`ed ' ye and ' him serve ' ye ' flee`s the ' Pharaoh ' as serve from

' word ' on I ' and heart ' there ' not ' which and ' 21 from house`ly the ' to

field`ed in ' and purchase`ed ' ye and ' him serve ' ye ' forsake as and ' Jehovah

' on ' are hand ' ye ' permit`ed ' Moses ' to ' Jehovah ' say as and ' 22

' on ' from as Mizra ' land ' all in ' hail ' became as and ' heaven`s the

' land in ' field`ed the ' grass ' all ' on and ' cattle`ed the ' on and ' ground the

' heaven`s the ' on ' and staff from ' ye ' Moses ' extent and ' 23 from as Mizra

' land`ed ' fire ' enter you and ' hail and ' ing`thunder`ing ' gave ' Jehovah and

' became as and ' (24 from as Mizra ' land ' on ' hail ' Jehovah ' rain as and
especially ' honour ' hail the ' middle`ing in ' you at streak from ' fire and ' hail
' it hundred ' from as Mizra ' land ' all in ' and your`ed ' be`s ' not ' which '
' land ' all in ' hail the ' struck and ' (25 nation`ing of ' whom`ed the
' cattle`ed ' till and ' men from ' field`ed in ' which ' all ' ye ' from as Mizra
' tree ' all ' ye and ' hail the ' smitten`ed ' field`ed the ' grass ' all ' ye and
' as son ' there ' which ' has I`ll ' land in ' only ' (26 buy ' field`ed the
' Moses of ' call as and ' Pharaoh ' send as and ' (27 hail ' be`s ' not ' Israel
just`s the ' Jehovah ' move the ' as you sin ' them as to ' say as and ' Aaron of and
' to ' and pray`s the ' (28 from as evil`ness the ' as people and ' as whither and '
' from as Allah ' ing`thunder`ing ' whom`ing the from ' increase and ' Jehovah
' (29 stand of ' has and yield`s you ' not and ' from are ye ' send`ed I and ' hail and
' ye ' too ashe ' town`s the ' ye ' as grip are ' Moses ' him to ' say as and
' hail the and ' shall forbare as ' ing`thunder`ing the and ' Jehovah ' to ' as palm
' (30 land the ' Jehovah of ' for ' perceive ' purpose of ' till`ing ' be`s as ' not
' shall dread you ' suspend ' for ' as you known ' are as serve and ' ye`ed and
' flaw`ed the and ' (31 from as Allah ' Jehovah ' as master ' around from
' flaw`ed the and ' Abib ' Barley`ed the ' for ' he and strike ' Barley`ed the and
' for ' and strike ' not ' you shorn the and ' wheat`ed the and ' (32 of hill
' town`s the ' ye ' Pharaoh ' affirm ' Moses ' out and ' (33 be`th ' you and dusk`s
ing`thunder`ing the ' and forbare as and ' Jehovah ' to ' him palm ' Chariot as and
Pharaoh ' look as and ' (34 land`ed ' are liguid ' not ' rain the and ' hail the and '
' add and ' ing`thunder`ing the and ' rain the and ' hail the ' forbare ' for '
' strength as and ' (35 him serve and ' that`ing ' and heart ' honour as and ' sin of
' word ' which are ' Israel ' as son ' ye ' send ' not and ' Pharaoh ' heart

Moses ' hand in ' Jehovah

' as whither ' for ' Pharaoh ' to ' came ' Moses ' to ' Jehovah ' say as and ' 1
' purpose of ' him serve ' heart ' ye and ' and heart ' ye ' as you honor the
' report you ' purpose of and ' 2 and approach in ' to`ed ' as ing`evidence ' twosome
' as you endeavour scared ' which ' ye ' are son ' son and ' are son ' as ear in
' height ' as you there ' which ' as ing`evidence ' ye and ' from as Mizra in
' came as and ' 3 your as Allah ' Jehovah ' as whither ' for ' complete known and
' here ' Pharaoh ' him to ' and you say as and ' Pharaoh ' to ' Aaron and ' Moses
' you refuse ' extent ' till ' from as Obara the ' as Allah ' Jehovah ' say
' for ' 4 as has serve as and ' as people ' ye ' send ' around from ' answer`ing of
' came`s from ' as behold`th ' as people ' ye ' send of ' ye`ed ' refuse ' mother
' has eye ' ye ' conceal`ed and ' 5 are border`ing in ' increase`ed I ' tomorrow
' ye ' eat and ' land the ' ye ' you see of ' all him ' not and ' land the
eat and ' hail the ' has from ' relate ' you remain has the ' escape`ed the ' preserve
' sprout the ' tree the ' fruit ' all ' ye and ' land the ' grass ' all ' ye '
all ' house`ly and ' are house`ly ' and fill and ' 6 field`ed the ' has from ' relate
' see ' not ' which ' from as Mizra ' all ' house`ly and ' are as serve '
' day as from ' are as you and father ' you and father and ' are as you and father
' came as and ' this the ' day as the ' till ' ground`ed the ' on ' complete him the
Jehovah ' say ' here ' him to ' and say as and ' Pharaoh ' to ' Aaron and ' Moses
' answer`ing of ' you refuse ' extent ' till ' from as Obara the ' as Allah '
' refuse ' mother ' for ' as has serve as and ' as people ' ye ' send ' around from
' tomorrow ' came`s from ' as behold`th ' as people ' ye ' send of ' ye`ed
' land the ' has eye ' ye ' conceal`ed and ' are border`ing in ' increase`ed I
' preserve ' ye ' eat and ' land the ' ye ' you see of ' finish ' not and
' ye ' eat and ' hail the ' has from ' relate ' you remain has the ' escape`ed the

' relate ' mop the ' tree the ' fruit ' all ' ye and ' land the ' grass ' all
' all ' house`ly and ' are house`ly ' and fill and ' field`ed the ' has from
' see ' not ' which ' from as Mizra ' all ' house`ly and ' are as serve
' day as from ' are as you and father ' you and father and ' are as you and father
' turn as and ' this the ' day as the ' till ' ground`ed the ' on ' complete him the
' till ' him to ' Pharaoh ' as serve ' and say as and ' 7 Pharaoh ' affirm ' out and
' from as person the ' ye ' send ' snare from of ' our of ' this ' be`s as ' extent
' for ' perceive ' suspend the ' them as Allah ' Jehovah ' ye ' and serve as and
to ' Aaron ' ye and ' Moses ' ye ' carry him and ' 8 from as Mizra ' the perish
' Jehovah ' ye ' and serve ' follow ' them as to ' say as and ' Pharaoh '
' Moses ' say as and ' 9 from as enter the ' as from and ' who ' your as Allah
' our as son in ' walk has ' our as elder in and ' our as youth in
' for ' walk has ' our herd in and ' our flock in ' our as daughter`th`ing in and
' Jehovah ' so ' be`s as ' them as to ' say as and ' 10 our of ' Jehovah ' solemn
' see ' from are children ' ye and ' from are ye ' send I ' which are ' your people
' oh ' follow ' so ' not ' 11 your as turn ' over ' evil`ed ' for
' from ye ' ye`ed ' for ' Jehovah ' ye ' and serve and ' from as strong the
' 12 Pharaoh ' around ' each ' from ye ' and exact as and ' from as seek from
' land ' on ' are hand ' ye ' permit`ed ' Moses ' to ' Jehovah ' say as and
' eat as and ' from as Mizra ' land ' on ' went and ' locust`ed in ' from as Mizra
' which ' tree the ' fruit ' all ' ye and ' land the ' grass ' all ' ye
' and hand ' and staff from ' ye ' Moses ' extent and ' 13 hail the ' remain`s the
' land in ' east`s ' spirit is ' lead ' Jehovah and ' from as Mizra ' land ' on
' be`s ' herd the ' the night`s the ' all and ' that`ing the ' day as the ' all
' went and ' 14 Locust`ed the ' ye ' help`ed ' east`s the ' spirit is and

border`ing ' all in ' rest as and ' from as Mizra ' land ' all ' on ' Locust`ed the

' so ' be`s ' not ' him before ' especially ' honour ' from as Mizra '

' 15 so ' be`s as ' not ' and as after and ' and your`ed ' increase`ed I

' land the ' dark you and ' land the ' all ' has eye ' ye ' conceal as and

which ' tree the ' fruit ' all ' ye and ' land the ' grass ' all ' ye ' eat as and

' tree in ' green ' all ' survive has ' not and ' hail the ' survive`s the '

' soon as and ' 16 from as Mizra ' land ' all in ' field`ed the ' grass in and

' Jehovah of ' as you sin ' say as and ' Aaron of and ' Moses of ' call of ' Pharaoh

sure ' as you sin ' oh ' and lift ' the time and ' 17 from walk and ' your as Allah

' repent as and ' your as Allah ' Jehovah ' to ' and pray`s the and ' move the '

' Pharaoh ' affirm ' out and ' 18 this the ' die`ing the ' ye ' only ' as on from

' sea ' spirit is ' Jehovah ' overthrow as and ' 19 Jehovah ' to ' pray as and

' and slap`ed as and ' Locust`ed the ' ye ' lift as and ' especially ' strength

' border`ing ' all in ' one ' increase`ed I ' remain has ' not ' join`ing ' sea`ed

' not and ' Pharaoh ' heart ' ye ' Jehovah ' strength as and ' 20 from as Mizra

permit`ed ' Moses ' to ' Jehovah ' say as and ' 21 Israel ' as son ' ye ' send

' land ' on ' dark ' became as and ' heaven`s the ' on ' are hand ' ye '

' and hand ' ye ' Moses ' extent and ' 22 dark the ' feel as and ' from as Mizra

' land ' all in ' dusk`ed ' dark ' became as and ' heaven`s the ' on

' him brother ' ye ' man I ' see ' not ' 23 from week ' you three ' from as Mizra

' all of and ' from week ' you three ' and as under from ' man I ' and rise ' not and

' call as and ' 24 from you sojourn from in ' light`ing ' be`s ' Israel ' as son

' ye ' and serve ' follow ' say as and ' Aaron of and ' Moses ' to ' Pharaoh

' also ' sat as ' from are herd and ' from are flock ' only ' Jehovah

' ye`ed ' also ' Moses ' say as and ' 25 your people ' bear ' from are children

' our as do and ' offer`ing and ' from as sacrifice ' and has hand in ' has set
' not ' our people ' bear ' our as purchase ' also and ' (26 our as Allah ' Jehovah of
' Jehovah ' ye ' serve of ' took has ' and her from ' for ' the spread ' remain you
Jehovah ' ye ' serve has ' what ' shaken ' not ' our brother`th and ' our as Allah
' heart ' ye ' Jehovah ' strength as and ' (27 there`ed ' and has came ' till '
' walk ' Pharaoh ' if ' say as and ' (28 from send of ' father`ed ' not and ' Pharaoh
day as in ' for ' around ' you see ' yield you ' to ' walk ' guard the ' as on from
' not ' you word ' so ' Moses ' say as and ' (29 die`ing you ' around ' are you see '
are as turn ' you see ' till`ing ' yield I

on ' came`s I ' one ' touch ' till`ing ' Moses ' to ' Jehovah ' say as and ' 1
' from are ye ' send as ' so ' as after and ' from as Mizra ' on and ' Pharaoh '
2 ' victual`ed ' from are ye ' exact as ' exact ' all`ed ' and send are ' victual`ed
' each ' man I ' and ask as and ' people the ' as ear in ' oh ' word
' as all and ' silver ' weapon ' he tend ' each ' Woman and ' and shepherd is
grace ' ye ' Jehovah ' give as and ' 3 as set has and ' you and raiment and ' gold
' from and ask`s the and ' from as Mizra ' as has eye in ' people the '
' land ' middle`ing in ' out ' as whither ' the night`s the ' you half are and
first`ing from ' from as Mizra ' land in ' first`ing ' all ' die and ' from as Mizra
' slave`ed the ' first`ing ' till and ' and throne ' on ' dwell the ' Pharaoh '
' cattle`ed ' all ' first`ing ' till and ' compassion`s the ' after ' which
' not ' like`ed ' which ' from as Mizra in ' great`ed ' cry`ed ' whom`ed the and
' Israel ' as son ' all of and ' yield you ' not ' like`ed and ' the you became has
' cattle`ed ' till and ' man I from of ' and tooth of ' dog ' maim as ' not
' from as Mizra ' between in ' Jehovah ' I made as ' which ' perceive ' purpose of
' especially ' great`ing ' Moses ' man that ' also ' Israel ' between in and
' as has eye in and ' Pharaoh ' as serve ' as has eye in ' from as Mizra ' land in
' as son ' Jehovah ' say ' here ' Pharaoh ' to ' Moses ' say as and ' people the
' as son ' ye ' send ' are as to ' say and ' Israel ' as first`ing
' ye ' kill ' Jehovah ' be`th ' and send of ' refuse you and ' as has serve as and
' Jehovah ' say ' here ' Moses ' say as and ' 4 are first`ing ' are son
' land ' middle`ing in ' issue him ' as whither ' the night`s the ' injure`s are
first`ing from ' from as Mizra ' land in ' first`ing ' all ' die and ' 5 from as Mizra
' slave`ed the ' first`ing ' till and ' and throne ' on ' dwell the ' Pharaoh '
' 6 cattle`ed ' all and ' first`ing ' till and ' compassion`s the ' after ' which

' which ' from as Mizra ' land ' all in ' great`ed ' cry`ed ' whom`ed the and
' 7 yield you ' not ' and your`ed and ' the you became has ' not ' and your`ed
man I from of ' and tooth of ' dog ' maim as ' not ' Israel ' as son ' all of and
' I made`ed as ' which ' has and perceive ' purpose of ' cattle`ed ' till and '
' and up as and ' 8 Israel ' between in and ' from as Mizra ' between in ' Jehovah
' say of ' vessel ' prostrate humble`ly the and ' Eli ' to`ed ' are as serve ' all
' so ' as after and ' are as foot in ' which ' people the ' all and ' ye`ed ' issue
Jehovah ' say as ' And ' 9 anger ' as choose ' Pharaoh ' affirm ' out and ' proceed
you and increase ' purpose of ' Pharaoh ' your as to ' hear as ' not ' Moses ' to '
ye ' concoct ' Aaron and ' Moses and ' 10 from as Mizra ' land in ' as you lip'ing '
' strength as and ' Pharaoh ' as before ' these`ed ' from as ing`wonder the ' all '
' Israel ' as son ' ye ' send ' not and ' Pharaoh ' heart ' ye ' Jehovah
and land from

from as Mizra ' land in ' Aaron ' to and ' Moses ' to ' Jehovah ' say as and ' 1
' shall head`s ' from as new the ' head ' relate ' this the ' new the ' 2 say of '
' all ' to ' oh ' and word ' 3 Year`ed the ' as new of ' relate ' that`ing
' this the ' new of ' ten`ing in ' say of ' Israel ' as son ' testimony
' you and father ' you house of ' resemble ' man I ' them of ' acquire as and
' whom`ing the from ' you house the ' less as ' mother and ' 4 you house of ' resemble
and you house ' to ' approach`ing the ' and nigh`s and ' that`ing ' take and ' Moses
' on ' plump you ' and eat ' as by ' man I ' you and soul ' you and amount in '
relate ' be`s as ' the Year ' son ' male ' from as complete ' resemble ' 5 Lamb the
' 6 and took you ' from as Goat the ' has from and ' from as sheep the ' has from '
' new of ' day as ' ten ' the four I ' till ' you guard from of ' relate ' be`s and
' Israel ' as son ' testimony ' assemble ' all ' and ye ' and slay and ' this the
' blood the ' has from ' and take and ' 7 from as twilight the ' between in
' on ' gaze`ing them ' on and ' you and post the ' twosome ' on ' and gave and
' ye ' and eat and ' 8 cattle ' and ye ' and eat as ' which ' from house`ly the
' on ' unleaven`ing and ' fire ' roast ' this the ' the night`s in ' flesh the
' oh ' and her from ' and eat you ' to ' 9 and eat`ed as ' from as poison`ing
' and head ' fire ' roast ' mother ' for ' Water in ' sodden from ' sodden`ing and
and her from ' and survive`s you ' not and ' 10 and approach ' on and ' him leg ' on
' abhorrence ' herd ' till ' and her from ' survive behold and ' herd ' till '
' your as give from ' and ye ' and eat you ' here are and ' 11 and burnt you
' your as stick and ' your as foot in ' your as shoe ' from as restrain
' that`ing ' pass ' has and hasten in ' and ye ' from you eat and ' your as hand in
this the ' the night`s in ' from as Mizra ' land in ' as you cross and ' 12 Jehovah of
' men from ' from as Mizra ' land in ' first`ing ' all ' as whom smitten and '

' do`ed I ' from as Mizra ' as Allah ' all in and ' cattle`ed ' till and
' loop`ing ' relate ' blood the ' be`s and ' 13 Jehovah ' as whither ' from as discern
' ye ' as whom look and ' there ' from ye ' which ' from house`ly the ' on
' from are in ' be`s as ' not and ' from are mosthigh ' as you pass and ' blood the
be`s and ' 14 from as Mizra ' land in ' as contrary`ing in ' you as anoint of ' defeat
and ye ' from you solemn and ' shall is remember of ' relate ' this the ' day as the '
' from on`ing ' statute ' from are as generation of ' Jehovah of ' solemn '
' sure ' and eat you ' unleaven`ing ' from week ' you seven ' 15 and solemn`ed you
' from are house`ly from ' remain ' and desist`s you ' has and head`s the ' day as in
' Israel from ' that`s the ' soul the ' hew`ed shall ' leaven ' eat ' all ' for
' 16 as seven`s the ' day as ' till and ' has and head`s the ' day as from
' day as in and ' holy ' call from ' has and head`s the ' day as in and
' not ' the are fill ' all ' relate ' be`s as ' holy ' call from ' as seven`s the
' that`ing ' soul ' all of ' eat as ' which ' sure ' cattle ' success`ed
' ye ' from you guard and ' 17 relate ' success`ed ' and alone of
' as you issue alas ' this the ' day as the ' might in ' for ' the unleaven`ing the
' from you guard and ' from as Mizra ' land from ' from middle`s and mass ' ye
' statute ' from are as generation of ' this the ' day as the ' ye ' from dual`s and
' new of ' day as ' ten ' the four I in ' has and head`s in ' 18 from on`ing
' from as ten and ' one the ' day as ' till ' unleaven ' and eat you ' twilight in
' come as ' not ' remain ' from week ' you seven ' 19 twilight in ' new of
soul the ' hew`ed shall ' you leaven from ' eat ' all ' for ' from are house`ly in
20 land the ' at native in and ' guest in ' Israel ' you congregation ' that`s the '
' your as desist and from ' all in ' and eat you ' not ' you leaven from ' all '
' Israel ' as elder ' all of ' Moses ' call as and ' 21 unleaven`ing ' and eat you

' flock ' relate ' and took and ' and remove ' them as to ' say as and
' from you take and ' (22 pass the ' and slay and ' from are as you at family of
' threshold ' which ' blood in ' from you dip and ' hyssop`ing ' you bunch
' you and post the ' twosome ' haul and ' gaze`ing them ' on I ' from you fling and
man I ' and issue you ' not ' from ye and ' threshold ' which ' blood the ' has from
ye ' defeat of ' Jehovah ' cross and ' (23 herd ' till ' and you house ' open from '
' on and ' gaze`ing them ' on ' blood the ' ye ' look`ed and ' from as Mizra '
' not and ' open the ' on ' Jehovah ' pass and ' you and post the ' twosome
' (24 defeat of ' your house`ly ' to ' came`ing of ' you as anoint the ' permanent
' are as son of and ' walk ' law of ' this the ' word the ' ye ' from you guard and
' which ' land the ' to ' and came you ' for ' be`s and ' (25 from on`ing ' till
' ye ' from you guard and ' word ' which are ' relate ' Jehovah ' permanent
' and say as ' for ' be`s and ' (26 this the ' new in ' such the ' serve`ed the
' (27 relate ' such the ' serve`ed the ' what ' your as son ' your as to
' on ' pass ' which ' Jehovah of ' that`ing ' pass ' sacrifice ' from you say and
from as Mizra ' ye ' and defeat in ' from as Mizra in ' Israel ' as son ' house`ly
' people the ' and stoop as and ' shade`s the ' our house`ly ' ye and '
' Israel ' as son ' concoct as and ' and walk as and ' (28 prostate humble`ly as and
(29 concoct ' so ' Aaron ' ye and ' Moses ' ye ' Jehovah ' command`ed ' which are
' all ' smitten`ed ' Jehovah and ' the night`s the ' half in ' became as and '
' on ' dwell the ' Pharaoh ' first`ing from ' from as Mizra ' land in ' first`ing
' empty`ing the ' you house in ' which ' as carry the ' first`ing ' till ' and throne
' that`ing ' the night`s ' Pharaoh ' rise as and ' (30 cattle`ed ' first`ing ' all and
' great`ed ' cry`ed ' became you and ' from as Mizra ' all and ' him serve ' all and
' (31 die ' there ' whither`s ' which ' you house ' whither`s ' for ' from as Mizra in

' and rise`ing ' say as and ' the night`s ' Aaron of and ' Moses of ' call as and
' Israel ' as son ' also ' from ye ' also ' as people ' middle`ing from ' and issue
from are flock ' also ' (32 your as word are ' Jehovah ' ye ' and serve ' and all and
' and all and ' from you word ' which are ' and took ' from are herd ' also '
' on ' from as Mizra ' strength you and ' (33 near ' also ' from you bless and
' and say ' for ' land the ' has from ' from send of ' soon of ' people the
' suspend ' and flour ' ye ' people the ' lift as and ' (34 from as die ' and has all
' on ' from you and raiment in ' you and bundle ' from you remain from ' leaven as
' and ask as and ' Moses ' word are ' concoct ' Israel ' as son and ' (35 from ridge
' (36 you and raiment and ' gold ' as all and ' silver ' weapon ' from as Mizra from
' from as Mizra ' as has eye in ' people the ' grace ' ye ' gave ' Jehovah and
' leave as and ' (37 from as Mizra ' ye ' and pluck as and ' from and ask as and
' you and hundred ' six are ' the booth`ing ' Rameses from ' Israel ' as son
' also and ' (38 children from ' earnest ' from as strong the ' as foot`er ' thousand
' honour ' purchase`ed ' herd and ' flock and ' from ye ' on`ed ' increase ' twilight
' and issue`s alas ' which ' flour the ' ye ' now Then ' (39 especially
' for ' leaven ' not ' for ' unleaven`ing ' you and bake ' from as Mizra from
' also and ' the linger you no ' and all as ' not and ' from as Mizra from ' and exact
' Israel ' as son ' sojourn from and ' (40 them of ' concoct ' not ' hunt`ed
' land in and ' Canaan ' land in ' and carry as ' which ' from you and father and
(41 the Year ' you and hundred ' four I and ' the Year ' from as three ' from as Mizra
you and hundred ' four I and ' the Year ' from as three ' end from ' became as and '
' all ' and out ' this the ' day as the ' might in ' became as and ' the Year '
' from as guard ' the night`s ' (42 from as Mizra ' land from ' Jehovah ' you and mass
' that`ing ' from as Mizra ' land from ' from issue`s alas of ' Jehovah of ' that`ing

' Israel ' as son ' all of ' from as guard ' Jehovah of ' this the ' the night`s the

' Aaron ' to and ' Moses ' to ' Jehovah ' say as and ' 43 from ing`generation of

' 44 and in ' eat as ' not ' foreign ' son ' all ' pass the ' statute ' such

' and ye ' he circumcise and ' and silver ' you purchase ' man I ' serve ' all and

' 46 and in ' eat as ' not ' merry`s and ' sojourn you ' 45 and in ' eat as ' yet

' you house the ' has from ' issue`s and you ' not ' eat as ' one ' you house in

' and buy you ' not ' fast have and ' the outside`ing the ' flesh the ' has from

' for and ' 48 and ye ' and do as ' Israel ' testimony ' all ' 47 and in

' Jehovah of ' pass ' do`ed and ' guest ' from are ye ' guest`ing as

' and you concoct of ' approach as ' yet and ' male ' all ' if ' circumcise`ing the

' 49 and in ' eat as ' not ' foreskin ' all and ' land the ' at native are ' be`s and

' abide ' guest of and ' at native of ' be`s as ' sister ' the protect`ing

' which are ' Israel ' as son ' all ' concoct as and ' 50 your middle`ing in

' 51 concoct ' so ' Aaron ' ye and ' Moses ' ye ' Jehovah ' command`ed

' ye ' Jehovah ' issue`s alas ' this the ' day as the ' might in ' became as and

from you mass ' on ' from as Mizra ' land from ' Israel ' as son

THE TORAH SCROLL 13

' all ' vessel ' holy ' 2 say of ' Moses ' to ' Jehovah ' word as and ' 1

' Men in ' Israel ' as son in ' compassion ' all ' emit ' first`ing

' people the ' to ' Moses ' say as and ' 3 that`ing ' vessel ' cattle`ed in and

' and in ' from you out ' which ' this the ' day as the ' ye ' and is remember

hand ' strength in ' for ' from as serve ' you house from ' from as Mizra ' land from

4 ' leaven ' eat as ' not and ' victual`ed ' from are ye ' Jehovah ' issue`s alas '

' be`s and ' 5 blossom`s the ' new in ' from as spring as ' from ye and ' day as the

' as Canaan the ' land ' to ' are as Allah ' Jehovah ' are came`s as ' for

' as Girgash the and ' as Periz the and ' as Amar the and ' as Heth the and

' are as you father of ' swear too has ' which ' as Jebus the and ' as Hivite the and

' ye ' you serve and ' honey and ' milk ' you secrete ' land ' walk ' set of

' eat you ' from week ' you six ' 6 this the ' new in ' such the ' serve`ed the

' unleaven`ing ' 7 Jehovah of ' solemn ' as seven`s the ' day as in and ' unleaven`ing

' leaven ' walk ' look`ed as ' not and ' from week the ' you seven ' ye ' eat as

' you proclaim and ' 8 are border`ing ' all in ' remain ' walk ' look`ed as ' not and

' do`ed ' this ' cross`ing in ' say of ' that`ing the ' day as in ' are son of

' walk ' and be`s and ' 9 from as Mizra from ' as you issue in ' vessel ' Jehovah

' are as has eye ' between in ' has and male of and ' are as hand ' on ' loop`ing

' hand in ' for ' execute`s ' Jehovah ' you protect`ing ' be`s you ' purpose of

' you guard and ' 10 from as Mizra from ' Jehovah ' are issue`s alas ' the strength

11 the from week ' from as water`s ' the season from of ' such the ' law`ed the ' ye

' land ' to ' are as Allah ' Jehovah ' are came`s as ' for ' be`s and '

' are as you father of and ' walk ' swear too has ' which are ' as Canaan the

Jehovah of ' compassion ' emit ' all ' you cross the and ' 12 walk ' the give has and

' from as male the ' walk ' be`s as ' which ' cattle`ed ' eject ' emit ' all and '

' not ' mother and ' pale`ed ' pardon`ed ' heass`ing ' emit ' all and ' 13 Jehovah of
' are as son in ' ground ' first`ing ' all and ' and you stiffneck and ' our pardon`ed
' what ' say of ' tomorrow ' are son ' are ask as ' for ' be`s and ' 14 pardon`ed
' Jehovah ' and has spring`s the ' hand ' strength in ' him to ' you say and ' such
' for ' became as and ' 15 from as serve ' you house from ' from as Mizra from
' first`ing ' all ' Jehovah ' kill as and ' our send of ' Pharaoh ' hard`ed the
cattle`ed ' first`ing ' till and ' ground ' first`ing from ' from as Mizra ' land in
' compassion ' emit ' all ' Jehovah of ' sacrifice ' as whither ' so ' on '
' 16 release`ed I ' as son in ' ground ' first`ing ' all and ' from as male the
' the are as hand ' on ' loop`ing ' all ' and be`s and
' strength in ' for ' are as has eye ' between in ' you and put forehead`ing of and
' became as and ' 17 from as Mizra from ' Jehovah ' and has spring`s the ' hand
' way ' from as Allah ' comfort ' not and ' people the ' ye ' Pharaoh ' send in
' say ' for ' that`ing ' approach`ing ' for ' from as Philista ' land
' fight`ed from ' from sight`ing in ' people the ' comfort as ' turn ' from as Allah
people the ' ye ' from as Allah ' away as and ' 18 the from as Mizra ' and carry and
' as son ' lug ' from as five and ' join`ing ' sea ' is wilderness the ' way '
' bone`ing have ' ye ' Moses ' took as and ' 19 from as Mizra ' land from ' Israel
' as son ' ye ' Joseph ' swear`s too the ' seven the ' for ' and people ' Joseph
' from are ye ' from as Allah ' punish as ' punish ' say of ' Israel
' 20 from are ye ' victual`ed ' as bone have ' ye ' from whom on the and
' the end in ' which ' from ye in ' and encamp and ' you and castimage ' leave as and
' from day as ' them as before ' walk the ' Jehovah and ' 21 is wilderness the
' stand`ing in ' the night`s and ' way the ' from bring the of ' cloud ' stand`ing in
not ' 22 the night`s and ' from day as ' you walk of ' them of ' light`s the of ' fire

' fire the ' stand`ing and ' from day as ' cloud the ' stand`ing ' refrain`ing '

people the ' as before ' the night`s

' as son ' to ' word ' 2 say of ' Moses ' to ' Jehovah ' word as and ' 1
' you hole`s the ' edge ' as before ' and encamp and ' and carry`ing as and ' Israel
' north`ing ' marry ' as before ' sea the ' between in and ' great from ' between in
' as son of ' Pharaoh ' say and ' 3 sea the ' on ' and grace you ' and behalf
4 is wilderness the ' them as on ' close ' land in ' them ' from as ramble ' Israel
' them as after ' chase and ' Pharaoh ' heart ' ye ' as you strength and '
' and known and ' and of life ' all in and ' Pharaoh in ' honour`ed I and
' my told and ' 5 so ' concoct as and ' Jehovah ' as whither ' for ' from as Mizra
' mind ' overthrow as and ' people the ' shoot ' for ' from as Mizra ' king of
' such ' what ' and say as and ' people the ' on I ' him serve and ' Pharaoh
' bound as and ' 6 our serve from ' Israel ' ye ' and has send ' for ' our as do
' six ' took as and ' 7 and people ' took of ' and people ' ye and ' and ride ' ye
' from as Mizra ' ride ' all and ' choose`ing ' ride ' you and hundred
' heart ' ye ' Jehovah ' strength as and ' 8 fail ' on ' from as three`s and
' Israel ' as son ' as after ' chase as and ' from as Mizra ' king ' Pharaoh
' and chase as and ' 9 high`ed ' hand in ' from as spring as ' Israel ' as son and
' on ' from as grace ' from ye`ing ' and catch`s and ' them as after ' from as Mizra
on ' and of life and ' him Chariot and ' Pharaoh ' ride ' skip`ing ' all ' sea the
' Pharaoh and ' 10 north`ing ' marry ' as before ' you hole`s the ' edge '
' them as has eye ' ye ' Israel ' as son ' and lift as and ' approach`s the
and dread as and ' them as after ' from as go ' from as Mizra ' be`th and ' see as and
and say as and ' 11 Jehovah ' to ' Israel ' as son ' and cry as and ' especially '
' from as Mizra in ' from as bury ' whither`s ' no them ' Moses ' to '
' our of ' you as do ' such ' what ' word from in ' die`ing of ' and has you take
' which ' word the ' this ' forward`ing ' 12 from as Mizra from ' our spring`s the of

' and her from ' oh ' forbare ' say of ' from as Mizra in ' are as to ' our word
' ye ' serve ' our of ' good`ing ' for ' from as Mizra ' ye ' the serve shall
' to ' Moses ' say as and ' 13 word from in ' our die`ing from ' from as Mizra
' ye ' see and ' and in annihilate`s the ' and look as you ' to ' people the
which are ' for ' day as the ' relate ' success`ed ' which ' Jehovah ' you Jesus`ing
' has and yield`s you ' not ' day as the ' from as Mizra ' ye ' from you seen '
' relate ' fight as ' Jehovah ' 14 from on`ing ' till ' till`ing ' from sight`ing of
' what ' Moses ' to ' Jehovah ' say as and ' 15 shall devise`s you ' from ye and
' ye`ed and ' 16 leave as and ' Israel ' as son ' to ' word ' Eli ' cry you
' sea the ' on ' are hand ' ye ' staff has and ' are down ' ye ' from mountain
' sea the ' middle`ing in ' Israel ' as son ' and came as and ' and divide`ed and
' heart ' ye ' strength from ' as behold`th ' as whither and ' 17 the wither in
' Pharaoh in ' honour`ed I and ' them as after ' and came as and ' from as Mizra
all ' and known and ' 18 him chariot in and ' and ride in ' and of life ' all in and
' Pharaoh in ' as honour thus ' Jehovah ' as whither ' for ' from as Mizra '
' onward as and ' 19 him chariot in and ' and ride in ' and of life ' all in and
' Israel ' the camp ' as before ' enter the ' from as Allah the ' messenger from
' cloud the ' stand`ing ' onward as and ' them as after from ' walk as and
' between in ' came as and ' 20 them as after from ' stand as and ' them around from
' became as and ' Israel ' the camp ' between in and ' from as Mizra ' the camp
approach ' not and ' the night`s the ' ye ' channel and ' dark the and ' cloud the
' ye ' Moses ' extent and ' 21 the night`s the ' all ' this ' to ' this '
' spirit is in ' sea the ' ye ' Jehovah ' walk him and ' sea the ' on ' and hand
thus hole of ' sea the ' ye ' site and ' the night`s the ' all ' harsh`ed ' east`s
' Israel ' as son ' and came as and ' 22 Water the ' and divide as and '

’ the Ham`ing ’ them of ’ Water the and ’ the wither in ’ sea the ’ middle`ing in
’ from as Mizra ’ and chase as and ’ 23 from of left from and ’ from right`s from
’ and ride ’ Pharaoh ’ skip`ing ’ all ’ them as after ’ and came as and
’ you guard I in ’ became as and ’ 24 sea the ’ middle`ing ’ to ’ him Chariot and
’ stand`ing in ’ from as Mizra ’ the camp ’ to ’ Jehovah ’ gaze as and ’ herd the
’ bound as and ’ 25 from as Mizra ’ the camp ’ ye ’ them as and ’ cloud and ’ fire
’ you and honour`ing in ’ and lead`ed as and ’ him you ride from ’ revolve ’ ye
’ for ’ Israel ’ around from ’ the flee`ing I ’ from as Mizra ’ and say as and
to ’ Jehovah ’ say as and ’ 26 from as Mizra in ’ them of ’ fight has the ’ Jehovah
’ and carry`ing as and ’ sea the ’ on ’ are hand ’ ye ’ permit`ed ’ Moses ’
’ 27 him Chariot ’ on and ’ and ride ’ on ’ from as Mizra ’ on ’ Water the
’ sea the ’ dwell and ’ sea the ’ on ’ and hand ’ ye ’ Moses ’ extent and
’ from as go ’ from as Mizra and ’ and give hence of ’ herd the ’ you and before
’ middle`ing in ’ from as Mizra ’ ye ’ Jehovah ’ is keep as and ’ and you call of
ye and ’ ride the ’ ye ’ and conceal as and ’ Water the ’ and dwell and ’ 28 sea the
’ them as after ’ from as came the ’ Pharaoh ’ sick`s ’ all of ’ from as chariot the ’
’ Israel ’ as son and ’ 29 one ’ till ’ cattle ’ remain has ’ not ’ height`s
’ them of ’ Water the and ’ sea the ’ middle`ing in ’ the wither in ’ and walk the
Jehovah ’ deliver`s as and ’ 30 from of left from and ’ from right`s from ’ the Ham`ing
look as and ’ from as Mizra ’ hand from ’ Israel ’ ye ’ that`ing the ’ day as in ’
’ look as and ’ 31 sea the ’ you lip ’ on ’ die ’ from as Mizra ’ ye ’ Israel ’
’ Jehovah ’ do`ed ’ which ’ great`ed the ’ glorify`s ’ ye ’ Israel
’ Jehovah ’ ye ’ people the ’ and dread as and ’ from as Mizra in
and serve ’ Moses in and ’ Jehovah in ’ and believe`s as and

' the is gift the ' ye ' Israel ' as son and ' Moses ' is gift as ' yet ' (1
' for ' Jehovah of ' the is gift I ' say of ' and say as and ' Jehovah of ' such the
' forceful ' (2 height`s ' high`ed ' and ride and ' skip`ing ' haughty`ed ' haughty`ed
' Eli ' this ' the Joshua`ing of ' vessel ' became as and ' am ' you prune and
' Jehovah ' (3 and lament from high I and ' as father ' as Allah ' and lament`ing I and
' Pharaoh ' you ride from ' (4 name ' Jehovah ' fight`ed from in ' man I ' strong`ing
and ring ' him three`s ' choose from and ' height`s ' that knew ' and as host at and
' and descend ' and shorn`s as ' you and deep`ing ' (5 join`ing ' height`s '
' power in ' as big has ' Jehovah ' are right`s ' (6 stone ' like ' you ravine`ing in
' are pomp`ing ' increase in and ' (7 enemy and I ' dash you ' Jehovah ' are right`s
' (8 hard are ' and from eat as ' are parch`ing ' send you ' are as rise ' beat you
' wander ' like ' and settle ' Water ' and from is keep ' nose`s ' shoot`ing and
' say ' (9 sea ' heart in ' you and deep`ing ' and congeal ' from as gush
' as soul ' and from fill you ' strip ' part I ' drawal`s I ' chase I ' enemy and I
' you brink has ' (10 as hand ' and there as protect`ing ' as in hole ' earth`s
' Water in ' net fly`ing are ' and hover ' sea ' and shorn ' are shoot`ing
' who ' Jehovah ' from as route ' the with`ing are ' who ' (11 from as big`s
' do`ed ' you hymm ' terror has ' holy in ' as big has ' the with`ing are
' (13 land the ' and from worthless you ' are right`s ' contact`s ' (12 wonderful`ed
are harsh in ' you inherit ' you redeem ' and this ' people ' are bow in ' crush`s has
' shall tremble as and ' from as people ' and hear ' (14 are holy ' lament`ing ' to '
' as thousand`ing ' and amaze has ' yet ' (15 Philista ' as dwell ' hold ' sick`s
as dwell ' all ' horror has ' shiver ' and from hold as ' Moab ' as to`s ' Edom
' great`ing in and ' startle and ' die`ed hence ' them as on ' untemper ' (16 Canaan '
Jehovah ' are people ' cross as ' till ' has father are ' and from hand ' are seed`ing

' and from income`s ' 17 whom nest ' and this ' people ' cross as ' till '

you act ' are desist of ' so`ing from ' are you inherit ' blemish ' and flavor you and

' Jehovah ' 18 are as hand ' our so`ing ' Jehovah ' as master ' holy from ' Jehovah '

' Pharaoh ' skip`ing ' came ' for ' 19 till and ' from on`ing of ' king as

ye ' them as on ' Jehovah ' dwell and ' height`s ' him chariot in and ' and ride in

middle`ing in ' the wither in ' and walk the ' Israel ' as son and ' sea the ' who '

' Aaron ' you and brother ' the prophet`s the ' Miriam ' took you and ' 20 sea the '

' from as women the ' all ' flock`ed you and ' hand`ed in ' tambourine the ' ye

' them of ' low you and ' 21 you and dance in and ' from as tambourine in ' am after

' skip`ing ' haughty`ed ' haughty`ed ' for ' Jehovah of ' and is gift ' Miriam

' Israel ' ye ' Moses ' onward as and ' 22 height`s ' high`ed ' and ride and

' captain`ing ' word from ' to ' alas ing`out and ' join`ing ' Water

' and come ' not and ' word from in ' from week ' you three ' way ' and walk as and

Water ' laid`ing of ' and all as ' not and ' the you drop ' and came as and ' 23 Water

' 24 drop`ed ' there`ed ' call ' so ' on ' them ' Miriam ' for ' the drop from '

' 25 the drink has ' what ' say of ' Moses ' on ' people the ' and stop as and

' hurl as and ' tree ' Jehovah ' and look`ed him and ' Jehovah ' to ' cry as and

' law ' if ' there ' there ' Water the ' and sip as and ' Water the ' to

' hear`ing ' mother ' say as and ' 26 and test has ' there and ' discern from and

' him has eye in ' fit the and ' are as Allah ' Jehovah ' voice`ing of ' hear you

' all ' you guard and ' and as you command from of ' you ear the and ' do`ed you

' not ' from as Mizra in ' as you there ' which ' dance`ed the ' all ' and as law

' 27 are thither is ' Jehovah ' as whither ' for ' are as on ' there`s I

' ten`ed ' from twosome ' there and ' Elim`s in and ' the Elim`s ' and came as and

there ' and encamp and ' from as palmtree ' from as seven and ' Water ' you and low`s

Water the ' on '

' as son ' testimony ' all ' and came as and ' from as to`s from ' leave as and ' 1
' from as Ram`s ' between in ' which ' bush`s ' word from ' to ' Israel
' two the ' new of ' day as ' ten ' the five in ' as bush`s ' between in and
' testimony ' all ' and tarry`s and ' 2 from as Mizra ' land from ' from you issue of
and say as and ' 3 word from in ' Aaron ' on and ' Moses ' on ' Israel ' as son
Jehovah ' hand in ' our die`ing ' permanent ' who ' Israel ' as son ' them as to '
' flesh the ' repent`s ' on ' and has desist in ' from as Mizra ' land in '
' to ' and has ye ' from you issue alas ' for ' seven of ' fight ' our eat in
' this the ' assemble the ' all ' ye ' whom them of ' this the ' is wilderness the
' rain`s from ' as behold`th ' Moses ' to ' Jehovah ' say as and ' 4 hunger in
' and pickup and ' people the ' out and ' heaven`s the ' has from ' fight ' relate
' walk as the ' and bush whither ' purpose of ' and day as in ' day as ' word
' as six the ' day as in ' be`s and ' 5 not ' mother ' as you protect`ing in
' which ' on ' care`ed ' be`s and ' and came`s as ' which ' ye ' and stable`s and
' all ' to ' Aaron and ' Moses ' say as and ' 6 day as and ' day as ' and pickup as
' issue`s alas ' Jehovah ' for ' complete known and ' twilight ' Israel ' as son
' ye ' from whom look and ' herd and ' 7 from as Mizra ' land from ' from are ye
' Jehovah ' on ' your as you obstinate ' ye ' and hear in ' Jehovah ' honour`ing
Moses ' say as and ' 8 our as on ' and stop`ing you ' for ' what ' our brother`th and
' from bread and ' eat of ' flesh ' twilight in ' relate ' Jehovah ' set in '
' which ' your as you obstinate ' ye ' Jehovah ' hear in ' seven of ' is morn in
' not ' what ' our brother`th and ' and Mosthigh ' from as stop from ' from ye
to ' Moses ' say as and ' 9 Jehovah ' on ' for ' your as you obstinate ' our as on
' and approach ' Israel ' as son ' testimony ' all ' to ' say ' Aaron '
' became as and ' 10 your as you obstinate ' ye ' hear ' for ' Jehovah ' as before

' and turn as and ' Israel ' as son ' testimony ' all ' to ' Aaron ' word are

11 ' cloud in ' speak`ed ' Jehovah ' honour`ing ' be`th and ' is wilderness the ' to

' ye ' as you hear ' 12 say of ' Moses ' to ' Jehovah ' word as and

' between in ' say of ' them as to ' word ' Israel ' as son ' you and obstinate

' and swear too you ' is morn in and ' flesh ' and eat you ' from as twilight the

13 ' your as Allah ' Jehovah ' as whither ' for ' complete known and ' fight

' ye ' conceal you and ' privacy`ing the ' on you and ' twilight in ' became as and

' surround`s ' dew the ' you lay ' whom`ed the ' is morn in and ' camp`ed the

' around ' on ' be`th and ' dew the ' you lay ' on you and ' 14 camp`ed of

15 ' land the ' on ' is palm are ' thin ' shred at from ' thin ' is wilderness the

' him brother ' to ' man I ' and say as and ' Israel ' as son ' see as and

' Moses ' say as and ' that`ing ' what ' and known ' not ' for ' that`ing ' has from

16 ' eat`ed of ' relate ' Jehovah ' gave ' which ' fight the ' that`ing ' them as to

' man I ' and her from ' and pickup ' Jehovah ' command`ed ' which ' word the ' this

' from are as you soul ' report from ' you heap heap of ' sheaf ' and eat ' as by

' as son ' so ' concoct as and ' 17 and took you ' and tent in ' which of ' man I

' and mete as and ' 18 less`s from the and ' much`ed the ' and pickup as and ' Israel

' not ' less`s from the and ' much`ed the ' surplus`s the ' not and ' sheaf in

' Moses ' say as and ' 19 and pickup ' and eat ' as by ' man I ' lack`s the

' not and ' 20 herd ' till ' and her from ' survive`s as ' to ' man I ' them as to

till ' and her from ' from as person ' and survive`s as and ' Moses ' to ' and hear

them as on ' angry as and ' abhor as and ' from as moggot you ' elevate and ' herd '

' as palm ' man I ' is morn in ' is morn in ' and ye ' and pickup as and ' 21 Moses '

as six the ' day as in ' became as and ' 22 melt and ' sun the ' hot`ed and ' and eat

' all ' and came as and ' one of ' sheaf the ' two ' care`ed ' fight ' and pickup '

' say as and ' 23 Moses of ' and fortune`s as and ' till`ed the ' as lift`s has

' holy ' desist ' has and desist ' Jehovah ' word ' which ' that`ing ' them as to

' which ' ye and ' now ' now you ' which ' ye ' tomorrow ' Jehovah of

' relate ' and rest`s the ' surplus the ' all ' ye and ' and sodden ' and sodden you

herd the ' till ' and ye ' and rest`s as and ' 24 herd the ' till ' you guard from of

' not ' high`ed and ' abhor`s the ' not and ' Moses ' command`ed ' which are '

desist ' for ' day as the ' and eat`ed ' Moses ' say as and ' 25 and in ' whom`ed the

' 26 field`ed in ' and come`ed you ' not ' day as the ' Jehovah of ' day as the '

' desist ' as seven`s the ' day as in and ' and pickup`ed you ' from week ' you six

' and out ' as seven`s the ' day as in ' became as and ' 27 and in ' be`s as ' not

' Jehovah ' say as and ' 28 and come ' not and ' pickup of ' people the ' has from

' as you command from ' guard of ' from you refuse ' whither`ed ' till ' Moses ' to

desist the ' ye ' relate ' gave ' Jehovah ' for ' see ' 29 as you protect`ing and

' fight ' as six the ' day as in ' relate ' gave ' that`ing ' so ' on '

' man I ' out ' to and ' him under ' man I ' sparkle ' from as day as

' and desist as and ' 30 desist the ' as seven`s the ' day as in ' and place`ing from

' Israel ' you house ' and call as and ' 31 as seven`s the ' day as in ' people the

and flavor and ' son of ' fortune ' seed are ' that`ing and ' has from ' name ' ye

' which ' word the ' this ' Moses ' say as and ' 32 honey in ' you as wafer are '

' you guard from of ' and her from ' sheaf the ' and fill ' Jehovah ' command`ed

' which ' fight the ' ye ' and look as ' purpose of ' from are as generation of

' from are ye ' as issue`s alas in ' word from in ' from are ye ' as you eat the

' took ' Aaron ' to ' Moses ' say as and ' 33 from as Mizra ' land from

' has from ' sheaf the ' fill`ing ' there`ed ' give and ' sister ' you has vase

' you guard from of ' Jehovah ' as before ' and ye`ing ' rest`s the and

Moses ’ ye ’ to ’ Jehovah ’ command`ed ’ which are ’ (34 from are as generation of
you guard from of ’ testimony`ing the ’ as before ’ Aaron ’ and the rest`s as and ’
’ the Year ’ from as four I ’ has them ’ ye ’ and eat ’ Israel ’ as son and ’ (35
’ till ’ and eat ’ has them ’ ye ’ desist and has ’ land ’ to ’ cubit ’ till
’ the cook`s ’ urn do ’ sheaf the and ’ (36 Canaan ’ land ’ end`ed ’ to ’ cubit
that`ing

' bush`s ' is wilderness from ' Israel ' as son ' testimony ' all ' leave as and ' 1
' from as refresh`s in ' and encamp and ' Jehovah ' edge ' on ' them as march of
' people the ' contend and ' 2 people the ' laid`ing of ' Water ' whither`s and
' drink`ed has and ' Water ' our of ' and give`ed ' and say as and ' Moses ' people
' what and ' as stand ' has and increase`s you ' what ' Moses ' them of ' say as and
' Water of ' people the ' there ' thirsty as and ' 3 Jehovah ' ye ' try`ing you
' this ' what of ' and say as and ' Moses ' on ' people the ' tarry and
' as son ' ye and ' near ' whom them of ' from as Mizra from ' and give as on the
' say of ' Jehovah ' to ' Moses ' cry as and ' 4 thirsty in ' as purchase ' ye and
' 5 as has and throw and ' less ' till`ing ' this the ' people of ' do`ed I ' what
' ercort ' people the ' as before ' Obara ' Moses ' to ' Jehovah ' say as and
' and in ' group`s the ' which ' are down and ' Israel ' as elder from ' are ye
' as behold`th ' 6 you walk the and ' are hand in ' implicate ' channel the ' ye
' ing`desolate in ' boulder`ing the ' on ' there ' are as before ' stand
' drink`ed and ' Water ' and her from ' and out and ' boulder`ing in ' group`s the and
' 7 Israel ' as elder ' as has eye of ' Moses ' so ' do as and ' people the
increase`s ' on ' thus rebell and ' burden`ed ' place`ing the ' there ' call as and
' say of ' Jehovah ' ye ' from camouflage`ing ' on and ' Israel ' as son '
Amalek ' came as and ' 8 whither`s ' mother ' and has approach in ' Jehovah ' man the
' Moses ' say as and ' 9 from as refresh`s in ' Israel ' people ' fight as and '
' fight the ' spring ' from as person ' our of ' choose ' ed`Joshua`ing ' to
' hill`ed the ' head ' on ' settle ' for whither ' tomorrow ' Amalek in
' ed`Joshua`ing ' do as and ' 10 as hand in ' from as Allah the ' staff from and
' Aaron and ' Moses and ' Amalek in ' fight the of ' Moses ' if ' say ' which are
elevate`s ' which are ' be`s and ' 11 hill`ed the ' head ' to ' lug ' hole`ing and

' him hand ' rest`s as ' which are and ' Israel ' strong and ' him hand ' Moses '
' acquire as and ' from as my heavy ' Moses ' as hand and ' 12 Amalek ' strong and
' Aaron`ing and ' am on ' dwell and ' him under ' and site`s and ' stone
' victual`ed and ' one ' victual`ed ' him hand in ' and sustain ' hole`ing and
' 13 sun the ' came ' till ' the has steady ' him hand ' and became as and ' one
' drown and ' and people ' ye and ' Amalek ' ye ' ed`Joshua`ing ' defeat as and
' such ' write ' Moses ' to ' Jehovah ' say as and ' 14 desolate ' as by
' for ' ed`Joshua`ing ' as ear in ' there`s and ' report in ' shall is remember
' 15 heaven`s the ' under from ' Amalek ' male ' ye ' wipe`ed I ' wipe`ed
' 16 as flee ' Jehovah ' name ' call as and ' sacrifice from ' Moses ' son as and
Amalek in ' Jehovah of ' fight`ed from ' am ' throne ' on ' hand ' for ' say as and
evermore`ing and ' tread '

THE TORAH SCROLL 18

' all ' ye ' Moses ' inlaw ' Midian ' priest ' and preserve ' hear as and ' 1

' for ' and people ' Israel of and ' Moses of ' from as Allah ' do`ed ' which

' took as and ' 2 from as Mizra from ' Israel ' ye ' Jehovah ' issue`s alas

' after ' Moses ' wife ' the bird`ing ' ye ' Moses ' inlaw ' and preserve

' for ' Gershom ' one the ' there ' which ' am son ' two ' ye and ' 3 am send`ing

' one the ' there and ' 4 am foreign ' land in ' as whom became ' guest ' say

' as has security`s and ' as aid in ' as father ' as Allah ' for ' Eliezer

him son and ' Moses ' inlaw ' and preserve ' came as and ' 5 Pharaoh ' desolate from

' that`ing ' which ' is wilderness the ' to ' Moses ' to ' and wife and '

' Moses ' to ' say as and ' 6 from as Allah this ' mountain ' there ' grace`ed

' are wife and ' are as to ' came ' and preserve ' are inlaw ' as whither ' be`th

' and inlaw ' you call of ' Moses ' out and ' 7 people`ed ' am son ' two and

' man I ' and ask as and ' if ' moisten as and ' Moses of ' the and humble`ly as and

' 8 tent`ed the ' and came`ed as and ' from and peace of ' and evil`ed of

' Jehovah ' do`ed ' which ' all ' ye ' and inlaw of ' Moses ' report as and

' all ' ye ' Israel ' concern`ing ' on ' from as mizra of and ' Pharaoh of

' 9 Jehovah ' from shade as and ' way in ' from you come ' which ' travail`ed the

' Jehovah ' do`ed ' which ' the good`ing the ' all ' on ' and preserve ' dark Then

' say as and ' 10 from as Mizra ' hand from ' and shade`s the ' which ' Israel of

' hand from ' from are ye ' shade`s the ' which ' Jehovah ' bless`ing ' and preserve

' people the ' ye ' shade`s the ' which ' Pharaoh ' hand from and ' from as Mizra

' great`ing ' for ' as you known ' time`ed ' 11 from as Mizra ' hand ' under from

' insolent ' which ' word in ' for ' from as Allah the ' all from ' Jehovah

' on`ed ' Moses ' inlaw ' and preserve ' took as and ' 12 them as on

' all and ' Aaron ' came as and ' from as Allah of ' from as sacrifice and

' as before ' Moses ' inlaw ' people ' fight ' eat of ' Israel ' as elder from and

' Moses ' dwell and ' you tomorrow from ' became as and ' 13 from as Allah the

has from ' Moses ' on ' people the ' stand as and ' people the ' ye ' discern of

' all ' ye ' Moses ' inlaw ' look as and ' 14 twilight the ' till ' herd the '

' this the ' word the ' what ' say as and ' people of ' do`ed ' that`ing ' which

' are alone of ' sojourn as ' ye`ed ' why`ing ' people of ' do`ed ' ye`ed ' which

' till and ' herd the ' has from ' are as on ' settle ' people the ' all and

' Eli ' came`ing as ' for ' and inlaw of ' Moses ' say as and ' 15 twilight the

and came ' word ' them of ' be`s as ' for ' 16 from as Allah ' search of ' people the

' and shepherd is ' between in and ' man I ' between in ' as you discern and ' Eli '

' ye and ' from as Allah the ' as law ' ye ' and as knowledge alas and

' good`ing ' not ' him to ' Moses ' inlaw ' say as and ' 17 him you protect`ing

' also ' ye`ed ' also ' both ' foolish ' 18 do`ed ' ye`ed ' which ' word the

' word the ' with from ' honour ' for ' are people ' which ' this the ' people the

as voice`ing in ' hear ' time`ed ' 19 are alone of ' mark and do`ed ' able you ' not

' ye`ed ' be`ing ' are people ' from as Allah ' became as and ' are advice I '

' ye ' ye`ed ' brought the and ' from as Allah the ' split`ing ' people of

ye ' them ye ' the you warn the and ' 20 from as Allah the ' to ' from as word the

ye ' them of ' knowledge alas and ' you protect`ing the ' ye and ' from as law the '

shall do as ' which ' work`ed the ' ye and ' thus ' and walk as ' which ' way the '

' sick`s ' as person ' people the ' all from ' walk ' the select ' ye`ed and ' 21

' herein and ' profit ' as hateful ' faithful ' as person ' from as Allah ' as dread

' you and hundred ' as captain and ' from as thousand ' as captain ' them as on

' ye ' and discern and ' 22 you and ten ' as captain and ' from as five ' as captain

' great`ing the ' word the ' all ' be`s and ' time ' all in ' people the

them ' and discern as ' small the ' word the ' all and ' are as to ' has and came`s as
' ye ' mother ' 23 are ye ' and lift shall ' are as on from ' voice the and '
' you all as and ' from as Allah ' are command and ' do`ed you ' this the ' word the
came`ing as ' and place`ing ' on I ' this the ' people the ' all ' also and ' stand
' do as and ' and inlaw ' voice`ing of ' Moses ' hear as and ' 24 from and peace in '
' able I ' not ' people the ' to ' Moses ' say as and ' say ' which ' all
' your as Allah ' Jehovah ' from are ye ' arise ' as alone of ' for whither
as in star`ing are ' day as the ' from are behold and ' from are ye ' increase`ed the
' add ' from are as you father ' as Allah ' Jehovah ' increase of ' heaven`s the '
' from are ye ' bless as and ' from as move ' thousand ' from star ' from are mosthigh
' from are pressure ' as alone of ' lift I ' the sure`s ' relate ' word ' which are
' from as person ' relate ' ascribe ' from are increase`s and ' from as lift from
' your as tribe of ' from as known and ' from as understand`ing and ' from as wise
' good`ing ' and say as and ' and low as and ' your as head in ' from there`s I and
' as head ' ye ' took as and ' you concoct of ' you word ' which ' word the
' choose as and ' 25 from as known and ' from as wise ' from as person ' them as tribe
' from ye ' give as and ' Israel ' all from ' sick`s ' as person ' Moses
as captain and ' from as thousand ' as captain ' people the ' mosthigh ' from as head
' you and ten ' as captain and ' from as five ' as captain ' you and hundred '
' them as discern ' ye ' command as and ' them as tribe of ' from as officer and
' just ' from you tribe and ' your as brother ' between in ' and hear ' say of
not ' and guest ' between in and ' him brother ' between in and ' man I ' between in
' great`ing are ' small are ' discern from in ' inner`s ' and pasture`s you '
discern them ' for ' man I ' around from ' and guest`ing you ' not ' has and hear you
' from with ' hard`ed as ' which ' word the and ' that`ing ' from as Allah of '

' ye ' from ye ' command as and ' him you hear and ' Eli ' has and approach`s you
' ye ' and discern as and ' 25 ' shall do as ' which ' from as word the ' all
' hard`ed the ' great`ing the ' word the ' ye ' time ' all in ' people the
and discern`ing as ' small the ' word the ' all and ' Moses ' to ' has and came`s as
' to ' if ' walk as and ' and inlaw ' ye ' Moses ' send as and ' 27 them '
and land

' land from ' Israel ' as son ' you issue of ' as three`s the ' new in ' 1

2 as bush`s ' word from ' and came ' this the ' day as in ' from as Mizra

' as bush`s ' word from ' and came as and ' from as refresh`s from ' leave as and

3 mountain the ' over ' Israel ' there ' encamp and ' word from in ' and encamp and

' Jehovah ' him to ' call as and ' from as Allah the ' to ' on`ed ' Moses and '

' Jacob ' you house of ' say you ' here ' say of ' mountain the ' has from

' which ' ye ' from you seen ' from ye ' 4 Israel ' as son of ' my nation you and

' as wing ' on ' from are ye ' lift I and ' from as Mizra of ' as whom do

hear`ing ' mother ' the time and ' 5 Eli ' from are ye ' spawn`s and ' from as eagle

' as covenant`s ' ye ' from you guard and ' as voice`ing in ' and hear you '

' from as people the ' all from ' the special`ing ' vessel ' complete as became and

' you king from ' vessel ' and as he ' from ye and ' 6 land the ' all ' vessel ' for

' which ' from as word the ' to`ed ' holy`ing ' nation`ing and ' from as priest

' call as and ' Moses ' came as and ' 7 Israel ' as son ' to ' word you

' from as word the ' all ' ye ' them as before ' site and ' people the ' as elder of

' people the ' all ' and low as and ' 8 Jehovah ' and command`ed ' which ' these`ed

' dwell and ' the make ' Jehovah ' word ' which ' all ' and say as and ' together as

to ' Jehovah ' say as and ' 9 Jehovah ' to ' people the ' as word ' ye ' Moses

' cloud the ' thicket in ' are as to ' came ' for whither ' be`th ' Moses '

' against ' also and ' are people ' as word in ' people the ' hear as ' cross`ing in

people the ' as word ' ye ' Moses ' my told and ' from on`ing of ' and believe`s as

' people the ' to ' walk ' Moses ' to ' Jehovah ' say as and ' 10 Jehovah ' to '

11 from you raiment ' and immersion and ' tomorrow and ' day as the ' from you holy and

' day as in ' for ' as three`s the ' day as of ' from as ready`ing ' and became and '

' on I ' people the ' all ' as has eye of ' Jehovah ' descend ' as three`s the

' people the ' mountain the ' ye ' you border the and ' 12 as bush`s ' mountain
' offer`ing ' relate ' and guard the ' say you of ' people the ' to and ' surround`s
13 die him ' die`ing ' blemish ' touch the ' all ' and end`ed in ' touch and ' blemish
' look`ed as ' or ' throw as ' throw`ing ' for ' hand ' and in ' reach ' not '
' remove in ' am decide ' not ' man I ' mother ' cattle`ed ' mother ' dread`ed as
' has from ' Moses ' descend and ' 14 blemish ' lug as ' them`ed ' ing`produce the
' people the ' ye ' holy as and ' people the ' to ' mountain the
' him the ' people the ' to ' say as and ' 15 from you raiment ' and immersion as and
Woman ' to ' and address ' to ' from week the ' you three of ' from as ready`ing
' herd the ' you and became in ' as three`s the ' day as in ' became as and ' 16
' on ' honour ' cloud and ' from as glitter and ' ing`thunder`ing ' became as and
shudder as and ' especially ' strength ' is lip`ing the ' voice`ing and ' mountain the
' ye ' Moses ' issue him and ' 17 camp`ed in ' which ' people the ' all '
' camp`ed the ' has from ' from as Allah the ' you call of ' people the
' as bush`s ' mountain and ' 18 mountain the ' you as under in ' and reside whom and
' abhorrence ' Jehovah ' and Mosthigh ' descend ' which ' around from ' fail ' smoke
' all ' shudder as and ' has footstool the ' smoke are ' and smoke ' went and
ing`enter ' is lip`ing the ' voice`ing ' became as and ' 19 especially ' mountain the
and cloud as ' from as Allah the and ' word as ' Moses ' especially ' strength and '
head ' to ' as bush`s ' mountain ' on ' Jehovah ' descend and ' 20 voice`ing in '
' mountain the ' head ' to ' Moses ' to ' Jehovah ' call as and ' mountain the '
people in ' repeat ' up ' Moses ' to ' Jehovah ' say as and ' 21 Moses ' went and
' and her from ' fall and ' you see of ' Jehovah ' to ' and beat as ' turn '
' Jehovah ' to ' from as presence the ' from as priest the ' also and ' 22 increase
' to ' Moses ' say as and ' 23 Jehovah ' cattle ' grow as ' turn ' and holy you as

' as bush`s ' mountain ' to ' offer`ing of ' people the ' all him ' not ' Jehovah
mountain the ' ye ' border the ' say of ' and son ' testimony`ed the ' ye`ed ' for
' offer`s and ' up ' walk ' Jehovah ' him to ' say as and ' 24 and you holy and '
' to ' people the and ' from as priest the and ' are people ' Aaron and ' ye`ed
' descend and ' 25 height ' grow as ' turn ' Jehovah ' to ' offer of ' and beat as
them as to ' say as and ' people the ' to ' mountain the ' has from ' Moses

2 say of ' these`ed ' from as word the ' all ' ye ' from as Allah ' word as and ' 1
' land from ' are as you issue alas ' which ' are as Allah ' Jehovah ' for whither '
' walk ' be`s as ' not ' 3 from as serve ' you house from ' from as Mizra
' carve ' walk ' do`ed you ' not ' 4 around ' on ' from as after ' from as Allah
' land in ' which and ' above from ' heaven`s in ' which ' the portion`ing ' all and
' not ' 5 land of ' under from ' Water in ' which and ' under from
' for whither ' for ' from serve you ' not and ' them of ' the and humble`ly you
' on ' you and father ' low`ing ' punish ' jealous ' to ' are as Allah ' Jehovah
' 6 as hateful of ' from as four`s ' on and ' from as three`s ' on ' from as son
' as guard of and ' as love of ' from as thousand of ' bow ' do`ed and
' are as Allah ' Jehovah ' there ' ye ' lift you ' not ' 7 as you command from
' ye ' linger ' which ' ye ' Jehovah ' the blame as ' not ' for ' lift`ing of
' desist the ' day as ' ye ' guard`ing ' male`ing ' 8 lift`ing of ' name
' all ' dual`s and ' serve you ' from week ' you six ' 9 and holy`ed of
are as Allah ' Jehovah of ' desist ' as seven`s the ' day as and ' 10 are you are fill
' are son and ' ye`ed ' the are fill ' all ' and in ' do`ed you ' not '
' are guest and ' are you cattle and ' are faithful and ' are serve ' are daughter and
' ye ' Jehovah ' do`ed ' from week ' you six ' for ' 11 are as gate in ' which
' height ' which ' all ' ye and ' sea the ' ye ' land the ' ye and ' heaven`s the
' ye ' Jehovah ' bless ' so ' on ' as seven`s the ' day as in ' rest as and
' ye and ' are as father ' ye ' honour ' 12 and holy`ed as and ' desist the ' day as
' ground`ed the ' on ' are week ' has and lengthen`s as ' purpose of ' are mother
' not ' 14 murder you ' not ' 13 walk ' gave ' are as Allah ' Jehovah ' which
' 17 false ' till ' fellow in ' vouch`ed ' not ' 16 steal you ' not ' 15 adultery you
' fellow ' wife ' desire you ' not ' fellow ' you house ' desire you ' not

' and heass`ing and ' and ox`ing and ' and faithful and ' and serve and ' and field`ed
are as Allah ' Jehovah ' are came`s as ' for ' be`s and ' fellow of ' which ' all and
' the net`ness of ' there`ed ' came ' ye`ed ' which ' as Canaan the ' land ' to '
' from ye ' you field and ' you and great ' from as stone ' walk ' you rise the and
' as word ' all ' ye ' from as stone the ' on ' you write and ' field`s in
has desend the ' ye ' from are cross in ' be`s and ' such the ' the protect`ing the
' for whither ' which ' these`ed ' from as stone the ' ye ' and rise`s you '
you build and ' from as axe`s mountain in ' day as the ' from are ye ' command`ed from
from as stone ' sacrifice from ' are as Allah ' Jehovah of ' sacrifice from ' there '
' you and whole ' from as stone ' of iron ' them as on ' brandish`s ' not '
' offer`s the and ' are as Allah ' Jehovah ' sacrifice from ' ye ' the son you
' you sacrifice and ' are as Allah ' Jehovah of ' offer`ing ' and Mosthigh
' Jehovah ' as before ' you rejoice and ' there ' you eat and ' from as whole
' as after ' has desend the ' cross in ' that`ing the ' mountain the ' are as Allah
thus town in ' dwell the ' as Canaan the ' land in ' sun the ' came`ing from ' way
18 ' ridge ' split`ing ' ing`appear ' oak`ing ' beside ' heap heap the ' split`ing '
' voice`ing ' ye and ' ing`thunder`ing the ' ye ' hear ' people the ' all and
' mountain the ' ye and ' from as torch`s the ' ye ' from seen and ' is lip`ing the
get from ' and stand as and ' and low as and ' people the ' all ' see as and ' smoke
' our as Allah ' Jehovah ' and has show ' behold ' Moses ' to ' and say as and ' 19
' our hear ' and voice`ing ' ye and ' and great ' ye and ' and honour`ing ' ye
' word as ' for ' our as look ' this the ' day as the ' fire the ' middle`ing from
' die`ing has ' what of ' the time and ' life and ' ground the ' ye ' from as Allah
' from as add ' mother ' such the ' great`ed the ' fire the ' and has eat you ' for
' till`ing ' our as Allah ' Jehovah ' voice`ing ' ye ' hear of ' and us I

' voice`ing ' hear ' which ' flesh ' Circumcise ' who ' for ' and give from and
' fire the ' middle`ing from ' word from ' from as life ' from as Allah
' which ' all ' ye ' hear and ' ye`ed ' approach ' life as and ' and storeup`ing
' all ' ye ' our as to ' word you ' ye`ed and ' our as Allah ' Jehovah ' say as
' our as do and ' our hear and ' are as to ' our as Allah ' Jehovah ' word as ' which
' our people ' word as ' to and ' the hear has and ' our people ' ye`ed ' word
' people the ' to ' Moses ' say as and ' 20 die`ing has ' turn ' from as Allah the
' came ' from are ye ' camouflage`ing ' cross`ing in of ' for ' and look as you ' to
' your as turn ' on ' and you dread ' be`s you ' cross`ing in and ' from as Allah the
' Moses and ' get from ' people the ' stand as and ' 21 and sin you ' as except of
' word as and ' from as Allah the ' there ' which ' made is shelter ' to ' presence
' as word ' voice`ing ' ye ' as you hear ' say of ' Moses ' to ' Jehovah
which ' all ' and good`s the ' are as to ' and word ' which ' this the ' people the
' dread`ed of ' them of ' this ' from mind ' be`s and ' permanent ' who ' and word '
' purpose of ' from week the ' all ' as you command from ' ye ' guard of and ' near
from definite ' prophet`s ' from on`ing of ' them as son of and ' them of ' improve as
as word ' as set has and ' with`ing are ' them as brother ' approach from ' them of '
' and has command I ' which ' all ' ye ' them as to ' word and ' him animal '
' word as ' which ' him word ' to ' hear as ' not ' which ' man that ' be`s and
' prophet`s the ' sure ' and people from ' search I ' for whither ' as there in
' not ' which ' ye ' as there in ' word ' word of ' machete`s ' which
' from as Allah ' spice ' word as ' which and ' word of ' him whom command
' say you ' for and ' that`ing the ' prophet`s the ' die and ' from as after
' and word ' not ' which ' word the ' ye ' acknowledge has ' sure`s ' are mind in
' be`s as ' not ' Jehovah ' spice ' prophet`s the ' word as ' which ' Jehovah

' and word ' not ' which ' word the ' that`ing ' came`ing as ' not and ' word the
' strife`ing ' not ' prophet`s the ' and word ' 22 has and proud in ' Jehovah
' your as tent of ' relate ' and carry`ing ' them of ' say ' walk ' and her from
' all ' ye ' are as to ' the word I and ' as stand ' stand ' talk ' ye`ed and
from teach you ' which ' from as discern them and ' from as law the ' command`ed them
' the net`ness of ' them of ' gave ' for whither ' which ' land in ' concoct and '
to ' word ' say you of ' here ' Moses ' to ' Jehovah ' word as and ' say as and
' heaven`s the ' has from ' for ' from you seen ' from ye ' Israel ' as son '
' silver ' as Allah ' near ' smoke`ing you ' not ' 23 your people ' as you word
' ground`ed ' sacrifice from ' 24 relate ' and do you ' not ' gold ' as Allah and
ye and ' are as offer ' ye ' and Mosthigh ' you sacrifice and ' vessel ' do`ed you
' all in ' are herd from and ' ye and ' are flock from ' ye ' are as whole '
' there`ed ' as there ' ye ' from you is as remember I ' which ' place`ing the
' sacrifice from ' mother and ' 25 are as you bless and ' are as to ' came`ing I
for ' wrought`s ' has ye`ed ' the son you ' not ' vessel ' do`ed you ' from as stone
' on`ed you ' not and ' 26 profane`ed you and ' am on ' you wave the ' are desolate '
' are skin`ing ' the rent ' not ' which ' as sacrifice from ' on ' offer`ing from in
and as on I

' for ' 2 them as before ' there`s you ' which ' from as discern them ' to`ed and ' 1
you as seven in and ' are serve as ' from two ' six ' as Obara ' serve ' the nest you
' came`ing as ' material`s in ' mother ' 3 reason ' as free of ' out '
' and wife ' the out and ' that`ing ' Woman ' marry ' mother ' out ' material`s in
' if ' bore`ed as and ' Woman ' if ' permanent ' him master ' mother ' 4 and people
' be`s you ' am bore as and ' Woman the ' daughter`th`ing ' or ' from as son
say as ' say ' mother and ' 5 material`s in ' out ' that`ing and ' am master of
' as son ' ye and ' as wife ' ye and ' as master ' ye ' as you love ' serve the '
from as Allah the ' to ' him master ' and man direct and ' 6 as free ' proceed ' not
puncture and ' the post`ing the ' to ' or ' door the ' to ' and man direct and '
' 7 from on`ing of ' and serve and ' puncture from in ' and ear ' ye ' him master '
' issue you ' not ' the from not ' and daughter ' ye ' man I ' sale as ' for and
' as has eye in ' that`s ' evil`ed ' mother ' 8 from as serve the ' you issue are
' people of ' release`ed the and ' betroth`ed the ' not ' which ' am master
' mother and ' 9 thus ' and fabric in ' sale`ed of ' rule as ' not ' as foreign
' daughter`th`ing the ' discern from are ' the has betroth`s as ' and son of
' the remain ' if ' took as ' you after ' mother and ' 10 nihil ' success`ed
' to`ed ' three ' mother and ' 11 withdraw as ' not ' the answer and ' the garment`ing
' with`ed ' 12 silver ' whither`s ' reason ' the out and ' nihil ' success`ed ' not
' hunt`ed ' not ' which and ' 13 die him ' die`ing ' die and ' man I
place`ing ' walk ' as you there and ' and hand of ' whither`ed ' from as Allah the and
' on ' man I ' machete`s ' for and ' 14 there`ed ' flee`ing as ' which '
our took you ' as sacrifice from ' affirm ' tote`ed in ' and kill of ' and shepherd is
' 16 die him ' die`ing ' and mother and ' him father ' with`ed and ' 15 die`ing of '
' 17 die him ' die`ing ' and hand in ' come shall ' and sale and ' man I ' steal and

' for and ' 18 die him ' die`ing ' and mother and ' him father ' accurse from and

' ye ' man I ' and smitten`ed and ' from as person ' has and contend`s

' fall and ' die`ing as ' not and ' ferocity came ' or ' stone in ' and shepherd is

' on ' outside`ing in ' walk he the and ' rise`ing as ' mother ' 19 lay from of

' permanent ' and desist ' only ' here them ' blame`ed and ' and you stay from

' or ' and serve ' ye ' man I ' struck`ed ' for and ' 20 decease as ' decease and

' die him ' die`ing ' and hand ' under ' die and ' tribe in ' and faithful ' ye

' stand as ' from as day as ' or ' day as ' mother ' sure ' 21 avenge as ' avenge

from as person ' and strive ' for and ' 22 that`ing ' and silver ' for ' rise as ' not

' not and ' am bore as and ' and out and ' mountain`ed ' Woman ' and body has and '

' and Mosthigh ' whom too as ' which are ' fine as ' fine`ing ' harm`ing ' be`s as

be`s as ' harm`ing ' mother and ' 23 from as praise in ' gave and ' Woman the ' marry

under ' Year ' has eye ' under ' has eye ' 24 soul ' under ' soul ' set`ed has and '

' under ' am pierce from ' 25 foot ' under ' foot ' hand ' under ' hand ' Year '

' 26 the is trade ' under ' the is trade ' wound ' under ' wound ' am pierce from

' has eye ' ye ' or ' and serve ' has eye ' ye ' man I ' struck`ed ' for and

' 27 and has eye ' under ' and has send as ' as free of ' he humble and ' and faithful

' as free of ' made`s as ' and faithful ' Year ' or ' and serve ' Year ' mother and

' captain`ing ' stab ' struck`ed ' for and ' 28 and tooth ' under ' and has send as

' throw`ing ' die and ' Woman ' ye ' or ' man I ' ye ' cattle`ed ' all ' or

' and flesh ' ye ' eat as ' not and ' cattle`ed the ' Ox`ing the ' throw as

' captain`ing ' mother and ' 29 emission`s ' cattle`ed the ' Ox`ing the ' on in and

till alas and ' from and three ' past`ing from ' that`s ' gore ' with`ed ' cattle`ed

' Woman ' or ' man I ' die`s the and ' our guard as ' not and ' him on neighbor '

' 30 die him ' and as on in ' also and ' throw you as ' cattle`ed the ' Ox`ing the

and soul ' has and ransom ' gave and ' and Mosthigh ' you man`ing ' ing`atone ' mother
' stab ' struck`ed ' son ' or ' 31 and Mosthigh ' you man`ing ' which ' accord '
' mother ' 32 if ' success`ed ' this the ' discern from are ' stab ' daughter ' or
' silver ' mother`ed ' or ' cattle`ed the ' Ox`ing the ' stab ' middle`ed ' serve
' ox`ing the and ' and as master of ' permanent ' from as weigh ' from as three
' or ' empty`ing ' man I ' open as ' for and ' 33 throw you as ' cattle`ed the and
' fall and ' and screen as ' not and ' empty`ing ' man I ' pasture`ed as ' for
' marry ' 34 cattle`ed ' all ' or ' heass`ing ' or ' captain`ing ' there`ed
' be`s as ' die since ' him on in of ' carry`s as ' silver ' whole as ' empty`ing the
' ye ' and you cattle ' all ' or ' man I ' captain`ing ' hurt ' for and ' 35 if
' die and ' and you cattle ' all ' ye ' or ' and shepherd is ' captain`ing
' and silver ' ye ' halve and ' life the ' Ox`ing the ' ye ' and sale and
' for ' acknowledge has ' or ' 36 has halve as ' die the ' ye ' also and
' from three ' past`ing from ' that`s ' gore ' with`ed ' cattle`ed the ' captain`ing
' cattle`ed ' captain`ing ' whole as ' whole ' and as on in ' our guard as ' not and
if ' be`s as ' die since ' cattle`ed ' Ox`ing the ' under

' and butcher and ' resemble ' or ' captain`ing ' man I ' steal as ' for and ' 1
' four I and ' Ox`ing the ' under ' whole as ' herd ' the five ' and sale ' or
' steal the ' come as ' you is burglary in ' mother ' 2 Lamb the ' under ' flock
the appear ' mother ' 3 from as blood ' if ' whither`s ' die and ' and smitten`ed and
' mother ' whole as ' whole ' if ' from as blood ' and Mosthigh ' sun the '
' come you ' come the ' mother ' 4 and you steal in ' sale shall ' if ' whither`s
till ' resemble ' till ' heass`ing ' till ' Ox`ing from ' steal`ed the ' and hand in
' for and ' 5 whole as ' from two ' one ' from as life ' cattle`ed ' all '
' the burn`s ' ye ' send and ' vineyard ' or ' field`ed ' man I ' burn`s as
' and field`ed from ' whole as ' whole ' after ' field`ed in ' burn and
' improve from ' swear'ed as ' field`ed the ' all ' mother and ' he income`ing are
fire ' issue you ' for ' 6 whole as ' and vineyard ' improve from and ' and field`ed
or ' stalk the ' or ' man forture ' eat has and ' from as end`ing ' the come and '
' for and ' 7 the burn`s the ' ye ' burn`s them ' whole as ' whole ' field`ed the '
' guard of ' from as all ' or ' silver ' and shepherd is ' to ' man I ' permanent
' whole as ' steal the ' come as ' mother ' man that ' you house from ' steal has and
marry ' approach shall ' steal the ' come as ' not ' mother and ' 8 from two ' one
' and hand ' send ' not ' mother ' from as Allah the ' to ' you house the '
' on ' trespass ' word ' all ' on ' 9 and shepherd is ' you are fill in
' all ' on ' raiment`ed ' on ' resemble ' on ' heass`ing ' on ' captain`ing
' Jehovah ' till ' this ' that`ing ' for ' say as ' which ' perish`ed the
' and has evil`ness`s as ' which ' them two ' word ' came`ing as ' from as Allah the
' for and ' 10 and evil`ed of ' from two ' one ' whole as ' from as Allah the
' or ' captain`ing ' or ' heass`ing ' and shepherd is ' to ' man I ' permanent
' or ' remain has ' or ' die and ' guard of ' cattle`ed ' all ' or ' resemble

' be`s you ' Jehovah ' you seven`ing ' 11 look`ed ' whither`s ' carry`ed has
' you are fill in ' and hand ' send ' not ' mother ' them two ' between in
steal ' mother and ' 12 whole as ' not and ' and as on in ' take and ' and shepherd is
' torn as ' torn ' mother ' 13 him on in of ' whole as ' and people from ' steal as '
' ask as ' for and ' 14 whole as ' not and ' torn`ed the ' till ' and the came as
' and as on in ' die ' or ' remain shall ' and shepherd is ' affirm ' man I
' and people ' and as on in ' mother ' 15 whole as ' whole ' and people ' whither`s
' for and ' 16 and merry in ' came and ' that`ing ' merry`s ' mother ' whole as ' not
' lay and ' betroth`ed ' not ' which ' the bride`ing ' man I ' expansion`ed
' mother and ' 17 resemble I of ' if ' the has soon as ' mountain from ' people`ed
' soon are ' weight as ' silver ' if ' the set of ' am father ' refuse as ' refuse
' lay ' all ' 19 the life you ' not ' the witchcraft from ' 18 you bride`ing the
' from as Allah of ' sacrifice ' 20 die him ' die`ing ' cattle`ed ' people
not ' guest and ' 21 and alone of ' Jehovah of ' as zero in ' curse as ' from as after
' from whom became ' from as guest ' for ' our affict you ' not and ' the has mark '
shall low you ' not ' orphan`ing and ' the widow I ' all ' 22 from as Mizra ' land in
Eli ' cry as ' cry ' mother ' for ' and ye ' vouch`ed ' low`ed ' mother ' for ' 23
' as you kill and ' nature ' hole`ed and ' 24 and you cry ' hear I ' hear and '
' you and window I ' your as women ' and became and ' desolate in ' from are ye
' ye ' the stack ' silver ' mother ' 25 from as orphan`ing ' your as son and
' not ' the lend ' if ' be`s you ' not ' are people ' poor the ' ye ' as people
' ye ' country you ' country ' mother ' 26 seize ' and Mosthigh ' and has deposite`s
' for ' 27 if ' and has carry`s you ' sun the ' came ' till ' fellow ' you raiment
' ing`nake of ' and you raiment ' that`s ' the alone of ' the garment`ing ' that`s
' for ' as you hear and ' Eli ' cry as ' for ' be`s and ' lay as ' height`ed

' help`s and ' accurse you ' not ' from as Allah ' 28 for whither ' favor`ing
' after you ' not ' are teardrop and ' are you fill ' 29 figure ' not ' are people in
' are captain`ing of ' do`ed you ' so ' 30 vessel ' has set ' are as son ' first`ing
' and mother ' people ' be`s as ' from week ' you seven ' and flock of and
' holy ' as person and ' 31 vessel ' our give you ' as eight`s the ' day as in and
' and eat you ' not ' torn`ed ' field`ed in ' flesh and ' vessel ' shall became you
and ye ' shall hurl`s you ' dog of ' hurl the

THE TORAH SCROLL 23

' people ' are hand ' impose`s ' to ' lift`ing ' hear ' lift you ' not ' 1

' as after ' be`s you ' not ' 2 violence ' till ' you and became of ' evil`ness

' increase`ing ' on ' vouch`ed ' not and ' you tend of ' from as increase

' not ' weak and ' 3 bend`ing the of ' from as increase ' as after ' bend`ing has of

are enemy I ' captain`ing ' entreat you ' for ' 4 and increase`s in ' magnificent you

' carry the ' seduce`ed ' and you cattle ' all ' or ' and heass`ing ' or '

under ' crouch ' are hateful ' heass`ing ' saw`ed ' for ' 5 if ' and has carry`s you

' forsake you ' forsake ' if ' forsake from ' you forbear and ' and lift from '

' are has and destitute ' discern from ' stretch`ed ' not ' 6 and people

to ' just`s and ' emission`s and ' get you ' false ' word from ' 7 and increase`s in

' for ' implicate ' not ' hire and ' 8 evil`ness ' just`s I ' not ' for ' kill you '

' as word ' subvert as and ' from as observe ' as has eye ' is blind as ' hire the

' from you known ' from ye and ' and affict you ' not ' guest and ' 9 from as just`s

' land in ' from whom became ' from as guest ' for ' abide ' soul ' ye

' you gather and ' are land ' ye ' seed you ' from two ' six and ' 10 from as Mizra

he let and ' the has remit you ' you as seven`s the and ' 11 the you income`ing ' ye

' eat you ' from preserve and ' are people ' as has and destitute ' and eat and '

' are as vineyard of ' do`ed you ' so ' field`ed the ' you life

' are as work ' do`ed you ' from week ' you six ' 12 are as olivet`s of and

' are serve ' rest`ing as ' purpose of ' desist you ' as seven`s the ' day as in and

' are Ox`ing ' are you cattle ' all and ' with`ing are ' are faithful and

' all in and ' 13 guest the and ' are you mother ' son ' soul as and ' are heass and

' from as Allah ' there and ' and guard you ' your as to ' as you say ' which

' three ' 14 reverse`s ' on ' hear as ' not ' and male`s you ' not ' from as after

unleaven`ing the ' solemn ' ye ' 15 Year`ed in ' vessel ' solemn you ' from as foot

' which are ' unleaven`ing ' eat you ' from week ' you seven ' guard you '
you out ' and in ' for ' blossom`s the ' new ' season from of ' are as whom command
' solemn and ' 16 from as only ' around ' and look as ' not and ' from as Mizra from '
solemn and ' field`ed in ' seed you ' which ' are as work ' as first`ing ' reap`s the
' are as work ' ye ' are gather in ' Year`ed the ' you issue in ' gather the '
' all ' look`ed as ' Year`ed in ' from as move ' three ' 17 field`ed the ' has from
' not ' 18 Jehovah ' master the ' Ark`ing the ' around ' to ' are male`ing
' milk ' tarry`s ' not and ' as sacrifice ' blood ' leaven ' on ' sacrifice you
came`s you ' are you ground ' as first`ing ' you as head ' 19 herd ' till ' as solemn
' mike in ' kid ' sodden you ' not ' are as Allah ' Jehovah ' you house '
' that`s ' cross`ed and ' forget ' sacrifice are ' such ' do`ed ' for ' and mother
' as messenger from ' send ' for whither ' be`th ' 20 Jacob ' as Allah of
' place`ing the ' to ' are came`s the of and ' way in ' are guard of ' are as before
and voice`ing in ' hear and ' and as turn from ' guard the ' 21 as you stable ' which
' for ' from are trepass of ' linger ' not ' for ' and in ' constant ' to '
' and hear you ' hear ' mother ' for ' 22 and approach in ' as there
' word I ' which ' all ' ye ' from dual`s and ' and as voice`ing in
' ye ' as you boulder and ' are as enemy I ' ye ' as you father`s and
are came`s the and ' are as before ' as messenger from ' bear ' for ' 23 are as bundle
' as Girgash the and ' as Heth the and ' as Amar the and ' as Canaan the ' to '
' 24 him you slash the and ' as Jebus the and ' as Hivite the and ' as Periz the and
' not and ' from serve you ' not and ' them as Allah of ' the and humble`ly you ' not
' is carry and ' from beat you ' beat ' for ' them as work are ' do`ed you
' Jehovah ' ye ' complete serve and ' 25 them as you altar ' is carry you
' are as Water ' ye and ' are from bread ' ye ' bless and ' your as Allah

' be`s you ' not and ' (26 are approach from ' the of wipe ' as you repent the and
' are week ' report from ' ye ' are land in ' the exterminate and ' the bereave from
' ye ' as die the and ' are as before ' send I ' as die hence ' ye and ' (27 fill I
' all ' ye ' as set has and ' cattle ' income`ing ' which ' people the ' all
' leper`ed the ' ye ' as you send and ' (28 stiffneck ' are as to ' are as enemy I
' ye and ' as Amar the ' ye and ' as Canaan the ' ye ' the exact and ' are as before
' ye and ' as Periz the ' ye and ' as Girgashite the ' ye and ' as Heth the
' not ' (29 are as before from ' as Jebus`ing the ' ye and ' as Hivite the
land the ' be`s you ' turn ' sister ' Year`ed in ' are around from ' and has exact I
less ' (30 field`ed the ' you life ' are as on ' the increase and ' the from there '
' the sew ' which ' till ' are around from ' and has exact I ' less '
' Water ' are border`ing ' ye ' twosome and ' (31 land the ' ye ' you inherit and
' till ' is wilderness from and ' from as Philista ' sea ' till and ' join`ing
' land the ' as sojourn as ' ye ' from are hand in ' donkey ' for ' river the
' them of ' hew you ' not ' (32 are around from ' and complete`s exact and
' turn ' are land in ' and carry as ' not ' (33 covenant`s ' them as Allah of and
' for ' them as Allah ' ye ' serve you ' for ' vessel ' are ye ' and sin`s as
snare from of ' walk ' and be`s as

freewill ' Aaron and ' ye`ed ' Jehovah ' to ' on`ed ' say ' Moses ' to and ' 1
Israel ' as elder from ' from as seven and ' Ithamar and ' Eleazar ' Abihu and '
and alone of ' Moses ' presence and ' 2 get from ' from whom and humble`ly the and '
' lug as ' not ' people the and ' and too told ' not ' them and ' Jehovah ' to '
as word ' all ' ye ' people of ' report as and ' Moses ' came as and ' 3 and people
' people the ' all ' and low as and ' from as discern them ' all ' ye and ' Jehovah '
' word ' which ' from as word the ' all ' and say as and ' one ' voice`ing
' Jehovah ' as word ' all ' ye ' Moses ' write as and ' 4 the make ' Jehovah
' mountain the ' under ' sacrifice from ' son as and ' is morn in ' ridge as and
' ten ' from two of ' establish`ed from ' from as stone ' ten`ed ' from twosome and
' Israel ' as son ' as youth ' ye ' send as and ' 5 Israel ' as tribe
' from as whole ' from as sacrifice ' and sacrifice as and ' offer`ing ' and went and
' as outside ' Moses ' took as and ' 6 herd ' as son ' from as Bullock ' Jehovah of
' on ' sprinkle ' blood the ' half and ' ' site and ' blood the
' as ear in ' call as and ' covenant`s the ' report ' took as and ' 7 sacrifice them
' hear has ' Jehovah ' word ' which ' all ' and say as and ' people the
' and sprinkle`ed as and ' blood the ' ye ' Moses ' took as and ' 8 do`ed has and
' hew ' which ' covenant`s the ' blood ' be`th ' say as and ' people the ' on
Moses ' went and ' 9 these`ed ' from as word the ' all ' on ' your people ' Jehovah
' from as seven and ' Ithamar and ' Eleazar ' Abihu and ' freewill ' Aaron and '
' under and ' Israel ' as Allah ' ye ' see as and ' 10 Israel ' as elder from
' heaven`s the ' might are and ' report`s the ' you son of ' work`ed are ' him foot
' and hand ' send ' not ' Israel ' as son ' as beside`s ' to and ' 11 clean`ing of
' 12 and drink as and ' and eat as and ' from as Allah the ' ye ' and vision as and
' be`ing and ' mountain`ed the ' Eli ' on`ed ' Moses ' to ' Jehovah ' say as and

' from as stone the ' ing`tablet`ing ' ye ' walk ' the give I and ' there
' as you write ' which ' command`ed them and ' the protect`ing the and
' ed`Joshua`ing and ' Moses ' rise as and ' 13 from you mountain`ing of
to and ' 14 from as Allah the ' mountain ' to ' Moses ' went and ' and minister from
live`ing ' which ' till ' spoil`ed ' our of ' sparkle ' say ' from as elder the '
' marry ' who ' your people ' hole`ing and ' Aaron ' be`th and ' your as to '
' mountain the ' to ' Moses ' went and ' 15 them as to ' adduce ' from as word
' honour`ing ' nigh as and ' 16 mountain the ' ye ' cloud the ' conceal as and
' you six ' cloud the ' and conceal`ed as and ' as bush`s ' mountain ' on ' Jehovah
middle`ing from ' as seven`s the ' day as in ' Moses ' to ' call as and ' from week
' head in ' you eat ' fire are ' Jehovah ' honour`ing ' appear`ed and ' 17 cloud the '
' Moses ' came as and ' 18 Israel ' as son ' as has eye of ' mountain the
' Moses ' became as and ' mountain the ' to ' went and ' cloud the ' middle`ing in
the night`s ' from as four I and ' day as ' from as four I ' blemish

1 2 ' as son ' to ' word ' say of ' Moses ' to ' Jehovah ' word as and '
which ' man I ' all ' each ' the oblation`ing ' vessel ' acquire as and ' Israel
3 ' such and ' as you oblation`ing ' ye ' and took you ' and heart ' and impel as '
' silver and ' gold ' spy from ' and took you ' which ' the oblation`ing the
4 two ' you have hang`ing and ' has from stony and ' you perfect and ' copper has and
5 ' from as Ram`s ' ing`skin`ing and ' from as Goat and ' six and '
6 ' hate`s ' as tree and ' from as badger ' ing`skin`ing and ' from as ground from
' anoint`ed the ' eight of ' from as there in and ' light`ing from of ' eight and
7 ' as stone and ' onyx ' as stone and ' from as aroma the ' you perfume of and
8 ' holy from ' vessel ' concoct and ' pocket of and ' gird`ing of ' from as fill
9 ' look`ed from ' as whither ' which ' accord ' your middle`ing in ' as you nigh and
' ye and ' Tabernacle the ' you as similar ' ye ' blemish ' are ye`ing
10 ' and whom do and ' and do`ed you ' so and ' and vessel are ' all ' you as similar
mother`ed and ' and lengthen ' half and ' from extent I ' hate`s ' as tree ' Ark`ing
11 ' and you rise`ing ' half and ' mother`ed and ' and large ' half and '
' outside`ing from and ' you house from ' clean`ing ' gold ' and ye ' whom espy and
12 ' surround`s ' gold ' stranger ' and Mosthigh ' dual`s and ' and has espy you
four I ' on ' set`ed has and ' gold ' you and ring ' four I ' if ' you cast and
' sister the ' and rib ' on ' you and ring ' twosome and ' him you move '
13 ' as alone ' dual`s and ' you two the ' and rib ' on ' you and ring ' twosome and
14 ' ye ' brought the and ' gold ' from ye ' whom espy and ' hate`s ' as tree
' arise of ' Ark`ing the ' you and rib ' on ' you and ring in ' from as alone the
15 ' and became as ' Ark`ing the ' you and ring in ' cattle ' Ark`ing the ' ye
16 ' to ' set`ed has and ' and her from ' and correct`ing ' not ' from as alone the
17 ' dual`s and ' are as to ' donkey ' which ' testimony`ing the ' ye ' Ark`ing the

' the lengthen ' half and ' from extent I ' clean`ing ' gold ' you atone
' from two ' dual`s and ' 18 and large`ed ' half and ' mother`ed and
you coast ' two from ' from ye ' do`ed you ' fashion`ed ' gold ' from as Cherub`ing
victual`ed ' the end from ' one ' mantle`ing ' and do`ed as and ' 19 you atone the '
' you atone the ' has from ' victual`ed ' the end from ' one ' mantle`ing and '
' 20 him you coast ' two ' on ' from as Cherub`ing the ' ye ' and do you
' the above of ' from as wing ' as excrement ' from as Cherub`ing the ' and became and
' man I ' them around and ' you atone the ' on ' them as wing in ' from as veneer
' around ' and became as ' you atone the ' to ' him brother ' one ' to ' one
Ark`ing the ' on ' you atone the ' ye ' set`ed has and ' 21 from as Cherub`ing the
' testimony`ing the ' ye ' has set ' Ark`ing the ' to and ' the above of from '
' there ' walk ' as testimony and shall ' 22 are as to ' donkey ' which
' two ' son`s from ' you atone the ' above ' are ye ' as you word and
' all ' ye ' testimony`ing the ' Ark`ing ' on ' which ' from as Cherub`ing the
' dual`s and ' 23 Israel ' as son ' to ' are ye`ing ' command`ed I ' which
' mother`ed and ' and lengthen ' from extent I ' hate`s ' as tree ' has send
' and ye ' whom espy and ' 24 and you rise`ing ' half and ' mother`ed and ' and large
dual`s and ' 25 surround`s ' gold ' stranger ' if ' dual`s and ' clean`ing ' gold
' gold ' stranger ' dual`s and ' surround`s ' span ' you is fasten ' if '
' you and ring ' four I ' if ' dual`s and ' 26 surround`s ' and you is fasten of
' quarter`ing the ' four I ' on ' you and ring the ' ye ' set`ed has and ' gold
the has became`s you ' you is fasten the ' point of ' 27 him foot ' four I of ' which
' ye ' arise of ' from as alone of ' from house`ly of ' you and ring the '
' hate`s ' as tree ' from as alone the ' ye ' dual`s and ' 28 has send the
' 29 has send the ' ye ' cattle ' and lift shall ' gold ' from ye ' whom espy and

' him you as bowl and ' him you spoon and ' him you dish ' ye ' dual`s and
do`ed you ' clean`ing ' gold ' cattle ' and sculpture ' which ' him you pitcher and
' as before ' inner`s ' fight ' has send the ' on ' set`ed has and ' 30 from ye '
' fashion`ed ' clean`ing ' gold ' you taper`ing ' dual`s and ' 31 continual`s
am is knop ' am hill`s ' am end and ' am soft ' the taper`ing the ' ye ' do`ed you
' from as nest ' six`ed and ' 32 and became as ' her`ed from ' am bud and '
one the ' drain`ed ' the taper`ing ' money ' three`ed ' am drain ' from as spring as
' three`ed ' 33 two the ' drain`ed ' the taper`ing ' money ' three`ed and '
' bud and ' is knop ' one the ' the stalk ' from as nut from ' from as hill`s
' is knop ' one the ' the stalk ' from as nut from ' from as hill`s ' three`ed and
' from as spring became ' from as nest the ' you six of ' do`ed you ' so ' bud and
' from as hill`s ' the four I ' the taper`ing in and ' 34 the taper`ing the ' has from
' two ' under ' is knop and ' 35 am bud and ' am is knop ' from as nut from
' from as nest the ' two ' under ' is knop and ' her`ed from ' from as nest the
' her`ed from ' from as nest the ' two ' under ' is knop and ' her`ed from
36 the taper`ing the ' has from ' from as spring became ' from as nest the ' you six of
' all`ed ' and became as ' her`ed from ' from you and nest and ' them as is knop '
' am you lamp ' ye ' dual`s and ' 37 clean`ing ' gold ' sister ' fashion`ed
' on I ' and light`s the and ' am you lamp ' ye ' whom on`ed the and ' the seven
' gold ' am you and crush from and ' am take from and ' 38 the around ' Obara
' all ' ye and ' ye`ed ' do`ed as you ' clean`ing ' gold ' circle ' 39 clean`ing
' complete as similar in ' do`ed and ' look`ed and ' 40 these`ed ' from vessal are the
blemish ' look`ed from ' ye`ed ' which

' six ' you and have curtain ' ten ' do`ed you ' Tabernacle the ' ye and ' (1
' two ' you have hang`ing and ' has from stony and ' you perfect and ' twist from
' lenghten ' (2 from ye ' do`ed you ' reckon ' do`ed from ' from as Cherub`ing
large and ' cubit`ed ' from as ten and ' eight`ed ' sister the ' the have curtain the
all of ' sister ' mete`ed ' sister the ' the have curtain the ' cubit`ed ' four I '
' you and have curtain the ' five and ' (3 you and have curtain the '
' the sister ' to ' sister ' Woman ' you and connect ' the has became`s you
Woman ' you and connect ' the has became`s you ' you and have curtain the ' five and
' on ' you perfect ' loop`ing of ' dual`s and ' (4 the sister ' to ' sister '
' you connect from in ' the end from in ' sister the ' the have curtain the ' you lip
' the shall end`s the ' the have curtain the ' you lip in ' do`ed you ' so and
' do`ed you ' loop`ing of ' from as five ' (5 you two the ' you connect from in
' do`ed you ' loop`ing of ' from as five and ' sister the ' the have curtain in
' you two the ' you connect from in ' which ' the have curtain the ' the end in
' (6 the sister ' to ' sister ' Woman ' loop`ing of the ' you and front`s from
' ye ' you connect and ' gold ' as pin ' from as five ' dual`s and
' from as pin in ' the sister ' to ' sister ' Woman ' you and have curtain the
from as Goat ' you and have curtain ' dual`s and ' (7 one ' Tabernacle the ' be`s and
' you and have curtain ' ten`ed ' as you do ' Tabernacle the ' on ' tent of '
' from as three ' sister the ' the have curtain the ' lenghten ' (8 from ye ' do`ed you
' sister the ' the have curtain the ' large ' you and cubit`ed ' four I and ' cubit`ed
you connect and ' (9 you and have curtain the ' ten`ed ' as dual of ' sister ' mete`ed
' six ' ye and ' earnest ' you and have curtain the ' five ' ye '
' the have curtain the ' ye ' you fold and ' earnest ' you and have curtain the
' loop`ing of ' dual`s and ' (10 tent the ' around ' split`ing ' to ' whom six the

the shall end`s the ’ sister the ’ the have curtain the ’ you lip ’ on ’ from as five
’ you lip ’ on ’ do`ed you ’ loop`ing of ’ from as five and ’ you connect from in ’
’ as pin ’ dual`s and ’ (11 you two the ’ you connect the ’ the have curtain the
loop`ing of in ’ from as pin the ’ ye ’ brought the and ’ from as five ’ copper has
surplus the ’ exceed and ’ (12 one ’ be`s and ’ tent the ’ ye ’ you connect and ’
’ the have curtain the ’ as outside ’ tent the ’ you and have curtain in ’
’ maid`ed and ’ (13 Tabernacle the ’ as after ’ on I ’ exceed you ’ you surplus the
’ lengthen in ’ surplus in ’ victual`ed ’ maid`ed and ’ victual`ed
Tabernacle the ’ sidle ’ on ’ exceed`ing ’ be`s as ’ tent the ’ you and have curtain
’ conceal`ed from ’ dual`s and ’ (14 and garment`ing of ’ victual`ed and ’ victual`ed ’
’ conceal`ed from and ’ from as ground from ’ from as Ram`s ’ ing`skin`ing ’ tent of
’ ye ’ dual`s and ’ (15 the above of from ’ from as badger ’ ing`skin`ing
’ ten ’ (16 from as stand ’ hate`s ’ as tree ’ Tabernacle of ’ from as board the
’ half and ’ mother`ed and ’ one the ’ board the ’ lenghten ’ faithful`ing
’ board of ’ esteem`ing ’ twosome ’ (17 one the ’ board the ’ large ’ mother`ed the
’ so ’ the sister ’ to ’ sister ’ Woman ’ you and interval from ’ one the
’ ye ’ dual`s and ’ (18 Tabernacle the ’ as board ’ all of ’ do`ed you
’ quarter of ’ from as board ’ from as ten ’ Tabernacle of ’ from as board the
’ do`ed you ’ silver ’ as master ’ from as four I and ’ (19 right`ed you ’ south`ed
’ board the ’ under ’ from as master ’ two ’ from as board the ’ from as ten ’ under
’ board the ’ under ’ from as master ’ two and ’ him stake as ’ twosome of ’ one the
’ you two the ’ Tabernacle the ’ rib of and ’ (20 him stake as ’ twosome of ’ one the
’ (21 from as board ’ from as ten ’ do`ed you ’ the north`ing ’ quarter of
’ under ’ from as master ’ two ’ silver ’ them as master ’ from as four I and
’ (22 one the ’ board the ’ under ’ from as master ’ two and ’ one the ’ board the

(23 ' from as board ' six`ed ' do`ed you ' sea`ed ' Tabernacle the ' as you soft of and
' Tabernacle the ' you and corner from of ' do`ed you ' from as board ' two and
(24 ' below`ed from ' from as twin ' and became as and ' from as you soft in
you ring the ' to ' and head ' on I ' from as twin ' and became as ' and alike and
' you and corner them ' two of ' them two of ' be`s as ' so ' sister the '
(25 ' them as master and ' from as board ' eight`ed ' and became and ' and became as
board the ' under ' from as master ' two ' from as master ' ten ' six`ed ' silver
(26 dual`s and ' one the ' board the of ' under ' from as master ' two and ' one the '
' rib ' as board of ' the five ' hate`s ' as tree ' from as shoot`s '
(27 ' rib ' as board of ' from as shoot`s ' the five and ' one the ' Tabernacle the
' rib ' as board of ' from as shoot`s ' the five and ' you two the ' Tabernacle the
(28 column`ing sacred ' shoot`s the and ' sea`ed ' from as you soft of ' Tabernacle the
' to ' end`ed ' has from ' shoot`s from ' from as board the ' middle`ing in '
(29 ' ye and ' gold ' the espy you ' from as board the ' ye and ' end`ed
' from as shoot`s of ' integrity`s ' gold ' do`ed you ' them as you ring
(30 ' ye ' you rise the and ' gold ' from as shoot`s the ' ye ' whom espy and
(31 ' blemish ' whom look the ' which ' and discern from are ' Tabernacle the
' you have hang`ing and ' has from stony and ' you perfect ' veil put ' dual`s and
' ye`ed ' and do`ed as ' reckon ' do`ed from ' twist from ' six and ' two
(32 ' as stand`ing ' the four I ' on ' ye`ed ' set`ed has and ' from as Cherub`ing
' the four I ' on ' gold ' them as hook ' gold ' from as espy from ' hate`s
(33 from as pin the ' under ' veil put the ' ye ' set`ed has and ' silver ' as master
' Ark`ing ' ye ' veil put of ' you house from ' there`ed ' brought the and '
' between in ' relate ' veil put the ' the separate`s the and ' testimony`ing the
(34 ' ye ' set`ed has and ' from as holy the ' holy ' between in and ' holy the

35 ' from as holy the ' holy in ' testimony`ing the ' Ark`ing ' on ' you atone the
' ye and ' veil put of ' outside`ing from ' has send the ' ye ' herein and
' Tabernacle the ' rib ' soft ' on ' has send the ' behalf ' the taper`ing the
' the north`ing ' rib ' on ' has set ' has send the ' ye and ' right`ed you
' hate`s ' as tree ' you perfume ' perfume`s from ' sacrifice from ' dual`s and
four`ing ' and large ' mother`ed and ' and lengthen ' mother`ed ' and ye ' do`ed you
' him you horn ' and her from ' and you rise`ing ' from as you mother and ' be`s as '
him net stedfast ' ye and ' nail ' ye ' clean`ing ' gold ' and ye ' whom espy and
' gold ' stranger ' if ' dual`s and ' him you horn ' ye and ' surround`s '
' under from ' if ' do`ed you ' gold ' you and ring ' twosome and ' surround`s
' and sidle ' two ' on ' do`ed you ' him you rib ' twosome ' on ' and stranger of
' cattle ' and ye ' arise of ' from as alone of ' from house`ly of ' and became and
from ye ' whom espy and ' 36 hate`s ' as tree ' from as alone the ' ye ' dual`s and
Ark`ing ' on ' which ' veil put the ' as before ' and ye ' set`ed has and ' gold '
' perfume`s the and ' there`ed ' walk ' season I ' which ' testimony`ing the '
' is morn in ' is morn in ' from as aroma ' you perfume ' Aaron ' and Mosthigh
' and has perfume`s as ' you and lamp the ' ye ' and good`s the in
' between in ' you and lamp the ' ye ' Aaron ' offer`ing the in and
' as before ' continual`s ' you perfume ' the has perfume`s as ' from as twilight the
' you perfume ' and Mosthigh ' lug you ' not ' from are as generation of ' Jehovah
' and crowd you ' not ' libation and ' bestow`ed and ' on`ed and ' stranger`ed
' Year`ed in ' sister ' him you horn ' on ' Aaron ' atone and ' and Mosthigh
' atone as ' Year`ed in ' sister ' from as atone`ing the ' you sin ' blood from
' that`ing ' from as holy ' holy ' from are as generation of ' and Mosthigh
' you perfect ' tent the ' open of ' castimage ' dual`s and ' Jehovah of

do`ed from ' twist from ' six and ' two ' you have hang`ing and ' has from stony and

' hate`s ' as stand`ing ' the five ' castimage of ' dual`s and ' 37 fabricate '

' you cast and ' gold ' them as hook ' clean`ing ' gold ' from ye ' whom espy and

copper has ' as master ' the five ' them of

' faithful`ing ' five ' hate`s ' as tree ' sacrifice them ' ye ' dual`s and ' 1
' sacrifice them ' be`s as ' four`ing ' large ' faithful`ing ' five and ' lenghten
' on ' him you horn ' dual`s and ' 2 and you rise`ing ' faithful`ing ' three and
' him you horn ' the has became`s you ' and her from ' him angle ' four I
' and has cinder ' and as urn had ' dual`s and ' 3 copper has ' and ye ' whom espy and
' and as you clasp from and ' and as you sprinkle from and ' and as shovel and
' 4 copper has ' do`ed you ' and vessel are ' all of ' and as you as wipe and
on ' dual`s and ' copper has ' net`ness ' do`ed from ' sieve from ' if ' dual`s and
him you coast ' four I ' on ' copper has ' you and ring ' four I ' net`ness the '
' below`ed from ' sacrifice them ' ride are ' under ' ye`ed ' set`ed has and ' 5
' dual`s and ' 6 sacrifice them ' as outside ' till ' net`ness the ' whom`ed the and
' whom espy and ' hate`s ' as tree ' as alone ' sacrifice from of ' from as alone
' you and ring in ' him alone the ' ye ' brought alas and ' 7 copper has ' from ye
' sacrifice them ' you and rib ' twosome ' on ' from as alone the ' and became and
' which are ' and ye ' do`ed you ' ing`tablet`ing ' hollow`ing ' 8 and ye ' arise in
' yard ' ye ' dual`s and ' 9 and do as ' so and ' blemish ' are ye ' look`ed the
six ' yard of ' from as sling ' right`ed you ' south`ed ' quarter of ' Tabernacle the
' 10 sister the ' thither`ed of ' lenghten ' cubit`ed ' hundred`ed ' twist from '
' copper has ' from as ten ' them as master and ' from as ten ' and as stand`ing and
' so and ' 11 silver ' them as delight and ' from as stand the ' them as hook
' cubit`ed ' hundred`ed ' from as sling ' lengthen in ' the north`ing ' quarter of
' from as ten ' them as master and ' from as ten ' them as stand`ing and ' lenghten
' 12 silver ' them as delight and ' from as stand the ' them as hook ' copper has
mother`ed ' from as five ' from as sling ' sea`ed ' quarter of ' yard the ' large and
' large and ' 13 copper has ' ten`ed ' them as master and ' ten`ed ' them as stand '

14 ' mother`ed ' from as five ' emerge`ed from ' east`ed ' quarter of ' yard the
' them as stand`s ' shoulder of ' from as sling ' mother`ed ' ten`ed ' five and
' shoulder of and ' 15 copper has ' three`ed ' them as master and ' three`ed
three`ed ' them as stand`s ' from as sling ' mother`ed ' ten`ed ' five ' you two the
' castimage ' yard the ' gate of and ' 16 copper has ' three`ed ' them as master and '
' you have hang`ing and ' has from stony and ' you perfect ' mother`ed ' from as ten
' them as stand`ing and ' fabricate ' do`ed from ' twist from ' six and ' two
' as stand`ing ' all ' 17 copper has ' the four I ' them as master and ' the four I
' silver ' them as hook ' silver ' from as delight from ' surround`s ' yard the
' cubit`ed ' hundred`ed ' yard the ' lenghten ' 18 copper has ' them as master and
' faithful`ing ' five ' the rise`ing and ' from as five in ' from as five ' large and
' all of ' ye ' dual`s and ' 19 copper has ' them as master and ' twist from ' six
all and ' him stake as ' all in and ' and you serve ' all in ' Tabernacle the ' weapon
' you perfect ' as fabric ' dual`s and ' copper has ' yard the ' stake as '
20 holy in ' cattle ' minister of ' two ' you have hang`ing and ' has from stony and
' are as to ' acquire as and ' Israel ' as son ' ye ' command`ed you ' ye`ed and '
lamp ' offer`ing the of ' light`ing from of ' set`s are ' remember ' olivet`s ' eight
' which ' veil put of ' outside`ing from ' ing congregate ' tent in ' 21 continual`s '
' twilight from ' him son and ' Aaron ' and ye ' pile as ' testimony`ing the ' on
from are as generation of ' from on`ing ' statute ' Jehovah ' as before ' herd ' till
Israel ' as son ' each '

1 ' ye and ' are as brother ' Aaron ' ye ' are as to ' approach the ' ye`ed and '
' vessel ' and priest of ' Israel ' as son ' middle`ing from ' and ye ' him son
2 ' Aaron ' as son ' Ithamar and ' Eleazar ' Abihu and ' freewill ' Aaron
' honour`ing of ' are as brother ' Aaron of ' holy ' as fabric ' dual`s and
3 which ' heart ' as wise ' all ' to ' word you ' ye`ed and ' you is renown of and
' Aaron ' as fabric ' ye ' concoct and ' wise`ed ' spirit is ' him you fill '
4 ' which ' from as fabric the ' to`ed and ' vessel ' and priest of ' and holy of
' embroider you ' you coat and ' of rode and ' gird`ing and ' pocket ' shall do as
' Aaron of ' holy ' as fabric ' concoct and ' belt`s I and ' you turban from
5 ' and took as ' them and ' vessel ' and priest of ' him son of and ' are as brother
' ye and ' has from stony the ' ye and ' you prefect the ' ye and ' gold the ' ye
6 ' ye ' concoct and ' six the ' ye and ' two the ' you have hang`ing the
' you have hang`ing and ' has from stony and ' you perfect ' gold ' gird`ing the
7 ' you and shoulder ' twosome ' reckon ' do`ed from ' twist from ' six and ' two
8 ' connect as and ' him you coast ' two ' on I ' if ' be`s as ' you and connect
' and her from ' and work`ed are ' and Mosthigh ' which ' and you gird ' reckon and
' two ' you have hang`ing and ' has from stony and ' you perfect ' gold ' be`s as
9 ' onyx the ' as stone ' twosome ' ye ' you take and ' twist from ' six and
10 ' six`ed ' Israel ' as son ' you name ' ye ' them as on ' you open and
' six`ed the ' you name ' ye and ' sister the ' stone the ' on ' from you name from
11 ' from you bore mark are ' you two the ' stone the ' on ' from as survive has the
' twosome ' ye ' open you ' ing`signet ' as open`ing ' stone ' devise ' do`ed from
' you and ing`arrange ' Israel ' as son ' you name ' on ' from as stone the
12 twosome ' ye ' herein and ' from ye ' do`ed you ' gold ' you and embroider from
' as stone ' gird`ing the ' you and shoulder ' on ' from as stone the '

' ye ' Aaron ' help and ' Israel ' as son of ' be`th ' shall is remember
' him you shoulder ' twosome ' on ' Jehovah ' as before ' from you name
twosome and ' (14 gold ' you and embroider from ' dual`s and ' (13 shall is remember of
' from ye ' do`ed you ' you and border from ' clean`ing ' gold ' you and is root '
' you and wrap the ' you and is root ' ye ' set`ed has and ' wrap`ing ' do`ed from
' do`ed from ' discern from ' pocket ' dual`s and ' (15 you and embroider them ' on
' you perfect ' gold ' our do you ' gird`ing the ' work`ed are ' reckon
do`ed you ' twist from ' six and ' two ' you have hang`ing and ' has from stony and
' span and ' and lengthen ' span ' made`ing are ' be`s as ' four`ing ' (16 and ye '
from as row`ing ' the four I ' stone ' you fill ' and in ' you fill and ' (17 and large
' (18 one the ' row`ing the ' carbuncle and ' the topaz ' ground ' row`ing ' stone '
row`ing the and ' (19 from diamond and ' report`s ' emerald ' two the ' row`ing the and
' row`ing the and ' (20 dream`ed I and ' sparkle ' Jacinth ' as three`s the '
' you and ing`arrange ' lip`ed as and ' onyx and ' beryl`s you ' as four`s the
' (21 from ye and split in ' and became as ' gold ' you and from as embroider from
' Israel ' as son ' you name ' on ' the has became`s you ' from as stone the and
on ' man I ' ing`signet ' as open`ing ' from you name ' on ' ten`ed ' from twosome
' on ' dual`s and ' (22 tribe ' ten ' from two of ' the has became`s you ' name '
' gold ' wrap`ing ' do`ed from ' you and border ' you and is root ' pocket the
' you and embroider from ' twosome ' pocket the ' on ' dual`s and ' (23 clean`ing
' twosome ' ye ' set`ed has and ' gold ' you and ring ' twosome and ' gold
' ye ' set`ed has and ' (24 pocket the ' you coast ' two ' on ' you and ring the
' on I ' you and ring the ' twosome ' on ' gold the ' you and wrap ' twosome
' twosome ' you coast the ' twosome ' ye and ' (25 pocket the ' you coast
' set`ed has and ' you and embroider them ' twosome ' on ' has set ' you and wrap the

' dual`s and ' 26 him turn ' split`ing ' to ' gird`ing the ' you and shoulder ' on
' you coast ' two ' on ' from ye ' herein and ' gold ' you and ring ' twosome
' gird`ing the ' connect ' Obara ' on I ' which ' and you lip ' on ' pocket the
' from ye ' set`ed has and ' gold ' you and ring ' twosome ' dual`s and ' 27 he house
' split`ing from ' below`ed from ' gird`ing the ' you and shoulder ' twosome ' on
28 gird`ing the ' reckon of ' above from ' and you connect from ' point of ' him turn
' you ring ' to ' and you ring from ' pocket the ' ye ' and attach as and '
' reckon ' on ' you and became of ' you perfect ' lace`s in ' gird`ing the
' help and ' 29 gird`ing the ' above ' pocket the ' shove as ' not and ' gird`ing the
' on ' discern them ' pocket in ' Israel ' as son ' you name ' ye ' Aaron
Jehovah ' as before ' shall is remember of ' holy the ' to ' and came in ' and heart
' ye and ' from as light`ing the ' ye ' dual`s and ' the continual`s '
' ye ' discern them ' pocket ' to ' set`ed has and ' 30 from as complete the
' heart ' on ' and became and ' from as complete the ' ye and ' from as light`ing the
discern from ' ye ' Aaron ' help and ' Jehovah ' as before ' and came in ' Aaron
' 31 the continual`s ' Jehovah ' as before ' and heart ' on ' Israel ' as son '
be`s and ' 32 you perfect ' of vessal are ' gird`ing the ' above`s ' ye ' dual`s and
' surround`s ' and edge of ' be`s as ' lip`ed ' and middle`ing in ' and head ' edge '
' 33 rend as ' not ' if ' be`s as ' I corselet`ed ' as palm ' stony ' do`ed from
has from stony and ' you perfect ' as pomegranate`ing ' and hem too ' on ' dual`s and
' and hem too ' on ' twist from ' six and ' two ' you have hang`ing and '
' 34 surround`s ' from middle`ing in ' gold ' as bell`ing put and ' surround`s
' gold ' bell`ing put ' pomegranate`ing and ' gold ' bell`ing put
' be`s and ' 35 surround`s ' above`s the ' as peace`ing ' on ' pomegranate`ing and
' to ' and came in ' and voice`ing ' hear has and ' minister of ' Aaron ' on

36 ' die`ing as ' not and ' and you issue in and ' Jehovah ' as before ' holy the
as open`ing ' and Mosthigh ' you open and ' clean`ing ' gold ' flower`s ' dual`s and
37 ' lace`s ' on ' and ye ' herein and ' Jehovah of ' holy ' ing`signet '
' around ' split`ing ' to ' you turban them ' on ' be`s and ' you perfect
38 ' Aaron ' help and ' Aaron ' brow ' on ' be`s and ' be`s as ' you turban them
' Israel ' as son ' and holy`s as ' which ' from as holy the ' low`ing ' ye
' continual`s ' and brow ' on ' be`s and ' them as holy ' you and present ' all of
39 ' you coat the ' you embroider and ' Jehovah ' as before ' them of ' accept`ing of
' do`ed from ' do`ed you ' belt`s I and ' six ' you turban from ' dual`s and ' six
40 ' dual`s and ' you and coat ' do`ed you ' Aaron ' as son of and ' fabricate
' them of ' do`ed you ' you and have bonnet and ' from as belt`s I ' them of
41 ' Aaron ' ye ' from ye ' you arm the and ' you is renown of and ' honour`ing of
you fill and ' from ye ' you anoint and ' and ye ' him son ' ye and ' are as brother
42 ' do`ed and ' vessel ' and priest and ' from ye ' you holy and ' energy ' ye '
' nake`ed ' flesh ' you and conceal of ' alone ' as breeche from ' them of
43 on ' and became and ' and became as ' from as soft ' till and ' from as give they
' or ' ing`congregate ' tent ' to ' from came in ' him son ' on and ' Aaron '
and linger ' not and ' holy in ' minister of ' sacrifice them ' to ' from accost in
him after ' and seed of and ' if ' from on`ing ' statute ' and die and ' low`ing '

' from ye ' holy of ' them of ' do`ed you ' which ' word the ' this and ' 1

' from as Ram`s and ' herd ' son ' one ' apart ' took of ' vessel ' priest of

' unleaven`ing ' cake`ing and ' unleaven`ing ' from bread and ' 2 they full ' from two

' from as anoint ' unleaven`ing ' as slim`s and ' eight in ' you and mingle`ing

' set`ed has and ' 3 from ye ' do`ed you ' from as wheat ' flour ' eight in

' exult in ' from ye ' you approach the and ' one ' exalt ' on ' from ye`ing

' ye and ' Aaron ' ye and ' 4 from as Ram`s the ' two ' ye and ' broken ' ye and

' you wash and ' ing`congregate ' tent ' open ' to ' approach`s you ' him son

' you arm the and ' from as fabric the ' ye ' you take and ' 5 Water in ' from ye

' belt`s I ' and ye ' you retain and ' you coat the ' ye ' Aaron ' ye

' set`ed has and ' gird the ' above`s the ' ye and ' ' and ye ' you arm the and

' if ' you gird and ' pocket the ' ye and ' gird`ing the ' ye and ' and Mosthigh

' and head ' on ' you turban them ' herein and ' 6 gird`ing the ' reckon in

' 7 you turban them ' on ' holy the ' consecrate ' ye ' set`ed has and

' and head ' on ' you cast and ' anoint`ed the ' eight ' ye ' you take and

' from you arm the and ' approach`s you ' him son ' ye and ' 8 and ye ' you anoint and

' him son and ' Aaron ' from as belt`s I ' from ye ' you retain and ' 9 you and coat

priest`ed ' them of ' whom`ed the and ' you and have bonnet ' them of ' you saddle and

' 10 him son ' friend`s ' Aaron ' hand ' you fill and ' from on`ing ' statute of '

' tent ' open ' Jehovah ' as before ' broken ' ye ' you approach the and

head ' on ' them as hand ' ye ' him son and ' Aaron ' laid and ' ing`congregate

' tent ' open ' Jehovah ' as before ' broken ' ye ' you slay and ' 11 broken '

' on ' set`ed has and ' broken ' blood from ' you take and ' 12 ing`congregate

pour you ' blood the ' all ' ye and ' are finger came ' sacrifice them ' you and horn

' milk the ' all ' ye ' you take and ' 13 sacrifice them ' position`ing ' to '

' honour the ' on ' you perserve the ' ye and ' approach the ' ye ' amount`ed the
' behold as on ' which ' milk the ' ye and ' whom`ing total ' twosome ' ye and
' ye and ' broken ' flesh ' ye and ' 14 the sacrifice them ' you perfume the and
' outside`ing from ' abhorrence ' burnt you ' and excrement ' ye and ' and town`ing
' implicate ' one the ' Ram`s the ' ye and ' 15 that`s ' you sin ' camp`ed of
Ram`s the ' head ' on ' them as hand ' ye ' him son and ' Aaron ' and laid and
' and blood ' ye ' you take and ' Ram`s the ' ye ' you slay and ' 16
' Ram`s the ' ye and ' 17 surround`s ' sacrifice them ' on ' you sprinkle and
' him leg and ' and approach ' you wash and ' him dismember of ' dismember you
' you perfume the and ' 18 and head ' on and ' him dismenber ' on ' set`ed has and
smell`s ' Jehovah of ' that`ing ' on`ed ' the sacrifice them ' Ram`s the ' all ' ye
' Ram`s the ' ye ' you take and ' 19 Jehovah of ' that`ing ' Woman ' odor`ing has '
' head ' on ' them as hand ' ye ' him son and ' Aaron ' laid and ' two the
' and blood from ' you take and ' Ram`s the ' ye ' you slay and ' 20 Ram`s the
him son ' ear ' tip`ing ' on and ' Aaron ' ear ' tip`ing ' on ' set`ed has and
' on and ' whom right`s the ' energy ' thick`ing ' on and ' whom right`s the '
on ' blood the ' ye ' you sprinkle and ' whom right`s the ' from foot ' thick`ing
' anoint`ed the ' eight from ' you take and ' 21 surround`s ' sacrifice them '
' eight from and ' sacrifice them ' on ' which ' blood the ' has from and
' on and ' him fabric ' on and ' Aaron ' on ' olivet`s the and ' anoint`ed the
' that`ing ' and you holy and ' and ye ' him son ' as fabric ' on and ' him son
' 22 and ye ' him son ' as fabric ' ye and ' him son ' ye and ' him fabric ' ye and
' ye and ' rump`ed the and ' ye ' milk the ' Ram`s the ' has from ' you take and
' you ing`preserve ' ye and ' approach the ' ye ' amount`ed the ' milk the
' which ' milk the ' ye and ' whom`ing total ' twosome ' ye and ' honour the

’ from as fill ’ Ram`s ’ for ’ right`s the ’ moisten`ing ’ ye and ’ behold as on
’ sister ’ eight ’ fight ’ cake and ’ sister ’ fight ’ circle and ’ 23 that`ing
’ 24 Jehovah ’ as before ’ which ’ unleaven`ing the ’ path ’ one ’ slim`s and
’ him son ’ as palm ’ on and ’ Aaron ’ as palm ’ on ’ total ’ herein and
you take and ’ 25 Jehovah ’ as before ’ the wave`ing you ’ from ye ’ you wave the and
’ on ’ the sacrifice them ’ you perfume the and ’ from hand from ’ from ye ’
’ that`ing ’ Woman ’ Jehovah ’ as before ’ odor`ing has ’ smell`s of ’ on`ed the
’ from as fill the ’ Ram`s from ’ vision`ed the ’ ye ’ you take and ’ 26 Jehovah of
’ as before ’ the wave`ing you ’ and ye ’ you wave the and ’ Aaron of ’ which from
’ vision`ed ’ ye ’ you holy and ’ 27 widow`ed ’ walk ’ be`s and ’ Jehovah
wave alas ’ which ’ the oblation`ing the ’ moisten`ing ’ ye and ’ the wave`ing scared
’ Aaron of ’ which from ’ from as fill the ’ Ram`s from ’ residue the ’ which and ’
’ law of ’ him son of and ’ Aaron of ’ be`s and ’ 28 him son of ’ which from and
’ that`ing ’ the oblation`ing ’ for ’ Israel ’ as son ’ each ’ from on`ing
’ as sacrifice from ’ Israel ’ as son ’ each ’ be`s as ’ the oblation`ing and
’ holy the ’ as fabric and ’ 29 Jehovah of ’ from you oblation`ing ’ them as whole
’ cattle ’ anoint`ed of ’ him after ’ him son of ’ and became as ’ Aaron of ’ which
’ from arm as ’ from week ’ you seven ’ 30 energy ’ ye ’ height ’ fill of and
’ tent ’ to ’ came`ing as ’ which ’ him son from ’ him under ’ priest the
’ from as fill the ’ Ram`s ’ ye and ’ 31 holy in ’ minister of ’ ing`congregate
eat and ’ 32 holy`ing ’ place`ing in ’ and flesh ’ ye ’ you sodden and ’ implicate
’ which ’ fight the ’ ye and ’ Ram`s the ’ flesh ’ ye ’ him son and ’ Aaron ’
’ atone ’ which ’ from ye ’ and eat and ’ 33 ing`congregate ’ tent ’ open ’ exult in
’ not ’ stranger and ’ from ye ’ holy of ’ energy ’ ye ’ height ’ fill of ’ cattle
’ flesh from ’ survive as ’ mother and ’ 34 them ’ holy ’ for ’ eat as

ye ' you burnt and ' herd the ' till ' fight the ' has from and ' from as fill the

dual`s and ' 35 that`ing ' holy ' for ' eat as ' not ' abhorrence ' survive behold '

' here ye ' as whom command ' which ' accord ' star`ed ' him son of and ' Aaron of '

' you sin ' Bullock and ' 36 energy ' ye ' fill you ' from week ' you seven

' on ' you sin and ' from as atone`ing the ' on ' day as of ' do`ed you

and holy of ' and ye ' you anoint and ' and Mosthigh ' are atone in ' sacrifice them

and ye ' you holy and ' sacrifice them ' on ' atone you ' from week ' you seven ' 37

' touch the ' all ' from as holy ' holy ' sacrifice them ' be`s and '

sacrifice them ' on ' do`ed you ' which ' this and ' 38 holy as ' sacrifice from in

' offer ' continual`s ' day as of ' from two ' the Year ' as son ' from as mutton '

' ye and ' is morn in ' do`ed you ' one the ' mutton the ' ye ' 39 continual`s

' 40 from as twilight the ' between in ' do`ed you ' two the ' mutton the

' hin`s ' whom four`s ' set`s are ' eight in ' mingle`ing ' flour ' has and ten and

' ye and ' 41 one the ' mutton of ' between`s ' hin`s ' whom four`s ' libation and

you bestrow are ' from as twilight the ' between in ' do`ed you ' two the ' mutton the

odor has ' smell`s of ' and nihil ' do`ed you ' him the libation are and ' herd the '

' open ' from are as generation of ' continual`s ' offer ' 42 Jehovah of ' Woman '

there`ed ' relate ' season I ' which ' Jehovah ' as before ' ing`congregate ' tent

' as testimony has and ' as you search has and ' 43 there ' are as to ' word of '

' 44 as honour`ing in ' and holy has and ' Israel ' as son of ' there`ed

' ye and ' sacrifice them ' ye and ' ing`congregate ' tent ' ye ' as you holy and

' as you nigh and ' 45 vessel ' priest of ' holy I ' him son ' ye and ' Aaron

46 from as Allah of ' them of ' as whom became and ' Israel ' as son ' middle`ing in

' which ' them as Allah ' Jehovah ' as whither ' for ' and known and '

' as nigh of ' from as Mizra ' land from ' from ye ' as you issue alas them as Allah ' Jehovah ' as whither ' from middle`ing in

' hate`s ' as tree ' you perfume ' prefume from ' sacrifice from ' dual`s and ' 1
four`ing ' and large ' mother`ed and ' and lengthen ' mother`ed ' 2 and ye ' do`ed you
' 3 him you horn ' and her from ' and tall ' from as you mother and ' be`s as '
him net stedfast ' ye and ' nail ' ye ' clean`ing ' gold ' and ye ' whom espy and
' gold ' stranger ' if ' dual`s and ' him you horn ' ye and ' surround`s '
' under from ' if ' do`ed you ' gold ' you ring ' twosome and ' 4 surround`s
' and sidle ' two ' on ' do`ed you ' him you rib ' twosome ' on ' and stranger of
' 5 cattle`ed ' and ye ' arise of ' from as alone of ' from house`ly of ' be`s and
' from ye ' whom espy and ' hate`s ' as tree ' from as alone the ' ye ' dual`s and
' Ark ' on ' which ' veil put the ' as before ' and ye ' set`ed has and ' 6 gold
' which ' testimony the ' on ' which ' you atone the ' as before ' testimony the
' Aaron ' and Mosthigh ' perfume`s the and ' 7 there`ed ' walk ' season I
' ye ' and good`s became in ' is morn in ' is morn in ' from as aroma ' you perfume
you lamp the ' ye ' Aaron ' offer thus and ' 8 the has perfume`s as ' you lamp the
continual`s ' you perfume ' the has perfume`s as ' from as twilight the ' between in '
' and Mosthigh ' lug you ' not ' 9 from are as generation of ' Jehovah ' as before '
' not ' libation and ' bestow`ed and ' on`ed and ' stranger`ed ' you perfume
' sister ' him you horn ' on ' Aaron ' atone and ' 10 and Mosthigh ' and crowd you
atone as ' Year`ed in ' sister ' from as atone the ' you sin ' blood from ' Year`ed in
' that`ing ' from as holy ' holy ' from are as generation of ' and Mosthigh '
' lift you ' for ' 12 say of ' Moses ' to ' Jehovah ' word as and ' 11 Jehovah of
' man I ' and gave and ' them as my appoint of ' Israel ' as son ' head ' ye
' be`s as ' not and ' from ye ' my appoint in ' Jehovah of ' and soul ' ing atone
' cross the ' all ' and give as ' this ' 13 from ye ' my appoint in ' defeat ' cattle
' holy the ' weigh in ' weigh the ' you half from ' from as my appoint the ' on

you half from ' weigh the ' that`ing ' guest`ed ' from as ten ' holy the ' weigh and
' on ' cross the ' all ' 14 Jehovah of ' the oblation`ing ' weigh the '
' above`ed and ' the Year ' from as ten ' son from ' from as my appoint the
increase`ed as ' not ' ten`s the ' 15 Jehovah ' you oblation`ing ' ye ' and give as
' ye ' set of ' weigh the ' whom outside they ' less`s as ' not ' weak the and '
' you take and ' 16 from are as you soul ' on ' atone of ' Jehovah ' you oblation`ing
' set`ed has and ' Israel ' as son ' each ' from as atone`ing the ' silver ' ye
' Israel ' as son of ' be`s and ' ing`congregate ' tent ' you serve ' on ' and ye
17 from are as you soul ' on ' atone of ' Jehovah ' as before ' shall is remember of
' Laver`ing ' dual`s and ' 18 say of ' Moses ' to ' Jehovah ' word as and '
' and ye ' set`ed has and ' the wash of ' copper has ' and so and ' copper has
set`ed has and ' sacrifice them ' between in and ' ing`congregate ' tent ' between in
' ye ' him son and ' Aaron ' and her from ' and wash and ' 19 Water ' there`ed '
ing`congregate ' tent ' to ' from came in ' 20 them as foot ' ye and ' them as hand
' to ' from accost in ' or ' and die`ing as ' not and ' Water ' and wash as '
and wash and ' 21 Jehovah of ' Woman ' perfume`s the of ' minister of ' sacrifice them
' whom`ed the and ' and die`ing as ' not and ' them as foot and ' them as hand '
' 22 from ing`generation of ' and seed of and ' if ' from on`ing ' statute ' them of
' walk ' took ' ye`ed and ' 23 say of ' Moses ' to ' Jehovah ' word as and
has and cinnamon and ' you and hundred ' five ' pure`ing Myrrh ' head ' heaven`s in
' the nest and ' from as you hundred and ' from as five ' and whom smash ' spice '
' five ' stoop`ed and ' 24 from as you hundred and ' from as five ' spice
' 25 behold's ' olivet`s ' eight and ' holy the ' weigh in ' you and hundred
' you ointment from ' ointment ' holy ' you anoint ' eight ' and ye ' dual`s and
' you anoint and ' 26 be`s as ' holy ' you anoint ' eight ' ointment ' do`ed from

’ 27 testimony`ing the ’ Ark`ing ’ ye and ’ ing`congregate ’ tent ’ ye ’ and in
’ the taper`ing the ’ ye and ’ and vessel are ’ all ’ ye and ’ has send the ’ ye and
’ ye and ’ 28 you perfume the ’ sacrifice from ’ ye and ’ vessel`ed are ’ all ’ ye and
’ Laver`ing the ’ ye and ’ and vessel are ’ all ’ ye and ’ on`ed the ’ sacrifice from
’ from as holy ’ holy ’ and became and ’ from ye ’ you holy and ’ 29 and so ’ ye and
’ him son ’ ye and ’ Aaron ’ ye and ’ 30 holy as ’ cattle ’ touch the ’ all
’ as son ’ to and ’ 31 vessel ’ priest of ’ from ye ’ you holy and ’ anoint you
vessel ’ this ’ be`s as ’ holy ’ you anoint ’ eight ’ say of ’ word you ’ Israel
’ ing`sculpture ’ not ’ ground ’ flesh ’ on ’ 32 from are as generation of ’
’ that`ing ’ holy ’ and your`ed ’ and do you ’ not ’ and you equal from in and
’ and your`ed ’ ointment as ’ which ’ man I ’ 33 relate ’ be`s as ’ holy and
’ you foreign and ’ stranger ’ on ’ and her from ’ permanent ’ which and
from as aroma ’ walk ’ took ’ Moses ’ to ’ Jehovah ’ say as and ’ 34 him people from
’ the white`ing and ’ from as aroma ’ am has milk and ’ you roar and ’ prophesy ’
’ you perfume ’ ye`ed ’ dual`s and ’ 35 be`s as ’ alone in ’ alone ’ remember`ed
’ 36 holy ’ clean`ing ’ you salt from ’ ing`ointment ’ do`ed from ’ ointment
’ as before ’ and numb`ed ’ set`ed has and ’ eminent ’ and numb`ed ’ you sky and
’ there`ed ’ walk ’ season I ’ which ’ ing`congregate ’ tent in ’ testimony`ing the
do`ed you ’ which ’ you perfume the and ’ 37 relate ’ be`s you ’ from as holy ’ holy
’ relate ’ be`s you ’ holy ’ relate ’ and do you ’ not ’ the you equal from in ’
’ thus ’ smell`s the of ’ like`ed ’ success`ed ’ which ’ man I ’ 38 Jehovah of
him people from ’ you foreign and

THE TORAH SCROLL 31

Ex 31:1-31:15

spice ' as you call ' look`ed ' 2 say of ' Moses ' to ' Jehovah ' word as and ' 1
' 3 Judah ' below`ed ' hole`ing ' son ' as light`ing ' son ' Bezaleel '
the similar`ing in and ' the wise in ' from as Allah ' spirit is ' and ye ' fill I and
' you reckon from ' reckon of and ' 4 the are fill ' all in and ' knowledge in and '
' you devise in and ' 5 copper has in and ' silver in and ' gold in ' you concoct of
' all in ' you concoct of ' tree ' you devise in and ' you fill of ' stone
' Aholiad ' ye ' and ye ' as set has ' be`th ' as whither and ' 6 the are fill
as set has ' heart ' wise ' all ' heart in and ' judge ' below`ed ' Ahisamach ' son
' tent ' ye ' 7 are as whom command ' which ' all ' ye ' concoct and ' wise`ed '
' you atone the ' ye and ' testimony`ing of ' Ark`ing the ' ye and ' ing`congregate
' has send the ' ye and ' 8 tent the ' weapon ' all ' ye and ' and Mosthigh ' which
' ye and ' clean`ed the ' the taper`ing the ' ye and ' and vessel are ' all ' ye and
' ye and ' 9 you perfume the ' sacrifice from ' ye and ' vessel`ed are ' all
' Laver`ing the ' ye and ' and vessel are ' all ' ye and ' on`ed the ' sacrifice from
holy the ' as fabric ' ye and ' survivor the ' as fabric ' ye and ' 10 and so ' ye and
' ye and ' 11 priest of ' him son ' as fabric ' ye and ' priest the ' Aaron of '
' accord ' holy of ' from as aroma the ' you perfume ' ye and ' anoint`ed the ' eight
to ' Jehovah ' word as and ' say as and ' 12 and do as ' are as whom command ' which
' sure ' say of ' Israel ' as son ' to ' word ' ye`ed and ' 13 say of ' Moses '
' as between in ' that`s ' ye`ing ' for ' and guard you ' as you desist ' ye
' as whither ' for ' knowledge of ' from are as generation of ' your as between in and
holy ' for ' desist the ' ye ' from you guard and ' 14 from are holy from ' Jehovah
' do`ed the ' all ' for ' die him ' die`ing ' am of sick from ' relate ' that`s '
' approach from ' that`s the ' soul the ' hew`ed shall ' the are fill ' thus
' day as in and ' the are fill ' success`ed ' from week ' you six ' 15 the as people

' do`ed the ' all ' Jehovah of ' holy ' has and desist ' desist ' as seven`s the
as son ' and guard and ' 16 die him ' die`ing ' desist the ' day as in ' the are fill
' desist the ' ye ' you concoct of ' desist the ' ye ' Israel '
between in and ' as between in ' 17 from on`ing ' covenant`s ' from ing`generation of
' from week ' you six ' for ' from on`ing of ' that`s ' ye`ing ' Israel ' as son '
' day as in and ' land the ' ye and ' heaven`s the ' ye ' Jehovah ' do`ed
' Moses ' to ' give as and ' 18 soul as and ' desist ' as seven`s the
' ing`tablet ' two ' ye ' as bush`s ' blemish ' and ye ' word of ' mark and accord
' finger I in ' from as write`ing ' from as stone ' ing`tablet ' testimony`ing the
from as Allah

1 ' has from ' you up of ' Moses ' six in ' for ' people the ' look as and '
him to ' and say as and ' Aaron ' on ' people the ' assemble as and ' mountain the
' our as before ' and walk as ' which ' from as Allah ' our of ' do`ed ' rise`ing '
from as Mizra ' land from ' and has rapture ' which ' man that ' Moses ' this ' for
2 ' Aaron ' them as to ' say as and ' if ' be`s ' what ' and has known ' not '
' your as women ' as ear in ' which ' gold the ' as jewelry ' ye ' and break
3 ' Eli ' and came`s the and ' your as daughter`th and ' your as son
' which ' gold the ' as jewelry ' ye ' people the ' all ' and break whom and
4 ' from hand from ' took as and ' Aaron ' to ' and came`s as and ' them as ear in
' castimage`ed ' calf ' and do`ed as and ' engrave in ' and ye ' mould and
' reinstate`ing the ' which ' Israel ' are as Allah ' to`ed ' and say as and
5 ' sacrifice from ' son as and ' Aaron ' look as and ' from as Mizra ' land from
6 ' tomorrow ' Jehovah of ' solemn ' say as and ' Aaron ' call as and ' him before
' and adduce and ' offer`ing ' and went and ' you tomorrow from ' and ridge`s as and
' and rise as and ' and drink and ' eat of ' people the ' dwell and ' from as whole
7 ' for ' up ' walk ' say of ' Moses ' to ' Jehovah ' word as and ' laught of
8 ' wrong ' from as Mizra ' land from ' offer`s the ' which ' are people ' eradicate
them of ' concoct ' complete as command ' which ' way the ' has from ' mountain from
' if ' and sacrifice as and ' if ' prostate humble`ly as and ' castimage`ed ' calf '
' reinstate`ing the ' which ' Israel ' are as Allah ' to`ed ' and say as and
9 ' as you seen ' Moses ' to ' Jehovah ' say as and ' from as Mizra ' land from
10 that`ing ' stiffneck ' hard`ed ' people ' be`th and ' this the ' people the ' ye
from eat and ' cattle ' nature ' delay and ' vessel ' the rest`s the ' the time and '
' Aaron in and ' great`ing ' nation`ing of ' are ye`ing ' do`ed I and '
' praise whom and ' and destory`s the of ' especially ' Jehovah ' anger`th you the

' Jehovah ' around ' ye ' Moses ' wait and ' 11 Aaron ' till in ' Moses
' are people in ' nose ' the delay ' Jehovah ' what of ' say as and ' him Allah
' great`ing ' power in ' from as Mizra ' land from ' you spring the ' which
and say as ' what of ' 12 am and permit ' seed`ing in and ' the strength ' hand in and
' from ye ' kill of ' from spring`s the ' evil`ed in ' say of ' from as Mizra '
' ground`ed the ' around ' above ' from you and witness and ' from as mountain in
' evil`ed the ' on ' comfort the and ' nose ' has and tomorrow ' carry`ing
' Israel of and ' Jacob of and ' Isaac of ' Abraham of ' male`ing ' 13 are people of
' word you and ' against ' them of ' you swear too has ' which ' are as serve
' from are seed ' ye ' increase`ed I ' increase`ed the ' them as to
' which ' such the ' land the ' all and ' heaven`s the ' as in star`ing are
' 14 from on`ing of ' the and inherit and ' from are seed of ' donkey ' as you say
' you concoct of ' word ' which ' evil`ed the ' on ' Jehovah ' comfort as and
' mountain the ' has from ' Moses ' descend and ' turn as and ' 15 and people of
' ing`tablet ' and hand in ' testimony`ing the ' ing`tablet ' two and
' them ' victual`ed and ' victual`ed ' them as cross ' two from ' from as write`ing
' them`ed ' from as Allah ' do`ed from ' ing`tablet the and ' 16 from as write`ing
' on ' etch`ing ' that`ing ' from as Allah ' write from ' write them and
' people the ' voice`ing ' ye ' ed`Joshua`ing ' hear as and ' 17 ing`tablet the
' 18 camp`ed in ' fight`ed from ' voice`ing ' Moses ' to ' say as and ' evil`ed in
' whither`s and ' the strong`ing ' answer`ing ' voice`ing ' whither`s ' say as and
' for whither ' you and low`ing ' voice`ing ' the defeat`ing ' answer`ing ' voice`ing
' look as and ' camp`ed the ' to ' approach ' which are ' became as and ' 19 hear
' Moses ' anger ' delay and ' you and dance and the ' ye and ' calf the ' ye
' from ye ' buy as and ' ing`tablet the ' ye ' him hand from ' hurl as and

’ concoct ’ which ’ calf the ’ ye ’ took as and ’ 20 mountain the ’ you as under in

’ thin ’ which ’ till ’ and grind`ed as and ’ abhorrence ’ and burnt`ed as and

’ 21 Israel ’ as son ’ ye ’ moisten as and ’ Water the ’ around ’ on ’ sneeze and

’ this the ’ people the ’ walk ’ do`ed ’ what ’ Aaron ’ to ’ Moses ’ say as and

to ’ Aaron ’ say as and ’ 22 great`ed ’ sin`ed ’ and Mosthigh ’ brought the ’ for

’ for ’ people the ’ ye ’ you known ’ ye`ed ’ as master ’ anger ’ delay ’

from as Allah ’ our of ’ do`ed ’ vessel ’ and say as and ’ 23 that`ing ’ hair`ing in

’ which ’ man that ’ Moses ’ this ’ for ’ our as before ’ and walk as ’ which ’

’ be`s ’ what ’ and has known ’ not ’ from as Mizra ’ land from ’ and has rapture

’ and give as and ’ and break you the ’ gold ’ kind ’ them of ’ say and ’ 24 if

’ 25 this the ’ calf the ’ out and ’ abhorrence ’ and hurl`ed I and ’ vessel

’ for ’ that`ing ’ hair`ing ’ for ’ people the ’ ye ’ Moses ’ look as and

Moses ’ stand as and ’ 26 them as ascend ’ and disgrace`ed of ’ Aaron ’ and hair`ed

’ and gather as and ’ Eli ’ Jehovah of ’ who ’ say as and ’ camp`ed the ’ gate in ’

’ Jehovah ’ say ’ here ’ them of ’ say as and ’ 27 Levi ’ as son ’ all ’ him to

’ and soft ’ on ’ and desolate ’ man I ’ and there`s ’ Israel ’ as Allah

and kill and ’ camp`ed in ’ gate of ’ gate from ’ and carry`ing and ’ and cross and

ye ’ man I and ’ and shepherd is ’ ye ’ man I and ’ him brother ’ ye ’ man I ’

’ fell and ’ Moses ’ word are ’ Levi ’ as son ’ concoct as and ’ 28 and approach's ’

’ from as thousand ’ you three are ’ that`ing the ’ day as in ’ people the ’ has from

’ Jehovah of ’ day as the ’ your as hand ’ and fill ’ Moses ’ say as and ’ 29 man I

’ from are mosthigh ’ set of and ’ him brother in and ’ and son in ’ man I ’ for

’ Moses ’ say as and ’ you tomorrow from ’ became as and ’ 30 bless`ed ’ day as the

’ the time and ’ great`ed ’ sin`ed ’ from you sin ’ from ye ’ people the ’ to

’ 31 your as you sin ’ till in ’ the atone I ’ as maybe I ’ Jehovah ’ to ’ on`ed I

' sin ' thou`th ' be`th ' say as and ' Jehovah ' to ' Moses ' dwell and
' as Allah ' them of ' concoct as and ' great`ed ' sin`ed ' this the ' people the
' mother and ' lift ' from you sin ' lift you ' mother ' the time and ' 32 gold
' say as and ' 33 you write ' which ' are report from ' oh ' as camp ' whither`s
as report from ' and camp I ' vessel ' sin ' which ' who ' Moses ' to ' Jehovah
as you word ' which ' on I ' people the ' ye ' rest`ed ' walk ' the time and ' 34
' day as in and ' are as before ' bear ' as messenger from ' be`th and ' walk '
Jehovah ' hurt and ' 35 from you sin ' them as on ' as you punish and ' as punish`ing
' do`ed ' which ' calf the ' ye ' concoct ' which ' on ' people the ' ye '
Aaron

1 ' victual`ed ' on`ed ' walk ' say of ' Moses ' to ' Jehovah ' word as and '

' to ' from as Mizra ' land from ' offer`s the ' which ' people the and ' ye`ed

' Jacob of and ' Isaac of ' Abraham of ' as you swear too has ' which ' land the

2 ' are as before ' as you send and ' the has give I ' are seed of ' say of

' as Amar the and ' as Canaan the ' ye ' as you exact and ' messenger from

' as Hivite the ' as Periz the and ' as Girgash the and ' as Heth the and

3 ' not ' for ' honey and ' milk ' you secrete ' land ' to ' as Jebus the and

' turn ' ye`ed ' stiffneck ' hard`ed ' people ' for ' are approach in ' on`ed I

4 this the ' mischief ' word the ' ye ' people the ' hear as and ' way in ' are eat

5 ' and Mosthigh ' and as till ' man I ' and drink ' not and ' and mourn you as and '

' from ye ' Israel ' as son ' to ' say ' Moses ' to ' Jehovah ' say as and

' are approach in ' on`ed I ' one ' hour ' stiffneck ' hard`ed ' people

' are as on from ' are as till ' up alas ' the time and ' are as whom all and

6 ' Israel ' as son ' and pluck whom and ' walk ' do`ed I ' what ' the know and

7 ' ye ' took as ' Moses and ' in hole`ing ' mountain from ' from as till ' ye

' has from ' get the ' camp`ed of ' outside`ing from ' if ' staff has and ' tent the

' all ' and be`s and ' ing`congregate ' tent ' if ' call and ' camp`ed the

' which ' ing`congregate ' tent ' to ' and out ' Jehovah ' as seek from

8 tent the ' to ' Moses ' you issue are ' be`s and ' camp`ed of ' outside`ing from

' and tent ' open ' man I ' and settle and ' people the ' all ' and rise`ing as '

9 ' be`s and ' tent`ed the ' and came ' till ' Moses ' as after ' and scan`s the and

' stand and ' cloud the ' stand`ing ' descend ' tent`ed the ' Moses ' came`ing are

10 people the ' all ' and look`ed and ' Moses ' people ' word and ' tent the ' open

' all ' and rise and ' tent the ' open ' stand ' cloud the ' stand`ing ' ye '

11 ' word and ' and tent ' open ' man I ' prostrate humble`ly the and ' people the

' man I ' word as ' which are ' inner`s ' to ' inner`s ' Moses ' to ' Jehovah
' and minister from and ' camp`ed the ' to ' sojourn ' and shepherd is ' to
tent the ' middle`ing from ' refrain`ing ' not ' youth ' Nun ' son ' ed`Joshua`ing
on the ' Eli ' say ' ye`ed ' look`ed ' Jehovah ' to ' Moses ' say as and ' 12
' ye ' as give acknowledge the ' not ' ye`ed and ' this the ' people the ' ye '
' spice ' are as knowledge as ' you say ' ye`ed and ' as people ' send you ' which
' oh ' mother ' the time and ' 13 as has eye in ' grace ' you come ' also and
' ye ' oh ' as has acknowledge the ' are as has eye in ' grace ' as you come
' are as has eye in ' grace ' come I ' purpose of ' are know and ' are as way
' around ' say as and ' 14 this the ' nation`ing the ' are people ' for ' look`ed and
' whither`s ' mother ' him to ' say as and ' 15 walk ' as bring the and ' and walk as
height`ed and ' 16 victual`ed ' and has on you ' to ' from as enter the ' are as turn
' are as has eye in ' grace ' as you come ' for ' although`ing ' acknowledge as '
' our people ' are you walk in ' forward`ing ' are people and ' as whither
' which ' people the ' all from ' are people and ' as whither ' and has as made shall
' ye ' also ' Moses ' to ' Jehovah ' say as and ' 17 ground`ed the ' around ' on
' grace ' you come ' for ' do`ed I ' you word ' which ' this the ' word the
' ye ' oh ' as has look the ' say as and ' 18 spice ' are know and ' as has eye in
' on ' as good`ing ' all ' cross`s I ' as whither ' say as and ' 19 are honour`ing
' as incline and ' are as before ' Jehovah ' spice ' as you call and ' are as turn
' 20 compassion I ' which ' ye ' as you compassion and ' grace I ' which ' ye
' not ' for ' around ' ye ' you see of ' able you ' not ' say as and
' place`ing ' be`th ' Jehovah ' say as and ' 21 life and ' ground the ' as has look as
' cross in ' be`s and ' 22 boulder`ing the ' on ' you settle and ' near
as hedge and ' boulder`ing the ' you and pick`s in ' are as herein and ' as honour`ing

' as palm ' ye ' as you repent the and ' 23 as Obara ' till ' are as on ' as palm '

and look as ' not ' around and ' as after ' ye ' sight`s and

' ing`tablet ' two ' walk ' carve ' Moses ' to ' Jehovah ' say as and ' 1
' ing`tablet the ' on ' as you write and ' from as has and head`s are ' from as stone
' ing`tablet the ' on ' him the ' which ' from as word the ' ye
is morn of ' ready`ing ' be`ing and ' 2 you is carry ' which ' from as has head`s the
' vessel ' you settle and ' as bush`s ' mountain ' to ' is morn in ' offer`s and '
' are people ' went`ed ' not ' man I and ' 3 mountain the ' head ' on ' there
' flock the ' also and ' mountain the ' all in ' look`ed as ' to ' man I ' also and
' 4 that`ing the ' mountain the ' split`ing ' to ' and sore ' to ' herd the and
from as has and head`s are ' from as stone ' ing`tablet ' two ' Moses ' carve Then
' as bush`s ' mountain ' to ' went and ' is morn in ' Moses ' ridge as and '
' two ' and hand in ' took as and ' and ye ' Jehovah ' command`ed ' which are
' reside whom and ' cloud in ' Jehovah ' descend and ' 5 from as stone ' ing`tablet
on ' Jehovah ' cross as and ' 6 Jehovah ' spice ' call as and ' there ' and people
' favor`ing and ' compassion`ing ' to ' Jehovah ' Jehovah ' call as and ' him turn '
' bow ' obey ' 7 faithful and ' bow ' increase and ' toward`s ' lenghten
' blame`ed and ' sin`ed and ' trepass and ' low`ing ' help ' from as thousand of
' from as son ' on ' you and father ' low`ing ' punish ' the blame as ' not`ing
' 8 from as four`s ' on and ' from as three`s ' on ' from as son ' as son ' on and
' 9 the and humble`ly as and ' land`ed ' stoop as and ' Moses ' soon as and
' as master ' are as has eye in ' grace ' as you come ' oh ' mother ' say as and
' stiffneck ' hard`ed ' people ' for ' and has approach in ' as master ' oh ' bear
' our as you sin of and ' our as low`ing of ' you forgive and ' that`ing
over ' covenant`s ' hew ' for whither ' be`th ' say as and ' 10 our you inherit and
and create has ' not ' which ' you and wonderful has ' do`ed I ' are people ' all '
' all ' look`ed and ' from nation`ing the ' all in and ' land the ' all in '

' for ' Jehovah ' do`ed from ' ye ' and approach in ' ye`ed ' which ' people the
walk ' guard`ing ' 11 are people ' do`ed ' as whither ' which ' that`ing ' terror has
' exact ' as behold`th ' day as the ' are command from ' for whither ' which ' ye '
' as Heth the and ' as Amar the and ' as Canaan the ' ye ' are around from
' 12 as Jebus the and ' as Hivite the and ' as Periz the and ' as Girgash the and
' which ' land the ' sojourn as of ' covenant`s ' hew you ' turn ' walk ' guard the
for ' 13 are approach in ' snare from of ' be`s as ' turn ' and am on ' came ' ye`ed
them as you altar ' ye and ' shall annihlate you ' them as you sacrifice from ' ye '
' not ' for ' 14 shall hew you ' and them as which ' ye and ' shall is carry you '
' to ' name ' jealous ' Jehovah ' for ' after ' divinity ' the and humble`ly you
' land the ' sojourn as of ' covenant`s ' hew you ' turn ' 15 that`ing ' jealous
' them as Allah of ' and sacrifice and ' them as Allah ' as after ' and diver and
' you take and ' 16 and sacrifice from ' you eat and ' walk ' call and
' as after ' him daughter`th ' and diver and ' are as son of ' him daughter`th from
behold as Allah ' as after ' are as son ' ye ' and diver the and ' behold as Allah
' solemn ' ye ' 18 walk ' do`ed you ' not ' castimage`ed ' as Allah ' 17
' unleaven`ing ' eat you ' from week ' you seven ' guard you ' unleaven`ing the
' for ' blossom`s the ' new ' season from of ' are as whom command ' which are
' emit ' all ' 19 from as Mizra from ' you out ' and in ' blossom`s the ' new in
' captain`ing ' emit ' male`s you ' are as purchase ' all and ' vessel ' compassion
' not ' mother and ' pale`ed ' pardon`ed ' heass`ing ' emit and ' 20 Lamb and
' are as son in ' ground ' first`ing ' all and ' and you stiffneck and ' and pardon`ed
' from week ' you six ' 21 from as only ' around ' and look as ' not and ' pardon`ed
reap`s in and ' devise`s in ' desist you ' as seven`s the ' day as in and ' serve you
' as first`ing ' walk ' do`ed you ' you and seven ' solemn and ' 22 desist you '

’ 23 Year`ed the ’ you course`ing ’ gather`s the ’ solemn and ’ from as wheat ’ reap`s
’ around ’ ye ’ are male`ing ’ all ’ look`ed as ’ Year`ed in ’ from as move ’ three
’ occupy`s I ’ for ’ 24 Israel ’ as Allah ’ Jehovah ’ master the ’ Ark`ing the
’ ye ’ as you large the and ’ are around from ’ from as increase ’ from nation`ing
’ are offer`ing in ’ are land ’ ye ’ man I ’ desire as ’ not and ’ are border`ing
’ from as move ’ three ’ are as Allah ’ Jehovah ’ around ’ ye ’ sight`ing the of
’ not and ’ as sacrifice ’ blood ’ leaven ’ on ’ slay you ’ not ’ 25 Year`ed in
’ as first`ing ’ you as head ’ 26 pass the ’ solemn ’ sacrifice ’ is morn of ’ tarry`s
’ sodden you ’ not ’ are as Allah ’ Jehovah ’ you house ’ came`s you ’ are you ground
walk ’ write ’ Moses ’ to ’ Jehovah ’ say as and ’ 27 and mother ’ mike in ’ kid
these`ed ’ from as word the ’ edge ’ on ’ for ’ these`ed ’ from as word the ’ ye ’
’ there ’ became as and ’ 28 Israel ’ ye and ’ covenant`s ’ are ye ’ as hew ’
’ from as four I and ’ day as ’ from as four I ’ Jehovah ’ people ’ as before
’ on ’ write as and ’ drink`ed ’ not ’ Water and ’ eat ’ not ’ fight ’ the night`s
’ 29 from as word the ’ you ten ’ covenant`s the ’ as word ’ ye ’ ing`tablet the
ing`tablet ’ two and ’ as bush`s ’ mountain from ’ Moses ’ you up in ’ became as and
’ mountain the ’ has from ’ and subdue in ’ Moses ’ and hand in ’ testimony`ing the ’
30 and ye ’ and word in ’ him turn ’ town`ing ’ horn ’ for ’ known ’ not ’ Moses and
’ be`th and ’ Moses ’ ye ’ Israel ’ as son ’ all and ’ Aaron ’ look as and ’
call as and ’ 31 him to ’ accost from ’ and dread as and ’ him turn ’ town`ing ’ horn
’ all and ’ Aaron ’ him to ’ and dwell and ’ Moses ’ them as to ’
’ as after and ’ 32 them as to ’ Moses ’ word as and ’ till`ed in ’ from as help`s the
’ ye ’ from command as and ’ Israel ’ as son ’ all ’ him to ’ and presence ’ so
Moses ’ finish and ’ 33 as bush`s ’ blemish ’ and ye ’ Jehovah ’ word ’ which ’ all
’ came in and ’ 34 the cloak ’ him turn ’ on ’ give as and ’ from ye ’ word from ’

' cloak`ed the ' ye ' correct`s ' and ye ' word of ' Jehovah ' as before ' Moses
' all ' ye ' Israel ' as son ' to ' word and ' out and ' and you issue ' till
' Moses ' around ' ye ' Israel ' as son ' see and ' 35 and command`ed as ' which
' ye ' Moses ' carry`s the and ' Moses ' around ' town`ing ' horn ' for
and ye ' word of ' and came ' till ' him turn ' on ' cloak`ed the

say as and ' Israel ' as son ' testimony ' all ' ye ' Moses ' assemble as and ' 1
' Jehovah ' command`ed ' which ' from as word the ' to`ed ' them as to '
' the are fill ' do`ed you ' from week ' you six ' 2 from ye ' you concoct of
' has and desist ' desist ' holy ' relate ' be`s as ' as seven`s the ' day as in and
' not ' 3 die him ' the are fill ' and in ' do`ed the ' all ' Jehovah of
4 ' desist the ' day as in ' your as ing`desist from ' all in ' fire ' and burn`s you
' this ' say of ' Israel ' as son ' testimony ' all ' to ' Moses ' say as and
' from are ye from ' and took ' 5 say of ' Jehovah ' command`ed ' which ' word the
' ye ' the came`s as ' and heart ' freewill`s ' all ' Jehovah of ' the oblation`ing
you perfect and ' 6 copper has and ' silver and ' gold ' Jehovah ' you oblation`ing
7 ' from as Goat and ' six and ' two ' you have hang`ing and ' has from stony and '
from as badger ' ing`skin`ing and ' from as ground from ' from as Ram`s ' ing`skin and
' from as there in and ' light`ing from of ' eight and ' 8 hate`s ' as tree and '
' as stone and ' 9 from as aroma the ' you perfume of and ' anoint`ed the ' eight of
' all and ' 10 pocket of and ' gird`ing of ' from as fill ' as stone and ' onyx
' which ' all ' ye ' concoct`ed as and ' and came as ' from are in ' heart ' wise
' ye and ' and tent ' ye and ' Tabernacle the ' ye ' 11 Jehovah ' command`ed
' him shoot`s ' ye and ' him board ' ye and ' him pin ' ye and ' and conceal`ed from
' ye and ' Ark`ing the ' ye ' 12 him master ' ye and ' him stand`s ' ye and
' ye ' 13 castimage the ' veil put ' ye and ' you atone the ' ye ' him alone
' fight ' ye and ' and vessel are ' all ' ye and ' him alone ' ye and ' has send the
' all ' ye and ' light`ing them ' you taper`ing ' ye and ' 14 from as turn the
' ye and ' 15 light`ing them ' eight ' ye and ' am you lamp ' ye and ' vessel`ed are
anoint`ed the ' eight ' ye and ' him alone ' ye and ' you perfume the ' sacrifice from
open of ' open the ' castimage ' ye and ' from as aroma the ' you perfume ' ye and '

' sieve from ' ye and ' on`ed the ' sacrifice from ' ye ' 15 Tabernacle the '
' and vessel are ' all ' ye and ' him alone ' ye and ' if ' which ' copper has the
' ye and ' yard the ' as sling ' ye ' 17 and so ' ye and ' Laver`ing the ' ye
' ye ' 18 yard the ' gate ' castimage ' ye and ' am master ' ye and ' and am stand
' ye and ' yard the ' stake`ing as ' ye and ' Tabernacle the ' stake`ing as
' holy in ' minister of ' survivor the ' as fabric ' ye ' 19 them as preserve from
him son ' as fabric ' ye and ' priest the ' Aaron of ' holy the ' as fabric ' ye and
' as before from ' Israel ' as son ' testimony ' all ' and out and ' 20 priest of '
' and heart ' and lift has ' which ' man I ' all ' and came`s as and ' 21 Moses
' and came`s the ' and ye ' and spirit is ' the freewill ' which ' man I ' all and
' ing`congregate ' tent ' you are fill of ' Jehovah ' you oblation`ing ' ye
' and came`s as and ' 22 holy the ' as fabric of and ' and you serve ' all of and
' heart ' freewill`s ' all ' from as women the ' on ' from as person the
' all ' bead are and ' calf's ' you ring and ' jewelry and ' chain ' and came`s the
' gold ' you wave`ing you ' wave`s the ' which ' man I ' all and ' gold ' weapon
' you perfect ' and ye ' come has ' which ' man I ' all and ' 23 Jehovah of
' from as Goat and ' six and ' two ' you have hang`ing and ' has from stony and
' from as badger ' ing`skin and ' from as ground from ' from as Ram`s ' ing`skin and
' copper has and ' silver ' you oblation`ing ' Miriam ' all and ' 24 and came`s the
' come has ' which ' all and ' Jehovah ' you oblation`ing ' ye ' and came`s the
25 and came`s the ' serve`ed the ' you are fill ' all of ' hate`s ' as tree ' and ye
and came`s as and ' and spun`ed ' am hand in ' heart ' you wise ' Woman ' all and '
' ye and ' has from stony the ' ye and ' you prefect the ' ye ' the spin '
' from as women the ' all and ' 26 six the ' ye and ' two the ' you have hang`ing the
' ye ' spun`ing ' the wise in ' has ye`ed ' thick of ' help ' which

onyx the ' as stone ' ye ' and came`s the ' from help`s the and ' (27 from as Goat the
' ye and ' (28 pocket of and ' gird`ing of ' from as fill the ' as stone ' ye and '
' eigth of and ' bitter`ing the of ' eight the ' ye and ' from as spice the
' man I ' all and ' (29 from as aroma the ' you perfume of and ' anoint`ed the
' all of ' came`s the of ' from heart ' from ye ' freewill ' which ' Woman and
' hand in ' you concoct of ' Jehovah ' command`ed ' which ' the messenger from the
say as and ' (30 Jehovah of ' the freewill ' Israel ' as son ' and came`s the ' Moses
' Bezaleel ' spice ' Jehovah ' call ' see ' Israel ' as son ' to ' Moses '
' and ye ' fill as and ' (31 Judah ' below`ed ' hole`ing ' son ' as light`ing ' son
' knowledge in and ' the similar`ing in and ' the wise in ' from as Allah ' spirit is
' you concoct of ' you and reckon from ' reckon of and ' (32 the are fill ' all in and
' stone ' you devise in and ' (33 copper has in and ' silver in and ' gold in
' you are fill ' all in ' you concoct of ' tree ' you devise in and ' you fill of
' that`ing ' and heart in ' gave ' you and instruct`ing and ' (34 you and reckon from
' you wise ' from ye ' fill ' (35 judge ' below`ed ' Ahisamach ' son ' Aholiab and
' fabricate and ' reckon and ' devise ' you are fill ' all ' you concoct of ' heart
' two the ' you have hang`ing in and ' has from strony in and ' you perfect in
' as reckon and ' the messenger from the ' all ' as concoct ' strony and ' six in and
you and reckon from

' which ' heart ' wise ' man I ' all and ' Aholiab and ' Bezaleel ' do`ed and ' 1
' knowledge of ' the similar`ing and ' wise`ed ' cattle`ed ' Jehovah ' gave
' which ' all of ' holy the ' you serve ' you are fill ' all ' ye ' you concoct of
Aholiad ' to and ' Bezaleel ' to ' Moses ' call as and ' 2 Jehovah ' command`ed
' wise`ed ' Jehovah ' gave ' which ' heart ' wise ' man I ' all ' to and '
' to ' approach`ed of ' and heart ' and lift has ' which ' all ' and heart in
' as before from ' acquire as and ' 3 ye`ed ' you concoct of ' the messenger from the
' as son ' and came`s the ' which ' the oblation`ing the ' all ' ye ' Moses
them and ' ye`ed ' you concoct of ' holy the ' you serve ' you are fill of ' Israel
' 4 is morn in ' is morn in ' the freewill ' till`ing ' him to ' and came`s the '
' all ' ye ' from as do the ' from as wise the ' all ' and came`s as and
' them`ed ' which ' and you are fill from ' man I ' man I ' holy the ' you are fill
' say of ' Moses ' to ' and word as and ' and say as and ' 5 from as do
' serve`ed the ' enough from ' came`s the of ' people the ' from as much
' 6 ye`ed ' you concoct of ' Jehovah ' command`ed ' which ' the are fill of
' say of ' camp`ed in ' voice`ing ' and cross`s as and ' Moses ' command as and
' the are fill ' till`ing ' concoct`ed as ' to ' Woman and ' man I
' 7 came`s the from ' people the ' finish`er and ' holy the ' you oblation`ing of
' the messenger from the ' all of ' blood`s ' whom`ed the ' the are fill the and
as wise ' all ' concoct as and ' 8 and is as sacred`ing and ' ye`ed ' you concoct of
' concoct ' Tabernacle the ' ye ' the messenger from the ' as function in ' heart '
' you perfect and ' twist from ' six ' you and have curtain ' ten
' do`ed from ' from as Cherub`ing ' two ' you have hang`ing and ' has from stony and
eight`ed ' sister the ' the have curtain the ' lenghten ' 9 from ye ' do`ed ' reckon
' the have curtain the ' cubit`ed ' four I ' large and ' cubit`ed ' from as ten and '

connect as and ' 10 you and have curtain the ' all of ' sister ' mete`ed ' sister the
' five and ' sister ' to ' sister ' you and have curtain the ' five ' ye '
' do as and ' 11 sister ' to ' sister ' connect ' you and have curtain the
' sister the ' the have curtain the ' you lip ' on ' you perfect ' loop`ing of
' you lip in ' do`ed ' so and ' you connect from in ' the end from
' 12 you two the ' you connect from in ' the shall end`s the ' the have curtain the
' sister the ' the have curtain in ' do`ed ' loop`ing of ' from as five
' which ' the have curtain the ' the end in ' do`ed ' loop`ing of ' from as five and
' sister ' loop`ing of the ' you and front`s from ' you two the ' you connect from in
' ye ' connect as and ' gold ' as pin ' from as five ' do as and ' 13 sister ' to
' became as and ' from as pin in ' sister ' to ' sister ' you and have curtain the
tent of ' from as Goat ' you and have curtain ' do as and ' 14 one ' Tabernacle the
from ye ' do`ed ' you and have curtain ' ten`ed ' as you do ' Tabernacle the ' on '
' cubit`ed ' from as three ' sister the ' the have curtain the ' lenghten ' 15
' mete`ed ' sister the ' the have curtain the ' large ' faithful`ing ' four I and
' ye ' connect as and ' 16 you and have curtain the ' ten`ed ' as dual of ' sister
you and have curtain the ' six ' ye and ' earnest ' you and have curtain the ' five
' you lip ' on ' from as five ' loop`ing of ' do as and ' 17 earnest '
' you connect from in ' the shall end`s the ' sister the ' the have curtain the
' the have curtain the ' you lip ' on ' do`ed ' loop`ing of ' from as five and
' from as five ' copper has ' as pin ' do as and ' 18 you two the ' you connect the
' do as and ' 19 one ' you and became of ' tent the ' ye ' connect of
' from as ground from ' from as Ram`s ' you town`ing ' tent of ' conceal`ed from
do as and ' 20 the above of from ' from as badger ' ing`skin`ing ' conceal`ed from and
' 21 from as stand ' hate`s ' as tree ' Tabernacle of ' from as board the ' ye '

' half and ' mother`ed and ' one the ' board the ' lenghten ' faithful`ing ' ten
' board of ' esteem`ing ' twosome ' (22 one the ' board the ' large ' mother`ed the
' all of ' do`ed ' so ' sister ' to ' sister ' you and interval from ' one the
' Tabernacle of ' from as board the ' ye ' do as and ' (23 Tabernacle the ' as board
' (24 right`ed you ' south`ed ' quarter of ' from as board ' from as ten
' from as ten ' under ' do`ed ' silver ' as master ' from as four I and
twosome of ' one the ' board the ' under ' from as master ' two ' from as board the
twosome of ' one the ' board the ' under ' from as master ' two and ' him stake as '
' quarter of ' you two the ' Tabernacle the ' rib of and ' (25 him stake as '
' from as four I and ' (26 from as board ' from as ten ' do`ed ' the north`ing
' one the ' board the ' under ' from as master ' two ' silver ' them as master
' as you soft of and ' (27 one the ' board the ' under ' from as master ' two and
from as board ' two and ' (28 from as board ' six`ed ' do`ed ' sea`ed ' Tabernacle the
' (29 from as you soft in ' Tabernacle the ' you and corner from of ' do`ed '
' and became as ' and alike and ' below`ed from ' from as ing`twin ' and became and
' do`ed ' so ' sister the ' you ring the ' to ' and head ' to ' from as twin
' eight`ed ' and became and ' (30 you and corner them ' two of ' them two of
two ' from as master ' ten ' six`ed ' silver ' them as master and ' from as board
' (31 one the ' board the ' under ' from as master ' two ' from as master '
' rib ' as board of ' the five ' hate`s ' as tree ' as shoot`s ' concoct as and
rib ' as board of ' from as shoot`s ' the five and ' (32 sister the ' Tabernacle the
rib ' as board of ' from as shoot`s ' the five and ' you two the ' Tabernacle the '
' shoot`s the ' ye ' do as and ' (33 sea`ed ' from as you soft of ' Tabernacle the '
end`ed ' has from ' from as board the ' middle`ing in ' shoot of ' column`ing sacred
' ye and ' gold ' espy`ed ' from as board the ' ye and ' (34 end`ed ' to '

’ espy as and ’ from as shoot`s of ’ integrity`s ’ gold ’ do`ed ’ them as you ring
you perfect ’ veil put the ’ ye ’ do as and ’ 35 gold ’ from as shoot`s the ’ ye
’ twist from ’ six and ’ two ’ you have hang`ing and ’ has from stony and ’
’ nihil ’ do as and ’ 36 from as Cherub`ing ’ ye`ed ’ do`ed ’ reckon ’ do`ed from
gold ’ them as hook ’ gold ’ from espy as and ’ hate`s ’ as stand`ing ’ the four I
’ castimage ’ do as and ’ 37 silver ’ as master ’ the four I ’ them of ’ cast and ’
two ’ you have hang`ing and ’ has from stony and ’ you perfect ’ tent the ’ open of
the five ’ him stand`ing ’ ye and ’ 38 fabricate ’ do`ed from ’ twist from ’ six and ’
’ gold ’ them as delight and ’ them as head ’ the espy and ’ them as hook ’ ye and ’
copper has ’ the five ’ them as master and

THE TORAH SCROLL 37

Ex 37:1-37:14

’ from extent I ’ hate`s ’ as tree ’ Ark`ing the ’ ye ’ Bezaleel ’ do as and ’ 1
’ mother`ed and ’ and large ’ half and ’ mother`ed and ’ and lengthen ’ half and
’ clean`ing ’ gold ’ and espy`ed as and ’ 2 and you rise`ing ’ half and
’ gold ’ stranger ’ if ’ do as and ’ outside`ing from and ’ you house from
’ four I ’ on ’ gold ’ you and ring ’ four I ’ if ’ cast and ’ 3 surround`s
twosome and ’ sister the ’ and rib ’ on ’ you and ring ’ twosome and ’ him you move
’ as tree ’ as alone ’ do as and ’ 4 you two the ’ and rib ’ on ’ you and ring ’
’ from as alone the ’ ye ’ came as and ’ 5 gold ’ from ye ’ espy as and ’ hate`s
’ Ark`ing the ’ ye ’ arise of ’ Ark`ing the ’ you and rib ’ on ’ you and ring in
’ half and ’ from extent I ’ clean`ing ’ gold ’ you atone ’ do as and ’ 6 cattle
’ two ’ do as and ’ 7 and large`ed ’ half and ’ mother`ed and ’ and lengthen`ed
’ you coast ’ two from ’ from ye ’ do`ed ’ fashion`ed ’ gold ’ from as Cherub`ing
’ mantle`ing and ’ victual`ed ’ the end from ’ one ’ mantle`ing ’ 8 you atone the
’ ye ’ do`ed ’ you atone the ’ has from ’ victual`ed ’ the end from ’ one
’ and became as and ’ 9 and as you and coast ’ two from ’ from as Cherub`ing the
’ from as veneer ’ the above of ’ from as wing ’ as excrement ’ from as Cherub`ing the
’ to ’ one ’ man I ’ them around and ’ you atone the ’ on ’ them as wing in
from as Cherub`ing the ’ around ’ him the ’ you atone the ’ to ’ him brother ’ one
’ from extent I ’ hate`s ’ as tree ’ has send the ’ ye ’ do as and ’ 10
and you rise`ing ’ half and ’ mother`ed and ’ and large ’ mother`ed and ’ and lengthen
’ gold ’ stranger ’ if ’ do as and ’ clean`ing ’ gold ’ and ye ’ espy as and ’ 11
’ do as and ’ surround`s ’ span ’ you is fasten ’ if ’ do as and ’ 12 surround`s
’ four I ’ if ’ cast and ’ 13 surround`s ’ and you is fasten of ’ gold ’ stranger
’ four I ’ on ’ you and ring the ’ ye ’ give as and ’ gold ’ you and ring
’ you is fasten the ’ point of ’ 14 him foot ’ four I of ’ which ’ quarter`ing the

' ye ' arise of ' from as alone of ' integrity`s ' you and ring the ' him the

' hate`s ' as tree ' from as alone the ' ye ' do as and ' 15 has send the

ye ' do as and ' 16 has send the ' ye ' arise of ' gold ' from ye ' espy as and

' ye and ' him you dish ' ye ' has send the ' on ' which ' from vessal are the '

' which ' you pitcher the ' ye and ' him you as bowl ' ye and ' him you spoon

' the taper`ing the ' ye ' do as and ' 17 clean`ing ' gold ' cattle ' ing`sculpture

' am soft ' the taper`ing the ' ye ' do`ed ' fashion`ed ' clean`ing ' gold

' 18 him the ' her`ed from ' am bud and ' am is knop ' am hill`s ' am end and

' money ' three`ed ' am drain ' from as spring as ' from as nest ' six`ed and

drain`ed ' the taper`ing ' money ' three`ed and ' one the ' drain`ed ' the taper`ing

' one the ' the stalk ' from as nut from ' from as hill`s ' three`ed ' 19 two the '

' the stalk ' from as nut from ' from as hill`s ' three`ed and ' bud and ' is knop

' from as nest the ' you six of ' so ' bud and ' is knop ' one

' the taper`ing in and ' 20 the taper`ing the ' has from ' from as spring became

' 21 am bud and ' am is knop ' from as nut from ' from as hill`s ' the four I

' under ' is knop and ' her`ed from ' from as nest the ' two ' under ' is knop and

from as nest the ' two ' under ' is knop and ' her`ed from ' from as nest the ' two

' 22 her`ed from ' from as out the ' from as nest the ' you six of ' her`ed from '

fashion`ed ' all`ed ' him the ' her`ed from ' from you and nest and ' them as is knop

the seven ' am you lamp ' ye ' do as and ' 23 clean`ing ' gold ' sister ' one '

' gold ' circle ' 24 clean`ing ' gold ' am you crush from and ' am take from and '

' ye ' do as and ' 25 vessel`ed are ' all ' ye and ' ye`ed ' do`ed ' clean`ing

' and lengthen ' mother`ed ' hate`s ' as tree ' you perfume the ' sacrifice from

' and you rise`ing ' from as you mother and ' four`ing ' and large ' mother`ed and

' clean`ing ' gold ' and ye ' espy as and ' 26 him you horn ' him the ' and her from

' him you horn ' ye and ' surround`s ' him net stedfast ' ye and ' nail ' ye
' you and ring ' twosome and ' 27 surround`s ' gold ' stranger ' if ' do as and
' him you rib ' twosome ' on ' and stranger of ' under from ' if ' do`ed ' gold
' and ye ' arise of ' from as alone of ' from house`ly of ' and sidle ' two ' on
' espy as and ' hate`s ' as tree ' from as alone the ' ye ' do as and ' 28 cattle
' ye and ' holy ' anoint`ed the ' eight ' ye ' do as and ' 29 gold ' from ye
ointment ' do`ed from ' clean`ing ' from as aroma the ' you perfume

' five ' hate`s ' as tree ' on`ed the ' sacrifice from ' ye ' do as and ' 1
' four`ing ' and large ' faithful`ing ' five and ' and lengthen ' faithful`ing
' on ' him you horn ' do as and ' 2 and you rise`ing ' faithful`ing ' three and
' and ye ' espy as and ' him you horn ' him the ' and her from ' him angle ' four I
' ye ' sacrifice them ' weapon ' all ' ye ' do as and ' 3 copper has
' you and sprinkle them ' ye and ' from as shovel the ' ye and ' you and repent`s the
' and vessel are ' all ' you and crush them ' ye and ' you and fork them ' ye and
' do`ed from ' sieve from ' sacrifice from of ' do as and ' 4 copper has ' do`ed
' 5 and half ' till ' below`ed from ' and ride are ' under ' copper has ' net`ness
' sieve from of ' you coast the ' four I in ' you and ring ' four I ' cast and
' ye ' do as and ' 6 from as alone of ' integrity`s ' copper has the
' 7 copper has ' from ye ' espy as and ' hate`s ' as tree ' from as alone the
' you and rib ' on ' you and ring in ' from as alone the ' ye ' came as and
' do`ed ' ing`tablet`ing ' hollow`ing ' cattle ' and ye ' arise of ' sacrifice them
' and so ' ye and ' copper has ' Laver`ing the ' ye ' do as and ' 8 and ye
' tent ' open ' and mass ' which ' you and mass the ' you and appear in ' copper has
right`ed you ' south`ed ' quarter of ' yard the ' ye ' do as and ' 9 ing`congregate
' 10 cubit`ed ' hundred`ed ' twist from ' six ' yard the ' as sling '
' copper has ' from as ten ' them as master and ' from as ten ' and them as stand`ing
' quarter of and ' 11 silver ' them as delight and ' from as stand`ing the ' as hook
' from as ten ' them as stand`ing ' cubit`ed ' hundred`ed ' the north`ing
' from as stand`ing the ' as hook ' copper has ' from as ten ' them as master and
' from as sling ' sea`ed ' quarter of and ' 12 silver ' them as delight and
' ten`ed ' them as master and ' ten`ed ' them as stand`ing ' cubit`ed ' from as five
quarter of and ' 13 silver ' them as delight`ing and ' from as stand`ing the ' as hook

' five ' from as sling ' 14 mother`ed ' from as five ' emerge`ed from ' east`ed '
' three`ed ' them as stand`ing ' shoulder the ' to ' mother`ed ' ten`ed
' victual`ed ' you two the ' shoulder of and ' 15 three`ed ' them as master and
' mother`ed ' ten`ed ' five ' from as sling ' yard the ' gate of ' victual`ed and
' as sling ' all ' 16 three`ed ' them as master and ' three`ed ' them as stand`ing
' from as master the and ' 17 twist from ' six ' surround`s ' yard the
' from as stand`ing the ' them as hook ' copper has ' from as stand`ing of
them and ' silver ' them as head ' as and espy and ' silver ' them as delight`ing and
castimage and ' 18 yard the ' as stand`ing ' all and ' silver ' from as delight from '
' has from stony and ' you perfect ' fabricate ' do`ed from ' yard the ' gate '
' mother`ed ' from as ten and ' twist from ' six and ' two ' you have hang`ing and
' as sling ' point of ' faithful`ing ' five ' large in ' the rise`ing and ' lenghten
' the four I ' them as master and ' the four I ' them as stand`ing and ' 19 yard the
' them as head ' as and espy and ' silver ' them as hook ' copper has
' Tabernacle of ' stake`ing became ' all and ' 20 silver ' them as delight and
' Tabernacle the ' as punish`ing ' to`ed ' 21 copper has ' surround`s ' yard of and
' you serve ' Moses ' edge ' on ' punish ' which ' testimony`ing the ' Tabernacle
' Bezaleel and ' 22 priest the ' Aaron ' son ' Ithamar ' hand in ' from Levi the
' all ' ye ' do`ed ' Judah ' below`ed ' hole`ing ' son ' as light`ing ' son
' son ' Aholiad ' and ye and ' 23 Moses ' ye ' Jehovah ' command`ed ' which
' you perfect in ' fabricate and ' reckon and ' devise ' judge ' below`ed ' Ahisamach
' all ' 24 six in and ' two the ' you have hang`ing in and ' has from strony in and
' holy the ' you are fill ' all in ' the are fill of ' as concoct the ' gold the
' circle ' from as ten and ' nine ' the wave`ing scared ' gold ' became as and
' 25 holy the ' weigh in ' weigh ' from as three and ' you and hundred ' seven and

seven and ' thousand and ' circle ' each ' till`ed the ' as punish`ing ' silver and
(25 holy the ' weigh in ' weigh ' from as seven and ' the five and ' you and hundred '
' holy the ' weigh in ' weigh the ' you half from ' you heap heap of ' divide '
the Year ' from as ten ' son from ' from as my appoint the ' on ' cross the ' all of
' you three and ' thousand ' you and hundred ' six of ' above`ed and '
' became as and ' (27 from as five and ' you and hundred ' five and ' from as thousand
' ye and ' holy the ' as master ' ye ' metal of ' silver the ' circle ' each
' circle the ' you hundred of ' from as master the ' each ' veil put the ' as master
' you and hundred the ' seven and ' thousand the ' ye and ' (28 master of ' circle
' from as stand`ing of ' from as hook ' do`ed ' from as seven and ' the five and
' copper has and ' (29 from ye ' delight and ' them as head ' the espy and
' four I and ' from as thousand and ' circle ' from as seven ' the wave`ing scared
' tent ' open ' as master ' ye ' thus ' do as and ' (30 weigh ' you and hundred
' sieve from ' ye and ' copper has the ' sacrifice from ' ye and ' ing`congregate
' weapon ' all ' ye and ' sacrifice from of ' if ' which ' copper has the
' as master ' ye and ' surround`s ' yard the ' as master ' ye and ' (31 sacrifice them
' all ' ye and ' Tabernacle the ' stake`ing as ' all ' ye and ' yard the ' gate
surround`s ' yard the ' stake`ing as

' you have hang`ing and ' has from strony the and ' you prefect the ' has from and ' 1
' concoct as and ' holy in ' minister of ' survivor ' as fabric ' concoct ' two the
' Jehovah ' command`ed ' which are ' Aaron of ' which ' holy the ' as fabric ' ye
' you perfect ' gold ' gird`ing the ' ye ' concoct as and ' 2 Moses ' ye
' 3 twist from ' six and ' two ' you have hang`ing and ' has from stony and
' from as lace`s ' and utmost and ' gold the ' as sheet ' ye ' and expense as and
' middle`ing in and ' you prefect the ' middle`ing in ' you concoct of
' two the ' you have hang`ing the ' middle`ing in and ' has from stony the
' concoct`ed ' you and shoulder ' 4 reckon ' do`ed from ' six the ' middle`ing in and
' reckon and ' 5 connect ' and as you and coast ' two ' on ' you and connect ' if
' and work`ed are ' that`ing ' and her from ' and Mosthigh ' which ' and you gird
' six and ' two ' you have hang`ing and ' has from stony and ' you perfect ' gold
' concoct as and ' 6 Moses ' ye ' Jehovah ' command`ed ' which are ' twist from
' gold ' you and embroider from ' you ing`arrange ' onyx the ' as stone ' ye
' 7 Israel ' as son ' you name ' on ' ing`signet ' as open`ing ' you and open from
' as stone ' gird the ' you and shoulder ' on ' from ye ' name as and
' ye ' Jehovah ' command`ed ' which are ' Israel ' as son of ' shall is remember
' work`ed are ' reckon ' do`ed from ' pocket the ' ye ' concoct as and ' 8 Moses
' you have hang`ing and ' has from stony and ' you perfect ' gold ' gird`ing the
' ye ' concoct`ed ' made`ing are ' be`s ' four`ing ' 9 twist from ' six and ' two
' 10 made`ing are ' and large ' span and ' and lengthen ' span ' pocket the
' ground ' row`ing ' stone ' as row`ing ' the four I ' and in ' and fill as and
' two the ' row`ing the and ' 11 one the ' row`ing the ' carbuncle and ' the topaz
Jacinth ' as three`s the ' row`ing the and ' 12 from diamond and ' report`s ' emerald
onyx ' beryl`s you ' as four`s the ' row`ing the and ' 13 dream`ed I and ' sparkle '

from you fill in ' gold ' you and embroider from ' you ing`arrange ' lip`ed as and '
from twosome ' be`th ' Israel ' as son ' you name ' on ' from as stone the and ' 14
' name ' on ' man I ' ing`signet ' as open`ing ' from you name ' on ' ten`ed '
you and is root ' pocket the ' on ' concoct as and ' 15 tribe ' ten ' from two of
' concoct as and ' 16 clean`ing ' gold ' wrap`ing ' do`ed from ' you and border '
' gold ' you and ring ' twosome and ' gold ' you and embroider from ' twosome
' you coast ' two ' on ' you and ring the ' twosome ' ye ' and give as and
' on ' gold the ' you and wrap the ' twosome ' ye ' and give as and ' 17 pocket the
' twosome ' ye and ' 18 pocket the ' you coast ' on ' you and ring the ' twosome
' twosome ' on ' and gave ' you and wrap the ' twosome ' you coast the
' you and shoulder ' on ' from and permanent and ' you and embroider them
you and ring ' twosome ' concoct as and ' 19 him turn ' split`ing ' to ' gird`ing the
' and you lip ' on ' pocket the ' you coast ' two ' on ' and site`s and ' gold '
twosome ' concoct as and ' 20 he house ' gird`ing the ' connect ' Obara ' to ' which
' you and shoulder ' twosome ' on ' from and permanent and ' gold ' you and ring '
' point of ' him turn ' split`ing from ' below`ed from ' gird`ing the
' and attach as and ' 21 gird`ing the ' reckon of ' above from ' and you connect from
' lace`s in ' gird`ing the ' you ring ' to ' him you ring from ' pocket the ' ye
' shove as ' not and ' gird`ing the ' reckon ' on ' you and became of ' you perfect
Moses ' ye ' Jehovah ' command`ed ' which are ' gird`ing the ' above ' pocket the
' which are ' from as complete the ' ye and ' highland`s the ' ye ' concoct as and '
' above`s the ' ye ' concoct as and ' 22 Moses ' ye ' Jehovah ' command`ed
' edge and ' 23 you perfect ' of vessal are ' stony ' do`ed from ' gird the
' and edge of ' lip`ed ' I corselet`ed ' as palm ' and middle`ing in ' above`s the
' above`s the ' as peace`ing ' on ' concoct as and ' 24 rend as ' not ' surround`s

' two ' you have hang`ing and ' has from stony and ' you perfect ' as pomegranate`ing
and give as and ' clean`ing ' gold ' as bell`ing put ' concoct as and ' 25 twist from
on ' from as pomegranate`ing the ' middle`ing in ' from as bell`ing put the ' ye '
26 from as pomegranate the ' middle`ing in ' surround`s ' above`s the ' as peace`ing '
' gold ' bell`ing put ' pomegranate`ing and ' gold ' bell`ing put '
' minister of ' surround`s ' above`s the ' as peace`ing ' on ' pomegranate`ing and
' ye ' concoct as and ' 27 Moses ' ye ' Jehovah ' command`ed ' which are
' ye and ' 28 him son of and ' Aaron of ' stony ' do`ed from ' six ' you coat the
' ye and ' six ' you and have bonnet the ' as shake ' ye and ' six ' you turban them
' six ' belt`s I the ' ye and ' 29 twist from ' six ' alone the ' as breeche from
' two ' you have hang`ing and ' has from stony and ' you perfect and ' twist from
' 30 Moses ' ye ' Jehovah ' command`ed ' which are ' fabricate ' do`ed from
' clean`ing ' gold ' holy the ' consecrate ' flower`s ' ye ' concoct as and
' holy ' ing`signet ' as open`ing ' write from ' and Mosthigh ' and write as and
' on ' set of ' you perfect ' lace`s ' and Mosthigh ' and give as and ' 31 Jehovah of
Moses ' ye ' Jehovah ' command`ed ' which are ' the above of from ' you turban them
' ing`congregate ' tent ' Tabernacle the ' you serve ' all ' perfect and ' 32
ye ' Jehovah ' command`ed ' which are ' accord ' Israel ' as son ' concoct as and
Moses ' to ' Tabernacle the ' ye ' and came`s as and ' 33 concoct ' so ' Moses '
him shoot`s ' him board ' him pin ' and vessel are ' all ' ye and ' tent the ' ye '
' ing`skin`ing ' conceal`ed from ' ye and ' 34 and them base I and ' him stand and '
ing`skin`ing ' conceal`ed from ' ye and ' from as ground from the ' from as Ram`s the
' Ark`ing ' ye ' 35 castimage the ' veil put ' ye and ' from as badger the '
' ye ' 36 you atone the ' ye and ' him alone ' ye and ' testimony`ing the
' 37 from as turn the ' fight ' ye and ' and vessel are ' all ' ye and ' has send the

' you and lamp ' am you lamp ' ye and ' clean`ed the ' the taper`ing the ' ye
' 38 light`ing them ' eight ' ye and ' vessel`ed are ' all ' ye and ' pile`ed them
' ye and ' anoint`ed the ' eight ' ye and ' gold the ' sacrifice from ' ye and
' ye ' 39 tent the ' open ' castimage ' ye and ' from as aroma the ' you perfume
if ' which ' copper has the ' sieve from ' ye and ' copper has the ' sacrifice from
ye and ' Laver`ing the ' ye ' and vessel are ' all ' ye and ' him alone ' ye and '
am master ' ye and ' am stand`ing ' ye and ' yard the ' as sling ' ye ' 40 and so '
' and am preserve from ' ye and ' yard the ' gate of ' castimage the ' ye and '
' tent of ' Tabernacle the ' you serve ' weapon ' all ' ye and ' am stake as ' ye and
' ye and ' holy in ' minister of ' survivor the ' as fabric ' ye ' 41 ing`congregate
' him son ' as fabric ' ye and ' priest the ' Aaron of ' holy the ' as fabric
concoct ' so ' Moses ' ye ' Jehovah ' command`ed ' which ' accord ' 42 priest of
all ' ye ' Moses ' look as and ' 43 serve`ed the ' all ' ye ' Israel ' as son '
' command`ed ' which are ' ye`ed ' concoct ' be`th and ' the messenger from the '
Moses ' from ye ' bless as and ' concoct ' so ' Jehovah

’ new the ’ day as in ’ 2 say of ’ Moses ’ to ’ Jehovah ’ word as and ’ 1
’ tent ’ Tabernacle the ’ ye ’ rise`s you ’ new of ’ one in ’ has and head`s the
’ testimony`ing the ’ Ark`ing ’ ye ’ there ’ herein and ’ 3 ing`congregate
’ ye ’ brought the and ’ 4 veil put the ’ ye ’ Ark`ing the ’ on ’ booth and
’ ye ’ brought the and ’ and pile ’ ye ’ you pile and ’ has send the
’ ye ’ set`ed has and ’ 5 am you lamp ’ ye ’ offer`s the and ’ the taper`ing the
’ testimony`ing the ’ Ark`ing ’ as before ’ you perfume of ’ gold the ’ sacrifice from
’ ye ’ set`ed has and ’ 6 Tabernacle of ’ open the ’ castimage ’ ye ’ herein and
’ tent ’ Tabernacle the ’ open ’ as before ’ on`ed the ’ sacrifice from
’ tent ’ between in ’ Laver`ing the ’ ye ’ set`ed has and ’ 7 ing`congregate
’ 8 Water ’ there ’ set`ed has and ’ sacrifice them ’ between in and ’ ing`congregate
’ castimage ’ ye ’ set`ed has and ’ surround`s ’ yard the ’ ye ’ herein and
’ you anoint and ’ anoint`ed the ’ eight ’ ye ’ you take and ’ 9 yard the ’ gate
’ and ye ’ you holy and ’ and in ’ which ’ all ’ ye and ’ Tabernacle the ’ ye
’ ye ’ you anoint and ’ 10 holy ’ be`s and ’ and vessel are ’ all ’ ye and
’ ye ’ you holy and ’ and vessel are ’ all ’ ye and ’ on`ed the ’ sacrifice from
you anoint and ’ 11 from as holy ’ holy ’ sacrifice them ’ be`s and ’ sacrifice them
’ 12 and ye ’ you holy and ’ and so ’ ye and ’ Laver`ing the ’ ye ’
’ tent ’ open ’ to ’ him son ’ ye and ’ Aaron ’ ye ’ you approach the and
’ ye ’ you arm the and ’ 13 Water in ’ from ye ’ you wash and ’ ing`congregate
’ you holy and ’ and ye ’ you anoint and ’ holy the ’ as fabric ’ ye ’ Aaron
you arm the and ’ approach`s you ’ him son ’ ye and ’ 14 vessel ’ priest and ’ and ye
ye ’ you anoint ’ which are ’ from ye ’ you anoint and ’ 15 you and coat ’ from ye ’
’ you and became of ’ whom`ed the and ’ vessel ’ and priest and ’ them as father ’
’ 16 from ing`generation of ’ from on`ing ’ you priest of ’ from you anoint ’ them of

(17 do`ed ' so ' and ye ' Jehovah ' command`ed ' which ' accord ' Moses ' do as and
' you two the ' Year`ed in ' has and head`s the ' new in ' became as and '
Tabernacle the ' rise alas ' new of ' one in ' from as Mizra from ' from you issue of
' him master ' ye ' give as and ' Tabernacle the ' ye ' Moses ' rise as and ' (18
' ye ' rise as and ' him shoot`s ' ye ' give as and ' him board ' ye ' site and
site and ' Tabernacle the ' on ' tent the ' ye ' Chariot as and ' (19 him stand`ing
' which are ' the above of from ' and Mosthigh ' tent the ' conceal`ed from ' ye '
' ye ' give as and ' took as and ' (20 Moses ' ye ' Jehovah ' command`ed
' on ' from as alone the ' ye ' site and ' Ark`ing the ' to ' testimony`ing the
' Ark`ing the ' on ' you atone the ' ye ' give as and ' Ark`ing the
' Tabernacle the ' to ' Ark`ing the ' ye ' came as and ' (21 the above of from
' Ark`ing ' on ' sculpture and ' castimage the ' veil put ' ye ' site and
' site and ' (22 Moses ' ye ' Jehovah ' command`ed ' which are ' testimony`ing the
' soft ' on ' ing`congregate ' tent in ' has send the ' ye ' give as and
' pile as and ' (23 veil put of ' outside`ing from ' the north`ing ' Tabernacle the
Jehovah ' command`ed ' which are ' Jehovah ' as before ' fight ' pile ' and Mosthigh
' ing`congregate ' tent in ' the taper`ing the ' ye ' site and ' (24 Moses ' ye '
' ye ' went and ' (25 south`ed ' Tabernacle the ' soft ' on ' has send the ' behalf
' ye ' Jehovah ' command`ed ' which are ' Jehovah ' as before ' you and lamp the
' ing`congregate ' tent in ' gold the ' sacrifice from ' ye ' site and ' (26 Moses
' you perfume ' and Mosthigh ' perfume as and ' (27 veil put the ' as before
Moses ' ye ' Jehovah ' command`ed ' which are ' Jehovah ' as before ' from as aroma
' ye and ' (29 Tabernacle of ' open the ' castimage ' ye ' site and ' (28
' tent ' Tabernacle the ' open ' as before ' there ' on`ed the ' sacrifice from
bestow`ed the ' ye and ' on`ed the ' ye ' and Mosthigh ' went and ' ing`congregate

' ye ' site and ' 30 Moses ' ye ' Jehovah ' command`ed ' which are '
sacrifice them ' between in and ' ing`congregate ' tent ' between in ' Laver`ing the
' and her from ' and wash as and ' 31 the wash of ' Water ' there`ed ' give as and '
' 32 them as foot ' ye and ' them as hand ' ye ' him son and ' Aaron and ' Moses
' to ' from you approach in and ' ing`congregate ' tent ' to ' from came in
' 33 Moses ' ye ' Jehovah ' command`ed ' which are ' and wash as ' sacrifice them
' sacrifice from of and ' Tabernacle of ' surround`s ' yard the ' ye ' rise as and
all ' ye ' Moses ' finish and ' yard the ' gate ' castimage ' ye ' give as and
' tent ' ye ' cloud the ' conceal as and ' 34 the messenger from the '
not and ' 35 Tabernacle the ' ye ' fill ' Jehovah ' honour`ing and ' ing`congregate
' nigh ' for ' ing`congregate ' tent ' to ' came`ing of ' Moses ' finish '
36 Tabernacle the ' ye ' fill ' Jehovah ' honour`ing and ' cloud the ' and Mosthigh
' as son ' leave as ' Tabernacle the ' above ' cloud the ' offer`ing the in and '
' cloud the ' went`ed ' not ' mother and ' 37 them as march ' all in ' Israel
' Jehovah ' cloud ' for ' 38 and offer`ing the ' day as ' till ' leave as ' not and
' the night`s ' and in ' be`s you ' fire and ' from day as ' Tabernacle the ' on
. ' them as march ' all in ' Israel ' you house ' all ' as has eye of

' tent from ' him to ' Jehovah ' word as and ' Moses ' to ' call as and (1
' you say and ' Israel ' as son ' to ' word ' (2 say of ' ing`congregate
' Jehovah of ' has approach ' from with ' approach`s as ' for ' ground ' them as to
' flock the ' has from and ' herd the ' has from ' cattle`ed the ' has from
and has approach ' on`ed ' mother ' (3 your as has approach ' ye ' and approach`s you
open ' to ' and has approach`s as ' from as complete ' male ' herd the ' has from '
' as before ' and accept`ing of ' and ye ' approach`s as ' ing`congregate ' tent '
' run`ed has and ' on`ed the ' head ' on ' and hand ' ye ' laid and ' (4 Jehovah
' as before ' herd the ' son ' ye ' slay and ' (5 and Mosthigh ' atone of ' if
' ye ' from as priest the ' Aaron ' as son ' and approach`s the and ' Jehovah
' surround`s ' sacrifice them ' on ' blood the ' ye ' and sprinkle and ' blood the
' on`ed the ' ye ' pull`s the and ' (6 ing`congregate ' tent ' open ' which
' Aaron ' as son ' and gave and ' (7 am dismember of ' ye`ed ' dismember and
on ' from as tree ' and pile and ' sacrifice them ' on ' fire ' from as priest the
' ye ' from as priest the ' Aaron ' as son ' and pile and ' (8 fire the '
from as tree the ' on ' fat the ' ye and ' head the ' ye and ' from as dismember the
' and approach and ' (9 sacrifice them ' on ' which ' fire the ' on ' which '
total ' ye ' priest the ' perfume`s the and ' Water in ' and wash as ' him leg and
Jehovah of ' odor`ing has ' smell`s ' Woman ' that`ing ' on`ed ' the sacrifice them '
' Jehovah of ' and has approach ' on`ed ' flock the ' has from ' mother and ' (10
' male ' on`ed of ' from as Goat the ' has from ' or ' from as sheep the ' has from
' ing`congregate ' tent ' open ' to ' and has approach`s as ' from as complete
' sacrifice them ' soft ' on ' and ye ' slay and ' (11 and ye ' approach`s as
' Aaron ' as son ' and sprinkle and ' Jehovah ' as before ' the north`ing
' (12 surround`s ' sacrifice them ' on ' and blood ' ye ' from as priest the

and fat ' ye and ' and head ' ye and ' him dismember of ' and ye ' and dismember and
fire the ' on ' which ' from as tree the ' on ' from ye ' priest the ' pile and '
13 ' wash as ' from as leg the and ' approach the and ' sacrifice them ' on ' which '
' perfume`s the and ' total ' ye ' priest the ' approach`s the and ' Water in
14 ' Jehovah of ' odor has ' smell`s ' Woman ' that`ing ' on`ed ' the sacrifice them
' Jehovah of ' and has approach ' on`ed ' fly`ing the ' has from ' mother and
' as son ' has from ' or ' from as turtledove the ' has from ' approach`s the and
15 ' priest the ' and approach`s the and ' and has approach ' ye ' the Dove`ing the
' perfume`s the and ' and head ' ye ' wring and ' sacrifice them ' to
15 sacrifice them ' cold`s ' on I ' and blood ' come`ed has and ' the sacrifice them
' hurl`s the and ' the you discharge in ' and you appear ' ye ' wriggle`s and '
17 ' statisfy the ' place`ing ' to ' east`ed ' sacrifice them ' beside ' ye`ed
' perfume`s the and ' separate`s as ' not and ' and as wing in ' and ye ' cloven and
' on ' which ' from as tree the ' on ' the sacrifice them ' priest the ' and ye
Jehovah of ' odor has ' smell`s ' Woman ' that`ing ' on`ed ' fire the

1 ' flour ' Jehovah of ' bestow`ed ' has approach ' approach`s you ' for ' soul and '
' am on ' gave and ' eight ' am on ' cast and ' and has approach ' be`s as
2 ' Aaron ' as son ' to ' the came`s the and ' that`s ' bestow`ed ' the son`ing of
' flour`ed from ' and grasp ' fill ' there from ' grasp and ' from as priest the
' priest the ' perfume`s the and ' the you white`ing ' all ' on ' eigth`ed from and
3 ' Jehovah of ' odor has ' smell`s ' Woman ' the sacrifice them ' he male I ' ye
' him son of and ' Aaron of ' bestow`ed the ' has from ' you Turtedove and behold and
4 ' approach`s you ' for and ' Jehovah ' as fire from ' from as holy ' holy
' unleaven`ing ' cake`ing ' flour ' flame`ing ' the batch ' bestow`ed ' has approach
5 eight in ' from as anoint ' unleaven`ing ' as slim`s and ' eight in ' you mingle`ing
' flour ' are has approach ' you pan the ' on ' bestow`ed ' mother and '
6 ' from as bit ' ye`ed ' piece`ing ' be`s you ' find`ed ' eight in ' the mingle`ing
7 ' you bestow`ed ' mother and ' that`s ' bestow`ed ' eight ' am on ' you cast and
8 ' brought the and ' do`ed you ' eight in ' flour ' are has approach ' you fry from
' Jehovah of ' to`ed from ' success`ed ' which ' bestow`ed the ' ye
sacrifice them ' to ' the also`s the and ' priest the ' to ' the approach`s the and
9 ' he male I ' ye ' bestow`ed the ' has from ' priest the ' palace`s and '
10 ' Jehovah of ' odor has ' smell`s ' Woman ' the sacrifice them ' perfume`s the and
' him son of and ' Aaron of ' bestow`ed the ' has from ' you Turtedove and behold and
11 ' which ' bestow`ed the ' all ' Jehovah ' as fire from ' from as holy ' holy
' remain ' all ' for ' leaven ' do`ed you ' not ' Jehovah of ' and approach`s you
' and her from ' and approach`s you ' and perfume`s you ' not ' honey ' all and
12 ' from ye ' and approach`s you ' you as head ' has approach ' Jehovah of ' Woman
13 ' odor has ' smell`s of ' lug as ' not ' sacrifice them ' to and ' Jehovah of
' not and ' salt you ' salt in ' are as you bestow ' has approach ' all and

' on ' are as you bestow ' above ' are as Allah ' covenant`s ' salt ' desist`s you
' approach`s you ' mother and ' 14 salt ' approach`s you ' are as has approach ' all
exact ' abhorrence ' as toast ' Abib ' Jehovah of ' from as first`ing ' you bestow
' 15 are as first'ing ' you bestow ' ye ' approach`s you ' of vineyard '
' bestow`ed ' the son`ing of ' am on ' herein and ' eight ' am on ' set`ed has and
' exact`ed from ' he male I ' ye ' priest the ' perfume`s the and ' 16 that`s
Jehovah of ' Woman ' the you white`ing ' all ' on ' eigth`ed from and

' has from ' mother ' and has approach ' from as whole ' sacrifice ' mother and ' 1
' the female ' mother ' male ' mother ' approach`s from ' that`ing ' herd the
2 ' ye ' laid and ' Jehovah ' as before ' and has approach`s as ' from as complete
' tent ' open ' and slay and ' and has approach ' head ' on ' and hand
' ye ' from as priest the ' Aaron ' as son ' and sprinkle and ' ing`congregate
3 sacrifice from ' approach`s the and ' surround`s ' sacrifice them ' on ' blood the
' ye ' amount`ed the ' milk the ' ye ' Jehovah of ' Woman ' from as whole the '
4 ' ye and ' approach the ' on ' which ' milk the ' all ' ye and ' approach the
' on ' which ' behold as on ' which ' milk the ' ye and ' whom`ing total ' twosome
' on ' honour the ' on ' you ing`perserve the ' ye and ' from as trust the
5 ' as son ' and ye ' and perfume`s the and ' the has correct`s ' whom`ing total
' from as tree the ' on ' which ' on`ed the ' on ' the sacrifice them ' Aaron
odor has ' smell`s ' Woman ' sacrifice them ' on ' which ' fire the ' on ' which
6 ' sacrifice of ' and has approach ' flock the ' has from ' mother and ' Jehovah of '
' from as complete ' the female ' or ' male ' Jehovah of ' from as whole the
7 ' ye ' approach`s from ' that`ing ' sheep ' mother ' and has approach`s as
8 ' laid and ' Jehovah ' as before ' and ye ' approach`s the and ' and has approach
' as before ' and ye ' slay and ' and has approach ' head ' on ' and hand ' ye
' and blood the ' ye ' Aaron ' as son ' and sprinkle and ' ing`congregate ' tent
9 ' sacrifice from ' approach`s the and ' surround`s ' sacrifice them ' on
' the from as complete ' am these ' and milk ' Jehovah of ' Woman ' from as whole the
ye ' amount`ed the ' milk the ' ye and ' the has correct`s ' tree`ed the ' point of
10 ' ye and ' approach the ' on ' which ' milk the ' all ' ye and ' approach the '
' on ' which ' behold as on ' which ' milk the ' ye and ' whom`ing total ' twosome
' on ' honour the ' on ' you ing`perserve the ' ye and ' from as trust the

’ priest the ’ and perfume`s the and ’ 11 the has correct`s ’ whom`ing total
’ harsh ’ mother and ’ 12 Jehovah of ’ Woman ’ fight ’ the sacrifice them
’ ye ’ laid and ’ 13 Jehovah ’ as before ’ and approach`s the and ’ and has approach
’ ing`congregate ’ tent ’ as before ’ and ye ’ slay and ’ and head ’ on ’ and hand
’ on ’ and blood ’ ye ’ from as priest the ’ Aaron ’ as son ’ and sprinkle and
’ and has approach ’ and her from ’ approach`s the and ’ 14 surround`s ’ sacrifice them
ye and ’ approach the ’ ye ’ amount`ed the ’ milk the ’ ye ’ Jehovah of ’ Woman
whom`ing total ’ twosome ’ ye and ’ 15 approach the ’ on ’ which ’ milk the ’ all ’
’ from as trust the ’ on ’ which ’ behold as on ’ which ’ milk the ’ ye and ’
’ whom`ing total ’ on ’ honour the ’ on ’ you ing`perserve the ’ ye and
fight ’ the sacrifice them ’ priest the ’ from perfume`s the and ’ 16 the has correct`s
statute ’ 17 Jehovah of ’ milk ’ all ’ Jehovah of ’ odor has ’ smell`s of ’ Woman ’
’ all ’ your as desist and from ’ all in ’ from are as generation of ’ from on`ing ’
and eat you ’ not ’ blood ’ all and ’ milk

' as son ' to ' word ' 2 say of ' Moses ' to ' Jehovah ' word as and ' 1
' unleaven`ing ' all from ' mistake`ed in ' sin you ' for ' soul ' say of ' Israel
' you brother from ' do`ed and ' the has as suffice ' not ' which ' Jehovah
' you guilty of ' sin as ' anoint`s the ' priest the ' mother ' 3 be`th from
' son ' apart ' sin ' which ' and you sin ' on ' approach`s the and ' people the
broken ' ye ' came`s the and ' 4 you sin of ' Jehovah of ' from as complete ' herd
' ye ' laid and ' Jehovah ' as before ' ing`congregate ' tent ' open ' to '
5 Jehovah ' as before ' broken ' ye ' slay and ' broken ' head ' on ' and hand
blood from ' and hand ' ye ' fill ' which ' anoint`s the ' priest the ' take and '
' dip and ' 6 ing`congregate ' tent ' to ' and ye ' came`s the and ' broken '
' blood the ' has from ' this the and ' blood in ' and finger I ' ye ' priest the
' around ' ye ' Jehovah ' as before ' and finger came ' from as move ' seven
' on ' blood the ' has from ' priest the ' gave and ' 7 holy the ' veil put
Jehovah ' as before ' from as aroma the ' you perfume ' sacrifice from ' you and horn
' pour as ' broken ' blood the ' all ' ye and ' ing`congregate ' tent in ' which '
' tent ' open ' which ' on`ed the ' sacrifice from ' position`ing ' to
' elevate`s ' you sin the ' apart ' milk ' all ' ye and ' 8 ing`congregate
' ye and ' approach the ' on ' ye ' amount`ed the ' milk the ' ye ' and her from
' whom`ing total ' twosome ' ye and ' 9 approach the ' on ' which ' milk the ' all
ye and ' from as trust the ' on ' which ' behold as on ' which ' milk the ' ye and
the has correct`s ' whom`ing total ' on ' honour the ' on ' you ing`perserve the '
' from as whole the ' sacrifice ' Ox`ing from ' residue as ' which are ' 10
' ye and ' 11 on`ed the ' sacrifice from ' on ' priest the ' from perfume`s the and
' him leg ' on and ' and head ' on ' and flesh ' all ' ye and ' broken ' town`ing
' broken ' all ' ye ' and issue`s alas and ' 12 and excrement and ' and approach and

' pour ' on I ' clean`ing ' place`ing ' to ' camp`ed of ' outside`ing from ' to
' on ' abhorrence ' from as tree the ' on ' and ye ' and burnt and ' statisfy the
' Israel ' testimony ' all ' mother and ' 13 burnt as ' statisfy the ' pour
' concoct and ' assemble the ' as purpose`s ' word ' eternal has and ' transgress as
' the has as suffice ' not ' which ' Jehovah ' unleaven`ing ' all from ' sister
' am on ' and sin ' which ' you sin the ' acknowledge`ed shall ' 14 and guilty and
' from as complete ' herd ' son ' apart ' assemble the ' and approach`s the and
' 15 ing`congregate ' tent ' as before ' and ye ' and came`s the and ' you sin of
' broken ' head ' on ' them as hand ' ye ' till`ed the ' as elder ' and laid and
' 16 Jehovah ' as before ' broken ' ye ' slay and ' Jehovah ' as before
' tent ' to ' broken ' blood from ' anoint`s the ' priest the ' came`s the and
blood the ' has from ' and finger I ' ye ' priest the ' dip and ' 17 ing`congregate
' Jehovah ' as before ' from as move ' seven ' blood the ' has from ' this the and '
' permanent ' blood the ' has from and ' 18 holy the ' veil put the ' around ' ye
' from as aroma the ' you perfume ' sacrifice them ' you and horn ' on ' priest the
' all ' ye and ' ing`congregate ' tent in ' which ' Jehovah ' as before ' which
open ' which ' on`ed the ' sacrifice from ' position`ing ' to ' pour as ' blood the
' and her from ' elevate`s ' and milk ' all ' ye and ' 19 ing`congregate ' tent '
' do`ed ' which are ' apart of ' do`ed and ' 20 the sacrifice them ' perfume`s the and
priest the ' them as on ' atone and ' if ' success`ed ' so ' you sin the ' apart of
' to ' broken ' ye ' issue`s alas and ' 21 them of ' forgive has and '
broken ' ye ' burnt ' which are ' and ye ' burnt and ' camp`ed of ' outside`ing from
' lift`s has ' which ' 22 that`s ' assemble the ' you sin ' has and head`s the '
which ' him Allah ' Jehovah ' unleaven`ing ' all from ' sister ' do`ed and ' sin as
' acknowledge the ' or ' 23 guilty and ' mistake`ed in ' the has as suffice ' not '

' ye ' came`s the and ' thus ' sin ' which ' and you sin ' him to
' laid and ' 24 from as complete ' male ' from as Goat ' gate`s ' and has approach
' place`ing in ' and ye ' slay and ' gate`s the ' head ' on ' and hand ' ye
' 25 that`s ' you sin ' Jehovah ' as before ' on`ed the ' ye ' and slay as ' which
' on ' gave and ' and finger came ' you sin the ' blood from ' priest the ' take and
' to ' pour as ' and blood ' ye and ' on`ed the ' sacrifice from ' you and horn
perfume`s as ' and milk ' all ' ye and ' 26 on`ed the ' sacrifice from ' position`ing
' atone and ' the from as whole the ' sacrifice ' milk are ' the sacrifice them '
' mother and ' 27 if ' forgive has and ' and you sin from ' priest the ' and Mosthigh
' the daul`ing in ' land the ' affirm ' mistake`ed in ' sin you ' sister ' soul
' the has as suffice ' not ' which ' Jehovah ' unleaven`ing ' all from ' sister
' sin ' which ' and you sin ' him to ' acknowledge the ' or ' 28 guilty and
' from as Goat ' you gate`s ' and has approach ' ye ' came`s the and ' am on
' laid and ' 29 sin ' which ' and you sin ' on ' the from as complete ' the female
' you sin the ' ye ' slay and ' you sin the ' head ' on ' and hand ' ye
' priest the ' take and ' 30 on`ed the ' ye ' and slay as ' which ' place`ing in
' sacrifice from ' you and horn ' on ' gave and ' and finger came ' blood`ed from
' sacrifice them ' position`ing ' to ' pour as ' blood`ed ' all ' ye and ' on`ed the
' chasten the ' which are ' correct`s ' the milk ' all ' ye and ' 31 on`ed the
' priest the ' perfume`s the and ' from as whole the ' sacrifice ' above ' milk the
' and Mosthigh ' atone and ' Jehovah of ' odor has ' smell`s of ' the sacrifice them
' came`s as ' mutton ' sheep`ed ' mother and ' 32 if ' forgive has and ' priest the
the has came`s as ' the from as complete ' the female ' you sin of ' and has approach
' ye`ed ' slay and ' you sin the ' head ' on ' and hand ' ye ' laid and ' 33
' take and ' 34 on`ed the ' ye ' and slay as ' which ' place`ing in ' you sin of

’ on ’ gave and ’ and finger came ’ you sin the ’ blood from ’ priest the
’ to ’ pour as ’ blood`ed ’ all ’ ye and ’ on`ed the ’ sacrifice from ’ you and horn
’ correct`s ’ the milk ’ all ’ ye and ’ 35 on`ed the ’ sacrifice them ’ position`ing
’ from as whole the ’ sacrifice from ’ sheep the ’ milk ’ chasten as ’ which are
’ as fire ’ on ’ the sacrifice them ’ from ye ’ priest the ’ perfume`s the and
sin ’ which ’ and you sin ’ on ’ priest the ’ and Mosthigh ’ atone and ’ Jehovah
if ’ forgive has and ’

till ’ that`ing and ’ to`ed ’ voice`ing ’ hear`ed and ’ sin you ’ for ’ soul and ’ (1
’ help and ’ fortune`s as ’ not`ing ’ mother ’ known ’ or ’ look`ed ’ or ’
or ’ unclean ’ word ’ all in ’ reach ’ which ’ for ’ soul ’ or ’ (2 and low`ing
’ cattle`ed ’ you foolish in ’ or ’ unclean`ed ’ the life ’ you foolish in ’
and her from ’ eternal has and ’ unclean ’ breed ’ you foolish in ’ or ’ unclean`ed
’ you unclean in ’ faint ’ for ’ or ’ (3 guilty and ’ unclean ’ that`ing and ’
’ eternal has and ’ thus ’ unclean as ’ which ’ and you unclean ’ all of ’ ground
’ for ’ soul ’ or ’ (4 guilty and ’ known ’ that`ing and ’ and her from
’ or ’ mischief`s of ’ from as you lip in ’ pronounce of ’ swear too you
’ the seven`ing in ’ ground the ’ pronounce as ’ which ’ all of ’ improve`s the of
’ you brother of ’ guilty and ’ known ’ that`ing and ’ and her from ’ eternal has and
’ to`ed from ’ you brother of ’ guilty as ’ sin as ’ for ’ be`s and ’ (5 to`ed from
’ ye ’ came`s the and ’ (6 am on ’ sin ’ which ’ ye ’ the endure`ing the and
has from ’ the female ’ sin ’ which ’ and you sin ’ on ’ Jehovah of ’ and guilty
’ atone and ’ you sin of ’ from as Goat ’ you gate`s ’ or ’ sheep`ed ’ flock the ’
forgive has and ’ sin ’ which ’ and you sin from ’ on ’ priest the ’ and Mosthigh
came`s the and ’ resemble ’ enough ’ and hand ’ reach`s ’ not ’ mother and ’ (7 if ’
two ’ or ’ from as protect ’ twosome ’ sin ’ which ’ and guilty ’ on ’ ye ’
’ (8 on`ed of ’ one and ’ you sin of ’ one ’ Jehovah of ’ the Dove`ing ’ as son ’
’ which ’ ye ’ approach`s the and ’ priest the ’ to ’ from ye ’ came`s the and
’ and head ’ ye ’ priest the ’ wring and ’ the has and head ’ you sin of
blood from ’ this the and ’ (9 separate`s as ’ not and ’ and stiffneck ’ split`ing from
’ blood in ’ remain behold and ’ sacrifice them ’ cold`s ’ on I ’ you sin the ’
’ ye and ’ (10 that`s ’ you sin ’ sacrifice them ’ position`ing ’ to ’ come`ed as
’ and Mosthigh ’ atone and ’ discern from are ’ on`ed ’ success`ed ’ two the

mother and ’ 11 if ’ forgive has and ’ sin ’ which ’ and you sin from ’ priest the
’ two of ’ or ’ from as protect ’ twosome of ’ and hand ’ drawal`s you ’ not ’
’ sin ’ which ’ and has approach ’ ye ’ came`s the and ’ the Dove`ing ’ as son
’ eight ’ am on ’ site`s ’ cast ’ not ’ you sin of ’ flour ’ the cook`s ’ urn do
’ 12 that`s ’ you sin ’ for ’ the son`ing of ’ am on ’ permanent ’ not and
’ her`ed from ’ priest the ’ grasp and ’ priest the ’ to ’ the came`s the and
’ the sacrifice them ’ perfume`s the and ’ he male I ’ ye ’ and grasp ’ fill`ing
priest the ’ and Mosthigh ’ atone and ’ 13 that`s ’ you sin ’ Jehovah ’ as fire ’ on
’ to`ed from ’ you brother from ’ sin ’ which ’ and you sin ’ on ’
’ word as and ’ 14 bestow`ed are ’ priest of ’ whom`ed the and ’ if ’ forgive has and
’ sin`ed and ’ above ’ above you ’ for ’ soul ’ 15 say of ’ Moses ’ to ’ Jehovah
’ and guilty ’ ye ’ came`s the and ’ Jehovah ’ as holy from ’ mistake`ed in
’ silver ’ are pile in ’ flock the ’ has from ’ from as complete ’ Ram`s ’ Jehovah of
’ sin ’ which ’ ye and ’ 16 guilty of ’ holy the ’ weigh in ’ from as weigh
’ and Mosthigh ’ Joseph ’ and you five`s ’ ye and ’ whole as ’ holy the ’ has from
’ Ram`s in ’ and Mosthigh ’ atone as ’ priest the and ’ priest of ’ and ye ’ gave and
’ sin you ’ for ’ sister ’ soul ’ mother and ’ 17 if ’ forgive has and ’ guilty the
’ not ’ which ’ Jehovah ’ unleaven`ing ’ all from ’ sister ’ he do and
’ 18 and low`ing ’ help and ’ guilty and ’ known ’ not and ’ the has as suffice
’ are pile in ’ flock the ’ has from ’ from as complete ’ Ram`s ’ came`s the and
’ on ’ priest the ’ and Mosthigh ’ atone and ’ priest the ’ to ’ guilty of
’ forgive has and ’ known ’ not ’ that`ing and ’ mistake ’ which ’ and you mistake
Jehovah of ’ guilty ’ guilty ’ that`ing ’ guilty ’ 19 if

' sin you ' for ' soul ' 2 say of ' Moses ' to ' Jehovah ' word as and ' 1
' has and punish in ' and whom people in ' lie and ' Jehovah in ' above ' above`ed and
' ye ' oppress ' or ' tear in ' or ' hand ' you deposite`ing in ' or
on ' swear has and ' thus ' lie and ' the perish ' come ' or ' 3 and whom people
' sin of ' ground the ' success`ed ' which ' all from ' sister ' on ' false '
' ye ' carry`s the and ' guilty and ' sin as ' for ' be`s and ' 4 be`th in
' or ' oppress ' which ' oppress the ' ye ' or ' tear ' which ' tear`ed the
' ye ' or ' and ye ' punish the ' which ' has and punish the ' ye
' swear too as ' which ' word ' all from ' or ' 5 come ' which ' perish`ed the
' him you five`s and ' and head in ' and ye ' whole and ' false of ' and Mosthigh
' day as in ' and has give as ' if ' that`ing ' which of ' and Mosthigh ' add
' Ram`s ' Jehovah of ' came`s as ' and guilty ' ye and ' 6 and you guilty
priest the ' to ' guilty of ' are pile in ' flock the ' has from ' from as complete
' forgive has and ' Jehovah ' as before ' priest the ' and Mosthigh ' atone and ' 7
' 8 thus ' guilty`ed of ' success`ed ' which ' all from ' sister ' on ' if
' Aaron ' ye ' command`ed ' 9 say of ' Moses ' to ' Jehovah ' word as and
on`ed the ' that`s ' on`ed the ' you protect`ing ' such ' say of ' him son ' ye and
' till ' the night`s the ' all ' sacrifice them ' on ' fuel`ed from the ' on '
' priest the ' arm and ' 10 and in ' fuel you ' sacrifice them ' fire and ' herd the
' and flesh ' on ' arm as ' alone ' as breeche from and ' alone ' and mete
' on`ed the ' ye ' fire the ' eat you ' which ' statisfy the ' ye ' palace`s and
' ye ' pull and ' 11 sacrifice them ' beside ' name and ' sacrifice them ' on
' ye ' issue`s alas and ' from as after ' from as fabric ' arm and ' him fabric
' 12 clean`ing ' place`ing ' to ' camp`ed of ' outside`ing from ' to ' statisfy the
' extinguish`ed ' not ' and in ' fuel you ' sacrifice them ' on ' fire the and

' pile and ' is morn in ' is morn in ' from as tree ' priest the ' am on ' burn and
' (13 from as whole the ' as milk ' am on ' perfume`s the and ' on`ed the ' am on
' (14 extinguish`ed ' not ' sacrifice them ' on ' fuel you ' continual`s ' fire
' as son ' ye`ed ' and approach`s the ' bestow`ed the ' you protect`ing ' such and
' palace`s and ' (15 sacrifice them ' around ' to ' Jehovah ' as before ' Aaron
' ye and ' eigth`ed from and ' bestow`ed the ' flour from ' and grasp in ' and numb`ed
' perfume`s the and ' bestow`ed the ' on ' which ' the white`ing the ' all
' (16 Jehovah of ' he male I ' odor has ' smell`s ' Woman ' the sacrifice them
' him son and ' Aaron ' and eat as ' her`ed from ' you Turtedove and behold and
ing`congregate ' tent ' yard in ' holy`ing ' place`ing in ' eat you ' unleaven`ing
' ye`ed ' as set has ' from part ' leaven ' batter`ed ' not ' (17 the and eat as '
guilty are and ' you sin are ' that`s ' from as holy ' holy ' Jehovah ' as fire from
' from on`ing ' law ' the has eat as ' Aaron ' as son in ' male ' all ' (18
' cattle ' faint ' which ' all ' Jehovah ' as fire from ' from are as generation of
' has approach ' this ' (20 say of ' Moses ' to ' Jehovah ' word as and ' (19 holy as
' day as in ' Jehovah of ' and approach`s as ' which ' him son and ' Aaron
' continual`s ' the bestow of ' flour ' the cook`s ' urn do ' and ye ' anoint the
' (21 from as twilight the ' between in ' he half from and ' is morn in ' he half from
' the has came`s you ' you baken from ' do`ed you ' eight in ' you pan the ' on
' odor has ' smell`s ' approach`s you ' from as bit ' you bestow ' as ing`pie`s
success`ed ' him son from ' him under ' anoint`s the ' priest the and ' (22 Jehovah of
all and ' (23 perfume`s you ' of vessal are ' Jehovah of ' from on`ing ' law ' ye`ed '
' word as and ' (24 eat you ' not ' be`s you ' of vessal are ' priest ' you bestow '
' him son ' to and ' Aaron ' to ' word ' (25 say of ' Moses ' to ' Jehovah
' slay you ' which ' place`ing in ' you sin the ' you protect`ing ' such ' say of

' from as holy ' holy ' Jehovah ' as before ' you sin the ' slay you ' on`ed the

' place`ing in ' the has eat as ' ye`ed ' sin them ' priest the ' 26 that`s

' faint ' which ' all ' 27 ing`congregate ' tent ' yard in ' eat you ' holy`ing

' fabric the ' on ' blood`ed from ' splash`ed ' which and ' holy as ' the flesh in

' 28 holy`ing ' place`ing in ' immersion whom ' and am on ' splash`ed ' which

' mother and ' is carry as ' and in ' sodden you ' which ' devise ' as all and

all ' 29 Water in ' rinse and ' dribbles and ' sodden`ed ' copper has ' vessal are in

' 30 that`s ' from as holy ' holy ' ye`ed ' eat as ' from as priest in ' male '

' tent ' to ' blood`ed from ' came`ing as ' which ' you sin ' all and

burnt you ' abhorrence ' eat you ' not ' holy in ' atone of ' ing`congregate

2 ' that`ing ' from as holy ' holy ' guilty the ' you protect`ing ' such and ' 1
' ye ' and slay as ' on`ed the ' ye ' and slay as ' which ' place`ing in
3 ' surround`s ' sacrifice them ' on ' sprinkle as ' and blood ' ye and ' guilty the
' ye and ' am these ' ye ' and her from ' approach`s as ' and milk ' all ' ye and
' which ' milk the ' all ' ye and ' approach the ' ye ' amount`ed the ' milk the
which ' milk the ' ye and ' whom`ing total ' twosome ' ye and ' 4 approach the ' on
' you ing`perserve the ' ye and ' from as trust the ' on ' which ' behold as on '
' perfume`s the and ' 5 the has correct`s ' whom`ing total ' on ' honour the ' on
6 that`ing ' guilty ' Jehovah of ' Woman ' the sacrifice them ' priest the ' from ye
eat as ' holy`ing ' place`ing in ' and has eat as ' from as priest in ' male ' all '
' the protect`ing ' guilty are ' you sin are ' 7 that`ing ' from as holy ' holy '
' 8 be`s as ' if ' and in ' atone as ' which ' priest the ' them of ' sister
' on`ed the ' town`ing ' man I ' offer ' ye ' approach`s them ' priest the and
' which ' bestow`ed ' all and ' 9 be`s as ' if ' priest of ' approach`s the ' which
' on and ' you fry from in ' the make ' all and ' furnace`ing in ' batter`ed
' all and ' 10 be`s you ' if ' ye`ed ' approach`s them ' priest of ' you pan the
' Aaron ' as son ' all of ' desolate`ed and ' eight in ' the mingle`ing ' bestow`ed
' sacrifice ' you protect`ing ' such and ' 11 him brother are ' man I ' be`s you
' on ' mother ' 12 Jehovah of ' and approach`s as ' which ' from as whole the
' sacrifice ' on ' approach`s the and ' and has approach`s as ' the endure`ing
' eight in ' you and mingle ' unleaven`ing ' cake`ing ' the endure`ing the
you baken from ' flour and ' eight in ' from as anoint ' unleaven`ing ' as slim`s and
' leaven ' fight ' cake ' on ' 13 eight in ' you and mingle ' cake`ing '
' 14 him whole ' you endure`ing ' sacrifice ' on ' and has approach ' approach`s as
the oblation`ing ' has approach ' all from ' one ' and her from ' approach`s the and

' if ' from as whole the ' blood ' ye ' sprinkle the ' priest of ' Jehovah of '
' day as in ' him whole ' you endure`ing ' sacrifice ' flesh and ' 15 be`s as
' 16 herd ' till ' and her from ' rest`s as ' not ' eat as ' and has approach
' day as in ' and has approach ' sacrifice ' the freewill ' or ' vow ' mother and
' you tomorrow from and ' eat as ' and sacrifice ' ye ' and approach`s the
' flesh from ' survive behold and ' 17 eat as ' and her from ' survive behold and
' mother and ' 18 burnt as ' abhorrence ' as three`s the ' day as in ' sacrifice the
' as three`s the ' day as in ' him whole ' sacrifice ' flesh from ' eat as ' eat the
adominable`ing ' if ' reckon as ' not ' and ye ' approach`s them ' approve`ed ' not
' 19 lift you ' the low`ing ' and her from ' you eat the ' soul the and ' be`s as '
' abhorrence ' eat as ' not ' unclean ' all in ' faint ' which ' flesh the and
which ' soul the and ' 20 flesh ' eat as ' clean`ing ' all ' flesh the and ' burnt as
' Jehovah of ' which ' from as whole the ' sacrifice from ' flesh ' eat you '
' that`s the ' soul the ' hew`ed shall ' and Mosthigh ' and you unclean and
' you unclean in ' unclean ' all in ' reach ' for ' soul and ' 21 am people from
eat and ' unclean ' breed ' all in ' or ' unclean`ed ' cattle`ed in ' or ' ground
' hew`ed shall ' Jehovah of ' which ' from as whole the ' sacrifice ' flesh from '
' Moses ' to ' Jehovah ' word as and ' 22 am people from ' that`s the ' soul the
' captain`ing ' milk ' all ' say of ' Israel ' as son ' to ' word ' 23 say of
' milk and ' the foolish ' milk and ' 24 and eat you ' not ' Goat and ' sheep and
' not ' eat and ' the messenger from the ' all of ' success`ed ' torn`ed
' which ' cattle`ed the ' has from ' milk ' eat ' all ' for ' 25 and eat`ed you
' soul the ' hew`ed shall ' Jehovah of ' Woman ' her`ed from ' and approach`s as
' all in ' and eat you ' not ' blood ' all and ' 26 am people from ' you eat the
' soul the ' all and ' 27 cattle`ed of and ' fly`ing of ' your as desist and from

' that`s the ' soul the ' hew`ed shall ' blood ' all ' eat you ' which
to and ' word ' (29 say of ' Moses ' to ' Jehovah ' word as and ' (28 am people from
' sacrifice ' ye ' approach`s them ' say of ' word you ' Israel ' as son '
' Jehovah of ' and has approach ' ye ' came`s as ' Jehovah of ' him whole
' as fire ' ye ' the has as came`s you ' him hand ' (30 him whole ' sacrifice from
' ye ' and has came`s as ' vision`ed the ' on ' milk the ' ye ' Jehovah
' (31 Jehovah ' as before ' the wave`ing you ' and ye ' wave`s the of ' vision`ed the
' be`s and ' the sacrifice them ' milk the ' ye ' priest the ' perfume`s the and
' right`s the ' moisten`ing ' ye and ' (32 him son of and ' Aaron of ' vision`ed the
' (33 your as whole ' as sacrifice from ' priest of ' the oblation`ing ' and give you
as son from ' milk the ' ye and ' from as whole the ' blood ' ye ' approach`s them
' ye ' for ' (34 widow`ed ' right`s the ' moisten`ing ' be`s you ' if ' Aaron '
' the oblation`ing the ' moisten`ing ' ye and ' the wave`ing scared ' vision`ed
' them as whole ' as sacrifice from ' Israel ' as son ' each ' as you take
from on`ing ' law of ' him son of and ' priest the ' Aaron of ' from ye ' give I and
' you anoint and ' Aaron ' you anoint ' such ' (35 Israel ' as son ' each '
' from ye ' and approach`s the ' day as in ' Jehovah ' as fire from ' him son
' them of ' set of ' Jehovah ' command`ed ' which ' (36 Jehovah of ' priest of
from on`ing ' statute ' Israel ' as son ' each ' from ye ' and anoint ' day as in
' the bestow of and ' on`ed of ' the protect`ing the ' such ' (37 from generation of '
' sacrifice of and ' from as fill`ing of and ' guilty of and ' you sin of and
' blemish ' Moses ' ye ' Jehovah ' command`ed ' which ' (38 from as whole the
approach`s the of ' Israel ' as son ' ye ' and you command ' day as in ' as bush`s
as bush`s ' word from in ' Jehovah of ' them as has approach ' ye '

ye and ' Aaron ' ye ' took ' (2 say of ' Moses ' to ' Jehovah ' word as and ' (1
' anoint`ed the ' eight ' ye and ' from as fabric the ' ye and ' and ye ' him son '
' exalt ' ye and ' from as Ram`s the ' two ' ye and ' you sin the ' apart ' ye and
tent ' open ' to ' assemble the ' till`ed the ' all ' ye and ' (3 unleaven`ing the
' and ye ' Jehovah ' command`ed ' which are ' Moses ' do as and ' (4 ing`congregate '
say as and ' (5 ing`congregate ' tent ' open ' to ' till`ed the ' assemble you and
' Jehovah ' command`ed ' which ' word the ' this ' till`ed the ' to ' Moses '
' him son ' ye and ' Aaron ' ye ' Moses ' approach as and ' (6 you concoct of
you coat the ' ye ' and Mosthigh ' give as and ' (7 Water in ' from ye ' wash as and
' above`s the ' ye ' and ye ' arm as and ' belt came ' and ye ' restrain as and '
' and ye ' restrain as and ' gird`ing the ' ye ' and Mosthigh ' give as and
' and Mosthigh ' site and ' (8 and in ' if ' gird as and ' gird`ing the ' reckon in
' from as light`ing the ' ye ' pocket the ' to ' give as and ' pocket the ' ye
and head ' on ' you turban them ' ye ' site and ' (9 from as complete the ' ye and
ye ' him turn ' split`ing ' to ' you turban them ' on ' give as and ' site and '
' Jehovah ' command`ed ' which are ' holy the ' consecrate ' gold the ' flower`s '
anoint as and ' anoint`ed the ' eight ' ye ' Moses ' took as and ' (10 Moses ' ye
' (11 from ye ' holy as and ' and in ' which ' all ' ye and ' Tabernacle the ' ye '
' from as move ' seven ' sacrifice them ' on ' and her from ' splash and
' ye and ' and vessel are ' all ' ye and ' sacrifice them ' ye ' anoint as and
' eight from ' cast and ' (12 from holy of ' and so ' ye and ' Laver`ing the
' (13 and holy of ' and ye ' anoint as and ' Aaron ' head ' on ' anoint`ed the
' you and coat ' from arm as and ' Aaron ' as son ' ye ' Moses ' approach as and
' them of ' saddle as and ' from as belt I ' from ye ' restrain as and
adduce and ' (14 Moses ' ye ' Jehovah ' command`ed ' which are ' you and have bonnet

' ye ' him son and ' Aaron ' lay as and ' you sin the ' apart ' ye '
' took as and ' slay as and ' 15 you sin the ' apart ' head ' on ' them as hand
' sacrifice them ' you and horn ' on ' give as and ' blood the ' ye ' Moses
blood the ' ye and ' sacrifice them ' ye ' sin as and ' and finger came ' surround`s
' atone of ' and holy`ed as and ' sacrifice them ' position`ing ' to ' cast '
' approach the ' on ' which ' milk the ' all ' ye ' took as and ' 16 and Mosthigh
' ye and ' whom`ing total ' twosome ' ye and ' honour the ' you ing`preserve ' ye and
' broken ' ye and ' 17 the sacrifice them ' Moses ' perfume as and ' behold as milk
' burnt ' and excrement ' ye and ' and flesh ' ye and ' and town`ing ' ye and
ye ' Jehovah ' command`ed ' which are ' camp`ed of ' outside`ing from ' abhorrence
and lay as and ' on`ed the ' Ram`s ' ye ' adduce and ' approach as and ' 18 Moses '
' 19 Ram`s the ' head ' on ' them as hand ' ye ' him son and ' Aaron '
' sacrifice them ' on ' blood the ' ye ' Moses ' sprinkle as and ' slay as and
' perfume as and ' him dismember of ' dismember ' Ram`s the ' ye and ' 20 surround`s
' 21 fat the ' ye and ' from as dismember the ' ye and ' head the ' ye ' Moses
' perfume as and ' Water in ' wash ' from as leg the ' ye and ' approach the ' ye and
smell`s of ' that`ing ' on`ed ' the sacrifice them ' Ram`s the ' all ' ye ' Moses
ye ' Jehovah ' command`ed ' which are ' Jehovah of ' that`ing ' Woman ' odor has '
from as fill the ' Ram`s ' two the ' Ram`s the ' ye ' approach as and ' 22 Moses '
' head ' on ' them as hand ' ye ' him son and ' Aaron ' and lay as and '
on ' give as and ' and blood from ' Moses ' took as and ' slay as and ' 23 Ram`s the
' and hand ' thick`ing ' on and ' whom right`s the ' Aaron ' ear ' tip`ing '
' approach as and ' 24 whom right the ' and foot ' thick`ing ' on and ' whom right the
tip`ing ' on ' blood the ' has from ' Moses ' give as and ' Aaron ' as son ' ye
' on and ' whom right the ' energy ' thick`ing ' on and ' whom right the ' from ear '

' blood the ' ye ' Moses ' sprinkle as and ' whom right the ' from foot ' thick`ing
' ye and ' milk the ' ye ' took as and ' 25 surround`s ' sacrifice them ' on
' ye and ' approach the ' on ' which ' milk the ' all ' ye and ' am these
' ye and ' whom`ing total ' twosome ' ye and ' honour the ' you ing`preserve
' exult from and ' 26 right`s the ' moisten`ing ' ye and ' behold as milk
' sister ' find`ed ' cake ' took of ' Jehovah ' as before ' which ' unleaven`ing the
' on ' site and ' one ' slim`s and ' sister ' eight ' fight ' cake and
total ' ye ' give as and ' 27 right`s the ' moisten`ing ' on and ' from as milk the
' from ye ' wave as and ' him son ' as palm ' on and ' Aaron ' as palm ' on '
' above ' from ye ' Moses ' took as and ' 28 Jehovah ' as before ' the wave`ing you
' from as fill ' on`ed the ' on ' the sacrifice them ' perfume as and ' them as palm
' took as and ' 29 Jehovah of ' that`ing ' Woman ' odor has ' smell`s of ' them
' as before ' the wave`ing you ' alas wave`s as and ' vision`ed the ' ye ' Moses
' which are ' widow`ed ' be`s ' Moses of ' from as fill the ' Ram`s from ' Jehovah
' eight from ' Moses ' took as and ' 30 Moses ' ye ' Jehovah ' command`ed
splash and ' sacrifice them ' on ' which ' blood the ' has from and ' anoint`ed the
' as fabric ' on and ' him son ' on and ' him fabric ' on and ' Aaron ' on '
' ye and ' him fabric ' ye and ' Aaron ' ye ' holy as and ' and ye ' him son
' to ' Moses ' say as and ' 31 and ye ' him son ' as fabric ' ye and ' him son
' tent ' open ' flesh the ' ye ' and sodden ' him son ' to and ' Aaron
ye and ' and ye ' and eat you ' there and ' holy the ' place`ing in ' ing`congregate
' as whom command ' which are ' from as fill the ' exult in ' which ' fight the '
' flesh in ' survive behold and ' 32 and eat`ed as ' him son and ' Aaron ' say of
' tent ' open from and ' 33 and burnt you ' abhorrence ' from bread in and
' day as ' till ' from week ' you seven ' and issue you ' not ' ing`congregate

' ye ' fill as ' from week ' you seven ' for ' your as fill ' week ' you fill
' Jehovah ' command`ed ' this the ' day as in ' do`ed ' which are ' 34 your as hand
' ing`congregate ' tent ' open and ' 35 from are mosthigh ' atone of ' you concoct of
' from week ' you seven ' the night`s and ' from day as ' and inhabitant
for ' and die`ing you ' not and ' Jehovah ' you guard from ' ye ' from you guard and
' all ' ye ' him son and ' Aaron ' do as and ' 36 as whom command ' so '
Moses ' hand in ' Jehovah ' command`ed ' which ' from as word the

THE TORAH SCROLL 9

' Aaron of ' Moses ' call ' as eight`s the ' day as in ' became as and ' (1
' took ' Aaron ' to ' say as and ' (2 Israel ' as elder of and ' him son of and
' they full ' on`ed of ' Ram`s and ' you sin of ' herd ' son ' calf ' walk
' Israel ' as son ' as elder ' to and ' (3 Jehovah ' as before ' approach the and
' calf and ' you sin of ' from as Goat ' gate`s ' and took ' say of ' word you
' Ram`s and ' Ox`ing and ' (4 on`ed of ' they full ' the Year ' as son ' mutton and
the mingle`ing ' bestow`ed and ' Jehovah ' as before ' sacrifice of ' from as whole of
' acquire as and ' (5 your as to ' speak`ed ' Jehovah ' day as the ' for ' eight in '
' ing`congregate ' tent ' around ' to ' Moses ' command`ed ' which ' ye
(6 ' Jehovah ' as before ' and stand as and ' till`ed the ' all ' and approach as and
smoke`ing you ' Jehovah ' command`ed ' which ' word the ' this ' Moses ' say as and
' to ' Moses ' say as and ' (7 Jehovah ' honour`ing ' your as to ' look`ed as and '
' ye and ' are you sin ' ye ' do`ed and ' sacrifice them ' to ' approach ' Aaron
' ye ' do`ed and ' people the ' till in and ' are till in ' atone and ' are offer
' command`ed ' which are ' from till in ' atone and ' people the ' has approach
' ye ' slay as and ' sacrifice them ' to ' Aaron ' approach as and ' (8 Jehovah
' ye ' Aaron ' as son ' and approach as and ' (9 if ' which ' you sin the ' calf
' on ' give as and ' blood in ' and finger I ' dip as and ' him to ' blood the
' position`ing ' to ' cast ' blood the ' ye and ' sacrifice them ' you and horn
' ye and ' whom`ing total ' ye and ' milk the ' ye and ' (10 sacrifice them
perfume`s the ' you sin the ' has from ' honour the ' has from ' you ing`perserve the
' ye and ' (11 Moses ' ye ' Jehovah ' command`ed ' which are ' the sacrifice them '
(12 camp`ed of ' outside`ing from ' abhorrence ' burnt ' flies`ing ' ye and ' flesh the
' him to ' Aaron ' as son ' and come`s as and ' on`ed the ' ye ' slay as and '
(13 ' surround`s ' sacrifice them ' on ' and sprinkle`ed as and ' blood the ' ye

' head the ' ye and ' am dismember of ' him to ' and come`s the ' on`ed the ' ye and

' approach the ' ye ' wash as and ' (14 the sacrifice them ' on ' perfume as and

' (15 the sacrifice them ' on`ed the ' on ' perfume as and ' from as leg the ' ye and

' gate`s ' ye ' took as and ' people the ' has approach ' ye ' approach`s as and

' and sin`ed as and ' and slay`ed as and ' people of ' which ' you sin the

' do`ed as and ' on`ed the ' ye ' approach`s as and ' (16 has and head`s are

' fill as and ' bestow`ed the ' ye ' approach`s as and ' (17 discern from are

offer ' alone of from ' sacrifice them ' on ' perfume as and ' her`ed from ' him palm

' sacrifice ' Ram`s the ' ye and ' Ox`ing the ' ye ' slay as and ' (18 herd the '

' ye ' Aaron ' as son ' and come`s as and ' people of ' which ' from as whole the

' (19 surround`s ' sacrifice them ' on ' and sprinkle`ed as and ' him to ' blood the

' Ram`s the ' has from and ' Ox`ing the ' has from ' from as milk the ' ye and

honour the ' you ing`preserve and ' whom`ing total and ' amount`ed the and ' am these

' you and vision the ' on ' from as milk the ' ye ' and site`s and ' (20

you and vision the ' ye and ' (21 the sacrifice them ' from as milk the ' perfume as and

' the wave`ing you ' Aaron ' wave`s the ' right`s the ' moisten`ing ' ye and '

' (22 Moses ' ye ' Jehovah ' command`ed ' which are ' Jehovah ' as before

' from bless as and ' people the ' to ' and hand ' ye ' Aaron ' lift as and

' (23 from as whole the and ' on`ed the and ' you sin the ' you and work ' descend and

' and out and ' ing`congregate ' tent ' to ' Aaron and ' Moses ' came as and

' to ' Jehovah ' honour`ing ' look`ed as and ' people the ' ye ' and bless as and

' eat you and ' Jehovah ' as before from ' fire ' issue you and ' (24 people the ' all

' see as and ' from as milk the ' ye and ' on`ed the ' ye ' sacrifice them ' on

them around ' on ' and fell and ' and shout as and ' people the ' all

' man I ' Abihu and ' freewill ' Aaron ' as son ' acquire as and ' 1
' behold as on ' and site`s and ' fire ' thick ' and give as and ' and you crush from
' stranger`ed ' fire ' Jehovah ' as before ' and approach`s as and ' you perfume
' as before from ' fire ' issue you and ' 2 from ye ' command`ed ' not ' which
' 3 Jehovah ' as before ' and die as and ' from ye`ing ' eat you and ' Jehovah
' say of ' Jehovah ' word ' which ' that`ing ' Aaron ' to ' Moses ' say as and
' honour I ' people the ' all ' around ' on and ' holy I ' as approach in
' to and ' ask as from ' to ' Moses ' call as and ' 4 Aaron ' blood as and
' them as to ' say as and ' Aaron ' teat ' Uzziel ' as son ' Elizaphan
' to ' holy the ' around ' each ' your as brother ' ye ' and lift ' and approach
from ye ' and from linger and ' and approach as and ' 5 camp`ed of ' outside`ing from
Moses ' word ' which are ' camp`ed of ' outside`ing from ' to ' from you coat in '
' Ithamar ' to and ' Eleazar ' to and ' Aaron ' to ' Moses ' say as and ' 6
and rip you ' not ' your as fabric and ' and hair you ' to ' your as head ' him son
' angry as ' till`ed the ' all ' on and ' and die`ing you ' not and '
' ye ' and against as ' Israel ' you house ' all ' your as brother and
' ing`congregate ' tent ' open from and ' 7 Jehovah ' burnt ' which ' burnt`ed the
Jehovah ' you anoint ' eight ' for ' has and die`ing you ' turn ' and issue you ' not
' Jehovah ' word as and ' 8 Moses ' word are ' concoct as and ' from are mosthigh '
' ye`ed ' impose`ed ' to ' merry and ' between`s ' 9 say of ' Aaron ' to
' not and ' ing`congregate ' tent ' to ' from are came in ' are ye ' are as son and
' 10 from are as generation of ' from on`ing ' statute ' and die`ing you
' sick the ' between in and ' holy the ' between in ' separate`s the of and
' 11 clean`ing the ' between in and ' unclean the ' between in and
' from as law the ' all ' ye ' Israel ' as son ' ye ' you and instruct`ing and

' Moses ' word as and ' 12 Moses ' hand in ' them as to ' Jehovah ' word ' which
' him son ' Ithamar ' to and ' Eleazar ' to and ' Aaron ' to
' you survive has the ' bestow`ed the ' ye ' and took ' from as survive has the
' sacrifice them ' beside ' unleaven`ing ' the and eat and ' Jehovah ' as fire from
' place`ing in ' ye`ed ' from you eat and ' 13 that`s ' from as holy ' holy ' for
' Jehovah ' as fire from ' that`s ' are as son ' law and ' are law ' for ' holy`ing
' ye and ' the wave`ing scared ' vision`ed ' ye and ' 14 as whom command ' so ' for
ye`ed ' clean`ing ' place`ing in ' and eat you ' the oblation`ing the ' moisten`ing
' law and ' are law ' for ' are ye ' are as daugther`th and ' are as son and '
' 15 Israel ' as son ' as whole ' as sacrifice from ' and gave ' are as son
' on ' the wave`ing scared ' vision'ed and ' the oblation`ing the ' moisten`ing
' the wave`ing you ' wave`s the of ' and came`s as ' from as milk the ' as fire
are as daughter`th of and ' are as son of and ' walk ' be`s and ' Jehovah ' as before
' ye and ' 16 Jehovah ' command`ed ' which are ' from on`ing ' law of ' are ye '
' burnt`ing ' be`th and ' Moses ' search ' search ' you sin the ' gate`s
' Aaron ' as son ' Ithamar ' on and ' Eleazar ' on ' angry as and
' ye ' from you eat ' not ' why`ing ' 17 say of ' from as survive has the
' that`s ' from as holy ' holy ' for ' holy the ' place`ing in ' you sin the
' atone of ' till`ed the ' low`ing ' ye ' arise of ' relate ' gave ' ye`ed and
' blood`ed ' ye ' entree the ' not ' behold ' 18 Jehovah ' as before ' them as on
' holy in ' ye`ed ' and eat you ' eat`ing ' the from around ' holy the ' to
' behold ' Moses ' to ' Aaron ' word as and ' 19 as whom command ' which are
' from offer ' ye and ' from you sin ' ye ' and approach`s the ' day as the
' as you eat and ' to`ed are ' near ' the has call you and ' Jehovah ' as before
' hear as and ' 20 Jehovah ' as has eye in ' improve as the ' day as the ' you sin

him has eye in ' improve as and ' Moses

2 them as to ' say of ' Aaron ' to and ' Moses ' to ' Jehovah ' word as and ' 1

' which ' life`ed the ' such ' say of ' Israel ' as son ' to ' and word '

' all ' 3 land the ' on ' which ' cattle`ed the ' all from ' and eat you

' you and spread ' twosome ' cloven ' you cloven and ' the spread ' you spread`s from

this ' ye ' sure ' 4 and eat you ' ye`ed ' cattle`ed in ' guest`ed ' you and above

spread`ed the ' as spread`s they and ' guest`ed the ' as on they ' and eat you ' not '

' the spread and ' that`ing ' guest`ed ' on`ed from ' for ' wean the ' ye '

' ye and ' 5 relate ' that`ing ' unclean ' spread`s from ' and has whither`s

' not ' the spread and ' that`ing ' guest`ed ' on`ed from ' for ' has lip the

' for ' you in stream the ' ye and ' 6 relate ' that`ing ' unclean ' spread`s as

' the spread`s the ' not ' the spread and ' that`s ' guest`ed ' you on from

' spread`s from ' for ' Swine`s the ' ye and ' 7 relate ' that`s ' unclean`ed

' guest`ed ' that`ing and ' the spread ' cloven ' cloven and ' that`ing ' the spread

' not ' from flesh from ' 8 relate ' that`ing ' unclean ' guest`ing as ' not

' them ' from as unclean ' and reach ' not ' from you foolish in and ' and eat you

' which ' all ' Water in ' which ' all from ' and eat you ' this ' ye and ' 9 relate

' from as sea in ' Water in ' drink scales and ' fin`s had ' if

if ' whither`s ' which ' all and ' 10 and eat you ' from ye ' from as inherit in and

' from as inherit in and ' from as sea in ' Water in ' drink scales and ' fin`s had '

Water in ' which ' life`ed the ' soul ' all from and ' Water the ' breed ' all from

' from flesh from ' relate ' and became as ' detest and ' 11 relate ' them ' detest '

' which ' all and ' 12 and detest you ' from you foolish ' ye and ' and eat you ' not

relate ' that`ing ' detest ' Water in ' drink scales and ' fin`s had ' if ' whither`s

' and eat whom ' not ' fly`ing the ' has from ' and detest you ' to`ed ' ye and ' 13

' ye and ' spread the ' ye and ' captain has the ' ye ' them ' detest

' 15 the has kind ' hence`ed the ' ye and ' same`ed the ' ye and ' 14 am diver have the
' ye and ' low`ed as the ' daughter ' ye and ' 16 and has kind ' twilight ' all ' ye
' discharge the ' ye and ' emaciate the ' ye and ' violence`ing you the
' ye and ' hurl the ' ye and ' cup are the ' ye and ' 17 and the has kind
ye and ' you vomit the ' ye and ' you there give the ' ye and ' 18 lip`ing between the
' the has kind ' enrage`ed the and ' the bow`s the ' ye and ' 19 comfort`ed the '
' breed ' all and ' 20 put of swoop the ' ye and ' you palm`s menstrate the ' ye and
ye ' sure ' 21 relate ' that`ing ' detest ' four I ' on ' enter the ' fly`ing the
' four I ' on ' enter the ' fly`ing the ' breed ' all from ' and eat you ' this '
' on ' cattle ' leap of ' him foot of ' above from ' from as leg ' not`ing ' which
' Locust`ed the ' ye ' and eat you ' lag ' to`ed ' ye ' 22 land the
' ye and ' and the has kind ' from rock the ' ye and ' and the has kind
' 23 and the has kind ' peak at the ' ye and ' and the has kind ' of will hole the
' detest ' from as foot ' four I ' if ' which ' fly`ing the ' breed ' all and
' touch the ' all ' and unclean you ' to`ed of and ' 24 relate ' that`ing
' help the ' all and ' 25 twilight the ' till ' unclean as ' from you foolish in
unclean and ' Water in ' wash and ' him fabric ' immersion as ' from you foolish from
you spread`s from ' that`s ' which ' cattle`ed the ' all of ' 26 twilight the ' till '
' guest'ed and ' you cloven ' the has whither`s ' cloven`ed and ' the spread '
' touch the ' all ' relate ' them ' from as unclean ' on`ed from ' the has whither`s
' all in ' him palm ' gush ' on ' walk and be ' all and ' 27 unclean as ' cattle
' all ' relate ' them ' from as unclean ' four I ' on ' you enter the ' life`ed the
' help the and ' 28 twilight the ' till ' unclean as ' from you foolish in ' touch the
' till ' unclean and ' him fabric ' immersion as ' from you foolish from ' ye
unclean the ' relate ' this and ' 29 relate ' them`ed ' from as unclean ' twilight the

' Mouse the and ' my sick the ' land the ' on ' breed the ' breed in '
' power the and ' the blame I the and ' 30 and the has kind ' establish the and
' to`ed ' 31 you from swarm the and ' down at the and ' the I gum the and
' cattle ' touch the ' all ' breed the ' all in from ' relate ' from as unclean the
' made as ' which ' all and ' 32 twilight the ' till ' unclean as ' from die`s in
or ' tree ' weapon ' all from ' unclean as ' from die`ing in ' lag ' and Mosthigh
' success`ed ' which ' weapon ' all ' moisten ' or ' town`ing ' or ' fabric '
' twilight the ' till ' unclean and ' came`ing as ' Water in ' cattle ' the are fill
' to ' lag ' made as ' which ' devise ' weapon ' all and ' 33 clean and
' and ye and ' unclean as ' and middle`ing in ' which ' all ' and middle`ing
' came`ing as ' which ' eat as ' which ' eat the ' all from ' 34 and buy you
' belong`ed ' which ' moisten`ed from ' all and ' unclean as ' Water ' and Mosthigh
' from you foolish from ' made as ' which ' all and ' 35 unclean as ' weapon ' all in
' and annihilate as ' from as pasture`s and ' flame`ing ' unclean as ' and Mosthigh
' sure ' 36 relate ' and became as ' from as unclean and ' them ' from as unclean
' clean`ing ' be`s as ' Water ' the ditch ' empty`ing and ' Water ' low`s from
' made as ' for and ' 37 unclean as ' from you foolish in ' touch and
' clean`ing ' seed as ' which ' seed`ing ' seed ' all ' on ' from you foolish from
' fall and ' seed the ' on ' Water ' permanent ' for and ' 38 that`ing
' for and ' 39 relate ' that`ing ' unclean ' and Mosthigh ' from you foolish from
' eat`ed of ' relate ' that`s ' which ' cattle`ed the ' has from ' die`ing as
' eat the and ' 40 twilight the ' till ' unclean as ' the you foolish in ' touch the
' till ' unclean and ' him fabric ' immersion as ' the you foolish in from
' him fabric ' immersion as ' the you foolish ' ye ' help the and ' twilight the
' on ' breed the ' breed the ' all and ' 41 twilight the ' till ' unclean and

' on ' walk and be ' all ' 42 eat as ' not ' that`ing ' detest ' land the
' the much ' all ' till ' four I ' on ' walk and be ' all and ' abdomen`ing
' not ' land the ' on ' breed the ' breed the ' all of ' from as foot
' ye ' and detest you ' to ' 43 them ' detest ' for ' from and eat you
' and unclean you ' not and ' breed the ' breed the ' all in ' from are as you soul
' Jehovah ' as whither ' for ' 44 height ' from you unclean has and ' cattle
for ' from as holy ' complete as became and ' from you holy sacred and ' your as Allah
' from are as you soul ' ye ' and unclean you ' not and ' as whither ' holy`ing '
' Jehovah ' as whither ' for ' 45 land the ' on ' crawl the ' breed the ' all in
' whom the of ' from as Mizra ' land from ' from are ye ' above`ed the ' your as Allah
' holy`ing ' for ' from as holy ' complete as became and ' from as Allah of ' relate
' all and ' fly`ing the and ' cattle`ed the ' you protect`ing ' such ' 46 as whither
' soul the ' all of and ' Water in ' you crawl the ' life`ed the ' soul the
' unclean the ' between in ' separate`s the of ' 47 land the ' on ' you breed the
' you eat has the ' life`ed the ' between in and ' clean`ing the ' between in and
eat you ' not ' which ' life`ed the ' between in and

THE TORAH SCROLL 12

Lev 12:1-12:8

' as son ' to ' word ' 2 say of ' Moses ' to ' Jehovah ' word as and ' 1
' male ' bore`ed as and ' seed`s you ' for ' Woman ' say of ' Israel
' the decree`ing ' impurity ' week are ' from week ' you seven ' unclean`ed and
' flesh ' ye ' split`ing as ' as eight`s the ' day as in and ' 3 unclean you
' from week ' you three and ' day as ' from as three and ' 4 and you foreskin
' to and ' reach ' not ' holy ' all in ' clean`ed ' as blood in ' inhabitant
' mother and ' 5 clean`ed ' week ' you fill ' till ' income`ing ' not ' holy them
' decree`ed so ' from as seven`ing ' unclean`ed and ' bore you ' the female
' as blood ' on ' inhabitant ' from week ' you six and ' day as ' from as six and
' daughter of ' or ' son of ' clean`ed ' week ' you fill in and ' 6 clean`ed
' or ' the Dove`ing ' son and ' on`ed of ' and you year ' son ' mutton ' came`s you
' 7 priest the ' to ' ing`congregate ' tent ' open ' to ' you sin of ' protect
' priest the ' am on ' atone and ' Jehovah ' as before ' and approach`s the and
you bore became ' you protect`ing ' such ' am blood ' source`ing from ' clean`ed and
' hand`ed ' come you ' not ' mother and ' 8 female`ed of ' or ' is remember of '
' as son ' two ' or ' from as protect ' twosome ' take`ed and ' resemble ' enough
' am on ' atone and ' on`ed of ' one and ' you sin of ' one ' the Dove`ing
clean`ed and ' priest the

' ground ' 2 say of ' Aaron ' to and ' Moses ' to ' Jehovah ' word as and ' 1
' you blemish ' or ' you scab ' or ' arise ' and flesh ' burn`ing ' be`s as ' for
' to ' came alas and ' you leper ' touch of ' and flesh ' burn`ing ' be`s and
' 3 from as priest the ' him son from ' one ' to ' or ' priest the ' Aaron
' barley and ' flesh the ' burn`ing ' touch the ' ye ' priest the ' look`ed and
' valley ' touch the ' appear`ed and ' son of ' overthrow ' have plague in
' and look`ed and ' that`ing ' you leper ' touch ' and flesh ' alter have from
' that`s ' white`ed ' you blemish ' mother and ' 4 and ye ' unclean and ' priest the
' flies`ing ' has from ' look`ed from ' whither`s ' valley and ' and flesh ' burn`ing
' ye ' priest the ' close`s the and ' son of ' overthrow ' not ' Barley`ed and
' day as in ' priest the ' and look`ed and ' 5 from week ' you seven ' touch the
extremity`ed ' not ' him has eye in ' stand ' touch the ' be`th and ' as seven`s the
' from week ' you seven ' priest the ' and close`s the and ' burn`ing ' touch the '
you two ' as seven`s the ' day as in ' and ye ' priest the ' look`ed and ' 6 you two
' burn`ing ' touch the ' extremity`ed ' not and ' touch the ' here`ed ' be`th and '
' him fabric ' immersion and ' that`s ' you scab from ' priest the ' and clean and
burn`ing ' you scab them ' the extremity you ' extremity`ed ' mother and ' 7 clean and
' the look shall ' and you clean of ' priest the ' to ' and sight the ' as after '
he extremity ' be`th and ' priest the ' look`ed and ' 8 priest the ' to`ed ' you two
' 9 that`s ' you leper ' priest the ' and unclean and ' burn`ing ' you scab them '
priest the ' to ' came alas and ' Men in ' be`s you ' for ' you leper ' touch and
that`s and ' burn`ing ' white`ed ' arise ' be`th and ' priest the ' look`ed and ' 10
' 11 arise in ' life ' flesh ' crush`s from and ' son of ' gate ' reverse`ed the '
' and unclean and ' and flesh ' burn`ing ' that`s ' sleep and has ' you leper
' mother and ' 12 that`ing ' unclean ' for ' and has close as ' not ' priest the

' ye ' you leper the ' garment`ed and ' burn`ing ' you leper the ' bud you ' bud`ing
' all of ' him foot ' till and ' and head from ' touch the ' town`ing ' all
' be`th and ' priest the ' look`ed and ' (13 priest the ' as has eye ' look`ed from
' touch the ' ye ' clean and ' and flesh ' all ' ye ' you leper the ' garment`ed
' sight`ing the ' day as in and ' (14 that`ing ' clean`ing ' son of ' overthrow ' fail
' flesh the ' ye ' priest the ' look`ed and ' (15 unclean as ' life ' flesh ' and in
' you leper ' that`ing ' unclean ' life the ' flesh the ' and unclean and ' life the
' reverse the shall ' life the ' flesh the ' carry`ing as ' for ' or ' (16 that`s
be`th and ' priest the ' and look`ed and ' (17 priest the ' to ' came and ' Laban of
touch the ' ye ' priest the ' clean and ' Laban of ' touch the ' reverse the has '
' botch`s ' and burn ' and in ' be`s as ' for ' flesh and ' (18 that`ing ' clean`ing '
or ' white`ed ' arise ' botch`s the ' place`ing in ' be`s and ' (19 decease has and
' (20 priest the ' to ' the look shall ' you blood Men ' white`ed ' you blemish '
flies`ing ' has from ' depth ' and look`ed from ' be`th and ' priest the ' look`ed and
' touch ' priest the ' and unclean and ' son of ' overthrow ' and gate`ed and '
' the has look as ' mother and ' (21 the bud ' botch`s in ' that`s ' you leper
' deth`ed and ' son of ' gate ' thus ' whither`s ' be`th and ' priest the
and close`s the and ' here`ed ' that`s and ' flies`ing ' has from ' the has whither`s
' extremity`ed ' mother and ' (22 from week ' you seven ' priest the '
(23 that`ing ' touch ' and ye ' priest the ' unclean and ' burn`ing ' the extremity you
' he extremity ' not ' you blemish the ' stand you ' am under ' mother and '
flesh ' or ' (24 priest the ' and clean and ' that`s ' botch`s the ' you increase did
' crush`s from ' whom`ed the and ' fire ' you scorch ' and burn ' be`s as ' for '
' (25 white`ed ' or ' you blood Men ' white`ed ' you blemish ' epidermis`ed the
' son of ' gate ' overthrow`ed has ' be`th and ' priest the ' ye`ed ' look`ed and

' that`s ' you leper ' flies`ing ' has from ' valley ' appear`ed and ' you blemish in
' you leper ' touch ' priest the ' and ye ' unclean and ' the bud ' epidermis`ed in
' whither`s ' be`th and ' priest the ' the has look as ' mother and ' 26 that`s
' has from ' the has whither`s ' deth`ed and ' son of ' gate ' you blemish in
' you seven ' priest the ' and close`s the and ' here`ed ' that`s and ' flies`ing
' mother ' as seven`s the ' day as in ' priest the ' and look`ed and ' 27 from week
' and ye ' priest the ' unclean and ' burn`ing ' the extremity you ' extremity`ed
' you blemish the ' stand you ' am under ' mother and ' 28 that`s ' you leper ' touch
' epidermis`ed the ' arise ' here`ed ' that`s and ' burn`ing ' he extremity ' not
' epidermis`ed the ' you increase did ' for ' priest the ' and clean and ' that`s
' head in ' touch ' and in ' be`s as ' for ' Woman ' or ' man I and ' 29 that`s
' be`th and ' touch the ' ye ' priest the ' look`ed and ' 30 beard it in ' or
thin ' orange ' gate ' and in and ' flies`ing ' has from ' valley ' and look`ed from
or ' head the ' you leper ' that`ing ' scurf ' and ye ' priest the ' unclean and '
scurf the ' touch ' ye ' priest the ' look`ed as ' for and ' 31 that`s ' elder the '
' flies`ing ' has from ' valley ' and look`ed from ' whither`s ' be`th and '
touch ' ye ' priest the ' close`s the and ' and in ' whither`s ' black ' barley and
touch the ' ye ' priest the ' look`ed and ' 32 from week ' you seven ' scurf the '
' not and ' scurf the ' extremity`ed ' not ' be`th and ' as seven`s the ' day as in '
' valley ' whither`s ' scurf the ' appear`ed and ' orange ' gate ' and in ' be`s
' shave as ' not ' scurf the ' ye and ' shave you the and ' 33 flies`ing ' has from
34 you two ' from week ' you seven ' scurf the ' ye ' priest the ' close`s the and
' as seven`s the ' day as in ' scurf the ' ye ' priest the ' look`ed and '
' and look`ed from and ' burn`ing ' scurf the ' extremity`ed ' not ' be`th and
' priest the ' and ye ' clean and ' flies`ing ' has from ' valley ' and has whither`s

' extremity`ed ' mother and ' 35 clean and ' him fabric ' immersion and
and look`ed and ' 36 and you clean ' as after ' burn`ing ' scurf the ' extremity`ed as
' is morn as ' not ' burn`ing ' scurf the ' extremity`ed ' be`th and ' priest the '
' mother and ' 37 that`ing ' unclean ' orange the ' gate of ' priest the
' and in ' sprout ' black ' barley and ' scurf the ' stand ' him has eye in
' 38 priest the ' and clean and ' that`ing ' clean`ing ' scurf the ' decease has
' you and blemish ' from flesh ' burn`ing ' be`s as ' for ' Woman ' or ' man I and
' burn`ing ' be`th and ' priest the ' look`ed and ' 39 you and white ' you and blemish
' that`ing ' freckle ' you and white ' you alas are ' you and blemish ' from flesh
' and head ' furbish as ' for ' man I and ' 40 that`ing ' clean`ing ' burn`ing ' bud
' him turn ' quarter from ' mother and ' 41 that`ing ' clean`ing ' that`ing ' bald
be`s as ' for and ' 42 that`ing ' clean`ing ' that`ing ' bare ' and head ' furbish as
' you leper ' blood Men ' son of ' touch ' and you bare in ' or ' and you bald in '
' look`ed and ' 43 and you bare in ' or ' and you bald in ' that`s ' you bud
' you blood Men ' white`ed ' touch the ' arise ' be`th and ' priest the ' and ye`ed
' town`ing ' you leper ' appear`ed are ' and you bare in ' or ' and you bald in
' unclean ' that`ing ' unclean ' that`ing ' leper`ing ' man I ' 44 flesh
leper`ing the and ' 45 and have plague ' and head in ' priest the ' and has unclean as
' from as rip`ing ' and became as ' him fabric ' touch the ' and in ' which '
unclean and ' the swoop`er as ' moustache ' on and ' hair`ing ' be`s as ' and head and
' unclean as ' and in ' touch the ' which ' week ' all ' 46 call as ' unclean '
' camp`ed of ' outside`ing from ' dwell ' single ' that`ing ' unclean
' you leper ' touch ' and in ' be`s as ' for ' fabric the and ' 47 and carry and from
' or ' twosome in ' or ' 48 from as flaw ' fabric in ' or ' woollen ' fabric in
' all in ' or ' burn`ing ' or ' woollen of and ' from as flaw of ' twilight in

' blood Men ' or ' only only as ' touch the ' be`s and ' 49 town`ing ' you are fill
' all in ' or ' twilight in ' or ' twosome in ' or ' burn`ing ' or ' fabric in
' ye ' look`ed the and ' that`ing ' you leper ' touch ' town`ing ' weapon
' ye ' close`s the and ' touch the ' ye ' priest the ' look`ed and ' 50 priest the
' day as in ' touch the ' ye ' look`ed and ' 51 from week ' you seven ' touch the
or ' twosome in ' or ' fabric in ' touch the ' extremity`ed ' for ' as seven`s the
' flies`ing ' success`ed ' which ' all of ' burn`ing ' or ' twilight in '
' 52 that`ing ' unclean ' touch the ' you bitter from ' you leper ' the are fill of
' ye ' or ' as drink the ' ye ' or ' fabric the ' ye ' burnt and
' weapon ' all ' ye ' or ' from as flaw in ' or ' woollen in ' twilight the
you bitter from ' you leper ' for ' touch the ' and in ' be`s as ' which ' flies`ing
' priest the ' look`ed as ' mother and ' 53 burnt you ' abhorrence ' that`s '
' or ' twosome in ' or ' fabric in ' touch the ' extremity`ed ' not ' be`th and
' priest the ' command`ed and ' 54 town`ing ' weapon ' all in ' or ' twilight in
' and close`s the and ' touch the ' and in ' which ' ye ' and immersion and
' as after ' priest the ' look`ed and ' 55 you two ' from week ' you seven
' ye ' touch the ' overthrow ' not ' be`th and ' touch the ' ye ' immersion the
' abhorrence ' that`ing ' unclean ' extremity`ed ' not ' touch the and ' him has eye
and you bare in ' or ' and you bald in ' that`s ' you crush put ' and has burnt you
' as after ' touch the ' here`ed ' be`th and ' priest the ' look`ed ' mother and ' 56
' or ' fabric the ' has from ' and ye ' and rend and ' and ye ' and immersion the
twilight the ' has from ' or ' as drink the ' has from ' or ' flies`ing ' has from
' or ' twosome in ' or ' fabric in ' till`ing ' saw`ed ' mother and ' 57
' abhorrence ' that`s ' you bud ' town`ing ' weapon ' all in ' or ' twilight in
' or ' fabric the and ' 58 touch the ' and in ' which ' ye ' and has burnt you

’ which ’ flies`ing ’ weapon ’ all ’ or ’ twilight the ’ or ’ as drink the
59 clean and ’ you two ’ immersion and ’ touch the ’ lag ’ chasten ’ immersion you
’ or ’ woollen the ’ fabric ’ you leper the ’ touch ’ you protect`ing ’ such ’
’ weapon ’ all ’ or ’ twilight the ’ or ’ as drink the ’ or ’ from as flaw the
and unclean of ’ or ’ and clean of ’ town`ing

' be`s you ' such ' (2 say of ' Moses ' to ' Jehovah ' word as and ' (1
' to ' came alas and ' and you clean ' day as in ' leper them ' you protect`ing
' camp`ed of ' outside`ing from ' to ' priest the ' out and ' (3 priest the
has from ' you leper the ' touch ' decease has ' be`th and ' priest the ' look`ed and
' clean from of ' and take and ' priest the ' command`ed and ' (4 leper`ing the '
' cedar ' tree and ' you and clean ' you and life ' from as bird`ing ' twosome
' priest the ' command`ed and ' (5 hyssop`ing and ' you have hang`ing ' two and
' on ' devise ' weapon ' to ' sister the ' bird`ing the ' ye ' and slay and
' ye`ed ' took as ' life`ed the ' bird`ing the ' ye and ' (6 from as life ' Water
' ye and ' you have hang`ing the ' two ' ye and ' cedar the ' tree ' ye and
' life`ed the ' bird`ing the ' ye and ' from ye`ing ' dip and ' Hyssop`ing the
' (7 from as life the ' Water the ' on ' the slay`ing the ' bird`ing the ' blood in
' from as move ' seven ' you leper the ' has from ' clean them ' on ' this the and
' around ' on ' life`ed the ' bird`ing the ' ye ' send and ' and clean and
' ye ' shave and ' him fabric ' ye ' clean them ' immersion and ' (8 field`ed the
' to ' came`ing as ' after and ' clean and ' Water in ' wash and ' and barley ' all
' (9 from week ' you seven ' and tent of ' outside`ing from ' dwell and ' camp`ed the
' ye ' and barley ' all ' ye ' shave as ' as seven`s the ' day as in ' be`s and
' all ' ye and ' him has eye ' top`ing ' ye and ' and beard it ' ye and ' and head
' ye ' wash and ' him fabric ' ye ' immersion and ' shave as ' and barley
two ' took as ' as eight`s the ' day as in and ' (10 clean and ' Water in ' and flesh
' sister ' the footstool and ' the Year ' as son ' they`s full ' from as mutton '
' from as has ten ' three`ed and ' the from as complete ' the you year ' daughter
' (11 one ' eight ' log and ' eight in ' the mingle`ing ' bestow`ed ' flour
from ye and ' clean them ' man that ' ye ' clean them ' priest the ' stand`s the and

' priest the ' take and ' 12 ing`congregate ' tent ' open ' Jehovah ' as before '
log ' ye and ' guilty of ' and ye ' approach`s the and ' one the ' mutton the ' ye
' 13 Jehovah ' as before ' the wave`ing you ' from ye ' wave`s the and ' eight the '
' ye ' and slay as ' which ' place`ing in ' mutton the ' ye ' slay and
' you sin are ' for ' holy the ' place`ing in ' on`ed the ' ye and ' you sin the
take and ' 14 that`ing ' from as holy ' holy ' priest of ' that`ing ' guilty the are
' tip`ing ' on ' priest the ' gave and ' guilty the ' blood from ' priest the '
whom right the ' and hand ' thick`ing ' on and ' whom right the ' clean them ' ear
log from ' priest the ' take and ' 15 whom right the ' and foot ' thick`ing ' on and '
' dip and ' 16 whom of left the ' priest the ' palm ' on ' cast and ' eight the '
' which ' eight the ' has from ' whom right the ' and finger I ' ye ' priest the
' eight the ' has from ' this the and ' whom of left the ' and palm ' on
protect as from and ' 17 Jehovah ' as before ' from as move ' seven ' and finger came
' tip`ing look ' on ' priest the ' permanent ' and palm ' on ' which ' eight the '
whom right the ' and hand ' thick`ing ' on and ' whom right the ' clean them ' ear
' 18 guilty the ' blood ' on ' whom right the ' and foot ' thick`ing ' on and '
' on ' permanent ' priest the ' palm ' on ' which ' eight in ' survive behold and
' 19 Jehovah ' as before ' priest the ' and Mosthigh ' atone and ' clean them ' head
' clean them ' on ' atone and ' you sin the ' ye ' priest the ' do`ed and
' am on the and ' 20 on`ed the ' ye ' slay as ' after and ' and you unclean from
' the sacrifice them ' bestow`ed the ' ye and ' on`ed the ' ye ' priest the
' 21 clean and ' priest the ' and Mosthigh ' atone and ' Jehovah ' as before
take and ' you drawal from ' and hand ' whither`s and ' that`ing ' weak ' mother and
' and Mosthigh ' atone of ' the wave`ing you of ' guilty ' one ' mutton '
' log and ' the bestow of ' eight in ' mingle`ing ' one ' flour ' has and ten and

' the Dove`ing ' as son ' two ' or ' from as protect ' twosome and ' 22 eight
23 on`ed ' one the and ' you sin ' one ' be`s and ' and hand ' drawal`s you ' which
' to ' and you clean of ' as eight`s the ' day as in ' from ye ' came`s the and '
take and ' 24 Jehovah ' as before ' ing`congregate ' tent ' open ' to ' priest the
wave`s the and ' eight the ' log ' ye and ' guilty the ' mutton ' ye ' priest the '
ye ' slay and ' 25 Jehovah ' as before ' the wave`ing you ' priest the ' from ye '
' gave and ' guilty the ' blood from ' priest the ' take and ' guilty the ' mutton '
' and hand ' thick`ing ' on and ' whom right the ' clean them ' ear ' tip`ing ' on
' has from and ' 26 whom right the ' and foot ' thick`ing ' on and ' whom right the
' 27 whom of left the ' priest the ' palm ' on ' priest the ' cast ' eight the
' eight the ' has from ' whom right the ' and finger came ' priest the ' this the and
' as before ' from as move ' seven ' whom of left the ' and palm ' on ' which
' and palm ' on ' which ' eight the ' has from ' priest the ' gave and ' 28 Jehovah
' and hand ' thick`ing ' on and ' whom right the ' clean them ' ear ' tip`ing ' on
' place`ing ' on ' whom right the ' and foot ' thick`ing ' on and ' whom right the
' on ' which ' eight the in ' has from ' survive behold and ' 29 guilty the ' blood
' and Mosthigh ' atone of ' clean them ' head ' on ' permanent ' priest the ' palm
' has from ' one the ' ye ' do`ed and ' 30 Jehovah ' as before
' which from ' the Dove`ing the ' as son ' has from ' or ' from as turtledove the
one the ' ye ' and hand ' drawal`s you ' which ' ye ' 31 and hand ' drawal`s you
' priest the ' atone and ' bestow`ed the ' on ' on`ed ' one the ' ye and ' you sin '
and in ' which ' you protect`ing ' such ' 32 Jehovah ' as before ' clean them ' on
' 33 and you clean in ' and hand ' drawal`s you ' not ' which ' you leper ' touch '
' for ' 34 say of ' Aaron ' to and ' Moses ' to ' Jehovah ' word as and
' relate ' gave ' as whither ' which ' Canaan ' land ' to ' and came you

' land ' you house in ' you leper ' touch ' as set has and ' hold`ed of
' proclaim`s and ' you house the ' if ' which ' came and ' (35 from are you hold
' (36 you house in ' vessel ' speak`ed ' have plague are ' say of ' priest of
' suspend in ' you house the ' ye ' and turn and ' priest the ' command`ed and
all ' unclean as ' not and ' touch the ' ye ' you see of ' priest the ' came`ing as
' you see of ' priest the ' came`ing as ' so ' as after and ' you house in ' which '
' be`th and ' touch the ' ye ' priest the ' look`ed and ' (37 you house the ' ye
' you and raise moisten ' you house the ' you and herd`s ' touch the
has from ' depth ' has am appear and ' you and blood Men ' or ' you and only only as
' open ' to ' you house the ' has from ' priest the ' out and ' (38 is stedfast the '
' (39 from week ' you seven ' you house the ' ye ' close`s the and ' you house the
' be`th and ' look`ed and ' as seven`s the ' day as in ' priest the ' sojourn
' command`ed and ' (40 you house the ' you and herd`s ' touch the ' extremity`ed
' touch the ' thick ' which ' from as stone the ' ye ' and change and ' priest the
place`ing ' to ' town`s of ' outside`ing from ' to ' has ye`ed ' and hurl`s the and
' surround`s ' you house from ' and corner as ' you house the ' ye and ' (41 unclean '
' outside`ing from ' to ' and end`s the ' which ' dust the ' ye ' and pour and
' from as stone ' and take and ' (42 unclean ' place`ing ' to ' town`s of
' dust and ' from as stone the ' under ' to ' and came`s the and ' you and after
' mother and ' (43 you house the ' ye ' and plaster and ' and took as ' after
' ye ' and change ' after ' you house in ' bud and ' touch the ' carry`ing as
as after and ' you house the ' ye ' you coast the ' as after and ' from as stone the
' bud ' be`th and ' look`ed and ' priest the ' came and ' (44 plaister`ing the '
' that`ing ' you appear from ' you leper ' you house in ' touch the ' extremity`ed
ye ' you house the ' ye ' and overpower and ' (45 that`ing ' unclean ' you house in

' you house the ' dust ' all ' ye and ' him tree ' ye and ' him stone '
unclean ' place`ing ' to ' town`s of ' outside`ing from ' to ' and issue`s alas and
' and ye ' close`s the ' week ' all ' you house the ' to ' came the and ' 46
ye ' immersion as ' you house in ' lay the and ' 47 twilight the ' till ' unclean as
' 48 him fabric ' ye ' immersion as ' you house in ' eat the and ' him fabric '
' bud ' not ' be`th and ' look`ed and ' priest the ' came`ing as ' came ' mother and
' ye ' plaster the ' as after ' you house in ' touch the ' extremity`ed
' decease has ' for ' you house the ' ye ' priest the ' clean and ' you house the
' twosome ' you house the ' ye ' sin of ' and take and ' 49 touch the
50 hyssop`ing and ' you have hang`ing ' two and ' cedar ' tree and ' from as bird`ing
Water ' on ' devise ' weapon ' to ' sister the ' bird`ing the ' ye ' slay and '
' two ' ye and ' cedar the ' tree ' ye ' take and ' 51 from as life '
life`ed the ' bird`ing the ' ye and ' Hyssop`ing the ' ye and ' you have hang`ing the
' water`s in and ' the slay`ing the ' bird`ing the ' blood in ' from ye ' dip and '
' 52 from as move ' seven ' you house the ' to ' this the and ' from as life the
' water`s in and ' bird`ing the ' blood in ' you house the ' ye ' sin and
' cedar the ' tree in and ' life`ed the ' bird`ing in and ' from as life the
' ye ' send and ' 53 hyssop`ing in and ' you have hang`ing the ' two in and
' around ' to ' town`s of ' outside`ing from ' to ' life`ed the ' bird`ing the
' such ' 54 clean and ' you house the ' on ' atone and ' field`ed the
' 55 scurf of and ' you leper the ' touch ' all of ' the protect`ing the
' you scab of and ' arise of and ' 56 you house of and ' fabric the ' you leper of and
day as in and ' unclean the ' day as in ' you and instruct`ing ' 57 you blemish of and
you leper the ' you protect`ing ' such ' clean`ing the '

’ and word ’ 2 say of ’ Aaron ’ to and ’ Moses ’ to ’ Jehovah ’ word as and ’ 1
’ for ’ man I ’ man I ’ them as to ’ from you say and ’ Israel ’ as son ’ to
such and ’ 3 that`ing ’ unclean ’ and secrete`ing ’ and flesh from ’ secrete ’ be`s as
’ ye ’ and flesh ’ spittle ’ and secrete`ing in ’ and you unclean ’ be`s you ’
’ and secrete`ing from ’ and flesh ’ from as crush the ’ or ’ and secrete`ing
’ or ’ and flesh ’ secrete ’ week ’ all ’ against ’ that`ing ’ and you unclean
4 ’ that`s ’ and you unclean ’ and secrete`ing from ’ and flesh ’ from as crush the
’ secrete the ’ and Mosthigh ’ lay as ’ which ’ lay them ’ nosering`s as ’ all
5 ’ unclean as ’ and Mosthigh ’ dwell ’ which ’ as all the ’ all and ’ unclean as
’ wash and ’ him fabric ’ immersion as ’ and lay from in ’ faint ’ which ’ man I and
’ as all the ’ on ’ dwell the and ’ 6 twilight the ’ till ’ unclean and ’ Water in
’ wash and ’ him fabric ’ immersion as ’ secrete the ’ and Mosthigh ’ dwell ’ which
’ flesh in ’ touch the and ’ 7 twilight the ’ till ’ unclean and ’ Water in
’ till ’ unclean and ’ Water in ’ wash and ’ him fabric ’ immersion as ’ secrete the
’ immersion and ’ clean`ing in ’ secrete the ’ green ’ for and ’ 8 twilight the
’ all and ’ 9 twilight the ’ till ’ unclean and ’ Water in ’ wash and ’ him fabric
’ all and ’ 10 unclean as ’ secrete the ’ and Mosthigh ’ ride as ’ which ’ ride them
’ twilight the ’ till ’ unclean as ’ him under ’ be`s as ’ which ’ all in ’ touch the
’ Water in ’ wash and ’ him fabric ’ immersion as ’ from ye`ing ’ lift and behold and
secrete the ’ and in ’ faint ’ which ’ all and ’ 11 twilight the ’ till ’ unclean and
’ wash and ’ him fabric ’ immersion and ’ Water in ’ rinse ’ not ’ and as hand and ’
faint ’ which ’ devise ’ as all and ’ 12 twilight the ’ till ’ unclean and ’ Water in
Water in ’ rinse as ’ tree ’ weapon ’ all and ’ is carry as ’ secrete the ’ and in ’
’ if ’ report and ’ and secrete`ing from ’ secrete the ’ clean as ’ for and ’ 13
’ wash and ’ him fabric ’ immersion and ’ and you clean of ’ from week ’ you seven

' day as in and ' 14 clean and ' from as life ' Water in ' and flesh ' ye
' as son ' two ' or ' from as protect ' twosome ' if ' took as ' as eight`s the
ing`congregate ' tent ' open ' to ' Jehovah ' as before ' came and ' the Dove`ing
' one ' priest the ' from ye ' do`ed and ' 15 priest the ' to ' from gave and '
' as before ' priest the ' and Mosthigh ' atone and ' on`ed ' one the and ' you sin
' and her from ' issue you ' for ' man I and ' 16 and secrete`ing from ' Jehovah
' till ' unclean and ' and flesh ' all ' ye ' Water in ' wash and ' seed ' you lay
' be`s as ' which ' town`ing ' all and ' fabric ' all and ' 17 twilight the
' till ' unclean and ' Water in ' immersion and ' seed ' you lay ' and Mosthigh
' seed ' you lay ' ye`ed ' the man I ' lay as ' which ' Woman and ' 18 twilight the
' for ' Woman and ' 19 twilight the ' till ' and unclean and ' Water in ' and wash and
you seven ' the flesh in ' the secrete`ing ' be`s as ' blood ' secrete`ed ' be`s you
' unclean as ' thus ' touch the ' all and ' impurity`ed in ' be`s you ' from week '
' impurity`ed in ' and Mosthigh ' lay you ' which ' all and ' 20 twilight the ' till
' all and ' 21 unclean as ' and Mosthigh ' inhabitant ' which ' all and ' unclean as
' Water in ' wash and ' him fabric ' immersion as ' lay`ed from in ' touch the
' as all the ' all in ' touch the ' all and ' 22 twilight the ' till ' unclean and
' Water in ' wash and ' him fabric ' immersion as ' and Mosthigh ' inhabitant ' which
' or ' that`s ' lay them ' on ' mother and ' 23 twilight the ' till ' unclean and
and in ' and touch in ' and Mosthigh ' desist as ' that`s ' which ' as all the ' on
' the man I ' lay as ' lay ' mother and ' 24 twilight the ' till ' unclean as '
you seven ' unclean as and ' and Mosthigh ' impurity`ed ' the became you and ' ye`ed
' 25 unclean as ' and Mosthigh ' lay as ' which ' lay them ' all and ' from week '
' from week ' blood`ed ' secrete`ing ' secrete`ing as ' for ' Woman and
' on ' secrete`ing you ' for ' or ' impurity`ed ' time ' weary ' from as increase

' impurity`ed ' week are ' the you unclean ' secrete`ing ' week ' all ' impurity`ed
and Mosthigh ' lay you ' which ' lay them ' all ' 26 that`s ' unclean`ed ' be`s you
' nihil ' be`s as ' impurity`ed ' lay from are ' the secrete`ing ' week ' all '
' be`s as ' unclean ' and Mosthigh ' inhabitant ' which ' as all the ' all and
' unclean as ' height ' ing`touch the ' all and ' 27 impurity`ed ' you unclean are
twilight the ' till ' unclean and ' Water in ' wash and ' him fabric ' immersion and
you seven ' nihil ' report`ed and ' the secrete`ing from ' clean`ed ' mother and ' 28
' implicate ' as eight`s the ' day as in and ' 29 clean you ' after and ' from week '
' the Dove`ing ' as son ' two ' or ' from as protect ' twosome ' nihil
' tent ' open ' to ' priest the ' to ' from ye`ing ' the came`s the and
' ye and ' you sin ' one the ' ye ' priest the ' do`ed and ' 30 ing`congregate
' Jehovah ' as before ' priest the ' am on ' atone and ' on`ed ' one the
' as son ' ye ' complete warn the and ' 31 the you unclean ' secrete`ing from
' from you unclean in ' and die`ing as ' not and ' from you unclean from ' Israel
' such ' 32 from middle`ing in ' which ' as tabernacle ' ye ' from unclean in
seed ' you lay ' and her from ' issue you ' which and ' secrete the ' you protect`ing
' secrete the and ' impurity`ed in ' menstruate`ed the and ' 33 thus ' unclean`ed of '
' which ' man I of and ' the female of and ' is remember of ' and secrete`ing ' ye
unclean`ed ' people ' lay as

1 ' as son ' two ' die`ing ' as after ' Moses ' to ' Jehovah ' word as and '
2 ' say as and ' and die as and ' Jehovah ' as before ' from you approach in ' Aaron
' to and ' are as brother ' Aaron ' to ' word ' Moses ' to ' Jehovah
' to ' veil put of ' you house from ' holy the ' to ' time ' all in ' came`ing as
' for ' die`ing as ' not and ' Ark`ing the ' on ' which ' you atone the ' around
3 to ' Aaron ' came`ing as ' such in ' you atone the ' on I ' cat`ed ' cloud in
4 ' on`ed of ' Ram`s and ' you sin of ' herd ' son ' Bullock in ' holy the '
' and became as ' alone ' as breeche from and ' arm as ' holy ' alone ' you coat and
' you turban from in and ' restrain as ' alone ' belt`s came and ' and flesh ' on
' all ' ye ' Water in ' wash and ' them ' holy ' as fabric ' turban as ' alone
5 ' took as ' Israel ' as son ' testimony ' each and ' from arm and ' and flesh
6 ' on`ed of ' one ' Ram`s and ' you sin of ' from as Goat ' as gate`s ' two
' atone and ' if ' which ' you sin the ' apart ' ye ' Aaron ' approach`s the and
7 ' two ' ye ' take and ' and you house ' till in and ' and till in
' tent ' open ' Jehovah ' as before ' from ye ' stand`s the and ' from as gate`s the
8 ' from as gate`s the ' two ' on ' Aaron ' gave and ' ing`congregate
9 gone goat of ' one ' ing`lot and ' Jehovah of ' one ' ing`lot ' you and ing`lot
' and Mosthigh ' on`ed ' which ' gate`s the ' ye ' Aaron ' approach`s the and '
10 on`ed ' which ' gate`s the and ' you sin ' and do`ed and ' Jehovah of ' ing`lot the
Jehovah ' as before ' life ' stand`s as ' gone goat of ' ing`lot the ' and Mosthigh '
11 ' word`ed them ' gone goat of ' and ye ' send of ' and Mosthigh ' atone of '
' atone and ' if ' which ' you sin the ' apart ' ye ' Aaron ' approach`s the and
' you sin the ' apart ' ye ' slay and ' and you house ' till in and ' and till in
12 ' above ' fire ' as ember ' crush`ed them ' fill`ing ' take and ' if ' which
' you perfume ' and as fist ' fill`ing and ' Jehovah ' as before from ' sacrifice them

gave and ' 13 veil put of ' you house from ' came`s the and ' thin`ed ' from as aroma
' conceal`ed and ' Jehovah ' as before ' fire the ' on ' you perfume the ' ye '
' testimony`ing the ' on ' which ' you atone the ' ye ' you perfume the ' cloud
' this the and ' broken ' blood from ' take and ' 14 die`ing as ' not and
' as before and ' east`ed ' you atone the ' around ' on I ' and finger came
' blood the ' has from ' from as move ' seven ' splash`ed ' you atone the
' people of ' which ' you sin the ' gate`s ' ye ' slay and ' 15 and finger came
' do`ed and ' veil put of ' you house from ' to ' and blood ' ye ' came`s the and
' and ye ' this the and ' broken ' blood of ' do`ed ' which are ' and blood ' ye
' holy the ' on ' atone and ' 16 you atone the ' as before and ' you atone the ' on
' all of ' them as trepass from and ' Israel ' as son ' you unclean from
' from ye ' nigh the ' ing`congregate ' tent of ' success`ed ' so and ' from you sin
' tent in ' be`s as ' not ' ground ' all and ' 17 from you unclean ' middle`ing in
atone and ' and you issue ' till ' holy in ' atone of ' and came in ' ing`congregate
Israel ' assemble ' all ' till in and ' and you house ' till in and ' and till in '
' atone and ' Jehovah ' as before ' which ' sacrifice them ' to ' out and ' 18
gave and ' gate`s the ' blood from and ' broken ' blood from ' take and ' and Mosthigh
' and Mosthigh ' this the and ' 19 surround`s ' sacrifice them ' you and horn ' on '
' and clean and ' from as move ' seven ' and finger came ' blood the ' has from
' atone from ' the all and ' 20 Israel ' as son ' you unclean from ' and holy and
' sacrifice them ' ye and ' ing`congregate ' tent ' ye and ' holy the ' ye
' ye ' Aaron ' laid and ' 21 life the ' gate`s the ' ye ' approach`s the and
' the endure`ing the and ' life the ' gate`s the ' head ' on ' him hand ' twosome
' all ' ye and ' Israel ' as son ' you and low`ing ' all ' ye ' and Mosthigh
' head ' on ' from ye ' gave and ' from you sin ' all of ' them as trespass

' help and ' 22 word`ed them ' as time ' man I ' hand in ' send and ' gate`s the
' desert`ed ' land ' to ' from you low`ing ' all ' ye ' and Mosthigh ' gate`s the
' tent ' to ' Aaron ' came and ' 23 word from in ' gate`s the ' ye ' send and
' arm ' which ' alone the ' as fabric ' ye ' pull and ' ing`congregate
' ye ' wash and ' 24 there ' from rest`s the and ' holy the ' to ' and came in
' him fabric ' ye ' arm and ' holy`ing ' place`ing in ' Water in ' and flesh
' atone and ' people the ' offer ' ye and ' and offer ' ye ' do`ed and ' out and
perfume`s as ' you sin the ' milk ' ye and ' 25 people the ' till in and ' and till in
' gone goat of ' gate`s the ' ye ' send them and ' 26 the sacrifice them '
' as after and ' Water in ' and flesh ' ye ' wash and ' him fabric ' immersion as
' ye and ' you sin the ' apart ' ye and ' 27 camp`ed the ' to ' came`ing as ' so
' holy in ' atone of ' from blood ' ye ' entree the ' which ' you sin the ' gate`s
ye ' abhorrence ' and burnt and ' camp`ed of ' outside`ing from ' to ' issue`s him
' burnt the and ' 28 from excrement ' ye and ' from flesh ' ye and ' from ing`skin '
' Water in ' and flesh ' ye ' wash and ' him fabric ' immersion as ' from ye
' relate ' whom`ed the and ' 29 camp`ed the ' to ' came`ing as ' so ' as after and
' new of ' ten`ing in ' as seven`s the ' new in ' from on`ing ' statute of
and do you ' not ' the are fill ' all and ' from are as you soul ' ye ' and low you
' day as in ' for ' 30 your middle`ing in ' abide ' guest the and ' at native the '
' all from ' from are ye ' clean of ' from are mosthigh ' atone as ' this the
' has and desist ' desist ' 31 and clean you ' Jehovah ' as before ' your as you sin
' statute ' from are as you soul ' ye ' from whom low and ' relate ' that`ing
' which and ' and ye ' anoint as ' which ' priest the ' atone as and ' 32 from on`ing
' ye ' arm and ' him father ' under ' priest of ' and hand ' ye ' fill as
' holy from ' ye ' atone and ' 33 holy the ' as fabric ' alone the ' as fabric

’ atone as ’ sacrifice them ’ ye and ’ ing`congregate ’ tent ’ ye and ’ holy the
34 ’ atone as ’ assemble the ’ people the ’ all ’ on and ’ from as priest the ’ on and
as son ’ on ’ atone of ’ from on`ing ’ statute of ’ relate ’ such ’ whom`ed the and
’ which are ’ do as and ’ Year`ed in ’ sister ’ from you sin ’ all from ’ Israel ’
Moses ’ ye ’ Jehovah ’ command`ed

to and ' Aaron ' to ' word ' 2 say of ' Moses ' to ' Jehovah ' word as and ' 1
' this ' them as to ' you say and ' Israel ' as son ' all ' to and ' him son '
you house from ' man I ' man I ' 3 say of ' Jehovah ' command`ed ' which ' word the
camp`ed in ' harsh ' or ' sheep ' or ' captain`ing ' slay as ' which ' Israel '
' tent ' open ' to and ' 4 camp`ed of ' outside`ing from ' slay as ' which ' or '
' or ' on`ed ' and ye ' you concoct of ' and came`s the ' not ' ing`congregate
' odor has ' smell`s of ' from are accept`ing of ' Jehovah of ' from as whole
' not ' ing`congregate ' tent ' open ' to and ' outside`ing in ' and slay`ed as and
' as before ' Jehovah of ' has approach ' and approach`s the of ' and came`s the
' pour ' blood ' that`ing the ' man I of ' reckon as ' blood ' Jehovah ' Tabernacle
purpose of ' 5 and people ' approach from ' that`ing the ' man that ' you foreign and
them ' which ' them as sacrifice ' ye ' Israel ' as son ' and came`s as ' which '
' from and came`s the and ' field`ed the ' around ' on ' from as sacrifice '
' priest the ' to ' ing`congregate ' tent ' open ' to ' Jehovah of
' 6 from ye`ing ' Jehovah of ' from as whole ' as sacrifice ' and sacrifice and
which ' Jehovah ' sacrifice from ' on ' blood the ' ye ' priest the ' sprinkle and
' smell`s of ' milk the ' perfume`s the and ' ing`congregate ' tent ' open '
' ye ' till`ing ' and sacrifice as ' not and ' 7 Jehovah of ' odor has
' them as after ' from as diver ' them ' which ' from gate`s of ' them as sacrifice
' 8 from ing`generation of ' them of ' such ' be`s you ' from on`ing ' statute
' has from and ' Israel ' you house from ' man I ' man I ' say you ' them as to and
' success`ed ' went`ed ' which ' from middle`ing in ' guest`ing as ' which ' abide
' not ' ing`congregate ' tent ' open ' to and ' 9 sacrifice ' or ' on`ed
man that ' you foreign and ' Jehovah of ' and ye ' you concoct of ' and has came`s as
' Israel ' you house from ' man I ' man I and ' 10 him people from ' that`ing the '

’ which ’ from middle`ing in ’ guest`ing as ’ which ’ abide ’ abide ’ has from and
ye ’ you eat the ’ soul in ’ around ’ ye ’ as set has and ’ blood ’ all ’ eat as
’ soul ’ for ’ 11 people`ed ’ approach from ’ ye`ed ’ as hew the and ’ blood the ’
’ on ’ relate ’ and as set has ’ as whither and ’ that`ing ’ blood in ’ flesh the
’ that`ing ’ blood the ’ for ’ from are as you soul ’ on ’ atone of ’ sacrifice them
’ soul ’ all ’ Israel ’ as son of ’ as you say ’ so ’ on ’ 12 atone as ’ soul in
not ’ your middle`ing in ’ abide ’ guest the and ’ blood ’ eat you ’ not ’ from with
’ Israel ’ you house from ’ as son from ’ man I ’ man I and ’ 13 blood ’ eat as ’
’ hunt`s ’ hunt`ing as ’ which ’ your middle`ing in ’ abide ’ abide ’ has from and
’ and blood ’ ye ’ pour and ’ eat as ’ which ’ fly`ing ’ or ’ the life
and soul in ’ and blood ’ flesh ’ all ’ soul ’ for ’ 14 dust in ’ and conceal`ed and
and eat you ’ not ’ flesh ’ all ’ blood ’ Israel ’ as son of ’ say and ’ that`ing ’
’ 15 hew as ’ him eat ’ all ’ that`ing ’ and blood ’ flesh ’ all ’ soul ’ for ’
’ at native in ’ torn`ed and ’ the foolish ’ eat you ’ which ’ soul the ’ all and
till ’ unclean and ’ Water in ’ wash and ’ him fabric ’ immersion and ’ guest in and
not ’ and flesh and ’ immersion as ’ not ’ mother and ’ 16 clean and ’ twilight the ’
and low`ing ’ help and ’ wash as ’

' as son ' to ' word ' (2 say of ' Moses ' to ' Jehovah ' word as and ' (1

' (3 your as Allah ' Jehovah ' as whither ' them as to ' you say and ' Israel

' not ' thus ' from you dwell ' which ' from as Mizra ' land ' work`ed are

' came`s from ' as whither ' which ' Canaan ' land ' work`ed are and ' and do you

' not ' them as statute in and ' and do you ' not ' there`ed ' from are ye

' as statute`ing ' ye and ' and do you ' as discern from ' ye ' (4 and walk you

' (5 your as Allah ' Jehovah ' as whither ' cattle ' you walk of ' and guard you

' which ' as discern from ' ye and ' as statute`ing ' ye ' from you guard and

' (6 Jehovah ' as whither ' cattle ' the life and ' ground the ' from ye ' success`ed

' and approach you ' not ' and flesh ' remain ' all ' to ' man I ' man I

' are as father ' skin`ing ' (7 Jehovah ' as whither ' nake`ed ' you and heap of

' the rent ' not ' that`s ' are mother ' the rent ' not ' are mother ' skin`ing and

' skin`ing ' the rent ' not ' are as father ' wife ' skin`ing ' (8 the skin`ing

' or ' are as father daughter ' are sister`ing ' skin`ing ' (9 that`s ' are as father

outside`ing ' you bore when ' or ' you house ' you bore when ' are mother ' daughter

' or ' are son ' daughter ' skin`ing ' (10 has the skin`ing ' the rent ' not '

be`th ' are skin`ing ' for ' has skin`ing ' the rent ' not ' are daughter ' daughter

' are as father ' you bore when ' are as father ' wife ' daughter ' skin`ing ' (11

' skin`ing ' (12 the skin`ing ' the rent ' not ' that`s ' are sister`ing

(13 that`s ' are as father ' remain ' the rent ' not ' are as father ' you and brother

' remain ' for ' the rent ' not ' are mother ' you and brother ' skin`ing '

' the rent ' not ' are as father ' as brother ' skin`ing ' (14 that`s ' are mother

' skin`ing ' (15 that`s ' are aunt ' approach you ' not ' and wife ' to and

' the rent ' not ' that`s ' are son ' wife ' the rent ' not ' are daughterinlaw

' skin`ing ' the rent ' not ' are as brother ' wife ' skin`ing ' (16 the skin`ing

' the rent ' not ' the daughter and ' Woman ' skin`ing ' 17 that`s ' are as brother
' implicate ' not ' daughter`ed ' daughter ' ye and ' son`ed ' daughter ' ye
Woman and ' 18 that`s ' wick`ed ' be`th ' the remain ' the skin`ing ' you and heap of
' you and heap of ' bundle of ' implicate ' not ' he and brother ' on I '
' impurity in ' Woman ' to and ' 19 am life in ' am on ' the skin`ing
' to and ' 20 the skin`ing ' you and heap of ' approach you ' not ' the you unclean
' unclean`ed of ' seed of ' are you lay ' has set ' not ' are whom people ' wife
' not and ' king of ' cross`s the of ' has set ' not ' are seed from and ' 21 thus
' male ' ye and ' 22 Jehovah ' as whither ' are as Allah ' there ' ye ' profane you
' all in and ' 23 that`s ' the abominate you ' Woman ' as lay from ' lay you ' not
' not ' Woman and ' thus ' unclean`ed of ' are you lay ' has set ' not ' cattle`ed
' to ' 24 that`ing ' both ' the four of ' cattle`ed ' as before ' stand you
' and unclean has ' to`ed ' all in ' for ' to`ed ' all in ' and unclean you
' 25 from are around from ' send from ' as whither ' which ' from nation`ing the
' spue`s and ' am on ' the low`ing ' punish I and ' land the ' unclean you and
' as statute`ing ' ye ' from ye ' from you guard and ' 26 am dwell ' ye ' land the
you and abominate you the ' all from ' and do you ' not and ' as discern from ' ye and
' complete ' your middle`ing in ' abide ' guest the and ' at native the ' these`ed '
' these ' you abominate you the ' all ' ye ' for ' 27 land ' ye ' and possess you
unclean you and ' your as before ' which ' land the ' as person ' complete ' concoct
' from are unclean in ' from are ye ' land the ' spue`s ' not and ' 28 land the '
' 29 your as before ' which ' nation`ing the ' ye ' vomit`ed ' which are ' ye`ed
' these`ed ' you and abominate you the ' all from ' success`ed ' which ' all ' for
' 30 from people ' approach from ' you concoct the ' you and soul the ' and hew shall
' you and do ' as except of ' as you guard from ' ye ' from you guard and

' your as before ' and do has ' which ' you and abominate you the ' statute`ing from

your as Allah ' Jehovah ' as whither ' for ' cattle ' and unclean you ' not and

testimony ' all ' to ' word ' (2 say of ' Moses ' to ' Jehovah ' word as and ' (1
' for ' and as he ' from as holy ' them as to ' you say and ' Israel ' as son '
' and mother ' man I ' (3 your as Allah ' Jehovah ' as whither ' holy`ing
' and guard you ' as you and desist ' ye and ' and look as you ' him father and
' to ' and turn you ' to ' (4 your as Allah ' Jehovah ' as whither
' relate ' and do you ' not ' castimage`ed ' as Allah and ' from as thing`s the
' sacrifice ' and sacrifice you ' for and ' (5 your as Allah ' Jehovah ' as whither
' (6 and sacrifice`ed you ' from are accept`ing of ' Jehovah of ' from as whole
' survive behold and ' you tomorrow from and ' eat as ' from are sacrifice ' day as in
' eat the ' mother and ' (7 burnt as ' abhorrence ' as three`s the ' day as ' till
(8 approve`ed ' not ' that`ing ' adominable`ing ' as three`s the ' day as in ' eat as
' profane ' Jehovah ' holy ' ye ' for ' linger ' and low`ing ' and as eat and '
ye ' from are reap in and ' (9 am people from ' that`s the ' soul the ' hew`ed shall
' reap of ' are field ' quarter ' all`ed you ' not ' from are land ' reap`s '
of on`ing you ' not ' are vineyard and ' (10 pickup you ' not ' are reap`s ' pickup and
forsake you ' guest of and ' poor of ' pickup you ' not ' are vineyard ' berry and '
' not and ' and steal you ' not ' (11 your as Allah ' Jehovah ' as whither ' from ye '
' not and ' (12 and whom people in ' man I ' and false you ' not and ' and lie you
' there ' ye ' you profane and ' false of ' as there in ' and swear too you
not and ' fellow ' ye ' oppress you ' not ' (13 Jehovah ' as whither ' are as Allah
' not ' (14 herd ' till ' are ye ' merry`s ' you act ' stop`s you ' not ' tear you '
' stumble`ing from ' has set ' not ' town`ing ' as before and ' devise ' accurse you
the concoct you ' not ' (15 Jehovah ' as whither ' are as Allah from ' you look as and
' not and ' weak ' around ' lift you ' not ' discern from in ' on`ing '
are whom people ' ye ' discern you ' just in ' great`ing ' around ' magnificent you

blood ' on ' stand you ' not and ' are as people in ' attach`s ' walk you ' not ' 16
' are as brother ' ye ' hateful you ' not ' 17 Jehovah ' as whither ' fellow '
' not and ' are whom people ' ye ' reprove`s you ' reprove the ' are mind in
' grudge`ing ' not and ' vengeance`ing ' not ' 18 sin ' and Mosthigh ' lift you
' as whither ' with`ing are ' fellow of ' you love and ' are people ' as son ' ye
four`s you ' not ' are you cattle ' and guard you ' as statute`ing ' ye ' 19 Jehovah
' fabric and ' from as restrict ' seed you ' not ' are field and ' from as restrict '
' for ' man I and ' 20 are as on ' went`ed ' not ' it has linsey ' from as restrict
' you put defame ' the slave ' that`s and ' seed ' you lay ' Woman ' ye ' lay as
' gave ' not ' am free ' or ' he release has ' not ' release`ed the and ' man I of
' 21 the free ' not ' for ' and you day as ' not ' if ' be`s you ' city in ' nihil
' tent ' open ' to ' Jehovah of ' and guilty ' ye ' came`s the and
Ram`s in ' priest the ' and Mosthigh ' atone and ' 22 guilty ' Ram`s ' ing`congregate
' sin ' which ' and you sin ' on ' Jehovah ' as before ' guilty the '
' and came you ' for and ' 23 sin ' which ' and you sin from ' if ' forgive has and
' from you foreskin and ' eat from ' tree ' all ' from you plant and ' land the ' to
' relate ' be`s as ' from two ' three ' and fruit ' ye ' and you foreskin
' and be`s as ' whom four`s the ' Year`ed in and ' 24 eat as ' not ' from as foreskin
' Year`ed in and ' 25 Jehovah of ' from as glory`ing ' holy ' and fruit ' all
' relate ' yeild`s the of ' and fruit ' ye ' and eat you ' whom five`s the
on ' and eat you ' not ' 26 your as Allah ' Jehovah ' as whither ' and you income`ing
' not ' 27 and has low`ing you ' not and ' and serpent you ' not and ' blood the '
quarter ' ye ' and eradicate`s you ' not and ' your head ' quarter ' and round`s you
' and give you ' not ' soul of ' the incision and ' 28 from are beard it '
' from are in ' and give you ' not ' picture picture ' you write and ' your flesh in

' are daughter ' ye ' profane you ' to ' 29 Jehovah ' as whither
' land the ' fill`ed and ' land the ' divers`ed you ' not and ' the whore`ing the of
and look as you ' as holy from and ' and guard you ' as you desist ' ye ' 30 wick`ed
' you and father`ing the ' to ' and turn you ' to ' 31 Jehovah ' as whither '
' cattle ' unclean`ed of ' and seek you ' to ' from as ghost`ing became ' to and
' vengeance`ing ' the carry`s ' around from ' 32 your as Allah ' Jehovah ' as whither
as whither ' are as Allah from ' you look as and ' elder ' around ' generation the and
' not ' your land in ' guest ' from are ye ' guest`ing as ' for and ' 33 Jehovah '
' abide ' relate ' be`s as ' from with ' at native are ' 34 and ye ' and give`ing
' from as guest ' for ' with`ing are ' if ' you love and ' from are ye ' abide
' 35 your as Allah ' Jehovah ' as whither ' from as Mizra ' land in ' from whom became
' weight from in ' mete`ed in ' discern from in ' on`ing ' and do you ' not
' just ' bit hence ' just ' as stone ' just ' as ear from ' 36 the juice`ing in and
' your as Allah ' Jehovah ' as whither ' relate ' be`s as ' just ' behold`s and
' 37 from as Mizra ' land from ' from are ye ' as you issue alas ' which
' as discern from ' all ' ye and ' as statute`ing ' all ' ye ' from you guard and
And ' Jehovah ' as whither ' from ye ' from dual`s and

' Israel ' as son ' to and ' (2 say of ' Moses ' to ' Jehovah ' word as and (1

' Israel ' you house from ' as son`s from ' man I ' man I ' say you ' word you

' and seed from ' permanent ' which ' Israel in ' abide ' abide ' has from and

' (3 stone in ' and council`ed as ' land the ' people ' die him ' die`ing ' king of

' as hew the and ' that`ing the ' man I in ' around ' ye ' donkey ' as whither and

' king of ' gave ' and seed from ' for ' and people ' approach from ' and ye

as holy ' there ' ye ' profane of and ' as holy from ' ye ' unclean ' purpose of

' ye ' land the ' people ' and eternal`s as ' eternal the ' mother and ' (4

' and seed from ' and set in ' that`ing the ' man that ' has from ' them as has eye

ye ' as whither ' as you there and ' (5 and ye ' die`s the ' as except of ' king of

' as hew the and ' and you slave from in and ' that`ing the ' man I in ' around '

' as after ' whore`ing of ' him after ' from as diver the ' all ' ye and ' and ye

' to ' turn`ed you ' which ' soul the and ' (6 from people ' approach from ' king the

' whore`ing of ' from as ghost`ing became ' to and ' you and father`ing the

as hew the and ' that`s the ' soul in ' around ' ye ' as set has and ' them as after

' from you holy sacred and ' (7 and people`ed ' approach from ' and ye`ed '

' Jehovah ' as whither ' holy`ing ' for ' from as holy ' complete as became and

' from dual`s and ' as statute`ing ' for ' ye ' from you guard and ' (8 your as Allah

which ' man I ' man I ' for ' (9 from are holy from ' Jehovah ' as whither ' from ye

' die him ' die`ing ' and mother ' ye and ' him father ' ye ' accurse as '

' which ' man I and ' (10 and in ' him blood ' accurse ' and mother and ' him father

' wife ' ye ' adultery as ' which ' man I ' wife ' ye ' adultery as

' (11 you adultery the and ' adultery the ' die him ' die`ing ' and shepherd is

' him father ' skin`ing ' him father ' wife ' ye ' lay as ' which ' man I and

man I and ' (12 height ' them as blood ' them two ' and you day as ' die`ing ' heap`ed

' them two ' and you day as ' die`ing ' and daugtherinlaw ' ye ' lay as ' which '
' ye ' lay as ' which ' man I and ' 13 height ' them as blood ' concoct ' both
and you day as ' die`ing ' concoct ' the abominate you ' Woman ' as lay from ' male
Woman ' ye ' took as ' which ' man I and ' 14 height ' them as blood ' them two '
' and ye ' and burnt as ' abhorrence ' that`s ' wick`ed ' mother`ed ' ye and '
' man I and ' 15 your middle`ing in ' wick`ed ' be`s you ' not and ' has ye`ed and
' ye and ' die him ' die`ing ' cattle`ed in ' and you lay ' permanent ' which
' all ' to ' approach you ' which ' Woman and ' 16 and kill you ' cattle`ed the
' ye and ' Woman the ' ye ' you kill and ' ye`ed ' the four of ' cattle`ed
' man I and ' 17 height ' them as blood ' and you day as ' die`ing ' cattle`ed the
' daughter ' or ' him father ' daughter ' and sister`ing ' ye ' took as ' which
' ye ' saw`ed ' that`s and ' the skin`ing ' ye ' look`ed and ' and mother
from people ' as son ' as has eye of ' and hew shall ' that`ing ' bow ' and skin`ing
' which ' man I and ' 18 linger ' and low`ing ' heap`ed ' and sister`ing ' skin`ing '
' ye ' the skin`ing ' ye ' the heap and ' thank`ing ' Woman ' ye ' lay as
' am blood ' source`ing ' ye ' he heap ' that`s and ' nake`ed the ' the source`ing
' skin`ing and ' 19 from people ' approach from ' them two ' and hew shall
for ' the rent ' not ' are mother ' sister`ing and ' are as father ' you and brother
which ' man I and ' 20 and linger ' from low`ing ' nake`ed the ' and remain ' ye '
' from sin ' heap`ed ' and uncle ' skin`ing ' ye ' and aunt ' ye ' lay as '
ye ' took as ' which ' man I and ' 21 and you day as ' from as raise`s ' and linger
' heap`ed ' him brother ' skin`ing ' that`s ' wander`ed ' him brother ' wife '
' as statute ' all ' ye ' from you guard and ' 22 and became as ' from as raise`s
' spue`s ' not and ' from ye ' from dual`s and ' as discern from ' all ' ye and
' there`ed ' from are ye ' came`s from ' as whither ' which ' from are ye ' land the

’ from nation`ing the ’ statute in ’ and walk you ’ not and ’ 23 thus ’ desist of
’ to`ed ’ all ’ ye ’ for ’ from are around from ’ send from ’ as whither ’ which
and possess you ’ from ye ’ relate ’ say and ’ 24 height ’ did aversion and ’ concoct
’ net`ness of ’ relate ’ the has give I ’ as whither and ’ from you ground ’ ye ’
your as Allah ’ Jehovah ’ as whither ’ honey and ’ milk ’ you secrete ’ land ’ ye`ed
’ 25 from as people the ’ has from ’ from are ye ’ as you separate the ’ which ’
unclean`ed of ’ clean`ed the ’ cattle`ed the ’ between in ’ from you separate the and
and detest you ’ not and ’ clean`ing of ’ unclean the ’ fly`ing the ’ between in and ’
’ which ’ all in and ’ fly`ing in and ’ cattle`ed in ’ from are as you soul ’ ye ’
’ 26 unclean`ed of ’ relate ’ as you separate the ’ which ’ ground`ed the ’ crawl you
Jehovah ’ as whither ’ holy`ing ’ for ’ from as holy ’ vessel ’ complete as became and
’ you and became of ’ from as people the ’ has from ’ from are ye ’ separate`s I and ’
’ father`ing ’ cattle ’ be`s as ’ which ’ for ’ Woman ’ or ’ man I and ’ 27 vessel
’ from as son came ’ and you day as ’ die`ing ’ as ghost`ing as ’ or
height ’ them as blood ’ from ye ’ and council whom

as son ' from as priest the ' to ' say ' Moses ' to ' Jehovah ' say as and ' 1
2 ' him people in ' unclean as ' not ' soul of ' them as to ' you say and ' Aaron '
' him father of ' him to ' approach`ing the ' and remain of ' mother ' for
3 ' him brother of and ' and daughter of and ' and son of and ' and mother of and
' which ' him to ' the approach`ing the ' the bride`ing the ' and sister`ing of and
' marry ' unclean as ' not ' 4 unclean as ' nihil ' man I of ' whom`ed the ' not
' from head in ' bald`ed ' the bald as ' not and ' 5 and sick the of ' him people in
' not ' from flesh in and ' and shave as ' not ' from beard it ' quarter and
them as Allah of ' and became as ' from as holy ' 6 you incision`ed ' and incision as
' as fire ' ye ' for ' them as Allah ' there ' ye ' and profane as ' not and '
' and became and ' from as approach`s from ' them ' them as Allah ' fight ' Jehovah
' and took as ' not ' the profane and ' the divers`ing ' Woman ' 7 from as holy
holy`ing ' for ' and took as ' not ' the man I from ' the expatriate`ing ' Woman and
' are as Allah ' fight ' ye ' for ' and you holy and ' 8 him Allah of ' that`ing '
as whither ' holy`ing ' for ' walk ' be`s as ' holy`ing ' approach`s from ' that`ing
' begin ' for ' priest ' man I ' daughter and ' 9 from are holy from ' Jehovah '
burnt you ' abhorrence ' you profane from ' that`s ' am father ' ye ' whore`ing of
' on ' narrow him ' which ' him brother from ' great`ing the ' priest the and ' 10
' ye ' arm of ' and hand ' ye ' fill and ' anoint`ed the ' eight ' and head
rip as ' not ' him fabric and ' hair as ' not ' and head ' ye ' from as fabric the
' him father of ' came`ing as ' not ' die ' you and soul ' all ' on and ' 11
' out ' not ' holy them ' has from and ' 12 unclean as ' not ' and mother of and
' eight ' consecrate ' for ' him Allah ' holy from ' ye ' profane as ' not and
' that`ing and ' 13 Jehovah ' as whither ' and Mosthigh ' him Allah ' you anoint
' the exact`ing and ' the widow I ' 14 took as ' am bride`ing in ' Woman

' mother ' for ' took as ' not ' to`ed ' ye ' the divers`ing and ' the profane and
15 ' profane as ' not and ' Woman ' took as ' him people from ' the bride`ing
16 word as and ' and holy from ' Jehovah ' as whither ' for ' him people in ' and seed
17 ' man I ' say of ' Aaron ' to ' word ' say of ' Moses ' to ' Jehovah '
' not ' they`ing ' and in ' be`s as ' which ' from ing`generation of ' are seed from
18 ' all ' for ' him Allah ' fight ' approach`s the of ' self`s of ' approach as
town`ing ' man I ' approach as ' not ' they`ing ' and in ' be`s as ' which ' man I
19 ' which ' man I ' or ' deform`ing ' or ' curse`ing ' or ' pass ' or '
20 ' or ' crookbacht ' or ' hand ' buy ' or ' foot ' buy ' and in ' be`s as
or ' you tetter ' or ' scurvy ' or ' him has eye in ' of cataract ' or ' thin
21 seed from ' they`ing ' and in ' which ' man I ' all ' testicle ' emasculate`ing '
' as fire ' ye ' approach`s the of ' adduce`s ' not ' priest the ' Aaron '
' adduce ' not ' him Allah ' fight ' ye ' and in ' they`ing ' Jehovah
22 ' from as holy the ' as holy from ' him Allah ' fight ' approach`s the of
23 ' not ' veil put the ' to ' sure ' eat as ' from as holy the ' has from and
' and in ' they`ing ' for ' adduce ' not ' sacrifice them ' to and ' came`s as
' Jehovah ' as whither ' for ' as holy from ' ye ' profane as ' not and
24 ' to and ' him son ' to and ' Aaron ' to ' Moses ' word as and ' from holy from
Israel ' as son ' all

to and ' Aaron ' to ' word ' 2 say of ' Moses ' to ' Jehovah ' word as and ' 1
' not and ' Israel ' as son ' as holy from ' and consecrate as and ' him son '
' vessel ' from as holy from ' them ' which ' as holy ' there ' ye ' and profane as
man I ' all ' from are as generation of ' them as to ' say ' 3 Jehovah ' as whither
' which ' from as holy the ' to ' from are seed ' all from ' approach as ' which '
' and Mosthigh ' and you unclean and ' Jehovah of ' Israel ' as son ' and holy`s as
' 4 Jehovah ' as whither ' as before from ' that`s the ' soul the ' hew`ed shall
' secrete ' or ' leper`ing ' that`ing and ' Aaron ' seed from ' man I ' man I
' all in ' touch the and ' clean as ' which ' till ' eat as ' not ' from as holy in
5 seed ' you lay ' and her from ' issue you ' which ' man I ' or ' soul ' unclean
if ' unclean as ' which ' unclean ' breed ' all in ' faint ' which ' man I ' or '
' soul ' 6 and you unclean ' all of ' if ' unclean as ' which ' Men in ' or '
' eat as ' not and ' twilight the ' till ' unclean`ed and ' and in ' reach ' which
came and ' 7 Water in ' and flesh ' wash ' mother ' for ' from as holy the ' has from
' for ' from as holy the ' has from ' eat as ' after and ' clean and ' sun the '
' and eat as ' not ' torn`ed and ' the foolish ' 8 that`ing ' and from bread
' ye ' and guard and ' 9 Jehovah ' as whither ' thus ' unclean`ed of
' and die and ' sin ' and Mosthigh ' and linger ' not and ' as you guard from
all and ' 10 from holy from ' Jehovah ' as whither ' and profane`ed as ' for ' and in
' not ' merry`s and ' priest ' sojourn you ' holy ' eat as ' not ' stranger '
' and silver ' has money ' soul ' nest`ed as ' for ' priest and ' 11 holy ' eat as
' and eat as ' them ' and you house ' as bore`s as and ' and in ' eat as ' that`ing
' stranger ' man I of ' be`s you ' for ' priest ' daughter and ' 12 and from bread in
' daughter and ' 13 eat you ' not ' from as holy the ' you oblation`ing in ' that`s
' whither`s ' seed and ' the exact`ing and ' the widow I ' be`s you ' for ' priest

' am youth`ing are ' am father ' you house ' to ' carry`ed and ' nihil
(14 and in ' eat as ' not ' stranger ' all and ' eat you ' am father ' from bread from
' and you five`s ' add and ' mistake`ed in ' holy ' eat as ' for ' man I and '
' and profane as ' not and ' (15 holy the ' ye ' priest of ' gave and ' and Mosthigh
' (16 Jehovah of ' and elevate`s ' which ' ye ' Israel ' as son ' as holy ' ye
' ye ' from eat in ' guilty`ed ' low`ing ' from ye`ing ' and lift`s the and
Jehovah ' word as and ' (17 from holy from ' Jehovah ' as whither ' for ' them as holy
all ' to and ' him son ' to and ' Aaron ' to ' word ' (18 say of ' Moses ' to '
' you house from ' man I ' man I ' them as to ' you say and ' Israel ' as son '
' approach`s as ' which ' Israel in ' abide ' abide ' has from and ' Israel
which ' from you and freewill ' all of and ' them as vow ' all of ' and has approach
' from are accept`ing of ' (19 on`ed of ' Jehovah of ' and approach`s as '
all ' (20 from as Goat in and ' from as sheep in ' is morn in ' male ' from as complete
' accept`ing of ' not ' for ' and approach`s you ' not ' they`ing ' and in ' which '
' from as whole ' sacrifice ' approach`s as ' for ' man I and ' (21 relate ' be`s as
' or ' is morn in ' or ' the freewill of ' or ' vow ' I made of ' Jehovah of
' not ' they`ing ' all and ' accept`ing of ' be`s as ' from as complete ' flock in
' or ' maim`ing ' or ' is and carry ' or ' you town`ing ' (22 and in ' be`s as
' to`ed ' and approach`s you ' not ' you tetter ' or ' scurvy ' or ' you mix as
' sacrifice them ' on ' lag ' and give you ' not ' Woman and ' Jehovah of
' the freewill ' deficent`ing and ' deform`ing ' Lamb and ' Ox`ing and ' (23 Jehovah of
' bruise`ing and ' (24 approve`ed ' not ' vow of and ' and ye ' the concoct you
' Jehovah of ' and approach`s you ' not ' hew`ing and ' scurf`ing and ' pound`ing and
' not ' foreign ' son ' hand from and ' (25 and do you ' not ' your land in and
' for ' to`ed ' all from ' your as Allah ' fight ' ye ' and approach`s you

' 26 relate ' and approve ' not ' height ' they`ing ' cattle ' from as eradicate from
or ' sheep ' or ' captain`ing ' 27 say of ' Moses ' to ' Jehovah ' word as and
' and mother ' under ' from week ' you seven ' be`s and ' bore him ' for ' harsh '
' has approach of ' approve`ed ' forward`ed and ' as eight`s the ' day as from and
' and son ' ye and ' and ye ' resemble ' or ' Ox`ing and ' 28 Jehovah of ' Woman
' sacrifice ' and sacrifice you ' for and ' 29 one ' day as in ' and slay you ' not
' 30 and sacrifice`ed you ' from are accept`ing of ' Jehovah of ' the endure`ing
' till ' and her from ' and survive`s you ' not ' eat as ' that`ing the ' day as in
' as you command from ' ye ' from you guard and ' 31 Jehovah ' as whither ' herd
ye ' and profane you ' not and ' 32 Jehovah ' as whither ' from ye ' from dual`s and
' Israel ' as son ' middle`ing in ' as you holy has and ' as holy ' there '
' from are ye ' issue`s and them ' 33 from are holy from ' Jehovah ' as whither
as whither ' from as Allah of ' relate ' you and became of ' from as Mizra ' land from
Jehovah '

' as son ' to ' word ' (2 say of ' Moses ' to ' Jehovah ' word as and ' (1
' which ' Jehovah ' as season from ' them as to ' you say and ' Israel
' (3 as season from ' them ' to`ed ' holy ' as call from ' from ye ' and call you
' as seven`s the ' day as in and ' the are fill ' the work you ' from week ' you six
' and do you ' not ' the are fill ' all ' holy ' call from ' has and desist ' desist
' to`ed and ' (4 your as desist and from ' all in ' Jehovah of ' that`ing ' desist
' from ye ' and call you ' which ' holy ' as call from ' Jehovah ' as season from
day as ' ten ' the four I in ' has and head`s the ' new in ' (5 from season from in
the five in and ' (6 Jehovah of ' pass ' from as twilight the ' between in ' new of '
' Jehovah of ' unleaven`ing the ' solemn ' this the ' new of ' day as ' ten '
has and head`s the ' day as in ' (7 and eat you ' unleaven`ing ' from week ' you seven
' not ' serve`ed ' you are fill ' all ' relate ' be`s as ' holy ' call from '
' you seven ' Jehovah of ' Woman ' from you approach the and ' (8 and do you
' you are fill ' all ' holy ' call from ' as seven`s the ' day as in and ' from week
' (10 say of ' Moses ' to ' Jehovah ' word as and ' (9 and do you ' not ' serve`ed
' and came you ' for ' them as to ' you say and ' Israel ' as son ' to ' word
' ye ' from you reap and ' relate ' gave ' as whither ' which ' land the ' to
' from are reap`s ' you as head ' sheaf the ' ye ' from brought the and ' the reap`s
' Jehovah ' as before ' sheaf the ' ye ' wave`s the and ' (11 priest the ' to
' and has wave`s as ' desist the ' you tomorrow from ' from are accept`ing of
' sheaf the ' ye ' from are wave`s the ' day as in ' from dual`s and ' (12 priest the
' (13 Jehovah of ' on`ed of ' and you year ' son ' from as complete ' mutton
' eight in ' the mingle`ing ' flour ' from as has ten ' two ' and you bestow and
' between`s ' and as libation`ed and ' odor has ' smell`s ' Jehovah of ' Woman
' not ' of vineyard and ' parch and ' from bread and ' (14 hin`s ' whom four`s

' from are came`s the ' till ' this the ' day as the ' might ' till ' and eat you
' from on`ing ' statute ' your as Allah ' has approach ' ye
' from you report and ' 15 your as desist and from ' all in ' from are as generation of
' ye ' from are came`s the ' day as from ' desist the ' you tomorrow from ' relate
' complete`ing full ' you and desist ' seven ' the wave`ing scared ' sheaf
' you seven`s the ' desist the ' you tomorrow from ' till ' 16 the has became`s you
' bestow`ed ' from you approach the and ' day as ' from as five ' and report you
' fight ' and came`s you ' from are as desist and they ' 17 Jehovah of ' new`ed
' flour ' from as has ten ' two ' cake`ing ' from twosome ' the wave`ing you
' 18 Jehovah of ' from as first`ing ' the revolve`s you ' leaven ' the has became`s you
they full ' from as mutton ' you seven ' fight the ' on ' from you approach the and
' from as Ram`s and ' one ' herd ' son ' Bullock and ' the Year ' as son '
' from you bestow and ' Jehovah of ' on`ed ' and became as ' they full ' from two
' from dual`s and ' 19 Jehovah of ' odor has ' smell`s ' Woman ' them as libation and
' as son ' from as mutton ' two and ' you sin of ' one ' from as Goat ' gate`s
from ye ' priest the ' wave`s the and ' 20 from as whole the ' sacrifice of ' the Year
' on ' Jehovah ' as before ' the wave`ing you ' from as first`ing the ' fight on '
' 21 priest of ' Jehovah of ' and became as ' holy ' from as mutton the ' two
' be`s as ' holy ' call from ' this the ' day as the ' might in ' from you call and
' from on`ing ' statute ' and do you ' not ' serve`ed ' you are fill ' all ' relate
from are reap in and ' 22 from are as generation of ' your as desist and from ' all in
' are field ' quarter ' all`ed you ' not ' from are land ' reap`s ' ye '
guest of and ' poor of ' pickup you ' not ' are reap`s ' pickup and ' are reap in and
' word as And ' 23 your as Allah ' Jehovah ' as whither ' from ye ' forsake you '
' say of ' Israel ' as son ' to ' word ' 24 say of ' Moses ' to ' Jehovah

' has and desist ' relate ' be`s as ' new of ' one in ' as seven`s the ' new in

' you are fill ' all ' 25 holy ' call from ' the gatekeeper`ing ' shall is remember

' 26 Jehovah of ' Woman ' from you approach the and ' and do you ' not ' serve`ed

' new of ' ten`ing in ' sure ' 27 say of ' Moses ' to ' Jehovah ' word as and

holy ' call from ' that`ing ' from as atone the ' day as ' this the ' as seven`s the

' from are as you soul ' ye ' from whom low and ' relate ' be`s as '

' not ' the are fill ' all and ' 28 Jehovah of ' Woman ' from you approach the and

' from as atone`ing ' day as ' for ' this the ' day as the ' might in ' and do you

for ' 29 your as Allah ' Jehovah ' as before ' from are mosthigh ' atone of ' that`ing

' this the ' day as the ' might in ' vouch`ed ' not ' which ' soul the ' all '

' all ' do`ed you ' which ' soul the ' all and ' 30 am people from ' hew`ed shall

' ye ' as you perish the and ' this the ' day as the ' might in ' the are fill

' the are fill ' all and ' 31 the as people ' approach from ' that`ing the ' soul the

' all in ' from are as generation of ' from on`ing ' statute ' and do you ' not

' relate ' that`ing ' has and desist ' desist ' 32 your as desist and from

' twilight in ' new of ' the nine in ' from are as you soul ' ye ' from whom low and

' word as and ' 33 from are desist ' and desist you ' twilight ' till ' twilight from

' say of ' Israel ' as son ' to ' word ' 34 say of ' Moses ' to ' Jehovah

' solemn ' this the ' as seven`s the ' new of ' day as ' ten ' the five in

' day as in ' 35 Jehovah of ' from week ' you seven ' booth`ing the

' not ' serve`ed ' you are fill ' all ' holy ' call from ' has and head`s the

' Jehovah of ' the fire ' and approach`s you ' from week ' you seven ' 36 and do you

' from walk ' be`s as ' holy ' call from ' as eight`s the ' day as in

' all and ' that`s ' you festival ' Jehovah of ' the fire ' from you approach the and

' Jehovah ' as season from ' to`ed ' 37 and do you ' not ' serve`ed ' you are fill

fire`ed ’ approach`s the of ’ holy ’ as call from , from ye ’ and call you ’ which
’ word ’ from as crowd has and ’ sacrifice ’ bestow`ed and ’ on`ed ’ Jehovah of ’
’ Jehovah ’ you and desist ’ alone of from ’ (38 and day as in ’ day as
’ all ’ earnest from and ’ your as you and present ’ all ’ earnest from and
and give you ’ which ’ your as you and freewill ’ all ’ earnest from and ’ your as vow
’ as seven`s the ’ new of ’ day as ’ ten ’ the five in ’ sure ’ (39 Jehovah of ’
solemn ’ ye ’ and solemn you ’ land the ’ you income`ing ’ ye ’ from are gather in
’ has and desist ’ has and head`s the ’ day as in ’ from week ’ you seven ’ Jehovah ’
’ from walk ’ from you take and ’ (40 has and desist ’ as eight`s the ’ day as in and
’ you and palm ’ magnificent ’ tree ’ fruit ’ has and head`s the ’ day as in
’ inherit ’ as twilight and ’ wrap`ing ’ tree ’ as twig and ’ from as palmtree
(41 from week ’ you seven ’ your as Allah ’ Jehovah ’ as before ’ from you rejoice and
’ from week ’ you seven ’ Jehovah of ’ solemn ’ and ye ’ from you solemn and ’
’ new in ’ from are as generation of ’ from on`ing ’ statute ’ Year`ed in
’ and inhabitant ’ booth`ing in ’ (42 and ye ’ and solemn you ’ as seven`s the
’ and carry as ’ Israel in ’ at native the ’ all ’ from week ’ you seven
’ booth`ing in ’ for ’ your as generation ’ and known ’ purpose of ’ (43 booth`ing in
’ from ye`ing ’ as issue`s alas in ’ Israel ’ as son ’ ye ’ as desist and the
’ word as and ’ (44 your as Allah ’ Jehovah ’ as whither ’ from as Mizra ’ land from
Israel ’ as son ’ to ’ Jehovah ’ as season from ’ ye ’ Moses

' as son ' ye ' command`ed ' (2 say of ' Moses ' to ' Jehovah ' word as and ' (1
' set`s are ' remember ' olivet`s ' eight ' are as to ' acquire as and ' Israel
' outside`ing from ' (3 continual`s ' lamp ' offer`ing the of ' light`ing from of
' and ye ' pile as ' ing`congregate ' tent in ' testimony`ing the ' veil put of
' Jehovah ' as before ' herd ' till ' twilight from ' him son and ' Aaron
' on ' (4 from are as generation of ' from on`ing ' statute ' continual`s
' as before ' you and lamp the ' ye ' pile as ' clean`ed the ' the taper`ing the
' ye`ed ' broil`s and ' flour ' you take and ' (5 herd ' till ' continual`s ' Jehovah
' block`ed ' be`s as ' from as has ten ' two ' cake`ing ' ten`ed ' from twosome
' six ' you and pile from ' from twosome ' from ye`ing ' herein and ' (6 sister the
' (7 Jehovah ' as before ' clean the ' has send the ' on ' you pile them
whom`ed the and ' remember`ed ' the son`ing of ' you pile them ' on ' set`ed has and
' day as in ' (8 Jehovah of ' Woman ' the is remember I of ' from bread of '
' Jehovah ' as before ' and has pile as ' desist the ' day as in ' desist the
' (9 from on`ing ' covenant`s ' Israel ' as son ' each ' continual`s
' place`ing in ' the and eat and ' him son of and ' Aaron of ' whom`ed the and
' law ' Jehovah ' as fire from ' if ' that`s ' from as holy ' holy ' for ' holy`ing
man I ' son ' that`ing and ' whom Israel ' Woman ' son ' out And ' (10 from on`ing
' son ' camp`ed in ' and strive and ' Israel ' as son ' middle`ing in ' as Mizra '
' Woman the ' son ' press and ' (11 as Israel the ' man that and ' whom Israel the
' and ye ' and came`s as and ' accurse as and ' there the ' ye ' whom Israel the
' as word ' daughter ' whom whole`ing ' and mother ' there and ' Moses ' to
' them of ' excrement of ' guard from in ' and the rest`s as and ' (12 judge ' below`ed
' (14 say of ' Moses ' to ' Jehovah ' word as And ' (13 Jehovah ' edge ' on
' camp`ed of ' outside`ing from ' to ' accurse them ' ye ' issue`s alas

' and head ' on ' them as hand ' ye ' from as hear the ' all ' and laid and
' Israel ' as son ' to and ' 15 till`ed the ' all ' and ye ' and council and
' help and ' him Allah ' accurse as ' for ' man I ' man I ' say of ' word you
' council`ing ' die him ' die`ing ' Jehovah ' there ' in blame and ' 16 and sin
' at native are ' guest are ' till`ed the ' all ' and in ' and council as
' soul ' all ' struck`ed ' for ' man I and ' 17 die him ' there the ' and in blame in
' the has whole as ' cattle`ed ' soul ' with`ed and ' 18 die him ' die`ing ' ground
and whom people in ' they`ing ' permanent ' for ' man I and ' 19 soul ' under ' soul
' has eye ' buy ' under ' buy ' 20 if ' success`ed ' so ' do`ed ' which are '
' Men in ' they`ing ' permanent ' which are ' Year ' under ' Year ' has eye ' under
' with`ed and ' the has whole as ' cattle`ed ' with`ed and ' 21 and in ' gave as ' so
' guest are ' relate ' be`s as ' one ' discern from ' 22 die him ' ground
word as and ' 23 your as Allah ' Jehovah ' as whither ' for ' be`s as ' at native are
to ' accurse them ' ye ' and issue`s him and ' Israel ' as son ' to ' Moses '
' as son and ' stone ' and ye ' and council as and ' camp`ed of ' outside`ing from '
Moses ' ye ' Jehovah ' command`ed ' which are ' concoct ' Israel

' word ' 2 say of ' as bush`s ' blemish ' Moses ' to ' Jehovah ' word as and ' 1
' to ' and came you ' for ' them as to ' you say and ' Israel ' as son ' to
' desist ' land the ' desist`ed and ' relate ' gave ' as whither ' which ' land the
' from as Year ' six and ' are field ' seed you ' from two ' six ' 3 Jehovah of
' 4 the you income`ing ' ye ' you gather and ' are vineyard ' prune you
' land of ' be`s as ' has and desist ' desist ' you as seven`s the ' Year`ed in and
prune you ' not ' are vineyard and ' seed you ' not ' are field ' Jehovah of ' desist
' as grape ' ye and ' reap`ing you ' not ' are reap`s ' as scab`s ' ye and ' 5
' 6 land of ' be`s as ' has and desist ' sleep ' is clip ' not ' are consecrate`s
are as serve of and ' walk ' eat`ed of ' relate ' land the ' desist ' whom`ed the and
' are as sojourn you of and ' are as merry`s of and ' are as Maid of and '
' which ' life`ed of and ' are you cattle of and ' 7 are people ' from as guest the
are of ' you report and ' 8 eat of ' the you income`ing ' all ' be`s you ' are land in
' seven ' from as Year ' seven ' from as Year ' you and desist ' seven '
' you and desist ' seven ' week ' are of ' and became and ' from as move
' you cross the and ' 9 the Year ' from as four I and ' nine ' from as Year the
' new of ' ten`ing in ' as seven`s the ' new in ' the gatekeeper`ing ' is lip`ing
' all in ' is lip`ing ' and cross`s you ' from as atone`ing the ' day as in
' the Year ' from as five the ' you Year ' ye ' from you holy and ' 10 from are land
' ing`produce ' am sojourn as ' all of ' land in ' pure`ing ' from you call and
' and you hold ' to ' man I ' from you carry and ' your of ' be`s you ' that`ing
' that`ing ' ing`produce ' 11 and inhabitant`ing ' and you at family ' to ' man I and
' and seed you ' not ' your of ' be`s you ' the Year ' from as five the ' you Year
' ye ' and is clip ' not and ' am scab`s ' ye ' and reap you ' not and
' your of ' be`s you ' holy ' that`ing ' ing`produce ' for ' 12 am consecrate`s

' you Year in ' 13 the you income`ing ' ye ' and eat you ' field`ed the ' has from
' 14 and you hold ' to ' man I ' and carry`ing you ' such the ' ing`produce the
' hand from ' nest`ed ' or ' are whom people of ' sale from ' and sale you ' for and
report from in ' 15 him brother ' ye ' man I ' and give`ing ' to ' are whom people
' are whom people ' each ' the nest you ' ing`produce the ' after ' from as Year '
' increase ' as by ' 16 are of ' sale as ' you income`ing ' as Year ' report from in
' less ' as by and , and you purchase ' increase`ed you ' from as Year the
you income`ing ' report from ' for ' and you purchase ' less`s you ' from as Year the
' ye ' man I ' and give`ing ' not and ' 17 are of ' sale ' that`ing '
' Jehovah ' as whither ' for ' are as Allah from ' you look as and ' and whom people
as discern from ' ye and ' as statute`ing ' ye ' from whom do and ' 18 your as Allah
' land the ' on ' from you dwell and ' from ye ' from whom do and , and guard you '
' seven of ' from you eat and ' the fruit ' land the ' gave`ed and ' 19 safe of
' eat has ' what ' and say you ' for and ' 20 am on ' safe of ' from you dwell and
' gather has ' not and ' seed has ' not ' behold ' you as seven`s the ' Year`ed in
your of ' as you bless ' ye ' as whom command and , 21 and has you income`ing ' ye
' the you income`ing the ' ye ' the you do and ' whom six the ' Year`ed in '
' Year`ed the ' ye ' from you seed and ' 22 from as Year the ' three of
' Year as ' the you income`ing the ' has from ' from you eat and ' whom eight`s the
' the you income`ing ' came`ing ' till ' whom nine the ' Year`ed the ' till
' for ' you bone`s of ' sale you ' not ' land the and ' 23 Year as ' and eat you
as stand ' from ye ' from as sojourn you and ' from as guest ' for ' land the ' vessel
' 25 land of ' and give you ' redeem`ed ' from are you hold ' land ' all in and ' 24
' came and ' and you hold from ' sale and ' are as brother ' are impoverish ' for and
him brother ' sale from ' ye ' redeem and ' him to ' approach`ing the ' and redeem

and hand ' the drawal`s the and ' redeem ' if ' be`s as ' not ' for ' man I and ' 26
' as Year ' ye ' reckon and ' 27 and you redeem ' enough are ' come and ,
if ' sale ' which ' man I of ' surplus the ' ye ' carry`s the and , and sale from
' enough ' and hand ' come`ed ' not ' mother and , 28 and you hold of ' sojourn '
' till ' and ye ' nest`ed the ' hand in ' and sale from ' be`s and ' if ' carry`s the
' 29 and you hold of ' sojourn ' ing`produce in ' out and ' ing`produce the ' you Year
' the Ham`ing ' town`s ' sojourn from ' you house ' sale as ' for ' man I and
' and sale from ' you Year ' complete ' till ' and you redeem ' whom`ed the and
' till ' redeem as ' not ' mother and ' 30 and you redeem ' be`s you ' from week
' you house the ' rise and ' the from as complete ' the Year ' if ' you and fill
' nest`ed of ' set`ing forever of ' the Ham`ing ' if ' which ' town`s in ' which
' house`ly and ' 31 ing`produce in ' out ' not ' him generation of ' and ye
' on ' surround`s ' the Ham`ing ' them of ' whither`s ' which ' from as yard the
' if ' be`s you ' redeem`ed ' and reckon`ed as ' land the ' field`ed
' as town ' house`ly ' from Levi the ' as town and ' 32 out ' ing`produce in and
' which and ' 33 from Levi of ' be`s you ' from on`ing ' you redeem ' from you hold
' town`s and ' you house ' sale from ' out and ' from Levi the ' has from ' redeem as
' that`s ' from Levi the ' as town ' house`ly ' for ' ing`produce in ' and you hold
' exact from ' field`ed and ' 34 Israel ' as son ' middle`ing in ' from you hold
35 them of ' that`s ' from on`ing ' you hold ' for ' and sale as ' not ' them as town
' are people ' and hand ' staff from and ' are as brother ' are impoverish ' for and '
' are as brother ' life and ' sojourn you and ' guest ' and in ' you strength the and
' whom increase you and ' seize ' and ye from ' took you ' to ' 36 are people
ye ' 37 are people ' are as brother ' life and ' are as Allah from ' you look as and
' not ' whom increase you height and ' seize in ' if ' give you ' not ' are silver '

' which ' your as Allah ' Jehovah ' as whither ' (38 are eat ' give you

ye ' your of ' set of ' from as Mizra ' land from , from are ye ' as you issue alas

' for and ' (39 from as Allah of ' your of ' you and became of ' Canaan ' land '

serve you ' not ' are of ' sale shall ' are people ' are as brother ' are impoverish

are people ' be`s as ' sojourn you are ' merry`s are ' (40 serve ' you serve ' and in '

' out and ' (41 are people ' serve as ' ing`produce the ' you Year ' till '

' to ' sojourn ' and people ' him son and ' that`ing ' are people from

' for ' (42 carry`ing as ' and as you father ' you hold ' to and , and you slave from

' from as Mizra ' land from , from ye ' as you issue alas ' which ' them ' as serve

fracture in ' and in ' up`ed you ' not ' (43 serve ' you sale from ' and sale as ' not

are as you mother`ed and ' are as serve and ' (44 are as Allah from ' you look as and '

' which ' from nation`ing the ' each ' are of ' and became as ' which '

' (45 mother`ed and ' serve ' and nest`ed you ' them from ' your as you surround`s

' your people ' from as guest the ' from as sojourn you the ' as son from ' also and

' which ' your people ' which ' from you slave they and , and nest`ed you ' them from

' (46 hold`ed of ' your of ' and became and ' your land in ' and bore`s and the

net`ness of ' your as after ' your as son of ' from ye ' from you inherit you the and

' from are as brother in and , and serve`s you ' cattle ' from on`ing of ' hold`ed '

(47 are brute ' and in ' up`ed you ' not ' him brother in ' man I ' Israel ' as son

' with and ' are people ' sojourn you and ' guest ' hand ' drawal`s you ' for and '

' are people ' sojourn you ' and guest of ' sale shall ' and people ' are as brother

' redeem`ed ' sale has ' as after ' (48 guest ' you slave from ' is cast of ' or

' and uncle ' or ' (49 and has redeem as ' him brother from ' one ' if ' be`s you

' and flesh ' remain from ' or ' and has redeem as ' and uncle ' son ' or

' and hand ' the drawal`s the ' or ' and has redeem as ' and you at family from

' and sale the ' you year from ' and nest`ed ' people ' reckon and ' 50 redeem shall
' and sale from ' silver ' be`s and ' ing`produce the ' you Year ' till ' if
mother ' 51 and people ' be`s as ' merry`s ' week are ' from as Year ' report from in
' carry`s as ' has edge`ed of ' from as Year in ' you and increase ' till`ing '
' remain has ' less ' mother and , 52 and you purchase ' silver from ' and you redeem
' edge are ' if ' reckon and ' ing`produce the ' you Year ' till ' from as Year in
Year`ed in ' the Year ' merry`s are ' 53 and you redeem ' ye ' carry`s as ' him year
' 54 are as has eye of ' are brute ' our up as ' not ' and people ' be`s as '
' ing`produce the ' you Year in ' out and ' to`ed in ' redeem as ' not ' mother and
' Israel ' as son ' vessel ' for ' 55 and people ' him son and ' that`ing
land from , from ye`ing ' as you issue alas ' which ' them ' as serve ' from as serve
your as Allah ' Jehovah ' as whither ' from as Mizra '

1 ' not ' altar`ed and ' carve and ' from as thing`s ' relate ' and do you ' not '
' and give you ' not ' hedge`s from ' stone and ' relate ' and rise`s you
' Jehovah ' as whither ' for ' am on ' you and humble`ly the of ' your land in
2 ' as holy from and ' and guard you ' as you desist ' ye ' your as Allah
3 ' and walk you ' as statute in ' mother ' Jehovah ' as whither ' and look as you
4 ' from ye ' from dual`s and ' and guard you ' as you command from ' ye and
' land the ' the give has and ' from time in ' from are as tifon ' as set has and
5 drawal`s the and ' and fruit ' permanent ' field`ed the ' tree and ' the produce`ing
' ye ' drawal`s as ' boulder`s in and ' boulder`s in ' ye ' thresh`s ' relate '
' from you dwell and ' seven of ' your from bread ' from you eat and ' seed the
6 ' land in ' from and peace ' as set has and ' your land in ' safe of
' the life ' as desist the and ' shudder`s from ' whither`s and ' from you lay and
7 ' your land in ' cross you ' not ' desolate and ' land the ' has from ' evil`ed
' your as before ' and fall and ' your as enemy I ' ye ' complete chase and
8 ' the hundred and ' hundred`ed ' the five ' from with ' and chase and ' desolate of
' your as enemy I ' and fall and ' and chase as ' thus increase ' from with
9 as you fruit the and ' your as to ' as whom turn and ' desolate of ' your as before
ye ' as you rise`s the and ' from are ye ' as whom increase the and ' from are ye '
10 ' has joy has ' slept ' from you eat and ' from are ye ' as covenant`s '
11 ' as set has and ' and issue`s and you ' new ' around from ' year as and
12 ' from are ye ' as soul ' loathe you ' not and ' your middle`ing in ' as tabernacle
' relate ' as whom became and ' your middle`ing in ' as you are tent the and
13 ' as whither ' people of ' vessel ' and as he ' from ye and ' from as Allah of
' land from ' from are ye ' as you issue alas ' which ' your as Allah ' Jehovah
' buy`ed I and ' from as serve ' them of ' whom`ing the from ' from as Mizra

you him from rise`ing ' from are ye ' are to`ing and ' from are on`ing ' you and down
' all ' ye ' and do you ' not and ' vessel ' and hear you ' not ' mother and ' 14
' and reject you ' as statute in ' mother and ' 15 these`ed ' unleaven`ing the
' as except of ' from are soul ' loathe you ' as discern from ' ye ' mother and
' ye ' from fracture the of ' as you command from ' all ' ye ' you and do
' relate ' such ' do`ed I ' as whither ' anger ' 16 as covenant`s
' you emaciate the ' ye ' amaze`ed ' from are mosthigh ' as you punish the and
' you bear`s from and ' from as has eye ' you fail from ' you imflame the ' ye and
' and eat`ed and ' from are seed ' only`s of ' from you seed and ' soul
' from you defeat and ' from are in ' around ' as set has and ' 17 your as enemy I
' your as hateful ' from are in ' and up and ' your as enemy I ' as before
to`ed ' till ' mother and ' 18 from are ye ' chase ' whither`s and ' from you flee and
seven ' from are ye ' correct`ed of ' as you add and ' vessel ' and hear you ' not '
' has and haughty ' ye ' as you is carry and ' 19 your as you sin ' on '
' ye and ' of iron are ' your as there ' ye ' as set has and ' from are harsh
' not and ' wise are ' only`s of ' complete and ' 20 serpent`ed are ' from are land
land the ' field`ed the ' tree and ' the produce`ing ' ye ' from are land ' has set
' repair ' as people ' and walk you ' mother and ' 21 and fruit ' permanent ' not '
' from are mosthigh ' as you add and ' vessel ' hear of ' and father you ' not and
' ye ' from are in ' as you send the and ' 22 your as you sin are ' seven ' with`ed
' ye ' the hew`s the and ' from are ye ' bereave`ed and ' field`ed the ' you life
23 your as way ' and blow and ' from are ye ' the less`s the and ' from are you cattle
' from you walk the and ' vessel ' and chasten you ' not ' the route ' mother and '
' as whither ' anger ' also ' as you walk the and ' 24 and repair ' as people
' also ' from are ye ' as whom smitten and ' repair in ' hotspring in ' your people

' as you came`s the and ' 25 your as you sin ' on ' seven ' as whither
' covenant`s ' avenge ' you avenge ' desolate ' from are mosthigh
' word ' as you send and ' your as town ' to ' from you gather has and
' as is carry in ' 26 enemy and I ' hand in ' from set has and ' your middle`ing in
' your from bread ' from as women ' ten ' now and ' fight ' down`ed ' relate
' weight`ing from in ' your from bread ' and carry`s the and ' one ' furnace`ing in
' not ' such in ' mother and ' 27 and swear too you ' not and ' from you eat and
' 28 repair in ' as people ' from you walk the and ' vessel ' and hear you
' as you correct and ' repair ' hotspring in ' your people ' as you walk the and
from you eat and ' 29 your as you sin ' on ' seven ' as whither ' anger ' from are ye
' 30 and eat you ' your as daughter`th ' flesh and ' your as son ' flesh '
' ye ' as hew the and ' your as you height ' ye ' as you destory the and
' as carcase ' on ' your as carcase ' ye ' as set has and ' your as totem
' ye ' as set has and ' 31 from are ye ' as soul ' loathe`ed and ' your as sake`ing
' your as holy from ' ye ' as fragrance`ing the and ' the desolate ' your as town
' as fragrance the and ' 32 from are odour has ' smell`s in ' smell`s I ' not and
' your as enemy I ' am on ' and from there and ' land the ' ye ' as whither
' from nation`ing in ' native`ed ' from are ye and ' 33 thus ' from as sojourn became
' from are land ' whom`ed the and ' desolate ' your as after ' as you only`s the and
run`ed you ' yet ' 34 the desolate ' and became as ' your as town and ' the from there
land in ' from ye and ' there`ed the ' week ' all ' am you desist ' ye ' land the '
' ye ' decide`ed the and ' land the ' desist you ' yet ' your as enemy I '
' not ' which ' ye ' desist you ' guilty`ed the ' week ' all ' 35 am you desist
' 36 am on ' from are desist in ' your as you desist in ' desist`ed
' faintness ' as you came the and ' from are in ' from as remain has the and

voice`ing ' from ye ' chase and ' them as enemy I ' you and land in ' from in heart in
' and fall and ' desolate ' you flee`ing from ' and flee and ' shaken ' on`ed '
as turn from are ' him brother in ' man I ' and stumble and ' (37 chase ' whither`s and
' the rise`ing you ' relate ' be`s you ' not and ' whither`s ' chase and ' desolate '
eat`ed and ' from nation`ing in ' from you perish and ' (38 your as enemy I ' as before
' from are in ' from as remain has the and ' (39 your as enemy I ' land ' from are ye '
' anger and ' them are as enemy I ' you and land in ' from low`ing in ' and stink as
' (40 and stink as ' from ye ' from you and father ' you and low`ing in
from you and father ' low`ing ' ye and ' from low`ing ' ye ' and endure`ing the and
' and walk the ' which ' anger and ' house ' and on from ' which ' from on from in '
' repair in ' from people ' walk I the ' as whither ' anger ' (41 repair in ' as people
humiliate as ' yet ' or ' them as enemy I ' land in ' from ye ' as you came the and
' (42 from low`ing ' ye ' and approve ' yet and ' of town the ' from mind '
' ye ' anger and ' Jacob`ing ' as covenant`s ' ye ' as you is remember and
is remember I ' Abraham ' as covenant`s ' ye ' anger and ' Isaac ' as covenant`s
' lag ' forsake you ' land the and ' (43 is remember I ' land the and '
' them and ' lag ' guilty`ed the in ' am you desist ' ye ' decide`ed you and
' as discern from in ' because in and ' because ' from low`ing ' ye ' and approve
' also ' anger and ' (44 from soul ' the loathe ' as statute ' ye and ' and reject
' not ' them as enemy I ' you and land in ' complete him the in ' such
' from daughterinlaw`ing of ' from as you loathe ' not and ' from as you reject
' (45 them as Allah ' Jehovah ' as whither ' for ' from ye ' as covenant`s ' broken of
' which ' from as has and head`s ' covenant`s ' them of ' as you is remember and
' as has eye of ' from as Mizra ' land from ' from ye ' as you issue alas
' as whither ' from as Allah of ' them of ' you and became of ' from nation`ing the

' from as discern them and ' from as law the ' to`ed ' Jehovah 45

' and between in ' Jehovah ' gave ' which ' you and protect`ing the and

Moses ' hand in ' as bush`s ' blemish ' Israel ' as son ' between in and

’ as son ’ to ’ word ’ 2 say of ’ Moses ’ to ’ Jehovah ’ word as and ’ 1
’ are pile in ’ vow ’ I made as ’ for ’ man I ’ them as to ’ you say and ’ Israel
from as ten ’ son from ’ male the ’ are pile ’ be`s and ’ 3 Jehovah of ’ you and soul
’ are pile ’ be`s and ’ the Year ’ from as six ’ son ’ till and ’ the Year ’
’ the female ’ mother and ’ 4 holy the ’ weigh in ’ silver ’ weigh ’ from as five
’ son from ’ mother and ’ 5 weigh ’ from as three ’ are pile ’ be`s and ’ that`s
’ are pile ’ be`s and ’ the Year ’ from as ten ’ son ’ till and ’ from two ’ five
6 from as weigh ’ you ten ’ the female of and ’ from as weigh ’ from as ten ’ male the
’ be`s and ’ from as Year ’ five ’ son ’ till and ’ new ’ son from ’ mother and ’
are pile ’ the female of and ’ silver ’ from as weigh ’ the five ’ male the ’ are pile
’ from as six ’ son from ’ mother and ’ 7 silver ’ from as weigh ’ you three ’
’ ten ’ the five ’ are pile ’ be`s and ’ male ’ mother ’ above`ed and ’ the Year
’ with ’ mother and ’ 8 from as weigh ’ you ten`ed ’ the female of and ’ weigh
’ priest the ’ as before ’ and stand`s the and ’ are pile from ’ that`ing
’ hand ’ drawal`s you ’ which ’ edge ’ on ’ priest the ’ and ye ’ pile`s the and
’ which ’ cattle`ed ’ mother and ’ 9 priest the ’ and has pile`s as ’ vow the
’ give as ’ which ’ all ’ Jehovah of ’ has approach ’ her`ed from ’ and approach`s as
’ not and ’ and has change`s as ’ not ’ 10 holy ’ be`s as ’ Jehovah of ’ and her from
’ mother and ’ good`ing in ’ evil ’ or ’ evil in ’ good`ing ’ and ye ’ drop`s as
’ that`ing ’ be`s and ’ cattle`ed in ’ cattle`ed ’ drop`s as ’ drop the
’ cattle`ed ’ all ’ mother and ’ 11 holy ’ be`s as ’ and you drop`s you and
’ has approach ’ her`ed from ’ and approach`s as ’ not ’ which ’ unclean`ed
’ 12 priest the ’ as before ’ cattle`ed the ’ ye ’ stand`s the and ’ Jehovah of
’ evil ’ between in and ’ good`ing ’ between in ’ ye`ed ’ priest the ’ pile`s the and
the our redeem as ’ redeem ’ mother and ’ 13 be`s as ’ so ’ priest the ’ are pile are

ye ' holy`s as ' for ' man I and ' 14 are pile ' on ' and whom five`s ' add and '
' between in ' priest the ' and pile`s the and ' Jehovah of ' holy ' and you house '
so ' priest the ' and ye ' pile`s as ' which are ' evil ' between in and ' good`ing
' and you house ' ye ' redeem as ' holy`s them ' mother and ' 15 rise`ing as '
mother and ' 16 if ' be`s and ' him on ' are pile ' silver ' you as five`s ' add and
are pile ' be`s and ' Jehovah of ' man I ' holy`s as ' and you hold ' field`ed from '
' weigh ' from as five in ' from as Barley ' drop at ' seed ' and seed ' as by '
' and field`ed ' holy`s as ' ing`produce the ' you year from ' mother and ' 17 silver
' holy`s as ' ing`produce the ' after ' mother and ' 18 rise`ing as ' are pile are
' edge ' on ' silver the ' ye ' priest the ' and of ' reckon and , and field`ed
' ing`produce the ' you Year ' till ' you and ing`leap the ' from as Year the
' ye ' you redeem as ' redeem ' mother and ' 19 are pile from ' withdraw has and
are pile ' silver ' you five`s ' ye ' add and , and ye ' holy`s them ' field`ed the
field`ed the ' ye ' redeem as ' not ' mother and ' 20 and of ' rise and ' him on '
' redeem as ' not ' after ' man I of ' field`ed the ' ye ' sale ' mother and '
' holy ' ing`produce in ' and you issue in ' field`ed the ' be`s and ' 21 till`ing
' 22 and you hold ' be`s you ' priest of ' curse the ' field`ed are ' Jehovah of
' field`ed from ' not ' which ' and you purchase ' field`ed ' ye ' mother and
' priest the ' if ' reckon and ' 23 Jehovah of ' man I ' holy`s as ' and you hold
' gave and ' ing`produce the ' you Year ' till ' are pile the ' you and amount ' ye
' you Year in ' 24 Jehovah of ' holy ' that`ing the ' day as in ' are pile the ' ye
' and ye from ' and nest`ed ' which of ' field`ed the ' carry`ing as ' ing`produce the
' weigh in ' be`s as ' are pile ' all and ' 25 land the ' you hold ' if ' which of
which ' first`ing ' sure ' 26 weigh the ' be`s as ' guest`ed ' from as ten ' holy the
' mother ' and ye ' man I ' holy`s as ' not ' cattle`ed in ' Jehovah of ' first as '

' cattle`ed in ' mother and ' 27 that`ing ' Jehovah of ' Lamb ' mother ' Ox`ing
' and as on ' and you five`s ' add and ' are pile in ' release`ed and ' unclean`ed the
' curse ' all ' sure ' 28 are pile in ' sale shall ' redeem as ' not ' mother and
' men from ' and of ' which ' all from ' Jehovah of ' man I ' curse as ' which
' not and ' sale as ' not ' and you hold ' field`ed from and ' cattle`ed and
' all ' 29 Jehovah of ' that`ing ' from as holy ' holy ' curse ' all ' redeem as
' die`ing ' liberate`ed ' not ' Men the ' has from ' curse as ' which ' curse
' fruit from and ' land the ' seed from ' land the ' ten from ' all and ' 30 die him
' redeem ' mother and ' 31 Jehovah of ' holy ' that`ing ' Jehovah of ' tree the
' all and ' 32 him on ' add ' and you five`s ' and ten they ' man I ' redeem as
' tribe the ' under ' cross as ' which ' all ' flock and ' herd ' ten from
good`ing ' between in ' herd as ' not ' 33 Jehovah of ' holy ' be`s as ' as ten`s the
' our drop`s as ' drop the ' mother and ' our drop`s as ' not and ' evil of '
' 34 redeem as ' not ' holy ' be`s as ' and you drop`s you and ' that`ing ' be`s and
' to ' Moses ' ye ' Jehovah ' command`ed ' which ' you command from the ' to`ed
' as bush`s ' mountain in ' Israel ' as son

’ tent in ’ as bush`s ’ word from in ’ Moses ’ to ’ Jehovah ’ word as and 1

’ you two the ’ Year`ed in ’ two the ’ new of ’ one in ’ ing`congregate

’ head ’ ye ’ and lift ’ 2 say of ’ from as Mizra ’ land from ’ from you issue of

’ you house of ’ complete and at family of ’ Israel ’ as son ’ testimony ’ all

’ 3 from you heap heap of ’ male ’ all ’ you name ’ is number in ’ from you father

’ Israel in ’ mass ’ out ’ all ’ above`ed and ’ the Year ’ from as ten ’ son from

’ 4 Aaron and ’ ye`ed ’ from you mass of ’ from ye ’ and my appoint you

’ head ’ man I ’ below`ed ’ man I ’ man I ’ and became as ’ from are ye and

’ you name ’ to`ed and ’ 5 that`ing ’ and as you father ’ you house of

mould`ing of I ’ Reuben of ’ from are ye ’ and stand as ’ which ’ from as person the

almight as boulder`ing ’ son ’ to as whole ’ Simeon of ’ 6 light`ing almight ’ son ’

to gave ’ Issachar of ’ 8 freewill as people ’ son ’ pocket`ing has ’ Judah of ’ 7

’ as son of ’ 10 s`window ’ son ’ father as to ’ Zebulun of ’ 9 is gain`ing ’ son ’

’ Manasse`ed of ’ gloref`ing as people ’ son ’ Elishama ’ Ephraim of ’ Joseph

’ son ’ judge as father ’ Benjamim`s of ’ 11 boulder`ing release’ed ’ son ’ to as wean

’ which of ’ 13 almight as people ’ son ’ aid as brother ’ Dan of ’ 12 as Gideon`ing

15 to and menstruate ’ son ’ add of I ’ Gad of ’ 14 has disturb ’ son ’ to as entreat

’ till`ed the ’ as call`s ’ to`ed ’ 16 has low`s ’ son ’ sore brother ’ Naphtali of ’

Israel ’ as thousand ’ as head ’ from you and father ’ you and down ’ as lift`s has

’ these`ed ’ from as person the ’ ye ’ Aaron and ’ Moses ’ took as and ’ 17 them ’

and assemble`s the ’ till`ed the ’ all ’ ye and ’ 18 you name in ’ and female ’ which

’ complete and at family ’ on ’ and bore as whom and ’ two the ’ new of ’ one in ’

from as ten ’ son from ’ you name ’ is number in ’ from you and father ’ you house of

’ command`ed ’ which are ’ 19 from you heap heap of ’ above`ed and ’ the Year ’

’ 20 as bush`s ’ word from in ’ from my appoint as and ’ Moses ’ ye ’ Jehovah

’ from you bore and you ’ Israel ’ first`ing ’ Reuben ’ as son ’ and became as and

’ is number in ’ from you and father ’ you house of ’ complete and at family of

’ the Year ’ from as ten ’ son from ’ from you heap heap of ’ male ’ all ’ you name

’ Reuben ’ below`ed ’ them as my appoint ’ 21 mass ’ out ’ all ’ above`ed and

’ as son of ’ 22 you and hundred ’ five and ’ thousand ’ from as four I and ’ six`ed

’ you house of ’ complete and at family of ’ from you bore and you ’ Simeon

’ you name ’ is number in ’ them and as my appoint ’ from you and father

above`ed and ’ the Year ’ from as ten ’ son from ’ male ’ all ’ from you heap heap of

’ nine`ed ’ Simeon ’ below`ed ’ them as my appoint ’ 23 mass ’ out ’ all ’

’ fortune ’ as son of ’ 24 you and hundred ’ three and ’ thousand ’ from as five and

from you and father ’ you house of ’ complete and at family of ’ from you bore and you

’ all ’ above`ed and ’ the Year ’ from as ten ’ son from ’ you name ’ is number in ’

’ the five ’ fortune ’ below`ed ’ them as my appoint ’ 25 mass ’ out

’ 26 from as five and ’ you and hundred ’ six and ’ thousand ’ from as four I and

’ complete and at family of ’ from you bore and you ’ Judah ’ as son of

from as ten ’ son from ’ you name ’ is number in ’ from you and father ’ you house of

’ below`ed ’ them as my appoint ’ 27 mass ’ out ’ all ’ above`ed and ’ the Year ’

’ 28 you and hundred ’ six and ’ thousand ’ from as seven and ’ the four I ’ Judah

’ complete and at family of ’ from you bore and you ’ Issachar ’ as son of

from as ten ’ son from ’ you name ’ is number in ’ from you and father ’ you house of

’ below`ed ’ them as my appoint ’ 29 mass ’ out ’ all ’ above`ed and ’ the Year ’

30 you and hundred ’ four I and ’ thousand ’ from as five and ’ the four I ’ Issachar

’ complete and at family of ’ from you bore and you ’ Zebulun ’ as son of ’

from as ten ’ son from ’ you name ’ is number in ’ from you and father ’ you house of

’ below`ed ’ them as my appoint ’ 31 mass ’ out ’ all ’ above`ed and ’ the Year ’

32 ' you and hundred ' four I and ' thousand ' from as five and ' the seven ' Zebulun
' from you bore and you ' Ephraim ' as son of ' Joseph ' as son of
' is number in ' from you and father ' you house of ' complete and at family of
33 ' mass ' out ' all ' above`ed and ' the Year ' from as ten ' son from ' you name
' five and ' thousand ' from as four I ' Ephraim ' below`ed ' them as my appoint
' from you bore and you ' Manasse`ed ' as son of ' 34 you and hundred
' is number in ' from you and father ' you house of ' complete and at family of
35 ' mass ' out ' all ' above`ed and ' the Year ' from as ten ' son from ' you name
' thousand ' from as three and ' from two ' Manasse`ed ' below`ed ' them as my appoint
' from you bore and you ' Benjamim`s ' as son of ' 36 from as you hundred and
' is number in ' from you and father ' you house of ' complete and at family of
37 ' mass ' out ' all ' above`ed and ' the Year ' from as ten ' son from ' you name
' thousand ' from as three and ' the five ' Benjamim`s ' below`ed ' them as my appoint
' from you bore and you ' judge ' as son of ' 38 you and hundred ' four I and
' is number in ' from you and father ' you house of ' complete and at family of
39 ' mass ' out ' all ' above`ed and ' the Year ' from as ten ' son from ' you name
' thousand ' from as six and ' from two ' judge ' below`ed ' them as my appoint
' from you bore and you ' which ' as son of ' 40 you and hundred ' seven and
' is number in ' from you and father ' you house of ' complete and at family of
41 ' mass ' out ' all ' above`ed and ' the Year ' from as ten ' son from ' you name
' thousand ' from as four I and ' one ' which ' below`ed ' them as my appoint
' from you bore and you ' Naphtali ' as son ' 42 you and hundred ' five and
' is number in ' from you and father ' you house of ' complete and at family of
43 ' mass ' out ' all ' above`ed and ' the Year ' from as ten ' son from ' you name
' thousand ' from as five and ' three`ed ' Naphtali ' below`ed ' them as my appoint

' punish ' which ' from as my appoint the ' to`ed ' 44 you and hundred ' four I and

' man I ' man I ' ten ' from two ' Israel ' as help`s and ' Aaron and ' Moses

' from you him you father ' you house of ' below`ed ' one ' below`ed ' one

' Israel ' as son ' as punish`ing ' all ' and became as and ' 45 him the

the Year ' from as ten ' son from ' from you father ' you house of ' from you mass of

' all ' and became as and ' 46 Israel in ' mass ' out ' all ' above`ed and '

' you three and ' thousand ' you and hundred ' six ' from as my appoint the

from Levi the and ' 47 from as five and ' you and hundred ' five and ' from as thousand

from middle`ing in ' and my appoint you the ' not ' from you and father ' below`ed '

' down`ed ' ye ' sure ' 49 say of ' Moses ' to ' Jehovah ' word as and ' 48

middle`ing in ' lift you ' not ' from head ' ye and ' my appoint you ' not ' Levi the

' on ' from Levi the ' ye ' punish the ' ye`ed and ' 50 Israel ' as son '

which ' all ' on and ' and vessel are ' all ' on and ' testimony`ing the ' Tabernacle

and vessel are ' all ' ye and ' Tabernacle the ' ye ' and linger ' them`ed ' if '

' 51 and encamp ' Tabernacle of ' surround`s and ' and the minister as ' them and '

you and prove and ' from Levi the ' and ye ' and up`s him ' Tabernacle the ' go in and

' stranger the and ' from Levi the ' and ye ' and rise`s as ' Tabernacle the '

' on ' man I ' Israel ' as son ' and grace and ' 52 die him ' approach the

' 53 from you mass of ' and flag ' and hand ' on ' man I and ' and camp`ed

' testimony`ing the ' Tabernacle of ' surround`s ' and encamp ' from Levi the and

' and guard and ' Israel ' as son ' testimony ' on ' angry ' be`s as ' not and

' 54 testimony`ing the ' Tabernacle ' you guard from ' ye ' from Levi the

' ye ' Jehovah ' command`ed ' which ' accord ' Israel ' as son ' concoct as and

concoct ' so ' Moses

1 2 on ' man I ' say of ' Aaron ' to and ' Moses ' to ' Jehovah ' word as and '
' and encamp ' from you and father ' you house of ' evidence`ing in ' and as flag '
3 ' and encamp ' ing`congregate ' tent of ' surround`s ' over from ' Israel ' as son
' Judah ' the camp ' flag ' emerge`ed from ' east`ed ' from as bivouac and
' son ' pocket`ing has ' Judah ' as son of ' help`s and ' from you mass of
4 ' the four I ' them and as my appoint and ' and mass and ' freewill as people
5 ' from as bivouac and ' you and hundred ' six and ' thousand ' from as seven and
son ' to gave ' Issachar ' as son of ' help`s and ' Issachar ' down`ed ' and Mosthigh
6 from as five and ' the four I ' and as my appoint and ' and mass and ' is gain`ing '
7 ' help`s and ' Zebulun ' staff from and ' you and hundred ' four I and ' thousand '
8 ' and mass and ' s`window ' son ' father as to ' Zebulun ' as son of
' four I and ' thousand ' from as five and ' the seven ' and as my appoint and
9 ' each ' Judah ' camp`ed of ' from as my appoint the ' all ' you and hundred
four I and ' from as thousand ' you six and ' thousand ' from as eight and ' thousand
10 ' flag ' leave as ' the has and head`s ' from you mass of ' you and hundred '
' as son of ' help`s and ' from you mass of ' right`ed you ' Reuben ' the camp
11 ' and mass and ' light`ing almight ' son ' mould`ing of I ' Reuben
' five and ' thousand ' from as four I and ' six`ed ' and as my appoint and
12 ' Simeon ' down`ed ' and Mosthigh ' from as bivouac`ing and ' you and hundred
13 ' almight as boulder`ing ' ' son ' to as whole ' Simeon ' as son of ' help`s and
' thousand ' from as five and ' nine`ed ' them and as my appoint and ' and mass and '
14 ' as son of ' help`s and ' fortune ' staff from and ' you and hundred ' three and
15 ' them and as my appoint and ' and mass and ' Reuel ' son ' add of I ' fortune
' you and hundred ' six and ' thousand ' from as four I and ' the five
16 ' each ' Reuben ' camp`ed of ' from as my appoint the ' all ' from as five and

' you and hundred ' four I and ' thousand ' from as five and ' one and ' thousand
' onward has and ' 17 leave as ' from as Year and ' from you mass of ' from as five and
you and camp the ' middle`ing in ' from Levi the ' the camp ' ing`congregate ' tent
them as flag of ' and hand ' on ' man I ' leave as ' so ' and encamp ' which are '
as son of ' help`s and ' sea`ed ' from you mass of ' Ephraim ' the camp ' flag ' 18
' and mass and ' 19 gloref`ing as people ' son ' Elishama ' Ephraim '
20 you and hundred ' five and ' thousand ' from as four I ' them and as my appoint and
' Manasse`ed ' as son of ' help`s and ' Manasse`ed ' down`ed ' him on and '
' and mass and ' 21 boulder`ing release'ed ' son ' to as wean
' thousand ' from as three and ' from two ' them and as my appoint and
' as son of ' help`s and ' Benjamim`s ' staff from and ' 22 from as you hundred and
' and mass and ' 23 as Gideon`ing ' son ' judge as father ' Benjamim`s
' four I and ' thousand ' from as three and ' the five ' them and as my appoint and
' each ' Ephraim ' camp`ed of ' from as my appoint the ' all ' 24 you and hundred
' from you mass of ' the hundred and ' from as thousand ' you eight and ' thousand
' the north`ing ' judge ' the camp ' flag ' 25 leave as ' from as three and
' son ' aid as brother ' judge ' as son of ' help`s and ' from you mass of
' from two ' them and as my appoint and ' and mass and ' 26 almight as people
' from as bivouac and ' 27 you and hundred ' seven and ' thousand ' from as six and
' to as entreat ' which ' as son of ' help`s and ' which ' down`ed ' and Mosthigh
' one ' them and as my appoint and ' and mass and ' 28 has disturb ' son
' staff from and ' 29 you and hundred ' five and ' thousand ' from as four I and
30 ' has low`s ' son ' sore brother ' Naphtali ' as son of ' help`s and ' Naphtali
' thousand ' from as five and ' three`ed ' them and as my appoint and ' and mass and
' judge ' camp`ed of ' from as my appoint the ' all ' 31 you and hundred ' four I and

' six and ' thousand ' from as five and ' swear`ed too and ' thousand ' each

' to`ed ' (32 them as flag of ' leave as ' the has after of ' you and hundred

' all ' from you and father ' you house of ' Israel ' as son ' as punish`ing

' you and hundred ' six ' from you mass of ' you and camp the ' as punish`ing

' you and hundred ' five and ' from as thousand ' you three and ' thousand

middle`ing in ' and my appoint you the ' not ' from Levi the and ' (33 from as five and

' (34 Moses ' ye ' Jehovah ' command`ed ' which are ' Israel ' as son '

' ye ' Jehovah ' command`ed ' which ' accord ' Israel ' as son ' concoct as and

' man I ' and go ' so and ' them as flag of ' and grace ' so ' Moses

and as you father ' you house ' on ' him you at family of

' Jehovah ' word ' day as in ' Moses and ' Aaron ' you bore and you ' to`ed and ' (1
' Aaron ' as son ' you name ' to`ed and ' (2 as bush`s ' blemish ' Moses ' ye
you name ' to`ed ' (3 Ithamar and ' Eleazar ' Abihu and ' freewill ' first`ing the
energy ' fill ' which ' from as anoint the ' from as priest the ' Aaron ' as son '
' Jehovah ' as before ' Abihu and ' freewill ' die as and ' (4 priest of '
' word from in ' Jehovah ' as before ' stranger`ed ' fire ' from approach`s the in
' Eleazar ' priest as and ' them of ' him the ' not ' from as son and ' as bush`s
to ' Jehovah ' word as and ' (5 them as father ' Aaron ' around ' on ' Ithamar and
' you stand the and ' Levi ' down`ed ' ye ' approach the ' (6 say of ' Moses '
' (7 and ye ' and minister and ' priest the ' Aaron ' as before ' and ye
' all ' you guard from ' ye and ' and you guard from ' ye ' and guard and
' you serve ' ye ' serve of ' ing`congregate ' tent ' as before ' till`ed the
' ing`congregate ' tent ' weapon ' all ' ye ' and guard and ' (8 Tabernacle the
' you serve ' ye ' serve of ' Israel ' as son ' you guard from ' ye and
' him son of and ' Aaron of ' from Levi the ' ye ' set`ed has and ' (9 Tabernacle the
each ' middle`ing from ' and vessel ' them`ed ' from as gave`ing ' from as gave`ing
' my appoint you ' him son ' ye and ' Aaron ' ye and ' (10 Israel ' as son '
(11 die him ' approach the ' stranger the and ' from you priest ' ye ' and guard and
' be`th ' as whither and ' (12 say of ' Moses ' to ' Jehovah ' word as and '
all ' under ' Israel ' as son ' middle`ing from ' from Levi the ' ye ' as you take
' them ransom`ing ' Israel ' as son in from ' compassion ' emit ' first`ing '
' all ' vessel ' for ' (13 from Levi the ' vessel ' and became and ' and became as
' from as Mizra ' land in ' first`ing ' all ' as whom smitten ' day as in ' first`ing
cattle`ed ' till ' men from ' Israel in ' first`ing ' all ' vessel ' as you holy the
' to ' Jehovah ' word as and ' (14 Jehovah ' as whither ' and became as ' vessel '

’ Levi ’ as son ’ ye ’ punish ’ 15 say of ’ as bush`s ’ word from in ’ Moses
son from ’ male ’ all ’ complete and at family of ’ from you and father ’ you house of
’ Moses ’ from ye ’ punish as and ’ 16 from my appoint you ’ above`ed and ’ new ’
’ to`ed ’ and became as and ’ 17 and command`ed ’ which are ’ Jehovah ’ edge ’ on
’ 18 Merari and ’ Kohath and ’ Gershon`ing ’ complete there in ’ Levi ’ as son
’ as son of ’ complete and at family of ’ Gershon`ing ’ as son ’ you name ’ to`ed and
’ from sheaf ’ complete and at family of ’ Kohath ’ as son and ’ 19 as hear and
’ Merari ’ as son and ’ 20 Uzziel and ’ Hebron`ing ’ noon as and
’ them ’ to`ed ’ as feel`ing and ’ as dance ’ complete and at family of
Gershon`ing of ’ 21 from you and father ’ you house of ’ Levi the ’ you and at family
’ them ’ to`ed ’ as hear the ’ you at family and ’ as white the ’ you at family ’
’ is number in ’ them as my appoint and ’ 22 as Gershon`ing the ’ you and at family
’ you seven ’ them as my appoint ’ above`ed and ’ new ’ son from ’ male ’ all
’ as Gershon`ing the ’ you at family ’ 23 you and hundred ’ five and ’ from as thousand
’ father ’ you house ’ help`s and ’ 24 sea`ed ’ and encamp ’ Tabernacle the ’ as after
’ as son ’ and guard from and ’ 25 divinity ’ son ’ add of I ’ as Gershon`ing of
’ tent the and ’ Tabernacle the ’ ing`congregate ’ tent in ’ Gershon`ing
’ 26 ing`congregate ’ tent ’ open ’ castimage and ’ and conceal`ed from and
’ on ’ which ’ yard the ’ open ’ castimage ’ ye and ’ yard the ’ as sling and
’ him preserve from ’ ye and ’ surround`s ’ sacrifice them ’ on and ’ Tabernacle the
’ as Amram the ’ you at family ’ Kohath of and ’ 27 and you serve ’ all of
’ as Hebron`ing the ’ you at family and ’ as Izhar the ’ you at family and
as Kohath the ’ you and at family ’ them ’ to`ed ’ as Uzziel the ’ you at family and
’ you eight ’ above`ed and ’ new ’ son from ’ male ’ all ’ is number in ’ 28
holy the ’ you guard from ’ as guard ’ you and hundred ’ six and ’ from as thousand

' Tabernacle the ' soft ' on ' and encamp ' Kohath ' as son ' you at family ' 29
' you and at family of ' father ' you house ' help`s and ' 30 right`ed you
Ark`ing the ' from you guard from and ' 31 Uzziel ' son ' Elizaphan ' as Kohath the
' you and sacrifice from the and ' the taper`ing the and ' table too the and '
' castimage the and ' cattle ' and minister as ' which ' holy the ' as all and
' help`s and ' 32 and from you serve ' all and ' and so and ' Laver`ing the and
you my appoint ' priest the ' Aaron ' son ' Eleazar ' from Levi the ' as lift`s has
' Mahli the ' you at family ' Merari of ' 33 holy the ' you guard from ' as guard '
' 34 Merari ' you and at family ' them ' to`ed ' Mushi the ' you at family and
above`ed and ' new ' son from ' male ' all ' is number in ' them as my appoint and
' you house ' help`s and ' 35 from as you hundred and ' from as thousand ' you six '
' wait`s father ' son ' to as boulder'ing ' Merari ' you and at family of ' father
' you my appoint and ' 36 the north`ing ' and encamp ' Tabernacle the ' soft ' on
' and as smell`s in and ' Tabernacle the ' as board ' Merari ' as son ' you guard from
' all and ' and vessel are ' all and ' and base I and ' and as stand`ing and
' them as master and ' surround`s ' yard the ' as stand`ing and ' 37 and you serve
' ye ' from as bivouac and ' 38 them as preserve from and ' from stake as and
' ing`congregate ' tent ' as before ' east`ed ' Tabernacle the ' as before
' you guard from ' from as guard ' him son and ' Aaron and ' Moses ' emerge`ed from
' approach the ' stranger the and ' Israel ' as son ' you guard from of ' holy them
Aaron and ' Moses ' punish ' which ' from Levi the ' as punish`ing ' all ' 39 die him
' new ' son from ' male ' all ' complete and at family of ' Jehovah ' edge ' on '
to ' Jehovah ' say as and ' 40 thousand ' from as ten and ' from two ' above`ed and
new ' son from ' Israel ' as son of ' male ' first`ing ' all ' punish ' Moses '
' you take and ' 41 from you name ' report from ' ye ' lift and ' above`ed and '

' first`ing ' all ' under ' Jehovah ' as whither ' vessel ' from Levi the ' ye
first`ing ' all ' under ' from Levi the ' you cattle ' ye and ' Israel ' as son in
' which are ' Moses ' punish as and ' (42 Israel ' as son ' you cattle in '
' (43 Israel ' as son in ' first`ing ' all ' ye ' and ye ' Jehovah ' command`ed
' son from ' you name ' is number in ' male ' first`ing ' all ' and became as and
' thousand ' from as ten and ' from two ' them as my appoint of ' above`ed and ' new
' Jehovah ' word as and ' (44 from as you hundred and ' from as seven and ' three`ed
' first`ing ' all ' under ' from Levi the ' ye ' took ' (45 say of ' Moses ' to
' from you cattle ' under ' from Levi the ' you cattle ' ye and ' Israel ' as son in
' ye and ' (45 Jehovah ' as whither ' from Levi the ' vessel ' and became and
' from as you hundred the and ' from as seven the and ' three`ed the ' as ramson`ing
' (47 Israel ' as son ' as first`ing from ' from Levi the ' on ' from as surplus the
' weigh in ' you heap heap of ' from as weigh ' you five ' you five ' you take and
' set`ed has and ' (48 weigh the ' guest`ed ' from as ten ' implicate ' holy the
cattle ' from as surplus the ' as ramson`ing ' him son of and ' Aaron of ' silver the
' each ' from ransom`ing the ' silver ' ye ' Moses ' took as and ' (49
' as first`ing ' each ' (50 from Levi the ' as ramson`ing ' on ' from as surplus the
' from as six and ' the five ' silver the ' ye ' took of ' Israel ' as son
' give as and ' (51 holy the ' weigh in ' thousand and ' you and hundred ' three and
edge ' on ' him son of and ' Aaron of ' from ransom`ing the ' silver ' ye ' Moses
Moses ' ye ' Jehovah ' command`ed ' which are ' Jehovah '

' help ' 2 say of ' Aaron ' to and ' Moses ' to ' Jehovah ' word as and ' 1
' Levi ' as son ' middle`ing from ' Kohath ' as son ' head ' ye
' son from ' 3 from you and father ' you house of ' complete and at family of
' the Year ' from as five ' son ' till and ' above`ed and ' the Year ' from as three
4 ing`congregate ' tent in ' the are fill ' you concoct of ' mass of ' came the ' all
' holy ' ing`congregate ' tent in ' Kohath ' as son ' you serve ' such '
' camp`ed the ' go in ' him son and ' Aaron ' came and ' 5 from as holy the
' ye ' thus ' and conceal and ' castimage the ' veil put ' ye ' and up`s alas and
' as and conceal ' and Mosthigh ' and gave and ' 6 testimony`ing the ' Ark`ing
' of vessal are ' fabric ' and Mosthigh ' and excrement and ' badger ' town`ing
' has send ' on and ' 7 him alone ' name and ' the above of from ' you perfect
' and gave and ' you perfect ' fabric ' and excrement as ' from as turn the
' ye and ' you and palm the ' ye and ' you and dish the ' ye ' and Mosthigh
' from bread and ' libation the ' you and hard ' ye and ' whom`ing bowl the
' fabric ' them as on ' and excrement and ' 8 be`s as ' and Mosthigh ' continual`s the
' and ye ' and conceal and ' two ' you have hang`ing ' as and conceal
and take and ' 9 him alone ' ye ' name and ' badger ' town`ing ' conceal`ed from in
' light`ing them ' you taper`ing ' ye ' and conceal and ' you perfect ' fabric '
' ye and ' am dismay`s from ' ye and ' am take from ' ye and ' am you lamp ' ye and
and gave and ' 10 cattle ' nihil ' and minister as ' which ' eight`ed ' weapon ' all
' badger ' town`ing ' conceal`ed from ' to ' vessel`ed are ' all ' ye and ' ye`ed '
' gold the ' sacrifice from ' on and ' 11 down`ing the ' on ' and gave and
' and ye ' and conceal and ' you perfect ' fabric ' and excrement as
and take and ' 12 him alone ' ye ' name and ' badger ' town`ing ' conceal`ed from in
holy in ' cattle ' and minister as ' which ' you survivor the ' weapon ' all ' ye '

' from ye`ing ' and conceal and ' you perfect ' fabric ' to ' and gave and '

' 13 down`ing the ' on ' and gave and ' badger ' town`ing ' conceal`ed from in

fabric ' and Mosthigh ' and excrement and ' sacrifice them ' ye ' and has thresh and

' which ' and vessel are ' all ' ye ' and Mosthigh ' and gave and ' 14 blue light '

' ye and ' you and crush them ' ye ' cattle ' and Mosthigh ' and minister as

all ' you and sprinkle them ' ye and ' from as shovel the ' ye and ' you and fork them

' as and conceal ' and Mosthigh ' and excrement and ' sacrifice them ' weapon '

' blue light ' fabric ' and take and ' him alone ' name and ' badger ' town`ing

' from ye ' and gave and ' and so ' ye and ' Laver`ing the ' ye ' and conceal and

' 15 down`ing the ' on ' and gave and ' badger ' town`ing ' conceal`ed from ' to

' ye and ' holy the ' ye ' you and conceal of ' him son and ' Aaron ' the all and

' and came as ' so ' as after and ' camp`ed the ' go in ' holy the ' weapon ' all

' and die and ' holy the ' to ' and faint ' not and ' arise of ' Kohath ' as son

' 16 ing`congregate ' tent in ' Kohath ' as son ' and lift from ' to`ed

' light`ing them ' eight ' priest the ' Aaron ' son ' Eleazar ' you my appoint and

' eight and ' continual`s the ' Manahath and ' from as aroma the ' you perfume and

' and in ' which ' all and ' Tabernacle the ' all ' you my appoint ' anoint`ed the

Aaron ' to and ' Moses ' to ' Jehovah ' word as and ' 17 him all in and ' holy in

' as Kohath the ' you at family ' tribe ' ye ' and hew`s you ' to ' 18 say of '

' him spirit ' them of ' concoct ' such and ' 19 from Levi the ' middle`ing from

' from as holy the ' holy ' to ' ye ' from accost in ' and die`ing as ' not and

' on ' man I ' man I ' from ye`ing ' name and ' and came as ' him son and ' Aaron

' you see of ' and came as ' not and ' 20 and lift from ' to and ' and you serve

' to ' Jehovah ' word as and ' 21 and die and ' holy the ' ye ' worthless are

' them ' also ' Gershon`ing ' as son ' head ' ye ' help ' 22 say of ' Moses

' son from ' (23 complete and at family of ' from you and father ' you house of
' the Year ' from as five ' son ' till and ' above`ed and ' the Year ' from as three
serve`ed ' serve of ' mass ' mass of ' came the ' all ' from ye`ing ' my appoint you
as Gershon`ing the ' you at family ' you serve ' such ' (24 ing`congregate ' tent in '
' you and have curtain ' ye ' and lift shall ' (25 lift from of and ' serve of '
' and conceal`ed from ' ing`congregate ' tent ' ye and ' Tabernacle the
ye and ' the above of from ' and Mosthigh ' which ' badger the ' conceal`ed from and
' yard the ' as sling ' ye and ' (26 ing`congregate ' tent ' open ' castimage '
on and ' Tabernacle the ' on ' which ' yard the ' gate ' open ' castimage ' ye and
' all ' ye and ' them as preserve from ' ye and ' surround`s ' sacrifice them '
and serve and ' them of ' success`ed ' which ' all ' ye and ' from you serve ' weapon
' as son ' you serve ' all ' be`s you ' him son and ' Aaron ' edge ' on ' (27
' from you serve ' all of and ' from lift from ' all of ' as Gershon`ing the
from lift from ' all ' ye ' you guard from in ' them as on ' from you my appoint and
' tent in ' as Gershon`ing the ' as son ' you at family ' you serve ' such ' (28
' Aaron ' son ' Ithamar ' hand in ' from you guard from and ' ing`congregate
' you house of ' complete and at family of ' Merari ' as son ' (29 priest the
' from as three ' son from ' (30 from ye ' my appoint you ' from you and father
' the Year ' from as five ' son ' till and ' above`ed and ' the Year
tent ' you serve ' ye ' serve of ' mass of ' came the ' all ' from my appoint you
' all of ' from lift from ' you guard from ' such and ' (31 ing`congregate '
' Tabernacle the ' as board ' ing`congregate ' tent in ' from you serve
' as stand`ing and ' (32 and base I and ' and as stand`ing and ' and as smell`s in and
' from stake as and ' them as master and ' surround`s ' yard the
' from you serve ' all of and ' them as all ' all of ' them as preserve from and

' you guard from ' weapon ' all ' ye ' and my appoint you ' you name in and
' all of ' Merari ' as son ' you at family ' you serve ' such ' 33 from lift from
' Aaron ' son ' Ithamar ' hand in ' ing`congregate ' tent in ' from you serve
' till`ed the ' as help`s and ' Aaron and ' Moses ' punish as and ' 34 priest the
' you house of and ' complete and at family of ' as Kohath the ' as son ' ye
till and ' above`ed and ' the Year ' from as three ' son from ' 35 from you and father
' tent in ' the serve of ' mass of ' came the ' all ' the Year ' from as five ' son '
complete and at family of ' them as my appoint ' and became as and ' 36 ing`congregate
' to`ed ' 37 from as five and ' you and hundred ' seven and ' from as thousand '
' tent in ' serve the ' all ' as Kohath the ' you at family ' as punish`ing
hand in ' Jehovah ' edge ' on ' Aaron and ' Moses ' punish ' which ' ing`congregate
complete and at family of ' Gershon`ing ' as son ' enough and appoint and ' 38 Moses '
' the Year ' from as three ' son from ' 39 from you and father ' you house of and '
' mass of ' came the ' all ' the Year ' from as five ' son ' till and ' above`ed and
' them as my appoint ' and became as and ' 40 ing`congregate ' tent in ' the serve of
' from as thousand ' from you and father ' you house of ' complete and at family of
' as punish`ing ' to`ed ' 41 from as three and ' you and hundred ' six and
' ing`congregate ' tent in ' serve the ' all ' Gershon`ing ' as son ' you at family
enough and appoint and ' 42 Jehovah ' edge ' on ' Aaron and ' Moses ' punish ' which
' you house of ' complete and at family of ' Merari ' as son ' you at family '
till and ' above`ed and ' the Year ' from as three ' son from ' 43 from you and father
' tent in ' the serve of ' mass of ' came the ' all ' the Year ' from as five ' son '
complete and at family of ' them as my appoint ' and became as and ' 44 ing`congregate
' as punish`ing ' to`ed ' 45 from as you hundred and ' from as thousand ' you three '
' edge ' on ' Aaron and ' Moses ' punish ' which ' Merari ' as son ' you at family

Moses ’ punish ’ which ’ from as my appoint the ’ all ’ 46 Moses ’ hand in ’ Jehovah
’ from Levi the ’ ye ’ Israel ’ as help`s and ’ Aaron and ’
’ son from ’ 47 from you and father ’ you house of and ’ complete and at family of
’ the Year ’ from as five ’ son ’ till and ’ above`ed and ’ the Year ’ from as three
’ tent in ’ swell ’ you serve and ’ serve`ed ’ you serve ’ serve of ’ came the ’ all
’ you eight ’ them as my appoint ’ and became as and ’ 48 ing`congregate
’ edge ’ on ’ 49 from as eight and ’ you and hundred ’ five and ’ from as thousand
’ on ’ man I ’ man I ’ Moses ’ hand in ’ from ye`ing ’ punish ’ Jehovah
’ which are ’ and as my appoint and ’ and lift from ’ on and ’ and you serve
Moses ’ ye ’ Jehovah ’ command`ed

' as son ' ye ' command`ed ' say of ' Moses ' to ' Jehovah ' word as and '

' all and ' leper`ing ' all ' camp`ed the ' has from ' and send as and ' Israel

' the female ' till and ' male from ' soul of ' unclean ' all and ' secrete

' not and ' from and send you ' camp`ed of ' outside`ing from ' to ' and send you

from middle`ing in ' nigh ' as whither ' which ' them as camp ' ye ' and unclean as

' to ' from ye`ing ' and send as and ' Israel ' as son ' so ' concoct as and '

' so ' Moses ' to ' Jehovah ' word ' which are ' camp`ed of ' outside`ing from

' say of ' Moses ' to ' Jehovah ' word as and ' Israel ' as son ' concoct

' and do as ' for ' Woman ' or ' man I ' say of ' Israel ' as son ' to ' word

' guilty`ed and ' Jehovah in ' above ' above of ' ground the ' you sin ' all from

' which ' from you sin ' ye ' and endure`ing the and ' that`s the ' soul the

' and you five`s and ' and head in ' and guilty ' ye ' carry`s the and ' concoct

' whither`s ' mother and ' if ' guilty ' which of ' gave and ' and Mosthigh ' add

carry and them ' guilty the ' him to ' guilty the ' carry`s the of ' redeem ' man I of

' which ' from as atone`ing the ' Ram`s ' alone of from ' priest of ' Jehovah of '

' as holy ' all of ' the oblation`ing ' all and ' and Mosthigh ' and in ' atone as

' be`s as ' if ' priest of ' and approach`s as ' which ' Israel ' as son

' permanent ' which ' man I and ' be`s as ' if ' and as holy ' ye ' man I and

' say of ' Moses ' to ' Jehovah ' word as and ' be`s as ' if ' priest of

' for ' man I ' man I ' them as to ' you say and ' Israel ' as son ' to ' word

' ye`ed ' man I ' lay and ' above ' and in ' above`ed and ' and wife ' revolt`ed

' the man I ' as purpose`s ' eternal`ed has and ' seed ' you lay

' thus ' whither`s ' till and ' unclean`ed has ' that`s and ' the is camouflage and

' spirit is ' and Mosthigh ' cross and ' handle`ed has ' not ' that`s and

' or ' unclean`ed has ' that`s and ' and wife ' ye ' jealous and ' jealous`ed

' and wife ' ye ' jealous and ' jealous`ed ' spirit is ' and Mosthigh ' Obara
' and wife ' ye ' man that ' came`s the and ' 15 unclean`ed has ' not ' that`s and
' urn do ' am on ' the has approach ' ye ' came`s the and ' priest the ' to
' not and ' eight ' and am on ' cast ' not ' from as Barley ' mill ' the cook`s
' that`s ' you jealous ' you bestow ' for ' the son`ing of ' and am on ' permanent
' approach`s the and ' 16 low`ing ' you male from ' shall is remember ' you bestow
' take and ' 17 Jehovah ' as before ' the stand`s the and ' priest the ' ye`ed
dust the ' has from and ' devise ' vessal are in ' from as holy ' Water ' priest the
gave and ' priest the ' took as ' Tabernacle the ' have floor in ' be`s as ' which '
' as before ' Woman the ' ye ' priest the ' stand`s the and ' 18 Water the ' to '
' ye ' am palm ' on ' gave and ' Woman the ' head ' ye ' hair and ' Jehovah
' hand in and ' that`s ' you jealous ' you bestow ' has and male the ' you bestow
' 19 from as execrate them ' from as bitter the ' who ' and became as ' priest the
' not ' mother ' Woman the ' to ' say and ' priest the ' ye`ed ' seven`s the and
' under ' unclean`ed ' whom betray ' not ' mother and ' are ye ' man I ' lay
' from as execrate them ' from as bitter the ' as they ' innocent the ' are man I
' for and ' are man I ' under ' whom betray ' for ' ye and ' 20 these`ed
' and you lay ' ye ' against ' man I ' give as and ' you unclean has
' Woman the ' ye ' priest the ' seven`s the and ' 21 are man I ' as beyond in from
' permanent ' resemble I of ' priest the ' say and ' these`ed ' you seven`ing in
' are people ' middle`ing in ' the seven`ing of and ' to`ed of ' are ye`ing ' Jehovah
' 22 mass'ed ' are womb ' ye and ' you fall ' are soft ' ye ' Jehovah ' set in
' brusie`s in ' these`ed ' from as execrate them ' Water the ' and came and
believe ' Woman the ' say`ed and ' soft ' fall of and ' womb ' you and establish of
' report in ' priest the ' these`ed ' oath`ing the ' ye ' write and ' 23 believe '

’ ye ’ moisten`ed the and ’ 24 from as bitter the ’ who ’ to ’ wipe`ed and
’ and came and ’ from as execrate them ’ from as bitter the ’ who ’ ye ’ Woman the
’ take and ’ 25 from as bitter of ’ from as execrate them ’ Water the ’ thus
’ you jealous the ’ you bestow ’ ye ’ Woman the ’ hand from ’ priest the
’ approach`s the and ’ Jehovah ’ as before ’ bestow`ed the ’ ye ’ wave`s the and
’ has from ’ priest the ’ grasp and ’ palace`s and ’ 26 sacrifice them ’ to ’ ye`ed
after and ’ the sacrifice them ’ perfume`s the and ’ he male I ’ ye ’ bestow`ed the
ye ’ moisten`ed the and ’ 27 Water the ’ ye ’ Woman the ’ ye ’ moisten`ed as ’
’ above ’ above you and ’ unclean`ed has ’ mother ’ whom`ed the and ’ Water the ’
’ from as execrate them ’ Water the ’ thus ’ and came and ’ the man came
’ soft`ed ’ fall`ed and ’ the womb ’ he establish and ’ from as bitter of
not ’ mother and ’ 28 people`ed ’ approach in ’ to`ed of ’ Woman the ’ whom`ed the and
’ sprout`ed and ’ that`s ’ clean`ed and ’ Woman the ’ unclean`ed has ’
’ which ’ you jealous the ’ you protect`ing ’ such ’ 29 seed ’ the seed has and
which ’ man I ’ or ’ 30 unclean`ed has and ’ the man I ’ under ’ Woman ’ revolt`ed
’ and wife ’ ye ’ jealous and ’ jealous`ed ’ spirit is ’ and Mosthigh ’ cross you ’
’ nihil ’ do`ed and ’ Jehovah ’ as before ’ Woman the ’ ye ’ stand`s the and
man that ’ blame`ed and ’ 31 such the ’ the protect`ing the ’ all ’ ye ’ priest the
the low`ing ’ ye ’ lift you ’ that`s the ’ Woman the and ’ low`ing from ’

' as son ' to ' word ' 2 say of ' Moses ' to ' Jehovah ' word as and ' 1
' I made as ' for ' Woman ' or ' man I ' them as to ' you say and ' Israel
' has who`s ' 3 Jehovah of ' is contemn the of ' consecrate`s ' vow ' vow of
belong`ed ' not ' merry ' leaven and ' between`s ' leaven ' is contemn as ' merry and
' from as grape and ' belong`ed ' not ' from as grape ' you remain from ' all and '
' and consecrate ' week ' all ' 4 eat as ' not ' from as wither and ' hot`s of
from as has maim from ' has intoxicate the ' vine from ' success`ed ' which ' all from
razor ' and consecrate ' vow ' week ' all ' 5 eat as ' not ' inclose ' till and '
' which ' from week the ' you fill ' till ' and head ' on ' cross as ' not '
6 and head ' gate ' hair ' great ' be`s as ' holy`ing ' Jehovah of ' is contemn as
' not ' die ' soul ' on ' Jehovah of ' and is contemn the ' week ' all '
and sister of and ' him brother of ' and mother of and ' him father of ' 7 came`ing as
on ' him Allah ' consecrate ' for ' from die`ing in ' them of ' unclean as ' not '
' 9 Jehovah of ' that`ing ' holy`ing ' and consecrate ' week ' all ' 8 and head '
' unclean and ' from instant ' moment in ' and Mosthigh ' die ' die`ing as ' for and
day as in ' and you clean ' day as in ' and head ' shave and ' and consecrate ' head
' came`s as ' as eight`s the ' day as in and ' 10 and has shave as ' as seven`s the '
' priest the ' to ' the Dove`ing ' as son ' two ' or ' from as protect ' twosome
you sin of ' one ' priest the ' do`ed and ' 11 ing congregate ' tent ' open ' to
soul the ' on ' sin ' which from ' and Mosthigh ' atone and ' on`ed of ' one and '
' is contemn the and ' 12 that`ing the ' day as in ' and head ' ye ' holy and '
' son ' mutton ' came`s the and ' and consecrate ' week ' ye ' Jehovah of
' and fell ' from as has and head`s the ' from week the and ' guilty of ' and you year
' consecrate`s the ' you protect`ing ' such and ' 13 and consecrate ' unclean ' for
' open ' to ' and ye ' came`s as ' and consecrate ' week ' you fill ' day as in

Jehovah of ' and has approach ' ye ' approach`s the and ' 14 ing`congregate ' tent
' on`ed of ' one ' from as complete ' and you year ' son ' mutton '
' the from as complete ' the you year ' daughter ' sister ' the footstool and
' exult and ' 15 from as whole of ' from as complete ' one ' Ram`s and ' you sin of
' as slim`s and ' eight in ' you mingle`ing ' cake`ing ' flour ' unleaven`ing
them as libation and ' from you bestow and ' eight in ' from as anoint ' unleaven`ing
' ye ' do`ed and ' Jehovah ' as before ' priest the ' approach`s the and ' 16
' sacrifice ' success`ed ' Ram`s the ' ye and ' 17 and offer ' ye and ' and you sin
' priest the ' do`ed and ' unleaven`ing the ' exalt ' on ' Jehovah of ' from as whole
' consecrate`s the ' shave and ' 18 and as libation ' ye and ' and you bestow ' ye
' ye ' take and ' and consecrate ' head ' ye ' ing`congregate ' tent ' open
' under ' which ' fire the ' on ' gave and ' and consecrate ' head ' gate
' seed`ing the ' ye ' priest the ' take and ' 19 from as whole the ' sacrifice
Osier the ' has from ' sister ' find`ed ' cake and ' Ram`s the ' has from ' sodden`ed
' consecrate`s the ' as palm ' on ' gave and ' one ' find`ed ' slim`s and '
from ye`ing ' wave`s the and ' 20 and consecrate ' ye ' and shave you the ' as after
priest of ' that`ing ' holy ' Jehovah ' as before ' the wave`ing you ' priest the '
' moisten`ing ' on and ' the wave`ing scared ' vision`ed ' on ' be`s as '
such ' 21 between`s ' consecrate`s the ' belong`ed ' after and ' the oblation`ing the
' and has approach ' evermore as ' which ' consecrate`s the ' you protect`ing '
' and hand ' drawal`s you ' which ' alone of from ' and consecrate ' on ' Jehovah of
' you protect`ing ' on ' success`ed ' so ' evermore as ' which ' and vow ' as palm
' to ' word ' 23 say of ' Moses ' to ' Jehovah ' word as and ' 22 and consecrate
Israel ' as son ' ye ' and bless you ' here ' say of ' him son ' to and ' Aaron
' channel`s ' 25 are guard as and ' Jehovah ' are bless as ' 24 them of ' say`ing '

' him turn ' Jehovah ' linger ' 25 are grace as and ' are as to ' him turn ' Jehovah

' as there ' ye ' and there`s and ' 27 from and peace ' walk ' site and ' are as to

from bless I ' as whither and ' Israel ' as son ' on

' ye ' rise`s the of ' Moses ' you and all ' day as in ' became as and ' 1

' all ' ye and ' and ye ' holy as and ' and ye ' anoint as and ' Tabernacle the

' and vessel are ' all ' ye and ' sacrifice them ' ye and ' and vessel are

' as lift`s has ' and approach`s as and ' 2 from ye ' holy as and ' from anoint as and

' as lift`s has ' them ' from you as father ' you house ' as head ' Israel

' 3 from as my appoint the ' on ' from as stand the ' them ' you and down the

' six ' Jehovah ' as before ' from has approach ' ye ' and came`s as and

' two ' on ' the calf ' herd ' ten ' from as Year and ' establish ' you and calf

' from ye`ing ' and approach`s as and ' one of ' Ox`ing and ' from as help`s the

took ' 5 say of ' Moses ' to ' Jehovah ' say as and ' 4 Tabernacle the ' as before

' ing`congregate ' tent ' you serve ' ye ' serve of ' and became and ' spy from '

and you serve ' as palm ' man I ' from Levi the ' to ' from ye`ing ' set`ed has and

' give as and ' herd the ' ye and ' you and calf the ' ye ' Moses ' took as and ' 6

' ye and ' you and calf the ' twosome ' ye ' 7 from Levi the ' to ' from ye`ing

' 8 from you serve ' as palm ' Gershon`ing ' as son of ' gave ' herd the ' you four I

' gave ' herd the ' you eight ' ye and ' you and calf the ' you four I ' ye and

' Aaron ' son ' Ithamar ' hand in ' from you serve ' as palm ' Merari ' as son of

' holy the ' you serve ' for ' gave ' not ' Kohath ' as son of and ' 9 priest the

' from as help`s the ' and approach`s as and ' 10 and linger ' shoulder in ' them as on

' and ye ' anoint the ' day as in ' sacrifice them ' you dedicate ' ye

' as before ' from has approach ' ye ' from as help`s the ' and approach`s as and

' one ' lift`s has ' Moses ' to ' Jehovah ' say as and ' 11 sacrifice them

' ye ' and approach`s as ' day as of ' one ' lift`s has ' day as of

' became as and ' 12 sacrifice them ' you dedicate of ' from has approach

' and has approach ' ye ' has and head`s the ' day as in ' approach`s them

' 13 Judah ' below`ed ' freewill as people ' son ' pocket`ing has
' the hundred and ' from as three ' sister ' silver ' you dish ' and has approach and
' weigh in ' weigh ' from as seven ' silver ' one ' sprinkle from ' the weigh from
' eight in ' the mingle`ing ' flour ' from as fill ' them two ' holy the
apart ' 15 you perfume ' fill`ed ' gold ' ten`ed ' sister ' palm ' 14 the bestow of
' and you year ' son ' one ' mutton ' one ' Ram`s ' herd ' son ' one '
' sacrifice of and ' 17 you sin of ' one ' from as Goat ' gate`s and ' 16 on`ed of
' from as hegoat`ing ' the five ' from as Ram`s ' from two ' herd ' from as whole the
' has approach ' this ' the five ' the Year ' as son ' from as mutton ' the five
' approach`s the ' two the ' day as in ' 18 freewill as people ' son ' pocket`ing has
' ye ' approach`s the ' 19 Issachar ' lift`s has ' is gain`ing ' son ' to gave
' the hundred and ' from as three ' sister ' silver ' you dish ' and has approach
' weigh in ' weigh ' from as seven ' silver ' one ' sprinkle from ' the weigh from
' eight in ' the mingle`ing ' flour ' from as fill ' them two ' holy the
apart ' 21 you perfume ' fill`ed ' gold ' ten`ed ' sister ' palm ' 20 the bestow of
' and you year ' son ' one ' mutton ' one ' Ram`s ' herd ' son ' one '
' sacrifice of and ' 23 you sin of ' one ' from as Goat ' gate`s and ' 22 on`ed of
' from as hegoat`ing ' the five ' from as Ram`s ' from two ' herd ' from as whole the
' has approach ' this ' the five ' the Year ' as son ' from as mutton ' the five
as son of ' lift`s has ' as three`s the ' day as in ' 24 is gain`ing ' son ' to gave
' you dish ' and has approach and ' 25 s`window ' son ' father as to ' Zebulun '
' sprinkle from ' the weigh from ' the hundred and ' from as three ' sister ' silver
' them two ' holy the ' weigh in ' weigh ' from as seven ' silver ' one
' sister ' palm ' 26 the bestow of ' eight in ' the mingle`ing ' flour ' from as fill
' Ram`s ' herd ' son ' one ' apart ' 27 you perfume ' fill`ed ' gold ' ten`ed

from as Goat ' gate`s and ' 28 on`ed of ' and you year ' son ' one ' mutton ' one
' from two ' herd ' from as whole the ' sacrifice of and ' 29 you sin of ' one '
' as son ' from as mutton ' the five ' from as hegoat`ing ' the five ' from as Ram`s
' 30 s`window ' son ' father as to ' has approach ' this ' the five ' the Year
son ' mould`ing of I ' Reuben ' as son of ' lift`s has ' as four`s the ' day as in
' sister ' silver ' you dish ' and has approach and ' 31 light`ing almight '
' silver ' one ' sprinkle from ' the weigh from ' the hundred and ' from as three
' flour ' from as fill ' them two ' holy the ' weigh in ' weigh ' from as seven
' gold ' ten`ed ' sister ' palm ' 32 the bestow of ' eight in ' the mingle`ing
' mutton ' one ' Ram`s ' herd ' son ' one ' apart ' 33 you perfume ' fill`ed
' one ' from as Goat ' gate`s and ' 34 on`ed of ' and you year ' son ' one
from as Ram`s ' from two ' herd ' from as whole the ' sacrifice of and ' 35 you sin of
' the Year ' as son ' from as mutton ' the five ' from as hegoat`ing ' the five '
' 36 light`ing almight ' son ' mould`ing of I ' has approach ' this ' the five
' son ' to as whole ' Simeon ' as son of ' lift`s has ' as five`s the ' day as in
' sister ' silver ' you dish ' and has approach and ' 37 almight as boulder`ing
' silver ' one ' sprinkle from ' the weigh from ' the hundred and ' from as three
' flour ' from as fill ' them two ' holy the ' weigh in ' weigh ' from as seven
' gold ' ten`ed ' sister ' palm ' 38 the bestow of ' eight in ' the mingle`ing
' mutton ' one ' Ram`s ' herd ' son ' one ' apart ' 39 you perfume ' fill`ed
' one ' from as Goat ' gate`s and ' 40 on`ed of ' and you year ' son ' one
from as Ram`s ' from two ' herd ' from as whole the ' sacrifice of and ' 41 you sin of
' the Year ' as son ' from as mutton ' the five ' from as hegoat`ing ' the five '
' 42 almight as boulder`ing ' son ' to as whole ' has approach ' this ' the five
' son ' add of I ' fortune ' as son of ' lift`s has ' as six the ' day as in

' sister ' silver ' you dish ' and has approach and ' 43 to and menstruate
' silver ' one ' sprinkle from ' the weigh from ' the hundred and ' from as three
' flour ' from as fill ' them two ' holy the ' weigh in ' weigh ' from as seven
' gold ' ten`ed ' sister ' palm ' 44 the bestow of ' eight in ' the mingle`ing
' mutton ' one ' Ram`s ' herd ' son ' one ' apart ' 45 you perfume ' fill`ed
' one ' from as Goat ' gate`s and ' 46 on`ed of ' and you year ' son ' one
from as Ram`s ' from two ' herd ' from as whole the ' sacrifice of and ' 47 you sin of
' the Year ' as son ' from as mutton ' the five ' from as hegoat`ing ' the five '
' day as in ' 48 to and menstruate ' son ' add of I ' has approach ' this ' the five
' son ' Elishama ' Ephraim ' as son of ' lift`s has ' as seven`s the
' sister ' silver ' you dish ' and has approach and ' 49 gloref`ing as people
' silver ' one ' sprinkle from ' the weigh from ' the hundred and ' from as three
' flour ' from as fill ' them two ' holy the ' weigh in ' weigh ' from as seven
' gold ' ten`ed ' sister ' palm ' 50 the bestow of ' eight in ' the mingle`ing
' mutton ' one ' Ram`s ' herd ' son ' one ' apart ' 51 you perfume ' fill`ed
' one ' from as Goat ' gate`s and ' 52 on`ed of ' and you year ' son ' one
from as Ram`s ' from two ' herd ' from as whole the ' sacrifice of and ' 53 you sin of
' the Year ' as son ' from as mutton ' the five ' from as hegoat`ing ' the five '
' 54 gloref`ing as people ' son ' Elishama ' has approach ' this ' the five
' son ' to as wean ' Manasse`ed ' as son of ' lift`s has ' as eight`s the ' day as in
' sister ' silver ' you dish ' and has approach and ' 55 ' boulder`ing release'ed '
' silver ' one ' sprinkle from ' the weigh from ' the hundred and ' from as three
' flour ' from as fill ' them two ' holy the ' weigh in ' weigh ' from as seven
' gold ' ten`ed ' sister ' palm ' 56 the bestow of ' eight in ' the mingle`ing
' mutton ' one ' Ram`s ' herd ' son ' one ' apart ' 57 you perfume ' fill`ed

' one ' from as Goat ' gate`s and ' 58 on`ed of ' and you year ' son ' one

from as Ram`s ' from two ' herd ' from as whole the ' sacrifice of and ' 59 you sin of

' the Year ' as son ' from as mutton ' the five ' from as hegoat`ing ' the five '

' 60 ' boulder`ing release`ed ' ' son ' to as wean ' has approach ' this ' the five

' judge as father ' Benjamim`s ' as son of ' lift`s has ' as nine`s the ' day as in

' sister ' silver ' you dish ' and has approach and ' 61 as Gideon`ing ' son

' silver ' one ' sprinkle from ' the weigh from ' the hundred and ' from as three

' flour ' from as fill ' them two ' holy the ' weigh in ' weigh ' from as seven

' gold ' ten`ed ' sister ' palm ' 62 the bestow of ' eight in ' the mingle`ing

' mutton ' one ' Ram`s ' herd ' son ' one ' apart ' 63 you perfume ' fill`ed

' one ' from as Goat ' gate`s and ' 64 on`ed of ' and you year ' son ' one

from as Ram`s ' from two ' herd ' from as whole the ' sacrifice of and ' 65 you sin of

' the Year ' as son ' from as mutton ' the five ' from as hegoat`ing ' the five '

day as in ' 66 as Gideon`ing ' son ' judge as father ' has approach ' this ' the five

' son ' aid as brother ' judge ' as son of ' lift`s has ' as ten`s the '

' sister ' silver ' you dish ' and has approach and ' 67 almight as people

' silver ' one ' sprinkle from ' the weigh from ' the hundred and ' from as three

' flour ' from as fill ' them two ' holy the ' weigh in ' weigh ' from as seven

' gold ' ten`ed ' sister ' palm ' 68 the bestow of ' eight in ' the mingle`ing

' mutton ' one ' Ram`s ' herd ' son ' one ' apart ' 69 you perfume ' fill`ed

' one ' from as Goat ' gate`s and ' 70 on`ed of ' and you year ' son ' one

from as Ram`s ' from two ' herd ' from as whole the ' sacrifice of and ' 71 you sin of

' the Year ' as son ' from as mutton ' the five ' from as hegoat`ing ' the five '

' 72 almight as people ' son ' aid as brother ' has approach ' this ' the five

' which ' as son of ' lift`s has ' day as ' ten ' as you do ' day as in

' silver ' you dish ' and has approach and ' 73 has disturb ' son ' to as entreat
' one ' sprinkle from ' the weigh from ' the hundred and ' from as three ' sister
' from as fill ' them two ' holy the ' weigh in ' weigh ' from as seven ' silver
gold ' ten`ed ' sister ' palm ' 74 the bestow of ' eight in ' the mingle`ing ' flour
' mutton ' one ' Ram`s ' herd ' son ' one ' apart ' 75 you perfume ' fill`ed '
' one ' from as Goat ' gate`s and ' 76 on`ed of ' and you year ' son ' one
from as Ram`s ' from two ' herd ' from as whole the ' sacrifice of and ' 77 you sin of
' the Year ' as son ' from as mutton ' the five ' from as hegoat`ing ' the five '
' day as in ' 78 has disturb ' son ' to as entreat ' has approach ' this ' the five
' son ' sore brother ' Naphtali ' as son of ' lift`s has ' day as ' ten ' from two
' from as three ' sister ' silver ' you dish ' and has approach and ' 79 has low`s
' from as seven ' silver ' one ' sprinkle from ' the weigh from ' the hundred and
' the mingle`ing ' flour ' from as fill ' them two ' holy the ' weigh in ' weigh
you perfume ' fill`ed ' gold ' ten`ed ' sister ' palm ' 80 the bestow of ' eight in
' son ' one ' mutton ' one ' Ram`s ' herd ' son ' one ' apart ' 81
' 83 you sin of ' one ' from as Goat ' gate`s and ' 82 on`ed of ' and you year
' the five ' from as Ram`s ' from two ' herd ' from as whole the ' sacrifice of and
this ' the five ' the Year ' as son ' from as mutton ' the five ' from as hegoat`ing
' you dedicate ' such ' 84 has low`s ' son ' sore brother ' has approach '
' Israel ' as lift`s has ' each ' and ye ' anoint the ' day as in ' sacrifice them
from two ' silver ' as sprinkle from ' ten`ed ' from twosome ' silver ' you and dish
' from as three ' 85 ten`ed ' from twosome ' gold ' you and palm ' ten '
' from as seven and ' silver the ' sister the ' dish`ed the ' the hundred and
' from as thousand ' from vessal are the ' silver ' all ' one the ' sprinkle them
' gold ' you and palm ' 86 holy the ' weigh in ' you and hundred ' four I and

’ palm the ’ ten`ed ’ ten`ed ’ you perfume ’ you and fill ’ ten`ed ’ from twosome
the hundred and ’ from as ten ’ you and palm the ’ gold ’ all ’ holy the ’ weigh in
’ from as Ram`s ’ from as Bullock ’ ten ’ from two ’ on`ed of ’ herd the ’ all ’ 87
’ ten ’ from two ’ the Year ’ as son ’ from as mutton ’ ten ’ from two
88 you sin of ’ ten ’ from two ’ from as Goat ’ as gate`s and ’ from you bestow and
’ the four I and ’ from as ten ’ from as whole the ’ sacrifice ’ herd ’ all and ’
’ from as six ’ from as hegoat`ing ’ from as six ’ from as Ram`s ’ from as Bullock
’ you dedicate ’ such ’ from as six ’ the Year ’ as son ’ from as mutton
’ to ’ Moses ’ came in and ’ 89 and ye ’ anoint the ’ as after ’ sacrifice them
’ voice`ing the ’ ye ’ hear as and ’ and ye ’ word of ’ ing`congregate ’ tent
’ Ark`ing ’ on ’ which ’ you atone the ’ above ’ him to ’ word from
him to ’ word as and ’ from as Cherub`ing the ’ two ’ son`s from ’ testimony`ing the

' Aaron ' to ' word ' 2 say of ' Moses ' to ' Jehovah ' word as and ' 1
split`ing ' to ' you and lamp the ' ye ' are offer`ing thus ' him to ' you say and
' 3 you and lamp the ' you seven ' and light`s as ' the taper`ing the ' around '
on`ed the ' the taper`ing the ' around ' split`ing ' to ' Aaron ' so ' do as and
' this and ' 4 Moses ' ye ' Jehovah ' command`ed ' which are ' am you lamp '
' till ' am soft ' till ' gold ' fashion`ed ' the taper`ing the ' do`ed from
ye ' Jehovah ' look`ed the ' which ' appear`ed are ' that`s ' fashion`ed ' am bud
' to ' Jehovah ' word as and ' 5 the taper`ing the ' ye ' do`ed ' so ' Moses '
Israel ' as son ' middle`ing from ' from Levi the ' ye ' took ' 6 say of ' Moses
' from clean of ' them of ' do`ed you ' here and ' 7 from ye ' you clean and '
' all ' on ' razor ' and cross`s the and ' you sin ' who ' them as on ' this the
' and take and ' 8 and clean the and ' them as fabric ' and immersion and ' from flesh
' eight in ' the mingle`ing ' flour ' and you bestow and ' herd ' son ' apart
' you approach the and ' 9 you sin of ' implicate ' herd ' son ' two ' Bullock and
' you assemble the and ' ing`congregate ' tent ' as before ' from Levi the ' ye
' ye ' you approach the and ' 10 Israel ' as son ' testimony ' all ' ye
' ye ' Israel ' as son ' and laid and ' Jehovah ' as before ' from Levi the
' ye ' Aaron ' wave`s the and ' 11 from Levi the ' on ' them as hand
' Israel ' as son ' each ' Jehovah ' as before ' the wave`ing you ' from Levi the
' from Levi the and ' 12 Jehovah ' you serve ' ye ' serve of ' and became and
' do`ed and ' from as Bullock the ' head ' on ' them as hand ' ye ' and laid as
' on ' atone of ' Jehovah of ' on`ed ' one the ' ye and ' you sin ' one the ' ye
' Aaron ' as before ' from Levi the ' ye ' you stand the and ' 13 from Levi the
Jehovah of ' the wave`ing you ' from ye ' you wave the and ' him son ' as before and
Israel ' as son ' middle`ing from ' from Levi the ' ye ' you separate the and ' 14

' and came as ' so ' as after and ' 15 from Levi the ' vessel ' and became and '
you clean and ' ing`congregate ' tent ' you serve ' ye ' serve of ' from Levi the
' from as gave ' for ' 16 the wave`ing you ' from ye ' you wave the and ' from ye '
' all ' under ' Israel ' as son ' middle`ing from ' vessel ' them`ed ' from as gave
' as you take ' Israel ' as son from ' all ' compassion ' you emit ' first`ing
Men in ' Israel ' as son in ' first`ing ' all ' vessel ' for ' 17 vessel ' from ye
' land in ' first`ing ' all ' as whom smitten ' day as in ' cattle`ed in and '
' ye ' took I and ' 18 vessel ' from ye ' as you holy the ' from as Mizra
' the give I and ' 19 Israel ' as son in ' first`ing ' all ' under ' from Levi the
' middle`ing from ' him son of and ' Aaron of ' from as gave ' from Levi the ' ye
' tent in ' Israel ' as son ' you serve ' ye ' serve of ' Israel ' as son
' be`s as ' not and ' Israel ' as son ' on ' atone of and ' ing`congregate
' 20 holy the ' to ' Israel ' as son ' accost in ' defeat ' Israel ' as son in
' Israel ' as son ' testimony ' all and ' Aaron and ' Moses ' do as and
' from Levi of ' Moses ' ye ' Jehovah ' command`ed ' which ' accord ' from Levi of
' from Levi the ' and sin whom and ' 21 Israel ' as son ' them of ' concoct ' so
' from ye ' Aaron ' wave as and ' them as fabric ' and immersion as and
' Aaron ' them as on ' atone as and ' Jehovah ' as before ' the wave`ing you
' ye ' serve of ' from Levi the ' and came ' so ' as after and ' 22 from clean of
' as before and ' Aaron ' as before ' ing`congregate ' tent in ' from you serve
' from Levi the ' on ' Moses ' ye ' Jehovah ' command`ed ' which are ' him son
such ' 24 say of ' Moses ' to ' Jehovah ' word as and ' 23 them of ' concoct ' so
above`ed and ' the Year ' from as ten and ' five ' son from ' from Levi of ' which '
' 25 ing`congregate ' tent ' you serve in ' mass ' mass of ' came`ing as '
' serve`ed the ' mass from ' carry`ing as ' the Year ' from as five ' son from and

' tent in ' him brother ' ye ' minister and ' 26 till`ing ' serve as ' not and
star`ed ' serve as ' not ' the serve and ' you guard from ' guard of ' ing`congregate
from you guard height ' from Levi of ' the concoct you '

' Year`ed in ' as bush`s ' word from in ' Moses ' to ' Jehovah ' word as and ' 1
' new in ' from as Mizra ' land from ' from you issue of ' you two the
pass the ' ye ' Israel ' as son ' concoct as and ' 2 say of ' has and head`s the
' this the ' new in ' day as ' ten ' the four I in ' 3 him ing`congregation in '
' him ing`congregation in ' and ye ' concoct whom ' from as twilight the ' between in
' 4 and ye ' and do you ' and as discern from ' all are and ' and as statute ' accord
' 5 pass the ' you concoct of ' Israel ' as son ' to ' Moses ' word as and
day as ' ten ' the four I in ' has and head`s in ' pass the ' ye ' concoct as and
' accord ' as bush`s ' word from in ' from as twilight the ' between in ' new of '
' 6 Israel ' as son ' concoct ' so ' Moses ' ye ' Jehovah ' command`ed ' which
' soul of ' from as unclean ' him the ' which ' from as person ' and became as and
7 that`ing the ' day as in ' pass the ' you concoct of ' and all as ' not and ' ground
' day as in ' Aaron ' as before and ' Moses ' as before ' and approach as and '
and us I ' him to ' them`ed the ' from as person the ' and say as and ' that`ing the
' as except of ' withdraw has ' what of ' ground ' soul of ' from as unclean '
' him ing`congregation in ' Jehovah ' has approach ' ye ' approach`s the
' and stand ' Moses ' them as to ' say as and ' 8 Israel ' as son ' middle`ing in
' Jehovah ' word as and ' 9 relate ' Jehovah ' command`ed as ' what ' hear`ed I and
man I ' man I ' say of ' Israel ' as son ' to ' word ' 10 say of ' Moses ' to
' or ' relate ' the get`ing ' way in ' or ' soul of ' unclean ' be`s as ' for '
' two the ' new in ' 11 Jehovah of ' pass ' do`ed and ' from are as generation of
' and do as ' from as twilight the ' between in ' day as ' ten ' the four I in
' not ' 12 and eat`ed as ' from as prison`ing and ' unleaven`ing ' on ' and ye
and is carry as ' not ' fast have and ' herd ' till ' and her from ' and remain`s as
which ' man that and ' 13 and ye ' and do as ' pass the ' statute ' accord ' and in '

' you concoct of ' forbear and ' be`s ' not ' way in and ' clean`ing ' that`ing '
has approach ' for ' am people from ' that`s the ' soul the ' hew`ed shall ' pass the
' linger ' and sin ' him ing`congregation in ' approach`s the ' not ' Jehovah '
do`ed and ' guest ' from are ye ' guest`ing as ' for and ' 14 that`ing the ' man that
' so ' him discern from are and ' pass the ' statute are ' Jehovah of ' pass '
' at native of and ' guest of and ' relate ' be`s as ' sister ' law`ed ' success`ed
' conceal`ed ' Tabernacle the ' ye ' from as drape`ing ' day as in and ' 15 land the
' twilight in and ' testimony`ing the ' tent of ' Tabernacle the ' ye ' cloud the
' so ' 16 herd ' till ' fire ' appear`ed are ' Tabernacle the ' on ' be`s as
the night`s ' fire ' appear`ed and ' and screen as ' cloud the ' continual`s ' be`s as
' so ' as after and ' tent the ' above ' cloud the ' offer`ing the ' as by and ' 17
cloud the ' there ' nigh as ' which ' place`ing in and ' Israel ' as son ' leave as
' leave as ' Jehovah ' edge ' on ' 18 Israel ' as son ' and encamp ' there '
' which ' week ' all ' and encamp ' Jehovah ' edge ' on and ' Israel ' as son
' lengthen`s thus and ' 19 and encamp ' Tabernacle the ' on ' cloud the ' nigh as
' and guard and ' from as increase ' from week ' Tabernacle the ' on ' cloud the
' joy`s ' 20 leave as ' not and ' Jehovah ' you guard from ' ye ' Israel ' as son
' on ' Tabernacle the ' on ' is number in ' from week ' cloud the ' be`s as ' which
' which ' joy`s ' 21 leave as ' Jehovah ' edge ' on and ' and encamp ' Jehovah ' edge
' cloud the ' the on shall ' herd ' till ' twilight from ' cloud the ' be`s as
' the on shall ' the night`s and ' from day as ' or ' leave has and ' is morn in
from week ' or ' new ' or ' from as day as ' or ' 22 leave has and ' cloud the
' and Mosthigh ' nigh of ' Tabernacle the ' on ' cloud the ' lengthen`s thus '
' and offer`ing thus and ' leave as ' not and ' Israel ' as son ' and encamp
leave as ' Jehovah ' edge ' on and ' and encamp ' Jehovah ' edge ' on ' 23 leave as

' hand in ' Jehovah ' edge ' on ' and guard ' Jehovah ' you guard from ' ye '

Moses

' twosome ' walk ' do`ed ' 2 say of ' Moses ' to ' Jehovah ' word as and ' 1
walk ' and became and ' from ye ' do`ed you ' fashion`ed ' silver ' you and is Cymbal
and slap and ' 3 you and camp the ' ye ' march of and ' till`ed the ' call from of '
' tent ' open ' to ' till`ed the ' all ' are as to ' and season shall ' thick '
' and season shall ' and slap as ' crush came ' mother and ' 4 ing`congregate
' 5 Israel ' as thousand ' as head ' from as help`s the ' are as to
' you and camp the ' leave has and ' the gatekeeper`ing ' from you slap and
' you two ' the gatekeeper`ing ' from you slap and ' 6 east`ed ' from as bivouac
' right`ed you ' the north`ing ' from as bivouac ' you and camp the ' leave has and
' ye ' assemble`s thus and ' 7 them as march of ' and slap as ' the gatekeeper`ing
' Aaron ' as son and ' 8 and gatekeeper`s ' not and ' and slap you ' assemble the
' relate ' and became and ' you and is Cymbal in ' and slap as ' from as priest the
' and came you ' for and ' 9 from are as generation of ' from on`ing ' statute of
' from are ye ' is boulder the ' phenomenon ' on ' your land in ' fight`ed from
' from you is remember shall ' you and is Cymbal in ' from you have mountain and
10 your as enemy I from ' from you deliver shall ' your as Allah ' Jehovah ' as before
' as head in and ' your as season from in and ' your as you rejoice ' day as in and '
on and ' your as offer ' on ' you and is Cymbal in ' from you slap and ' your as new
' shall is remember of ' relate ' and became and ' your as whole ' as sacrifice '
' your as Allah ' Jehovah ' as whither ' your as Allah ' Jehovah ' as before
blemish ' desist ' relate ' increase ' say of ' Moses ' to ' Jehovah ' word as and
as Amar the ' mountain ' and came and ' relate ' and situate ' and turn ' this the '
' south in ' depth`ed in and ' blemish ' goad`ed in ' and as nigh ' all ' to and '
' till ' has and white the and ' as Canaan the ' land ' sea the ' pure`ing in and
your as before ' as set has ' see ' Euphrates ' river ' great`ing the ' river the

' which ' land the ' ye ' and occupy ' and came ' land the ' ye '
' Isaac of ' Abraham of ' from are as you father of ' as you swear too has
Year`ed in ' became as and ' 11 them as after ' from seed of ' set of ' Jacob of and
' cloud the ' on`ed has ' new in ' from as ten in ' two the ' new in ' you two the '
' Israel ' as son ' leave as and ' 12 testimony`ing the ' Tabernacle ' above
' cloud the ' nigh as and ' as bush`s ' is wilderness from ' them as march of
' edge ' on ' the has and head`s in ' leave as and ' 13 has I apart ' word from in
' Judah ' as son ' the camp ' flag ' onward as and ' 14 Moses ' hand in ' Jehovah
' son ' pocket`ing has ' and mass ' on and ' from you mass of ' the has and head`s in
son ' to gave ' Issachar ' as son ' down`ed ' mass ' on and ' 15 freewill as people
' father as to ' Zebulun`ing ' as son ' down`ed ' mass ' on and ' 16 is gain`ing '
' as son ' leave has and ' Tabernacle the ' up alas and ' 17 s`window`ing ' son
' onward has and ' 18 Tabernacle the ' as lift has ' Merari ' as son and ' Gershon`ing
' and mass ' on and ' from you mass of ' Reuben ' as son ' the camp ' flag
' as son ' down`ed ' mass ' on and ' 19 light`ing almight ' son ' mould`ing of I
' mass ' on and ' 20 ' almight as boulder`ing ' ' son ' to as whole ' Simeon
' leave has and ' 21 to and menstruate ' son ' add of I ' fortune ' as son ' down`ed
' ye ' and rise`s the and ' holy them ' as lift has ' from as Kohath the
' as son ' the camp ' flag ' onward has and ' 22 cubit ' till ' Tabernacle the
' son ' Elishama ' and mass ' on and ' from you mass of ' Ephraim
to as wean ' Manasse`ed ' as son ' down`ed ' mass ' on and ' 23 gloref`ing as people
' Benjamim`s ' as son ' down`ed ' mass ' on and ' 24 boulder`ing release'ed ' son '
as son ' the camp ' flag ' onward has and ' 25 as Gideon`ing ' son ' judge as father
' on and ' from you mass of ' you and camp the ' all of ' gather from ' judge '
down`ed ' mass ' on and ' 26 ' almight as people ' ' son ' aid as brother ' and mass

' down`ed ' mass ' on and ' (27 has disturb ' son ' to as entreat ' which ' as son '
' as son ' as march ' to`ed ' (28 has low`s ' son ' sore brother ' Naphtali ' as son
' ing`cherish of ' Moses ' say as and ' (29 leave as and ' from you mass of ' Israel
' to ' and us I ' from as go ' Moses ' inlaw ' as Midian`s the ' Reuel ' son
' walk`ed ' relate ' donkey ' and ye ' Jehovah ' say ' which ' place`ing the
' on ' good`ing ' word ' Jehovah ' for ' walk ' and has good the and ' and has ye
' as land ' to ' mother ' for ' walk I ' not ' him to ' say as and ' (30 Israel
' forsake you ' oh ' to ' say as and ' (31 walk I ' as you bore and from ' to and
' word from in ' our as incline ' you known ' so ' on ' for ' and has ye
' walk you ' for ' be`s and ' (32 from as has eye of ' our of ' whom became and
Jehovah ' improve`s as ' which ' that`ing the ' good`ing the ' be`s and ' our people
Jehovah ' mountain from ' leave as and ' (33 walk ' and has good the and ' our people '
' go ' Jehovah ' covenant`s ' shout`ing I and ' from week ' you three ' way '
' them of ' protect`ing of ' from week ' you three ' way ' them as before
' from go in ' from day as ' them as on ' Jehovah ' cloud and ' (34 the bestow`ing
' say as and ' Ark`ing the ' go in ' became as and ' (35 camp`ed the ' has from
' are as enemy I ' and drive`ing as and ' Jehovah ' the rise`ing ' Moses
the bestow`ing in and ' (36 are around from ' are as hateful from ' and flee`ing as and
Israel ' as thousand ' you and many ' Jehovah ' the carry`ing ' say as '

' as ear in ' evil ' from as complain you from are ' people the ' became as and ' 1

' fire ' height ' burn you and ' now ' delay and ' Jehovah ' hear as and ' Jehovah

' to ' people the ' cry as and ' 2 camp`ed the ' the end in ' eat you and ' Jehovah

' 3 fire the ' quench you and ' Jehovah ' to ' Moses ' praise whom and ' Moses

' burn`ed ' for ' burn`ed you ' that`ing the ' place`ing the ' there ' call as and

' and approach in ' which ' doorpost gather the and ' 4 Jehovah ' fire ' height

' Israel ' as son ' also ' and wept and ' and dwell and ' lust`ed ' and lust the

' ye ' and has is remember ' 5 flesh ' and has eat`s as ' who ' and say as and

' ye ' reason ' from as Mizra in ' eat has ' which ' squirm`ed the

' Leek`s the ' ye and ' from as at Melon the ' ye and ' from as Cucumber`ing the

' the time and ' 6 from as Chive the ' ye and ' from as Onion the ' ye and

' has them ' to ' as zero in ' all ' whither`s ' wither`ed ' and has soul

' and has eye and ' that`ing ' fortune ' seed are ' Manna the and ' 7 our as has eye

' and pickup and ' people the ' deviate ' 8 at separate the ' has eye are

' and sodden and ' the mortar`ing in ' collapse ' or ' from as shoot ' and grind and

flavor are ' and flavor ' be`s and ' you and bake ' and ye ' concoct and ' pot`ing in

' the night`s ' camp`ed the ' on ' dew the ' you up in and ' 9 eight the ' sweet '

' people the ' ye ' Moses ' hear as and ' 10 and Mosthigh ' has them ' descend

' anger ' delay and ' and tent ' open of ' man I ' him you at family of ' against`ed

' Moses ' say as and ' 11 evil ' Moses ' as has eye in and ' especially ' Jehovah

' not ' what of and ' are serve of ' you evil the ' what of ' Jehovah ' to

' all ' swell ' ye ' there`s of ' are as has eye in ' grace ' as you come

' all ' ye ' as net`s the ' for whither the ' 12 mosthigh ' this the ' people the

' say you ' for ' and am you bore as ' for whither ' mother ' this the ' people the

' ye ' believe the ' linger ' which are ' are bosom at in ' and lift`ed ' Eli

’ 13 him you father of ’ as you swear too has ’ which ’ ground`ed the ’ on ’ suck the
’ for ’ this the ’ people the ’ all of ’ set of ’ flesh ’ vessel ’ whither`s from
’ 14 the eat has and ’ flesh ’ our of ’ give`ed ’ say of ’ mosthigh ’ and against as
’ people the ’ all ’ ye ’ arise of ’ as alone of ’ for whither ’ able I ’ not
’ do`ed ’ ye`ed ’ star`ed ’ mother and ’ 15 apportion from ’ honour ’ for ’ this the
’ grace ’ as you come ’ mother and ’ kill ’ oh ’ as murmur the ’ vessel
to ’ Jehovah ’ say as and ’ 16 as you evil in ’ cat`ed ’ to and ’ are as has eye in
’ Israel ’ as elder from ’ man I ’ from as seven ’ vessel ’ the gather ’ Moses ’
’ him ing`officer and ’ people the ’ as elder ’ them ’ for ’ you known ’ which
there ’ and reside you since ’ ing`congregate ’ tent ’ to ’ from ye ’ you take and
’ there ’ are people ’ as you word and ’ as you desend and ’ 17 are people ’
’ are as on ’ which ’ spirit is the ’ has from ’ as you beside the and
’ people the ’ lift from in ’ are ye ’ and lift shall ’ them as on ’ as you there and
’ say you ’ people the ’ to and ’ 18 are alone of ’ ye`ed ’ lift you ’ not and
’ from whom against ’ for ’ flesh ’ from you eat and ’ tomorrow of ’ and holy sacred
’ good`ing ’ for ’ flesh ’ and has eat`s as ’ who ’ say of ’ Jehovah ’ as ear in
19 from you eat and ’ flesh ’ relate ’ Jehovah ’ gave and ’ from as Mizra in ’ our of
’ not and ’ from as day as ’ not and ’ has and eat you ’ one ’ day as ’ not ’
day as ’ from as ten ’ not and ’ from week ’ ten`ed ’ not and ’ from week ’ the five
be`s and ’ from are anger from ’ out ’ which ’ till ’ from week ’ new ’ till ’ 20
’ which ’ Jehovah ’ ye ’ from you reject ’ for ’ because ’ disgust`ed of ’ relate ’
’ this ’ what of ’ say of ’ him before ’ and against you and ’ from are approach in
’ you and hundred ’ six ’ Moses ’ say as and ’ 21 from as Mizra from ’ and has out
’ and approach in ’ for whither ’ which ’ people the ’ as foot`er ’ thousand
’ 22 from week ’ new ’ and eat and ’ them of ’ donkey ’ flesh ’ you say ’ ye`ed and

' ye ' mother ' them of ' come and ' them of ' slay as ' herd the and ' flock the
' say as and ' (23 them of ' come and ' them of ' gather as ' sea the ' as squirm ' all
saw`ed ' time`ed ' ye`ed ' reap you ' Jehovah ' glorify`s ' Moses ' to ' Jehovah
to ' word as and ' Moses ' out and ' (24 not ' mother ' as word ' are call as the '
' man I ' from as seven ' gather as and ' Jehovah ' as word ' ye ' people the '
' (25 tent the ' you surround`s ' from ye ' stand as and ' people the ' as elder from
' has from ' beside as and ' him to ' word as and ' cloud in ' Jehovah ' descend and
' man I ' from as seven ' on ' give as and ' and Mosthigh ' which ' spirit is the
' spirit is the ' them as on ' rest`ing are ' became as and ' from as elder the
' two ' and remain Then ' (26 and gather as ' not and ' and prophet whom and
' two the ' there and ' Eldad ' one the ' there ' camp`ed in ' from as person
' them`ed and ' spirit is the ' them as on ' rest you and ' ing`Medad
' and prophet whom and ' tent`ed the ' and out ' not and ' from as write`ing in
Eldad ' say as and ' Moses of ' my told and ' youth the ' run as and ' (27 camp`ed in
ed`Joshua`ing ' low as and ' (28 camp`ed in ' from as prophet you from ' ing`Medad and '
' as master ' say as and ' him choose`s from ' Moses ' you juice ' Nun ' son '
vessel ' ye`ed ' jealous them ' Moses ' if ' say as and ' (29 from restrict ' Moses
' for ' from as prophet`s ' Jehovah ' people ' all ' permanent ' as from and '
' Moses ' gather as and ' (30 them as on ' and spirit is ' ye ' Jehovah ' permanent
' go ' spirit is and ' (31 Israel ' as elder and ' that`ing ' camp`ed the ' to
too extend and ' sea the ' has from ' from as guail ' shear as and ' Jehovah ' each
' here ' day as ' are way and ' here ' day as ' way are ' camp`ed the ' on I '
land the ' around ' on ' from as faithful are and ' camp`ed the ' you and surround`s
' all and ' that`ing the ' day as the ' all ' people the ' rise as and ' (32
' ye ' and gather as and ' you tomorrow the ' day as the ' all and ' the night`s the

' and slay as and ' from as heass ' ten`ed ' gather ' less`s them ' privacy`ing the
' flesh the ' 33 camp`ed the ' you and surround`s ' slay`ing ' them of
' Jehovah ' anger and ' hew as ' suspend ' them two ' between in ' and has till`ing
' increase`ed ' with`ed ' people in ' Jehovah ' struck and ' people in ' hole`ed
' that`ing the ' place`ing the ' there ' ye ' call as and ' 34 especially
' people the ' ye ' and bury ' there ' for ' lust`ed the ' you and bury
' people the ' and go ' lust`ed the ' Kibroth`ing from ' 35 from as lust them
Hazeroth`ing in ' and became as and ' you and yard the

' Woman the ' concern`ing ' on ' Moses in ' Aaron and ' Miriam ' word you and ' 1
' 2 took of ' whom Cush ' Woman ' for ' took of ' which ' whom Cush the
' also ' forward`ing ' Jehovah ' word ' Moses in ' sure ' only the ' and say as and
' blind`th ' Moses ' man that and ' 3 Jehovah ' hear as and ' word ' and son
' 4 ground`ed the ' around ' on ' which ' ground the ' all from ' especially
' to and ' Aaron ' to and ' Moses ' to ' from instant ' Jehovah ' say as and
and out and ' ing`congregate ' tent ' to ' from are you three ' and issue ' Miriam
' stand as and ' cloud ' stand`ing in ' Jehovah ' descend and ' 5 from you three '
' 6 them two ' and out and ' Miriam and ' Aaron ' call as and ' tent the ' open
' from are prophet`s ' be`s as ' mother ' as word ' oh ' and hear ' say as and
' word I ' dream`ing in and ' ing`perceive I the ' him to ' appear`ed in ' Jehovah
' believe has ' as you house ' all in ' Moses ' as serve ' so ' not ' 7 and in
' not and ' appear`ed in and ' and in ' word I ' talk ' to ' talk ' 8 that`ing
' not ' why`ing and ' scan`s as ' Jehovah ' you portion`ing and ' you riddle`s
' Jehovah ' anger ' delay and ' 9 Moses in ' as serve in ' word of ' from sight as
' be`th and ' tent the ' above ' repent ' cloud the and ' 10 walk as and ' height
' Miriam ' to ' Aaron ' turn as and ' snow are ' you leper from ' Miriam
' house ' Moses ' to ' Aaron ' say as and ' 11 you leper from ' be`th and
' and has slack has ' which ' you sin ' our as on ' impose`s ' oh ' to ' as master
' which ' die are ' be`s you ' oh ' to ' 12 and has sin ' which and
and flesh ' as outside ' eat as and ' and mother ' compassion from ' and you issue in
' oh ' decease ' oh ' to ' say of ' Jehovah ' to ' Moses ' cry as and ' 13
' green ' green ' am father and ' Moses ' to ' Jehovah ' say as and ' 14 nihil
you seven ' close you ' from week ' you seven ' taunt you ' forward`ing ' am turn in
' 15 gather you ' after and ' camp`ed of ' outside`ing from ' from week '

' from week ' you seven ' camp`ed of ' outside`ing from ' Miriam ' close you and
' after and ' 16 Miriam ' gather`ed the ' till ' and go ' not ' people the and
has I apart ' word from in ' and encamp and ' Hazeroth`ing from ' people the ' and go
' mountain ' till ' from ye in ' Israel ' as son of ' Moses ' say as and '
' gave ' look`ed ' our of ' gave ' our as Allah ' Jehovah ' which ' as Amar the
which are ' vemon ' on`ed ' land the ' ye ' are as before ' are as Allah ' Jehovah
to and ' look as you ' to ' walk ' are as you father ' as Allah ' Jehovah ' word '
' send`ed has ' and say as and ' Moses ' to ' and approach as and ' under '
' land the ' ye ' our of ' and ration as and ' our as before ' from as person
' thus ' on`ed has ' which ' way the ' ye ' word ' and has ye ' and carry`s as and
' improve as and ' behold as on ' prophet`ing ' which ' from as town the ' ye and
Moses ' as has eye in ' word the

' from as person ' walk ' send ' (2 say of ' Moses ' to ' Jehovah ' word as and ' (1
' gave ' as whither ' which ' Canaan ' land ' ye ' and protect`ing as and
and as you father ' below`ed ' one ' man I ' one ' man I ' Israel ' as son of
' Moses ' from ye ' send as and ' (3 cattle ' lift`s has ' all ' and send you '
' from as person ' taunt ' Jehovah ' edge ' on ' has I apart ' is wilderness from
' below`ed ' from you name ' to`ed and ' (4 them`ed ' Israel ' as son ' as head
' son ' discern ' Simeon ' below`ed ' (5 male`ing ' son ' hear`ing ' Reuben
' below`ed ' (7 turn`ed as ' son ' dog ' Judah ' below`ed ' (6 as light`ing
' son ' ed`Joshua`ing ' Ephraim ' below`ed ' (8 Joseph ' son ' redeem as ' Issachar
' below`ed ' (10 decease`ing ' son ' as escape ' Benjamim`s ' below`ed ' (9 Nun
' below`ed ' Joseph ' below`ed ' (11 as found`ing ' son ' to as fortune ' Zebulun
' son ' to as people ' judge ' below`ed ' (12 as skip`ing ' son ' kid ' Manasse`ed
' below`ed ' (14 to are who ' son ' demolish`ing ' which ' below`ed ' (13 as wean
' to and haughty ' fortune ' below`ed ' (15 as tunic and ' son ' as in rest ' Naphtali
' Moses ' send ' which ' from as person the ' you name ' to`ed ' (16 as with`s ' son
' Nun ' son ' Hoshua of ' Moses ' call as and ' land the ' ye ' protect`ing of
' land ' ye ' protect`ing of ' Moses ' from ye ' send as and ' (17 ed`Joshua`ing
' ye ' from whom on and ' south in ' this ' lug ' them as to ' say as and ' Canaan
' ye and ' that`s ' what ' land the ' ye ' from whom look and ' (18 mountain the
' less the ' puny`ed ' that`ing ' strength the ' am on ' dwell the ' people the
' dwell ' that`ing ' which ' land the ' what and ' (19 increase ' mother ' that`ing
' from as town the ' what and ' evil`ed ' mother ' that`s ' the good`ing the ' thus
' mother`ing ' from as camp in the ' be`th in ' sojourn as ' that`ing ' which
mother ' that`s ' the has there the ' land the ' what and ' (20 from as defence height
' whither`s ' mother ' tree ' thus ' man the ' secret`ed '

' land the ' fruit from ' from you take and ' from you strength you the and
' and went and ' 21 from as grape ' whom`ing first`ing ' week ' from week the and
' land the ' ye ' and protect`ing as and ' and came as and ' and walk as and
' 22 hotspring`ed ' came`ing of ' large ' till ' thorn ' is wilderness from
' there and ' Hebron`ing ' till ' and came as and ' south in ' and went and
' blame have the ' as bore`s as ' as virgin you and ' as six ' has from as brother
' migrate ' as before ' he son has ' from two ' seven ' has and connect and
' of and testicle ' inherit ' till ' and came as and ' 23 from as Mizra
' from as grape ' of and testicle and ' the prune`ing ' there from ' and hew as and
' has from and ' from as Year in ' down`ing in ' and lift`ed as and ' one
' place`ing of ' 24 from as fig the ' has from and ' from as pomegranate`ing the
' concern`ing ' on ' of and testicle ' inherit ' and call ' that`ing the
' 25 Israel ' as son ' there from ' and hew ' which ' of and testicle the
from as four I ' end from ' land the ' ye ' protect`ing from ' and carry`ing as and
' Aaron ' to and ' Moses ' to ' and came as and ' and walk as and ' 26 day as '
' has I apart ' word from ' to ' Israel ' as son ' testimony ' all ' to and
' till`ed the ' all ' ye and ' word ' from ye`ing ' and carry`s as and ' the holy
and say as and ' if ' and report as and ' 27 land the ' fruit ' ye ' from see as and
' you secrete ' also and ' and has you send ' which ' land the ' to ' and has came '
' harsh ' for ' however ' 28 the fruit ' this and ' that`s ' honey and ' milk
' splendor`ing in ' from as town the and ' land in ' dwell the ' people the
' our as look ' blame have the ' as bore as ' also and ' especially ' you and great
' as Heth the and ' south the ' land in ' sojourn as ' Amalek ' 29 there
' blemish ' sojourn as ' as Amar the and ' as Jebus the and ' as Hivite the and
' 30 has desend the ' hand ' on and ' sea the ' on ' dwell ' as Canaan the and

' on`ed ' if ' say as and ' Moses ' on I ' people the ' ye ' dog ' hush Then
' (31 nihil ' able has ' all him ' for ' ye`ed ' and has possess and ' on`ed has
' able has ' not ' and say ' and people ' lug ' which ' from as person the and
' (32 and her from ' that`ing ' strength ' for ' people the ' to ' offer`ing of
' as son ' to ' ye`ed ' joyful ' which ' land the ' slander ' and issue`s him and
ye`ed ' protect`ing of ' thus ' and has cross ' which ' land the ' say of ' Israel
' which ' people the ' all and ' that`s ' am sojourn as ' you eat ' land '
' our as look ' there and ' (33 wide`ing ' as person ' the middle`ing in ' our as look
be`s shall ' from as fall the ' has from ' donate ' as son ' from as fall`s the ' ye
' our as became ' so and ' from as shortgrasshopper are ' our as has eye in '
' them as tent in ' Israel ' as son ' and murmur as and ' them as has eye in
' and has spring`s the ' and has ye ' Jehovah ' you hateful in ' and say as and
' as Amar the ' hand in ' and has ye ' set of ' from as Mizra ' land from
' our as brother and ' from as on ' and us I ' whither`ed ' and has destory`s the of
' great`ing ' people ' say of ' and has in heart ' ye ' and burden`s the
' you and defence and ' you and great ' from as town ' and her from ' increase and
' say as and ' (34 there ' our as look ' from as Anak ' as son ' also and ' heaven`s in
' not and ' has and afraid you ' not ' Israel ' as son of ' burden`ed
' your as before ' enter the ' your as Allah ' Jehovah ' lag ' shall dread you
' from are ye ' do`ed ' which ' accord ' relate ' fight as ' that`ing
which ' you seen ' which ' is wilderness in and ' your as low`s of ' from as Mizra in
' and son ' ye ' man I ' linger ' which are ' are as Allah ' Jehovah ' are help '
' till ' from are came ' till ' from you walk the ' which ' way the ' all in
' your whither`s ' this the ' word in the and ' this the ' place`ing the
' your as before ' enter the ' your as Allah ' Jehovah in ' from as believe from

’ abhorrence ’ from are incline the of ’ place`ing ’ relate ’ protect`ing of ’ way in

’ thus ’ and walk you ’ which ’ way in ’ fron are sight the of ’ the night`s

from day as ’ cloud in and

THE TORAH SCROLL 14

Num 14:1-14:12

’ from Voice`ing ’ ye ’ and give as and ’ till`ed the ’ all ’ lift you and ’ 1
’ on ’ and stop as and ’ 2 that`ing the ’ the night`s in ’ people the ’ and wept and
’ them as to ’ and say as and ’ Israel ’ as son ’ all ’ Aaron ’ on and ’ Moses
word from in ’ or ’ from as Mizra ’ land in ’ and has die ’ if ’ till`ed the ’ all
’ and has ye ’ came`s from ’ Jehovah ’ what of and ’ 3 and has die ’ if ’ this the ’
’ our children and ’ our as women ’ desolate in ’ fall of ’ such the ’ land the ’ to
’ the carry`ing ’ our of ’ good`ing ’ forward`ing ’ spoil of ’ and became as
’ head ’ gave`ed ’ him brother ’ to ’ man I ’ and say as and ’ 4 the from as Mizra
’ on ’ Aaron and ’ Moses ’ fell and ’ 5 the from as Mizra ’ the carry`ing has and
’ 6 Israel ’ as son ’ testimony ’ assemble ’ all ’ as before ’ them around
’ has from ’ turn`ed as ’ son ’ Caled and ’ Nun ’ son ’ ed`Joshua`ing and
and say as and ’ 7 them as fabric ’ and rend ’ land the ’ ye ’ from as area`ing the
’ which ’ land the ’ say of ’ Israel ’ as son ’ testimony ’ all ’ to ’
especially ’ land the ’ the good`ing ’ ye`ed ’ protect`ing of ’ thus ’ and has cross
’ and has ye ’ came`s the and ’ Jehovah ’ and son ’ please ’ mother ’ 8 especially ’
’ that`s ’ which ’ land ’ our of ’ the give has and ’ such the ’ land the ’ to
’ and rebel you ’ to ’ Jehovah in ’ sure ’ 9 honey and ’ milk ’ you secrete
and has fight ’ for ’ land the ’ people ’ ye ’ and look as you ’ to ’ from ye and
’ to ’ and has ye ’ Jehovah and ’ them as on from ’ image ’ repent ’ them ’
from ye ’ council`ing of ’ till`ed the ’ all ’ and say as and ’ 10 from and dread you
’ ing`congregate ’ tent in ’ speak`ed ’ Jehovah ’ honour`ing and ’ from as son came ’
’ till ’ Moses ’ to ’ Jehovah ’ say as and ’ 11 Israel ’ as son ’ all ’ to
’ whither`ed ’ till and ’ this the ’ people the ’ as has blaspleme as ’ whither`ed
’ as whom do ’ which ’ evidence`ing the ’ all in ’ house ’ and believe`s as ’ not
’ do`ed I and ’ and has occupy`s I and ’ word in ’ and has sure ’ 12 and approach in

' great`ing ' nation`ing of ' are as father ' you house ' ye and ' are ye
' and hear and ' Jehovah ' to ' Moses ' say as and ' 13 and her from ' might`ing and
' this the ' people the ' ye ' are power in ' offer`s the ' for ' from as Mizra
and hear ' such the ' land the ' sojourn as ' to ' and say and ' 14 and approach from
' has eye ' which ' this the ' people the ' approach in ' Jehovah ' ye`ed ' for '
' them as on ' stand ' are cloud and ' Jehovah ' ye`ed ' speak`ed ' low`s in
' from day as ' them as before ' walk the ' ye`ed ' cloud ' stand in and
' people the ' ye ' die`ed the and ' 15 the night`s ' fire ' stand`ing in and
' and hear ' which ' from nation`ing the ' and say and ' one ' man I are ' this the
' came`s the of ' Jehovah ' you finish ' as except from ' 16 say of ' are hear ' ye
' them of ' swear too has ' which ' land the ' to ' this the ' people the ' ye
as master ' power ' oh ' great as ' the time and ' 17 word from in ' from slay as and
' increase and ' toward`s ' lenghten ' Jehovah ' 18 say of ' you word ' which are '
' blame`ed and ' trepass and ' sin`ed and ' low`ing ' help ' faithful and ' bow
on ' from as son ' on ' you and father ' low`ing ' punish ' the blame as ' not`ing
' low`ing of ' oh ' forgive ' 19 from as four`s ' on and ' from as three`s '
people of ' the you help ' which are and ' are bow ' great are ' this the ' people the
' Jehovah ' say as and ' 20 be`th ' till and ' from as Mizra from ' this the '
' as whither ' life ' from to`ing and ' 21 are as word are ' as you forgive
' all ' for ' 22 land the ' all ' ye ' Jehovah ' honour`ing ' fill as and
' ye and ' as honour`ing ' ye ' from as look the ' from as person the
' is wilderness in and ' from as Mizra in ' as whom do ' which ' as evidence`ing
' and hear ' not and ' from as move ' ten ' this ' near ' and flee as and
' which ' land the ' ye ' and look as ' mother ' 23 as voice`ing in
' all and ' them of ' set of ' from you and father of ' as you swear too has

' whom`ed the ' heel ' dog ' as serve and ' 24 see`ed as ' not ' as blaspheme from
' him you came`s the and ' as after ' fill as and ' and people ' you after ' spirit is
' 25 the has possess him ' and seed and ' there`ed ' came ' which ' land the ' to
' and turn ' tomorrow ' valley in ' sojourn as ' as Canaan the and ' as Amalek the and
Jehovah ' word as and ' 26 join`ing ' sea ' way ' word`ed them ' relate ' leave and
' till`ed of ' extent ' till ' 27 say of ' Aaron ' to and ' Moses ' to '
' ye ' mosthigh ' from as stop`s from ' them`ed ' which ' such the ' evil`ed the
' from as stop`s from ' them`ed ' which ' Israel ' as son ' you and obstinate
Jehovah ' state ' as whither ' life ' them as to ' say ' 28 as you hear ' mosthigh
' 29 relate ' do`ed I ' so ' as ear in ' from you word ' which are ' not ' mother '
' from are as punish ' all and ' your as carcase ' and fell ' this the ' word from in
' which ' above`ed and ' the Year ' from as ten ' son from ' your is number ' all of
land the ' to ' and came you ' from ye ' mother ' 30 mosthigh ' from you stop`s the
mother ' for ' thus ' from are ye ' nigh of ' as hand ' ye ' as you help ' which '
from are children and ' 31 Nun ' son ' ed`Joshua`ing and ' turn`ed as ' son ' dog '
' from ye ' as you came`s the and ' be`s as ' spoil of ' from you say ' which '
' 32 thus ' from you reject ' which ' land the ' ye ' and known and
' 33 this the ' word from in ' and fell ' from ye ' from are as carcase and
' from as four I ' word from in ' from as evil ' and became as ' your as son and
' complete ' till ' from are as ing`whore ' ye ' and lift shall ' the Year
' which ' from week the ' is number in ' 34 word from in ' your as carcase
' Year`ed of ' day as ' day as ' from as four I ' land the ' ye ' from you protect
' from as four I ' your as you low`ing ' ye ' and lift you ' Year`ed of ' day as
' Jehovah ' as whither ' 35 as you breach`ing ' ye ' complete known and ' the Year
' evil`ed the ' till`ed the ' all of ' do`ed I ' such ' not ' mother ' as you word

' this the ' word from in ' mosthigh ' from as season behold ' such the
' which ' from as person the and ' 36 and die`ing as ' there and ' and complete as
and stop`ing as and ' and dwell and ' land the ' ye ' protect`ing of ' Moses ' send
' on ' bear`ed ' issue`s alas of ' till`ed the ' all ' ye ' and Mosthigh '
' slander ' as issue and from ' from as person the ' and die as and ' 37 land the
' ed`Joshua`ing and ' 38 Jehovah ' as before ' pestilence`ed in ' evil`ed ' land the
from as person the ' has from ' and life ' turn`ed as ' son ' Caled and ' Nun ' son
' word as and ' 39 land the ' ye ' protect`ing of ' from as enter the ' them the '
' Israel ' as son ' all ' to ' these`ed ' from as word the ' ye ' Moses
' is morn in ' and ridge as and ' 40 especially ' people the ' and mourn you as and
' and behold`th ' say of ' mountain the ' head ' to ' and went and
' for ' Jehovah ' say ' which ' place`ing the ' to ' and has as on and
lug you ' not ' them of ' say ' Moses ' to ' Jehovah ' say as and ' and has sin
' not and ' from are approach in ' as has whither`s ' for ' and fight you ' not and '
this ' what of ' Moses ' say as and ' 41 your as enemy I ' as before ' and defeat you
proper`s you ' not ' that`s and ' Jehovah ' edge ' ye ' from as Obara ' from ye '
' not and ' from are approach in ' Jehovah ' whither`s ' for ' lug you ' to ' 42
' as Amalek the ' for ' 43 your as enemy I ' as before ' and defeat you
' for ' desolate in ' from you fall and ' your as before ' there ' as Canaan the and
' Jehovah ' be`s as ' not and ' Jehovah ' as after from ' from desist ' so ' on
' mountain the ' head ' to ' offer`ing of ' and fortress Then ' 44 your people
' approach from ' and feel ' not ' Moses and ' Jehovah ' covenant`s ' shout`ing I and
' dwell the ' as Canaan the and ' as Amalek the ' descend and ' 45 camp`ed the
' which are ' from ye ' and chase as and ' from you call of ' that`ing the ' blemish
' from and you struck and ' from and struck and ' from as word the ' the has as suffice

camp`ed the ' to ' and dwell and ' curse`ed the ' till

' as son ' to ' word ' (2 say of ' Moses ' to ' Jehovah ' word as and ' (1
' land ' to ' and came you ' for ' them as to ' you say and ' Israel
' from dual`s and ' (3 relate ' gave ' as whither ' which ' your as desist and from
vow`ed in ' or ' vow ' I made of ' sacrifice ' or ' on`ed ' Jehovah of ' Woman
Jehovah of ' odor has ' smell`s ' you concoct of ' from are as season from in ' or '
' approach`s the and ' (4 flock the ' has from ' or ' herd the ' has from '
' flour ' bestow`ed ' Jehovah of ' and has approach ' ye ' approach`s them
' has intoxicate and ' (5 eight ' hin`s ' whom four in ' mingle`ing ' has and ten
' or ' on`ed the ' on ' do`ed you ' hin`s ' whom four`s ' libation of
' bestow`ed ' do`ed you ' Ram`s of ' or ' (6 one the ' mutton of ' sacrifice of
' (7 hin`s ' whom three ' eight in ' the mingle`ing ' from as has ten ' two ' flour
' smell`s ' approach`s you ' hin`s ' whom three ' libation of ' has intoxicate and
' or ' on`ed ' herd ' son ' do`ed you ' for and ' (8 Jehovah of ' odor has
' (9 Jehovah of ' from as whole ' or ' vow ' I made of ' sacrifice
' three`ed ' flour ' bestow`ed ' herd the ' son ' on ' approach`s the and
' (10 hin`s ' as outside ' eight in ' mingle`ing ' from as has and ten
' Woman ' hin`s ' as outside ' libation of ' approach`s you ' has intoxicate and
or ' one the ' Ox`ing of ' success`ed ' star`ed ' (11 Jehovah of ' odor has ' smell`s
(12 from as Goat in ' or ' from as sheep in ' knead`ed ' or ' one the ' Ram`s of '
' one of ' and do you ' star`ed ' and do you ' which ' from is number are '
' to`ed ' ye ' star`ed ' success`ed ' at native the ' all ' (13 from is number are in
' for and ' (14 Jehovah of ' odor has ' smell`s ' Woman ' approach`s the of
' your middle`ing in ' which ' or ' guest ' from are ye ' guest`ing as
' Jehovah of ' odor has ' smell`s ' Woman ' do`ed and ' from are as generation of
relate ' sister ' law`ed ' assemble the ' (15 success`ed ' so ' and do you ' which are

from star ' from are as generation of ' from on`ing ' statute ' abide ' guest of and '
' sister ' the protect`ing ' 16 Jehovah ' as before ' be`s as ' guest are '
' 17 from are ye ' abide ' guest of and ' relate ' be`s as ' one ' discern from and
' Israel ' as son ' to ' word ' 18 say of ' Moses ' to ' Jehovah ' word as and
' as whither ' which ' land the ' to ' from are came in ' them as to ' you say and
from bread from ' from are eat in ' be`s and ' 19 there`ed ' from are ye ' came`s from
' you as head ' 20 Jehovah of ' the oblation`ing ' and oblation`s ' land the '
' the oblation`ing ' and oblation`s ' sick`ed ' from are you dough
' 21 ye`ed ' and oblation`s ' so ' threshingfloor ' you oblation`ing are
' the oblation`ing ' Jehovah of ' and give you ' your as you dough ' whom head from
' ye ' and do you ' not and ' transgress you ' for and ' 22 from are as generation of
ye ' 23 Moses ' to ' Jehovah ' word ' which ' these`ed ' unleaven`ing the ' all
' widow ' Moses ' hand in ' your as to ' Jehovah ' command`ed ' which ' all '
from are as generation of ' forward`ed and ' Jehovah ' command`ed ' which ' day as the
' mistake`ed of ' he do has ' till`ed the ' as purpose`s ' mother ' be`s and ' 24
smell`s of ' on`ed of ' one ' herd ' son ' apart ' till`ed the ' all ' concoct and
' discern from are ' and libation and ' and you bestow and ' Jehovah of ' odor has '
' on ' priest the ' atone and ' 25 you sin of ' one ' from as Goat ' gate`s and
' mistake`ed ' for ' them of ' forgive has and ' Israel ' as son ' testimony ' all
' Jehovah of ' Woman ' from has approach ' ye ' and came`s the ' them and ' that`s
' forgive has and ' 26 from you mistake ' on ' Jehovah ' as before ' from you sin and
' from middle`ing in ' abide ' guest of and ' Israel ' as son ' testimony ' all of
' sin you ' sister ' soul ' mother and ' 27 mistake`ed in ' people the ' all of ' for
you sin of ' the you year ' daughter ' harsh ' the approach`s the and ' mistake`ed in
' sin`ed in ' you mistake the ' soul the ' on ' priest the ' atone and ' 28

if ' forgive has and ' and Mosthigh ' atone of ' Jehovah ' as before ' mistake`ed in
from middle`ing in ' abide ' guest of and ' Israel ' as son in ' at native the ' 29
' 30 mistake`ed in ' do`ed of ' relate ' be`s as ' sister ' the protect`ing '
' at native the ' has from ' high`ed ' hand in ' do`ed you ' which ' soul the and
' hew`ed shall ' revile from ' that`ing ' Jehovah ' ye ' abide ' has from and
' word ' ye ' for ' 31 the as people ' approach from ' that`s the ' soul the
' hew you ' hew the ' broken ' him you command from ' ye and ' spoil`ed ' Jehovah
Israel ' as son ' and became as and ' 32 thus ' the low`ing ' that`s the ' soul the
' day as in ' from as tree ' forage from ' man I ' and come as and ' word from in '
' and ye ' from as spring them ' and ye ' and approach`s as and ' 33 desist the
' all ' to and ' Aaron ' to and ' Moses ' to ' from as tree ' forage from
' excrement ' not ' for ' guard from in ' and ye ' and rest`s as and ' 34 till`ed the
die him ' die`ing ' Moses ' to ' Jehovah ' say as and ' 35 if ' success`ed ' what
' till`ed the ' all ' from as son came ' and ye ' and council ' man that '
' till`ed the ' all ' and ye ' and issue`s him and ' 36 camp`ed of ' outside`ing from
from as son came ' and ye ' and council as and ' camp`ed of ' outside`ing from ' to
' say as and ' 37 Moses ' ye ' Jehovah ' command`ed ' which are ' die as and '
' you say and ' Israel ' as son ' to ' word ' 38 say of ' Moses ' to ' Jehovah
' as wing ' on ' whom`ing flower`s ' them of ' concoct and ' them as to
' whom flower`s ' on ' and gave and ' from ing`generation of ' them as fabric
' whom`ing flower`s of ' relate ' and be`s and ' 39 you perfect ' lace`s ' wing the
' unleaven`ing ' all ' ye ' from you is remember and ' and spy ' from whom look and
' as after ' ing`joyful you ' not and ' from ye ' from dual`s and ' Jehovah
' from as diver ' from ye ' which ' your as has eye ' as after and ' your in heart
' all ' ye ' from dual`s and ' and is remember you ' purpose of ' 40 them as after

(41 ’ your as Allah of ’ from as holy ’ complete as became and ’ as you command from
’ from are ye ’ as you issue alas ’ which ’ your as Allah ’ Jehovah ’ as whither
as whither ’ from as Allah of ’ relate ’ you and became of ’ from as Mizra ’ land from
your as Allah ’ Jehovah ’

' has decree and ' Levi ' son ' Kohath ' son ' Izhar ' son ' bald ' took as and ' 1
' as son ' swift ' son ' whither`ing and ' father as to ' as son ' high as father and
' as son from ' from as person and ' Moses ' as before ' and rise as and ' 2 Reuben
' till`ed ' as lift`s has ' from as you hundred and ' from as five ' Israel
Moses ' on ' and assemble as and ' 3 there ' as person ' ing`congregate ' as call`s
' all ' for ' relate ' increase ' them as to ' and say as and ' Aaron ' on and '
' why`ing and ' Jehovah ' from middle`ing in and ' from as holy ' taunt ' till`ed the
' on ' fell and ' Moses ' hear as and ' 4 Jehovah ' assemble ' on ' and help set
' say of ' and testimony ' all ' to and ' bald ' to ' word as and ' 5 him turn
' holy`ing the ' ye and ' if ' which ' ye ' Jehovah ' acknowledge`s as and ' herd
approach`s as ' and in ' choose as ' which ' ye and ' him to ' approach`s became and
' bald ' you and crush from ' relate ' and took ' concoct ' such ' 6 him to '
' and there`s and ' fire ' thick ' and give and ' 7 and testimony ' all and
' man that ' be`s and ' tomorrow ' Jehovah ' as before ' you perfume ' behold as on
' as son ' relate ' increase ' holy`ing the ' that`ing ' Jehovah ' choose as ' which
' 9 Levi ' as son ' oh ' and hear ' bald ' to ' Moses ' say as and ' 8 Levi
' from are ye ' Israel ' as Allah ' separate`s the ' for ' from with ' less the
' serve of ' him to ' from are ye ' approach`s the of ' Israel ' you congregation
' till`ed the ' as before ' stand of and ' Jehovah ' Tabernacle ' you serve ' ye
' are as brother ' all ' ye and ' are ye ' approach as and ' 10 from minister of
' ye`ed ' so of ' 11 priest`ed ' also ' from you seek and ' are ye ' Levi ' as son
' what ' Aaron and ' Jehovah ' on ' from as season behold ' are testimony ' all and
' call of ' Moses ' send as and ' 12 and Mosthigh ' and stop`ing you ' for ' that`ing
on`ed has ' not ' and say as and ' father as to ' as son ' Abiram of and ' Dathan of
honey and ' milk ' you secrete ' land from ' and give as on the ' for ' less the ' 13

' also ' our as on ' is burst you ' for ' word from in ' and give as them of '

(14 ' honey and ' milk ' you secrete ' land ' to ' not ' anger ' is burst the

' vineyard ' or ' field`ed ' you inherit ' our of ' has set and ' our you came`s the

(15 ' on`ed has ' not ' pick you ' them the ' from as person the ' as has eye the

' to ' pie ' to ' Jehovah ' to ' say as and ' especially ' Moses of ' delay and

' not and ' as you help ' lag ' one ' heass`ing ' not ' from you bestow

(16 ' ye`ed ' bald ' to ' Moses ' say as and ' lag ' one ' ye ' as bad the

' them and ' ye`ed ' Jehovah ' as before ' him the ' are testimony ' all and

(17 from set has and ' and you crush from ' man I ' and took and ' tomorrow ' Aaron and

man I ' Jehovah ' as before ' from you approach the and ' you perfume ' them as on '

' you and crush from ' from as you hundred and ' from as five ' and you crush from '

(18 ' man I ' acquire as and ' and you crush from ' man I ' Aaron and ' ye`ed and

' and site`s and ' fire ' thick ' them as on ' and give as and ' and you crush from

' ing`congregate ' tent ' open ' and stand as and ' you perfume ' them as on

(19 ' all ' ye ' bald ' them as on ' assemble as and ' Aaron and ' Moses and

' honour`ing ' look as and ' ing`congregate ' tent ' open ' to ' till`ed the

(20 to and ' Moses ' to ' Jehovah ' word as and ' till`ed the ' all ' to ' Jehovah

(21 ' such the ' till`ed the ' middle`ing from ' and separate the ' say of ' Aaron '

(22 and say as and ' them around ' on ' and fell and ' hour are ' from ye ' eat`ed and

' one ' man that ' flesh the ' all of ' you and spirit is the ' as Allah ' to '

(23 ' to ' Jehovah ' word as and ' angry you ' till`ed the ' all ' on and ' sin as

(24 ' and on the ' say of ' till`ed the ' to ' word ' say of ' Moses

(25 rise as and ' high as father and ' Dathan ' bald ' Tabernacle of ' surround`s from

' and walk as and ' high as father and ' Dathan ' to ' walk as and ' Moses '

(26 ' say of ' till`ed the ' to ' word as and ' Israel ' as elder ' him after

' from as evil`ness the ' from as person the ' as tent ' above ' oh ' and repent`ing
' and further ' turn ' them of ' which ' all in ' and reach ' to and ' these`ed
' Dathan ' bald ' Tabernacle ' above ' and went and ' 27 from you sin ' all in
' and out ' high as father and ' has decree and ' surround`s from ' high as father and
' them as son and ' them as women and ' them as tent ' open ' from as settle
' for ' has and perceive ' such in ' Moses ' say as and ' 28 from children and
' these`ed ' from as work the ' all ' ye ' you concoct of ' as has send ' Jehovah
' ground the ' all ' die`ing are ' mother ' 29 house of from ' not ' for
' punish as ' ground the ' all ' you my appoint and ' to`ed ' has and die`ing as
' create as ' the create`s ' mother and ' 30 as has send ' Jehovah ' not ' them as on
' from ye ' the worthless and ' edge`ed ' ye ' ground`ed the ' rid`ed and ' Jehovah
' the ask`ing ' from as life ' and up as and ' them of ' which ' all ' ye and
' ye ' these`ed ' from as person the ' and blaspheme ' for ' complete known and
' all ' ye ' word of ' mark and accord ' became as and ' 31 Jehovah
them as under ' which ' ground`ed the ' divide you and ' these`ed ' from as word the
' ye and ' from ye ' worthless you and ' edge`ed ' ye ' land the ' open you and ' 32
' all ' ye and ' Korah of ' which ' ground the ' all ' ye and ' them house`ly
from as life ' them of ' which ' all and ' them ' and up as and ' 33 property`ing the
' and perish as and ' land the ' them as on ' conceal you and ' the ask`ing '
' which ' Israel ' all and ' 34 assemble the ' middle`ing from
' turn ' and say ' for ' ing`crackle of ' sign ' them as you surround`s
' Jehovah ' each ' out`ed ' fire and ' 35 land the ' and has worthless you
' man I ' from as you hundred and ' from as five the ' ye ' eat you and
' Moses ' to ' Jehovah ' word as and ' 36 you perfume the ' as approach`s from
ye ' elevate and ' priest the ' Aaron ' son ' Eleazar ' to ' say ' 37 say of

' stranger`ed ' fire the ' ye and ' burnt`ed the ' son`s from ' you and crush them '
' from as sin the ' you and crush from ' ye ' 38 and holy ' for ' the forward
' char`s ' as expanse`ing ' from ye ' concoct and ' from you soul in ' these`ed
Jehovah ' as before ' from and approach`s the ' for ' sacrifice from of ' overlay`ing
39 ' Israel ' as son of ' loop`ing ' and became as and ' and holy as and '
' you and crush from ' ye ' priest the ' Aaron ' son ' Eleazar ' took as and
' from as burnt`ing the ' and approach`s the ' which ' copper has the
' shall is remember ' 40 sacrifice from of ' overlay`ing ' from and expense as and
' stranger ' man I ' approach as ' not ' which ' purpose of ' Israel ' as son of
' you perfume ' perfume`s the of ' that`ing ' Aaron ' seed from ' not ' which
' and testimony are and ' Korah are ' be`s as ' not and ' Jehovah ' as before
' all ' and stop as and ' 41 if ' Moses ' hand in ' Jehovah ' word ' which are
' Aaron ' on and ' Moses ' on ' you tomorrow from ' Israel ' as son ' testimony
' became as and ' 42 Jehovah ' people ' ye ' from die the ' from ye ' say of
to ' and turn as and ' Aaron ' on and ' Moses ' on ' till`ed the ' assemble thus
' look`ed as and ' cloud the ' and conceal`ed ' be`th and ' ing`congregate ' tent '
' tent ' around ' to ' Aaron and ' Moses ' came as and ' 43 Jehovah ' honour`ing
' advance the ' 45 say of ' Moses ' to ' Jehovah ' word as and ' 44 ing`congregate
' hour are ' from ye ' eat`ed and ' such the ' till`ed the ' middle`ing from
' took ' Aaron ' to ' Moses ' say as and ' 45 them around ' on ' and fell and
' sacrifice them ' above ' fire ' am on ' give and ' crush`ed them ' ye
atone and ' till`ed the ' to ' the soon ' walk alas and ' you perfume ' there`s and
' sick the ' Jehovah ' as before from ' angry the ' out ' for ' them as on '
to ' run as and ' Moses ' word ' which are ' Aaron ' took as and ' 47 defeat the
' people in ' defeat the ' sick the ' be`th and ' assemble the ' middle`ing '

(48 ' people the ' on ' atone as and ' you perfume the ' ye ' give as and

' from as life the ' between in and ' from as die the ' between in ' stand as and

' from as die the ' and became as and ' (49 pestilence`ed the ' festival you and

' you and hundred ' seven and ' thousand ' ten ' the four I ' pestilence`ed in

' to ' Aaron ' dwell and ' (50 bald ' word ' on ' from as die the ' alone of from

' pestilence`ed the and ' ing`congregate ' tent ' open ' to ' Moses

the festival has

' as son ' to ' word ' (2 say of ' Moses ' to ' Jehovah ' word as and ' (1
' each ' father ' you house of ' down`ed ' down`ed ' spy from ' ercort ' Israel
' ten ' from two ' from you and father ' you house of ' them as help`s ' all
' ye and ' (3 and staff from ' on ' write you ' name ' ye ' man I ' you and down
head of ' one ' down`ed ' for ' Levi ' down`ed ' on ' write you ' Aaron ' there
' ing`congregate ' tent in ' from bring the and ' (4 from you and father ' you house '
' be`s and ' (5 there`ed ' relate ' season I ' which ' testimony`ing the ' as before
' as hedge the and ' bud as ' and staff from ' and in ' choose I ' which ' man that
' them ' which ' Israel ' as son ' you and obstinate ' ye ' as on from
' as son ' to ' Moses ' word as and ' (6 from are mosthigh ' from as stop from
' help`s of ' down`ed ' them as help`s ' all ' him to ' and give as and ' Israel
' from two ' from you and father ' you house of ' one ' help`s of ' down`ed ' one
(7 from you and down ' middle`ing in ' Aaron ' staff from and ' you and down ' ten
' tent in ' Jehovah ' as before ' you and down the ' ye ' Moses ' rest as and '
to ' Moses ' came as and ' you tomorrow from ' became as and ' (8 testimony`ing the
' you house of ' Aaron ' down`ed ' bud ' be`th and ' testimony`ing the ' tent '
(9 from as nut ' wean as and ' flower`s ' flower as and ' bud ' issue him and ' Levi
' Jehovah ' as before from ' you and down the ' all ' ye ' Moses ' issue him and '
and staff from ' man I ' acquire as and ' see as and ' Israel ' as son ' all ' to
' Aaron ' down`ed ' ye ' carry the ' Moses ' to ' Jehovah ' say as and ' (10
' rebellion ' as son of ' loop`ing ' you guard from of ' testimony`ing the ' as before
' (11 and die`ing as ' not and ' as on from ' complete and stop you ' perfect and
' (12 do`ed ' so ' and ye ' Jehovah ' command`ed ' which are ' Moses ' do as and
' behold ' say of ' Moses ' to ' Israel ' as son ' and say as and
' all ' (13 and has perish ' and has all ' and has perish ' and has expire`ing

' maid ' die him ' Jehovah ' Tabernacle ' to ' approach`ing the ' approach the

expire`ing of ' and portion

' you house and ' are as son and ' ye`ed ' Aaron ' to ' Jehovah ' say as and ' 1

' ye`ed and ' holy them ' low`ing ' ye ' and lift you ' are ye ' are as father

2 ' from are you priest ' low`ing ' ye ' and lift you ' are ye ' are as son and

' are as father ' tribe ' Levi ' down`ed ' are as brother ' ye ' also and

' are and minister as and ' are as on ' If `ing as and ' are ye ' approach the

3 ' testimony`ing the ' tent ' as before ' are ye ' are as son and ' ye`ed and

to ' sure ' tent the ' all ' and guard from and ' are you guard from ' and guard and

' not and ' and approach as ' not ' sacrifice them ' to and ' holy the ' weapon '

' are as on ' if `ing has and ' 4 from ye ' also ' them ' also ' and die`ing as

' you serve ' all of ' ing`congregate ' tent ' you guard from ' ye ' and guard and

' from you guard and ' 5 your as to ' approach as ' not ' stranger and ' tent the

not and ' sacrifice them ' you guard from ' ye and ' holy the ' you guard from ' ye

' be`th ' as whither and ' 6 Israel ' as son ' on ' angry ' till`ing ' be`s as '

' as son ' middle`ing from ' from Levi the ' your as brother ' ye ' as you take

' ye ' serve of ' Jehovah of ' from as gave ' the present ' relate ' Israel

' are ye ' are as son and ' ye`ed and ' 7 ing`congregate ' tent ' you serve

' sacrifice them ' word ' all of ' from are you priest ' ye ' and guard you

' the present ' you serve ' complete serve and ' veil put of ' you house from of and

8 ' die him ' approach the ' stranger the and ' from are you priest ' ye ' donkey

' walk ' as set has ' be`th ' as whither and ' Aaron ' to ' Jehovah ' word as and

' Israel ' as son ' as holy ' all of ' as you oblation`ing ' you guard from ' ye

9 ' from on`ing ' law of ' are as son of and ' anoint`ed of ' from as set has ' walk

' all ' fire the ' has from ' from as holy the ' as holy from ' walk ' be`s as ' this

all of and ' from you sin ' all of and ' from you bestow ' all of ' from has approach

' holy ' vessel ' and carry`s as ' and guity`s as ' which ' from guilty '

' from as holy the ' holy in ' 10 are as son of and ' that`ing ' walk ' from as holy
this and ' 11 walk ' be`s as ' holy ' and ye ' eat as ' male ' all ' and has eat you
' as son ' you wave`ing you ' all of ' from present ' you oblation`ing ' walk '
' are as daughter`th of and ' are as son of and ' from as set has ' walk ' Israel
and ye ' eat as ' are you house in ' clean`ing ' all ' from on`ing ' law of ' are ye
' grain and ' possess`ing you ' milk ' all and ' Izhar ' milk ' all ' 12
' 13 from as set has ' walk ' Jehovah of ' and give as ' which ' from you as head
' Jehovah of ' and came`s as ' which ' from land in ' which ' all ' as first`ing
curse ' all ' 14 and has eat as ' are you house in ' clean`ing ' all ' be`s as ' walk
which ' flesh ' all of ' compassion ' emit ' all ' 15 be`s as ' walk ' Israel in '
sure ' walk ' be`s as ' cattle`ed in and ' Men in ' Jehovah of ' and approach`s as '
' first`ing ' ye and ' ground the ' first`ing ' ye ' pardon`ed ' release`ed '
new ' son from ' him and release and ' 16 pardon`ed ' unclean`ed the ' cattle`ed the
' holy the ' weigh in ' from as weigh ' you five ' silver ' are pile in ' pardon`ed '
' or ' captain`ing ' first`ing ' sure ' 17 that`ing ' guest`ed ' from as ten
ye ' them ' holy ' pardon`ed ' not ' harsh ' first`ing ' or ' sheep ' first`ing
' from milk ' ye and ' sacrifice them ' on ' sprinkle you ' from blood '
' from flesh and ' 18 Jehovah of ' odor has ' smell`s of ' Woman ' perfume`s you
' right`s the ' hip`ing and ' the wave`ing scared ' vision`ed are ' walk ' be`s as
and elevate`s ' which ' from as holy the ' you oblation`ing ' all ' 19 be`s as ' walk
' are as son of and ' walk ' as set has ' Jehovah of ' Israel ' as son '
' salt ' covenant`s ' from on`ing ' law of ' are ye ' are as daughter`th of and
' 20 are ye ' are seed of and ' walk ' Jehovah ' as before ' that`ing ' from on`ing
' part and ' inherit you ' not ' from land in ' Aaron ' to ' Jehovah ' say as and
' are part ' as whither ' from middle`ing in ' walk ' be`s as ' not

’ Levi ’ as son of and ’ 21 Israel ’ as son ’ middle`ing in ’ are you inherit and
’ lock ’ inherit`ed of ’ Israel in ’ ten from ’ all ’ as set has ’ be`th
’ tent ’ you serve ’ ye ’ from as serve ’ them ’ which ’ from you serve
’ to ’ Israel ’ as son ’ till`ing ’ and approach as ’ not and ’ 22 ing`congregate
’ Levi the ’ serve and ’ 23 die`ing of ’ sin ’ arise of ’ ing`congregate ’ tent
’ and linger ’ them and ’ ing`congregate ’ tent ’ you serve ’ ye ’ that`ing
’ middle`ing in and ’ from are as generation of ’ from on`ing ’ statute ’ from low`ing
’ ten from ’ ye ’ for ’ 24 inherit`ed ’ and inherit as ’ not ’ Israel ’ as son
’ the oblation`ing ’ Jehovah of ’ and elevate`s ’ which ’ Israel ’ as son
’ them of ’ as you say ’ so ’ on ’ inherit`ed of ’ from Levi of ’ and as set has
word as and ’ 25 inherit`ed ’ and inherit as ’ not ’ Israel ’ as son ’ middle`ing in
’ word you ’ from Levi the ’ to and ’ 26 say of ’ Moses ’ to ’ Jehovah ’
’ ye ’ Israel ’ as son ’ each ’ and took you ’ for ’ them as to ’ you say and
’ from are as you inherit in ’ spy from ’ relate ’ as set has ’ which ’ ten them
’ ten from ’ Jehovah ’ you oblation`ing ’ ye ’ and her from ’ from you high the and
’ from are you oblation`ing ’ relate ’ reckon has and ’ 27 ten them ’ has from
28 press the ’ has from ’ fill`ed are and ’ threshingfloor the ’ has from ’ grain are
’ all from ’ Jehovah ’ you oblation`ing ’ from ye ’ also ’ and oblation`s ’ so ’
’ Israel ’ as son ’ each ’ and took you ’ which ’ from are as you ten from
’ Aaron of ’ Jehovah ’ you oblation`ing ’ ye ’ and her from ’ from set has and
’ all ’ ye ’ and oblation`s ’ from are as you present ’ all from ’ 29 priest the
and her from ’ and holy from ’ ye ’ and milk ’ all from ’ Jehovah ’ you oblation`ing
and her from ’ and milk ’ ye ’ from are high`s thus ’ them as to ’ you say and ’ 30
’ threshingfloor ’ you income`ing are ’ from Levi of ’ reckon has and ’
’ place`ing ’ all in ’ and ye ’ from you eat and ’ 31 press ’ you income`ing are and

' lock ' relate ' that`ing ' merry ' for ' from are you house and ' from ye
' and lift you ' not and ' 32 ing`congregate ' tent in ' from are you serve
ye and ' and her from ' and milk ' ye ' from are high`s thus ' sin ' and Mosthigh
and die`ing you ' not and ' and profane you ' not ' Israel ' as son ' as holy '

' such ' 2 say of ' Aaron ' to and ' Moses ' to ' Jehovah ' word as and ' 1
to ' word ' say of ' Jehovah ' command`ed ' which ' the protect`ing the ' statute
' ground`ed ' apart`ed ' are as to ' acquire as and ' Israel ' as son '
on`ed ' not ' which and ' they`ing ' thus ' whither`s ' which ' the from as complete
' priest the ' Eleazar ' to ' ye`ed ' from set has and ' 3 on`ing ' am on '
' ye`ed ' slay and ' camp`ed of ' outside`ing from ' to ' ye`ed ' issue`s alas and
' and finger came ' blood`ed from ' priest the ' Eleazar ' take and ' 4 him before
' blood`ed from ' ing`congregate ' tent ' around ' behalf ' to ' this the and
ye ' and as has eye of ' bullock`ed the ' ye ' burnt and ' 5 from as move ' seven
' the excrement ' on ' blood`ed ' ye and ' flesh`ed ' ye and ' the town`ing '
' two and ' hyssop`ing and ' cedar ' tree ' priest the ' take and ' 6 burnt as
7 bullock`ed the ' you burnt ' middle`ing ' to ' hurl`s the and ' you have hang`ing
' Water in ' and flesh ' ye ' wash and ' priest the ' him fabric ' immersion and '
' till ' priest the ' unclean and ' camp`ed the ' to ' came`ing as ' after and
' Water in ' him fabric ' immersion as ' ye`ed ' burnt the and ' 8 twilight the
' 9 twilight the ' till ' unclean and ' Water in ' and flesh ' ye ' wash and
' rest`s the and ' bullock`ed the ' ashes ' ye ' clean`ing ' man I ' gather and
' whom`ed the and ' clean`ing ' place`ing in ' camp`ed of ' outside`ing from
' you sin ' wander`ed ' kind ' you guard from of ' Israel ' as son ' testimony of
' ye ' bullock`ed the ' ashes ' ye ' gather the ' immersion and ' 10 that`s
' as son of ' whom`ed the and ' twilight the ' till ' unclean and ' him fabric
' 11 from on`ing ' statute of ' from middle`ing in ' abide ' guest of and ' Israel
from week ' you seven ' unclean as and ' ground ' soul ' all of ' die in ' touch the
' day as in and ' as three`s the ' day as in ' and in ' sin whom ' that`ing ' 12
' day as in ' sin whom ' not ' mother and ' clean as and ' as seven`s the

touch the ' all ' 13 clean as ' not ' as seven`s the ' day as in and ' as three`s the
' ye ' sin whom ' not and ' die`ing as ' which ' ground the ' soul in ' die in '
Israel from ' that`s the ' soul the ' hew`ed shall ' unclean ' Jehovah ' Tabernacle
' be`s as ' unclean ' and Mosthigh ' sprinkle ' not ' wander`ed ' who ' for '
for ' ground ' the protect`ing the ' such and ' 14 and in ' and you unclean ' till`ing
tent in ' which ' all and ' tent the ' to ' came the ' all ' tent in ' die`ing as '
' which ' open`ing ' weapon ' all and ' 15 from week ' you seven ' unclean as '
' all and ' 16 that`ing ' unclean ' and Mosthigh ' lace`s and ' bracelet`s ' whither`s
die in ' or ' desolate ' of sick in ' field`ed the ' around ' on ' faint ' which
' 17 from week ' you seven ' unclean as ' bury in ' or ' ground ' might in ' or '
' and gave and ' you sin the ' you burnt ' dust from ' unclean of ' and take and
' hyssop`ing ' take and ' 18 weapon ' to ' from as life ' Water ' and Mosthigh
all ' on and ' tent the ' on ' this the and ' clean`ing ' man I ' Water in ' dip and
on and ' there ' him the ' which ' you and soul the ' on and ' from vessal are the '
' 19 bury in ' or ' die in ' or ' of sick in ' or ' might in ' touch the '
' as three`s the ' day as in ' unclean the ' on ' clean`ing the ' this the and
' as seven`s the ' day as in ' and sin and ' as seven`s the ' day as in and
' 20 twilight in ' clean and ' Water in ' wash and ' him fabric ' immersion and
' soul the ' hew`ed shall ' sin whom ' not and ' unclean as ' which ' man that and
' Jehovah ' holy from ' ye ' for ' assemble the ' middle`ing from ' that`s the
' 21 that`ing ' unclean ' and Mosthigh ' sprinkle ' not ' wander`ed ' who ' unclean
' who ' victual`ed and ' from on`ing ' statute of ' them of ' whom`ed the and
' wander`ed the ' who in ' touch the and ' him fabric ' immersion as ' wander`ed the
unclean the ' and in ' faint ' which ' all and ' 22 twilight the ' till ' unclean as
twilight the ' till ' unclean you ' you touch the ' soul the and ' unclean as '

' thorn ' word from ' till`ed the ' all ' Israel ' as son ' and came as and ' (1
there ' die you and ' holy in ' people the ' dwell and ' has and head`s the ' new in
' till`ed of ' Water ' be`s ' not and ' (2 there ' bury you and ' Miriam '
' people the ' contend and ' (3 Aaron ' on and ' Moses ' on ' and assemble as and
' and has expire`ing ' Levi and ' say of ' and say as and ' Moses ' people
' what of and ' (4 Jehovah ' as before ' our as brother ' expire`ing in
' this the ' is wilderness the ' to ' Jehovah ' assemble ' ye ' from you came the
' what of and ' (5 and has burn`s and ' and us I ' there ' die`ing of
' to ' and has ye ' came`s the of ' from as Mizra from ' and give as on the
' the Fig and ' seed ' place`ing ' not ' this the ' mischief ' place`ing the
' came as and ' (6 laid`ing of ' whither`s ' Water and ' pomegranate`ing and ' vine and
ing`congregate ' tent ' open ' to ' assemble the ' around from ' Aaron and ' Moses
them as to ' Jehovah ' honour`ing ' look as and ' them around ' on ' and fell and '
' down`ed the ' ye ' took ' (8 say of ' Moses ' to ' Jehovah ' word as and ' (7
' are as brother ' Aaron and ' ye`ed ' till`ed the ' ye ' assemble the and
' him Water ' gave and ' them as has eye of ' rock the ' to ' from you word and
' ye ' drunk`s the and ' rock the ' has from ' Water ' them of ' you spring the and
' down`ed the ' ye ' Moses ' took as and ' (9 from town`s in ' ye and ' till`ed the
Moses ' and assemble as and ' (10 and command`ed ' which are ' Jehovah ' as before from
' them of ' say as and ' rock the ' around ' to ' assemble the ' ye ' Aaron and '
' spring`s has ' this the ' rock the ' has them ' from as drop the ' oh ' and hear
' ye ' struck and ' and hand ' ye ' Moses ' elevate and ' (11 Water ' relate
' from as increase ' Water ' and out and ' from as move ' and staff from in ' rock the
' to ' Jehovah ' say as and ' (12 from town`s in and ' till`ed the ' drink you and
' house ' from you believe the ' not ' because ' Aaron ' to and ' Moses

' not ' so of ' Israel ' as son ' as has eye of ' as has holy`s the of
' which ' land the ' to ' this the ' assemble the ' ye ' and came`s you
' as son ' million ' which ' the much`s ' who ' them`ed ' (13) them of ' as set has
' as master ' Moses ' say as and ' height ' holy as and ' Jehovah ' ye ' Israel
are great ' ye ' are serve ' ye ' sight`ing the of ' you block ' ye`ed ' Jehovah
land in and ' heaven`s in ' all ' who ' which ' strength`ed the ' are hand ' ye and '
' cross I ' are as you strong`ing are and ' are as work are ' success`ed ' which '
' cross in ' which ' the good`ing the ' land the ' ye ' look`ed I and ' oh
' has and white the and ' this the ' good`ing the ' mountain the ' has desend the
' word ' yield you ' to ' walk ' increase ' Moses ' to ' Jehovah ' say as and
lift and ' cleft`ed the ' head ' to ' on`ed ' this the ' word in ' till`ing ' Eli
emerge`ed from and ' right`ed you and ' the north`ing and ' sea`ed ' are as has eye '
' has desend the ' ye ' cross you ' not ' for ' are as has eye in ' look`ed and '
' and strength`ed and ' Nun ' son ' ed`Joshua`ing ' ye ' command`ed and ' this the
' this the ' people the ' as before ' cross as ' that`ing ' for ' and harden`ed and
' (14) saw`ed ' which ' land the ' ye ' from ye ' inherit`s as ' that`ing and
' ye ' away`ing ' relate ' increase ' say of ' Moses ' to ' Jehovah ' word as and
' people the ' ye and ' the north`ing ' relate ' and turn ' this the ' mountain the
' your as brother ' border`ing in ' from as Obara ' from ye ' say of ' command`ed
from with ' and dread as and ' barley`s in ' from as sojourn became ' concoct ' as son
' not ' for ' height ' and guest set ' to ' especially ' from you guard has and '
for ' foot ' palm ' way from ' till ' the possess ' from land from ' relate ' donkey
' eat ' gate`s ' mountain ' ye ' as set has ' Esau of ' the possess '
' Water ' also and ' from you eat and ' silver in ' spy from ' and buy`s you
' send as and ' from you as drink and ' silver in ' spy from ' and pasture`s you

' say ' here ' Edom ' king ' to ' holy from ' from as messenger from ' Moses
' which ' travail`ed the ' all ' ye ' you known ' ye`ed ' Israel ' are as brother
carry has and ' the from as Mizra ' our as you father ' and up as and ' 15 our you come
' our of ' and evil`s as and ' from as increase ' from week ' from as Mizra in '
' Jehovah ' to ' cry has and ' 16 our as you father of and ' from as Mizra the
' our spring as and ' messenger from ' send as and ' our voice`ing ' hear as and
are border`ing ' end`ed ' town`s ' holy in ' and us I ' be`th and ' from as Mizra from
' field`ed in ' cross has ' not ' are land in ' oh ' cross`ed has ' 17
' king the ' way ' well`ing ' who ' the drink has ' not and ' vineyard in and
which ' till ' of and left and ' right`s ' marshal`ing ' permit`ed ' not ' walk has
' cross you ' not ' Edom ' him to ' say as and ' 18 are border`ing ' cross has '
' him to ' and say as and ' 19 are you call of ' proceed ' desolate in ' turn ' house
' are as Water ' mother and ' on`ed has ' the path in ' Israel ' as son
' only ' vineyard from ' as set has and ' as purchase and ' as whither ' the drink has
' cross you ' not ' say as and ' 20 cross`ed I ' as foot in ' word ' whither`s
the strength ' hand in and ' honour ' people in ' and you call of ' Edom ' out and
' and border`ing in ' Obara ' Israel ' ye ' gave ' Edom ' refuse as and ' 21
' and came as and ' holy from ' leave as and ' 22 him on from ' Israel ' extent and
' say as and ' 23 mountain the ' mountain ' till`ed the ' all ' Israel ' as son
border`ing ' on ' mountain the ' blemish ' Aaron ' to and ' Moses ' to ' Jehovah
' not ' for ' him people ' to ' Aaron ' gather as ' 24 say of ' Edom ' land '
' on ' Israel ' as son of ' as set has ' which ' land the ' to ' came`ing as
Aaron ' ye ' took ' 25 the much`s ' kind ' edge ' ye ' from you rebell ' which
' 26 mountain the ' mountain ' from ye ' on the and ' and son ' Eleazar ' ye and '
' ye ' from you arm the and ' him fabric ' ye ' Aaron ' ye ' you pull the and

' do as and ' 27 there ' die as and ' gather as ' Aaron and ' and son ' Eleazar
' mountain ' to ' and went`ed and ' Jehovah ' command`ed ' which are ' Moses
' ye ' Moses ' pull as and ' 28 till`ed the ' all ' as has eye of ' mountain the
' and son ' Eleazar ' ye ' from ye ' arm as and ' him fabric ' ye ' Aaron
' Moses ' descend and ' mountain the ' head in ' there ' Aaron ' die as and
' for ' till`ed the ' all ' see as and ' 29 mountain the ' has from ' Eleazar and
' all ' day as ' from as three ' Aaron ' ye ' and wept and ' Aaron ' expire`ing
Israel ' you house

' came ' for ' south the ' dwell ' Arad ' king ' as Canaan the ' hear as and ' 1
' dwell and ' Israel in ' fight as and ' from as area the ' way ' Israel
' Jehovah of ' vow ' Israel ' evermore as and ' 2 captive ' and her from
' as hand in ' this the ' people the ' ye ' has set ' gave ' mother ' say as and
' voice ing in ' Jehovah ' hear as and ' 3 them as town ' ye ' as you curse the and
them ye ' curse as and ' and hand in ' as Canaan the ' ye ' give as and ' Israel
' 4 curse ed ' place ing the ' there ' call as and ' them as town ' ye and '
' surround of ' join ing ' sea ' way ' mountain the ' mountain from ' leave as and
' word as and ' 5 way in ' people the ' soul ' reap you and ' Edom ' land ' ye
' and has you issue alas ' what of ' Moses in and ' from as Allah in ' people the
whither s ' for ' word from in ' die ing of ' from as Mizra from ' and give as on the
' from bread in ' end ed ' and has soul and ' Water ' whither s and ' fight '
' from as serpent the ' ye ' people in ' Jehovah ' send as and ' 6 of vile the
' people ' die as and ' people the ' ye ' and seize as and ' from as burnt the
' and say as and ' Moses ' to ' people the ' came as and ' 7 Israel from ' increase
' Jehovah ' to ' praise sacred ' jungle ' Jehovah in ' our word ' for ' and has sin
' Moses ' praise whom and ' serpent the ' ye ' our as on from ' repent as and
' walk ' do ed ' Moses ' to ' Jehovah ' say as and ' 8 people the ' till in
' seize ing the ' all ' be s and ' flee the ' on ' and ye ' there s and ' burnt ing
' copper has ' serpent ' Moses ' do as and ' 9 life and ' and ye ' look ed and
ye ' serpent the ' seize ' mother ' be s and ' flee the ' on ' and there ed as and
' 10 life and ' copper has the ' serpent ' to ' scan s the and ' man that '
leave as and ' 11 you and father in ' and encamp and ' Israel ' as son ' leave as and
' word from in ' from as Obara the ' eye s in ' and encamp and ' Oboth ing from '
to ' Jehovah ' say as and ' sun the ' emerge they ' Moab ' around ' on ' which

' for ' height ' guest set ' to and ' Moab ' ye ' besiege`ing ' to ' Moses '
' Lot ' as son of ' for ' the possess ' and land from ' walk ' donkey ' not
' and encamp and ' and go ' there from ' 12 the possess ' town ' ye ' as set has
' word ' ye`ed ' say of ' Moses ' to ' Jehovah ' word as and ' shrub ' inherit in
split`ing ' you appoach and ' town ' ye ' Moab ' border`ing ' ye ' day as the
' for ' height ' guest set ' to and ' from besiege`ing ' to ' Moab ' as son '
' as son of ' for ' the possess ' walk ' Moab ' as son ' land from ' donkey ' not
shrub ' inherit from ' and go as and ' there from ' 13 the possess ' am set has ' Lot
' ye ' which ' has and stream ' cross in from ' and encamp and '
' for ' as Amar the ' border`ing from ' spring as the ' is wilderness in the
' between in and ' Moab ' between in ' Moab ' border`ing ' has and stream
ye ' Jehovah ' you and fight from ' report in ' say as ' so ' on ' 14 as Amar the
' 15 has and stream ' from as inherit the ' ye and ' the join`ing in ' attain '
' town`s ' desist of ' permit`ed ' which ' from as inherit`s the ' which and
' that`s ' the well ' there from and ' 16 Moab ' border`ing of ' stay has and
' ye ' vessel ' the gather ' Moses ' to ' Jehovah ' say ' which ' well the
ye ' Israel ' is gift as ' yet ' 17 Water ' them of ' the give I and ' people the
' well ' 18 nihil ' blind`th ' well ' mosthigh ' such the ' the is gift the '
' people the ' as bear`s has ' conceive`ing are ' from as captain ' conceive`ing pure
19 the present ' is wilderness from and ' from you stay from in and ' pressibe from in
' 20 die`ing in ' to as inherit from and ' to as inherit ' the present from and '
' head ' Moab ' field`ed in ' which ' I nation the ' you and height from and
' say as and ' has and site`s the ' around ' on ' gaze`ed shall ' cleft`ed the
' inherit ' ye ' and word and ' leave ' and rise`ing ' Moses ' to ' Jehovah
shall reckon ' king ' Sihon`ing ' ye ' are hand in ' as set has ' look`ed ' Arnon

' and in ' strife the and ' vemon ' sick the ' and land ' ye and ' as Amar the '
' are startle ' ye ' sick I ' this the ' day as the ' fight`ed from
' heaven`s the ' all ' under ' from as people the ' around ' on ' are you dread and
' and sick and ' and tremble and ' are hear ' ye ' and hear as ' which
Sihon`ing ' to ' from as messenger from ' Israel ' send as and ' (21 are around from
' cross`ed I ' (22 say of ' from and peace ' as word ' as Amar the ' king '
' of left and ' right`s ' bound`ing ' not ' walk I ' king the ' way in ' are land in
' who ' the drink has ' not ' vineyard in and ' field`ed in ' permit`ed I ' not
' are border ' cross has ' which ' till ' walk has ' king the ' way in ' well
' silver in ' Water and ' as you eat and ' as has buy`s you ' silver in ' walk I
' which are ' as border in ' word`ed I ' only ' as whom drink and ' vessel ' has set
' barley`s in ' from as sojourn became ' concoct ' as son ' vessel ' concoct
Sihon`ing ' gave ' not and ' (23 burn ' from as sojourn became ' from as Moab the and
' Moses ' to ' Jehovah ' say as and ' and border`ing in ' Obara ' Israel ' ye '
' ye and ' Sihon`ing ' ye ' are as before ' set ' as you sick the ' look`ed
' gather as and ' and land ' ye ' net`ness of ' vemon ' sick the ' and land
word`ed them ' Israel ' you call of ' out and ' and people ' all ' ye ' Sihon`ing
Israel ' and struck`ed and ' (24 Israel in ' fight as and ' stamp`ed ' came as and '
' desolate ' as by ' and people ' all ' ye and ' him son ' ye and '
as son ' till ' spew ' till ' has stream from ' and land ' ye ' and possess as and
' Israel ' took as and ' (25 Ammon ' as son ' border`ing ' harsh ' for ' Ammon '
' watch ' all in ' Israel ' dwell and ' these`ed ' from as town the ' all ' ye
' shall reckon ' for ' (26 am you son ' all in and ' shall reckon in ' as Amar the
' fight has the ' that`ing and ' that`s ' as Amar the ' king ' Sihon`ing ' town`s
' and land ' all ' ye ' took as and ' has and head`s the ' Moab ' king in

' from as rule the ' and say as ' so ' on ' 27 Arnon ' till ' and hand from
28 Sihon`ing ' town`s ' has equal`ing you and ' the son you ' shall reckon ' him came
' Sihon`ing ' city`s from ' the bright ' shall reckon from ' out`ed ' fire ' for '
' walk ' hence`ing ' 29 Arnon ' die`ing in ' as on in ' Moab ' town ' the eat
' from as escape`s ' him son ' gave ' huge`ing ' people ' you perish ' Moab
' 30 Sihon`ing ' as Amar the ' king of ' desist`s in ' him you son and
' has and bear`s ' till ' shall reckon ' the perish ' substance has and
' dwell and ' 31 I in mete`s ' till ' which ' Nophah the ' till ' there`s has and
' foot of ' Moses ' send as and ' 32 as Amar the ' land in ' as town in ' Israel
' ye ' and occupy`s as and ' am you son ' and capture as and ' aid as ' ye
shameful the ' way ' and went and ' and turn as and ' 33 there ' which ' as Amar the
' all and ' that`ing ' from you call of ' shameful the ' king ' bake`ing ' out and '
' Moses ' to ' Jehovah ' say as and ' 34 as force I ' fight`ed from of ' and people
all ' ye and ' and ye ' as set has ' are hand in ' for ' and ye ' look as you ' to
' you as do ' which are ' if ' dual`s and ' and land ' ye and ' and people '
' 35 shall reckon in ' sojourn as ' which ' as Amar the ' king ' Sihon`ing of
' till ' and people ' all ' ye and ' him son ' ye and ' and ye ' and struck and
and land ' ye ' and possess as and ' survivor`s ' if ' remain`s the ' as zero in

’ Moab ’ you and in town in ’ and encamp and ’ Israel ’ as son ’ leave as and ’ 1

bird`ing ’ son ’ smooth in ’ look as and ’ 2 and moon`s ’ has descend of ’ cross from

’ Moab ’ guest as and ’ 3 as say of ’ Israel ’ do`ed ’ which ’ all ’ ye ’

’ awake and ’ that`ing ’ increase ’ for ’ especially ’ people the ’ around from

as elder ’ to ’ Moab ’ say as and ’ 4 Israel ’ as son ’ around from ’ Moab

’ all ’ ye ’ this the ’ assemble the ’ and are bread as ’ time`ed ’ Midian ’

’ field`ed the ’ green ’ ye ’ Ox`ing the ’ are bread are ’ our as you surround`s

send as and ’ 5 that`s the ’ time in ’ Moab of ’ king ’ bird`ing ’ son ’ Balak and

’ the protect`ing put ’ burn`ing ’ son ’ Balaam ’ to ’ from as messenger from ’

be`th ’ say of ’ if ’ call of ’ Ammon ’ as son ’ land ’ river the ’ on ’ which

’ has eye ’ ye ’ conceal`ed ’ be`th and ’ from as Mizra from ’ out ’ people ’

oh ’ walk`ed ’ the time and ’ 6 as split`ing from ’ dwell ’ that`ing and ’ land the

’ that`ing ’ might`ing ’ for ’ this the ’ people the ’ ye ’ vessel ’ light`ed ’

’ and has exact I and ’ and in ’ strike`ed ’ able I ’ as maybe I ’ apportion from

’ bless from ’ bless you ’ which ’ ye ’ as you known ’ for ’ land the ’ has from

’ Moab ’ as elder ’ and walk as and ’ 7 channel and ’ figure ’ which ’ ye and

to ’ and came as and ’ from hand in ’ them as determine and ’ Midian ’ as elder and

them as to ’ say as and ’ 8 smooth in ’ as word ’ him to ’ and word as and ’ Balaam ’

’ word ’ from are ye ’ as desist the and ’ the night`s the ’ talk ’ and stop`s ’

people ’ Moab ’ as captain ’ and dwell and ’ Eli ’ Jehovah ’ word as ’ which are

’ who`ed ’ say as and ’ Balaam ’ to ’ from as Allah ’ came as and ’ 9 Balaam ’

’ to ’ Balaam ’ say as and ’ 10 are people ’ these`ed ’ from as person the

’ 11 Eli ’ send ’ Moab ’ king ’ bird`ing ’ son ’ smooth in ’ from as Allah the

’ has eye ’ ye ’ conceal as and ’ from as Mizra from ’ out the ’ people the ’ be`th

able I ’ as maybe I ’ and ye ’ vessel ’ hollow`ed ’ walk`ed ’ the time and ’ land the

’ to ’ from as Allah ’ say as and ’ 12 him you exact and ’ and in ’ fight the of ’
’ for ’ people the ’ ye ’ figure ’ not and ’ them people ’ walk you ’ not ’ Balaam
’ to ’ say as and ’ is morn in ’ Balaam ’ rise as and ’ 13 that`ing ’ bless`ing
’ Jehovah ’ refuse ’ for ’ from are land ’ to ’ follow ’ smooth in ’ as captain
Moab ’ as captain ’ and rise`ing as and ’ 14 your people ’ walk the of ’ as set of
’ walk the ’ Balaam ’ refuse ’ and say as and ’ smooth in ’ to ’ and came as and ’
’ from as captain ’ send ’ smooth in ’ till`ing ’ add and ’ 15 our people
’ to ’ and came as and ’ 16 to`ed from ’ from as honour has and ’ from as increase
’ to ’ bird`ing ’ son ’ smooth in ’ say ’ here ’ if ’ and say as and ’ Balaam
’ especially ’ are honour I ’ honour ’ for ’ 17 Eli ’ walk the from ’ Timma ’ oh
vessel ’ hollow`ed ’ oh ’ the all and ’ do`ed I ’ Eli ’ say you ’ which ’ all and
as serve ’ to ’ say as and ’ Balaam ’ low as and ’ 18 this the ’ people the ’ ye ’
’ and you house ’ fill`ing ’ smooth in ’ vessel ’ permanent ’ mother ’ smooth in ’
’ as Allah ’ Jehovah ’ edge ’ ye ’ cross of ’ able I ’ not ’ gold ’ or ’ silver
’ oh ’ sparkle ’ the time and ’ 19 the great`ing ’ or ’ the small ’ you concoct of
’ Jehovah ’ add ’ what ’ the know and ’ the night`s the ’ from ye ’ also ’ spoil`ed
’ Balaam ’ to ’ from as Allah ’ messenger from ’ came as and ’ 20 as people ’ word
’ and came ’ walk ’ call of ’ mother ’ if ’ say as and ’ the night`s
’ which ’ word the ’ ye ’ sure and ’ from ye ’ walk ’ rise`ing ’ from as person the
’ is morn in ’ Balaam ’ rise as and ’ 21 do`ed you ’ and ye ’ are as to ’ word I
’ 22 Moab ’ as captain ’ people ’ walk as and ’ and has ye ’ ye ’ saddle as and
’ that`ing ’ ing`enter ’ for ’ from as Allah ’ Jehovah ’ anger ’ delay and
that`ing and ’ if ’ accurse of ’ way in ’ Jehovah ’ messenger from ’ reside whom and
’ look you and ’ 23 and people ’ him youth ’ two and ’ and has ye ’ on ’ ride ’
and desolate and ’ way in ’ settle ’ Jehovah ’ messenger from ’ ye ’ donkey`ing the

' way the ' has from ' donkey`ing the ' stretch and ' and hand in ' the extract`ing '
' donkey`ing the ' ye ' Balaam ' struck and ' field`ed in ' are hang and
' Jehovah ' messenger from ' stand as and ' 24 way the ' the slope`ing of
' fence and ' victual`ed ' fence ' from as vineyard the ' recess`ing from in
' Jehovah ' messenger from ' ye ' donkey`ing the ' look you and ' 25 victual`ed
to ' Balaam ' foot ' ye ' affict you and ' is stedfast the ' to ' affict you and
' messenger from ' Joseph and ' 26 the contrary`ing of ' add and ' is stedfast the '
' whither`s ' which ' boulder ' place`ing in ' stand as and ' cross`ing ' Jehovah
donkey`ing the ' look you and ' 27 of and left and ' right`s ' bend`ing has of ' way
' delay and ' Balaam ' under ' crouch you and ' Jehovah ' messenger from ' ye '
' open as and ' 28 stick in ' donkey`ing the ' ye ' struck and ' Balaam ' anger
' what ' Balaam ' to ' say you and ' donkey`ing the ' edge ' ye ' Jehovah
' 29 from as foot ' three ' this ' as has whom smitten ' for ' walk ' as whom do
man ' if ' house ' you endeavour sacred ' for ' donkey`ing of ' Balaam ' say as and
' say you and ' 30 are as you kill ' time`ed ' for ' as hand in ' desolate '
' which ' are donkey ' for whither ' forward`ing ' Balaam ' to ' donkey`ing the
' scarce be ' this the ' day as the ' till ' are till`ing from ' mosthigh ' you ride
' exile and ' 31 not ' say as and ' here ' walk ' you concoct of ' as you scarce the
Jehovah ' messenger from ' ye ' look as and ' Balaam ' as has eye ' ye ' Jehovah
' stoop as and ' and hand in ' the extract`ing ' and desolate and ' way in ' settle '
' messenger from ' him to ' say as and ' 32 now`s of ' the and humble`ly as and
' three`ing ' this ' are donkey ' ye ' group`s the ' what ' on ' Jehovah
' rush ' for ' are accurse of ' as grip as ' for whither ' be`th ' from as foot
' stretch and ' donkey`ing the ' as has saw and ' 33 as over of ' way the
around from ' contact`ed ' as maybe I ' from as foot ' three ' this ' as before from

' the ye`ing and ' as you kill ' as whom smitten ' here ye ' also ' time`ed ' for '
' Jehovah ' messenger from ' to ' Balaam ' say as and ' (34 as whom life the
' as you call of ' settle ' ye`ed ' for ' as you known ' not ' for ' as you sin
vessel ' the carry`ing I ' are as has eye in ' evil ' mother ' the time and ' way in
' people ' walk ' Balaam ' to ' Jehovah ' messenger from ' say as and ' (35
' are as to ' word I ' which ' word the ' ye ' however and ' from as person the
smooth in ' as captain ' people ' Balaam ' walk as and ' word of ' guard you ' and ye
to ' and you call of ' out and ' Balaam ' came ' for ' smooth in ' hear as and ' (36
' the end in ' which ' Arnon ' border`ing ' on ' which ' Moab ' town`s '
' send ' forward`ing ' Balaam ' to ' smooth in ' say as and ' (37 border`ing the
' Eli ' you walk the ' not ' what of ' walk ' call of ' are as to ' as you send
' to ' Balaam ' say as and ' (38 are honour ' able I ' not ' from believe the
' word ' able I ' able became ' time`ed ' are as to ' as brought ' be`th ' smooth in
' and ye ' as edge in ' from as Allah ' site`s ' which ' word the ' the noth`ing
alas came`s as and ' smooth in ' people ' Balaam ' walk as and ' (39 word of ' guard I
' flock and ' herd ' smooth in ' sacrifice as and ' (40 you halve ' city`s '
became as and ' (41 and ye ' which ' from as captain of and ' Balaam of ' send as and
die`ing in ' and went`ed and ' Balaam ' ye ' smooth in ' took as and ' is morn in '
people the ' end`ed ' ye ' there from ' look as and ' marry '

' spoil`ed ' vessel ' son`ed ' do`ed ' smooth in ' to ' Balaam ' say as and ' (1

' the seven ' spoil`ed ' vessel ' stable and ' you and sacrifice from ' the seven

' smooth in ' do as and ' (2 from as Ram`s ' swear`ed too and ' from as Bullock

' Ram`s and ' apart ' Balaam and ' smooth in ' went and ' Balaam ' word ' which are

' in annihilate`s the ' smooth in ' to ' Balaam ' say as and ' (3 sacrifice from in

' Jehovah ' call`ed as ' as maybe I ' the eat and ' are as offer`ing ' on

' as has look as ' what ' word and ' as you call of ' from as Allah

messenger from ' come as and ' (4 locate ' walk as and ' walk ' as you fortune the and

you seven ' ye ' him to ' say as and ' Balaam ' to ' from as Allah ' valve and '

' Ram`s and ' apart ' haul and ' as you pile ' you and sacrifice them '

' as animal ' word ' Jehovah ' messenger from ' site and ' (5 sacrifice from in

' (6 word you ' here and ' smooth in ' to ' carry`ing ' say as and ' Balaam

' all and ' that`ing ' him offer ' on ' settle ' be`th and ' him to ' dwell and

' highland ' has from ' say as and ' and rule ' lift as and ' (7 Moab ' as captain

' walk`ed ' east ' as mount from ' Moab ' king ' smooth in ' as grace has as

' hollow I ' what ' (8 Israel ' scorn`ed ' the all and ' Jacob ' vessel ' light`ed

' for ' (9 Jehovah ' and scorn ' not ' scorn I ' what and ' to ' hollow`ed ' not

' you and have bonnet and ' and has look I ' from as boulder`ing ' head from

from nation`ing in and ' nigh as ' single of ' people ' behold ' and has captain`ing I

' ye ' is number and ' Jacob ' dust ' her`ed ' who ' (10 reckon whom ' not '

' from as captain as ' die`ing ' as soul ' die`ing you ' Israel ' you four from

' to ' smooth in ' say as and ' (11 and your`ed ' as whom after ' became you and

' are as you take ' as enemy I ' hollow of ' vessel ' you as do ' what ' Balaam

' ye ' forward`ing ' say as and ' low as and ' (12 bless`ing ' you bless ' be`th and

' say as and ' (13 word of ' guard I ' and ye ' as edge in ' Jehovah ' site`s ' which

' which ' after ' place`ing ' to ' near ' oh ' walk ' smooth in ' him to
' not ' and all and ' saw`ed ' and the end ' however ' there from ' and has saw
14 ' field`ed ' alas took as and ' there from ' vessel ' and has hollow and ' saw`ed
' the seven ' son as and ' cleft`ed the ' head ' to ' from as espy
15 ' sacrifice from in ' Ram`s and ' apart ' went and ' you and sacrifice from
' are as offer`ing ' on ' here ' in annihilate`s the ' smooth in ' to ' say as and
16 to ' Jehovah ' messenger from ' call as and ' here ' call`ed I ' for whither and
smooth in ' to ' carry`ing ' say as and ' him animal ' word ' site and ' Balaam '
17 ' on ' settle ' and behold and ' him to ' came as and ' word you ' here and '
' smooth in ' him to ' say as and ' and ye ' Moab ' as captain and ' him offer
18 smooth in ' rise`ing ' say as and ' and rule ' lift as and ' Jehovah ' word ' what
19 ' to ' man I ' not ' bird`ing ' and son ' adorn ' the ear`s the ' hear`ed and '
' say ' that`ing the ' from regret as and ' ground ' son and ' deceive as and
20 bless of ' be`th ' the has substance`s ' not and ' word and ' success`ed ' not and
21 ' scan`s that ' not ' the has carry`s I ' not and ' bless I and ' as you take '
' him Allah ' Jehovah ' Israel in ' labour ' look`ed ' not and ' Jacob in ' low`ing I
22 ' from issue`s when ' to ' and in ' king ' you have joyful and ' and people
23 ' serpent ' not ' for ' if ' boost ' you put custom`ing ' from as Mizra from
' Jacob of ' say as ' while ' Israel in ' determine ' not and ' Jacob in
24 ' rise`ing as ' came`s all ' people ' behold ' to ' act ' what ' Israel of and
' blood and ' torn ' eat as ' till ' lay as ' not ' lift give as ' lion`ed are and
25 ' also ' Balaam ' to ' smooth in ' say as and ' belong`ed ' from as profane
26 and has bless you ' not ' bless`ing ' also and ' and has hollow you ' not ' hollow
' as you word ' forward`ing ' smooth in ' to ' say as and ' Balaam ' low as and '
from as Allah the ' Jehovah ' word as ' which ' word the ' all ' say of ' are as to

' oh ' walk`ed ' Balaam ' to ' smooth in ' say as and ' 27 do`ed I ' and ye '
' as has eye in ' fit as ' as maybe I ' after ' place`ing ' to ' are took I
' took as and ' 28 there from ' vessel ' and you hollow and ' from as Allah the
' around ' on ' gaze behold ' gape`ing the ' head ' Balaam ' ye ' smooth in
' vessel ' son`ed ' smooth in ' to ' Balaam ' say as and ' 29 has and site`s the
' spoil`ed ' vessel ' stable and ' you and sacrifice from ' the seven ' spoil`ed
' do as and ' 30 from as Ram`s ' swear`ed too and ' from as Bullock ' the seven
' Ram`s and ' apart ' went and ' Balaam ' word ' say ' which are ' smooth in
sacrifice from in the

' bless of ' Jehovah ' as has eye in ' good`ing ' for ' Balaam ' look as and ' (1
' you call of ' move in ' move are ' walk the ' not and ' Israel ' ye
' (2 him turn ' is wilderness the ' to ' drink as and ' from as serpent the
' nigh ' Israel ' ye ' look as and ' him has eye ' ye ' Balaam ' lift as and
' (3 from as Allah ' spirit is ' and Mosthigh ' became you and ' him tribe of
' burn`ing ' and son ' Balaam ' state ' say as and ' and rule ' lift as and
' to ' as say ' hear ' state ' (4 has eye the ' unveil ' strong the ' from oh and
' and uncover and ' fall ' the vision as ' almighty ' the vision from ' which
are as you tabernacle and ' Jacob ' are as tent ' and good ' what ' (5 from as has eye
' mosthigh ' you and garden are ' from as twirl ' from as inerit are ' (6 Israel '
' mosthigh ' from as ceder are ' Jehovah ' fix`ed has ' from as tent are ' river
' Water in ' and seed and ' and bucket from ' Water ' of splash ' (7 Water
' help set and ' and king ' ignite from ' elevate`ing and ' from as increase
' from as Mizra from ' and issue`s when ' and rest`ed ' to ' (8 and you and king
' him boulder ' from nation`ing ' eat as ' if ' boost ' you and put custom`ing
' lay ' leg ' (9 smash as ' him outside and ' gnaw as ' them as you might and
' are as bless from ' and has rise`s as ' who ' the wildcat`s are and ' the lion are
' smooth in ' anger ' delay and ' (10 execrate`ing ' are as execrate and ' bless`ing
' to ' smooth in ' say as and ' him palm ' ye ' clap as and ' Balaam ' to
' you bless ' be`th and ' walk ' as you call ' as enemy I ' hollow of ' Balaam
' to ' walk ' shoot ' the time and ' (11 from as move ' three ' this ' bless`ing
' are keep from ' be`th and ' are honour I ' honour ' as you say ' are place`ing
' forward`ing ' smooth in ' to ' Balaam ' say as and ' (12 honour`ing from ' Jehovah
say of ' as you word ' Eli ' you send ' which ' are as messenger from ' to ' also
' silver ' and you house ' fill`ing ' smooth in ' vessel ' permanent ' mother ' (13

' you concoct of ' Jehovah ' edge ' ye ' cross of ' able I ' not ' gold ' or
' Eli ' Jehovah ' word as ' which ' house of from ' evil`ed ' or ' the good`ing
14 ' as people of ' ing`enter ' as behold`th ' the time and ' word`ed I ' and ye
' this the ' people the ' success`ed ' which ' ye ' are advice`s I and ' walk`ed
15 ' and rule ' lift as and ' from week the ' you as after in ' are people of
' unveil ' strong the ' from oh and ' burn ' and son ' Balaam ' state ' say as and
16 ' knowledge ' known and ' to ' as say ' hear ' state ' has eye the
uncover`ing and ' fall ' the vision as ' almighty ' the vision from ' has and mosthigh
17 ' and has captain`ing I ' time`ed ' not and ' and has look I ' from as has eye '
' tribe ' rise and ' Jacob from ' in star`ing ' way ' approach`ing ' not and
Seth ' as son ' all ' is floor and ' Moab ' as quarter ' smash and ' Israel from
18 ' concoct ' gate`s ' the possess ' be`s and ' the possess ' Edom ' be`s and '
19 ' Jacob from ' descend and ' sick`s ' do`ed ' Israel and ' him enemy I
20 ' Amalek ' ye ' look as and ' town`s from ' survivor`s ' perish`s the and
' Amalek ' from nation`ing ' you as head ' say as and ' and rule ' lift as and
21 ' as nest`s the ' ye ' look as and ' perish ' adorn ' and whom after and
' there`s and ' are sojourn from ' has ye`s ' say as and ' and rule ' lift as and
22 ' what ' till ' Cain ' burn of ' be`s as ' mother ' for ' are nest ' rock in
23 who ' hence`ing ' say as and ' and rule ' lift as and ' are sojourn you ' which`ing
24 ' from as group ' hand from ' from spring`s as ' to ' and there from ' am decide '
' adorn ' that`ing ' also and ' Obara ' and low as and ' which`ing ' and low as and
25 ' and place`ing of ' dwell and ' walk as and ' Balaam ' rise as and ' perish
and way of ' walk the ' smooth in ' also and

THE TORAH SCROLL 25

' to ' whore`ing of ' people the ' wait and ' hate`s in ' Israel ' dwell and ' 1

' as sacrifice of ' people of ' the has call you and ' 2 Moab ' daughter`th`ing

' prostate humble`ly as and ' people the ' eat as and ' behold as Allah

' gape`ing ' marry of ' Israel ' as son from ' bracelet Then ' 3 has am Allah of

' Moses ' to ' Jehovah ' say as and ' 4 Israel in ' Jehovah ' anger ' delay and

' from as bracelet behold ' from as person the ' ye ' and kill as and ' say

' have drape`ing and ' people the ' as head ' all ' ye ' took ' gape`ing ' marry of

anger ' shout`ing at ' carry`ing as and ' sun the ' over ' Jehovah of ' from ye`ing

' Israel ' as discern ' to ' Moses ' say as and ' 5 Israel from ' Jehovah '

6 gape`ing ' marry of ' from as bracelet behold ' him person ' ye ' man I ' and kill

' to ' approach as and ' came ' Israel ' as son from ' man I ' be`th and '

' as has eye of and ' Moses ' as has eye of ' whom Midian the ' ye ' him brother

' tent ' open ' from as against ' them`ed and ' Israel ' as son ' testimony ' all

' Aaron ' son ' Eleazar ' son ' Phinehas ' look as and ' 7 ing`congregate

' spear ' took as and ' till`ed the ' middle`ing from ' rise as and ' priest the

' hollow`ed the ' to ' Israel ' man I ' as after ' came as and ' 8 and hand in

to ' Woman the ' ye and ' Israel ' man I ' ye ' them two ' ye ' bayonet as and

9 Israel ' as son ' above ' pestilence`ed the ' festival you and ' the you hollow '

' the four I ' pestilence`ed in ' from as die the ' and became as and '

' 11 say of ' Moses ' to ' Jehovah ' word as and ' 10 thousand ' from as ten and

' ye ' carry`s the ' priest the ' Aaron ' son ' Eleazar ' son ' Phinehas

' as you jealous ' ye ' and jealous in ' Israel ' as son ' above ' as you hot

' Israel ' as son ' ye ' as whom all ' not and ' from middle`ing in

' ye ' if ' gave ' as behold`th ' say ' so of ' 12 as you jealous in

him after ' and seed of and ' if ' whom`ed the and ' 13 from and peace ' as covenant`s

' him Allah of ' jealous ' which ' under ' from on`ing ' you priest ' covenant`s '
' Israel ' man that ' there and ' 14 Israel ' as son ' on ' atone as and
' son ' as prune ' whom Midian the ' ye ' smitten`ed ' which ' here them
' there and ' 15 as Simeon`ing of ' father ' you house ' lift`s has ' not`ing had
' boulder`ing ' daughter ' whom fierce ' whom Midian the ' here them ' Woman the
' word as and ' 16 that`ing ' Midian in ' father ' you house ' faithful`ing ' head
' from as Midian the ' ye ' and bundle ' 17 say of ' Moses ' to ' Jehovah
' relate ' them ' from as bundle ' for ' 18 from ye`ing ' from whom smitten and
' gape`ing ' word ' on ' relate ' and conspire ' which ' them as conspire in
' from sister`ing ' Midian ' lift`s has ' daughter ' whom fierce ' word ' on and
gape`ing ' word ' on ' pestilence`ed the ' day as in ' here them

Jehovah ' word as and ' say as and ' pestilence`ed the ' as after ' became as and ' 1
' 2 say of ' priest the ' Aaron ' son ' Eleazar ' to and ' Moses ' to '
' son from ' Israel ' as son ' testimony ' all ' head ' ye ' and lift
' all ' from you and father ' you house of ' above`ed and ' the Year ' from as ten
' priest the ' Eleazar and ' Moses ' word as and ' 3 Israel in ' mass ' out
' 4 say of ' and moon`s ' Jordan ' on ' Moab ' you twilight in ' from ye
' Jehovah ' command`ed ' which are ' above`ed and ' the Year ' from as ten ' son from
' land from ' from as spring became ' Israel ' as son and ' Moses ' ye
Enoch`ing ' Reuben ' as son and ' Israel ' first`ing ' Reuben ' 5 from as Mizra
6 as Pallu`ing the ' you at family ' Pallu`ing of ' as Enoch`ing the ' you at family '
' you at family ' as Carm of ' as Hezron`ing the ' you at family ' Hezron`ing of '
' and became as and ' as Reuben the ' you and at family ' to`ed ' 7 as Carm the
' seven and ' thousand ' from as four I and ' three`ed ' them as my appoint
' 9 father as to ' Pallu`ing ' as son and ' 8 from as three and ' you and hundred
' high as father and ' has decree and ' to and slumber ' father as to ' as son and
and object ' which ' till`ed the ' as call`s ' high as father and ' Dathan ' that`ing
' bald ' testimony in ' Aaron ' on and ' Moses ' on ' and season the '
land the ' open you and ' 10 Jehovah ' on ' from you season the in ' from blaze thus
till`ed the ' die`ing in ' land the ' from ye ' worthless you and ' edge`ed ' ye '
from as you hundred and ' from as five ' ye and ' bald ' ye and ' fire the ' eat in '
' 12 and die ' not ' bald ' as son and ' 11 flee`ing of ' and became as and ' man I '
' Nemuel of ' as Simeon`ing the ' complete and at family of ' Simeon ' as son
' Jachin of ' as Jamin the ' you at family ' Jamin of ' as Nemuel the ' you at family
' as Zerah the ' you at family ' Zerah of ' 13 as Jachin the ' you at family
' you and at family ' to`ed ' 14 as Saul the ' you at family ' ask`ing of

15 from as you hundred and ’ thousand ’ from as ten and ’ from two ’ as Simeon`ing the

’ you at family ’ has and espy of ’ complete and at family of ’ fortune ’ as son ’

’ you at family ’ Shuni of ’ Haggi the ’ you at family ’ Haggi of ’ as Zephon the

Eri the ’ you at family ’ Eri of ’ as ear the ’ you at family ’ Ozni of ’ 16 Shuni the

’ you at family ’ Areli`ing of ’ as Arvad the ’ you at family ’ as Arvad of ’ 17

’ fortune ’ as son ’ you and at family ’ to`ed ’ 18 Areli`ing the

’ 19 you and hundred ’ five and ’ thousand ’ from as four I ’ them as my appoint of

Canaan ’ land in ’ Onan and ’ town ’ die as and ’ Onan and ’ town ’ Judah ’ as son

the Shilo of ’ complete and at family of ’ Judah ’ as son ’ and became as and ’ 20

’ as Pharez the ’ you at family ’ Pharez of ’ as has Shilo the ’ you at family ’

’ grow ’ as son ’ and became as and ’ 21 as Zerah the ’ you at family ’ Zerah of

’ you at family ’ Hamuel of ’ as Hezron`ing the ’ you at family ’ Hezron`ing of

’ them as my appoint of ’ Judah ’ you and at family ’ to`ed ’ 22 as Hamuel the

’ as son ’ 23 you and hundred ’ five and ’ thousand ’ from as seven and ’ six`ed

’ as Tola the ’ you at family ’ Tola of ’ complete and at family of ’ Issachar

’ you at family ’ Jashub`ing of ’ 24 as has Pua the ’ you at family ’ the Pua of

’ to`ed ’ 25 as Shomron`ing the ’ you at family ’ has and guard of ’ as Jashub`ing the

’ from as six and ’ the four I ’ them as my appoint of ’ Issachar ’ you and at family

’ Zebulun ’ as son ’ 26 you and hundred ’ three and ’ thousand

’ Elon`ing of ’ as Sered the ’ you at family ’ Sered of ’ complete and at family of

’ 27 as Jahleel the ’ you at family ’ Jahleel of ’ as Elon`ing the ’ you at family

’ from as six ’ them as my appoint of ’ as Zebulun the ’ you and at family ’ to`ed

complete and at family of ’ Joseph ’ as son ’ 28 you and hundred ’ five and ’ thousand

’ you at family ’ Machir of ’ Manasse`ed ’ as son ’ 29 Ephraim and ’ Manasse`ed ’

’ Gilead of ’ Gilead ’ ye ’ bore`s and the ’ Machir and ’ as Machir the

' aid as brother ' Gilead ' as son ' to`ed ' 30 as Gilead the ' you at family
' 31 as Helek the ' you at family ' Helek of and ' as Ahiezer the ' you at family
' you at family ' Shechem and ' as Asriel`ing the ' you at family ' Asriel`ing and
' scout and ' as Shemida the ' you at family ' Shemida and ' 32 as Shechem the
if ' and be`s ' not ' scout ' son ' Zelophehad and ' 33 as scout the ' you at family
' daughter`th`ing ' there and ' daughter`th`ing ' mother ' for ' from as son '
' 34 run`ed you and ' the king ' partridge`ed ' keep`ed and ' the of wipe ' Zelophehad
' from two ' them as my appoint of and ' Manasse`ed ' you and at family ' to`ed
' as son ' to`ed ' 35 you and hundred ' seven and ' thousand ' from as five and
' you at family ' at of drink'ing of ' complete and at family of ' Ephraim
' Taham of ' as first he ' you at family ' first of ' as ing`Shuthelah the
' has town of ' Shuthelah ' as son ' to`ed and ' 36 as Taham the ' you at family
' Ephraim ' as son ' you and at family ' to`ed ' 37 as Eran the ' you at family
' five and ' thousand ' from as three and ' from two ' them as my appoint of
' as son ' 38 complete and at family of ' Joseph ' as son ' to`ed ' you and hundred
' as Bela the ' you at family ' Bela of ' complete and at family of ' Benjamim`s
as Ahiram the ' you at family ' Ahiram of ' as Ashbel the ' you at family ' Ashbel of
' you at family ' Hupham of ' as Shupham the ' you at family ' Shupham`ty of ' 39
' wander of ' worthless ' as son ' and became as and ' 40 as from pure`ing the
41 as Naaman the ' you at family ' Naaman of ' as Ard the ' you at family ' Naaman and
' them as my appoint and ' complete and at family of ' Benjamim`s ' as son ' to`ed '
' to`ed and ' 42 you and hundred ' six and ' thousand ' from as four I and ' the five
' you at family ' from humble'ing of ' complete and at family of ' judge ' as son
' 43 complete and at family of ' judge ' you and at family ' to`ed ' as Shuham the
' the four I ' them as my appoint of and ' as Shuham the ' you and at family ' all

' which ' as son ' 44 you and hundred ' four I and ' thousand ' from as six and
' the Jeshui of ' Jimnah the ' you at family ' Jimnah of ' complete and at family of
as son of ' 45 as Beriah the ' you at family ' Beriah of ' Jeshui the ' you at family
' you at family ' Malchiel of ' as Heber the ' you at family ' connect of ' Beriah '
' to`ed ' 47 abode ' which ' daughter ' there and ' 46 as Malchiel the
' three`ed ' them as my appoint of ' which ' as son ' you and at family
' Naphtali ' as son ' 48 you and hundred ' four I and ' thousand ' from as five and
' Guni of ' as Jahziel the ' you at family ' Jahziel of ' complete and at family of
' as Jezer the ' you at family ' Jezer of ' 49 Guni the ' you at family
' you and at family ' to`ed ' 50 as Salem`ing the ' you at family ' from and peace of
' the five ' them as my appoint and ' complete and at family of ' Naphtali
' to`ed ' 51 you and hundred ' four I and ' thousand ' from as four I and
' thousand and ' thousand ' you and hundred ' six ' Israel ' as son ' as punish`ing
' to ' Jehovah ' word as and ' 52 from as three and ' you and hundred ' seven and
' is number in ' inherit`ed in ' land the ' part you ' to`ed of ' 53 say of ' Moses
' less of and ' and you inherit ' increase`ed you ' increase of ' 54 you name
' permanent ' him my appoint ' as by ' man I ' and you inherit ' less`s you
' you name of ' land the ' ye ' part as ' ing`lot in ' sure ' 55 and you inherit
' ing`lot the ' edge ' on ' 56 and inherit whom ' from you and father ' you and down
' to`ed and ' 57 less of ' increase ' between in ' and you inherit ' part whom
' Gershon`ing of ' complete and at family of ' from Levi the ' as punish`ing
' as Kohath the ' you at family ' Kohath of ' as Gershon`ing the ' you at family
' as son ' you and at family ' to`ed ' 58 as Merari the ' you at family ' Merari of
' as Hebron`ing the ' you at family and ' as white the ' you at family ' Levi
' you at family and ' as Korah the ' you at family and ' Mahli the ' you at family and

' wife ' there and ' 59 from sheaf ' ye ' bore`s and the ' Kohath and ' Mushi the
' Levi of ' ye`ed ' bore`ed as ' which ' Levi ' daughter ' honour him ' from sheaf
ye and ' Moses ' ye and ' Aaron ' ye ' Amram of ' bore you and ' from as Mizra in
' ye and ' freewill ' ye ' Aaron of ' bore him and ' 60 from sister`ing ' Miriam '
' freewill ' die as and ' 61 Ithamar ' ye and ' Eleazar ' ye ' that`ing as father
' 62 Jehovah ' as before ' stranger`ed ' fire ' from approach`s the in ' Abihu and
' all ' thousand ' from as ten and ' three`ed ' them as my appoint ' and became as and
' and my appoint you the ' not ' for ' above`ed and ' new ' son from ' male
' inherit`ed ' them of ' gave ' not ' for ' Israel ' as son ' middle`ing in
' Eleazar and ' Moses ' as punish`ing ' to`ed ' 63 Israel ' as son ' middle`ing in
' you twilight in ' Israel ' as son ' ye ' and my appoint ' which ' priest the
' man I ' be`s ' not ' to`ed in and ' 64 and moon`s ' Jordan ' on ' Moab
' and my appoint ' which ' priest the ' Aaron and ' Moses ' as my and appoint from
' Jehovah ' say ' for ' 65 as bush`s ' word from in ' Israel ' as son ' ye
' lag ' survive has ' not and ' word from in ' and you day as ' die`ing ' them of
Nun ' son ' ed`Joshua`ing and ' turn`ed as ' son ' dog ' mother ' for ' man I

' son ' scout ' son ' Zelophehad ' daughter`th`ing ' the has approach you and ' 1
' son ' Manasse`ed ' you and at family of ' Manasse`ed ' son ' Machir ' son ' Gilead
' keep`ed and ' the of wipe ' him daughter`th ' you name ' to`ed and ' Joseph
' as before ' the has stand you and ' 2 run`ed you and ' Milcah and ' Hoghah and
' from help`s the ' as before and ' priest the ' Eleazar ' as before and ' Moses
' our as father ' 3 say of ' ing`congregate ' tent ' open ' till`ed the ' all and
' till`ed the ' middle`ing in ' be`s ' not ' that`ing and ' word from in ' die
die ' and sin in ' for ' bald ' testimony in ' Jehovah ' on ' from as season behold
' withdraw as ' what of ' 4 if ' and be`s ' not ' from as son and ' our as father '
' if ' whither`s ' for ' and you at family ' middle`ing from ' our as father ' there
' as brother ' middle`ing in ' inherit`ed ' that hold ' our of ' and give`ed ' son
' as before ' has discern from ' ye ' Moses ' approach as and ' 5 our as father
' so ' 7 say of ' Moses ' to ' Jehovah ' word as and ' say as and ' 6 Jehovah
' you hold ' them of ' has set ' gave ' you and word ' Zelophehad ' daughter`th`ing
' ye ' you cross the and ' them as father ' as brother ' middle`ing in ' inherit`ed
' has am father ' you inherit ' ye ' you cross as and ' has am father ' you inherit
' for ' man I ' say of ' word you ' Israel ' as son ' to and ' 8 behold of
' from you cross the and ' from set has and ' if ' whither`s ' son and ' die`ing as
' daughter ' if ' whither`s ' mother and ' 9 and daughter of ' and you inherit ' ye
whither`s ' mother and ' 10 him brother of ' and you inherit ' ye ' from set has and
' as brother of ' and you inherit ' ye ' from set has and ' from as brother ' if '
' him father of ' from as brother ' whither`s ' mother and ' 11 him father
him to ' approach`ing the ' and remain of ' and you inherit ' ye ' from set has and
' as son of ' whom`ed the and ' and ye`ed ' possess as and ' and you at family from '
' ye ' Jehovah ' command`ed ' which are ' discern from ' statute of ' Israel

to ' on`ed ' say of ' Moses ' to ' Jehovah ' word as and ' say as and ' 12 Moses
' which ' land the ' ye ' look`ed and ' this the ' from as Obara the ' mountain '
' you gather has and ' ye`ed ' the sight`s and ' 13 Israel ' as son of ' as set has
' Aaron ' gather has ' which are ' ye`ed ' also ' are as people ' to
' word from in ' as edge ' ye ' from you rebell ' which are ' 14 are as brother
' Water in ' as has holy`s the of ' till`ed the ' you in rebell in ' thorn
' 15 thorn ' word from ' holy ' you in rebell ' who ' them ' them as has eye of
' as Allah ' Jehovah ' punish as ' 16 say of ' Jehovah ' to ' Moses ' word as and
out ' which ' 17 till`ed the ' on ' man I ' flesh ' all of ' you and spirit is the
' which and ' them as before ' came`ing as ' which and ' them as before '
' testimony ' be`s you ' not and ' from came`s as ' which and ' from spring`s as
Jehovah ' say as and ' 18 evil`ed ' them of ' whither`s ' which ' flock are ' Jehovah
which ' man that ' Nun ' son ' ed`Joshua`ing ' ye ' walk ' took ' Moses ' to '
' 19 and Mosthigh ' are hand ' ye ' you laid and ' and in ' spirit is '
all ' as before and ' priest the ' Eleazar ' as before ' and ye ' you stand the and
set`ed has and ' 20 them as has eye of ' and ye ' whom`ed command and ' till`ed the '
' all ' shall hear as ' purpose of and ' and Mosthigh ' are glorify`ing from '
' stand as ' priest the ' Eleazar ' as before and ' 21 Israel ' as son ' testimony
' on ' Jehovah ' as before ' from as light`ing the ' discern from in ' if ' ask and
' all and ' that`ing ' came`ing as ' and talk`s ' on and ' and out ' and talk`s
which are ' Moses ' do as and ' 22 till`ed the ' all and ' and ye ' Israel ' as son
' ed`Joshua`ing ' ye ' took as and ' and ye ' Jehovah ' command`ed '
' all ' as before and ' priest the ' Eleazar ' as before ' alas stand as and
' and command`ed as and ' and Mosthigh ' him hand ' ye ' lay as and ' 23 till`ed the
are as has eye ' him to ' say as and ' Moses ' hand in ' Jehovah ' word ' which are

' from as king the ' two of ' Jehovah ' do`ed ' which ' ye ' sight`ing the '
' ye`ed ' which ' you and king them ' all of ' Jehovah ' success`ed ' so ' these`ed
' that`ing ' your as Allah ' Jehovah ' for ' from dread you ' not ' there`ed ' word
relate ' fight has the

' as son ' ye ' command`ed ' 2 say of ' Moses ' to ' Jehovah ' word as and ' 1
' as fire of ' as hot of ' as has approach ' ye ' them to ' you say and ' Israel
' vessel ' approach`s the of ' and guard you ' as odor has ' smell`s
' which ' Woman the ' this ' them of ' you say and ' 3 him ing`congregation in
' they full ' the Year ' as son ' from as mutton ' Jehovah of ' and approach`s you
' one the ' mutton the ' ye ' 4 continual`s ' offer`ed ' day as of ' from two
' between in ' do`ed you ' two the ' mutton the ' ye and ' is morn in ' do`ed you
' the bestow of ' flour ' the cook`s ' you as ten`s and ' 5 from as twilight the
continual`s ' offer ' 6 hin`s ' whom four`s ' set`s are ' eight in ' the mingle`ing
7 ' Jehovah of ' Woman ' odor has ' smell`s of ' as bush`s ' blemish ' am do the '
' crowd the ' holy in ' one the ' mutton of ' hin`s ' you four`s ' and libation and
' do`ed you ' two the ' mutton the ' ye and ' 8 Jehovah of ' merry ' libation
him libation are and ' herd the ' you bestrow are ' from as twilight the ' between in
desist the ' day as in and ' 9 Jehovah of ' odor has ' smell`s ' Woman ' do`ed you '
' two and ' they full ' the Year ' as son ' from as mutton ' two '
him libation and ' eight in ' the mingle`ing ' bestow`ed ' flour ' from as has and ten
' continual`s the ' offer ' on ' and desist in ' desist ' offer ' 10
' on`ed ' and approach`s you ' your as new ' as head in and ' 11 them as libation and
' one ' Ram`s and ' from two ' herd ' as son ' from as Bullock ' Jehovah of
' three`ed and ' 12 they full ' the seven ' the Year ' as son ' from as mutton
one the ' apart of ' eight in ' the mingle`ing ' bestow`ed ' flour ' from as has ten
' eight in ' the mingle`ing ' bestow`ed ' flour ' from as has ten ' two and '
' bestow`ed ' flour ' has and ten ' has and ten and ' 13 one the ' Ram`s of
Woman ' odor has ' smell`s ' on`ed ' one the ' mutton of ' eight in ' the mingle`ing
' apart of ' be`s as ' hin`s ' as outside ' them as libation and ' 14 Jehovah of '

mutton of ' hin`s ' whom four`s and ' Ram`s of ' hin`s ' whom three`s and ' one the
' as new of ' and new in ' new the ' offer ' such ' between`s ' one the '
' on ' Jehovah of ' you sin of ' one ' from as Goat ' gate`s and ' 15 Year`ed the
' new in and ' 16 them as and libation and ' concoct`ed as ' continual`s the ' offer
' 17 Jehovah of ' pass ' new of ' day as ' ten ' the four I in ' has and head`s the
' you seven ' solemn ' this the ' new of ' day as ' ten ' the five in and
call from ' has and head`s the ' day as in ' 18 and eat as ' unleaven`ing ' from week
' 19 and do you ' not ' serve`ed ' you are fill ' all ' holy '
' as son ' from as Bullock ' Jehovah of ' on`ed ' Woman ' from you approach the and
' as son ' from as mutton ' swear`ed too and ' one ' Ram`s and ' from two ' herd
' flour ' from you bestow and ' 20 relate ' and became as ' they full ' the Year
' two and ' apart of ' from as has and ten ' three`ed ' eight in ' the mingle`ing
' has and ten ' has and ten and ' 21 and do you ' Ram`s of ' from as has and ten
' gate`s and ' 22 from as mutton the ' you seven of ' one the ' mutton of ' do`ed you
' alone of from ' 23 from are mosthigh ' atone of ' you sin of ' one ' from as Goat
24 to`ed ' ye ' and do you ' continual`s the ' offer of ' which ' herd the ' offer
' Woman ' fight ' from week the ' you seven ' and do you ' day as of ' to`ed are '
' continual`s the ' you on`ing ' on ' Jehovah of ' odor has ' smell`s of
' as seven`s the ' day as in and ' 25 them as and libation and ' concoct`ed as
' not ' serve`ed ' you are fill ' all ' relate ' be`s as ' holy ' call from
' from are approach`s thus ' from as first`ing the ' day as in and ' 26 and do you
' holy ' call from ' from are as you seven in ' Jehovah of ' new`ed ' bestow`ed
' 27 and do you ' not ' serve`ed ' you are fill ' all ' relate ' be`s as
' Jehovah of ' odor has ' smell`s of ' Woman ' the on`ing ' from you approach the and
' from as mutton ' one ' Ram`s and ' from two ' herd ' as son ' from as Bullock

28 ' relate ' and became as ' they full ' the seven ' the Year ' as son
' from as has ten ' three`ed ' eight in ' the mingle`ing ' flour ' from you bestow and
29 ' one the ' Ram`s of ' from as has ten ' two and ' one the ' apart of
' you seven of ' one the ' mutton of ' has and ten ' has and ten and
' atone of ' you sin of ' one ' from as Goat ' gate`s and ' 30 from as mutton the
' alas you bestow and ' continual`s the ' offer ' alone of from ' 31 from are mosthigh
them as libation and ' relate ' and became as ' they full ' and do you

THE TORAH SCROLL 29

' be`s as ' holy ' call from ' new of ' one in ' as seven`s the ' new in and ' 1
' day as ' and do you ' not ' serve`ed ' you are fill ' all ' relate
' smell`s of ' on`ed ' from dual`s and ' 2 relate ' be`s as ' the gatekeeper`ing
from as mutton ' one ' Ram`s ' one ' herd ' son ' apart ' Jehovah of ' odor has
' flour ' from you bestow and ' 3 they full ' the seven ' the Year ' as son '
' two and ' apart of ' from as has ten ' three`ed ' eight in ' the mingle`ing
' mutton of ' one ' has and ten ' has and ten and ' 4 Ram`s of ' from as has ten
' one ' from as Goat ' gate`s and ' 5 from as mutton the ' you seven of ' one the
' new the ' offer ' alone of from ' 6 from are mosthigh ' atone of ' you sin of
' the you bestow and ' continual`s the ' offer and ' the you bestow and
' Woman ' odor has ' smell`s of ' from discern from are ' them as libation and
holy ' call from ' this the ' as seven`s the ' new of ' ten`ing in and ' 7 Jehovah of
' all and ' from are as you soul ' ye ' from whom low and ' relate ' be`s as '
' Jehovah of ' on`ed ' from you approach the and ' 8 and do you ' not ' the are fill
' one ' Ram`s and ' one ' herd ' son ' apart ' odor has ' smell`s
9 relate ' and became as ' they full ' the seven ' the Year ' as son ' from as mutton
' three`ed ' eight in ' the mingle`ing ' flour ' from you bestow and '
' 10 one the ' Ram`s of ' from as has ten ' two and ' apart of ' from as has and ten
' you seven of ' one the ' mutton of ' has and ten ' has and ten and
alone of from ' you sin of ' one ' from as Goat ' gate`s and ' 11 from as mutton the
' the you bestow and ' continual`s the ' offer and ' from as atone`ing the ' you sin '
' as seven`s the ' new of ' day as ' ten ' the five in and ' 12 them as libation and
not ' serve`ed ' you are fill ' all ' relate ' be`s as ' holy ' call from ' this the
' 13 from week ' you seven ' Jehovah of ' solemn ' from you solemn and ' and do you '
' Jehovah of ' odor has ' smell`s ' Woman ' on`ed ' from you approach the and

' from two ' from as Ram`s ' ten ' three`ed ' herd ' as son ' from as Bullock
' and became as ' they full ' ten ' the four I ' the Year ' as son ' from as mutton
' three`ed ' eight in ' the mingle`ing ' flour ' from you bestow and ' 14 relate
' from as Bullock the ' ten ' three`ed of ' one the ' apart of ' from as has ten
' 15 from as Ram`s the ' two of ' one the ' Ram`s of ' from as has ten ' two
' ten ' four`ed I of ' one the ' mutton of ' has and ten ' has and ten and
' one ' from as Goat ' gate`s and ' 16 them as libation and ' from as mutton the
' the you bestow and ' continual`s the ' offer ' alone of from ' you sin of
' herd ' as son ' from as Bullock ' two the ' day as in and ' 17 am libation and
' the Year ' as son ' from as mutton ' from two ' from as Ram`s ' ten ' from two
' them as libation and ' from you bestow and ' 18 they full ' ten ' the four I
' from is number in ' from as mutton of and ' from as Ram`s of ' from as Bullock of
' alone of from ' you sin of ' one ' from as Goat ' gate`s and ' 19 discern from are
day as in and ' 20 them as libation and ' the you bestow and ' continual`s the ' offer
' from two ' from as Ram`s ' ten ' as you do ' from as Bullock ' as three`s the '
' 21 they full ' ten ' the four I ' the Year ' as son ' from as mutton
' from as Ram`s of ' from as Bullock of ' them as libation and ' from you bestow and
' gate`s and ' 22 discern from are ' from is number in ' from as mutton of and
' continual`s the ' offer ' alone of from ' you sin of ' one ' from as Goat
' as four`s the ' day as in and ' 23 am libation and ' the you bestow and
' as son ' from as mutton ' from two ' from as Ram`s ' ten`ed ' from as Bullock
them as libation and ' from you bestow ' 24 they full ' ten ' the four I ' the Year
' from is number in ' from as mutton of and ' from as Ram`s of ' from as Bullock of '
' alone of from ' you sin of ' one ' from as Goat ' gate`s and ' 25 discern from are
' day as in and ' 26 am libation and ' the you bestow and ' continual`s the ' offer

from as mutton ’ from two ’ from as Ram`s ’ nine`ed ’ from as Bullock ’ as five`s the
’ from you bestow and ’ 27 they full ’ ten ’ the four I ’ the Year ’ as son ’
’ from as mutton of and ’ from as Ram`s of ’ from as Bullock of ’ them as libation and
’ one ’ from as Goat ’ gate`s and ’ 28 discern from are ’ from is number in
’ the you bestow and ’ continual`s the ’ offer ’ alone of from ’ you sin of
’ eight`ed ’ from as Bullock ’ as six the ’ day as in and ’ 29 am libation and
’ ten ’ the four I ’ the Year ’ as son ’ from as mutton ’ from two ’ from as Ram`s
’ from as Bullock of ’ them as libation and ’ from you bestow and ’ 30 they full
’ 31 discern from are ’ from is number in ’ from as mutton of and ’ from as Ram`s of
’ offer ’ alone of from ’ you sin of ’ one ’ from as Goat ’ gate`s and
’ day as in and ’ 32 am libation and ’ the you bestow and ’ continual`s the
’ from two ’ from as Ram`s ’ the seven ’ from as Bullock ’ as seven`s the
’ 33 they full ’ ten ’ the four I ’ the Year ’ as son ’ from as mutton
’ from as Ram`s of ’ from as Bullock of ’ from crow`ed has and ’ from you bestow and
’ gate`s and ’ 34 from discern from are ’ from is number in ’ from as mutton of and
’ continual`s the ’ offer ’ alone of from ’ you sin of ’ one ’ from as Goat
you festival ’ as eight`s the ’ day as in and ’ 35 am libation and ’ the you bestow and
’ 36 and do you ’ not ’ serve`ed ’ you are fill ’ all ’ relate ’ be`s you ’
’ apart ’ Jehovah of ’ odor has ’ smell`s ’ Woman ’ on`ed ’ from you approach the and
they full ’ the seven ’ the Year ’ as son ’ from as mutton ’ one ’ Ram`s ’ one
’ Ram`s of ’ apart of ’ them as libation and ’ from you bestow and ’ 37
’ gate`s and ’ 38 discern from are ’ from is number in ’ from as mutton of and
’ continual`s the ’ offer ’ alone of from ’ you sin of ’ one ’ from as Goat
’ Jehovah of ’ and do you ’ to`ed ’ 39 am libation and ’ the you bestow and
from are as you freewill and ’ your as vow from ’ earnest ’ from are as season from in

' from are as crow has of and ' from are as you bestow of and ' your as offer of '

' accord ' Israel ' as son ' to ' Moses ' say as and ' 40 from are as whole of and

Moses ' ye ' Jehovah ' command`ed ' which

' Israel ' as son of ' you and down the ' as head ' to ' Moses ' word as and ' (1
' for ' man I ' (2 Jehovah ' command`ed ' which ' word the ' this ' say of
' bound of ' the seven`ing ' seven the ' or ' Jehovah of ' vow ' evermore as
him mouth ' spring as the ' accord ' him word ' wait ' not ' and soul ' on ' bound
' bound`ed and ' Jehovah of ' vow ' promise ' for ' Woman and ' (3 success`ed '
' ye ' am father ' hear and ' (4 am youth in ' am father ' you house in ' bound
' devise`s the and ' the soul ' on ' bound`ed ' which ' am bound and ' am vow
' which ' am bound ' all and ' am vow ' all ' and rise and ' am father ' nihil
' prohibit`s ' deny`s ' mother and ' (5 and rise`ing as ' the soul ' on ' bound`ed
' which ' am bound and ' am vow ' all ' and hear ' day as in ' ye`ed ' am father
nihil ' forgive as ' Jehovah and ' and rise`ing as ' not ' the soul ' on ' bound`ed
' man I of ' be`s you ' him the ' mother and ' (6 ye`ed ' am father ' deny`s ' for '
' on ' bound`ed ' which ' am ordain ' pronounce from ' or ' am on ' am vow and
' nihil ' devise`s the and ' and hear ' day as in ' the man I ' hear and ' (7 the soul
' the soul ' on ' bound`ed ' which ' am bound and ' am vow ' all ' and rise and
' prohibit`s ' the man I ' hear ' day as in ' mother and ' (8 and rise`ing as
' ye and ' or ' am on ' which ' am vow ' ye ' broken and ' the ye`ing
' Jehovah and ' the soul ' on ' bound`ed ' which ' am ordain ' pronounce from
' which ' all ' the exact`ing and ' the widow I ' vow and ' (9 nihil ' forgive as
' you house ' mother and ' (10 am on ' rise`ing as ' the soul ' on ' bound`ed
' (11 the seven`ing in ' the soul ' on ' bound ' bound`ed ' or ' vow`ed ' the man I
' ye`ed ' deny`s ' not ' nihil ' devise`s the and ' the man I ' hear and
' on ' bound`ed ' which ' am bound ' all and ' am vow ' all ' and rise and
' the man I ' from ye ' erupt`s ' broken ' mother and ' (12 and rise`ing as ' the soul
' bound of and ' am vow of ' am ordain ' issue when ' all ' and hear ' day as in

' Jehovah and ' from broken`s ' the man I ' and rise`ing as ' not ' the soul
answer`ing of ' bound ' you seven`ing ' all and ' vow ' all ' 13 nihil ' forgive as
' 14 and has erupt`s ' the man I and ' and has rise`s as ' the man I ' soul '
' to ' day as from ' the man I ' nihil ' devise`s as ' devise`s the ' mother and
' am bound ' all ' ye ' or ' am vow ' all ' ye ' rise`s the and ' day as
' day as in ' nihil ' devise`s the ' for ' from ye ' rise`s the ' am on ' which
help and ' and hear ' as after ' from ye ' erupt`s ' broken ' mother and ' 15 and hear
Jehovah ' command`ed ' which ' from as law the ' to`ed ' 16 and the low`ing ' ye '
' father ' between in ' and wife of ' man I ' between in ' Moses ' ye '
am father ' you house in ' am youth in ' and daughter of

THE TORAH SCROLL 31

Num 31:1-31:14

' as son ' you avenge ' avenge ' (2 say of ' Moses ' to ' Jehovah ' word as and ' (1
are as people ' to ' gather you ' after and ' from as Midian the ' each ' Israel
' and change the ' say of ' people the ' to ' Moses ' word as and ' (3
' Midian ' on ' and became as and ' mass of ' from as person ' from are ye from
' thousand ' below`ed ' thousand ' (4 Midian in ' Jehovah ' you avenge ' set of
' (5 mass of ' and send you ' Israel ' you and down ' all of ' below`ed
ten ' from two ' below`ed ' thousand ' Israel ' as thousand from ' and commit Then
' thousand ' Moses ' from ye ' send as and ' (6 mass ' as change`ing ' thousand '
' priest the ' Eleazar ' son ' Phinehas ' ye and ' from ye ' mass of ' below`ed
' the gatekeeper`ing the ' you form cymbal and ' holy the ' as all and ' mass of
' Jehovah ' command`ed ' which are ' Midian ' on ' and mass Then ' (7 and hand in
' Midian ' as king ' ye and ' (8 male ' all ' and kill as and ' Moses ' ye
' ye and ' fabricate ' ye and ' hence`ing ' ye ' them as profane ' on ' and kill
' Midian ' as king ' you five ' four ' ye and ' hole`ing ' ye and ' boulder`ing
as son ' and dwell and ' (9 desolate in ' and kill ' burn`ing ' son ' Balaam ' ye and
' all ' ye and ' from children ' ye and ' Midian ' as women ' ye ' Israel '
' from of life ' all ' ye and ' from the purchase ' all ' ye and ' from you cattle
all ' ye and ' from you sojourn from in ' them as town ' all ' ye and ' (10 and plunder
strip the ' all ' ye ' acquire as and ' (11 abhorrence ' and burnt ' from you row`s '
' and came as and ' (12 cattle`ed in and ' Men in ' take`ing them ' all ' ye and '
' as son ' testimony ' all ' to and ' priest the ' Eleazar ' to and ' Moses ' to
' to ' strip the ' ye and ' take`ing them ' ye and ' as carry the ' ye ' Israel
' (13 Jericho ' Jordan ' on ' which ' Moab ' you twilight ' to ' camp`ed the
' as lift`s has ' all and ' priest the ' Eleazar and ' Moses ' and out and
angry as and ' (14 camp`ed of ' outside`ing from ' to ' from you call of ' till`ed the

' from as thousand the ' as captain ' of life the ' as punish`ing ' on ' Moses '
(15 fight`ed them ' mass from ' from as came the ' you and hundred the ' as captain and
the female ' all ' from whom life the ' what of ' Moses ' them as to ' say as and '
' commit of ' Balaam ' word in ' Israel ' as son of ' him the ' be`th ' be`th ' (16
' pestilence`ed the ' became you and ' gape`ing ' word ' on ' Jehovah in ' above
' children in ' male ' all ' and kill ' the time and ' (17 Jehovah ' testimony in
' all and ' (18 and kill ' male ' lay from of ' man I ' you known ' Woman ' all and
' male ' lay from ' and known ' not ' which ' from as women in ' children the
' outside`ing from ' relate ' and grace ' from ye and ' (19 relate ' and life the
' touch the ' all and ' soul ' kill ' all ' from week ' you seven ' camp`ed of
as seven`s the ' day as in and ' as three`s the ' day as in ' and sin set ' of sick in
town`ing ' weapon ' all and ' fabric ' all and ' (20 from are desist`s and ' from ye '
' (21 and sin set ' tree ' weapon ' all and ' from as Goat ' do`ed from ' all and '
' mass the ' as person ' to ' say ' priest the ' Eleazar ' say as and
' which ' the protect`ing the ' statute ' such ' fight`ed from of ' from as came the
silver the ' ye and ' gold the ' ye ' sure ' (22 Moses ' ye ' Jehovah ' command`ed
' ye and ' separate`s the ' ye and ' of iron the ' ye and ' copper has the ' ye and '
and cross`s you ' abhorrence ' came`ing as ' which ' word ' all ' (23 you ing`dust the
' which ' all and ' sin whom ' wander`ed ' who in ' sure ' clean and ' abhorrence '
' (24 Water in ' and cross`s you ' abhorrence ' came`ing as ' not
' as seven`s the ' day as in ' your as fabric ' from you immersion and
' say as and ' camp`ed the ' to ' and came you ' after and ' from you clean and
' from as came the ' mass the ' as person ' to ' priest the ' Eleazar
' command`ed ' which ' the protect`ing the ' statute ' such ' fight`ed from of
' ye and ' silver the ' ye and ' gold the ' ye ' sure ' Moses ' ye ' Jehovah

' ye and ' separate`s the ' ye and ' of iron the ' ye and ' copper has the

' and cross`s you ' abhorrence ' came`ing as ' which ' word ' all ' you ing`dust the

' which ' all and ' sin whom ' wander`ed ' who in ' sure ' clean and ' abhorrence

' from you immersion and ' Water in ' and cross`s you ' abhorrence ' came`ing as ' not

' after and ' from you clean and ' as seven`s the ' day as in ' your as fabric

26 say of ' Moses ' to ' Jehovah ' say as and ' 25 camp`ed the ' to ' and came you

' cattle`ed in and ' Men in ' as carry the ' take`ing them ' head ' ye ' lift '

' 27 till`ed the ' you and father ' as head and ' priest the ' Eleazar and ' ye`ed

' fight`ed them ' as handle ' between in ' take`ing them ' ye ' whom outside and

' 28 till`ed the ' all ' between in and ' mass of ' from as spring became

' fight`ed them ' as person ' each ' Jehovah of ' amount ' you high the and

' you and hundred the ' five from ' soul ' one ' mass of ' from as spring became

from as heass`ing the ' has from and ' herd the ' has from and ' ground the ' has from

' from whom outside they ' 29 cattle`ed the ' all from ' flock the ' has from and '

' you oblation`ing ' ye ' priest the ' Eeazar of ' set`ed has and ' and took you

' hold ' one ' implicate ' Israel ' as son ' whom outside they and ' 30 Jehovah

' herd the ' has from and ' ground the ' has from ' from as five the ' has from

cattle`ed the ' all from ' flock the ' has from and ' from as heass the ' has from and

' Tabernacle ' you guard from ' as guard ' from Levi of ' from ye ' set`ed has and '

' command`ed ' which are ' priest the ' Eleazar and ' Moses ' do as and ' 31 Jehovah

' spoil the ' preserve ' take`ing them ' became as and ' 32 Moses ' ye ' Jehovah

' thousand ' you and hundred ' six ' flock ' mass the ' people ' and plunder ' which

' herd and ' 33 from as thousand ' you five and ' thousand ' from as seven and

' one ' from as Heass and ' 34 thousand ' from as seven and ' from two

' from as women the ' has from ' ground ' soul and ' 35 thousand ' from as six and

' from two ' soul ' all ' male ' lay from ' and known ' not ' which
' part ' outside`ed them ' became you and ' (36 thousand ' from as three and
' you and hundred ' three ' flock the ' report from ' mass in ' from as spring became
five and ' from as thousand ' you seven and ' thousand ' from as three and ' thousand
flock the ' has from ' Jehovah of ' amount the ' became as and ' (37 you and hundred '
' six`ed ' herd the and ' (38 from as seven and ' the five ' you and hundred ' six '
' from two ' Jehovah of ' from amount and ' thousand ' from as three and
' five and ' thousand ' from as three ' from as Heass and ' (39 from as seven and
soul and ' (40 from as six and ' one ' Jehovah of ' from amount and ' you and hundred
' from two ' Jehovah of ' from amount and ' thousand ' ten ' six`ed ' ground '
you oblation`ing ' amount ' ye ' Moses ' give as and ' (41 soul ' from as three and
Moses ' ye ' Jehovah ' command`ed ' which are ' priest the ' Eeazar of ' Jehovah '
' Moses ' outside`ed ' which ' Israel ' as son ' whom outside they and ' (42
' you half from ' became you and ' (43 from as mass the ' from as person the ' has from
' thousand ' you and hundred ' three ' flock the ' has from ' till`ed the
' five and ' from as thousand ' you seven and ' thousand ' from as three and
' (45 thousand ' from as three and ' six`ed ' herd and ' (44 you and hundred
' (46 you and hundred ' five and ' thousand ' from as three ' from as Heass and
' Moses ' took as and ' (47 thousand ' ten ' six`ed ' ground ' soul and
' has from ' one ' hold the ' ye ' Israel ' as son ' whom outside they
give as and ' cattle`ed the ' has from and ' ground the ' has from ' from as five the
' Jehovah ' Tabernacle ' you guard from ' as guard ' from Levi the ' to ' from ye '
' to ' and approach as and ' (48 Moses ' ye ' Jehovah ' command`ed ' which are
' as captain ' mass the ' as thousand of ' which ' from as my appoint the ' Moses
to ' and say as and ' (49 you and hundred the ' as captain and ' from as thousand the

' fight`ed them ' as person ' head ' ye ' and lift has ' are as serve ' Moses '
' 50 man I ' and her from ' my appoint has ' not and ' and has hand in ' which
' weapon ' come ' which ' man I ' Jehovah ' has approach ' ye ' approach`s shall
' atone of ' bead are and ' calf`s ' you ring ' bracelet`s and ' pace`ed I ' gold
' Eleazar and ' Moses ' took as and ' 51 Jehovah ' as before ' our as you soul ' on
' 52 do`ed from ' weapon ' all ' spy from ' gold the ' ye ' priest the
' and high`s the ' which ' the oblation`ing the ' gold ' all ' became as and
' you and hundred ' seven and ' thousand ' ten ' six`ed ' Jehovah of
' each and ' from as thousand the ' as captain ' each ' weigh ' from as five and
if ' man I ' and plunder ' mass the ' as person ' 53 you and hundred the ' as captain
' each ' gold the ' ye ' priest the ' Eleazar and ' Moses ' took as and ' 54
' and came`s as and ' you and hundred the and ' from as thousand the ' as captain
' Israel ' as son of ' shall is remember ' ing`congregate ' tent ' to ' and ye
Jehovah ' as before

1 ' as son of and ' Reuben ' as son of ' be`s ' increase ' nest`ed from and '
see as and ' especially ' might`ing ' Manasse`ed the ' tribe ' half of and ' fortune
' place`ing the ' be`th and ' Gilead ' land ' ye and ' aid`s as ' land ' ye '
2 Reuben ' as son and ' fortune ' as son ' and came as and ' purchase`ed ' place`ing
' to and ' Moses ' to ' and say as and ' Manasse`ed the ' tribe ' half and '
3 ' say of ' till`ed the ' as lift`s has ' to and ' priest the ' Eleazar
' the leopard and ' aid as and ' has and bear`s and ' you and compass`s
' and germinate and ' therefore`ed and ' on`ed to and ' shall reckon and
4 ' testimony ' as before ' Jehovah ' smitten`ed ' which ' land the ' low`ing in and
5 ' purchase`ed ' are as serve of and ' that`s ' purchase`ed ' land ' Israel
ye ' permanent ' are as has eye in ' grace ' and has come ' mother ' and say as and
' and has cross`s you ' to and ' hold`ed of ' are as serve of ' such the ' land the '
6 ' as son of and ' Reuben ' as son of ' Moses ' say as and ' has desend the ' ye
' and came as ' your as brother the ' Manasse`ed the ' tribe ' half of and ' fortune
7 ' what of and ' talk ' and inhabitant ' from ye and ' fight`ed from of
' land the ' to ' cross from ' Israel ' as son ' heart ' ye ' has and breach`s
8 ' from are as you father ' concoct ' here ' Jehovah ' them of ' gave ' which
9 ' land the ' ye ' you see of ' creak in ' holy from ' from ye ' as send in
' land the ' ye ' see as and ' of and testicle ' inherit ' till ' and went and
' to ' came ' as except of ' Israel ' as son ' heart ' ye ' and prohibit`s and
10 ' Jehovah ' anger ' delay and ' Jehovah ' them of ' gave ' which ' land the
11 ' and look as ' mother ' say of ' swear too as and ' that`ing the ' day as in
' from as ten ' son from ' from as Mizra from ' from mosthigh the ' from as person the
' as you swear too has ' which ' ground`ed the ' ye ' above`ed and ' the Year
12 ' as after ' and fill ' not ' for ' Jacob of and ' Isaac of ' Abraham of

' son ' ed`Joshua`ing and ' as tracker the ' turn`ed as ' son ' dog ' as zero in
' Jehovah ' anger ' delay and ' (13 Jehovah ' as after ' and fill ' for ' Nun
' till ' the Year ' from as four I ' word from in ' from keep as and ' Israel in
' (14 Jehovah ' as has eye in ' mischief ' do`ed the ' magnificent`ing ' all ' complete
' you and increase you ' from are as you father ' under ' from you rise ' be`th and
anger ' shout`ing at ' on ' till`ing ' you and join of ' from as sin ' from as person
' and as after from ' has and inhabitant`ing ' for ' (15 Israel ' on I ' Jehovah '
' all of ' from you humble and ' word from in ' and rest`s the of ' till`ing ' add and
' you and fence ' and say as and ' him to ' and adduce and ' (16 this the ' people the
' from as town and ' talk ' our as purchase of ' the son has ' flock
' as before ' enrich`s ' change has ' our brother`th and ' (17 and has children of
' to ' from has came`s the ' mother ' which ' till ' Israel ' as son
' around from ' defence them ' as town in ' our children ' dwell and ' from place`ing
' till ' our house`ly ' to ' live`ing ' not ' (18 land the ' as sojourn as
not ' for ' (19 and you inherit ' ye ' man I ' Israel ' as son ' and inherit sacred
' for ' forward`ed and ' has descend of ' cross from ' from ye ' inherit has '
' has desend the of ' cross from ' our as to ' our you inherit ' came`ed
' ye ' smoke`ing you ' mother ' Moses ' them as to ' say as and ' (20 emerge`ed from
' Jehovah ' as before ' and change you ' mother and ' this the ' word the
' has desend the ' ye ' change`ing ' all ' relate ' cross and ' (21 fight`ed from of
and as turn from ' him enemy I ' ye ' and occupy`s the ' till ' Jehovah ' as before
' after and ' Jehovah ' as before ' land the ' footstool`ed has and ' (22
' Jehovah from ' from as emission`ing ' complete as became and ' has and inhabitant`ing
' hold`ed of ' relate ' such the ' land the ' whom`ed the and ' Isreal from and
from you sin ' be`th ' so ' smoke`ing you ' not ' mother and ' (23 Jehovah ' as before

24 ' from are ye ' come you ' which ' your as you sin ' and acknowledge ' Jehovah of '

' you and fence and ' your children of ' from as town ' relate ' and son

25 ' smoke`ing you ' from are as lip ' spring became and ' from are flock of

' tribe ' half and ' fortune ' as son and ' Reuben ' as son ' and say as and

' which are ' and do as ' are as serve ' say of ' Moses ' to ' Manasse`ed the

' our as purchase ' our as women and ' our children ' 26 command`ed from ' as master

27 ' Gilead the ' as town in ' there ' and became as ' our as you cattle ' all and

' Jehovah ' as before ' mass ' change`ing ' all ' and cross as ' are as serve and

Moses ' them of ' command as and ' 28 word ' as master ' which are ' fight`ed from of

' ye and ' Nun ' son ' ed`Joshua`ing ' ye and ' priest the ' Eleazar ' ye '

' say as and ' 29 Israel ' as son of ' you and down the ' you and father ' as head

fortune ' as son and ' Reuben ' as son ' and cross as ' mother ' them as to ' Moses

' all ' has desend the ' ye ' from are ye ' Manasse`ed the ' tribe ' half and '

land the ' footstool`ed has and ' Jehovah ' as before ' fight`ed from of ' change`ing

' Gilead the ' land ' ye ' them of ' from set has and ' your as before '

' from are ye ' from as change`ing ' and cross as ' not ' mother and ' 30 hold`ed of

' as son ' and low as and ' 31 Canaan ' land in ' your middle`ing in ' and hold shall

ye ' say of ' Manasse`ed the ' tribe ' half and ' fortune ' as son and ' Reuben

' and us I ' 32 the make ' so ' are as serve ' to ' Jehovah ' word ' which '

and give I and ' Canaan ' land ' Jehovah ' as before ' from as change`ing ' cross has

them of ' give as and ' 33 has descend of ' cross from ' our you inherit ' you hold '

' tribe ' half of and ' fortune ' as son and ' Reuben ' as son of ' Moses '

as Amar,the ' king ' Sihon`ing ' you king from ' ye ' Joseph ' son ' Manasse`ed the

' am town of ' land the ' shameful the ' king ' bake`ing ' you king from ' ye and '

' as son ' and son as and ' 34 surround`s ' land the ' watch ' you border`ing in

' 35 Aroer ' ye and ' you and compass ' ye and ' has and bear`s ' ye ' fortune
' aid`s as ' ye and ' from as has lip`ing ' you and compass ' ye and
' Haran ' you house ' ye and ' Nimrah ' you house ' ye and ' 36 the peak`ed as and
' and son ' Reuben ' as son and ' 37 flock ' you and fence and ' Mibzar ' watch
Nebo ' ye and ' 38 from as city`s ' ye and ' Elealeh ' ye and ' shall reckon ' ye
' therefore`ed ' ye and ' there ' you ing`arrange ' low`ing from ' marry ' ye and '
and son ' which ' from as town the ' you name ' ye ' you name in ' and call as and
' Gilead`ed ' Manasse`ed ' son ' Machir ' as son ' and walk as and ' 39
' 40 thus ' which ' as Amar the ' ye ' and occupy`s as and ' the and capture as and
' dwell and ' Manasse`ed ' son ' Machir of ' Gilead the ' ye ' Moses ' give as and
' ye ' capture as and ' walk the ' Manasse`ed ' son ' channel`s and ' 41 thus
' 42 channel`s ' crush`ing ' has ye`ed ' call as and ' them as Heth`ing
' am you son ' ye and ' own ' ye ' capture as and ' walk the ' at germinate and
name in ' Nobah ' nihil ' call as and

' land from ' and out ' which ' Israel ' as son ' as march ' to`ed ' 1
' write as and ' 2 Aaron and ' Moses ' hand in ' from you mass of ' from as Mizra
' Jehovah ' edge ' on ' them as march of ' them as spring from ' ye ' Moses
' Rameses from ' leave as and ' 3 them as spring from of ' them as march ' to`ed and
' new of ' day as ' ten ' the five in ' has and head`s the ' new in
' Israel ' as son ' and out ' pass the ' you tomorrow from ' has and head`s the
' from as Mizra and ' 4 from as Mizra ' all ' as has eye of ' high`ed ' hand in
' first`ing ' all ' cattle ' Jehovah ' smitten`ed ' which ' ye ' from as bury from
' as son ' leave as and ' 5 from as discern ' Jehovah ' do`ed ' them as Allah in and
' leave as and ' 6 booth`ing in ' and encamp and ' Rameses from ' Israel
is wilderness the ' the end in ' which ' from ye in ' and encamp and ' you crowd from
' which ' you hole`s the ' edge ' on ' and dwell and ' spy from ' leave as and ' 7
8 great from ' as before ' and encamp and ' north`ing ' marry ' around ' on
' middle`ing in ' and cross as and ' you hole`s the ' around from ' leave as and
' from week ' you three ' way ' and walk as and ' word`ed them ' sea the
the drop from ' leave as and ' 9 drop`ed in ' and encamp and ' from ye ' word from in
' ten`ed ' from twosome ' Elim`s in and ' the Elim`s ' and came as and '
there ' and encamp and ' from as palmtree ' from as seven and ' Water ' you and low`s
11 join`ing ' sea ' on ' and encamp and ' from as to`s from ' leave as and ' 10
12 bush`s ' word from in ' and encamp and ' join`ing ' Water ' leave as and
13 knock`ed in ' and encamp and ' bush`s ' is wilderness from ' leave as and
' leave as and ' 14 too god in ' and encamp and ' Dophkah from ' leave as and
' Water ' there ' be`s ' not and ' from refresh`s in ' and encamp and ' too god from
' and encamp and ' from as refresh`s from ' leave as and ' 15 laid`ing of ' people of
' as bush`s ' is wilderness from ' leave as and ' 16 as bush`s ' word from in

' Kibroth`ing from ' leave as and ' 17 lust`ed the ' you and bury in ' and encamp and
' Hazeroth`ing from ' leave as and ' 18 Hazeroth`ing in ' and encamp and ' lust`ed the
' and encamp and ' Rithmah from ' leave as and ' 19 the juniper in ' and encamp and
' and encamp and ' grow ' Ramanh`ing from ' leave as and ' 20 grow ' Ramanh`ing in
' 22 drip`ed in ' and encamp and ' Libnah`ing from ' leave as and ' 21 the white`ing in
' leave as and ' 23 Kohalath in ' and encamp and ' Rissah from ' leave as and
' mountain from ' leave as and ' 24 is lip ' blemish ' and encamp and ' Kohalath from
' Haradah from ' leave as and ' 25 the shudder in ' and encamp and ' is lip
' and encamp and ' Makheloth from ' leave as and ' 26 you tent from in ' and encamp and
' leave as and ' 28 old in ' and encamp and ' under from ' leave as and ' 27 under in
' Mithcah from ' leave as and ' 29 the sip in ' and encamp and ' Tarah from
' Hashmonah`ing from ' leave as and ' 30 Hashmonah`ing in ' and encamp and
' and encamp and ' Moseroth from ' leave as and ' 31 you and commit in ' and encamp and
choose ' and encamp and ' Joakan ' as son from ' leave as and ' 32 Joakan ' as son in
' fortune`ed fortune the ' tomorrow ' leave as and ' 33 fortune`ed fortune the '
' and encamp and ' Jotbathah from ' leave as and ' 34 he improve in ' and encamp and
' and encamp and ' Abronah from ' leave as and ' 35 the has cross in
and encamp and ' strong ' Ezion from ' leave as and ' 36 strong ' has and backbone in
and encamp and ' holy from ' leave as and ' 37 holy ' that`s ' thorn ' word from in '
' Aaron ' went and ' 38 Edom ' land ' the end in ' mountain the ' blemish '
' die as and ' Jehovah ' edge ' on ' mountain the ' mountain ' to ' priest the
' Israel ' as son ' you issue of ' from as four I the ' you Year in ' there
Aaron and ' 39 new of ' one in ' as five`s the ' new in ' from as Mizra ' land from
' blemish ' and die`ing in ' the Year ' each and ' from as ten and ' three ' son '
' dwell ' that`ing and ' Arad ' king ' as Canaan the ' hear as and ' 40 mountain the

' leave as and ' 41 Israel ' as son ' came`ing in ' Canaan ' land in ' south in
' leave as and ' 42 Zalmonah`ing in ' and encamp and ' mountain the ' mountain from
' s`Punon from ' leave as and ' 43 s`Punon in ' and encamp and ' Zalmonah`ing from
and encamp and ' Oboth`ing from ' leave as and ' 44 you and father in ' and encamp and
' leave as and ' 45 Moab ' border`ing in ' from as Obara the ' eye`s in '
' leave as and ' 46 fortune ' Dibon`ing in ' and encamp and ' from as Ije from
' has and eternal in ' and encamp and ' fortune ' Dibon`ing from
' the complete`s of bear ' Almon`ing from ' leave as and ' 47 the complete`s of bear
' 48 Nebo ' as before ' from as Obara the ' as mountain in ' and encamp and
' you twilight in ' and encamp and ' from as Obara the ' as soon ' leave as and
' has desend the ' on ' and encamp and ' 49 and moon`s ' Jordan ' on ' Moab
' you twilight in ' hate`s the ' mourn ' till ' you and site the ' you house from
' on ' Moab ' you twilight in ' Moses ' to ' Jehovah ' word as and ' 50 Moab
' you say and ' Israel ' as son ' to ' word ' 51 say of ' and moon`s ' Jordan
' land ' to ' has desend the ' ye ' from as Obara ' from ye ' for ' them as to
' land the ' as sojourn as ' all ' ye ' from you occupy the and ' 52 Canaan
' from whom`ing appease from ' all ' ye ' from you perish and ' from are around from
' all ' ye and ' and perish you ' complete and castimage ' as image ' all ' ye and
' land the ' ye ' from you occupy the and ' 53 and destory`s you ' from die in
net`ness of ' land the ' ye ' as set has ' relate ' for ' thus ' from you dwell and
' ing`lot in ' land the ' ye ' from you inherit you the and ' 54 ye`ed '
' ye ' and increase you ' increase of ' from are as you at family of
' which ' on I ' and you inherit ' ye ' less`s you ' less of and ' and you inherit
' you and down of ' be`s as ' if ' ing`lot the ' there`ed ' if ' out
' and occupy`s you ' not ' mother and ' 55 and inherit set ' from are as you father

' which ' be`s and ' from are around from ' land the ' as sojourn as ' all ' ye
from has target of and ' your as has eye in ' ridge`s of ' lag ' and survive`s you
' which ' land the ' on ' from are ye ' and is boulder and ' from are as hunt in '
' as liken`s ' which are ' be`s and ' 56 thus ' from as sojourn as ' from ye
relate ' do`ed I ' so ' them of ' you concoct of

' as son ' ye ' command`ed ' 2 say of ' Moses ' to ' Jehovah ' word as and ' 1
' land the ' to ' from as came ' from ye ' for ' them as to ' you say and ' Israel
' land ' inherit`ed in ' relate ' untemper ' which ' land the ' such ' Canaan
' south`ed ' quarter ' relate ' be`s and ' 3 am you border`ing of ' Canaan
border`ing ' relate ' be`s and ' Edom ' as hand ' on ' thorn ' is wilderness from
' relate ' converge and ' 4 east`ed ' salt the ' sea ' the end from ' south`ed '
' cross and ' from as approach have ' the above of ' south from ' border`ing the
' creak in ' holy of ' south from ' and you as spring you ' be`s and ' thorn`ed
' converge and ' 5 the has and might ' cross and ' big ' yard ' out and
' and be`s and ' from as Mizra ' inherit`ed ' the has and might from ' border`ing the
relate ' be`s as and ' sea`ed ' border`ing and ' 6 sea`ed the ' and you as spring you
border`ing ' relate ' be`s as ' this ' border`ing as and ' great`ing the ' sea the '
' has from ' the north`ing ' border`ing ' relate ' be`s as ' this and ' 7 sea`ed '
' 8 mountain the ' mountain ' relate ' lust you ' great`ing the ' sea the
' and be`s and ' hotspring`ed ' came`ing of ' lust you ' mountain the ' mountain from
' border`ing the ' out and ' 9 flank`ed ' border`ing the ' and you as spring you
' this ' has low`s ' yard ' and you as spring you ' and be`s and ' the has fragrant
' relate ' from you as lust the and ' 10 the north`ing ' border`ing ' relate ' be`s as
' descend and ' 11 the from lip ' has low`s ' yard from ' east`ed ' border`ing of
' low`s of ' east from ' fertile`ed that ' the from lip from ' border`ing the
' Chinnerath ' sea ' shoulder ' on I ' wipe`ed and ' border`ing the ' descend and
' and be`s and ' the has descend the ' border`ing the ' descend and ' 12 east`ed
' land the ' relate ' be`s you ' such ' salt the ' sea ' and as you spring you
' as son ' ye ' Moses ' command as and ' 13 surround`s ' am you border`ing of
ing lot in ' ye`ed ' and inherit set ' which ' land the ' such ' say of ' Israel

' half and ' you and down the ' you nine of ' set of ' Jehovah ' command`ed ' which '
' you house of ' as Reuben the ' as son ' down`ed ' and take ' for ' (14 down`ed the
' you house of ' kid the ' as son ' staff from and ' from you and father
(15 from you inherit ' and take ' Manasse`ed ' down`ed ' half and ' from you and father
' from you inherit ' and take ' down`ed the ' half and ' you and down the ' two '
' word as and ' (16 emerge`ed from ' east`ed ' and moon`s ' has descend of ' cross from
' which ' from as person the ' you name ' to`ed ' (17 say of ' Moses ' to ' Jehovah
ed`Joshua`ing and ' priest the ' Eleazar ' land the ' ye ' relate ' and inherit as
' down`ed from ' one ' lift`s has ' one ' help`s and ' (18 Nun ' son '
' you name ' to`ed and ' (19 land the ' ye ' inherit of ' and took you
' (20 turn`ed as ' son ' dog ' Judah ' below`ed ' from as person the
' (21 gloref`ing as people ' son ' Samuel ' Simeon ' as son ' the down of and
' as son ' the down of and ' (22 has and trust ' son ' Elidad ' Benjamim`s ' below`ed
' below`ed ' Joseph ' as son of ' (23 as exile ' son ' as morn ' lift`s has ' judge
' the down of and ' (24 grid`ing ' son ' to train ' lift`s has ' Manasse`ed ' as son
' the down of and ' (25 has discern ' son ' Kemuel ' lift`s has ' Ephraim ' as son
' the down of and ' (26 are claw ' son ' Elizaphan ' lift`s has ' Zebulun ' as son
' the down of and ' (27 Azzah ' son ' to as escape ' lift`s has ' Issachar ' as son
' (28 as whole ' son ' gloref`ing as brother ' lift`s has ' which ' as son
' son ' of I release`ed ' lift`s has ' Naphtali ' as son ' the down of and
' ye ' inherit of ' Jehovah ' command`ed ' which ' to`ed ' (29 gloref`ing as people
Canaan ' land in ' Israel ' as son

Jordan ' on ' Moab ' you twilight in ' Moses ' to ' Jehovah ' word as and ' 1
' and gave and ' Israel ' as son ' ye ' command`ed ' 2 say of ' and moon`s '
' desist of ' from as town ' from you hold ' you inherit from ' from Levi of
' and give you ' them as you surround`s ' from as town of ' exact from and
' desist of ' them of ' from as town the ' and became and ' 3 from Levi of
from property`ing of and ' from you cattle of ' and became as ' them as exact from and
' which ' from as town the ' as exact from and ' 4 from you life ' all of and '
' thousand ' the outside`ing and ' town`s the ' is wall ' from Levi of ' and give you
' ye ' town`s of ' outside`ing from ' complete mete and ' 5 surround`s ' mother`ed
' south`ed ' quarter ' ye and ' cubit`ed ' from as thousand ' east`ed ' quarter
cubit`ed ' from as thousand ' sea`ed ' quarter ' ye and ' cubit`ed ' from as thousand
' town`s the and ' cubit`ed ' from as thousand ' the north`ing ' quarter ' ye and '
6 ' from as town the ' as too guest from ' them walk ' be`s as ' this ' middle`ing in
watch ' six ' ye ' from Levi of ' and give you ' which ' from as town the ' ye and
' murder the ' there`ed ' flee`ing of ' and give you ' which ' deficient them '
' all ' 7 town`s ' from twosome and ' from as four I ' and give you ' them as on and
eight`ed and ' from as four I ' from Levi of ' and give you ' which ' from as town the
' which ' from as town the and ' 8 has am exact from ' ye and ' has ye`ed ' town`s '
and increase you ' dispute ' each ' Israel ' as son ' you hold from ' and give you
' which ' and you inherit ' as palm ' man I ' and less`s you ' less the ' each and '
Jehovah ' word as and ' 9 from Levi of ' and as town from ' permanent ' and inherit as
' you say and ' Israel ' as son ' to ' word ' 10 say of ' Moses ' to '
' land`ed ' to ' has desend the ' ye ' from as Obara ' from ye ' for ' them as to
' deficient from ' watch ' from as town ' relate ' from city`s the and ' 11 Canaan
' soul ' with`ed ' murder ' there`ed ' flee and ' relate ' the has became`s you

' deficient from of ' from as town the ' relate ' and became and ' 12 mistake`ed in
' as before ' and stand ' till ' murder the ' die him ' not and ' redeem from
six ' and give you ' which ' from as town the and ' 13 discern from of ' till`ed the
' three ' ye ' 14 relate ' the has became`s you ' deficient from ' watch '
' three ' ye and ' has descend of ' cross from ' and give you ' from as town the
' deficient from ' watch ' Canaan ' land in ' and give you ' from as town the
' sojourn you of and ' guest of and ' Israel ' as son of ' 15 the has became`s you
' these`ed ' from as town the ' six ' the has became`s you ' from middle`ing in
16 mistake`ed in ' soul ' with`ed ' all ' there`ed ' flee`ing of ' deficient from of
' murder ' die as and ' and smitten`ed ' of iron ' vessal are in ' mother and '
' which ' hand ' stone in ' mother and ' 17 murder the ' die him ' die`ing ' that`ing
' die`ing ' that`ing ' murder ' die as and ' and smitten`ed ' thus ' die`ing as
' which ' hand ' tree ' vessal are in ' mother and ' or ' 18 murder the ' die him
' die`ing ' that`ing ' murder ' die as and ' and smitten`ed ' and in ' die`ing as
murder the ' ye ' die`s as ' that`ing ' blood the ' redeem ' 19 murder the ' die him
' mother and ' 20 and has die`s as ' that`ing ' and in ' and entreat in '
' am hunt in ' and Mosthigh ' hurl`s the ' or ' and has expel as ' hateful`ed in
' die as and ' and hand in ' and smitten`ed ' the enemy came ' or ' 21 die as and
' die`s as ' blood the ' redeem ' that`ing ' murder ' here them ' die him ' die`ing
' weary ' moment in ' mother and ' 22 and in ' and entreat in ' murder the ' ye
' weary ' weapon ' all ' and Mosthigh ' hurl`s the ' or ' and expel`s ' the enemy I
' you see ' weary ' thus ' die`ing as ' which ' stone ' all in ' or ' 23 am hunt
' if ' enemy and I ' not ' that`ing and ' die as and ' and Mosthigh ' fell and
' between in ' till`ed the ' and discern and ' 24 and you evil ' seek from ' not and
' from as discern them ' on ' blood the ' redeem ' between in and ' here them

' murder the ' here them ' ye ' till`ed the ' and shade`s the and ' (25 these`ed
' to ' till`ed the ' and ye ' and carry`s the and ' blood the ' redeem ' hand from
' till ' thus ' dwell and ' there`ed ' flee ' which ' and deficient from ' town`s
holy the ' eight in ' and ye ' anoint ' which ' great`ing the ' priest the ' die`ing
' town`s ' border`ing ' ye ' murder the ' out ' out ' mother and ' (25
' redeem ' and ye ' come and ' (27 there`ed ' flee`ing as ' which ' and deficient from
' and deficient from ' town`s ' border`ing of ' outside`ing from ' blood the
for ' (28 blood ' if ' whither`s ' murder the ' ye ' blood the ' redeem ' murder and
' priest the ' die`ing ' till ' dwell ' and deficient from ' town`s in '
' carry`ing as ' great`ing the ' priest the ' die`ing ' as after and ' great`ing the
' relate ' to`ed ' and became and ' (29 and you hold ' land ' to ' murder the
' all in ' from are as generation of ' discern from ' statute of
murder as ' from as till ' as by ' soul ' with`ed ' all ' (30 your as desist and from
(31 die`ing of ' soul in ' the because ' not ' one ' till and ' murder the ' ye '
' evil`ness ' that`ing ' which ' murder ' soul of ' atone ' and took you ' not and '
flee`ing of ' atone ' and took you ' not and ' (32 die him ' die`ing ' for ' die`ing of
' till ' land in ' desist of ' carry`ing of ' and deficient from ' town`s ' to '
' ye ' and pollute`s you ' not and ' (33 great`ing the ' priest the ' die`ing
' that`ing ' blood the ' for ' thus ' from as dwell ' from ye ' which ' land the
' which ' blood of ' atone as ' not ' land of and ' land the ' ye ' pollute`s as
' and unclean you ' not and ' (34 and pour ' blood in ' mother ' for ' thus ' pour
nigh ' as whither ' which ' thus ' from as dwell ' from ye ' which ' land the ' ye
' as son ' middle`ing in ' nigh ' Jehovah ' as whither ' for ' the middle`ing in '
Israel

as son ' you and at family of ' you and father the ' as head ' and approach as and ' 1
' as son ' you and at family from ' Manasse`ed ' son ' Machir ' son ' Gilead '
' from as help`s the ' as before and ' Moses ' as before ' and word as and ' Joseph
' ye ' and say as and ' 2 Israel ' as son of ' you and father the ' as head
' inherit`ed in ' land the ' ye ' set of ' Jehovah ' command`ed ' as master
' set of ' Jehovah in ' command`ed ' as master and ' Israel ' as son of ' ing`lot in
' 3 him daughter`th of ' our as brother ' Zelophehad ' you inherit ' ye
' Israel ' as son ' as tribe ' as son from ' one of ' and became and
' you inherit from ' has you inherit ' the withdraw shall ' from as women of
' which ' down`ed the ' you inherit ' on ' the put flee`ing and ' our as you father
' 4 withdraw as ' our you inherit ' ing`lot from and ' them of ' the has became`s you
' the put flee`ing and ' Israel ' as son of ' ing`produce the ' be`s as ' mother and
' the has became`s you ' which ' down`ed the ' you inherit ' on ' has you inherit
' withdraw as ' our as you father ' down`ed ' you inherit from and ' them of
' edge ' on ' Israel ' as son ' ye ' Moses ' command as and ' 5 has you inherit
word the ' this ' 6 from as word ' Joseph ' as son ' down`ed ' so ' say of ' Jehovah
' good`ing of ' say of ' Zelophehad ' you and white ' Jehovah ' command`ed ' which '
' sure ' from as women of ' the has became`s you ' them as has eye in
' the has became`s you ' them as father ' down`ed ' you and at family of
' Israel ' as son of ' inherit`ed ' away you ' not and ' 7 from as women of
' down`ed ' you inherit in ' man I ' for ' down`ed ' to ' down`ed from
' daughter ' all and ' 8 Israel ' as son ' and cleave as ' and as you father
' one of ' Israel ' as son ' you and down from ' inherit`ed ' you possess
' purpose of ' resemble I of ' be`s you ' am father ' down`ed ' you and at family from
and as you father ' you inherit ' ye ' man I ' Israel ' as son ' and possess as

' for ' after ' down`ed ' to ' down`ed from ' inherit`ed ' away you ' not and ' 9
' 10 Israel ' as son ' you and down ' and cleave as ' and you inherit in ' man I
' daughter`th`ing ' concoct ' so ' Moses ' ye ' Jehovah ' command`ed ' which are
' Hoghah and ' keep`ed and ' the of wipe ' the has became`s you and ' 11 Zelophehad
has am uncle ' as son of ' Zelophehad ' daughter`th`ing ' run`ed you and ' Milcah and
' Joseph ' son ' Manasse`ed ' as son ' you and at family from ' 12 from as women of '
' down`ed ' on ' has you inherit ' became you and ' from as women of ' him the
from as discern them and ' unleaven`ing the ' to`ed ' 13 has am father ' you at family
' Israel ' as son ' to ' Moses ' hand in ' Jehovah ' command`ed ' which '
' and moon`s ' Jordan ' on ' Moab ' you twilight in

cross in ' Israel ' all ' to ' Moses ' word ' which ' from as word the ' to`ed 1
' between in ' join`ing ' split`ing ' thus town in ' word from in ' has desend the '
' enough and ' you and yard and ' Laban and ' untemper ' between in and ' has I apart
' gate`s ' mountain ' way ' ing`desolate from ' day as ' ten ' one ' 2 gold
' the Year ' from as four came ' became as and ' 3 creak in ' holy ' till
' as son ' to ' Moses ' word ' new of ' one in ' new ' ten ' as daul in
' as after ' 4 them as to ' and ye ' Jehovah ' command`ed ' which ' accord ' Israel
' sojourn as ' which ' as Amar the ' king ' Sihon`ing ' ye ' and you and smitten
' sojourn as ' which ' shameful the ' king ' bake`ing ' ye and ' shall reckon in
' Moab ' land in ' has desend the ' cross in ' 5 as force came ' you and Astar in
' 6 say of ' such the ' the protect`ing the ' ye ' well ' Moses ' of as that`ing
' increase ' say of ' ing`desolate in ' our as to ' word ' our as Allah ' Jehovah
and came and ' relate ' leave and ' and turn ' 7 this the ' blemish ' desist ' relate
' blemish ' thus town in ' and as nigh ' all ' to and ' as Amar the ' mountain '
' as Canaan the ' land ' sea the ' pure`ing in and ' south in and ' depth`ed in and
' 8 Euphrates ' river ' great the ' river the ' till ' has and white the and
and occupy ' and came ' land the ' ye ' your as before ' as set has ' and look`ed
from are as you father of ' Jehovah ' as you swear too has ' which ' land the ' ye '
' from seed of and ' them of ' set of ' Jacob of and ' Isaac of ' Abraham of '
' not ' say of ' that`s the ' time in ' your as to ' say and ' 9 them as after
' your as Allah ' Jehovah ' 10 from are ye ' arise ' as alone of ' able I
as in star`ing are ' day as the ' from are behold and ' from are ye ' increase`ed the
add ' from are you and father ' as Allah ' Jehovah ' 11 increase of ' heaven`s the '
from are ye ' bless as and ' from as move ' thousand ' from star ' from are mosthigh '
' as alone of ' lift I ' the sure`s ' 12 relate ' word ' which are '

relate ' ascribe ' 13 from are increase`s and ' from are burden and ' from are pressure
' from as known and ' from as understand`ing and ' from as wise ' from as person '
' near ' and low you and ' 14 your as head in ' from there`s I and ' your as tribe of
' 15 you concoct of ' you word ' which ' word the ' good`ing ' and say you and
' from as wise ' from as person ' your as tribe ' as head ' ye ' took I and
' from are mosthigh ' from as head ' from ye ' give I and ' from as known and
' as captain and ' you and hundred ' as captain and ' from as thousand ' as captain
' from as ing`officer and ' you and ten ' as captain and ' from as five
' time in ' from are as discern ' ye ' command`ed I and ' 16 your as tribe of
from you discern and ' your as brother ' between in ' and hear ' say of ' that`s the
' between in and ' him brother ' between in and ' man I ' between in ' just '
' small are ' discern from in ' inner`s ' and pasture`s you ' not ' 17 and guest
' man I ' around from ' and guest`ing you ' not ' has and hear you ' great`ing are
hard`ed as ' which ' word the and ' that`ing ' from as Allah of ' discern them ' for
' command`ed I and ' 18 him you hear and ' Eli ' has and approach`s you ' from with '
' which ' from as word the ' all ' ye ' that`s the ' time in ' from are ye
' all ' ye ' walk`ed has and ' ing`desolate from ' go`ed and ' 19 smoke`ing you
' which ' that`ing the ' look and behold and ' great`ing the ' is wilderness the
' Jehovah ' command`ed ' which are ' as Amar the ' mountain ' way ' from you seen
' say and ' 20 creak in ' holy ' till ' prophet`ing and ' and has ye ' our as Allah
' Jehovah ' which ' as Amar the ' mountain ' till ' from ye in ' your as to
' are as Allah ' Jehovah ' gave ' look`ed ' 21 our of ' gave ' our as Allah
' Jehovah ' word ' which are ' vemon ' on`ed ' land the ' ye ' are as before
' 22 under ' to and ' look as you ' to ' walk ' are as you father ' as Allah
' send`ed has ' and say you and ' from are all ' Eli ' shall approach you and

' land the ' ye ' our of ' and ration as and ' our as before ' from as person
' thus ' on`ed has ' which ' way the ' ye ' word ' and has ye ' and carry`s as and
' improve as and ' (23 has am to ' prophet`ing ' which ' from as town the ' ye and
from as person ' ten ' from two ' from with ' took I and ' word the ' as has eye in
' mountain`ed the ' and went and ' and turn as and ' (24 tribe of ' one ' man I '
' (25 ye`ed ' and foot as and ' of and testicle ' inherit ' till ' and came as and
our as to ' and cart`s as and ' land the ' fruit from ' from hand in ' acquire as and
' land the ' the good`ing ' and say as and ' word ' and has ye ' and carry`s as and '
' from you as father ' not and ' (26 our of ' gave ' our as Allah ' Jehovah ' which
' (27 your as Allah ' Jehovah ' edge ' ye ' and constant and ' offer`ing of
Jehovah ' you hateful in ' and say you and ' from are as tent in ' and murmur you and
and has ye ' set of ' from as Mizra ' land from ' and has spring`s the ' and has ye '
' and us I ' whither`ed ' (28 and has destory`s the of ' as Amar the ' hand in '
say of ' and has in heart ' ye ' and burden`s the ' our as brother and ' from as on
you and great ' from as town ' and her from ' from increase and ' great`ing ' people '
' our as look ' from as Anak ' as son ' also and ' heaven`s in ' you defence`ing and '
shall dread you ' not and ' has and afraid you ' not ' your as to ' say and ' (29 there
' that`ing ' your as before ' enter the ' your as Allah ' Jehovah ' (30 lag '
' from as Mizra in ' from are ye ' do`ed ' which ' accord ' relate ' fight as
' are help ' which ' you seen ' which ' is wilderness in and ' (31 your as low`s of
' all in ' and son ' ye ' man I ' linger ' which are ' are as Allah ' Jehovah
' place`ing the ' till ' from are came ' till ' from you walk the ' which ' way the
' from as believe from ' your whither`s ' this the ' word in the and ' (32 this the
protect`ing of ' way in ' your as before ' enter the ' (33 your as Allah ' Jehovah in
' the night`s ' abhorrence ' from are incline`ing the of ' place`ing ' relate '

’ cloud in and ’ thus ’ and walk you ’ which ’ way in ’ from are sight`ing the of
’ your as word ’ voice`ing ’ ye ’ Jehovah ’ hear as and ’ 34 from day as
’ man I ’ look`ed as ’ mother ’ 35 say of ’ swear too as and ’ angry as and
land the ’ ye ’ this the ’ mischief ’ magnificent`ing ’ these`ed ’ from as person in
from are as you father of ’ set of ’ as you swear too has ’ which ’ the good`ing the ’
’ the has look as ’ that`ing ’ turn`ed as ’ son ’ dog ’ as you despise`ing ’ 36
because ’ him son of and ’ thus ’ way ’ which ’ land the ’ ye ’ donkey ’ if and
’ Jehovah ’ anger`th you the ’ house ’ also ’ 37 Jehovah ’ as after ’ fill ’ which ’
’ 38 there`ed ’ income`ing ’ not ’ ye`ed ’ also ’ say of ’ from are sake in
’ came`ing as ’ that`ing ’ are as before ’ stand the ’ Nun ’ son ’ ed`Joshua`ing
’ ye ’ the has inherit`s as ’ that`ing ’ for ’ strength I ’ and ye ’ there`ed
’ be`s as ’ spoil of ’ from you say ’ which ’ from are children and ’ 39 Israel
’ evil and ’ good`ing ’ day as the ’ and known ’ not ’ which ’ your as son and
’ them and ’ the has give I ’ them of and ’ there`ed ’ and came as ’ them`ed
’ word`ed them ’ relate ’ leave and ’ and turn ’ from ye and ’ 40 the and possess as
’ and has sin ’ Eli ’ and say you and ’ and low you and ’ 41 join`ing ’ sea ’ way
’ accord ’ and has fight has and ’ on`ed has ’ and us I ’ our as Allah ’ Jehovah of
’ ye ’ man I ’ and gird you and ’ our as Allah ’ Jehovah ’ and has command ’ which
mountain`ed the ’ offer`ing of ’ and has became you and ’ and you fight from ’ weapon
’ not and ’ lug you ’ not ’ them of ’ say ’ Eli ’ Jehovah ’ say as and ’ 42
’ not and ’ from are approach in ’ as has whither`s ’ for ’ and fight you
’ your as to ’ the word I and ’ 43 your as enemy I ’ as before ’ and defeat you
’ your as Allah ’ Jehovah ’ edge ’ ye ’ and constant and ’ from you hear ’ not and
’ as Amar the ’ out and ’ 44 mountain`ed the ’ and on you and ’ s`insolent you and
’ that`ing the ’ blemish ’ dwell the ’ as Canaan the and ’ as Amalek the

the has as suffice ’ which are ’ from are ye ’ and chase as and ’ from are you call of

45 curse`ed ’ till ’ barley`s in ’ from are ye ’ and group as and ’ from as word the ’

’ hear ’ not and ’ Jehovah ’ as before ’ and against you and ’ and inhabitant and ’

’ 46 your as to ’ ear`s the ’ not and ’ from are voice`ing in ’ Jehovah

’ which ’ from week are ’ from as increase ’ from week ’ holy in ’ and inhabitant and

from you dwell

' which are ' join`ing ' sea ' way ' word`ed them ' go`ed and ' turn`ed has and ' 1

' from week ' gate`s ' mountain ' ye ' converge`ing and ' Eli ' Jehovah ' word

' relate ' increase ' 3 say of ' Eli ' Jehovah ' say as and ' 2 from as increase

4 ' the north`ing ' relate ' and turn ' this the ' mountain the ' ye ' away`ing

' border`ing in ' from as Obara ' from ye ' say of ' command`ed ' people the ' ye and

' barley`s in ' from as dwell the ' concoct ' as son ' your as brother

' to ' 5 especially ' from you guard has and ' from with ' and dread as and

' the possess ' from land from ' relate ' donkey ' not ' for ' height ' and guest set

' ye ' as set has ' Esau of ' the possess ' for ' foot ' palm ' way from ' till

from you eat and ' silver in ' spy from ' and buy`s you ' eat ' 6 gate`s ' mountain

from you as drink and ' silver in ' spy from ' and pasture`s you ' Water ' also and '

' are as hand ' do`ed from ' all in ' are bless ' are as Allah ' Jehovah ' for ' 7

' this ' this the ' great`ing the ' is wilderness the ' ye ' are you walk ' known

' you lack ' not ' are people ' are as Allah ' Jehovah ' the Year ' from as four I

' say of ' Edom ' king ' to ' from as messenger from ' send`ed I and ' word

not and ' vineyard in and ' field`ed in ' tender`ed ' not ' are land in ' cross`ed I

' tour`ing ' not ' walk has ' king the ' way ' empty`ing ' who ' the drink has '

not ' say as and ' are border`ing ' cross has ' which ' till ' of left and ' right`s

' 8 are you call of ' proceed ' desolate in ' turn ' house ' cross you '

from as sojourn became ' concoct ' as son ' our as brother ' each ' cross`ed has and

' shall as tree from and ' you to`s from ' thus town the ' way from ' barley`s in '

' 9 Moab ' word from ' way ' cross`ed has and ' turn`ed has and ' strong

' to and ' Moab ' ye ' besiege`ing ' to ' Eli ' Jehovah ' say as and

' and land from ' walk ' donkey ' not ' for ' fight`ed from ' height`ing ' guest set

' 10 the possess ' town ' ye ' as set has ' Lot ' as son of ' for ' the possess

' great`ing ' people ' thus ' and carry as ' from as turn of ' from week that
anger ' and reckon as ' from as decease ' 11 from as Anak are ' residue ' increase and
' them of ' and call as ' from as Moab the and ' from as Anak are ' them '
' from as hole the ' and carry as ' Barley`s in and ' 12 from as mother`s
' from and possess as ' concoct ' as son and ' from as turn of
' from and possess as and ' them around from ' Jehovah ' from and destory`s as and
' land of ' Israel ' do`ed ' which are ' them as under ' and dwell and
' and rise`ing ' the time and ' 13 them of ' Jehovah ' gave ' which ' and you possess
' ye ' cross`ed has and ' shrub ' inherit ' ye ' relate ' and cross and ' leave
' holy from ' and has walk the ' which ' from week the and ' 14 shrub ' inherit
' from as three ' shrub ' inherit ' ye ' and has cross ' which ' till ' creak in
' as person ' magnificent`ing ' all ' complete ' till ' the Year ' eight`ed and
' Jehovah ' swear too has ' which are ' camp`ed the ' approach from ' fight`ed them
' trouble of ' height ' whom`ed the ' Jehovah ' hand ' also and ' 15 them of
' which are ' became as and ' 16 accomplish ' till ' camp`ed the ' approach from
people the ' approach from ' die`ing of ' fight`ed them ' as person ' all ' similitude
' Obara ' ye`ed ' 18 say of ' Eli ' Jehovah ' word as and ' say as and ' 17
' you appoach and ' 19 town ' ye ' Moab ' border`ing ' ye ' day as the
' height ' guest set ' to and ' from besiege`ing ' to ' Ammon ' as son ' split`ing
' for ' the possess ' walk ' Ammon ' as son ' land from ' donkey ' not ' for
reckon you ' from as decease ' land ' 20 the possess ' am set has ' Lot ' as son of
' from as turn of ' thus ' and carry as ' from as decease ' that`s ' anger '
' from as turn of ' thus ' and sojourn call as ' from as Ammon`ing the and
' people ' 21 from as wick wick ' them of ' and call as ' from as Ammon the and
' from destory`s as and ' from as Anak are ' residue ' increase and ' great`ing

(22 them as under ' and dwell and ' from and possess as and ' them around from ' Jehovah
' barley`s in ' from as sojourn became ' concoct ' as son of ' do`ed ' which are '
' them around from ' as hole the ' ye ' destory`s the ' which
this the ' day as the ' till ' them as under ' and dwell and ' from and possess as and
harsh`ed ' till ' from as yard in ' from as sojourn became ' from eye`ing the and ' (23
' from destory`s the ' Caphtor`ing from ' from as spring became ' from as Caphtor '
' ye ' and cross and ' leave ' and rise`ing ' (24 them as under ' and dwell and
' king ' Sihon`ing ' ye ' are hand in ' as set has ' look`ed ' Arnon ' inherit
' strife the and ' vemon ' sick the ' and land ' ye and ' as Amar the ' shall reckon
' are startle ' set ' sick I ' this the ' day as the ' (25 fight`ed from ' and in
' heaven`s the ' all ' under ' from as people the ' around ' on ' are you dread and
' and sick and ' and tremble and ' are hear ' ye ' shall hear as ' which
' is wilderness from ' from as messenger from ' send`ed I and ' (26 are around from
' from and peace ' as word ' shall reckon ' king ' Sihon`ing ' to ' and and east
' bound`ing ' not ' walk I ' way in ' way in ' are land in ' cross`ed I ' (27 say of
' as you eat and ' as has buy`s you ' silver in ' eat ' (28 of and left and ' right`s
' cross`ed I ' only ' as whom drink and ' vessel ' has set ' silver in ' Water and
' concoct ' as son ' vessel ' concoct ' which are ' (29 as foot in
' from as sojourn became ' from as Moab the and ' barley`s in ' from as sojourn became
' which ' land the ' to ' has desend the ' ye ' cross I ' which ' till ' burn
' king ' Sihon`ing ' father`ed ' not and ' (30 our of ' gave ' our as Allah ' Jehovah
' Jehovah ' hard`ed the ' for ' and in ' and has cross`s the ' shall reckon
' purpose of ' and mind ' ye ' harden and ' and spirit is ' ye ' are as Allah
' Eli ' Jehovah ' say as and ' (31 this the ' day as are ' are hand in ' and set
' king ' Sihon`ing ' ye ' are as before ' set ' as you sick the ' look`ed

' net`ness of ' vemon ' sick the ' and land ' ye and ' as Amar the ' shall reckon
' all and ' that`ing ' our you call of ' Sihon`ing ' out and ' 32 and land ' ye
' Jehovah ' and give`ed as and ' 33 stamp`ed ' fight`ed from of ' and people
' ye and ' him son ' ye and ' and ye ' strike`ed and ' our as before ' our as Allah
' time in ' and as town ' all ' ye ' capture`ed has and ' 34 and people ' all
' complete from ' and as town ' all ' ye ' the curse`s has and ' that`s the
' 35 survivor`s ' and has remain the ' not ' children the and ' from as woman the and
' from as town the ' strip and ' our of ' and has plunder ' cattle`ed the ' only
' Arnon ' inherit ' you lip ' on ' which ' Aroer from ' 36 and has capture ' which
' whom`ed the ' not ' Gilead the ' till and ' inherit in ' which ' town`s the and
' Jehovah ' gave ' total ' ye ' and her from ' defend`ed ' which ' repair`ed
' as son ' land ' to ' only ' 37 and has hand in ' our as before ' our as Allah
' as town and ' spew the ' inherit ' hand ' all ' you approach ' not ' Ammon
our as Allah ' Jehovah ' and has command`ed ' which ' all and ' mountain the

king ' bake`ing ' out and ' shameful the ' way ' the on shall ' turn`ed has and ' 1
fight`ed from of ' and people ' all and ' that`ing ' our you call of ' shameful the '
' for ' and ye ' look as you ' to ' Eli ' Jehovah ' say as and ' 2 as force I '
' and land ' ye and ' and people ' all ' ye and ' and ye ' as set has ' are hand in
which ' as Amar the ' king ' Sihon`ing of ' you as do ' which are ' if ' dual`s and
' our as Allah ' Jehovah ' give as and ' 3 shall reckon in ' sojourn as '
' all ' ye and ' shameful the ' king ' bake`ing ' ye ' also ' and has hand in
' if ' remain`s the ' as zero in ' till ' and has strike`ed and ' and people
' that`s the ' time in ' and as town ' all ' ye ' capture`ed has and ' 4 survivor`s
from as six ' spy from ' and has take ' not ' which ' repair`ed ' whom`ed the ' not
' all ' 5 Bashan in ' bake`ing ' you king from ' clod them ' country ' all ' town`s '
' from as door ' be peak ' the Ham`ing ' splendor`ing in ' from as town ' to`ed
' 6 especially ' increase`ed the ' as Periz the ' as town from ' earnest ' bar`s and
' king ' Sihon`ing of ' our as do ' which are ' from ye`ing ' the curse`s has and
' from as women the ' complete from ' town`s ' all ' curse the ' shall reckon
' from as town the ' strip and ' cattle`ed the ' all and ' 7 children the and
land the ' ye ' that`s the ' time in ' took has and ' 8 our of ' and has plunder'ing
' has desend the ' cross in ' which ' as Amar the ' as king ' two ' hand from '
' from as s`Zidon ' 9 pomegranate`ing at ' mountain ' till and ' Arnon ' inherit from
' if ' and call as ' as Amar the and ' has as captain ' Hermon of ' and call as
' all and ' Gilead the ' all and ' fit`ing from the ' watch ' all ' 10 ice`s
' bake`ing ' you king from ' watch ' as force I and ' avenue`ed ' till ' shameful the
' remain has ' shameful the ' king ' bake`ing ' only ' for ' 11 Bashan in
' of iron ' bed ' and bed ' be`th ' from as decease the ' preserve from
' faithful`ing ' nine ' Ammon ' as son ' you increase in ' that`s ' the forward`ing

' ye and ' 12 man I ' you cubit ' the large ' faithful`ing ' four I and ' the lengthen
' which ' Aroer from ' that`s the ' time in ' and has possess ' such the ' land the
' him town and ' Gilead the ' mountain ' half and ' Arnon ' inherit ' you lip ' on
' all and ' Gilead the ' preserve and ' 13 as Gad of and ' as Reuben of ' as set has
' tribe ' half of ' as set has ' bake`ing ' you king from ' shameful the
' that`ing the ' shameful the ' all of ' clod them ' country ' all ' Manasse`ed the
' took of ' Manasse`ed ' son ' channel`s and ' 14 from as decease ' land ' call as
' as s`Geshur the ' border`ing ' till ' clod them ' country ' all ' ye
' shameful the ' ye ' name ' on ' from ye ' call as and ' as depression them and
' as set has ' Machir of and ' 15 this the ' day as the ' till ' channel`s ' crush`ing
' has from ' as set has ' as Gad of and ' as Reuben of and ' 16 Gilead the ' ye
border`ing and ' inherit the ' middle`ing ' Arnon ' inherit ' till and ' Gilead the
thus town the and ' 17 Ammon ' as son ' border`ing ' inherit the ' spew ' till and '
' sea ' till and ' net so from ' border`ing and ' the has descend the and '
' cleft`ed the ' you and brook ' under ' salt the ' sea ' thus town the
' say of ' that`s the ' time in ' from are ye ' command`ed I and ' 18 emerge`ed from
' such the ' land the ' ye ' relate ' gave ' your as Allah ' Jehovah
' your as brother ' as before ' and cross you ' from as change`ing ' the net`ness of
' from are children ' only ' 19 sick`s ' as son ' all ' Israel ' as son
increase ' purchase`ed ' for ' as you known ' your as purchase and ' your as women and
till ' 20 relate ' as set has ' which ' from are as town in ' and carry as ' relate '
' and possess as and ' from star ' your as brother of ' Jehovah ' rest`s as ' which '
' them of ' gave ' your as Allah ' Jehovah ' which ' land the ' ye ' them ' also
' which ' and you possess of ' man I ' from desist and ' has desend the ' cross in
that`s the ' time in ' as whom command ' Joshua`ing ' ye and ' 21 relate ' as set has

’ Jehovah ’ do`ed ’ which ’ all ’ ye ’ sight`ing the ’ are as has eye ’ say of ’
’ Jehovah ’ success`ed ’ so ’ these`ed ’ from as king the ’ two of ’ your as Allah
’ not ’ 22 there`ed ’ Obara ’ ye`ed ’ which ’ you and king them ’ all of
relate ’ fight has the ’ that`ing ’ your as Allah ’ Jehovah ’ for ’ from and dread you
’ as master ’ 24 say of ’ that`s the ’ time in ’ Jehovah ’ to ’ favor`ed ye and ’ 23
’ ye ’ are serve ’ ye ’ sight`ing the of ’ you and sick the ’ ye`ed ’ Jehovah
’ heaven`s in ’ to ’ who ’ which ’ strength`ed the ’ are hand ’ ye and ’ are great
25 are as you strong`ing are and ’ are as work are ’ success`ed ’ which ’ land in and
’ which ’ the good`ing the ’ land the ’ ye ’ look`ed I and ’ oh ’ cross`ed I ’
’ this the ’ good`ing the ’ mountain the ’ has desend the ’ cross in
’ from are purpose of ’ house ’ Jehovah ’ cross whom and ’ 26 has and white the and
’ to ’ walk ’ increase ’ Eli ’ Jehovah ’ say as and ’ Eli ’ hear ’ not and
’ head ’ to ’ on`ed ’ 27 this the ’ word in ’ till`ing ’ Eli ’ word ’ yield you
’ the north`ing and ’ sea`ed ’ are as has eye ’ lift and ’ cleft`ed the
’ not ’ for ’ are as has eye in ’ look`ed and ’ emerge`ed from and ’ right`ed you and
’ ed`Joshua`ing ’ ye ’ command and ’ 28 this the ’ has desend the ’ ye ’ cross you
’ as before ’ cross as ’ that`ing ’ for ’ and harden`ed and ’ and strength`ed and
’ land the ’ ye ’ from ye`ing ’ inherit`s as ’ that`ing and ’ this the ’ people the
gape`ing ’ you house ’ split`ing ’ I nation in ’ carry has and ’ 29 saw`ed ’ which

1 ' to and ' from as law the ' to ' hear ' Israel ' the time and '
you concoct of ' from are ye ' teach from ' for whither ' which ' from as discern them
' ye ' from you possess and ' from brought and ' shall life you ' purpose of '
2 ' relate ' gave ' from are as you father ' as Allah ' Jehovah ' which ' land the
' command`ed from ' for whither ' which ' word the ' on ' and yield`s you ' not
ye ' guard of ' and her from ' and withdraw you ' not and ' day as the ' from are ye
' command`ed from ' for whither ' which ' your as Allah ' Jehovah ' unleaven`ing '
3 ' Jehovah ' do`ed ' which ' ye ' sight`ing the ' your as has eye ' from are ye
' marry ' as after ' walk the ' which ' man that ' all ' for ' gape`ing ' marry in
4 ' are approach from ' are as Allah ' Jehovah ' and destory`s the ' gape`ing
' from as life ' your as Allah ' Jehovah in ' from as cleave the ' from ye and
5 ' from as law ' from are ye ' as you teach ' and look`ed ' day as the ' from are all
' as Allah ' Jehovah ' as has command ' which are ' from as discern from and
' from as came ' from ye ' which ' land the ' approach in ' so ' you concoct of
6 ' that`s ' for ' from dual`s and ' from you guard and ' the net`ness of ' there`ed
' from as people the ' as has eye of ' from are you son`s and ' from are you wise
only ' and say and ' these`ed ' from as law the ' all ' ye ' shall hear as ' which
7 ' this the ' great`ing the ' nation`ing the ' understand`ing and ' wise ' people '
' from as Allah ' if ' which ' great`ing ' nation`ing ' who ' for
' and has call ' all in ' our as Allah ' Jehovah are ' him to ' from as approach`ing
8 ' from as law ' if ' which ' great`ing ' nation`ing ' as from and ' him to
' such the ' the protect`ing the ' accord ' from just`s ' from as discern from and
9 walk ' guard the ' only ' day as the ' your as before ' gave ' for whither ' which
from as word the ' ye ' forget you ' turn ' especially ' are soul ' guard`ing and '
' are in heart from ' and correct`ing ' turn and ' are as has eye ' see ' which '

' are as son of ' from you acknowlege the and ' are as life ' week ' all
' Jehovah ' as before ' you stand ' which ' day as ' 10 are as son ' as son of and
' vessel ' assemble the ' Eli ' Jehovah ' say in ' ing`desolate in ' are as Allah
' has and teach as ' which ' as word ' ye ' from hear`s I and ' people the ' ye
' on ' from as life ' them ' which ' from week the ' all ' near ' dread`ed of
' shall approach you and ' 11 has and teach as ' them as son ' ye and ' ground`ed the
' till ' abhorrence ' burn ' is be and ' mountain the ' under ' has and stand you and
' Jehovah ' word as and ' 12 gloom have and ' cloud ' dark ' heaven`s the ' mind
' from ye ' from as word ' voice`ing ' fire the ' middle`ing from ' your as to
' from seen ' your whither`s ' the has simititude and ' from as hear
' and covenant`s ' ye ' relate ' my told and ' 13 voice`ing ' as you despise`ing
' from as word the ' you ten ' you concoct of ' from are ye ' command`ed ' which
' as ye and ' 14 from as stone ' ing`tablet ' two ' on ' from write as and
' from as law ' from are ye ' teach of ' that`s the ' time in ' Jehovah ' command`ed
' which ' land in ' from ye ' from are you concoct of ' from as discern from and
' from you guard has and ' 15 the net`ness of ' there`ed ' from as Obara ' from ye
' all ' from you seen ' not ' for ' from are as you soul of ' especially
' ing`desolate in ' your as to ' Jehovah ' word ' day as in ' the portion`ing
' from dual`s and ' has and eradicate you ' turn ' 16 fire the ' middle`ing from
' or ' male ' you as similar ' statue ' all ' you has simititude ' carve ' relate
' you as similar ' land in ' which ' cattle`ed ' all ' you as similar ' 17 the female
' all ' you as similar ' 18 heaven`s in ' fly`ing you ' which ' wing ' bird`ing ' all
' Water in ' which ' am squirm ' all ' you as similar ' ground`ed in ' crawl
' the heaven`s the ' are as has eye ' lift you ' turn and ' 19 land of ' under from
' from as in star`ing the ' ye and ' moon the ' ye and ' sun the ' ye ' sight`s and

' them of ' whom and humble`ly the and ' arc has and ' heaven`s the ' mass ' all
' all of ' from ye ' are as Allah ' Jehovah ' part ' which ' complete serve and
' took of ' from are ye and ' 20 heaven`s the ' all ' under ' from as people the
' of iron the ' pasture`ing from ' from are ye ' issue him and ' Jehovah
' day as are ' inherit`ed ' people of ' if ' you and became of ' from as Mizra from
' your as word ' on ' house ' anger`th you the ' Jehovah and ' 21 this the
as except of and ' has desend the ' ye ' as Obara ' as except of ' swear too as and
' gave ' are as Allah ' Jehovah ' which ' the good`ing the ' land the ' to ' came '
' such the ' land in ' die ' for whither ' for ' 22 inherit`ed ' walk
' from as Obara ' from ye and ' has desend the ' ye ' Obara ' as has whither`s
' 23 such the ' the good`ing the ' land the ' ye ' from you possess and
' Jehovah ' covenant`s ' ye ' and forget you ' turn ' relate ' and guard the
' carve ' relate ' from dual`s and ' your people ' hew ' which ' your as Allah
' for ' 24 are as Allah ' Jehovah ' are command ' which ' all ' you has simititude
' for ' 25 jealous ' to ' that`ing ' the eat ' fire ' are as Allah ' Jehovah
' from sleep and shall ' from as son ' as son and ' from as son ' and bore`s and you
all ' you has simititude ' carve ' from dual`s and ' from eradicate the and ' land in
' your as Allah ' Jehovah ' as has eye in ' mischief ' from dual`s and '
' ye ' day as the ' from are in ' as you till`s the ' 26 and provoke`s the of
mountain from ' has and perish you ' perish ' for ' land the ' ye and ' heaven`s the
' has desend the ' ye ' from as Obara ' from ye ' which ' land the ' above '
for ' am on ' from week ' has and lengthen`s you ' not ' the net`ness of ' there`ed
' from are ye ' Jehovah ' drive`s the and ' 27 shall destory you ' destory the '
' report from ' extent ' from you remain has and ' from as people in
' 28 there`ed ' from are ye ' Jehovah ' lead as ' which ' from nation`ing in

' tree ' ground ' as hand ' do`ed from ' from as Allah ' there ' complete serve and
' not and ' shall hear as ' not and ' shall look as ' not ' which ' stone and
' ye ' there from ' from you seek and ' 29 has and moon`s ' not and ' shall eat as
' all in ' and has search you ' for ' and you come and ' are as Allah ' Jehovah
' all ' are and come and ' walk ' defense ' 30 are soul ' all in and ' are in heart
' till ' desist and ' from week the ' you as after in ' these`ed ' from as word the
' to ' for ' 31 and voice`ing in ' you hear and ' are as Allah ' Jehovah
' not and ' are heal ' not ' are as Allah ' Jehovah ' compassion`ing
' are as you father ' covenant`s ' ye ' forget as ' not and ' are you corrupt as
' from week of ' oh ' ask ' for ' 32 them of ' swear too has ' which
' day as the ' widow ' are as before ' him the ' which ' from as has and head`s the
' end`ed from of and ' land the ' on ' ground ' from as Allah ' create ' which
' word are ' be`s ' behold ' heaven`s the ' end`ed ' till and ' heaven`s the
' people ' hear the ' 33 and your`ed ' hear has the ' or ' this the ' great`ing the
' fire the ' middle`ing from ' word from ' from as life ' from as Allah ' voice`ing
' from as Allah ' flee`ed the ' or ' 34 life as and ' ye`ed ' you hear ' which are
' nation`ing ' approach from ' nation`ing ' if ' you take ' came`ing of
' from as miracle from in and ' evidence`ing in ' you and burden in
' am and permit ' seed`ing in and ' the strength ' hand in and ' fight`ed from in and
' relate ' do`ed ' which ' accord ' from as great ' from hence drop`ing in and
' sight the ' ye`ed ' 35 your as low`s of ' from as Mizra in ' your as Allah ' Jehovah
' till`ing ' whither`s ' from as Allah the ' that`ing ' Jehovah ' for ' knowledge of
and voice`ing ' ye ' are hear`s the ' heaven`s the ' has from ' 36 and alone of from
the great`ing the ' and fire ' ye ' are show ' land the ' on and ' are correct of '
' for ' under and ' 37 fire the ' middle`ing from ' you hear ' and as word and '

' from and seed in ' choose as and ' are as you father ' ye ' love
' and power in and ' and around in ' are spring`s as and ' and them as after
' from nation`ing ' occupy`s the of ' 38 from as Mizra from ' great`ing the
' are around from ' with from ' from as might`ing and ' from as great
' day as are ' inherit`ed ' from land ' ye ' walk ' set of ' are came`s the of
' are in heart ' to ' desist`ing the and ' day as the ' you known and ' 39 this the
' on and ' above from ' heaven`s in ' from as Allah the ' that`ing ' Jehovah ' for
' and as law ' ye ' you guard and ' 40 till`ing ' whither`s ' under from ' land the
' day as the ' are command from ' for whither ' which ' him you command from ' ye and
' purpose of and ' are as after ' are as son of and ' walk ' improve as ' which
' are as Allah ' Jehovah ' which ' ground`ed the ' on ' from week ' lengthen`s you
' three ' Moses ' separate`s as ' yet ' 41 from week the ' all ' walk ' gave
' flee`ing of ' 42 sun the ' emerge from ' has desend the ' cross in ' from as town
' no in ' and shepherd is ' ye ' murder as ' which ' ing`murder the ' there`ed
' from and three ' past`ing from ' if ' hateful ' not ' that`ing and ' knowledge
ye ' 43 life and ' these`ed ' from as town the ' has from ' sister ' to ' flee and
' ye and ' as Reuben of ' fit`ing from the ' land in ' word from in ' ing`defence '
' Bashan in ' has heap`ing ' ye and ' as Gad of ' till heap in ' you and boost
as before ' Moses ' there ' which ' the protect`ing the ' such and ' 44 am Manasse of
' from as law the and ' testimony`ing the ' to`ed ' 45 Israel ' as son '
' Israel ' as son ' to ' Moses ' word ' which ' from as discern them and
' I nation in ' has desend the ' cross in ' 46 from as Mizra from ' from you issue in
which ' as Amar the ' king ' Sihon`ing ' land in ' gape`ing ' you house ' split`ing
' Israel ' as son and ' Moses ' smitten`ed ' which ' shall reckon in ' sojourn as '
' and land ' ye ' and possess as and ' 47 from as Mizra from ' from you issue in

' as Amar the ' as king ' two ' shameful the ' king ' bake`ing ' land ' ye and

' which ' Aroer from ' 48 sun the ' emerge from ' has desend the ' cross in ' which

' that`ing ' has and lift`s ' mountain ' till and ' Arnon ' inherit ' you lip ' on

' has desend the ' Obara ' thus town the ' all and ' 49 pomegranate`ing at

' under ' salt the ' sea ' thus town the ' sea ' till and ' emerge`ed from

cleft`ed the ' you and brook

' hear ' them as to ' say as and ' Israel ' all ' to ' Moses ' call as and ' 1
' which ' from as discern them ' ye and ' from as law the ' ye ' Israel
' from ye ' complete teach and ' day as the ' from are as ear in ' word ' for whither
our people ' hew ' our as Allah ' Jehovah ' 2 complete and do of ' from you guard and
' hew ' our as you and father ' ye ' not ' 3 ing`desolate in ' covenant`s '
' to`ed ' and us I ' and has ye ' for ' such the ' covenant`s the ' ye ' Jehovah
' word ' from around in ' inner`s ' 4 from as life ' and has all ' day as the ' talk
stand ' for whither ' 5 fire the ' middle`ing from ' blemish ' your people ' Jehovah
' that`s the ' time in ' your as between in and ' Jehovah ' between in '
' from sight as ' for ' Jehovah ' as word ' ye ' relate ' fortune`s the of
' for whither ' 6 say of ' blemish ' from whom on ' not and ' fire the ' around from
' from as Mizra ' land from ' are as you issue alas ' which ' are as Allah ' Jehovah
' from as Allah ' walk ' be`s as ' not ' 7 from as serve ' you house from
' all and ' carve ' walk ' do`ed you ' not ' 8 around ' on ' from as after
under from ' land in ' which and ' above from ' heaven`s in ' which ' the portion`ing
' the and humble`ly you ' not ' 9 land of ' under from ' Water in ' which and '
to ' are as Allah ' Jehovah ' for whither ' for ' from serve you ' not and ' them of
' on and ' from as son ' on ' you and father ' low`ing ' punish ' jealous '
' bow ' do`ed and ' 10 as hateful of ' from as four`s ' on and ' from as three`s
' not ' 11 him you command from ' as guard of and ' as love of ' from as thousand of
' not ' for ' lift`ing of ' are as Allah ' Jehovah ' there ' ye ' lift you
' 12 lift`ing of ' name ' ye ' linger ' which ' ye ' Jehovah ' the blame as
' are command ' which are ' and holy`ed of ' desist the ' day as ' ye ' guard`ing
' all ' dual`s and ' serve you ' from week ' you six ' 13 are as Allah ' Jehovah
are as Allah ' Jehovah of ' desist ' as seven`s the ' day as and ' 14 are you are fill

' are son and ' ye`ed ' the are fill ' all ' and in ' do`ed you ' not '
' are ox`ing and ' are faithful and ' are serve and ' are daughter and
are as gate in ' which ' are guest and ' are you cattle ' all and ' are heass`ing and
' (15 with`ing are ' are faithful and ' are serve ' rest`ing as ' purpose of '
' from as Mizra ' land in ' you became`s ' serve ' for ' you is remember and
' the strength ' hand in ' there from ' are as Allah ' Jehovah ' are spring`s as and
' are as Allah ' Jehovah ' are command ' so ' on ' am and permit ' seed`ing in and
' are as father ' ye ' honour ' (16 desist the ' day as ' ye ' you concoct of
' purpose of ' are as Allah ' Jehovah ' are command ' which are ' are mother ' ye and
' on ' walk ' improve as ' purpose of and ' are week ' has and lengthen`s as
(18 murder you ' not ' (17 walk ' gave ' are as Allah ' Jehovah ' which ' ground`ed the
fellow in ' vouch`ed ' not and ' (20 steal you ' not and ' (19 adultery you ' not and '
' desire you ' not and ' (21 fellow ' you house ' desire you ' not ' lift`ing ' till '
' and field`ed ' fellow ' you house ' the lust you ' not and ' fellow ' wife
' which ' all and ' and heass`ing and ' and Ox`ing ' and faithful and ' and serve and
' land ' to ' are as Allah ' Jehovah ' are came`s as ' for ' be`s and ' fellow of
you rise the and ' the net`ness of ' there`ed ' came ' ye`ed ' which ' as Canaan the
' field`s in ' from ye ' you field and ' you and great ' from as stone ' walk '
' the protect`ing the ' as word ' all ' ye ' from as stone the ' on ' you write and
' and rise`s you ' has desend the ' ye ' from are cross in ' be`s and ' such the
' command`ed from ' for whither ' which ' these`ed ' from as stone the ' ye
' there ' you build and ' from as axe`s mountain in ' day as the ' from are ye
' not ' (22 from as stone ' sacrifice from ' are as Allah ' Jehovah of ' sacrifice from
ye ' the son you ' you and whole ' from as stone ' of iron ' them as on ' brandish`s
offer`ing ' and Mosthigh ' offer`s the and ' are as Allah ' Jehovah ' sacrifice from '

there ' you eat and ' from as whole ' you sacrifice and ' are as Allah ' Jehovah of '
' that`ing the ' mountain the ' are as Allah ' Jehovah ' as before ' you rejoice and '
' land in ' sun the ' came`ing from ' way ' as after ' has desend the ' cross in
' beside ' heap heap the ' split`ing ' thus town in ' dwell the ' as Canaan the
word ' these`ed ' from as word the ' ye ' ridge ' split`ing ' ing`appear ' oak`ing
' fire the ' middle`ing from ' blemish ' from are assemble ' all ' to ' Jehovah '
' add ' not and ' great`ing ' voice`ing ' gloom have the and ' cloud the ' dark
Eli ' from give as and ' from as stone ' ing`tablet ' two ' on ' from write as and
' middle`ing from ' voice`ing the ' ye ' from are hear are ' became as and ' 23
' all ' Eli ' shall approach you and ' abhorrence ' burn ' is be and ' dark the
' behold ' and say you and ' 24 your as elder and ' your as tribe ' as head
' and great ' ye and ' and honour`ing ' ye ' our as Allah ' Jehovah ' and has show
' day as the ' fire the ' middle`ing from ' our hear ' and voice`ing ' ye and
life and ' ground the ' ye ' from as Allah ' word as ' for ' our as look ' this the
' fire the ' and has eat you ' for ' die`ing has ' what of ' the time and ' 25
' ye ' hear of ' and us I ' from as add ' mother ' such the ' great`ed the
' who ' for ' 26 and give from and ' till`ing ' our as Allah ' Jehovah ' voice`ing
' word from ' from as life ' from as Allah ' voice`ing ' hear ' which ' flesh ' all
' ye`ed ' approach ' 27 life as and ' and storeup`ing ' fire the ' middle`ing from
' ye`ed and ' our as Allah ' Jehovah ' say as ' which ' all ' ye ' hear and
' our as Allah ' Jehovah ' word as ' which ' all ' ye ' our as to ' word you
voice`ing ' ye ' Jehovah ' hear as and ' 28 our as do and ' our hear and ' are as to
as you hear ' Eli ' Jehovah ' say as and ' Eli ' from are word in ' your as word '
' are as to ' and word ' which ' this the ' people the ' as word ' voice`ing ' ye '
' be`s and ' permanent ' who ' 29 and word ' which ' all ' and good`s became

’ all ’ ye ’ guard of and ’ near ’ dread`ed of ’ them of ’ this ’ from mind

’ them of ’ improve as ’ purpose of ’ from week the ’ all ’ as you command from

’ and carry`ing ’ them of ’ say ’ walk ’ 30 from on`ing of ’ them as son of and

’ the word I and ’ as stand ’ stand ’ talk ’ ye`ed and ’ 31 your as tent of ’ relate

’ from as law the and ’ command`ed them ’ all ’ ye ’ are as to

’ which ’ land in ’ concoct and ’ from teach you ’ which ’ from as discern them and

’ from you guard and ’ 32 the net`ness of ’ them of ’ gave ’ for whither

not ’ from are ye ’ your as Allah ’ Jehovah ’ command`ed ’ which are ’ you concoct of

’ which ’ way the ’ all in ’ 33 of left and ’ right`s ’ and repent`ing you ’

’ purpose of ’ shall walk you ’ from are ye ’ your as Allah ’ Jehovah ’ command`ed

’ from week ’ from you lengthen the and ’ relate ’ good`ing and ’ shall life you

has and possess you ’ which ’ land in

' which ' from as discern them and ' from as law the ' command`ed them ' such and ' 1

' you concoct of ' from are ye ' teach of ' your as Allah ' Jehovah ' command`ed

purpose of ' 2 the net`ness of ' there`ed ' from as Obara ' from ye ' which ' land in

' all ' ye ' guard of ' are as Allah ' Jehovah ' ye ' look as you '

' are command from ' for whither ' which ' him you command from and ' and as statute

' are as life ' week ' all ' are son ' son and ' are son and ' ye`ed ' day as the

' Israel ' you hear and ' 3 are week ' has and lengthen`s as ' purpose of and

' which and ' walk ' improve as ' which ' you concoct of ' you guard and

' as Allah ' Jehovah ' word ' which are ' especially ' has and increase`ed you

' hear ' 4 honey and ' milk ' you secrete ' land ' walk ' are as you father

Jehovah ' ye ' you love and ' 5 one ' Jehovah ' our as Allah ' Jehovah ' Israel

' all in and ' are soul ' all in and ' are in heart ' all in ' are as Allah '

for whither ' which ' these`ed ' from as word the ' and became and ' 6 are especially

' from you sharpen and ' 7 are in heart ' on ' day as the ' are command from '

' are you house in ' are desist in ' height ' you word and ' are as son of

' 8 are rise`ing in and ' are lay in and ' way in ' are you walk in and

' and became and ' are as hand ' on ' loop`ing ' from you bind and

' on ' from you write and ' 9 are as has eye ' between in ' you and put forehead of

are came`s as ' for ' be`s and ' 10 are as gate in and ' are you house ' you and post

' swear too has ' which ' land the ' to ' are as Allah ' Jehovah '

' walk ' set of ' Jacob of and ' Isaac of ' Abraham of ' are as you father of

' 11 you built ' not ' which ' you and good`ing and ' you and great ' from as town

' you fill ' not ' which ' good`ing ' all ' from as fill ' from as daughter and

from as vineyard ' you slice ' not ' which ' from as slice`ing ' ing`covenant`ing and

' 12 you seven and ' you eat and ' you plant ' not ' which ' from as olivet`s and '

' which ' are as Allah ' Jehovah ' ye ' forget you ' turn ' walk ' guard the
' 13 from as serve ' you house from ' from as Mizra ' land from ' are issue`s alas
' name in and ' serve you ' and ye and ' look as you ' are as Allah ' Jehovah ' ye
' from as after ' from as Allah ' as after ' shall walk you ' not ' 14 swear too you
' for ' 15 from are as you and surround`s ' which ' from as people the ' as Allah from
' anger ' the delay ' turn ' are approach in ' are as Allah ' Jehovah ' jealous ' to
' around ' above ' are destory`s the and ' against ' are as Allah ' Jehovah
' which are ' your as Allah ' Jehovah ' ye ' and flee you ' not ' 16 ground`ed the
unleaven`ing ' ye ' has and guard you ' guard`ing ' 17 burden`ed in ' from whom flee
' 18 are command ' which ' him law and ' him testimony and ' your as Allah ' Jehovah '
' are as Allah ' Jehovah ' as has eye in ' good`ing the and ' fit the ' dual`s and
' land the ' ye ' you possess and ' brought and ' walk ' improve as ' purpose of
' 19 are as you father of ' Jehovah ' swear too has ' which ' the good`ing the
' word ' which are ' are around from ' are as enemy I ' all ' ye ' expel of
' what ' say of ' tomorrow ' are son ' are ask as ' for ' be`s and ' 20 Jehovah
' which ' from as discern them and ' from as law the and ' testimony`ing the
' are son of ' you say and ' 21 from are ye ' our as Allah ' Jehovah ' command`ed
' from as Mizra in ' Pharaoh of ' our as became ' from as serve
' 22 the strength ' hand in ' from as Mizra from ' Jehovah ' and has issue`s him and
' from as great ' from as you lip`ing and ' ing`evidence ' Jehovah ' give as and
' and you house ' all in and ' Pharaoh in ' from as Mizra in ' from as evil and
' purpose of ' there from ' issue`s alas ' and has ye`ing and ' 23 our as has eye of
' swear too has ' which ' land the ' ye ' our of ' set of ' and has ye ' came`s the
' you concoct of ' Jehovah ' and has command as and ' 24 our as you father of ' Jehovah
our as Allah ' Jehovah ' ye ' dread`ed of ' these`ed ' from as law the ' all ' ye

' and has you life the of and ' from week the ' all ' our of ' good`ing of '

' guard has ' for ' our of ' be`s you ' just`ed and ' 25 this the ' day as the are

' Jehovah ' as before ' such the ' command`ed them ' all ' ye ' you concoct of

and has command ' which are ' our as Allah

THE TORAH SCROLL 7

' ye`ed ' which ' land the ' to ' are as Allah ' Jehovah ' are came`s as ' for ' 1

' from as increase ' from nation`ing ' castout and ' the net`ness of ' there`ed ' came

' as Amar the and ' as Girgash the and ' as Heth the ' are around from

' as Jebus the and ' as Hivite the and ' as Periz the and ' as Canaan the and

2 with from ' from as might`ing and ' from as increase ' from nation`ing ' the seven

' from whom smitten and ' are as before ' are as Allah ' Jehovah ' from gave and '

' not and ' covenant`s ' them of ' hew you ' not ' from ye ' curse`s you ' curse the

' has set ' not ' are daughter ' height ' inlaw set ' not and ' 3 reason you

' correct`s ' for ' 4 are son of ' implicate ' not ' and daughter and ' and son of

' from as after ' from as Allah ' and serve and ' as after from ' are son ' ye

5 mountain from ' are destory`s the and ' from are in ' Jehovah ' anger ' hole`ed and

' them as you sacrifice from ' them of ' and do`ed you ' here ' mother ' for '

' shall is carry you ' them as you altar and ' shall annihlate you

' has and burnt you ' them as carve`s and ' has and cut you ' them as captain I and

jungle ' are as Allah ' Jehovah of ' ye`ed ' holy`ing ' people ' for ' 6 abhorrence

' people of ' if ' you and became of ' are as Allah ' Jehovah ' choose '

' around ' on ' which ' from as people the ' all from ' the special`ing

' delight ' from as people the ' all from ' from are much ' not ' 7 ground`ed the

' less the ' from ye ' for ' from are in ' choose as and ' from are in ' Jehovah

' from are ye ' Jehovah ' you love from ' for ' 8 from as people the ' all from

' swear too has ' which ' the swear`ing too the ' ye ' and guard from and

' hand in ' from are ye ' Jehovah ' issue`s alas ' from are as you father of

Pharaoh ' hand from ' from as serve ' you house from ' are liberate and ' the strength

' that`ing ' are as Allah ' Jehovah ' for ' you known and ' 9 from as Mizra ' king '

' covenant`s the ' guard ' believe has the ' these ' from as Allah the

' him you command from ' as guard of and ' and as love of ' my spare the and
' him turn ' on I ' and as hateful of ' from rule and ' 10 evermore`ing ' thousand of
' him turn ' on I ' and as hateful of ' after as ' not ' and perish`s the of
from as law the ' ye and ' command`ed them ' ye ' you guard and ' 11 if ' whole as
day as the ' are command from ' for whither ' which ' from as discern them ' ye and '
' ye ' has and hear you ' heel ' be`s and ' 12 complete and do of '
' from ye ' from dual`s and ' from you guard and ' these`ed ' from as discern them
' ye and ' covenant`s the ' ye ' walk ' are as Allah ' Jehovah ' guard and
' are love and ' 13 are as you father of ' swear too has ' which ' my spare the
' fruit and ' are womb ' fruit ' bless and ' are increase the and ' are bless and
' eject ' are is oil`ed and ' are possess you and ' are grain ' are you ground
' which ' ground`ed the ' on ' are flock ' you and Ashtar and ' are as thousand
' bless`ing ' 14 walk ' set of ' are as you father of ' Jehovah ' swear too has
' exterminate ' against ' be`s as ' not ' from as people the ' all from ' be`s you
' with from ' Jehovah ' wriggle`s and ' 15 are you cattle in and ' the exterminate and
' from pastoral the ' from as Mizra ' as menstruate from ' all and ' as sick ' all
' all in ' from gave and ' against ' from there`s as ' not ' you known ' which
' Jehovah ' which ' from as people the ' all ' ye ' you eat and ' 16 are as hateful
not and ' them as on ' are has eye ' spare`ing you ' not ' walk ' gave ' are as Allah
' for ' 17 walk ' that`ing ' snare from ' for ' them as Allah ' ye ' serve you '
' these`ed ' from nation`ing the ' from as increase ' are mind in ' say you
' look as you ' not ' 18 from occupy`s the of ' able I ' the sure`s ' apportion from
' are as Allah ' Jehovah ' do`ed ' which ' ye ' male you ' male ' lag
' you and great the ' estimate`ing the ' 19 from as Mizra ' all of and ' Pharaoh of
' from as miracle them and ' evidence`ing the and ' are as has eye ' see ' which

' which ' am and permit the ' seed`ing the and ' strength`ed the ' hand the and
are as Allah ' Jehovah ' success`ed ' so ' are as Allah ' Jehovah ' are issue`s alas
20 ' them around from ' dread ' ye`ed ' which ' from as people the ' all of '
' till ' height ' are as Allah ' Jehovah ' send as ' leper`ed the ' ye ' also and
21 ' are around from ' from as demolish has the and ' from as remain has the ' perish
are approach in ' are as Allah ' Jehovah ' for ' them around from ' afraid you ' not
' ye ' are as Allah ' Jehovah ' castout and ' 22 terror has and ' great`ing ' to '
able you ' not ' less ' less ' are as before from ' .these`ed ' from nation`ing the
' you life ' are as on ' increase`ed you ' turn ' mountain from ' from zero`ing are '
trouble and ' are as before ' are as Allah ' Jehovah ' from gave and ' 23 field`ed the
' them as king ' gave and ' 24 from destory`s the ' till ' great`ed ' the linger`ing '
' heaven`s the ' under from ' from there ' ye ' you perish the and ' are hand in
' are destory`s the ' till ' are as before in ' man I ' in annihilate`s as ' not
' not ' abhorrence ' has and burnt you ' them as Allah ' as carve`s ' 25 from ye
snare you ' turn ' walk ' you take and ' them as on ' gold and ' silver ' desire you
' not and ' 26 that`ing ' are as Allah ' Jehovah ' you abominate you ' for ' and in '
' curse ' whom became and ' are you house ' to ' the abominate you ' came`s you
' for ' and has abhor you ' abhor and ' and has detest you ' detest ' and your`ed
that`ing ' curse

1 ' day as the ' are command from ' for whither ' which ' command`ed them ' all '
' shall life you ' purpose of ' you concoct of ' has and guard you
' land the ' ye ' from you possess and ' from brought and ' from whom increase and
2 ' you is remember and ' from are as you father of ' Jehovah ' swear too has ' which
' this ' are as Allah ' Jehovah ' are led`s the ' which ' way the ' all ' ye
' are you and low ' purpose of ' word from in ' the Year ' from as four I
' guard you the ' are mind in ' which ' ye ' knowledge of ' are camouflage`ing of
3 ' are hunger as and ' are low as and ' not ' mother ' him you command from
' not and ' you known ' not ' which ' has them ' ye ' are eat`s as and
' not ' for ' are acknowledge`s the ' purpose of ' are as you father ' has and known
' all ' on ' for ' ground the ' am decide ' and alone of ' fight the ' on
4 ' not ' are you raiment ' ground the ' am decide ' Jehovah ' edge ' issue when
' this ' end`ed in ' not ' are as foot and ' are as on from ' zero`ed in
5 which are ' for ' are in heart ' people ' you known and ' the Year ' from as four I
6 ' are correct from ' are as Allah ' Jehovah ' and son ' ye ' man I ' correct as '
' you walk of ' are as Allah ' Jehovah ' unleaven`ing ' ye ' you guard and
7 ' are as Allah ' Jehovah ' for ' and ye ' dread`ed of and ' and as way in
' as inherit ' land ' the large and ' the good`ing ' land ' to ' are came`s from
' divide`ed in ' from as out ' you and deep`ing and ' you and low`s ' Water
8 ' the Fig and ' vine and ' Barley`ed and ' wheat`ed ' land ' mountain in and
9 ' not ' which ' land ' honey and ' eight ' olivet`s ' land ' pomegranate`ing and
' land ' thus ' all ' lack you ' not ' fight ' thus ' eat you ' you scarce from in
10 ' copper has ' slice you ' am mount from and ' of iron ' am stone ' which
' on ' are as Allah ' Jehovah ' ye ' you bless and ' you seven and ' you eat and
11 ' turn ' walk ' guard the ' walk ' gave ' which ' the good`ing the ' land the

’ guard ’ as except of ’ are as Allah ’ Jehovah ’ ye ’ forget you

’ for whither ’ which ’ him you law and ’ him discern from and ’ him you command from

’ you seven and ’ eat you ’ turn ’ 12 day as the ’ are command from

are herd and ’ 13 desist as and ’ the son you ’ from as good`ing ’ from as daughter and

’ walk ’ increase`ed as ’ gold and ’ silver and ’ respect`ing as ’ are flock and ’

you forget and ’ are in heart ’ residue ’ 14 increase`ed as ’ walk ’ which ’ all and

’ from as Mizra ’ land from ’ are spring`s from the ’ are as Allah ’ Jehovah ’ ye ’

’ great`ing the ’ word from in ’ are led`s from the ’ 15 from as serve ’ you house from

’ has and thirsty and ’ in exterminate and ’ burnt`ing ’ serpent ’ look and behold and

’ boulder`ing from ’ Water ’ walk ’ issue`s and them ’ Water ’ whither`s ’ which

’ not ’ which ’ word from in ’ has from ’ are eat`s from the ’ 16 man dream the

’ purpose of and ’ are you and low ’ purpose of ’ are as you father ’ has and known

’ you say and ’ 17 are whom after in ’ are improve the of ’ are camouflage`ing

’ ye ’ vessel ’ do`ed ’ as hand ’ fast have and ’ as power ’ are mind in

for ’ are as Allah ’ Jehovah ’ ye ’ you is remember and ’ 18 this the ’ of life the

purpose of and ’ sick`s ’ you concoct of ’ power ’ walk ’ has ligue the ’ that`ing ’

’ are as you father of ’ swear too has ’ which ’ and covenant`s ’ ye ’ rise`s the ’

’ mother ’ be`s and ’ 19 this the ’ day as are ’ Jacob of and ’ Isaac of ’ Abraham of

’ as after ’ you walk the and ’ are as Allah ’ Jehovah ’ ye ’ forget you ’ forget

’ whom and humble`ly the and ’ complete serve and ’ from as after ’ from as Allah

’ perish ’ for ’ day as the ’ from are in ’ as testimony the ’ them of

’ perish`s from ’ Jehovah ’ which ’ from nation`ing are ’ 20 has and perish you

’ has and hear you ’ not ’ heel ’ has and perish you ’ so ’ from are around from

your as Allah ’ Jehovah ’ voice`ing in

(1 ' has desend the ' ye ' day as the ' Obara ' ye`ed ' Israel ' hear '
' from as might`ing and ' from as great ' from nation`ing ' net`ness of ' came`ing of
(2 ' heaven`s in ' you and defence and ' you and great ' from as town ' with from
' you known ' ye`ed ' which ' from as Anak ' as son ' residue ' great`ing ' people
(3 ' donate ' as son ' as before ' in annihilate`s as ' who ' you hear ' ye`ed and
' cross the ' that`ing ' are as Allah ' Jehovah ' for ' day as the ' you known and
' that`ing and ' from destory`s as ' that`ing ' the eat ' fire ' are as before
from you perish the and ' from you occupy the and ' are as before ' from humilate`s as
(4 are mind in ' say you ' to ' walk ' Jehovah ' word ' which are ' mountain from '
' say of ' are as before from ' from ye ' are as Allah ' Jehovah ' expel`s in '
' land the ' ye ' net`ness of ' Jehovah ' as has came`s the ' as you just in
' Jehovah ' these`ed ' from nation`ing the ' you evil`ness in and ' such the
(5 ' fit in and ' are you just in ' not ' are around from ' from occupy`s from
you evil`ness in ' for ' from land ' ye ' net`ness of ' came ' ye`ed ' are in heart
' from occupy`s from ' are as Allah ' Jehovah ' these`ed ' from nation`ing the '
' which ' word the ' ye ' rise`s the ' purpose of and ' are around from
Jacob of and ' Isaac of ' Abraham of ' are as you father of ' Jehovah ' swear too has
' gave ' are as Allah ' Jehovah ' are you just in ' not ' for ' you known and ' (6
people ' for ' the net`ness of ' such the ' the good`ing the ' land the ' ye ' walk
(7 ' which ' ye ' forget you ' to and ' male`ing ' ye`ed ' stiffneck ' hard`ed '
' day as the ' widow ' word from in ' are as Allah ' Jehovah ' ye ' you angry the
' till ' from are came ' till ' from as Mizra ' land from ' from you out ' which
(8 ' Jehovah ' people ' from whom became ' from rebell from ' this the ' place`ing the
' anger`th whom and ' Jehovah ' ye ' from you angry the ' ing`desolate in and
(9 ' as offer`ing in ' from are ye ' destory`s the of ' from are in ' Jehovah

' ing`tablet ' from as stone the ' ing`tablet ' you take ' mountain`ed the
' blemish ' carry I and ' your people ' Jehovah ' hew ' which ' covenant`s the
as you eat ' not ' fight ' the night`s ' from as four I and ' day as ' from as four I
' two ' ye ' Eli ' Jehovah ' give as and ' 10 as whom drink ' not ' Water and '
' from as Allah ' finger I in ' from as write`ing ' from as stone the ' ing`tablet
your as Allah ' Jehovah ' word ' which ' from as word the ' accord ' them as on and
' 11 assemble the ' day as in ' fire the ' middle`ing from ' blemish ' your people '
the night`s ' from as four I and ' day as ' from as four I ' end from ' became as and
tablet`ing ' from as stone the ' ing`tablet ' two ' ye ' Eli ' Jehovah ' gave '
' mountain from ' up ' rise`ing ' Eli ' Jehovah ' say as and ' 12 covenant`s the '
' you spring the ' which ' are people ' eradicate ' for ' victual`ed
' which ' way the ' has from ' mountain from ' wrong ' from as Mizra from
' say as and ' 13 castimage`ed ' flag ' them of ' concoct ' complete as command
' be`th and ' this the ' people the ' ye ' as you seen ' say of ' Eli ' Jehovah
' apportion from ' puny ' 14 that`ing ' stiffneck ' hard`ed ' people
' heaven`s the ' under from ' from there ' ye ' wipe`ed I and ' from destory`s I and
15 and her from ' increase and ' might`ing ' nation`ing of ' are ye`ing ' do`ed I and
' burn ' is be and ' mountain the ' has from ' wander`ed and ' turn`ed I and '
' 16 as hand ' twosome ' on ' covenant`s the ' ing`tablet ' two and ' abhorrence
' from whom do ' your as Allah ' Jehovah of ' from you sin ' be`th and ' look`ed I and
' way the ' has from ' mountain from ' from you repent ' castimage`ed ' calf ' relate
' two in ' handle`ed I and ' 17 from are ye ' Jehovah ' command`ed ' which
' as hand ' twosome ' above ' your as grove and ' ing`tablet`ing the
' Jehovah ' as before ' fall`ed ye and ' 18 your as low`s of ' from is carry I and
' the night`s ' from as four I and ' day as ' from as four I ' the has and head`s are

' all ' on ' as whom drink ' not ' Water and ' as you eat ' not ' fight
' as has eye in ' mischief ' you concoct of ' from you sin ' which ' your as you sin
' cook ' around from ' as you fear ' for ' 19 and provoke`s the of ' Jehovah
' destory`s the of ' from are mosthigh ' Jehovah ' angry ' which ' hot`ed the and
' 20 that`ing the ' move in ' also ' Eli ' Jehovah ' hear as and ' from are ye
' and destory`s the of ' especially ' Jehovah ' anger`th you the ' Aaron in and
' ye and ' 21 that`s the ' time in ' Aaron ' till in ' also ' praise`ed ye and
' as you take ' calf the ' ye ' from whom do ' which ' your as you sin
' grind`ing ' and ye ' actual`ed and ' abhorrence ' and ye ' the burnt I and
' and dust ' ye ' the hurl`s I and ' dust of ' thin ' which ' till ' improve as the
burn`ed you in and ' 22 mountain the ' has from ' ing`descend the ' inherit the ' to
' from as angry from ' lust`ed the ' you and bury in and ' burden`ed in and '
holy from ' from are ye ' Jehovah ' send in and ' 23 Jehovah ' ye ' from whom became
' as set has ' which ' land the ' ye ' and occupy ' lug ' say of ' creak in '
' not and ' your as Allah ' Jehovah ' edge ' ye ' and constant and ' relate
' 24 and voice`ing in ' from you hear ' not and ' if ' from you believe the
' as testimony ' day as from ' Jehovah ' people ' from whom became ' from rebell from
' from as four I ' ye ' Jehovah ' as before ' fall`ed ye and ' 25 from are ye
as you fall you the ' which ' the night`s the ' from as four I ' ye and ' day as the
to ' praise`ed ye and ' 26 from are ye ' destory`s the of ' Jehovah ' say ' for '
' are people ' eradicate`s you ' to ' Jehovah ' as master ' say`ed and ' Jehovah '
' you spring the ' which ' are great in ' you ramson ' which ' are you inherit and
' are as serve of ' male`ing ' 27 strength`ed the ' are hand in ' from as Mizra from
' people the ' am hard ' to ' pie ' to ' Jacob of and ' Isaac of ' Abraham of
' and say as ' turn ' 28 and you sin ' to and ' and evil`ness ' to and ' this the

' as except from ' there from ' and has you issue alas ' which ' land the ' people

' word ' which ' land the ' to ' from ye ' came`s the of ' Jehovah ' you finish

' from spring`s the ' from ye`ing ' and you hateful from and ' them of

' are you inherit and ' are people ' them and ' 29 word from in ' from whom them of

' great`ing the ' are power in ' from as Mizra from ' you spring the ' which

am and permit the ' are seed`ing in and

' two ' walk ' carve ' Eli ' Jehovah ' say ' that`s the ' time in ' (1
' Eli ' on`ed and ' from as has and head`s are ' from as stone ' ing`tablet
' on ' write`ed I and ' (2 tree ' Ark`ing ' walk ' dual`s and ' mountain`ed the
ing`tablet`ing the ' on ' him the ' which ' from as word the ' ye ' ing`tablet the
' from you there and ' you is carry ' which ' from as has and head`s the '
' two ' carve`ed I and ' hate`s ' as tree ' Ark`ing ' do`ed I and ' (3 stream`ing in
' haul`ed and ' from as has and head`s are ' from as stone ' ing`tablet
' on ' write as and ' (4 as hand in ' ing`tablet`ing the ' two and ' mountain`ed the
' you ten ' ye ' has and head`s the ' write from are ' ing`tablet`ing the
' middle`ing from ' blemish ' your as to ' Jehovah ' word ' which ' from as word the
' (5 Eli ' Jehovah ' from give as and ' assemble the ' day as in ' fire the
' ye ' the guilty`s and ' mountain the ' has from ' wander`ed and ' turn`ed I and
' there ' and became as and ' as whom do ' which ' stream`ing in ' ing`tablet`ing the
' and go ' Israel ' as son and ' (6 Jehovah ' as has command ' which are
as son ' you well from ' and go ' Joakan ' as son in ' and encamp and ' Moseroth from
' and encamp and ' and go ' there from ' (7 the ing`commit ' Joakan '
' and go ' there from ' fortune`ed fortune the ' has from and ' fortune`ed fortune the
' and go ' there from ' Water ' as inherit ' land ' he improve in ' and encamp and
' and encamp and ' and go ' there from ' the has cross in ' and encamp and
' word from in ' and encamp and ' and go ' there from ' strong ' has and backbone in
' blemish ' and encamp and ' and go ' there from ' holy ' that`s ' thorn
' priest as and ' there ' bury as and ' Aaron ' there ' die as and ' mountain the
' Jehovah ' separate`s the ' that`s the ' time in ' (8 him under ' and son ' Eleazar
stand of ' Jehovah ' covenant`s ' Ark`ing ' ye ' arise of ' Levi the ' tribe ' ye
day as the ' till ' name in ' bless of and ' and minister of ' Jehovah ' as before '

' people ' the inherit and ' part ' Levi of ' be`s ' not ' so ' on ' 9 this the '
' Jehovah ' word ' which are ' and you inherit ' that`ing ' Jehovah ' him brother
' from week are ' blemish ' as you stand ' for whither and ' 10 if ' are as Allah
' from as four I and ' day as ' from as four I ' from as has and head`s the
not and ' that`ing the ' move in ' also ' Eli ' Jehovah ' hear as and ' the night`s
' Eli ' Jehovah ' say as and ' 11 are you corrupt the ' Jehovah ' father`ed '
' and came as and ' this the ' people the ' as before ' march of ' walk ' rise`ing
' as you swear too has ' which ' land the ' ye ' and possess as and
' Jehovah ' what ' Israel ' the time and ' 12 them of ' set of ' from you father of
Jehovah ' ye ' dread`ed of ' mother ' for ' are people from ' ask ' are as Allah
' and ye ' love`ed of and ' him way ' all in ' you walk of ' are as Allah '
' all in and ' are in heart ' all in ' are as Allah ' Jehovah ' ye ' serve of and
' ye and ' are as Allah ' Jehovah ' unleaven`ing ' ye ' guard of and ' 13 are soul
' good`ing of ' day as the ' are command from ' for whither ' which ' and as statute
' as there and ' heaven`s the ' are as Allah ' Jehovah of ' behold ' 14 walk
' are as you father in ' only ' 15 thus ' which ' all and ' land the ' heaven`s the
' from seed in ' choose as and ' from ye`ing ' love`ed of ' Jehovah ' delight
16 this the ' day as are ' from as people the ' all from ' from are in ' them as after
' your in heart ' you foreskin ' ye ' from you circumcise and '
' Jehovah ' for ' 17 till`ing ' and hard you ' not ' from are stiffneck and
' as master`ing and ' from as Allah the ' as Allah ' that`ing ' your as Allah
look and behold and ' strong`ing the ' great`ing the ' these ' from as master`ing the
' do`ed ' 18 hire ' took as ' not and ' inner`s ' linger ' not ' which '
' fight ' if ' set of ' guest ' love and ' widow`ed I and ' orphan`ing ' discern from
' from as guest ' for ' abide ' ye ' from you love and ' 19 raiment`ed and

' are as Allah ' Jehovah ' ye ' (20 from as Mizra ' land in ' from whom became
' name in and ' cleave you ' and in and ' serve you ' and ye and ' look as you
' are as Allah ' that`ing and ' are you worship you ' that`ing ' (21 swear too you
' you and terror behold ' ye and ' you and great the ' ye ' are ye ' do`ed ' which
and descend ' soul ' from as seven in ' (22 are as has eye ' see ' which ' these`ed
' Jehovah ' rug ' the time and ' the from as Mizra ' are as you father '
increase of ' heaven`s the ' as in star`ing are ' are as Allah

and you guard from ' you guard and ' are as Allah ' Jehovah ' ye ' you love and ' 1
' all ' him discern from and ' him you command from and ' him you law and '
' your as son ' ye ' not ' for ' day as the ' complete known and ' 2 from week the
' Jehovah ' chasten from ' ye ' see ' not ' which and ' and known ' not ' which
' ye and ' strength`ed the ' and hand ' ye and ' and great ' ye ' your as Allah
' him work ' ye and ' him ing`evidence ' ye and ' 3 am and permit the ' and seed`ing
' from as Mizra ' king ' Pharaoh of ' from as Mizra ' middle`ing in ' do`ed ' which
' from as Mizra ' host at of ' do`ed ' which and ' 4 and land ' all of and
' sea ' who ' ye ' drive`s the ' which ' and ride of and ' him horse`ing of
' from perish as and ' your as after ' from pursue in ' them around ' on ' join`ing
word from in ' relate ' do`ed ' which and ' 5 this the ' day as the ' till ' Jehovah
' do`ed ' which and ' 6 this the ' place`ing the ' till ' from are came ' till '
rid`ed ' which ' Reuben ' son ' father as to ' as son ' Abiram of and ' Dathan of
' ground the ' all ' ye and ' from worthless you and ' edge`ed ' ye ' land the '
' all ' ye and ' them as tent ' ye and ' them house`ly ' ye and ' Korah of ' which
' for ' 7 Israel ' all ' approach in ' them as foot in ' which ' substance`ing the
' great`ing the ' Jehovah ' do`ed from ' all ' ye ' sight`ing the ' your as has eye
' which ' command`ed them ' all ' ye ' from you guard and ' 8 do`ed ' which
' purpose of ' day as the ' from are ye ' are command`ed from ' for whither
' which ' land the ' ye ' from you possess and ' from brought and ' and strength you
purpose of and ' 9 the net`ness of ' there`ed ' from as came ' from as Obara ' from ye
' swear too has ' which ' ground`ed the ' on ' from week ' has and lengthen`s you '
' land ' from seed of and ' them of ' set of ' from are as you father of ' Jehovah
from as came ' them ye ' which ' land the ' for ' 10 honey and ' milk ' you secrete
' which ' that`s ' from as Mizra ' land are ' not ' the net`ness of ' there`ed '

’ drunk`s the and ’ are seed ’ ye ’ seed you ’ which ’ there from ’ from you out
’ from ye ’ which ’ land the and ’ 11 vegetation the ’ garden are ’ are as foot in
’ from as mountain ’ land ’ the net`ness of ’ there`ed ’ from as Obara
’ which ’ land ’ 12 Water ’ impose`ed ’ heaven`s the ’ rain of ’ you and divide and
’ Jehovah ’ as has eye ’ continual`s ’ ye`ed ’ search ’ are as Allah ’ Jehovah
’ you as after ’ till and ’ Year`ed the ’ whom head from ’ thus ’ are as Allah
as you command from ’ to ’ and hear you ’ hear ’ mother ’ be`s and ’ 13 Year`ed the
’ love`ed of ’ day as the ’ from are ye ’ command`ed from ’ for whither ’ which ’
’ your in heart ’ all in ’ and serve of and ’ your as Allah ’ Jehovah ’ ye
and time in ’ from are land ’ rain ’ as you gave and ’ 14 from are soul ’ all in and
’ are grain ’ you gather and ’ latter`ing from and ’ conceive him ’
’ are field in ’ grass ’ as you gave and ’ 15 are is oil`ed and ’ are possess you and
’ turn ’ relate ’ and guard the ’ 16 you seven and ’ you eat and ’ are you cattle of
’ complete serve and ’ from you repent and ’ your in heart ’ expansion`ed
’ 17 them of ’ from whom and humble`ly the and ’ from as after ’ from as Allah
heaven`s the ’ ye ’ boulder have and ’ from are in ’ Jehovah ’ anger ’ hole`ed and
’ ye ’ has set ’ not ’ ground`ed the and ’ rain ’ be`s as ’ not and ’
’ land the ’ above ’ the soon ’ from you perish and ’ the produce`ing
’ ye ’ from you there and ’ 18 relate ’ gave ’ Jehovah ’ which ’ the good`ing the
’ from you bind and ’ from are soul ’ on and ’ your in heart ’ on ’ to`ed ’ as word
’ you and put forehead of ’ and became and ’ your as hand ’ on ’ loop`ing ’ from ye
’ your as son ’ ye ’ from ye ’ complete teach and ’ 19 your as has eye ’ between in
’ way in ’ are you walk in and ’ are you house in ’ are desist in ’ height ’ word of
you and post`ing ’ on ’ from you write and ’ 20 are rise`ing in and ’ are lay in and
’ from are week ’ respect`ing as ’ purpose of ’ 21 are as gate in and ’ are house`ly ’

' Jehovah ' swear too has ' which ' ground`ed the ' on ' your as son ' week and
' on ' heaven`s the ' week are ' them of ' set of ' from are as you father of
command`ed them ' all ' ye ' has and guard you ' guard ' mother ' for ' 22 land the
' day as the ' from are ye ' command`ed from ' for whither ' which ' such the '
' you walk of ' your as Allah ' Jehovah ' ye ' love`ed of ' the you concoct of
' Jehovah ' occupy`s the and ' 23 and in ' cleave`ed the of and ' him way ' all in
' from are as before from ' these`ed ' from nation`ing the ' all ' ye
' from as might`ing and ' from as great ' from nation`ing ' from you possess and
and in ' from are foot ' palm ' way you ' which ' place`ing the ' all ' 24 with from
' has and white the and ' is wilderness the ' has from ' be`s as ' relate '
' shall after the ' sea the ' till and ' Euphrates ' river ' river the ' has from and
' man I ' in annihilate`s as ' not ' 25 from are border`ing ' be`s as
' Jehovah ' permanent ' from are I drop`ing and ' your startle ' your as before in
' thus ' and way you ' which ' land the ' all ' around ' on ' your as Allah
' your as before ' gave ' for whither ' look`ed ' 26 relate ' word ' which are
' which ' bless`ed the ' ye ' 27 accurse`ed and ' bless`ed ' day as the
for whither ' which ' your as Allah ' Jehovah ' unleaven`ing ' to ' has and hear you
' not ' mother ' accurse`ed the and ' 28 day as the ' from are ye ' command`ed from '
from you repent and ' your as Allah ' Jehovah ' unleaven`ing ' to ' has and hear you
' from are ye ' command`ed from ' for whither ' which ' way the ' has from '
' not ' which ' from as after ' from as Allah ' as after ' you walk of ' day as the
' to ' are as Allah ' Jehovah ' are came`s as ' for ' be`s and ' 29 from you known
ye ' set`ed has and ' the net`ness of ' there`ed ' came ' ye`ed ' which ' land the
' on ' accurse`ed the ' ye and ' from as axe`s ' mountain ' on ' bless`ed the '
as after ' has desend the ' cross in ' them`ed ' forward`ing ' 30 of in eye ' mountain

' dwell the ' as Canaan the ' land in ' sun the ' came`ing from ' way '

' the ing`appear ' as oak`ing ' beside ' heap heap the ' split`ing ' thus town in

' has desend the ' ye ' from as Obara ' from ye ' for ' 31 ridge ' split`ing

gave ' your as Allah ' Jehovah ' which ' land the ' ye ' net`ness of ' came`ing of

' 32 thus ' from you dwell and ' ye`ed ' from you possess and ' relate '

' all ' ye and ' from as law the ' all ' ye ' you concoct of ' from you guard and

day as the ' your as before ' gave ' for whither ' which ' from as discern them

' has and guard you ' which ' from as discern them and ' from as law the ' to`ed ' 1
' are as you father ' as Allah ' Jehovah ' gave ' which ' land in ' you concoct of
on ' from as life ' from ye ' which ' from week the ' all ' the net`ness of ' walk
' you and place`ing the ' all ' ye ' has and perish you ' perish ' 2 ground`ed the '
' from as possess ' from ye ' which ' from nation`ing the ' there ' and serve ' which
' from as high the ' from as mountain the ' on ' them as Allah ' ye ' from ye
' 3 has flourish ' tree ' all ' under and ' you and hill the ' on and
' complete is carry and ' them as you sacrifice from ' ye ' complete overthrow and
' abhorrence ' has and burnt you ' them as captain I and ' them as you altar ' ye
' ye ' from you perish and ' has and cut you ' them as Allah ' as carve`s and
' so ' smoke`ing you ' not ' 4 that`ing the ' place`ing the ' has from ' from there
' which ' place`ing the ' to ' mother ' for ' 5 your as Allah ' Jehovah of
' ye ' there`s of ' your as tribe ' all from ' your as Allah ' Jehovah ' choose as
' 6 there`ed ' from brought and ' and search you ' and nigh`s of ' there ' name
' ye and ' your as sacrifice and ' your as offer ' there`ed ' from brought the and
' slaughter as ' you oblation`ing ' ye and ' from are as you ten from
from are herd ' you and first and ' from are as you freewill and ' from are as vow and
' Jehovah ' as before ' there ' from you eat and ' 7 from are flock and '
' from ye ' your as hand ' send from ' all in ' from you rejoice and ' your as Allah
' not ' 8 are as Allah ' Jehovah ' are bless ' which ' from are house`ly and
' man I ' day as the ' talk ' from as do ' and us I ' which ' accord ' smoke`ing you
' to ' time`ed ' till ' from ye in ' not ' for ' 9 him has eye in ' fit the ' all
gave ' your as Allah ' Jehovah ' which ' inherit`ed the ' to and ' the rest`ing them
' from you dwell and ' has desend the ' ye ' from you cross and ' 10 relate '
' from are ye ' inherit`s from ' your as Allah ' Jehovah ' which ' land in

' surround`s from ' your as enemy I ' all from ' relate ' rest`s the and

' choose as ' which ' place`ing the ' be`s and ' 11 safe ' from you dwell and

' there`ed ' there ' name ' ye ' nigh of ' and in ' your as Allah ' Jehovah

' from are ye ' command`ed from ' for whither ' which ' all ' ye ' and came`s you

' from are as you ten from ' your as sacrifice and ' from are as you on`ing

' all and ' from are as you freewill and ' slaughter as ' you oblation`ing and

from you rejoice and ' 12 Jehovah of ' and promise ' which ' your as vow ' choose from

' your as son and ' from ye ' your as Allah ' Jehovah ' as before '

' from are as you mother`ed and ' your as serve and ' your as daughter`th and

' part ' if ' whither`s ' for ' your as gate in ' which ' Levi the and

are as offer ' on`ed you ' turn ' walk ' guard the ' 13 from are ye ' the inherit and

which ' place`ing in ' mother ' for ' 14 saw`ed ' which ' place`ing the ' all in '

' are as offer ' on`ed you ' there ' are as tribe ' one in ' Jehovah ' choose as '

only ' 15 are command from ' for whither ' which ' all ' ye ' do`ed you ' there and

' you bless are ' flesh ' you eat and ' sacrifice you ' are soul ' ye`ing ' all in '

' unclean the ' are as gate ' all in ' walk ' gave ' which ' are as Allah ' Jehovah

' blood the ' only ' 16 Ram are and ' roebuck are ' and has eat as ' clean`ing the and

able you ' not ' 17 Water are ' and has pour you ' land the ' on ' and eat you ' not

' are possess you and ' are grain ' ten from ' are as gate in ' eat of '

' all and ' are flock and ' are herd ' you and first and ' are is oil`ed and

' you oblation`ing and ' are as you freewill and ' promise ' which ' are as vow

' and has eat you ' are as Allah ' Jehovah ' as before ' mother ' for ' 18 are as hand

' ye`ed ' and in ' are as Allah ' Jehovah ' choose as ' which ' place`ing in

' Levi the and ' are faithful and ' are serve and ' are daughter and ' are son and

' are as Allah ' Jehovah ' as before ' you rejoice and ' are as gate in ' which

' ye ' forsake you ' turn ' walk ' guard the ' (19 are as hand ' send from ' all in
' Jehovah ' large`s as ' for ' (20 are you ground ' on ' are week ' all ' Levi the
' you say and ' walk ' word ' which are ' are border`ing ' ye ' are as Allah
' ye`ing ' all in ' flesh ' eat of ' are soul ' lust`ed ' for ' flesh ' the eat
' which ' place`ing the ' with from ' get as ' for ' (21 flesh ' eat you ' are soul
' there ' name ' ye ' has there`ing of ' are as Allah ' Jehovah ' choose as
' Jehovah ' gave ' which ' are flock from and ' are herd from ' you sacrifice and
' all in ' are as gate in ' you eat and ' are as whom command ' which are ' walk
' ye and ' roebuck the ' ye ' eat as ' which are ' sure ' (22 are soul ' ye`ing
' clean`ing the and ' against ' unclean the ' and has eat you ' so ' Ram`s the
' blood the ' eat ' as except of ' strength ' only ' (23 together as ' and has eat as
' people ' soul the ' eat you ' not and ' soul the ' that`ing ' blood the ' for
Water are ' and has pour you ' land the ' on ' and has eat you ' not ' (24 flesh the
' are as son of and ' walk ' improve as ' purpose of ' and has eat you ' not ' (25
' only ' (26 Jehovah ' as has eye in ' fit the ' do`ed you ' for ' are as after
brought and ' lift you ' are as vow and ' walk ' and became as ' which ' are as holy
' are as offer ' dual`s and ' (27 Jehovah ' choose as ' which ' place`ing the ' to '
blood and ' are as Allah ' Jehovah ' sacrifice from ' on ' blood the and ' flesh the
' are as Allah ' Jehovah ' sacrifice from ' on ' pour as ' are as sacrifice '
' all ' ye ' dual`s and ' you hear and ' guard`ing ' (28 eat you ' flesh the and
' day as the ' are command from ' for whither ' which ' these`ed ' from as word the
from on`ing ' till ' are as after ' are as son of and ' walk ' improve as ' purpose of
' Jehovah ' as has eye in ' good`ing the and ' fit the ' do`ed you ' for '
from nation`ing the ' ye ' are as Allah ' Jehovah ' hew`s as ' for ' (29 are as Allah
' are around from ' from ye`ing ' net`ness of ' there`ed ' came ' ye`ed ' which '

turn ' walk ' guard the ' 30 from land in ' desist as and ' from ye ' you possess and
' are around from ' from destory`s the ' as after ' them as after ' catch you '
' and serve as ' the sure`s ' say of ' them as Allah of ' search you ' turn and
' also ' so ' do`ed I and ' them as Allah ' ye ' these`ed ' from nation`ing the
all ' ye ' for ' are as Allah ' Jehovah of ' so ' do`ed you ' not ' 31 as whither
' for ' them as Allah of ' concoct ' hateful ' which ' Jehovah ' you abominate you '
abhorrence ' and burnt as ' them as daughter`th ' ye and ' them as son ' ye ' also
' for whither ' which ' word the ' all ' ye ' 32 them as Allah of '
' and guard you ' and ye ' day as the ' from are ye ' are command`ed from
' and withdraw you ' not and ' and Mosthigh ' and yield`s you ' not ' you concoct of
and her from

' dream`ing ' dream ' or ' prophet`s ' are approach in ' rise`ing as ' for ' 1
' ye`ing the ' came and ' 2 you lip`ing ' or ' ye`ing ' are as to ' gave and
' as after ' walk`ed has ' say of ' are as to ' word ' which ' you lip`ing the and
3 from serve has and ' from you known ' not ' which ' from as after ' from as Allah
' to ' or ' that`ing the ' prophet`s the ' as word ' to ' hear you ' not
' Jehovah ' flee`ed from ' for ' that`ing the ' dream`ing the ' ing`dream the
' ye ' from as love ' from are man the ' knowledge of ' from are ye ' your as Allah
4 from are soul ' all in and ' your in heart ' all in ' your as Allah ' Jehovah
' shall dread you ' and ye and ' shall walk you ' your as Allah ' Jehovah ' as after
' and voice`ing in and ' has and guard you ' him you command from ' ye and
5 shall cleave you ' and in and ' and serve you ' and ye and ' has and hear you
' that`ing the ' dream`ing the ' dream the ' or ' that`ing the ' prophet`s the and
' your as Allah ' Jehovah ' on ' repent`ed ' word ' for ' die him
are release the and ' from as Mizra ' land from ' from are ye ' has spring`s from the
' which ' way the ' has from ' are drawn`s the of ' from as serve ' you house from '
' mischief ' you burn and ' thus ' you walk of ' are as Allah ' Jehovah ' are command
or ' are as father ' son ' are as brother ' are entice`s ' for ' 6 are approach from
' wife ' or ' are daughter ' or ' are son ' or ' are mother ' son '
' say of ' demolish in ' are soul are ' which ' fellow ' or ' are bosom at
' not ' which ' from as after ' from as Allah ' the serve shall ' walk`ed has
' from as people the ' as Allah from ' 7 are as you father and ' ye`ed ' you known
' or ' are as to ' from as approach`ing the ' your as you surround`s ' which
' end`ed ' till and ' land the ' the end from ' with from ' from as get`ing the
' not and ' him to ' hear you ' not and ' him to ' want`ed ' not ' 8 land the
' not and ' pity you ' not and ' and Mosthigh ' are has eye ' spare`ing you

be`s you ' are hand ' and has kill you ' kill ' for ' 9 and Mosthigh ' conceal`ed you
' people the ' all ' friend`s ' and die`s the of ' the has and head`s in ' and in '
' seek ' for ' die and ' from as son came ' and you throw and ' 10 the has after in
' are spring`s from the ' are as Allah ' Jehovah ' above ' are drawn`s the of
' Israel ' all and ' 11 from as serve ' you house from ' from as Mizra ' land from
you concoct of ' till`ing ' and Joseph`s ' not and ' shall dread as and ' and hear as
' crush came ' hear you ' for ' 12 are approach in ' this the ' mischief ' word are '
' there ' desist of ' walk ' gave ' are as Allah ' Jehovah ' which ' are as town
' are approach from ' of worthless`s ' as son ' from as person ' and out ' 13 say of
' walk`ed has ' say of ' from town`s ' as sojourn as ' ye ' and drawn`s as and
' 14 from you known ' not ' which ' from as after ' from as Allah ' the serve shall
faithful ' be`th and ' improve as the ' you ask and ' you examine and ' you search and
are approach in ' such the ' abominate`ed you the ' he do has ' word the ' ready`ing '
' as by ' that`s the ' town`s the ' as sojourn as ' ye ' middle`ed ' smitten`ed ' 15
the you cattle ' ye and ' thus ' which ' all ' ye and ' ye`ed ' curse the ' desolate
' middle`ing ' to ' collect you ' strip`ed ' all ' ye and ' 16 desolate ' as by '
strip`ed ' all ' ye and ' town`s the ' ye ' abhorrence ' you burnt and ' the large
' from on`ing ' hang ' whom`ed the and ' are as Allah ' Jehovah of ' of vessal are '
' the noth`ing ' are hand in ' cleave as ' not and ' 17 till`ing ' the son you ' not
now ' has and tomorrow ' Jehovah ' carry`ing as ' purpose of ' curse the ' has from
' are increase the and ' are compassion and ' from as compassion ' walk ' gave and '
' voice`ing in ' hear you ' for ' 18 are as you father of ' swear too has ' which are
' which ' him you command from ' all ' ye ' guard of ' are as Allah ' Jehovah
' fit the ' you concoct of ' day as the ' are command from ' for whither
are as Allah ' Jehovah ' as has eye in ' good`ing the and

not and ' and gash set ' not ' your as Allah ' Jehovah of ' from ye ' from as son ' 1

' people ' for ' 2 die of ' your as has eye ' between in ' bald`ed ' and deposite`s '

' Jehovah ' choose ' jungle ' are as Allah ' Jehovah of ' ye`ed ' holy`ing

' all from ' the special`ing ' people of ' if ' you and became of ' are as Allah

all ' and eat you ' not ' 3 ground`ed the ' around ' on ' which ' from as people the

captain`ing ' and eat you ' which ' cattle`ed the ' such and ' 4 the abominate you '

' prominent and ' Ram`s ' 5 from as Goat ' Lamb and ' from as sheep ' Lamb and '

' 6 prune and ' as lust and ' s`statisfy`ing and ' wildgoat and ' heass`ing as and

' cloven ' you cloven and ' the spread ' you spread`s from ' cattle`ed ' all and

' ye`ed ' cattle`ed in ' guest`ed ' you on from ' you and spread ' twosome

' guest`ed the ' as on they ' and eat you ' not ' this ' ye ' sure ' 7 and eat you

' ye and ' wean the ' ye ' the cloven`ing the ' spread`ed the ' as spread`s they and

' them`ed ' guest`ed ' am above ' for ' has lip the ' ye and ' you in stream the

ye and ' 8 relate ' them ' from as unclean ' and spread`s the ' not ' the spread and

' cloven ' cloven and ' that`ing ' the spread ' spread`s from ' for ' Swine`s the '

' that`ing ' unclean ' the fear`ing ' not and ' guest`ed ' that`ing and ' the spread

' not ' from you foolish in and ' and eat you ' not ' from flesh from ' relate

' all ' Water in ' which ' all from ' and eat you ' this ' ye and ' 9 and reach

' which ' all and ' 10 and eat you ' drink scales and ' fin`s had ' if ' which

' unclean ' and eat you ' not ' drink scales and ' fin`s had ' if ' whither`s

' which ' this and ' 12 and eat you ' clean`ed ' bird`ing ' all ' 11 relate ' that`ing

' ye and ' spread the ' ye and ' captain has the ' ye ' lag ' and eat you ' not

' vulture the and ' hence`ed the ' ye and ' look`ed the and ' 13 am diver have the

' daughter ' ye and ' 15 and has kind ' twilight ' all ' ye and ' 14 the has kind

' ye and ' emaciate the ' ye and ' violence`ing you the ' ye and ' low`ed as the

15 ' cup are the ' ye and ' discharge the ' ye and ' and the has kind ' discharge the
17 ' you there give the ' ye and ' lip`ing between the ' ye and ' hurl the ' ye and
18 ' the bow`s the ' ye and ' comfort`ed the ' ye and ' you vomit the ' ye and
' ye and ' you palm`s menstrate the ' ye and ' the has kind ' enrage`ed the and
19 ' relate ' that`ing ' unclean ' fly`ing the ' breed ' all and ' put of swoop the
21 20 ' not ' and eat you ' clean`ing ' fly`ing ' all ' lag ' and eat whom ' not
' are as gate in ' which ' guest of ' the foolish ' all ' and eat you
' people ' for ' as foreign of ' the sale ' or ' eat`ed and ' the has give you
' mike in ' kid ' sodden you ' not ' are as Allah ' Jehovah of ' ye`ed ' holy`ing
22 ' are seed ' you income`ing ' all ' ye ' ten you ' ten ' and mother
23 as before ' you and eat and ' Year`ed in ' the Year ' field`ed the ' spring as the
are as Allah ' Jehovah ' choose as ' which ' place`ing in ' are as Allah ' Jehovah '
' are possess you ' are grain ' ten from ' there ' name ' ye ' nigh of '
' purpose of ' are flock and ' are herd ' you and first and ' are is oil`ed and
24 ' from week the ' all ' are as Allah ' Jehovah ' ye ' dread`ed of ' teach you
' and arise ' able you ' not ' for ' way the ' with from ' increase`ed as ' for and
are as Allah ' Jehovah ' choose as ' which ' place`ing the ' with from ' get as ' for
' Jehovah ' are bless as ' for ' there ' name ' ye ' nigh of ' there`ing of '
25 are hand in ' silver the ' splendor and ' silver in ' set`ed has and ' are as Allah
are as Allah ' Jehovah ' choose as ' which ' place`ing the ' to ' you walk the and '
26 ' are soul ' lust`ed ' which ' all in ' silver the ' set`ed has and ' and in '
which ' all in and ' merry in and ' has intoxicate in and ' flock in and ' is morn in
' are as Allah ' Jehovah ' as before ' there ' you eat and ' are soul ' are ask you '
27 ' which ' Levi the and ' are you house and ' ye`ed ' you rejoice and
' part ' if ' whither`s ' for ' and has forsake you ' not ' are as gate in

' issue`s and you ' from two ' three ' the end from ' 28 are people ' the inherit and
' that`s the ' Year`ed in ' are you income`ing ' ten from ' all ' ye
' if ' whither`s ' for ' Levi the ' came and ' 29 are as gate in ' and bring the and
' orphan`ing the and ' guest the and ' are people ' the inherit and ' part
' and have carry and ' and eat and ' are as gate in ' which ' widow`ed I the and
are as hand ' do`ed from ' all in ' are as Allah ' Jehovah ' are bless as ' purpose of
do`ed you ' which '

’ word ’ this and ’ 2 remit`ed ’ do`ed you ’ from two ’ seven ’ end from ’ 1
’ linger`ed ’ which ’ and hand ’ Moses ’ marry ’ all ’ remit`ing ’ remit`ed the
’ him brother ’ ye and ’ and shepherd is ’ ye ’ adduce`s ’ not ’ and shepherd is in
which and ’ address`s ’ as foreign the ’ ye ’ 3 Jehovah of ’ remit`ed ’ call ’ for
’ for ’ however ’ 4 are hand ’ remit you ’ are as brother ’ ye ’ walk ’ be`s as ’
’ are bless as ’ bless`ing ’ for ’ has and destitate ’ against ’ be`s as ’ not
’ walk ’ gave ’ are as Allah ’ Jehovah ’ which ’ land in ’ are as Allah ’ Jehovah
’ voice`ing in ’ hear you ’ hear`ing ’ mother ’ only ’ 5 the net`ness of ’ inherit`ed
command`ed them ’ all ’ ye ’ you and do of and ’ guard of ’ are as Allah ’ Jehovah
’ Jehovah ’ for ’ 6 day as the ’ are command from ’ for whither ’ which ’ such the ’
’ you pledge the and ’ walk ’ word ’ which are ’ are bless ’ are as Allah
’ you rule and ’ pledge you ’ not ’ ye`ed and ’ from as increase ’ from nation`ing
be`s as ’ for ’ 7 and rule as ’ not ’ jungle ’ from as increase ’ from nation`ing in
’ are as gate ’ you one in ’ are as brother ’ one from ’ has and destitate ’ against ’
ye ’ harden you ’ not ’ walk ’ gave ’ are as Allah ’ Jehovah ’ which ’ are land in
’ are as brother from ’ are hand ’ ye ’ shut are you ’ not and ’ are in heart ’
’ if ’ are hand ’ ye ’ open you ’ open ’ for ’ 8 has and destitute the
’ lack as ’ which ’ and lack from ’ enough ’ and has pledge`s you ’ pledge`s the and
’ are in heart ’ people ’ word ’ be`s as ’ turn ’ walk ’ guard the ’ 9 if
’ sleep ’ swear`ed too the ’ sleep ’ the approach`ing ’ say of ’ of worthless`s
’ are as brother in ’ are has eye ’ shepherd is and ’ remit`ed the
’ to ’ are as on ’ call and ’ if ’ has set ’ not and ’ has and destitute the
’ sore ’ not and ’ if ’ has set ’ gave`ing ’ 10 sin ’ against ’ be`s and ’ Jehovah
’ are bless as ’ this the ’ word the ’ sake in ’ for ’ if ’ are set in ’ are mind in
are as hand ’ send from ’ all in and ’ are as work ’ all in ’ are as Allah ’ Jehovah

on ' land the ' approach from ' has and destitute the ' forbare as ' not ' for ' 11
are hand ' ye ' open you ' open ' say of ' are command from ' for whither ' so '
' for ' 12 are land in ' are has destitute of and ' are poor of ' are as brother of '
' are serve and ' am cross the ' or ' as cross the ' are as brother ' walk ' sale as
' as free ' and has send you ' you as seven`s the ' Year`ed in and ' from two ' six
' not ' are people from ' as free ' and has send you ' for and ' 13 are people from
are flock from ' if ' donate`s you ' donate`s the ' 14 from only`s ' and has send you
' Jehovah ' are bless ' which are ' are press from and ' are threshingfloor from and '
' you became`s ' serve ' for ' you is remember and ' 15 if ' has set ' are as Allah
' so ' on ' are as Allah ' Jehovah ' are liberate and ' from as Mizra ' land in
be`s and ' 16 day as the ' this the ' word the ' ye ' are command from ' for whither
' are love ' for ' are people from ' proceed ' not ' are as to ' say as ' for '
' ye ' you take and ' 17 are people ' if ' good`ing ' for ' are you house ' ye and
' serve ' walk ' be`s and ' door in and ' and ear in ' set`ed has and ' puncture them
' not and ' 18 so ' do`ed you ' are you mother of ' anger and ' from on`ing
' are people from ' as free ' and ye ' are send in ' are as has eye in ' hard`ed as
' are bless and ' from two ' six ' are serve ' merry`s ' merry ' care`ed ' for
which ' first`ing the ' all ' 19 do`ed you ' which ' all in ' are as Allah ' Jehovah
' Jehovah of ' holy`s you ' male the ' are flock in and ' are herd in ' bore him '
' fleece you ' not and ' are Ox`ing ' first`ing in ' serve you ' not ' are as Allah
and has eat you ' are as Allah ' Jehovah ' as before ' 20 are flock ' first`ing ' ye
' ye`ed ' Jehovah ' choose as ' which ' place`ing in ' Year`ed in ' the Year '
town`ing ' or ' pass ' they`ing ' and in ' be`s as ' for and ' 21 are you house and
' Jehovah of ' and has sacrifice you ' not ' evil ' they`ing ' all ' or '
' clean`ing the and ' unclean the ' and has eat you ' are as gate in ' 22 are as Allah

eat you ' not ' and blood ' ye ' only ' 23 Ram are and ' roebuck are ' together as

Water are ' and has pour you ' land the ' on '

THE TORAH SCROLL 16

Deu 16:1-16:11

' Jehovah of ' pass ' dual`s and ' blossom`s the ' new ' ye ' guard`ing ' 1
' Jehovah ' are issue`s alas ' blossom`s the ' new in ' for ' are as Allah '
' pass ' you sacrifice and ' 2 the night`s ' from as Mizra from ' are as Allah
' choose as ' which ' place`ing in ' herd and ' flock ' are as Allah ' Jehovah of
' and eat you ' not ' 3 there ' name ' ye ' nigh of ' are as Allah ' Jehovah
' and Mosthigh ' and eat you ' from week ' you seven ' leaven ' and Mosthigh
' land from ' you out ' has and hasten in ' for ' poor ' fight ' unleaven`ing
' land from ' are you issue ' day as ' ye ' male you ' purpose of ' from as Mizra
' remain ' walk ' look`ed as ' not and ' 4 are as life ' week ' all ' from as Mizra
' has from ' tarry`s ' not and ' from week ' you seven ' are border`ing ' all in
' day as in ' from as twilight the ' between in ' sacrifice you ' which ' flesh the
' ye ' sacrifice of ' able you ' not and ' 5 is morn of ' has and head`s the
6 walk ' gave ' are as Allah ' Jehovah ' which ' are as gate ' you one in ' pass the
are as Allah ' Jehovah ' choose as ' which ' place`ing in the ' to ' mother ' for '
' pass the ' ye ' sacrifice you ' there ' there ' name ' ye ' nigh of '
' are you issue ' ing`congregate ' sun the ' came`ing are ' twilight in
' which ' place`ing in ' you eat and ' you sodden and ' 7 from as Mizra from
' is morn in ' you as turn and ' and in ' are as Allah ' Jehovah ' choose as
' unleaven`ing ' eat you ' from week ' you six ' 8 are as tent of ' you walk the and
' are as Allah ' Jehovah of ' you festival ' solemn ' as seven`s the ' day as in and
' you and seven ' the seven ' 9 serve`ed ' you are fill ' all ' do`ed you ' not
' report of ' begin ' rise`ed in ' crawl at ' are block from ' walk ' report you
' Jehovah of ' you and seven ' solemn ' dual`s and ' 10 you and seven ' the seven
' which are ' has set ' which ' are as hand ' you freewill ' estimate ' are as Allah
' Jehovah ' as before ' you rejoice and ' 11 are as Allah ' Jehovah ' are bless as

' are serve and ' are daughter and ' are son and ' ye`ed ' are as Allah
' guest the and ' are as gate in ' which ' Levi the and ' are faithful and
' place`ing in ' are approach in ' which ' widow`ed I the and ' orphan`ing the and
12 ' there ' name ' ye ' nigh of ' are as Allah ' Jehovah ' choose as ' which
' from as Mizra ' land in ' you became`s ' serve ' for ' you is remember and
' solemn ' 13 these`ed ' from as law the ' ye ' dual`s and ' you guard and
' are gather in ' from week ' you seven ' walk ' do`ed you ' booth`ing the
' are solemn in ' you rejoice and ' 14 are press from and ' are threshingfloor from
' are faithful and ' are serve and ' are daughter and ' are son and ' ye`ed
' which ' widow`ed I the and ' orphan`ing the and ' guest the and ' Levi the and
' are as Allah ' Jehovah of ' solemn you ' from week ' you seven ' 15 are as gate in
' are bless as ' for ' are as Allah ' Jehovah ' choose as ' which ' place`ing in
' do`ed from ' all in and ' are you income`ing ' all in ' are as Allah ' Jehovah
' from as move ' three`ing ' 16 rejoice ' sure ' whom became and ' are as hand
are as Allah ' Jehovah ' around ' ye ' are male`ing ' all ' look`ed as ' Year`ed in
' unleaven`ing the ' solemn in ' and in ' choose as ' which ' place`ing in '
' not and ' booth`ing the ' solemn in and ' you and seven the ' solemn in and
' you present are ' man I ' 17 from as only ' Jehovah ' around ' ye ' see`ed as
18 ' walk ' gave ' which ' are as Allah ' Jehovah ' you bless are ' and hand
' are as gate ' all in ' walk ' has set ' from as ing`officer and ' from as discern
' and discern and ' are as tribe of ' walk ' gave ' are as Allah ' Jehovah ' which
' discern from ' stretch`ed ' not ' 19 just ' discern from ' people the ' ye
' hire the ' for ' hire ' implicate ' not and ' inner`s ' pasture`s you ' not and
from as just`s ' as word ' subvert as and ' from as wise ' as has eye ' is blind as
' ye ' you possess and ' the life you ' purpose of ' chase you ' just ' just ' 20

' walk ' fix you ' not ' (21 walk ' gave ' are as Allah ' Jehovah ' which ' land the
' which ' are as Allah ' Jehovah ' sacrifice from ' beside ' tree ' all ' which`ed
' which ' establish`ed from ' walk ' rise`s you ' not and ' (22 walk ' do`ed you
are as Allah ' Jehovah ' hateful`ed

which ' Lamb and ' captain`ing ' are as Allah ' Jehovah of ' sacrifice you ' not ' 1
' you abominate you ' for ' evil ' word ' all ' they`ing ' and in ' be`s as '
' you one in ' are approach in ' come as ' for ' 2 that`ing ' are as Allah ' Jehovah
' Woman ' or ' man I ' walk ' gave ' are as Allah ' Jehovah ' which ' are as gate
' are as Allah ' Jehovah ' as has eye in ' mischief ' ye ' success`ed ' which
' from as Allah ' serve as and ' walk as and ' 3 and covenant`s ' cross of
' moon of ' or ' sun of and ' them of ' the and humble`ly as and ' from as after
' 4 him whom command ' not ' which ' heaven`s the ' mass ' all of ' or
be`th and ' improve as the ' you search and ' you hear and ' walk ' and proclaim`s and
' such the ' abominate`ed you the ' he do has ' word the ' ready`ing ' faithful '
' ye ' or ' that`ing the ' man that ' ye ' you spring the and ' 5 Israel in
' this the ' mischief ' word the ' ye ' concoct ' which ' that`s the ' Woman the
' from you throw and ' Woman the ' ye ' or ' man that ' ye ' are as gate ' to
on ' or ' from as till ' from two ' edge ' on ' 6 and die and ' from as son came
' edge ' on ' die him ' not ' die the ' die him ' from as till ' three`ed ' edge '
the has and head`s in ' and in ' be`s you ' from as till the ' hand ' 7 one ' till
' you burn and ' the has after in ' people the ' all ' friend`s ' and die`s the of '
discern from of ' word ' with from ' I made as ' for ' 8 are approach from ' mischief
' judge`s of ' judge`s ' between in and ' blood of ' blood ' between in '
' are as gate in ' you and increase`s ' as word ' touch of ' touch ' between in and
' Jehovah ' choose as ' which ' place`ing the ' to ' offer`s and ' you rise and
' from Levi the ' from as priest the ' to ' brought and ' 9 and in ' are as Allah
' them the ' from as sea in ' be`s as ' which ' ing`discern the ' to and
' 10 discern them ' word ' ye ' walk ' and proclaim`s and ' and you search and
' has from ' walk ' menstruate as told ' which ' word the ' edge ' on ' dual`s and

' are as Allah ' Jehovah ' choose as ' which ' that`ing the ' place`ing the
' edge ' on ' 11 order`ing as ' which ' accord ' you concoct of ' you guard and
' which ' discern them ' edge ' on and ' order`ing as ' which ' the protect`ing the
' which ' word the ' has from ' curve`ing ' not and ' do`ed you ' walk ' and say as
' which ' man that and ' 12 of left and ' right`s ' walk ' menstruate as told
stand the ' priest the ' to ' hear ' as except of ' has and proud in ' success`ed
ing`discern the ' to ' or ' are as Allah ' Jehovah ' ye ' there ' minister of '
' 13 Israel from ' mischief ' you burn and ' that`ing the ' man that ' die and '
' has and proud`s as ' not and ' and dread as and ' and hear as ' people the ' all and
' are as Allah ' Jehovah ' which ' land the ' to ' income`ing ' for ' 14 till`ing
' you say and ' thus ' the you dwell and ' the you possess and ' walk ' gave
' which ' from nation`ing the ' accord ' king ' mosthigh ' the there`s I
' choose as ' which ' king ' are as on ' there`s you ' there`s ' 15 as you surround`s
' there`s you ' are as brother ' approach from ' and in ' are as Allah ' Jehovah
which ' as foreign ' man I ' are as on ' set of ' able you ' not ' king ' are as on
' if ' increase`ed as ' not ' only ' 16 that`ing ' are as brother ' not '
' the from as Mizra ' people the ' ye ' carry`s as ' not and ' from as Horse`ing
' not ' relate ' say the ' Jehovah and ' skip`ing ' you and increase the ' purpose of
' not and ' 17 till`ing ' this the ' way in ' carry`ing of ' has and yield`s you
' silver and ' and mind ' correct`ing ' not and ' from as women ' if ' increase`ed as
' and desist are ' be`s and ' 18 especially ' if ' increase`ed as ' not ' gold and
' care`ed ' ye ' if ' write and ' and you king from ' throne ' on
' from as priest the ' as before from ' report ' on ' such the ' the protect`ing the
' week ' all ' and in ' call and ' and people ' whom`ed the and ' 19 from Levi the
' him Allah ' Jehovah ' ye ' dread`ed of ' teach as ' purpose of ' him life

’ ye and ’ such the ’ the protect`ing the ’ as word ’ all ’ ye ’ guard of
’ and mind ’ high`ing ’ as except of ’ 20 complete do of ’ these`ed ’ from as law the
’ command`ed them ’ has from ’ repent`ing ’ as except of and ’ him brother from
’ throne ’ on ’ from week ’ lengthen`s as ’ purpose of ’ of and left and ’ right`s
Israel ’ approach in ’ him son and ’ that`ing ’ and you king from

THE TORAH SCROLL 18

’ part ’ Levi ’ tribe ’ all ’ from Levi the ’ from as priest of ’ be`s as ’ not ’ 1
’ and you inherit and ’ Jehovah ’ as fire ’ Israel ’ people ’ the inherit and
’ him brother ’ approach in ’ if ’ be`s as ’ not ’ the inherit and ’ 2 shall eat as
be`s as ’ this and ’ 3 if ’ word ’ which are ’ and you inherit ’ that`ing ’ Jehovah
’ as sacrifice ’ each ’ people the ’ each ’ from as priest the ’ discern from ’
’ priest of ’ gave and ’ resemble ’ mother ’ captain`ing ’ mother ’ sacrifice the
are grain ’ you as head ’ 4 hollow`ed the and ’ from jawbone`s the and ’ seed'ing the
has set ’ are flock ’ shear ’ you as head and ’ are is oil`ed and ’ are possess you ’
’ are as tribe ’ all from ’ are as Allah ’ Jehovah ’ choose ’ and in ’ for ’ 5 if ’
’ bless of and ’ and minister of ’ are as Allah ’ Jehovah ’ as before ’ stand of
’ came`ing as ’ for and ’ 6 from week the ’ all ’ him son and ’ that`ing ’ name in
’ guest ’ that`ing ’ which ’ Israel ’ all from ’ are as gate ’ one from ’ Levi the
’ which ’ place`ing the ’ to ’ and soul ’ ye`ing ’ all in ’ came and ’ there
’ accord ’ him Allah ’ Jehovah ’ spice ’ minister and ’ 7 Jehovah ’ choose as
part ’ 8 Jehovah ’ as before ’ there ’ from as stand the ’ from Levi the ’ him brother
’ 9 you and father the ’ on ’ and as sale from ’ earnest ’ and eat as ’ part are ’
walk ’ gave ’ are as Allah ’ Jehovah ’ which ’ land the ’ to ’ came ’ ye`ed ’ for
’ from nation`ing the ’ you abominate you are ’ you concoct of ’ teach you ’ not ’
’ and daughter and ’ and son ’ cross`s from ’ against ’ come as ’ not ’ 10 them the
’ serpent from and ’ has low`ing from ’ from as determine ’ determine ’ abhorrence
’ father`ing ’ ask and ’ connect ’ connect and ’ 11 witchcraft from and
you abominate you ’ for ’ 12 from as die the ’ to ’ search and ’ as ghost`ing as and
you abominate you the ’ sake in and ’ to`ed ’ do`ed ’ all ’ are as Allah ’ Jehovah ’
’ from ye`ing ’ from occupy`s from ’ are as Allah ’ Jehovah ’ these`ed ’
’ 14 are as Allah ’ Jehovah ’ people ’ be`s you ’ from as complete ’ 13 are around from

' from as occupy as ' them ye ' which ' these`ed ' from nation`ing the ' for
and hear as ' from as determine the ' to and ' from as cloud them ' to ' from ye`ing
' prophet`s ' 15 are as Allah ' Jehovah ' walk ' gave ' so ' not ' ye`ed and '
Jehovah ' walk ' rise`s as ' as storeup`ing ' are as brother from ' are approach from
affirm ' you ask ' which ' accord ' 16 has and hear you ' him to and ' are as Allah '
not ' say of ' assemble the ' day as in ' ing`desolate in ' are as Allah ' Jehovah '
' fire the ' ye and ' as Allah ' Jehovah ' voice`ing ' ye ' hear of ' yield`s I '
' 17 faithful`ing ' not and ' till`ing ' cat`ed ' not ' such the ' great`ed the
' prophet`s ' 18 and word ' which ' and good`s became ' Eli ' Jehovah ' say as and
' with`ing are ' them as brother ' approach from ' them of ' from definite
' which ' all ' ye ' them as to ' word and ' him animal ' as word ' as set has and
him word ' to ' hear as ' not ' which ' man that ' be`s and ' 19 and has command I
sure ' 20 and people from ' search I ' for whither ' as there in ' word as ' which '
' which ' ye ' as there in ' word ' word of ' machete`s ' which ' prophet`s the '
' from as Allah ' spice ' word as ' which and ' word of ' him whom command ' not
' say you ' for and ' 21 that`ing the ' prophet`s the ' die and ' from as after
and word ' not ' which ' word the ' ye ' acknowledge has ' the sure`s ' are mind in
be`s as ' not and ' Jehovah ' spice ' prophet`s the ' word as ' which ' 22 Jehovah '
' and word ' not ' which ' word the ' that`ing ' came`ing as ' not and ' word the '
' strife`ing ' not ' prophet`s the ' and word ' has and proud in ' Jehovah
and her from

Made in the USA
Las Vegas, NV
23 March 2023

69579977R00305